IRRIGATION MANAGEMENT

VOLUME II

B.L. DARRA
C.S. RAGHUVANSHI

ATLANTIC PUBLISHERS AND DISTRIBUTORS

Published by
ATLANTIC PUBLISHERS AND DISTRIBUTORS
B-2, Vishal Enclave, Opp. Rajouri Garden, New Delhi-27
Phones 5413460, 5429987

Sales Office
4346/4C, Ansari Road, Darya Ganj,
New Delhi-110 002
Phones 3273880, 3285873, 3280451
Fax 91-11-3285873
e-mail gupta.atlantc@axcess.net.in

ISBN 81-7156-778-9

Typeset at
APD Computer Graphics, Delhi

Printed in India at
Mehra Offset Press, Delhi

PREFACE

One of the most challenging aspects of Irrigation Development today is that improving both the quality and quantity of human capital involved. So far the quality of human agents have remained underrated. Alfred Marshall described that "Knowledge is the most powerful engine of production;" it enables us to subdue nature and satisfy our demands.

The conventional priorities of Irrigation projects are more hardware including dams and canals to irrigate more crop lands. This require more involvement of professionals who are well educated/trained to understand each level of complex irrigation system. This is possible through the continual upgrading in the levels — of information, knowledge and skills of all involved in irrigated farming.

Irrigation Management includes the terms, irrigation water management and "On-farm water management." The irrigation system incorporates all the relevant disciplines and professions required to design and operate systems for increased agricultural production. This also includes all inputs and services complementary to water for increased crop production. This means that we should observe, analyze and keeping track of thinking or worrying about the irrigation system as a whole. This indicates a real need for interdisciplinary team approach for training and action programmes.

It is, therefore, essential to prepare the better personnel in the design, implementation, operation, utilization and maintenance of irrigation systems. The real need is for cadres of professionals who understand the system in relation to the agricultural production process. Irrigation development would be useful only when the professionals are fully equipped with the new criteria so as to work in hand to hand with farmers.

It is our experience in working with many professional groups that a system understanding is required by all professionals alongwith the specific disciplines training.

In keeping with system approach, professionals need to work together in teams to solve system problems. The training should have focus on the consequences of system performance on farms and farmers. In fact professionals learn more when they interact with farmers. The major priority should be given for human resource development with a focus on field orientation in training in various disciplines involved in irrigation management.

In view of this it was felt that a book having a manual cum descriptive design should be made available to the trainers and trainees of WALMIS/IMTIS. The concepts about the need to utilise the created potential as also to increase agricultural production per unit of land and water available within the system must be well understood through the well trained personnel.

These aspects of irrigation system *i.e.* increase the efficiency of water management by controlling water logging and erratic and inadequate irrigation near the tail ends besides excessive loss of water in the conveyance, distribution and application stages — of irrigation water have been highlighted in the present Vol. II. The understanding of basic disciplines was covered in Vol. I where soils, agronomy, extension and land management was discussed at length in view of various ecological and socio-economical and related aspects of agricultural economics.

The book elaborately describes the aspects of irrigation engineering related with plant growth and crop production — in various chapters to transfer the feasible technology for water management on the farm to the professionals.

It is hoped that the book would be found useful not only by the trainers of the WALMIES/IMTIS but also by the irrigation engineers, agricultural scientists as well as by the planners, designers, administrators, public representatives and above all by the representatives of farmers who are interacting directly with the beneficiaries.

B.L. DARRA
C.S. RAGHUVANSHI

CONTENTS

CHAPTER 1

SOIL AND THEIR IRRIGABILITY PATTERNS FOR EFFECTIVE IRRIGATION MANAGEMENT

1. Introduction

The economic feasibility as well as viability of any proposed irrigation project in its proposed command area is very essential for assessing the benefits and hazards under irrigated agriculture system. Besides other evaluation parameters, the most important is the expected behaviour or response of applied water to the different types or kinds of soils in the proposed command and their productivity potential for growing different crops. The most important parameter is the classification of soils of an area into various soil mapping units, and their land and irrigability ratings which would decide the beneficial impact of water to be supplied to the fields for growing various crops. The supply of definite quantity of water or for fixing a water duty allowance to avoid hazardous effects also depends on the aforesaid parameter. This warrants the detailed pre-irrigation soil survey of the proposed command prior to its irrigation.

The basic data related to the nature and kind of soils is obtained through soil survey. A soil survey is a procedure for orderly, systematic examination and classification of soils in the field location of soil boundaries and plotting them on a map. Soil survey also generates data which is useful for soil and land irrigability classification (Fig. 1.1).

2. Role of Soil Survey in Irrigation Management

Knowledge of soils within a potential irrigation area is essential for economic and technical reasons. The high cost of development of irrigated agriculture requires justification by assessment of risks and benefits and the design of irrigation schemes itself is dependent on detailed knowledge of soils in the irrigable area.

Following are the principal purposes of soil survey studies in irrigation management :

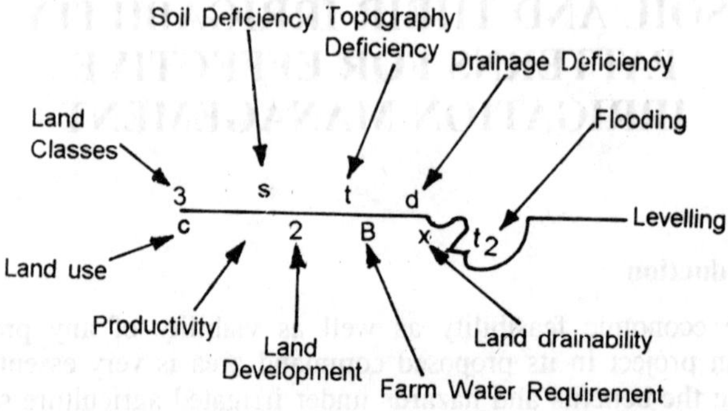

Fig. 1.1: Showing Climatic diagram of mapping symbols.

(i) to ensure selection of soils for irrigation that are productive (*i.e.* soil and land suitability for irrigation),

(ii) to aid in the location of canals and other irrigation work,

(iii) to determine irrigation needs of specific soil types,

(iv) to determine drainage needs of specific soil types,

(v) to determine land reclamation needs of specific soil types,

(vi) to determine overall land levelling needs,

(vii) to help in determining the size of farms,

(viii) to help in appraising land value for evaluating cost-benefit ratio in development programme,

(ix) to determine suitable cropping patterns in project area,

(x) to help in deciding irrigation schedule,

(xi) to calculate land/irrigation revenue through calculation of land rental values with the help of land capability classification of soil survey.

(xii) Calculation of coefficient of linear extensibility (COLE)

3. Soil Characteristics Relevant to Irrigation

The soil characteristics which are relevant to irrigation are given in Table 1.

TABLE 1.1

	Soil Characteristics	Investigation Requirements
(i)	Effective soil depth.	Field measurement at each observation site.
(ii)	Particle size distribution (soil texture)	Field assessment by surface feel at each observation site and also laboratory determination of representative profiles.
(iii)	Structure and stability of structure under irrigation	Field assessment from representative profile.
(iv)	Soil porosity	Field determination of bulk density for layers of representative profile. Layers of each mapping unit.
(v)	Infiltration rate (cumulative and basic)	A minimum of three replicated measurement of each mapping unit near profile site.
(vi)	Saturated hydraulic conductivity	Replicated field measurements in each mapping unit.
(vii)	Water retention characteristics	Field capacity, permanent wilting point, bulk density at profile site for each mapping unit.
(viii)	Depth to ground water	Systematic measurement in the field, deep borings or well observation.
(ix)	Salinity of soil and ground water	Systematic sampling for laboratory determination.
(x)	Cation exchange capacity (CEC) and exchangeable sodium percentage (ESP)	Laboratory determination of representative profile soil samples.
(xi)	Soil PH	Laboratory determination on representative profile samples.
(xii)	COLE	Coefficient of linear extensibility.

4. Kinds of Base Maps

The following are the types of base maps used in soil survey work :

(i) *Aerial Photographs* : Nearly all detailed soil mapping is done on aerial photographs. The greater and single advantage of aerial photograph as base map in soil survey work is that all minute details are shown which otherwise are beyond the reach of soil surveyor. Physical and cultural features of the ground are shown in an infinite details. Field boundaries, trees, bushes, rock outcrops, buildings, plant cover are known before actual plotting of soil boundaries. Studies in approximate delineation of soil boundaries can be undertaken in laboratory itself. It has both speed and accuracy of work. Stream, lakes and swamps that are difficult to plot accurately by ground methods are known in their minute details by aerial photographs. The scale used is 1:15000.

(ii) *Topographic Maps* : Topographic maps of high standards are generally used in soil surveys. These maps contain cultural and physical details accurately drawn and shown in these maps. According to needs of job the grades are marked on the survey maps for starting the survey.

I. MAPPING UNITS

The distinct features of land and variation in soil properties etc. are mapped on the above maps. The particular characteristics of any area mapped are called soil taxonomic or soil classifying unit and the same taxonomic units are grouped together and the boundaries of these homogeneous areas are delineated on a soil map. (Fig. 1.2)

The mapping unit consists of following factors grouped singularly and put on map.

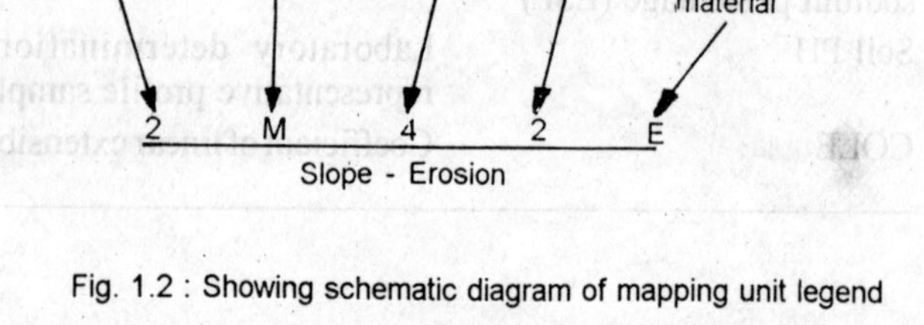

Fig. 1.2 : Showing schematic diagram of mapping unit legend

(i) *Soil Series* : This in a mapping unit represents morphological soil parameters. This indicates grouping of alike soils having similarity in their characteristics and behaviour on a landscape. The soils under the same series are supposed to be developed on the same parent material in the same environment soil series, in other words represent the properties of a contiguous *pedon** in the recognised *polypedon***. The informations are depicted regarding land use. The high density of observations are plotted using grid of 50m × 50m to 100m × 100m and are called intensive detailed soil survey while 200 m × 200 m to 400 m × 400 m are called semi-detailed surveys. The grid survey between 1000 m × 1000 m to 2000 m × 2000 m are called detailed reconnaissance or exploratory soil survey. In these the auger holes are taken at desired grid from a central

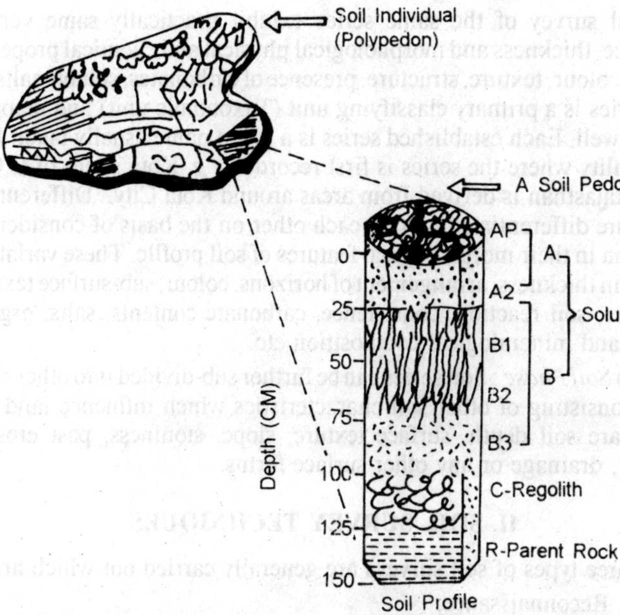

Fig. 1.3 : A Typical Soil Pedon
(Courtesy) Dr. R.I. Karle, New Delhi

*A pedon is the smallest volume that can be recognised as a soil individual smallest but representative of soil to be identified. It can be compared to unit cell of a crystal and has three dimensions. It has vertically demarcation between soil and "not soil" while laterally it has large area representing number of horizons and variability (Profile on other hand represents only vertical section).

**A group of alike pedons bounded in all directions by other pedons or material (non-soil) is called polypedon.

base line between regularly spaced straight traverses, entire area is covered and continuously marked or plotted. Soil series are in this way marked based on the typygying pedons already specified through profile examination in the area. The indication of soil phases with the standard series provides detailed information of the landscape.

The map scale is large for detailed soil surveys which are either of Sajra map scale usually 20" = 1 mile (1:8000 or 1:4000 or 1 cm =40 m) or base maps of 16"= 1 mile or 8" = 1 mile blown up to this scale from standard maps provided by Government of India called as survey map. The similar mapping units are delineated through soil boundaries which indicate their course having exactly same features. These maps contain all informations regarding natural, and cultural features such as streams, lakes, ditches, roads, buildings, railway roads etc. so that user can locate himself on the map and read out the desired informations precisely.

Soil survey of the same series exhibit practically same vertical sequence, thickness and morphological physical and chemical properties such as colour, texture, structure, presence of carbonates, soluble salts etc. Soil series is a primary classifying unit (Taxonomic unit) and mapping unit as well. Each established series is a given name usually taken from the locality where the series is first recorded *e.g.* Kota series of C.C.A. Kota, Rajasthan is derived from areas around Kota City. Different soil series are differentiated among each other on the basis of considerable variation in their morphological features of soil profile. These variations may be in thickness, arrangement of horizons, colour, sub-surface texture, structure, soil reaction, consistence, carbonate contents, salts, organic matter and mineralogical composition etc.

(ii) *Soil Phase* : Soil series can be further sub-divided into other small units consisting of other soil characteristics which influence land use. These are soil depth, surface texture, slope, stoniness, past erosion, salinity, drainage or any other surface forms.

II. SOIL SURVEY TECHNIQUES

Three types of soil surveys are generally carried out which are :

1. Reconnaissance,
2. Detailed Reconnaissance (semi-detailed), and
3. Detailed.

These depend upon the method, the intensity of survey and the resulting details and precision of mapping. In deciding the type of survey to be undertaken, the terrain features, time and personnel available for the survey and the purposes to which the surveyed land will be put to use, are some of the factors that will require to be considered.

Reconnaissance Survey

The scale of mapping used in this type of survey is 1" = 1 mile (1:63360) or 1:50,000 using the top-sheets of the survey of India as base maps or aerial photographs of similar scale. The field work will involve studies of profiles at intervals depending upon the soil heterogeneity. Auger sampling for every 1 to 1½ Km. is carried out to study the variations in profile characters *i.e.* change in colour, depth, texture, structure, nature of parent material or parent rock and related features are noted in the case of each of the profiles studies. Profile showing similar horizontal characters within narrowly defined limits are grouped together into SERIES. This is a classificational unit in which the mapping units in reconnaissance soil surveys are named after the place (location, village or town) where representative profiles were first recognized and described.

Due to the fact that more than one series occurs in a limited area mixed up in a manner which is difficult to distinguish in the scale of 1" = 1 mile or (1:50,000 scale) mapping. Therefore, under this type of survey, the mapping unit is a soil Association. The series occurring together in a regularly repeating geographic pattern are grouped together into an "Association". These surveys are used for planning and agricultural development, water shed development, afforestation etc.

Semi-Detailed and Detailed Survey

In this method a grid of 200 to 400 metres is chosen for semi-detailed while a grid of 100 metre for detailed survey on a scale map of 1 : 15840 or 1 : 7920 or 8" to 16" = 1 mile is used. The auger samples are collected at least upto 1 metre depth and max. to 150 cms. and as per established series of area soil mapping units or soil variety are marked at each grid and soil boundaries are delineated from which Irrigability or land capability classes are formed and demarcated on map for interpretation.

Bentchmark Soils

It is used for soil research purpose (Murthy, 1982).

III. SOIL VARIETAL CHARACTERISTICS RELEVANT TO IRRIGATION

The changes which are likely to occur in an area *e.g.* soil conditions (physical, chemical and biological) cropping patterns and environmental aspects and inter-related and sum total of these would be interpreted for either favourable or unfavourable influence after water application.

The soil characteristics which should be considered in the required planning are listed below as per their priorities :

(1) Selection of soils which would sustain irrigation as per their suitability.

(2) The total quantity of water as per specific soil types/series based on their available water storage capacity *i.e.* Network planning of distribution system as per soil conditions.

(3) The drainage needs of the proposed command in addition to natural drainage system existing.

(4) Diagnosis of salt effected area in pre-irrigation period and likely to be created in post-irrigation period, their reclamation and management.

(5) The extent of land levelling (cut-fills) in the demarcated areas and overall needs.

(6) The proposed cropping patterns based on soil type in different areas of the proposed command for higher and sustained agriculture production.

IV. SELECTION OF SOILS

The suitability of soils for different crops in relation to the proposed irrigation system planning depends upon following consideration :

(1) *Effective Soil Depth*

This is a soil mentle resting over parent material which could be either undifferentiated alluvium, hard pan (murrum layer) weathered (unconsolidated) or unweathered (consolidated) rock below where roots are unable to pass and even a permanently moistured saturated zone in which plant roots cannot survive.

The various soil depth classes recognised for this purpose in connection with soil survey are following :

(a)	Very Shallow	-	less than 7.5 cm.
(b)	Shallow	-	7.5 to 22.5 cm.
(c)	Medium deep	-	22.5 to 45.0 cm.
(d)	Deep	-	45 to 90 cm.
(e)	Very deep	-	more than 90 cm.

The area, therefore, can be classified into different soil depth classes and average area under each soil depth class be recorded.

(2) *Soil Texture*

It represents the distribution of particle size in different soils of the command. Three important particles sizes are being considered for assessing soil texture :

(i) Sand (2.0 to 0.02 mm dia as per International method).

(ii) Silt (0.02 to 0.002 mm dia as per International method).

(iii) Clay (0.002 mm and below).

The number of texture classes of surface and below by auger hole method upto 1 metre should be grouped as under after profile examinations in the area :

(1) Coarse textured soils *e.g.*, sandy, and loamy sand.

(2) Medium textured soils *e.g.* loam, silt loam and sandy loam.

(3) Fine textured soils *e.g.* sandyclay-loam, clay-loam, clayey, fatty clay, silty-clay etc.

Soil Structure : The natural arrangement and orientation of soil particles forming a soil aggregates of different shapes and sizes are termed as soil structure. The various soil structures recognised are :

(a) *Structureless* : (a) Single grain (*e.g.* sand) and (b) Massive (single grain particles clinging together with small amount of clay and organic matter but are without definite lines of cleavage).

(b) *With structure* : (a) Granular or crumb (rounded granules of soil aggregated in either uniform or irregular size and shape) and (b) Platty Soil aggregates having horizontal dimensions greater than vertical as in mica (Biotite, muscovite)

(c) *Blocky* : Soil aggregates conglomerating in (non-angular or angular) a shape having same horizontal and vertical dimensions.

(d) *Prismatic and Collumner*: Soil aggregates having vertically elongated shape as in prism. If elongated portions are rounded it is columner (common in sodic soils).

(3) *Structure Destroyed (puddle soil mess)*

The hydro-physical properties of soils are considerably affected by this parameter.

(4) *Available Water Capacity*

For designing efficient water delivery or distribution system for fixing frequency or interval of irrigation and depth etc. the available water capacity of the different established soil classes has to be worked out.

This term when represented on per cent basis is called available water per cent or A.W.P. It is a difference of moisture at field capacity (F.C.) minus moisture at permanent wilting point (PWP) for different soil classes. The AWP, Irrigation frequency and depth of water in a soil is expressed as cm/m soil depth which can be calculated by formula :

(i) $AWP = \dfrac{(FC-PWP) \times AV.BD \text{ of a soil class } (Pb) \times \text{depth } (D)}{100}$

(ii) Irrigation Interval, $i = \dfrac{P \times D \times AWP}{ETC}$

(iii) Application depth, $d = \dfrac{P \times D \times AWP}{Ea}$
Water or irrigation depth

Where i = irrigation in days

P = means allowable moisture depletion for particular soil

D = rootzone depth

Ea = application efficiency

ETC = crop evapotranspiration.

Illustration :

If P = 0.5, D (50%), D = 0.5 metre, AWP (Sa) = 200 mm/M.

Ea = 0.75 & ETC = 5 mm/day, then i=10 days and d = 67 mm.

The available soil moisture depletion to be allowed depends upon the crop growth stage and hence irrigation interval be fixed accordingly.

(5) *Infiltration Rate*

The basic (Ib) and cummulative infiltration must be determined at various locations in all the classes and average value for each class should be recorded.

(6) *Stream Size*

It has been suggested by Darra (1984) that for clayey soils, the stream size should be kept at 10 lits/sec for medium type and medium textured 15 lits/sec. for medium to medium coarse land, it may be kept 30 lit per second and for coarse texture upto 60 lits/sec (2 cusecs).

(7) *Permeability*

This term is now designated as hydraulic conductivity and can be determined in laboratory and in situation fields by auger hole test method in presence of water table or by pit method in absence of water table. The test be conducted for all soil classes and averaged for each class.

(8) *Soil Salinity and Sodicity*

The amount of salts, pH and exchangeable sodium per cent would determine the type of problem in the area and accordingly different soil classes affected may be regrouped for design of drainage system and leaching of salts for their suitability to irrigation and irrigation planning. The reclamation measures be done by gypsum/lime as per requirement and green manuring with dhaincha and salt resistant crops/paddy with special agronomical practices.

(9) *Water Quality*

The quality of under-ground and irrigation water must be tested prior to planning or clearance of wetting of any irrigation project. Also a periodic test of water quality be made to accommodate any change in future planning and maintained soil fertility and sustain land use in any type of soil in a command. For water quality rating see Table 1.10.

(10) *Natural Drainage*

Water logging is a common feature after a few years of canal irrigation if appropriate and adequate network drainage facilities under natural or otherwise are not developed simultaneously to the provision of irrigation distribution system. The system be planned as per soil conditions in different classes recognised and keeping in view the calcareous or gypsi-ferrous or gypsious sub-surface and sub-stratum or hard barrier strata of each soil class without which the drainage system created would be in effective.

(11) *Classification of Different Soil Classes into Irrigability Classes*

Five to six irrigable classes are made for command. These are :

(1) Class I or A = None to slight soil limitation (slope 1%, water table < 3 m).

(2) Class II or B = Moderate soil limitations either of soil, drainage, salt, topography and erosion for sustained used under irrigation (slope 1-3%, water table < 3 m).

(3) Class III or C — Severe above listed limitations for sustained (slope 3-5%), water table (< 3 m) use under irrigation.

(4) Class IV or D — Very severe soil limitations for sustained use under irrigation (slope 5 to 10%), Water table < 3 to 4 m).

(5) Class V or E (slope 7 to 15%) — Unsuitable for irrigation under

prevailing conditions but may be brought under irrigation by reclamation and management at high cost.

(6) Class VI or F — Totally unsuitable for irrigation due to poor soil cover, and rock out crops — Hence not considered for irrigability rating.

Accordingly aggregate index be found out and planning be made.

Land Development Needs

The irrigation is economical when applied to only I and II irrigability classes where slopes are not steeper. For gravity or flow irrigation system the ideal slopes is 0.3% to 0.4% in flow direction. However, by manipulating stream size and application method the soils upto 1.0% may be irrigated. The land levelling programme should be taken only on deep to very deep soils and should be avoided where soil depth is less than 0.50 metre. However, since 1" soil layer of top takes 300 to 1000 years to develop under natural conditions and 25 to 30 years under highly and intensive soil management practices the cuttings should be planned to bare minimum and emphasis should be on terrace making and contour cultivation, contour stripping cropping and other soil conservation measures for other class of soils as per details of soil survey.

Cropping Pattern

The deep rooted crops are recommended for classes I and II soils while perennial crops area should be restricted to 11 to 12% in class II. For other classes the cropping pattern should be worked out as per soil characteristics to have efficient use of irrigation water supplies as guided by soil survey reports and recommendations. Mehta and Shekhawat (1972) gave the cropping patterns of various crops based on the soil types available in Rajasthan keeping in view the soil survey mapping irrigability classes.

Lining

Lining should be as per soil characteristics for clayey textural soils rich in montmorillonite having high shrinkage, swelling and cracking. The pucca Katla, cement concrete, lining or high molecular wt. and high density plastic sheets should be used in irrigation and drainage systems. However, it is found that soda-ash (sodium carbonate of low grade or where alkali effluences are available) should be mixed with soil in 1:10 or 1:100 ratio and kneading be done with appropriate quantity of water as per local conditions. One cm to 2.5 cm thick layer lining after the soil has attained pH more than 9.0 has been found to be very useful lining material. The pervious soils with high infiltration rate should also be lined. However, where the basic infiltration rates of soil is between 6.5 to 12.5 cm/hr it needs lining to avoid seepage from the conveyance system. The soil survey provides these data for irrigation planning (Hitoshi-Fokuda Engineer from Tokyo, Japan suggested this).

LAND CLASS RATINGS

Land class ratings have been worked out by various workers on the basis of soil irrigability class (aggregate index), slope and depth to ground water etc. as discussed below.

Soil Rating for Irrigation

Soil is a natural live system having unique profile morphology and therefore, any single soil variety or the group of different soil varieties would give different response to the different crops with or without irrigation water. The expected response would also be different under different set of agricultural and irrigation operations. The response criteria is influenced by the inherent soil characteristics or properties and can be considered collectively for the interpretation of their likely behaviour. This overall behaviour of soil for land use is done through rating of soils on quantitative basis by assigning values to each soil property and then pooling these for interpretation.

The various workers have provided different approaches as discussed below :

Marbut and Barnes Approach

This method takes into account statistical information on yield history. This is being used by soil survey division, Bureau of Plant, Soils and Agricultural Engineering and United States Department of Agriculture, in soil survey reports.

Sigmond Approach (1938)

He emphasised the rating classification based on total dissolved salts in soil and water being used.

Morgan Approach (1939)

In this method Morgan grouped soils into five categories based on the degree of adaptation of land types to various crops, pastures and forests.

Powers et al. (1948) Approach

He considered the rate of productivity of soil types by assigning a top mark of 10 to the best soils.

Storie Approach (1948 and 1959)

He devised a soil rating chart for California soils in which each soil property of a soil profile and land feature is assigned a percentage value in terms of its influence on land utilization and its productivity. This classification is given below.

The Storie Index*

This method of soil rating, known as the Storie Index, is based on soil characteristics that govern the land's potential utilization and productive capacity. It is independent of other physical or economic factors that might determine the desirability of growing certain plants in a given location.

Essentially the present revision sets up a new factor C to evaluate slope; the original factor C is now designated as factor X.

Percentage values are assigned to the characteristics of the soil itself, including the soil profile (factor A); the texture of the surface soil (factor B); the slope (factor C); and conditions of the soil exclusive of profile, surface texture, and slope *e.g.* drainage, alkali content, nutrient level, erosion, and micro-relief (factor X). The most favourable or ideal conditions with respect to each factor are rated at 100 per cent. The percentage values or ratings for the four factors are then multiplied, and the result being the Storie Index rating of the soil.

The characteristics of the soil profile (factor A) are essentially the features of the sub-surface layers. For California purposes the soils have been divided into nine profile groups. For example, soils that are deep and readily pervious to roots and water (listed in profile group I in the soil-rating chart) are rated at 100 per cent. Profiles with dense clay sub-soils (listed in profile group IV on the soil-rating chart) are rated lower. Primary or residual soils (listed in profile groups VII, VIII and IX) are rated in accordance with the depth to bedrock.

Further, the soils are rated on the basis of the texture of the surface soils (designated as factor B). Medium textured soils, such as the loams

---

*Storie, R. Earl, and Walter W. Weir, *Manual for Identifying and Classifying California Soil Series*, 1948, with Supplement, 1958. Published by Associated Students' Store, Univ. of Calif., Berkeley.

and the silt loams, are rated highest; the extremes in texture, such as sands and clays, are lower.

Rating of the slope of the land is considered in factor C. Nearly level or gently sloping land is rated at 100 per cent. As the slope increases, the rating for this factor decreases. As shown in the soil-rating chart, single letters are used to indicate simple slopes, and double letters to indicate compound slopes. The per cent slope expresses the number of feet rise or fall for 100 feet horizontal distance.

Conditions exclusive of profile, soil texture, and slope are considered in factor X on the soil-rating chart. These conditions consist of drainage, alkali or salt content, general nutrient level, acidity, erosion, and micro-relief (surface regularity).

If conditions exist that are listed under ratings for each are treated amity they are multiplied in order to secure rating.

Rating the Soil for a Tract

The index for each soil type is stated separately, and then a rating for that is obtained by weighing each soil index in proportion of the acreage of that soil. As an example, using the soil map on the rating of the tract is determined as follows :

1. Index for the area YI-A (Yolo loam). This is a recent alluvial soil, deep, drained.

Factor A : Yolo series, profile group I.

Factor B : loam texture....

Factor C : Slope A, nearly level....

Factor X : no other modifying factors.

Index rating= 100% x 100% x 100% x 100%.

2. Index for Ac-BB (Antioch clay loam). This is a claypan terrace soil with unduraphy.

Factor A : Antioch series, profile group IV.

Factor B : clay loam texture....

Factor C : undulating topography....

Factor X : no other modifying factors....

Index rating = 60% × 85% × 95% × 100%.

Soil Grading

For simplification, six soil grades have been California by combining soils having rare rating as follows :

Grade I (excellent) : Soils that rate between 100 per cent which are suitable for crops, including alfalfa, orchard, tree crops.

Grade 2 (good) : Soils that rate between 80 per cent which are suitable for most crops are generally good to excellent.

Grade 3 (fair) : Soils that rate between 40 per cent and are generally of fair quality wide range of suitability than grades 1 and 2.

Gardner Approach (1945)

It was suggested by Gardner that soil pH, electrical conductivity and permeability are important factors and should be included as the criteria for classification of land and irrigation water.

Harris Approach (1948)

Harris worked out a system similar to that of Storie for Arizona soils which also takes into account the effects of water and climate. These factors were designated as the 'Basic land values'.

Mehta et al. Approach (1958)

The land rating system proposed by Storie was simplified by Mehta *et al.* (1958) for the soils of Chambal Command area and that of western area of Rajasthan. In this different profile characteristics have been assigned definite marks which are totalled together as against multiplying the percentage values of each factor to arrive at rating index. The total marks for all the soil factors combined are 100 which have been divided as below for each factor considering its importance in affecting crop growth under irrigation. The allocation of marks for profile is as follows :

Texture of soil	=	20
Total soluble salts	=	25
Permeability	=	20
pH	=	15
Exchangeable sodium	=	10
Non-capillary porosity	=	10

SOIL-RATING CHART*

(Storie Soil Index rating = factor A × factor B × factor C × factor X)

FACTOR A — Rating on character of Physical Profile

	Per cent
I. Soils on recent alluvial fans, flood plains, or other secondary deposits having undeveloped profiles	100
X-shallow phases (on consolidated material), 2 feet deep	50-60
X-shallow phases (on consolidated material), 3 feet deep	70
g-extremely gravelly subsoils	80-95
S-stratified clay subsoils	80-95
II. Soils on young alluvial fans, flood plains, or other secondary deposits having slightly developed profiles	95-100
X-shallow phases (on consolidated material), 2 feet deep.	50-60
X-shallow phases (on consolidated material), 3 feet deep	70
g-extremely gravelly subsoils	80-95
S-stratified clay subsoils	80-95
III. Soils on older alluvial fans, alluvial plains, or terraces having moderately developed profiles (moderately dense subsoils)	80-95
X-shallow phases (on consolidated material), 2 feet deep	40-60
X-shallow phases (on consolidated material), 3 feet deep	60-70
g-extremely gravelly subsoils	60-90
IV. Soils on older plains or terraces having strongly developed profiles (dense clay subsoils)	40-80
V. Soils on older plains or terraces having hardpan subsoil layers	
at less than 1 foot	5-20
at 1 to 2 feet	20-30
at 2 to 3 feet	30-40
at 3 to 4 feet	40-50
at 4 to 6 feet	50-80

(Contd.)

Soil-Rating Chart (*Contd.*)

		Per cent
VI.	Soils on older terraces and upland areas having dense clay subsoils resting on moderately consolidated or consolidated material	40-80
VII.	Soils on upland areas underlain by hard igneous bedrock at less than 1 foot	10-30
	at 1 to 2 feet	30-50
	at 2 to 3 feet	0-70
	at 3 to 4 feet	70-80
	at 4 to 6 feet	80-100
	at more than 6 feet	100
VIII.	Soils on upland areas underlain by consolidated sedimentary rocks	
	at less than 1 foot	100
	at 1 to 2 feet	30-50
	at 2 to 3 feet	50-70
	at 3 to 4 feet	70-80
	at 4 to 6 feet	80-100
	at more than 6 feet	100
IX.	Soils on upland areas underlain by softly consolidated material	
	at 1 to 2 feet	40-60
	at 2 to 3 feet	60-80
	at 3 to 4 feet	80-90
	at 4 to 6 feet	90-100
	at more than 6 feet	100

FACTOR B— Rating on basis of Surface Texture	Per cent
Medium textured :	
very fine sandy loam	100
fine sandy loam	100
loam	100
silt loam	100
sandy loam	95
loamy fine sand	90
silty clay loam	90
clay loam	85
Heavy-textured :	
silty clay	60-70
clay	50-60
Light or coarse-textured :	
coarse sandy loam	70-90
loamy sand	80
very fine sand	80
fine sand	65
sand	60
coarse sand	30-60
Gravelly :	
gravelly fine sandy loam	70-80
gravelly loam	60-80
gravelly silt loam	60-80
gravelly sandy loam	50-70
gravelly clay loam	60-80

gravelly clay	40-70
gravelly sand	20-30
Stony :	
stony fine sandy loam	70-80
stony loam	60-80
stony silt loam	60-80
stony sandy loam	50-70
stony clay loan	50-80
stony clay	40-70
stony sand	10-40

FACTOR C –Rating on the basis of slope

A—Nearly level (0 to 2%)	100
AA—Gently undulating (0 to 2%)	95–100
B—Gently sloping (3 to 8%)	95–100
BB—Undulating (3 to 8%)	85–100
C—Moderately sloping (9 to 15%)	80–95
CC—Rolling (9 to 15%)	80–95
D—Strongly sloping (16 to 30%)	70–80
DD—Hilly (16 to 30%)	70–80
E—Steep (30 to 45%)	30–50
F—Very steep (45% and over)	5–30

FACTOR X–Rating on conditions other than those in factors A, B and C

Drainage :	
well-drained	100
fairly well drained	80-90
moderately waterlogged	40-80
badly waterlogged	40-80
subject to overflow	variable
Alkali :	
alkali-free	100
slightly affected	60-95
moderately affected	30-60
moderately to strongly affected	15-30
strongly affected	5-15
Nutrient (fertility) level :	
high	100
fair	80-90
poor	40-80
very poor	variable
Acidity according to degree	
Erosion :	
none to slight	100

(*Contd.*)

Soil-Rating Chart *(Contd.)*

	Per cent
detrimental deposition :	
moderate sheet erosion	80-90
occasional shallow gullies	70-80
moderate sheet erosion with shallow gullies	60-70
deep gulies :	
moderate sheet erosion with deep gullies	40-60
severe sheet erosion	30-40
severe sheet erosion with shallow gullies	20-30
severe sheet erosion with deep gullies	10-20
very severe erosion	variable
moderate wind erosion	80-90
severe wind erosion	40-90
Microrelief :	
smooth	100
channels	60-80
hogwallows	40-60
low hummocks	30-40
high hummocks	20-30
dunes	10-20

Per cent

3. Index for Acl-CC (clay loam)

This is a brown upland soil from shale part redrock at a depth of 3 feet. Rolling moderate sheet erosion, with occasional group.

Factor A : Medium fine black soils
Factor B : Clay loam texture
Factor C : Rolling topography
Factor X : Moderate sheet erosion
with shal gullies

Index rating = 70% × 85% × 90% × 70% = 37

4. The index for the entire tract shown may then be calculated according to the soil, as follows :

Loam	100 × 10
Clay loam (medium clay)	48 × 5.5
Clay loam (more clay)	37 × 4.5

Index rating for the tract . . . $= \frac{1.430}{20} = 71.5\%$

Another System for Juding irrigtability of soils is as under (Dastane, 1969)

TABLE 1.2 (A)

Other Limits and Rating of Different Characters in Evaluating of Land for Irrigation Commands

Description	A		B		C		D		E	
	Available water holding capacity (mm) of top one meter layer		Minimum permeability of water in root profile mm/Gr.		Permeability of water ripe after introduction of irrigation Depth of water table in meters		Maximum soluble salt content per cent in root profile		Maximum exchangeable Sodium percentage in root profile	
	Limit	Marks	Limit	Marks	Limit	Marks	Limit	Marks	Limit	Marks
Excellent	>175	3	16-25	3	Below 3	3	<0.20	3	<5	3
Good	101-175	2	11-15 or 26-50	2	Below 2	2	0.20-0.30	2	6-10	2
Fair	26-100	1	6-100R 51-125	1	Below 1	1	0.30 0.50	1	11-15	1
Poor	<25	0	25 or >125	0	within one	0	>0.50	0	>15	0

Grand Score = A × B × C × D × E

After the marks are allotted to any proposed command area to be brought under irrigation, and the grand score obtained by multiplication of the marks for all A, B, C, D and E soil properties, the land can be further classified for its suitability by the Table 1.2 (B).

TABLE 1.2 (B)

Showing Classification of Land for Irrigation

Classification of Land

Irrigability Class	Description	Grand Score
I	Excellent	above 80
II	Good	50-60
III	Fair	16-49
IV	Poor	2-15
V	Unsuitable	0-1

However, in case of rice crop, percolation forms a major part as large as 60 to 70 per cent of total water requirement. For rice, therefore, land should be selected on the basis of mean daily percolation values during the crop growing season [See Table 1.2 (C)].

TABLE 1.2 (C)

Showing Land Evaluation for Rice Culture

Class	Percolation mm/may
Excellent	1.0-2.5
Good	2.5-5.0
Marginal	5.0-7.5
Unsuitable	>7.5

This method has also been found to be realistic and superior to traditional methods.

These allocations for a soil profile were further sub-divided into surface, sub-surface and substratum. Separate marks have been allotted for every factor in each profile zone and then sum of all or average of each gives marks for individual property and after aggregating will give rating of the whole soil profile. In fixing marks for different layers on horizons of the soil profile for any particular factor the likely impact of each under irrigation has been considered. Accordingly the distribution of marks for some factors is uniform for all the layers while in others it is different for different horizons. In fixing standard for each factor, local experience of the area was taken into account. The marks allotted for each factor are given in Table 1.3.

TABLE 1.3

Showing Distribution of Marks for Different Soil-Profile Horizons

Soil Properties	Total marks	Surface soil	Sub-soil	Sub-stratum	Nature of variation
Soil texture	20	8	7	5	Addition
Total soluble salts	25	10	8	7	-do-
Permeability	20	-	13	7	-do-
pH	15	15	15	15	Average
Exchangeable Sodium	10	10	10	10	-do-
Non-capillary porosity	10	10	10	10	-do-

These soil properties have been further sub-divided based on their further categorisation as described below. However, the per cent of stones and gravels if present in soil more than 10 to 20 per cent by volume of soil would have detrimental effect on root space and water relation on the surface. Shaw (1952) pointed out that the strata of sand and gravel mainly affect the air water and nutrient supply of the soil. *Gravels when present in considerable quantity affect the texture of the soil with respect to its irrigation behaviour.* As such a deduction in marks for different layers from the marks allotted to respective textural classes are suggested as given in Table 1.4 (A).

TABLE 1.4 (A)

Distribution of Marks

Texture : Total marks = 20

Textural class	Surface soil (8)	Sub-soil (7)	Substratum (5)
Clay	6	3	2
Clay loam	7	4	3
Silty clay loam	8	7	4
Loam	8	7	5
Sandy clay loam	7	5	6
Sandy loam	5	5	4
Sandy	3	2	1

MAPPING SOIL BOUNDARIES AND PREPARATION OF SOIL MAPS

The soil boundaries are indicative of grouping similar soil mapping units into one group. In reconnaissance survey the soil boundaries indicate apparent change in ground features supplemented with the pre-informations of representative soil profiles examined at that spot or elsewhere. Sometimes the two profile characters representing two soil series are mixed closely and at a short interval grid than fixed for survey. These are grouped together and soil-association comprising two or three and named accordingly.

In semi-detailed the soil boundaries are also inferred from surface evidence and profile observations. However, in intensive detailed survey the boundaries are delineated through actual traversing. The difference on ground features at each grid fixed or even lesser are marked on map.

TABLE 1.4 (B)

Deduction for Gravel from Textural Marks

Gravel per cent	Surface soil	Sub-soil	Substratum
0-20	2	1	-
20-30	5	3	2
30-50	7	5	3
More than 50	8	7	3

TABLE 1.4 (C)

Permeability : Total Marks 20

Soil class	Percolation rate inches per hr.	Sub-surface	Substratum
Very slow	Less than 0.06	7	3
Slow	0.06-0.14	10	6
Moderate	0.18-0.60	13	7
Moderately rapid	0.60-1.00	13	7
Rapid	1.0-2.0	10	5
Very rapid	More than 2.0	7	5

TABLE 1.4 (D)

Soluble Salts : Total Marks : 25

Soluble salt Per cent	Surface' soil		Sub-soil		Substratum	
	Heavy tex.	Coarse tex.	Heavy tex.	Coarse tex.	Heavy tex.	Coarse tex.
Less than 0.15	10	—	8	—	7	—
0.15-0.2	8	10	6	8	6	7
0.2-0.3	8	8	6	6	4	4
0.3-0.4	5	5	5	5	5	5
0.4-0.5	4	4	4	4	4	4
More than 0.5	2	2	3	3	3	3

TABLE 1.4 (E)

Soil Reaction (p^H) : Total Mark 15

pH	Surface soil		Sub-soil		Substratum	
	Heavy tex.	Coarse tex.	Heavy tex.	Coarse tex.	Heavy tex.	Coarse tex.
Below 8.0	15	—	15	—	15	—
8.0-8.5	13	15	13	15	13	15
8.5-9.0	10	10	10	10	10	10
More than 9.0	5	5	5	5	5	5

TABLE 1.4 (F)

Non-capillary Porosity : Total Marks 10

Non-capillary porosity	Surface soil (10)	Sub-soil (10)	Substratum (10)
0-5	2	2	2
5-10	4	4	4
10-20	6	6	6
Above 20	10	10	10
Above 50% of total porosity	4	4	4

TABLE 1.4 (G)

Exchangeable Sodium : Total Marks, 10

Exchangeable Sodium Per cent	Surface soil (10)		Sub-surface (10)		Substratum (10)	
	Heavy tex.	Coarse tex.	Heavy tex.	Coarse tex.	Heavy tex.	Coarse tex.
Less than 10	10	—	10	—	10	—
10-15	8	10	8	10	8	10
Above 15	6	8	6	8	6	8

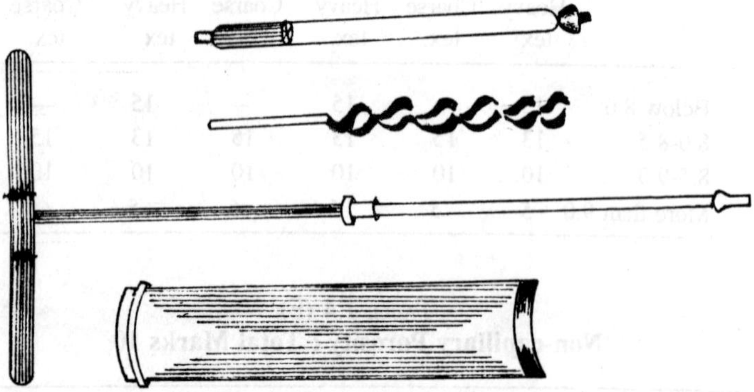

Fig.1.4 : Details of a Soil Probe with part of the tube cutaway for easier insertion inspection and removal. A screw type auger is also shown (Courtesy : OAK Field Apparatus Co.)

Fig.1.5 : Posthole auger. Augers of this type are often used for studying the distribution of Irrigation water in soil (Courtesy : Wan Brothers)

The difference or changes occurring in surface slope, erosion, vegetation and soil colour within a grid are sketched on the map to collect exact informations and from these boundary of variation in soil pattern is marked on the field. It is better to avoid interpolation between observations afterwards as that may provide biased interpretation.

The basis of intensive soil surveys is the occurrence of different soil characteristics in the control section of sub-surface depth ranging from 25-100 cms. Thus change in soil texture, colour, occurrence of carbonates, toughness of clays in sub-surface, structure change is the main basis of differentiation which may be reflected in this soil depth called control section. This depth also has been worked out on the occurrence of the parent material for example murrum layer in black soils. If this layer is below 90 cm to 1 metre the series unit is imposed to have full depth but if it is less than 1 metre than the notation 'p' is introduced in mapping unit and if parent material occurs in between 0 to 50 cm depth, it is marked 'p_1' and if between 50-100, it is marked as 'p_2', or the different series may be constituted if large area occurs in a given command or catchment.

In the beginning survey (when soil series is not standardised through soil correlation), the abbreviation 'A', 'B', 'C' for surface texture and 'a', 'b', 'c' for control texture are used for making soil mapping unit and depth is recorded as dn. However, it refers to depth notation 'd' as described below :

(i) At a depth less than 7.5 cm as d_1 = Very shallow

(ii) For depth between 7.5 - 22.5 cm as d_2 = Shallow

(iii) For depth between 22.5 - 445 cm as d_3 = Medium deep

(iv) For depth between 45 - 90 cms d_4 = Deep

(v) For depth between 90 cms & above as d_5 = Very deep

This differentiates the same textural class based on depth and separate mapping units are made. Similarly based on occurrence of carbonates, stonniness, consistance, structure ground slope and erosion, the different mapping units made are recorded on the map.

The representative soil profile (1 m x 1 m x 1.5 m) for each soil boundary should be opened up at appropriate location and examined for detailed morphological characteristics as given in proforma (Appendix). Near the profile site for each soil boundary specific soil tests *viz*. moisture content at field capacity by basin method, infiltration by double ring method should be conducted. Layerwise soil samples from profile should be collected to determine soil moisture content at permanent wilting point (PWP) by sunflower potted plants in the laboratory. The part of the samples be used for other analyses.

Interpretation

The data generated in soil survey should be interpretated to arrive at the following conclusions :

(1) Soil pattern *i.e.* soil and land irrigability classification (extent of irrigable area and their limitations).

(2) Drainage, saline, alkali and land development needs.

(3) Optimum water delivery frequency as decided from soil crop climate data.

(4) Suitable cropping pattern and crop classification.

(5) Design parameters for micro distribution system.

Soil and Land Irrigability Classifications

In any irrigation project, there are certain soil and land characteristics significant to the design and operation of irrigation system. Soil irrigability classification deals with evaluation of soils (Profile features) for their suitability to irrigation on the basis of quantitative limits of soil characteristics pertinent to irrigation. Land irrigability includes soil irrigable classes, topographic features (slope) and ground water position (depth to ground water table from surface) to decide overall suitability of land for sustained use under irrigation and to fix per cent perennials (x-limit) in the Command. Extent of irrigable area is also known from land irrigability classification. Soil survey reports should therefore, be

TABLE 1.5

Interpretation of Acreage Index

Overall aggregate index	Corresponding over all soil irrigability class	Meaning of corresponding soil irrigability class
5-4	A	None to slight soil limitations for sustained use under irrigation.
4-3	B	Moderate soil limitations for sustained use under irrigation.
3-2	C	Severe soil limitations for sustained use under irrigation
2-1	D	Very severe soil limitations for sustained use under irrigation
Less than 1	E	Not suitable for irrigation

TABLE 1.6
Case Study of Irrigability Class*

Soil Characteristics	Observed property	Soil irri-gable class	Points earned by irri-gable class	Credits or weight-age given	Total Points earned by soil property
Soil depth	more than 1 meter	A	5	5	5×5=25
Soil texture	Clay & silty clay	B	4	5	4×5=20
Soil structure	Angular blocky	B	4	3	4×3=12
Available water	200m/m	B	4	5	4×5=20
Infiltration rate	3cm/hr	A	5	4	5×4=20
Permeability	1 cm/hr	B	4	4	4×4=16
Salinity	ECe Millim phos/cm	A	5	3	5×3=15
Sodicity	ESP 10-14	A	5	3	5×3=15
Gravel	Nil	A	5	3	5×3=15
Total	—	—	—	35	158

∴ Total Points = 35

Aggregate Index = 158 ÷ 35 = 4.51

Hence, it is a class I or 'A' land. That means this land has none to slight limitations under irrigation (Table 5).

* It is a class I or A land that means no soil limitation for irrigation.

TABLE 1.7
Hypothetical Example to Calculate Aggregate Soil Irrigability Class

Soil characteristies	No. of credits allotted (B)	Observed soil property (C)	Irrigability class (D)	Points to irriga-ble (E)	Total points to each f=b X c
Effective soil depth	5	100 cm	A	5	25
Soil texture	5	Clayey	B	4	20
Soil structure	3	Massive sub-surface	E	1	3
Available water in effective soil depth	5	20cm	B	4	20
Basic infiltration rate	4	0.2cm/hr	D	2	8
Coarse fragments surface cover	3	Gravels 25%	B	4	12
Salinity	3	ECe=4.0 Millimpos cm	D	2	6
Sodicity	3	ESP=60	E	1	3
Total	35	...	...	...	101
Overall aggregate index	2.89	...	...	...	$\frac{101}{35} = 2.89$

interpreted for soil and land irrigability classification. These are also interpreted for fertility, fertilizer assessment, soil and water conservation, reclamation, restoration of waste land, ravines, degraded areas, recreation, wild life protection, urban development, waste disposal, town planning, tax assessment or mortgage of lands and flood controls etc.

TABLE 1.8

Modified Soil Irrigability Ratings (Palaskar and Varade 1985) for Different Soil Characteristics

Soil characteristic	Soil Rating Class				
	A	B	C	D	E
Effective soil depth	90cm very deep	45-90 cm deep	22.5-45 cm medium	7.5-22 cm shallow	7.5 cm very shallow
Soil texture group	Sil CI L	C, SIC, SC	SL.	L.S.	S.Si
Soil structure	Crumb Granular	Angular blocky S.An. blocky.	Platy	Columner prismatic	Massive single grain.
Av. Water capacity (AWP) in profile cm	21	21-14	14-7	7-2	2
Basic infiltration (Ib) rate (cm/hr)	0.7-3.5	3.5-6.5	6.5-12.5	0.3-0.7	12.5 or 0.3
Saturated hydraulic conductivity (cm/hr)	6-2	2-0.5	12.55-6.0	25-12.5 or 0.5-0.25	25 or 0.25
Salinity :					
(i) ECmmhos/cm of saturation extract	4.0	4-8	8-12	12-16	16
(ii) Per cent area effected (visual observations)	10	10-25	25-50	50-75	75
Soil Sodicity ESP	15	15-20	20-30	30-40	40
Surface covers :					
(a) Gravels 0.2 cm to 0.75 cm dia. by volume	15	15-35	35-50	50-70	70
(b) Rock out crops distance in meters	40	20-40	18-20	5-15	5
Erosion	Slight	Moderate	Medium gullies	Big gullies	Ratio

The design and operation of any irrigation system is dependent on certain soil and land characteristics. For irrigation projects, the prior study of representative soil profiles is essentially made to evaluate the response of soils under irrigation system. Based on these soil and land features, soil irrigability classification is worked out this evaluation provides the quantitative limits of soil nature in the forth coming irrigated areas. Suitability to irrigation and proposed cropping patterns in the soils of the areas would decide the economic and technical feasibility of the proposed irrigation project.

Land irrigability considers soil irrigable classes, topographic/ physiographic features *e.g.*, slope and ground water conditions *i.e.*, ground water table depth from the rootzone and soil surface. These factors decide overall suitability of land or its response, for attaining the sustained agricultural production when the area soils are brought under irrigation. This leads to fix percentage of perennials (limit) in the irrigated command. These studies help to assess the extent of irrigable area as well as area to be reserved for wild life, afforestation and recreation etc.

Detailed, Soil survey is conducted on the 16"=1 mile maps and soil boundaries are mapped. Based on these soil irrigable classes are worked out and mapped. The water distribution net work is accordingly designed to avoid deleterious effects of irrigation in near future.

Soil Irrigability Classification

There are five soil irrigability classes [Table 1.8(A)] which are important for soil evaluation studies under the flow irrigation and aerable cropping. These are described under the following table 1.8(A). The 6th one considered to be totally unsuitable for irrigation.

TABLE 1.8(A)

Soil Irrigable Class	Meaning
A	None to slight soil limitations for sustained use under irrigation.
B	Moderate soil limitations for sustained use under irrigation.
C	Severe soil limitations for sustained use under irrigation.
D	Very severe soil limitations for sustained use under irrigation.
E	Temporarily unsuitable for irrigation

The soil irrigable classes referred above are decided on the basis of criteria given in Table 1.8(B). The information furnished in this table is the modification proposed by Palaskar and Varade (1985) over the original criteria suggested by Rege, et al. (1974).

TABLE 1.8(B)

Modified Soil Irrigability Ratings for Different Soil Characteristics (Palaskar and Varade, 1985)

Soil Characteristics	Soil Irrigability Class				
	A	B	C	D	E
Effective Soil Depth (cm.)	>90 Very deep	45-90 deep	22.5-45 medium	7.5-22.5 shallow	<7.5 Very shallow
Soil Textural Group	Sil, CL L	C,SIC SC	SL	LS	S.SI.
Soil Structure	Crumb Granular	Angular blocky Sub-angular blocky	Platy	Columner, Prismatic	Massive, Single-grained
Available Water Capacity in effective profile depth (cm)	>21	21-14	14-7	7-2	<2
Basic infiltration rate (cm./hr.)	0.7-3.5	3.5-6.5	6.5-12.5	0.3-0.7	>12.5 <0.3
Saturated hydraulic conductivity (cm./hr.)	6-2	2-0.5	12.5-6	25-12.5 or 0.5-0.25	>25 or <0.25
Salinity :					
(i) EC, mmhos/cm. at 25°C of saturation extract	<4	4-8	8-12	12-16	>16
(ii) % area affected (Visual observations)	<10	10-25	25-50	50-75	>75
Soil sodicity (ESP)	<15	15-20	20-30	30-40	>40

(Contd.)

TABLE 1.8(B) (*Contd.*)

Soil Characteristics	Soil Irrigability Class				
	A	B	C	D	E
Surface covers :					
(a) Gravels (0.2 cm. to 7.5 cm. dia) % by Vol.	<15	15-35	35-55	50-70	>70
(b) Rock out-crops Dist. in meters	>40	20-40	15-20	5-15	<5
Erosion	Slight	Moderate	Medium gullies	Big gullies	Ravines

SIL = Silt loam, CL = Clay loam, L = Loam, C = Clay, SC = Sandy Clay, SIC = Silty Clay SL = Sandy loam, LS = Loamy Sand, S = Sandy, SI = Silt, ESP = Exchangeable Sodium Percentage.

Aggregate Soil Irrigability class is worked out as per the procedure explained in Table for a typical example and the aggregate. Soil Irrigability Index is interpreted from the information given in Table 1.8(C).

TABLE 1.8(C)

Typical Example to Determine Aggregate Soil Irrigability Class

Soil Characteritics	No. of credits allotted	Observed Soil property	Irriga-bility rating as per the modified criteria : Table1. 8(A)	Points allotted to irrigable class	Total points earned by respective soil chara-cteristics
(1)	(2)	(3)	(4)	(5)	(6)
Effective soil depth	5	100 cm	A	5	25
Soil texture	5	Clayey	B	4	20
Soil structure	3	Massive (Sub-surface)	E	1	3
Available water in effective soil depth	5	20 cm	B	4	20
Infiltration rate (Basic)	4	0.2 cm/hr	E	1	4
Saturated hydraulic conductivity	4	0.3 cm/hr	D	2	8
Coarse fragments or surface covers	3	Gravels, 25%	B	4	12

(*Contd.*)

TABLE 1.8(C) (*Contd.*)

(1)	(2)	(3)	(4)	(5)	(6)
Salinity	3	EC_e = 14 mmhos/cm	D	2	6
Sodicity	3	ESP = 60	E	1	3
Total	35		—	—	101
Overall (or Aggregate) index		2.89			$\frac{101}{35}$
Aggregate soil irrigability class, as decided from	—	—	C	—	
Table 1.8(C), using value 2.89			(Severe Soil Limitations for sustained use under irrigation)		

The project therefore, needs very careful implementation to achieve sustained crop production in long run.

TABLE 1.8(D)
Interpretation of Aggregate Index

Overall or Aggregate index	Corresponding overall soil irrigability class	Meaning of corresponding soil irrigability class
5-4	A	None to slight soil limitations for sustained use under irrigation.
4-3	B	Moderate soil limitations for sustained use under irrigation.
3-2	C	Severe soil limitations for sustained use under irrigation.
2-1	D	Very severe soil limitations for sustained use under irrigation.
Less than 1	E	Not suitable for irrigation.

Example :

Soil Irrigability Class of Irrigation Project

Soil Characteristics	Observed Property	Soil irrigability class	Points earned by irrigable class	Weightage given (Credits)	Total points earned by soil property
(1)	(2)	(3)	(4)	(5)	(6)
Soil depth	More than 1 m	A	5	5	25
Soil texture	Silty clay & clay	B	4	5	20
Soil structure	Angular blocky	B	4	3	12
Available water in effective profile depth	200 mm	B	4	5	20
Infiltration rate	3 cm/hr	A	5	4	20
Permeability (Conductivity)	1 cm/hr	B	4	4	16
Salinity	ECe = 1 mmhos/cm	A	5	3	15
Sodicity	ESP = 10-14	A	5	3	15
Gravels	NIL	A	5	3	15
Total :		—	—	35	158

$$\text{Aggregate irrigability index} = \frac{\text{Points earned}}{\text{Total points}} = \frac{158}{35} = 4.51$$

Aggregate irrigability class = A, meaning no soil limitations for irrigation.

Land Irrigability Classification

Six Land Irrigability classes are recognised which are decided on the basis of soil irrigable class, land slope and ground water position as per the criteria mentioned in Table 8(E). The definition of these six land irrigability classes is as follows :

Land Irrigability Class	Meaning
I	Land with no limitation.
II	Land with moderate limitations.
III	Land with severe limitations.
IV	Land with very severe limitations.
V	Temporarily unsuitable land.
VI	Land unsuitable for irrigation.

TABLE 1.8(E)

Criteria for Land Irrigability Classification

Characteristics	Land Classes					
	I	II	III	IV	V	VI
Soil Irrigability Class (Aggregate)	A	A or B	A or B or C	A or B or C or D	Temporary field needs investigation	E
Land slope (%)	Less than 1	1-3	3-5	5-10	10-15	More than 15
Depth of Ground-water table from G.L.	More than 3 m	2-3 m	2-1 m	Less than 1 m	—	—

Example :

(1) Soil Irrigability Class = A

(2) Land slope = 1.3%

(3) Ground Water depth = 5 m.

∴ Land Irrigability Class is II.

The 'X' limit (per cent area under perennials) is decided on the basis of Land Irrigability Classes. The 'X' limits are stated below :

Land Irrigability Class	'X' Limit
I	12-15%
II	9-12%
III	6-9%
IV	3-6%

Source :

Palaskar, M.S. and Varade, S.B. (1985), Suggested Modification in Soil Irrigability Classification, J. Maharashtra Agricultural Universities (Accepted).

Rege, N.D., Bali, Y.P. and Karale, R.L. (1974), Soil and Land Characteristics, their interpretation for Irrigability Classification, Soil Conservation Division, Ministry of Agriculture, New Delhi.

Special Course on Diagnostic Analysis (1985) DA Concepts and Techniques WALMI, Aurangabad (India).

Some Important Calculations for Irrigation Planning

1. Wt. of acre furrow slice lbs.

W = Wt of a cu.ft. of soil x 43560 x 6.67

(BDX Wt of 1 cuft H_2O) (62.4) (No.of sq.ft. per acres (Depth of furrow slice)

---

12 (Depth of Cu.ft. in inches)

Say BD = 1:32

$$W = \frac{1.32 \times 62.4 \times 43560 \times 6.67}{12}$$

2. To convert Lbs/cubic foot (surface) to inches of available water :

   Wt. of one cu.ft. of water ÷ 12 or 62.4 ÷ 12 = 5.2 inches of equivalent surface water.

3. One per cent of Org. matter in a soil = 0.8 lbs in a cu.ft. of silt loam soil

   Suppose Org. matter hold twice its weight as H_2O (water).

   Then 1% O.M. = (0.8 × 2) – 5.2 = 0.3 inches of water holding capacity per foot depth of soil.

4. 10 tons of manure = 5000 lbs of dry matter.

*The manure would hold twice its dry weight as water and increase W.H.C. of an acre furrow slice by 10000 – (5.2) c 43560 = 0.014 inches of water and only 50% of it is available. Thus addition of organic matter @ given above would hold 0.04 – 2 = 0.02" of H_2O which is negligible for conservation of moisture void ratio is increased

5. (A) *Type One Soil*

Suppose for any soil – Infiltration Rate = 0.25 inch/hr

Hence this soil would require a 2 inch rainfall to fall slowly over an 8 hour period if no run-off is to occur.

Or,

* 1 × 2 =2" water can be absorbed in 2 hours and if rainfall is also 2" in 2 hours, the run-off is NIL.

TABLE 1.9

Land Classification Specifications

Characteristics	Class 1-Arable	Class 2-Arable	Class3-Arable	Class : 4 F- Limited Arable	Class : 5- Limited Arable	Class : 6- Nonarable
SOIL						
Texture of surface (25 to 30 cms)	Sandy loam to to very Perme-able clay	Loamy sand to Permeable clay	Loamy sand to Permeable clay	Sandy loam slowly perme-able clay	Loamy sand slowly perme-able clay	Includes lands which do not meet the mini-mum requirements for other land classes and are not suitable for irrigation.
Sand gravel, able	36" plus-good friable soil of fine sandy loam to clay loam or 42" of sandy loam to sandy loam	24" plus-good friable soil of fine sandy loam or heavier or 30" of sandy loam to loam sand	78" plus good friable soil of fine sandy loam or heavier of 24" of lighter texture soil	None present	None present	This include lands having depth V. shallow to shallow, hardpan or sand, very gravelly, Kankar soil off the rivers banks, old channels not in use or to correction

						steepy slopes, and rocky lands or having an inadequate drain-age, not susceptible to delivery of irriga-tion water or desert sands or sand dunes, or coastal, severely salt affected, marshy or coastal mangroves or pasture land use.
Hardpan or rock	None	48" or deeper	36" plus	Not less than 30"	Not less than 18"	
Alkalinity	pH less than 8.3	pH less than 9.0	pH less than 9.0 in surface pH less than 9.5 in sub-soil	pH less than 9.0 pH less than 9.0	pH less than 9.0" surface pH less than 9.5"	
Salinity	Total salts do not exceed 0.2%	Total salts do not exceed 0.5%	Total salt do not exceed 0.5%	Total salts do not exceed 0.5%	Salts do sub-soil Total not exceed 10%	

TOPOGRAPHY

Relief	Smooth slopes upto 2% in general gradient in reasonable, large sized bodies sloping in the same plane	Smooth slopes up to 5% general gradient in reasonably large sized bodies sloping in the same plane or rougher slopes which are less than 4% in general gradient.	Smooth slopes upto 10% in general gradient in reasonably large sized bodies sloping in the same plane or rougher slope which are less than 8% in general gradient.	Rolling topography with slope 8 to 20% in general gradient suited generally only for sprinkler or pre-sprinkler system.	Nearly flat, mainly used to grazing or "Irrigated pasture."

MAP LEGENDS COLOURS FOR IRRIGABILITY OR LAND CAPABILITY

Class		Colour	Use
Class I	—	Light Green	Irrigable capability maps.
Class II	—	Yellow	
Class III	—	Red	
Class IV	—	Blue	
Class V	—	Dark Green	
Class VI	—	Orange	Only used in land capability maps.
Class VII	—	Brown	
Class VIII	—	Purple	

TABLE 1.10

Water Quality Rating as Proposed by Workers in India

(Pai and Mukkeri, 1979)

Nature of soil	Crops to be grown	Upper permissible safe limit of Ec of water for irrigation micromphos/cm.
Deep black soils and alluvial soils having clay content more than 30% fairly to well drained	Semi-tolerant crops Tolerant crops	1500 2000
Soils having clay content ranging from 20-30% internally well drained & good surface-drainage	Semi-tolerant crops Tolerant crops	2000 4000
Soils with 10-20% clay, internally well drained and good surface drainage	Semi-tolerant crops Tolerant crops	4000 6000
Soil with clay content less than 10% excellent internal and surface drainage	Tolerant crops	8000

If 2 inch rainfall occurs in 2 hours there would be absorption of water @ 0.25 inch/hr only 2 × 0.25 inch of water = 0.5"/hr.

i.e. Out of 2" only 0.5" is used, rest goes as run-off

Therefore, only 25% used, 75% wasted.

(B) *Type Two Soil*

I Rate = 1 inch/hour

Rainfall = 2" in 2 hours on the same day

6. *Mulches*

The mulch @ 1 to 3 tons/acre are effective for moisture conservation.

TABLE 1.11

Guide to Map Scale

Scale	Feet per inch	Inches per 1000 feet	Inches per mile	Miles per inch	Metres per inch	Acres per square inch	Square inches per acre	Square miles per square inch
1:500	41.67	24.00	126.72	0.008	12.70	0.040	25.091	0.00006
1:600	50.00	20.00	105.60	0.009	15.24	0.057	17.424	0.00009
1:1000	83.33	12.00	63.36	0.016	25.40	0.159	6.273	0.00025
1:1200	100.00	10.00	52.80	0.019	30.48	0.230	4.356	0.00036
1:1500	125.00	8.00	42.24	0.024	38.10	0.359	2.788	0.00056
1:2000	166.67	6.00	31.68	0.032	50.80	0.638	1.568	0.00100
1:2400	200.00	5.00	26.40	0.038	60.96	0.918	1.089	0.0014
1:2500	208.33	4.80	25.34	0.039	63.50	0.996	1.004	0.0016
1:3000	250.00	4.00	21.12	0.047	76.20	1.435	0.697	0.0022
1:4000	333.33	3.00	15.84	0.063	101.60	2.551	0.392	0.0040
1:5000	416.67	2.40	12.67	0.079	127.00	3.986	0.251	0.0062
1:6000	500.00	2.00	10.56	0.095	152.40	5.739	0.174	0.0090
1:7920	560.00	1.515	8.00	0.125	201.17	10.000	0.100	0.0156
1:8000	666.67	1.500	7.92	0.126	203.20	10.203	0.098	0.0159
1:9600	800.00	1.250	6.60	0.152	243.84	14.692	0.068	0.0230
1:10000	833.33	1.200	6.336	0.158	254.00	15.942	0.063	0.0249
1:12000	1000.00	1.000	5.280	0.189	304.80	22.957	0.044	0.0359
1:15000	1250.00	0.800	4.224	0.237	381.00	35.870	0.028	0.0560

1:15840	1320.00	0.758	4.000	0.250	402.34	40.000	0.025	0.0625
1:19200	1600.00	0.625	3.300	..	487.08	58.770	0.017	0.0918
1:20000	1666.67	0.600	3.168	..	408.00	63.769	0.016	0.0996
1:20120	1760.00	0.568	3.000	- -	530.45	71.111	0.014	0.1111
1:24000	2000.00	0.504	2.640	- -	609.00	91.827	.0111	0.1435
1:25000	2083.33	0.480	2.534	..	625.00	99.639	0.010	0.1557
1:31680	2640.00	0.379	2.000	..	604.07	160.00	0.006	0.2500
1:48000	4000.00	0.250	1.320	0.758	1219.20	367.309	0.003	0.5739
1:62500	5206.33	0.192	1.014	0.986	1587.50	622.744	0.0016	0.9730
1:63360	5260.00	0.189	1.000	1.000	1609.35	640.00	0.0016	1.00
1:00000	8333.33	0.120	0.634	1.578	2540.00	1594.225	0.0006	2.49
1:125000	10416.67	0.090	0.507	1.973	3175.01	2490.980	0.0004	3.89
1:126720	10560.00	0.095	0.500	2.000	3218.69	2560.000	0.0004	4.00
1:250000	20833.33	0.048	0.253	3.346	6150.01	9963.907	0.0001	15.57
1:253440	21120.00	0.047	0.250	4.000	6437.39	10244.202	0.0001	16.00
1:500000	41666.67	0.024	0.127	7.01	12700.02	39855.627	$\frac{0.4}{25}$	62.27
1:750000	62500.00	0.016	0.084	17.837	19050.04	89675.161	$\frac{0.4}{11}$	140.12
1:1000000	83333.33	0.012	0.063	12.783	25400.05	159422.507	$\frac{0.5}{62}$	249.10
Formulae	$\frac{\text{Scale}}{12}$	$\frac{12000}{\text{Scale}}$	$\frac{63360}{\text{Scale}}$	$\frac{\text{Scale}}{63,360}$	$\frac{\text{Feet per inch}}{0.3048006}$	$\frac{(\text{Scale})^2}{43560 \times 144}$	$\frac{4560 \times 144}{(\text{Scale})^2}$	$\frac{(\text{Feet per inch})^2}{(5280)^2}$

7. A level terrace 18 inches high can hold water back for a width of 300 ft on the 0.5% slope.

A terrace on a 6% slope with 18" of affective height can hold water back over an area of only 25 ft. width (*i.e.* 0.6%/0.5%)

12 times less width than 0.5% slope

$$\frac{300}{12} = 25$$

NOTE

For interest of readers detailed land classification is given in Table 1.9 and water quality rating in Table 1.10. It is also felt that for soil surveyors or those who work with maps, guide conversion scale may be useful as given in Table 1.11.

The few practical examples given in this chapter may be found useful during field working and planning.

CHAPTER 2

SURFACE WATER HYDROLOGY

STREAM DISCHARGE MEASURING

The different stream gauging methods have been employed to estimate the stream discharge in running canals, distributaries and minors etc. These are discussed below.

Area-Velocity Method

The flow rate (Q) through any conveying system/area is a product of mean velocity (V mean) of flow in a direction of the area (A). Thus

$$Q = AV \text{ mean}$$

If the total area of flow 'A' which is a sum total of small divided areas as shown in figure is multiplied with mean velocity (V mean) in that cross-section the above relationship may be expressed as :

$$Q = A_1V_1 \times A_2V_2......A_nV_n$$

where

n = number of small areas

$A_1....A_n$ = area of the small areas

$V_1...V_n$ = Mean velocity of flow in these small areas.

Area Computation

The individual and cumulative area estimation is done from the chart made for the area under flow section for the various points such as x_0, 0; x_1, y_1, x_2y_2,....x_6, 0 on the channel's perimeter may be determined from a given point on the surface of the stream in the direction normal to the flow direction. By assessing the stream perimeter across the flow the area of flow section *i.e.* A_1, A_2, A_3....A_6....in respect of a particular water level surface can be determined by any of standard method such as by graph, Simpson's rule or trapezoidal rule or by a planimeter. In case the depth distance is small (x_o, x_1, x_2..x_6), *e.g.* small minors, water courses etc., having small streams, the simplest field method by using a measuring tape held at 90° angle to the bank of conveyance system *i.e.* canal etc. The depths y_0, y_1, y_2 ...0 which may be measured from the water surface to the bed by knowing the corresponding points (plumbed from the tape) on the surface of water by means of sounding by a rod, pole or tape with some weight the end. In case of large streams and deep depths boats are used for sounding.

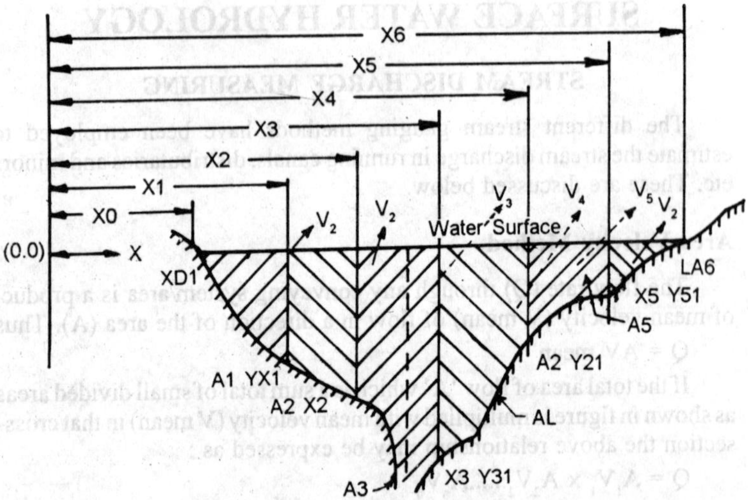

Fig. 2.1 : Cross Section of a Stream Indicating Mean Velocity of Flow in different zones

Mean Velocity Assessment : This is done by measuring velocity at different points along with depth lying half way between the boundaries of the respective areas (*e.g.* along the line xy for the area as given in Figure 2.1). The different longitudinal velocities (a_1 a_2 a_3...) as determined at various points (o_1, o_2, o_3 etc.) on axis xy may be plotted and joined by a smooth curve (dotted) ABY (Velocity at Y = 0 as it lies on a stationary bed). The mean velocity of flow V_3 is given by the width of an equivalent rectangle XYCD which has same area as that of ABYX. The velocity at point B is the same as the mean velocity V_3. The actual velocity is equal to about its mean value at 0.6 depth (XY) measured below the surface. The value of velocity in A_3 section at 0.6 depth would be (x_2y_2) mean velocity. This statement holds good provided the stream is regular and has smooth flow. In some case the velocity at 0.6 & 0.8 depths are recorded and average of these two velocities is considered as mean velocity *i.e.* $V_3 = \frac{1}{2}(\mu\, 0.6 + \mu\, 0.8)$. Thus mean velocity for each divided section/areas at mid-vertical section (xy) can be determined and total is computed for the entire system, as

$$Q = (A_1V_1 + A_2V_2 + \text{- - - - - - - - - - - - - - - -} + A_6V_6)$$

In case the area is large the mean velocity for which is required to be computed than the Isovel lines (the line representing the points of the same velocity in the area) may be drawn from the velocity measurements at different locations/points on the grid (of suitable interval) by direct interpolation. This is done just as contours are plotted by indirect method except that like RL values, velocity values are taken in Isovels. In Fig. 2.3 the Isovel lines for three velocities *viz.* 0.5, 1.0 and 1.5 m sec are drawn. The boundaries (annular area) of each Isovel bed line has 'O' value. These can be measured graphically or by planimeter. The total discharge through the channel section can be estimated by adding the discharge which passes through each annular area. Thus:

$$Q = \left[A_1 (1.5 + A_2 \frac{(1.5 + 1.0)}{2} + A_3 \frac{(1.0 + .5)}{2} + A_4 \frac{(0.5 + 0.0)}{2}\right]$$

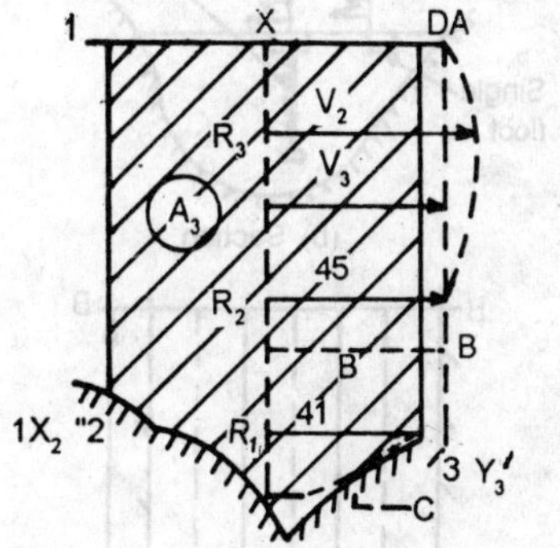

Fig. 2.2 : Distribution of longitudinal velocity along depth (XY)

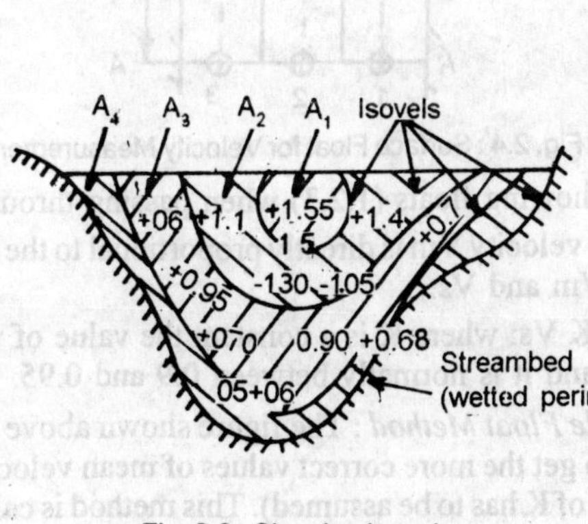

Fig. 2.3 : Showing Isovels

Velocity Measurement Methods

The measurement of velocity required for above procedure involves the measurement of longitudinal velocities at different points in the flow direction. The same may be determined by any of the methods given below :

(i) *Surface Float Method* : In this method a cross section in a channel or minor or canal system is first fixed up in between which velocity is to be determined as shown in Fig. 2.4 Considering only one float swimming across stream. At the time of start or passing of any float a stop watch may be started and stopped as soon as floats reach point or section marked or fixed as BB section. Say distance travelled by float between section AA and BB (L) in time t. Then surface velocity (V_s) is given by $V_s = \frac{L}{T}$.

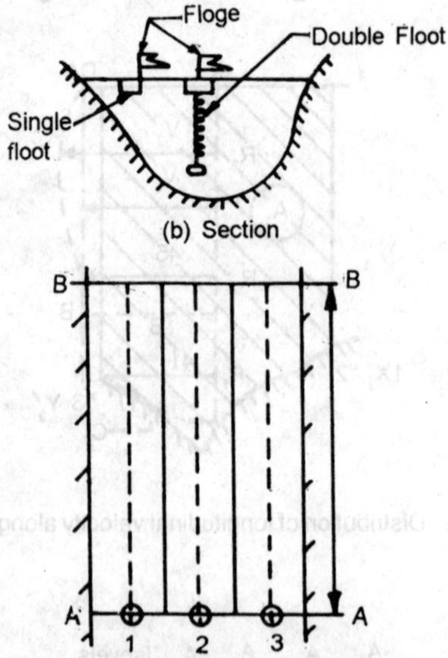

Fig. 2.4 : Surface Float for Velocity Measurement

Fig. 2.4 showing floats (1,2,3) when passing through Section AA.

The mean velocity Vm is directly proportional to the surface velocity Vs and thus Vm and Vs.

or Vm = K Vs: where K is a constant the value of which is always less than 1.0 and it is normally between 0.9 and 0.95.

(ii) *Double Float Method* : The figure shown above depicts 3 floats. This is done to get the more correct values of mean velocity (as by single float the value of K has to be assumed). This method is called double float or velocity rods method. These assemblies are designed in such a way that the distance between the top and the bottom parts adjust the movement which is nearly equal to the mean velocity of flow as determined by single float method.

Current Meters Methods

This method is an accurate and easier one to measure the flow velocity of the steams. The current meters are manufactured in two types namely :

(a) *Pygmy meters* : These are also called as price type or cup type. In this type the cups or bucket wheels attached to a shaft starts rotating as soon as dipped in the stream or flowing water. The axis of the plane or rotation is kept normal to the surface of water. The head-phone is

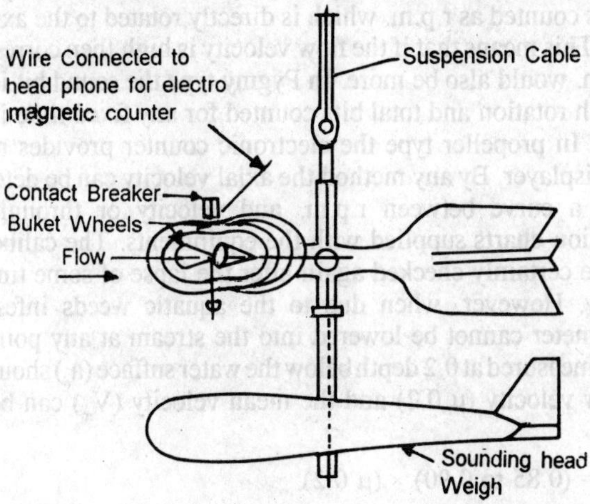

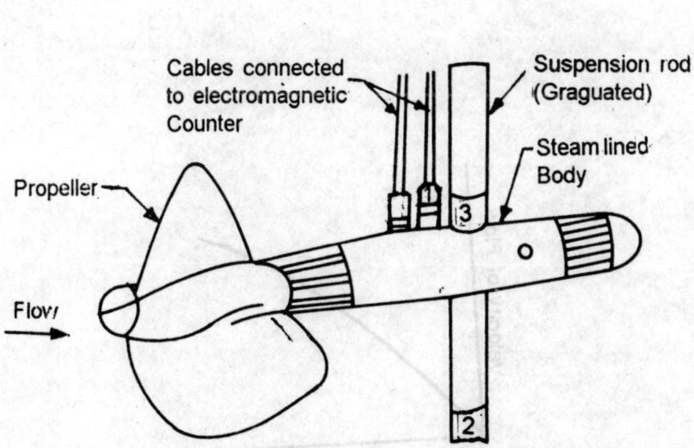

Fig. 2.5 : Showing a Pygmy Type and Propeller Type Current Meters.

attached by a wire for listening the contact sound with the help of electromagnetic counter. The contact breaker rod is also attached at the junction of the counter. The back end of bucket wheels is a tail shaped piece. This entire arrangement is supported on a rod to which suspension cable is attached which passes through an adapter at central portion of the meter. At base a sounding lead weight is also provided.

(b) *Propeller Type* : In this model the propeller is rotated by the flowing water with the mounting axis. The blades are kept rotated parallel to the direction of flow of water. The streamlined body supporting propellers at front has cables connected to the electromagnetic counter near the graduated suspension rod.

The movement of either cups or propeller in each model provides the rotations counted as r.p.m. which is directly rotated to the axial velocity of flow. This means that if the flow velocity is high then correspondingly the r.p.m. would also be more. In Pygmy type the sound bit is produced after each rotation and total bits counted for any fixed time interval are counted. In propeller type the electronic counter provides r.p.m. on a digital displayer. By any method the axial velocity can be determined by plotting a curve between r.p.m. and velocity or through standard caliberation charts supplied with the equipments. The caliberations or curves be certainly checked again after the lapse of some time interval regularly. However, when due to the aquatic weeds infestation the current meter cannot be lowered into the stream at any point then the velocity measured at 0.2 depth below the water sufface (a_o) should be taken as a flow velocity (μ 0.2) and the mean velocity (V_m) can be found as under :

$$V_m = (0.85 \text{ to } 0.90) \times (\mu\ 0.2)$$

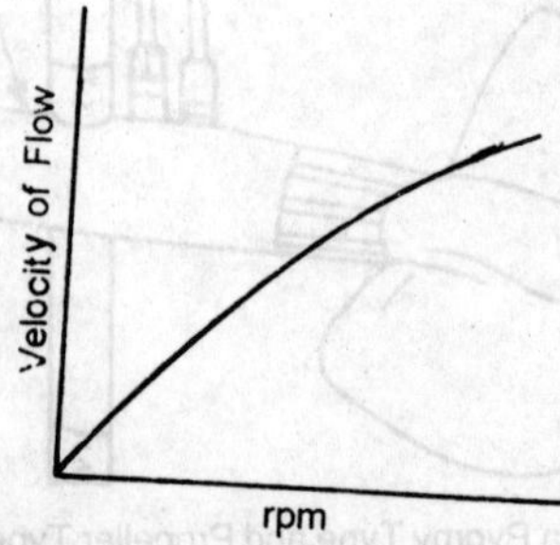

Fig. 2.6 : Caliberation Curve for a Current Meter

WATER LEVEL AND DISCHARGE RELATIONSHIP

The level of water in a flowing stream has a direct relationship with the quantum of flow. Thus lower the water level indicates lower quantity of water flowing through an outlet or a section of flowing water resources (canal or river) and higher level would discharge more water quantity. This relationship therefore, would be changed at the different stages of a flowing water due to variation in heat at different locations. If the readings of flow rate 'Q' is plotted against the water surface elevations (levels), a graphic relationship can be got. The discharge at various locations can be estimated by area-velocity method as outlined earlier and the measured values may be plotted as depicted in Fig. 2.8. From this graph the discharge 'Q', at any cross section (stage) 'X' of the stream can be worked out. The new relationship has to be regularly plotted after a lapse of some time because the variation in the section of channel may occur due to silting erosion of sides and bed along with other factors.

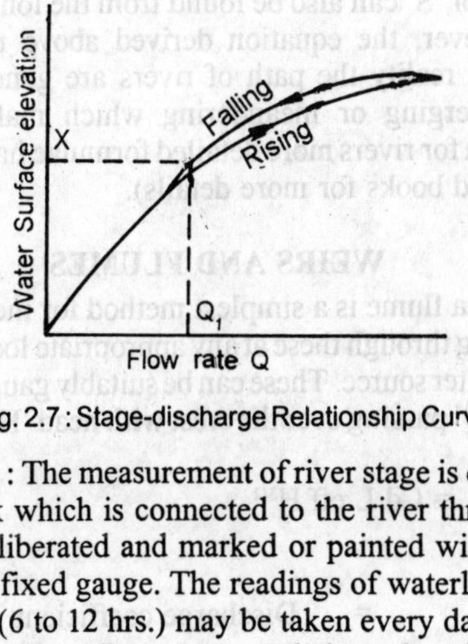

Fig. 2.7 : Stage-discharge Relationship Curve

River Gauges : The measurement of river stage is done by providing a well at the bank which is connected to the river through a pipe. The well sides are caliberated and marked or painted with standard scales which works as a fixed gauge. The readings of waterlevel in the well at the fixed interval (6 to 12 hrs.) may be taken every day either manually or mechanically with a float connected through a lever to a pointer (automatic gauge).

Stage-Fall Discharge Relationship

The rate of flow (Q) in cumecs (cubic meters per second) in a stream having a steady and uniform flow in a given section (L) can be given by Manning's equation :

$$Q = K/S$$

where K = conveyance and is equal to $1/n\ AR^{2/3}$

A = Area of flow section in square meters (m^2)

R = Hydraulic mean depth in meter and corresponds to A/P (P = wetted perimeter in meters)

n = Manning's roughness coefficient the value of which in hilly and rocky rough terrain ranges from 0.2 to 0.02 for flow through rocky rough area or alluvial bed respectively (consult standard books for all values).

S = longitudinal slope which can be determined by taking the values of the river stage at either end of the reach. However, if the flow is uniform, bed level slope and water surface slope are assumed to be equal. If E_1 and E_2 are the RL elevations of the water surface Q at the ends of the reach of length L then :

$$S = (E_1 - E_2)/L$$

The values of 'S' can also be found from the longitudinal section of river bed. However, the equation derived above represents an ideal condition but in reality the path of rivers are generally irregular *i.e.* contracting, diverging or meandering which makes the flow non-uniform. As such for rivers more detailed formulae have been worked out (consult Standard books for more details).

WEIRS AND FLUMES

The weir or a flume is a simplest method for measuring the stream discharge passing through these at any appropriate location in the section of the flowing water source. These can be suitably gauged after designing. The discharge 'Q' passing over the crest with head 'H' (in meter) is given by :

$$Q\ (\text{cumecs}) = Cd\ L\ eff\ H^{3/2}$$

Where

Cd = Discharge coefficient

L eff = Effective length of water way (total length of clear way minus the end contraction)

L eff = Bo - nt - 2 (nKp + Ka) H

Bo = Distance between the faces of two abutments

n = Number of piers

t = Thickness of each pier in meters

KP and KA = Coefficient of end contractions for piers and abutments respectively and found from geometry of pier as given below :

Va=Q'/B1) (P+h)

where Q' = Cd L eff $h^{3/2}$ (If Va/2g = 0, then Q' = Q)

Find H = (h + $Va^2/2g$) and Q = Cd L eff $H^{3/2}$

P = Height of weir above bed, B_1 = width of stream upstream.

DISCHARGE COEFFICIENTS (D.C.)

In case of weir or flume equation for measuring discharge except the values of discharge coefficient say 'Cd' other values are known. In weirs or flumes equations the dimensions of discharge coefficient are $m^{1/2}$/sec. The values of D.C. has a relationship with submergence ratio (S) and is given by S = h_2/h_1. The values of D.C. for free flow and different geometries of weirs and flumes are given in Table 2.1. The function of weir and flume is said to be free if 'S' actual submergence 'S' does not exceed a critical value say 'Scr'. If S > Scr it is submerged.

The coefficient of discharge when weir is submerged depends upon the extent of submergence beyond critical limit (Scr). This is also called as the modular limit.

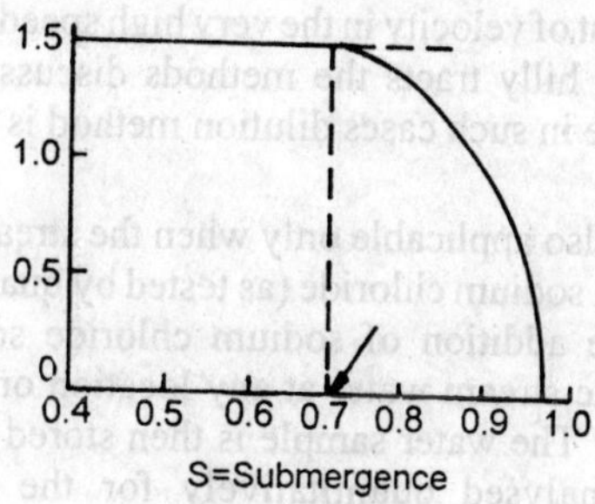

Fig. 2.8 : Showing Changes in Values of Cd with Submergence (S)

Example :

Supposing 100 per cent submergence of a weir and using standard tables of discharge coefficient find the discharge coefficient for values of critical submergence at value of 0.70 (70 per cent for a sharp crested weir).

Solution :

As per given condition of submergence (100%), we have $h_1 = h_2$ and therefore Discharge coefficient (Cd) = 0

TABLE 2.1

Values of Discharge Coefficient for Various Degrees of Submergence for Two-dimensional Flow

Structure	Discharge Coefficient (Cd')*	Cd	Submergence** limit (h_2/h_1)	Weir's Design sketch
Round nosed horizontal crested weir	0.544 (For R/H ≥ 0.11	1.705	0.700, 810, 92 (for vertical back face)	
Stream line weir	(L/H ≥ 1.94 (H/P < 0.9		0.790, 87, 0.97 (For sloping back face)	

*Rectangular 0.461
**Profile weir (constant)

Now given Scr. = 0.70

Hence value of Discharge coefficient (Cd) = 1.50

For S ≤ 0.70 and Cd = 0 for S= 1.0 (100%). Thus value of 'Cd' will vary from 0 to 1.5 when submergence varies from 70% to 100%.

Dilution Measurement Method

The measurement of velocity in the very high speed turbulent streams such as falling from hilly tracts the methods discussed above are not practicable and hence in such cases dilution method is used as described below.

This method is also applicable only when the stream size is not very large and is free from sodium chloride (as tested by quality analysis). The method employs the addition of sodium chloride solution of known strength say 'f' to the stream water at any location on upstream side at the constant rate (q). The water sample is then stored at any location at downstream and analysed quantitatively for the sodium chloride concentration (p) coming from upstream. If the flow rate of the stream is 'R' then

$$Pq = Q$$

Now the volume of salt added upstream location per unit time (rate) should be equal the volume of salt coming at the downstream location. Therefore :

$$Q = P/ \times q$$

Limitation of Method

(i) No water can be free from sodium chloride as such initial concentration of salt must be analysed first to get values of velocity flow. Thus if 'pi' is the initial salt concentration it must be deducted from the added salt concentration 'N'.

Hence $Pq = (p - pi)\,Q$

or $Q = \dfrac{P_q}{p - pi}$

(ii) The non-uniform addition of standard salt solution will not give uniform values of salt passing downstream and hence lot of error may be induced in calculations. As such the salt solution should be added after more dilution in the stream so that uniform salt concentration (N) reaches at all the points in stream.

There are many other methods now being used for measurement of flow velocity or streams gauging these are :

(i) Ultrasonic technique.

(ii) Electro-magnetic technique.

(iii) Radio-active tracer technique.

Hydrograph

In case it is necessary to observe the stage, velocity, flow (discharge) etc. for other characteristics of flowing water with respect to time the hydrograph technique is employed. The hydrograph provides the flow rate in relation to time in a graphical way (Fig. 2.9). The velocity of flow during the rainfall in a basin varies from time to time and it is maximum (peak value) (*i.e.* Q max at a certain time and reduces to original flow rate (Q minimum or Qo).

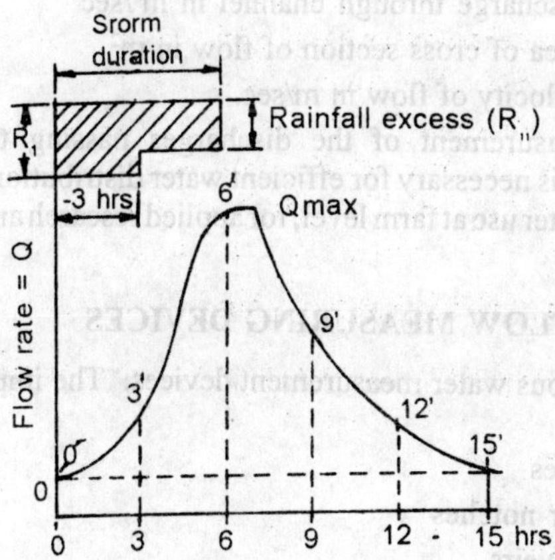

Fig. 2.9 : Flow Hydrograph at Station P resulting from a Storm in any Catchment

This is plotted to understand runoff at different intervals (The details of which are included on the Chapter of Runoff). The flow velocities at different locations be measured by the hydrograph.

Hydraulic Measurement of Open Channels

Manning Formula : The velocity of water flowing through an open channel is given by Manning's formula indicated below :

$$V = 1/n\ R^{2}/5\ S^{1/2}$$

Where

V = Velocity of water in m/sec

R = A/p

A = Area of cross section of flow in m^2

P = Wetted Perimeter in metres

S = Bed slope

n = Rugosity coefficient.

This equation is applicable to steady and uniform flow through channels. The value of 'n' depends upon the surface roughness of channels and many other factors. For good lined channels, it is taken as 0.02 and for unlined channels 0.03. Considerable variation in these values takes place. Once the velocity is worked out by using above equation, the discharge can be calculated by using the following continuity equation :

$$Q = AV$$

Where

Q = Discharge through channel in m^3/sec

A = Area of cross section of flow in m^2

V = Velocity of flow in m/sec.

The flow measurement of the discharges passing through the irrigation channels is necessary for efficient water distribution increasing the efficiency of water use at farm level, for applied research and for socio-economic factors.

FLOW MEASURING DEVICES

There are various water measurement devices. The important ones are :

1. 'V' - notches
2. Rectangular notches
3. Clipolletti weirs
4. Replogale flume

5. Parshall flume
6. Cut throat flume
7. Standing wave flume etc.

Out of these notches are cheapest devices but these cannot be used in a continuous channel without a drop in bed. Hence, a fall is necessary so as to have a clear overfall on the downstream side of notch. However, unlike the notches, the flumes are the devices which can be used in a continuous channel without a drop. Hence, they are very convenient to use in irrigation channels. Several types of flumes are indicated above. Out of these most popularly used are parshall flumes due to several advantages over the other flumes like (i) very high range of discharge measurements, (ii) easy to install, and (iii) relatively less loss of head and accuracy.

The detailed procedural working of parshall flume is given below.

Parshall Flumes

Introduction. In order to find out Water Conveyance Efficiency of a water course we have to first determine the extent of water loss through it. The purpose of an Irrigation Conveyance System is to convey water from the canal to the field being irrigated. Hence, any water which enters the system at the head, but does not reach the field is a loss. In simple terms total conveyance water loss through a water course, or a given length of water course, is the difference between the discharge at the head and at the tail. In order to find out the water loss through a water course, therefore, discharge or flow through it is required to be measured at the head and at the tail.

Process. Flow of water can be measured in a water course by using a flow-measuring device. This device can be a current meter or a flume. Generally, a pucca flume as a measuring device is constructed permanently at the measuring point, but portable flumes can also be used for flow measurements which have an added advantage of facilitating measurements at any other locations where a pucca permanent device is not constructed.

Equipment. Most suitable equipment for conducting flow measurements by means of portable measuring device is a parshall flume or a cut throat flume. Before coming to the method of measurements let us discuss details about these flumes.

Parshall Flume. Parshall designed a measuring device with which the discharge is obtained by measuring the loss in head caused by forcing a stream of water through a throat or converged section of a flume with a depressed bottom. The Parshall flume is based on the venturi principle for the measurement of flow in open channels. The flume consists of three principal sections : (1) A converging or contracting section at its upstream and leading to (2) a constricted section or throat, and (3) a diverging or expanding section downstream. The floor of the converging section is level, both longitudinally and transversely. The floor of the throat inclined downward, and the floor of the diverging section slopes upward.

The Parshall flume can be constructed in a wide range of sizes to measure discharge from a very small fraction of a cusec to more than 3000 cusecs. The width of the throat (W) is used to designate the size of the flume. The smaller size flumes, with throat width, 1 to 6 inches are generally used as portable flumes for measuring flows in small channels and water courses. Construction and installation tolerances for these small size flumes are highly critical and must be carefully controlled to assure satisfactory measurements. The larger size flumes with throat width upto 50 feet are adopted for the measurement of stream-flows of 10 to more than 3000 cusecs, by constructing a pucca structure. The ranges of discharges and appropriate standard dimensions for various throat widths are shown in Table 2.2 to 2.6. The lattered columns of the Table refer to the dimensions similarly identified in Figure 2.10.

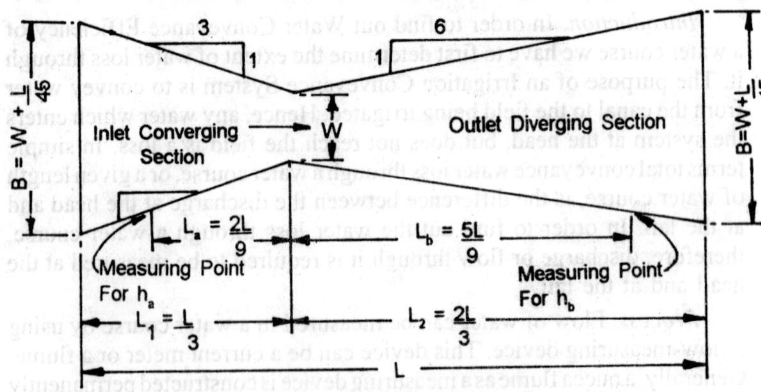

Fig. 2.10 : Parshall Flume

Discharge through the Parshall measuring flume can occur under either of two different conditions of flow (1) where there is no submergence, a condition called free-flow and (2) where the elevation of water surface downstream from the flume is high enough to retard the rate of discharge, a condition called submerged flow. To determine the rate of discharge two depth gauges (Ha and Hb) are provided (Fig. 2.11). Both gauges are set with zero points at the mean elevation of the crest of the flume.

A distinct advantage of the Parshall Flume is its ability to operate as a single-head device with a minimum loss of head. This ability permits its use in relatively shallow channels with flat grades. For a given discharge the loss in head through a Parshall flume is only about one-fourth of that required by a weir under similar free-flow conditions.

The degree or percentage of submergence is the ratio of the two measured heads, or Hb divided by Ha. Where this ratio does not exceed certain limits, the rate of flow of discharge is not affected by the elevation of the water surface downstream, and a free-flow condition exists. The free-flow limits of the ratio Hb/Ha vary with the widths of the throat and are tabulated as follows :

Width of Throat	Free flow limit of Hb/Ha
1 to 3 inches	0.5
6 to 9 inches	0.6
1 to 8 feet	0.7
10 to 50 feet	0.8

Tables for evaluating discharges in free-flow and submerged conditions are enclosed for various throat width W of Parshall flume.

TABLE 2.2

Free-flow Discharge Values for Parshall Measuring Flume

Head, H (feet)	Discharge, Q, for throat widths, W, of											
	3 inches	6 inches	9 inches	1 foot	1.5 feet	2 feet	3 feet	4 feet	5 feet	6 feet	7 feet	8 feet
	Second feet	Second feet	Second feet	Second feet	Second feet	Second feet	Second feet	Second feet	Second feet	Second feet	Second feet	Second feet
0.60	0.450	0.92	1.40	1.84	2.73	3.62	5.39	7.15	8.89	10.6	12.4	14.1
.61	.462	.94	1.44	1.88	2.80	3.72	5.83	7.34	9.13	10.9	12.7	14.5
.62	.474	.97	1.48	1.93	2.87	3.81	5.68	7.53	9.37	11.2	13.0	14.8
.63	.485	.99	1.51	1.98	2.95	3.91	5.82	7.72	9.61	11.5	13.4	15.2
.64	.497	1.02	1.55	2.03	3.02	4.01	5.97	7.91	9.85	11.8	13.7	15.6
.65	.509	1.04	1.59	2.08	3.09	4.11	6.12	8.11	10.1	12.1	14.1	16.0
.66	.522	1.07	1.63	2.13	3.17	4.20	6.26	8.31	10.3	12.4	14.4	16.4
.67	.534	1.10	1.66	2.18	3.24	4.30	6.41	8.51	10.6	12.7	14.8	16.8
.68	.546	1.12	1.70	2.23	3.31	4.40	6.56	8.71	10.8	13.0	15:1	17.2
.69	.558	1.15	1.74	2.28	3.39	4.50	6.71	8.91	11.1	13.3	15.5	17.6

.70	.571	1.17	1.78	2.33	3.46	4.60	6.86	9.11	11.4	13.6	15.8	18.0
.71	.584	1.20	1.82	2.38	3.54	4.70	7.02	9.32	11.6	13.9	16.2	18.5
.72	.597	1.23	1.86	2.43	3.62	4.81	7.17	9.53	11.9	14.2	16.6	18.9
.73	.610	1.26	1.90	2.48	3.69	4.91	7.33	9.74	12.1	14.5	16.9	19.3
.74	.623	1.28	1.94	2.53	3.77	5.02	7.49	9.95	12.4	14.9	17.3	19.7
.75	.636	1.31	1.98	2.58	3.85	5.12	7.65	10.2	12.7	15.2	17.7	20.1
.76	.649	1.34	2.02	2.63	3.93	5.23	7.81	10.4	12.9	15.5	18.0	20.6
.77	.662	1.36	2.06	2.68	4.01	5.34	7.97	10.6	13.2	15.8	18.4	21.0
.78	.675	1.39	2.10	2.74	4.09	5.44	8.13	10.8	13.5	16.2	18.8	21.5
.79	.689	1.42	2.14	2.80	4.17	5.55	8.30	11.0	13.8	16.5	19.2	21.9
.80	.702	1.45	2.18	2.85	4.26	5.66	8.46	11.3	14.0	16.8	19.6	22.4
.81	.716	1.48	2.22	2.90	4.34	5.77	8.63	11.5	14.3	17.2	20.0	22.8
.82	.730	1.50	2.27	2.96	4.42	5.88	8.79	11.7	14.6	17.5	20.4	23.3
.83	.744	1.53	2.31	3.02	4.50	6.00	8.96	11.9	14.9	17.8	20.8	23.7
.84	.757	1.56	2.35	3.07	4.59	6.11	9.13	12.2	15.2	18.2	21.2	24.2
.85	.771	1.59	2.39	3.12	4.67	6.22	9.30	12.4	15.5	18.5	21.6	24.6

Contd.

TABLE 2.2 (*Contd.*)

Head, H (feet)	Discharge, Q, for throat widths, W, of											
	3 inches	6 inches	9 inches	1 foot	1.5 feet	2 feet	3 feet	4 feet	5 feet	6 feet	7 feet	8 feet
	Second feet	Second feet	Second feet	Second feet	Second feet	Second feet	Second feet	Second feet	Second feet	Second feet	Second feet	Second feet
.86	.786	1.62	2.44	3.18	4.76	6.33	9.48	12.6	15.8	18.9	22.0	25.1
.87	.800	1.65	2.48	3.24	4.84	6.44	9.65	12.8	16.0	19.2	22.4	25.6
.88	.814	1.68	2.52	3.29	4.93	6.56	9.82	13.1	16.2	19.6	22.8	26.1
.89	.828	1.71	2.57	3.35	5.01	6.68	10.0	13.3	16.6	19.9	23.2	26.5
.90	.843	1.74	2.61	3.41	5.10	6.80	10.2	13.6	16.9	20.3	23.7	27.0
.91	.858	1.77	2.66	3.46	5.19	6.92	10.4	13.8	17.2	20.7	24.1	27.5
.92	.872	1.81	2.70	3.52	5.28	7.03	10.5	14.0	17.5	21.0	24.5	28.0
.93	.887	1.84	2.75	3.58	5.37	7.15	10.7	14.3	17.8	21.4	24.9	28.5
.94	.902	1.87	2.79	3.64	5.46	7.27	10.9	14.5	18.1	21.8	25.4	29.0
.95	.916	1.90	2.84	3.70	5.55	7.39	11.1	14.8	18.4	22.1	25.8	29.5
.96	.931	1.93	2.88	3.76	5.64	7.51	11.3	15.0	18.8	22.5	26.2	30.0
.97	.946	1.97	2.93	3.82	5.73	7.63	11.4	15.3	19.1	22.9	26.7	30.5
.98	.961	2.00	2.98	3.88	5.82	7.75	11.6	15.5	19.4	23.2	27.1	31.0
.99	.977	2.03	3.02	3.94	5.91	7.88	11.8	15.8	19.7	23.6	27.6	31.5

1.00	.992	2.06	3.07	4.00	6.00	8.00	12.0	16.0	20.0	24.0	28.0	32.0	
1.01	1.01	2.09	3.12	4.06	6.09	8.12	12.2	16.3	20.3	24.4	28.5	32.5	
1.02	1.02	2.12	3.17	4.12	6.19	8.25	12.4	16.5	20.6	24.8	28.9	33.0	
1.03	1.04	2.16	3.21	4.18	6.28	8.38	12.6	16.8	21.0	25.2	29.4	33.6	
1.04	1.05	2.19	3.26	4.25	6.37	8.50	12.8	17.0	21.3	25.6	29.8	34.1	
1.05	1.07	2.22	3.31	4.31	6.47	8.63	13.0	17.3	21.6	25.9	30.3	34.6	
1.06	1 09	2.26	3.36	4.37	6.56	8.76	13.2	17.5	21.9	26.3	30.7	35.1	
1.07	1.10	2.29	3.40	4.43	6.66	8.88	13.3	17.8	22.3	26.7	31.2	35.7	
1.08	1.12	2.32	3.45	4.50	6.75	9.01	13.5	18.1	22.6	27.1	31.7	36.2	
1.09	1.13	2.36	3.50	4.56	6.85	9.14	13.7	18.3	22.9	27.5	32.1	36.8	

TABLE 2.3

Free-Flow Discharge Values for Parshall Measuring Flume

Head,	Discharge, Q, for throat widths, W, of											
	3 inches	6 inches	9 inches	1 foot	1.5 feet	2 feet	3 feet	4 feet	5 feet	6 feet	7 feet	8 feet
H (feet)	Second feet	Second feet	Second feet	Second feet	Second feet	Second feet	Second feet	Second feet	Second feet	Second feet	Second feet	Second feet
0.10	0.028	0.05	0.09	0.11	0.15	--	--	--	--	--	--	--
.11	.033	.06	.10	.12	.18	--	--	--	--	--	--	--
.12	.037	.07	.12	.14	.21	--	--	--	--	--	--	--
.13	.042	.08	.14	.16	.24	--	--	--	--	--	--	--
.14	.047	.09	.15	.18	.27	--	--	--	--	--	--	--
.15	.053	.10	.17	.20	.30	0.42	0.61	--	--	--	--	--
.16	.058	.11	.19	.23	.34	.47	.68	--	--	--	--	--
.17	.064	.12	.20	.26	.38	.51	.75	--	--	--	--	--
.18	.070	.14	.22	.29	.42	.56	.82	--	--	--	--	--
.19	.076	.15	.24	.32	.46	.61	.89	--	--	--	--	--

.20	.082	.16	.26	.35	.51	.66	.97	1.26	1.55	—	—	—
.21	.089	.18	.28	.37	.55	.71	1.04	1.36	1.68	—	—	—
.22	.095	.19	.30	.40	.59	.77	1.12	1.47	1.31	—	—	—
.23	.102	.20	.32	.43	.63	.82	1.20	1.58	1.94	—	—	—
.24	.109	.22	.35	.46	.67	.88	1.28	1.69	2.08	—	—	—
.25	.117	.23	.37	.49	.71	.93	1.37	1.80	2.22	2.63	3.02	3.46
.26	.124	.25	.39	.51	.76	.99	1.46	1.91	2.36	2.80	3.25	3.68
.27	.131	.26	.41	.54	.80	1.05	1.55	2.03	2.50	2.97	3.44	3.90
.28	.138	.28	.44	.58	.85	1.11	1.64	2.15	2.65	3.15	3.65	4.13
.29	.146	.29	.46	.61	.90	1.18	1.73	2.27	2.80	3.33	3.85	4.37
.30	.154	.31	.49	.64	.94	1.24	1.82	2.39	2.96	3.52	4.08	4.62
.31	.162	.32	.51	.68	.99	1.30	1.92	2.52	3.12	3.71	4.30	4.88
.32	.170	.34	.54	.71	1.04	1.37	2.02	2.65	3.28	3.90	4.52	5.13
.33	.179	.36	.56	.74	1.09	1.44	2.12	2.78	3.44	4.10	4.75	5.39
.34	.187	.38	.59	.77	1.14	1.50	2.22	2.92	3.61	4.30	4.98	5.66
.35	.196	.39	.62	.80	1.19	1.57	2.32	3.06	3.78	4.50	5.22	5.93
.36	.205	.41	.64	.84	1.25	1.64	2.42	3.20	3.95	4.71	5.46	6.20

Contd.

TABLE 2.3 (*Contd.*)

Head,	Discharge, Q, for throat widths, W, of											
	3 inches	6 inches	9 inches	1 foot	1.5 feet	2 feet	3 feet	4 feet	5 feet	6 feet	7 feet	8 feet
H (feet)	Second feet	Second feet	Second feet	Second feet	Second feet	Second feet	Second feet	Second feet	Second feet	Second feet	Second feet	Second feet
.37	.216	.43	.67	.88	1.30	1.72	2.53	3.34	4.13	4.92	5.70	6.48
.38	.222	.45	.70	.92	1.36	1.79	2.64	3.48	4.31	5.13	5.95	6.76
.39	.231	.47	.73	.95	1.41	1.86	2.75	3.62	4.49	5.35	6.20	7.05
.40	.241	.48	.76	.99	1.47	1.93	2.86	3.77	4.68	5.57	6.46	7.34
.41	.250	.50	.78	1.03	1.53	2.01	2.97	3.92	4.86	5.80	6.72	7.64
.42	.260	.52	.81	1.07	1.58	2.09	3.08	4.07	5.05	6.02	6.98	7.94
.43	.269	.54	.84	1.11	1.64	2.16	3.29	4.22	5.24	6.25	7.25	8.24
.44	.279	.56	.87	1.15	1.70	2.24	3.32	4.38	5.43	6.48	7.52	8.55
.45	.289	.58	.90	1.19	1.76	2.32	3.44	4.54	5.63	6.72	7.80	8.87
.46	.299	.61	.94	1.23	1.82	2.40	3.56	4.70	5.83	6.96	8.08	9.19
.47	.309	.63	.97	1.27	1.88	2.48	3.68	4.86	6.03	7.20	8.36	9.51
.48	.319	.65	1.00	1.31	1.94	2.57	3.80	5.03	6.24	7.44	8.65	9.84
.49	.329	.67	1.03	1.35	2.00	2.65	3.92	5.20	6.45	7.69	8.94	10.2

.50	.339	.69	1.06	1.39	2.06	2.73	4.05	5.36	6.66	7.94	9.23	10.5
.51	.350	.71	1.10	1.44	2.13	2.82	4.18	5.53	6.87	8.20	9.53	10.9
.52	.361	.73	1.13	1.48	2.19	2.90	4.31	5.70	7.09	8.46	9.83	11.2
.53	.371	.76	1.16	1.52	2.25	2.99	4.44	5.88	7.30	8.72	10.1	11.5
.54	.382	.78	1.20	1.57	2.32	3.08	4.57	6.05	7.52	8.98	10.5	11.9
.55	.393	.80	1.23	1.62	2.39	3.17	4.70	6.23	7.74	9.25	10.8	12.2
.56	.404	.82	1.26	1.66	2.45	3.26	4.84	6.41	7.97	9.52	11.1	12.6
.57	.415	.85	1.30	1.70	2.52	3.35	4.98	6.59	8.20	9.79	11.4	13.0
.58	.427	.87	1.33	1.75	2.59	3.44	5.11	6.77	8.43	10.1	11.7	13.3
.59	.438	.89	1.37	1.80	2.66	3.53	5.25	6.96	8.66	10.4	12.0	13.7

TABLE 2.4

Dimensions and Capabilitis of the Parshall Measuring Flume for Various Throat Widths (W)

(Letters refer to dimensions. See Fig. 2.10)

Width	A		B		C		D		E		F	
Small	Ft.	In.	Ft.	In.	Ft.	In.	Ft.	In.	Ft.	In.	Ft.	In.
1-inch...	0	9-17/32	1	2	0	3-21/32	0	6-19/32	0	9	0	3
2-inch...	0	10-7/8	1	4	0	5-5/16	0	8-13/32	0	10	0	4-1/2
3-inch...	1	0-1/4	1	6	0	7	0	10-3/16	1	6	0	6
Intermediate												
6-inch...	1	4-5/16	2	0	1	3-1/2	1	3-5/8	2	0	1	0
9-inch...	1	11-1/8	2	10	1	3	1	10-5/8	2	6	1	0
1-foot...	3	0	4	4-7/8	2	0	2	9-1/4	3	0	2	0
1-1/2-feet	3	2	4	7-7/8	3	0	3	11-1/2	3	0	2	0
2-feet...	3	4	4	10-7/8	3	0	3	11-1/2	3	0	2	0
3-feet..	3	8	5	4-3/4	4	0	5	1-7/8	3	0	2	0
4-feet...	4	0	5	10-5/8	5	0	6	4-1/4	3	0	2	0

5-feet...	4	4	6	4-1/2	6	0	7	6-5/8	3	0	2	0
6-feet...	4	8	6	10-3/8	7	0	8	9	3	0	2	0
7-feet...	5	0	7	4-1/4	8	0	9	11-3/8	3	0	2	0
8-feet...	5	4	7	10-1/8	9	0	11	1-3/4	3	0	2	0
Large												
10-feet...	6	0	14	0	12	0	15	7-1/4	4	0	3	0
12-feet...	6	8	16	0	14	8	18	4-3/4	5	0	3	0
15-feet...	7	8	25	0	18	4	25	0	6	0	4	0
20-feet...	9	4	25	0	24	0	30	0	7	0	6	0

Contd.

TABLE 2.4 (*Contd.*)

Width	G		K	N		X	Y	Free-flow capacity Minimum	Free-flow capacity Maximum
	Ft.	In.	In.	Ft.	In.	In.	In.	Sec.-Ft	Sec.-Ft
Small									
1-inch...	0	8	3/4	0	1-1/8	5/16	1/2	0.01	0.20
2-inch...	0	10	7/8	0	1-11/16	5/8	1	.02	.50
3-inch...	1	0	1	0	2-1/4	1-1/2	.03	.03	1.00
Intermediate									
6-inch	2	0	3	0	4-1/2	2	3	.05	3.9
9-inch	1	6	3	0	4-1/2	2	3	.09	8.9
1-feet	3	0	3	0	9	2	3	.11	16.1
1-1/2-feet	3	0	3	0	9	2	3	.15	24.6
2-feet	3	0	3	0	9	2	3	.42	33.1
3-feet	3	0	3	0	9	2	3	.61	50.4
4-feet	3	0	3	0	9	2	3	1.3	67.9
5-feet	3	0	3	0	9	2	3	1.6	85.6

6-feet	3	0	3	0	9	2	3	2.6	103.5
7-feet	3	0	3	0	9	2	3	3.0	121.4
8-feet	3	0	3	0	9	2	3	3.5	139.5
Large									
10-feet	6	0	6	1	1-1/2	12	9	6.0	200.0
12-feet	8	0	6	1	1-1/2	12	9	8.0	350.0
15-feet	10	0	9	1	6	12	9	8.0	600.0
20-feet	12	0	12	2	3	12	9	10.0	1000.0

Cut Throat Flume : The cut-throat flume has been developed for operation under both free-flow and submerged flow conditions. These are being now widely used on account of their simplicity in construction as well as installation. The flume has a flat bottom, vertical walls and a zero-length throat section. The most obvious advantage of a cut-throat flume is economy of fabrication due to the flat bottom and elimination of the throat section *i.e.* only convergent inlet and divergent outlet. Another advantage is that every flume length has the same entrance and exit section lengths, which allows the same frames or patterns to be used for any desired throat width. Because of being flat bottomed and flume can be placed on the channel bed and also inside a lined channel.

The cut-throat flume can operate either as a free or submerged flow device. The figure illustrates the structural arrangement for fabrications of a cut-throat flume.

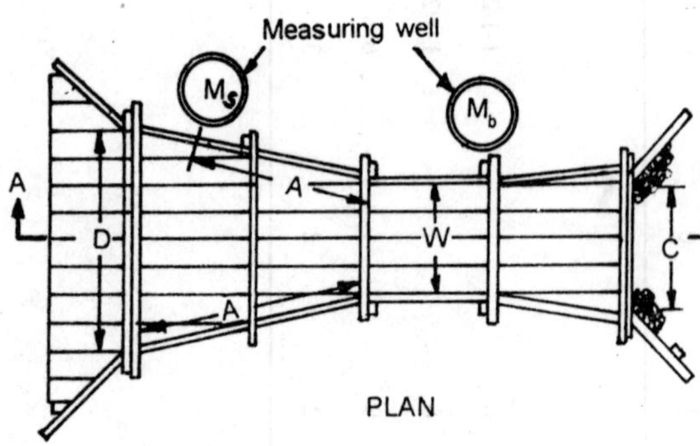

Fig. 2.11 : Cut throat flume

A. Flume Installation : *A Flume dimensions check up* : All flume dimensions must be measured to be sure that the flume has been constructed properly. If dimensions of the throat vary more than 1/16 inch, the flume should be rejected. Check also for general appearance of the flume. The walls should be vertical and perpendicular to the flat bottom. The converging and diverging sections should be fabricated according to specifications. Check all welded joints. If welds are improper the flume should be rejected.

B, Gauge Installation : Gauges and inlets to the stilling wells reading the upstream head (ha) as well as downstream head (hb) should be checked against the specifications. If the flume is equipped with stilling wells, check the water level next to the staff gauges as compared to the level in the stilling wells in standing water with the flume properly levelled. Incorrect installation will cause erroneous discharge readings.

C. Orientation for Levelling : If the flume must be installed in a channel with water flowing in it, make sure that two longitudinal and transverse locations on the flume top are parallel with two similar locations on the flume bottom. As close to the flume throat as possible, preferably on the converging section of the flume, place a short (about 6" long) carpenter's level in the transverse direction of the floor of the flume and bring the bubble to the level position. Likewise bring the flume to a level position in the longitudinal direction. Find the same transverse level position somewhere on the top of the flume, either in the throat region on the cross piece at the start of the converging section, or on the cross piece at the start of the diverting stream mark this position for later levelling the flume in flowing water. Likewise for longitudinal levelling, place the level on top of the walls of the converging or diverging section of the flume. Wherever the bubble comes to the centre, mark that position on top of the walls. Always use these two marked position to level the flume if it must be installed in flowing water, otherwise always use the floor of the flume to ensure that the flume is installed in a level position.

Check these predetermined positions occasionally with reference to the flume bottom, as the flume may become deformed with long continued use.

Installation and Operational Considerations : (1) Always remember that generally a watercourse has a flat gradient with very little free-board. Some time should therefore be taken to decide about the site for flume installation. With the cut-throat flume, good discharge measurements can be made, even under submerged flow conditions. However, submergence should not exceed 90% if possible. Higher submergence will reduce energy loss, but the problem of upstream section being overtopped could be minimised alternatively through careful installation and/or by building up the banks of the upstream channel. However, where conditions permit (Steep-gradient conditions with more free-board) installation should be for free flow conditions.

(2) The flume should be placed in the centre of the channel. It should be parallel to the direction of water flow in the channel.

(3) The sides and bottom and around the flume walls be properly sealed so that there are no leaks. Sandy conditions impose serious leak problems.

Plastic sheets/cloth used as a cut-off wall in the surrounding soil can be used to overcome this problem.

(4) Before recording readings of the upstream and downstream gauges, always check for leaks along the sides and underneath the flume. The inside bottom of the flume should be checked and cleared of any sediment or trash as this will cause ha to increase and result in an erroneous reading.

The following steps will help to a great extent to get a reasonably accurate measurement :

1. After the second flume is installed, make sure that one person is assigned to walk along the channel back to the first flume which has been installed near the inlet. This person should make note of spills, bank leaks, trading between the farmers, bank failures, water diversions into other branches, and anything special which might affect the discharge measurement at the second flume.

2. When the second flume is installed, the flow is reduced for the initial periods following installation. In flat gradient channels a lot of water is stored in the upstream section of the channel. Sufficient time should be allowed to dissipate this storage, otherwise this may lead to wrong results. Wait long enough after flume installations to achieve steady flow conditions. This can be noted when the flow rate becomes constant (the ha guage reading does not change with time) if there are no changes in the upstream section of the channel.

*The free flow discharge rate is given by

$$Q = C H_a^n$$

where Q is in m³/sec. H_a is measured in metres.

For sumberged flow both upstream and downstream head measurement are required and discharge Q is given by equation :

$$Q - \frac{C_s(H_a - H_b)^n}{(- \text{Long } s)^{ns}}$$

Where,

Q is the discharge rate in m^3/sec

H_a is the upstream head in m

H_b is the downstream head in m

n is the exponent of free flow

ns is the exponent of submerged flow

s is the submergence, H_b/H_a, in decimal form and

Cs is the submerged flow coefficient = Ks W1.025
Values of Ks and Ns are given in Table 2.5.

TABLE 2.5

Relationship Between Cut Throat-flume Length (l), Transition Submergence (s), Coefficients and Exponents for Free flow and Submerged Discharge

L	St	Free flow		Submerged flow	
metres	%	n	K	Ns	Ks
0.5	60.7	2.08	6.15	1.675	3.5
0.6	62.0	1.989	5.17	1.600	2.9
0.7	63.0	1.932	4.63	1.55	2.6
0.8	64.2	1.880	4.18	1.513	2.35
0.9	65.3	1.843	3.89	1.483	2.15
1.0	66.4	1.810	3.60	1.456	2.00
1.2	68.5	1.756	3.22	1.427	1.75
1.4	70.5	1.712	2.93	1.407	1.56
1.6	72.0	1.675	2.72	1.393	1.45
1.8	73.8	1.646	2.53	1.386	1.32
2.0	75.5	1.620	2.40	1.381	1.24
2.2	77.0	1.600	2.30	1.378	1.18
2.4	78.4	1.579	2.22	1.381	1.12
2.6	79.5	1.568	2.15	1.386	1.08
2.7	80.5	1.562	2.13	1.390	1.06

Water Delivery Efficiency

It is the rate of flow at the second flume (Q2) to the flow at the first flume (Q1) in a Water Course or any channel. The delivery efficiency is therefore given by equation :

Ed (%) = (Q2/Q1) x 100

Discharge calculations are illustrated by following examples :

Example I :

W = 20 cm

L = 180 cm

Ha = 25 cm

Hb = 10 cm

From Table 2.5 St - 73.8 so we have free flow (S.St) from Table 2.5

K = 2.53

C = $KW^{1.025}$ = 2.53 (0.20, 1.025 = 0.486)

From Table 2.5

N = 1.65

Q = $CH_a^{\ n}$ = $0.486 (.25)^{1.65}$ = $0.0493 m^3/sec$ = 49.3 lps

Example II :

W = 10 cm

L = 90 cm

H_a = 30 cm

H_b = 27 cm

S = 27/30 - 0.90 - 90%

From the Table 2.5 St = 65.3 per cent and small s is greater value, submerged flow exists and the discharge is given by :

$$Q = \frac{Cs\,(H_a - H_b)^n}{(-\log s)^n s} \quad \text{and}$$

$$Cs = KsW^{1.025}$$

From Table 2.5 :

Ks = 2.15, n = 1.843, Ns = 1.483

Cs = $2.15 (0.10)^{1.025}$ = 0.203

$$Q = \frac{0.203(0.30-0.27)\times 1.843}{(0.0458)} \quad 0.0307 m^3/sec.$$

= 30.7 lps.

TABLE 2.6

Free flow Calibrations for Selected Cut-throat Flumes
(Values listed are discharge in cfs.)

ha ft.	4IN× 3FT	8IN× 3FI	12IN× 3FI	16IN× 3FT	8IN× 6FT	16IN× 6FI	24IN× 6FT	32IN× 6FT	12IN× 9FT	24IN× 9FT	36IN× 9F	48IN× 9FT
.02	.00	.00	.00	.00	.00	.01	.01	.02	.01	.02	.02	.03
.04	.00	.01	.01	.02	.01	.03	.04	.05	.02	.05	.07	.10
.06	.01	.02	.03	.03	.02	.05	.07	.10	.04	.09	.13	.18
.08	.01	.03	.04	.06	.04	.08	.12	.16	.07	.14	.21	.28
.10	.02	.04	.07	.09	.06	.11	.17	.23	.10	.20	.30	.40
.12	.03	.06	.09	.12	.08	.15	.23	.31	.13	.26	.39	.53
.14	.04	.08	.12	.16	.10	.20	.30	.40	.16	.33	.50	.67
.16	.05	.10	.15	.21	.12	.25	.37	.50	.20	.41	.62	.83
.18	.06	.13	.19	.26	.15	.30	.45	.61	.24	.49	.74	1.00
.20	.08	.15	.23	.31	.17	.35	.54	.72	.28	.58	.88	1.18
.22	.09	.18	.28	.37	.20	.42	.63	.85	.33	.67	1.02	1.37
.24	.11	.21	.33	.44	.24	.48	.73	.98	.38	.77	1.16	1.56

Contd.

TABLE 2.6 (*Contd.*)

ha	4IN×	8IN×	12IN×	16IN×	8IN×	16IN×	24IN×	32IN×	12IN×	24IN×	36IN×	48IN×
ft.	3FT	3FI	3FI	3FT	6FT	6FI	6FT	6FT	9FT	9FT	9F	9FT
.26	.12	.25	.38	.51	.27	.55	.83	1.11	.43	.87	1.32	1.77
.28	.14	.29	.43	.58	.30	.62	.94	1.26	.48	.98	1.48	1.99
.30	.16	.32	.49	.66	.34	.69	1.05	1.41	.54	1.09	1.65	2.22
.32	.18	.36	.55	.74	.38	.77	1.17	1.57	.59	1.21	1.82	2.45
.34	.20	.41	.62	.83	.42	.85	1.29	1.73	.65	1.32	2.00	2.69
.36	.22	.45	.69	.92	.46	.93	1.42	1.90	.71	1.45	2.19	2.94
.38	.25	.50	.76	1.02	.50	1.02	1.55	2.08	.77	1.58	2.38	3.20
.40	.27	.55	.83	1.12	.55	1.11	1.69	2.26	.84	1.71	2.58	3.47
.42	.30	.60	.91	1.22	.59	1.20	1.83	2.45	.90	1.84	2.79	3.74
.44	.32	.66	.99	1.33	.64	1.30	1.97	2.65	.97	1.98	3.00	4.03
.46	.35	.71	1.08	1.44	.69	1.40	2.12	2.85	1.04	2.12	3.21	4.31
.48	.38	.77	1.17	1.56	.74	1.50	2.28	3.05	1.11	2.27	3.43	4.61
.50	.41	.83	1.26	1.68	.79	1.60	2.44	3.26	1.19	2.42	3.66	4.91
.52	.44	.89	1.35	1.81	.84	1.71	2.60	3.48	1.26	2.57	3.89	5.22
.54	.47	.96	1.45	1.94	.90	1.82	2.76	3.71	1.34	2.73	4.12	5.54
.56	.50	1.02	1.55	2.07	.95	1.93	2.94	3.93	1.42	2.89	4.36	5.86
.58	.54	1.09	1.65	2.21	1.01	2.05	3.11	4.17	1.50	3.05	4.61	6.19

.60	.57	1.16	1.76	2.36	1.07	2.16	3.29	4.41	1.58	3.21	4.86	6.53
.62	.61	1.23	1.87	2.50	1.12	2.28	3.47	4.65	1.65	3.38	5.11	6.87
.64	.64	1.31	1.98	2.65	1.18	2.40	3.66	4.90	1.74	3.55	5.37	7.22
.66	.68	1.38	2.09	2.81	1.25	2.53	3.85	5.15	1.83	3.73	5.64	7.58
.68	.72	1.46	2.21	2.97	1.31	2.66	4.04	5.41	1.92	3.91	5.91	7.94
.70	.76	1.54	2.33	3.13	1.37	2.79	4.24	5.68	2.01	4.09	6.18	8.31
.72	.80	1.62	2.46	3.29	1.44	2.92	4.44	5.95	2.10	4.27	6.46	8.68
.74	.84	1.71	2.59	3.47	1.50	3.05	4.64	6.22	2.19	4.46	6.74	9.06
.76	.88	1.79	2.72	3.64	1.57	3.19	4.85	6.50	2.28	4.65	7.03	9.44
.78	.92	1.88	2.85	3.82	1.64	3.33	5.06	6.78	2.38	4.84	7.32	9.83
.80	.97	1.97	2.98	4.00	1.71	3.47	5.28	7.07	2.47	5.03	7.61	10.23
.82	1.01	2.06	3.12	4.19	1.78	3.62	5.50	7.37	2.57	5.23	7.91	10.63
.84	1.06	2.15	3.27	4.38	1.85	3.76	5.72	7.66	2.67	5.43	8.21	11.04
.86	1.10	2.25	3.41	4.57	1.93	3.91	5.94	7.97	2.77	5.64	8.52	11.45
.88	1.15	2.35	3.56	4.77	2.00	4.06	6.17	8.27	2.87	5.84	8.83	11.87
.90	1.20	2.45	3.71	4.97	2.08	4.21	6.41	8.59	2.97	6.05	9.15	12.29
.92	1.25	2.55	3.86	5.17	2.15	4.37	6.64	8.90	3.07	6.26	9.47	12.72
.94	1.30	2.65	4.02	5.38	2.23	4.53	6.88	9.22	3.18	6.47	9.79	13.16
.96	1.35	2.76	4.17	5.59	2.31	4.69	7.12	9.55	3.28	6.69	10.11	13.60
.98	1.40	2.86	4.34	5.81	2.39	4.85	7.37	9.88	3.29	6.91	10.45	14.04
1.00	1.46	2.97	4.50	6.03	2.47	5.01	7.62	10.21	3.50	7.13	10.78	14.49

TABLE 2.7

Submerged Flow Calibrations for 8 in × 3 f Cut-throat Flume

(Values listed are discharge in cfs.)

$h_a - h_b$,ft

ha ft.	.02	.04	.06	.08	.10	.12	.14	.16	.18	.20	.22	.24	.26	.28	.30	.32	.34	.36	.38	.40
.02	.0	.0	.0	.0	.0	.0	.0	.0	.0	.0	.0	.0	.0	.0	.0	.0	.0	.0	.0	.0
.04	.0	.0	.0	.0	.0	.0	.0	.0	.0	.0	.0	.0	.0	.0	.0	.0	.0	.0	.0	.0
.06	.0	.0	.0	.0	.0	.0	.0	.0	.0	.0	.0	.0	.0	.0	.0	.0	.0	.0	.0	.0
.08	.0	.0	.0	.0	.0	.0	.0	.0	.0	.0	.0	.0	.0	.0	.0	.0	.0	.0	.0	.0
.10	.0	.0	.0	.0	.0	.0	.0	.0	.0	.0	.0	.0	.0	.0	.0	.0	.0	.0	.0	.0
.12	.1	.1	.1	.1	.1	.1	.1	.1	.1	.1	.1	.1	.1	.1	.1	.1	.1	.1	.1	.1
.14	.1	.1	.1	.1	.1	.1	.1	.1	.1	.1	.1	.1	.1	.1	.1	.1	.1	.1	.1	.1
.16	.1	.1	.1	.1	.1	.1	.1	.1	.1	.1	.1	.1	.1	.1	.1	.1	.1	.1	.1	.1
.18	.1	.1	.1	.1	.1	.1	.1	.1	.1	.1	.1	.1	.1	.1	.1	.1	.1	.1	.1	.1
.20	.1	.1	.2	.2	.2	.2	.2	.2	.2	.2	.2	.2	.2	.2	.2	.2	.2	.2	.2	.2
.22	.1	.2	.2	.2	.2	.2	.2	.2	.2	.2	.2	.2	.2	.2	.2	.2	.2	.2	.2	.2
.24	.2	.2	.2	.2	.2	.2	.2	.2	.2	.2	.2	.2	.2	.2	.2	.2	.2	.2	.2	.2
.26	.2	.2	.2	.2	.2	.2	.2	.2	.2	.2	.2	.2	.2	.2	.2	.2	.2	.2	.2	.2

.28	.2	.2	.3	.3	.3	.3	.3	.3	.3	.3	.3	.3	.3	.3	.3	.3	.3	.3	.3	.3
.30	.2	.3	.3	.3	.3	.3	.3	.3	.3	.3	.3	.3	.3	.3	.3	.3	.3	.3	.3	.3
.32	.3	.3	.3	.4	.4	.4	.4	.4	.4	.4	.4	.4	.4	.4	.4	.4	.4	.4	.4	.4
.34	.3	.3	.4	.4	.4	.4	.4	.4	.4	.4	.4	.4	.4	.4	.4	.4	.4	.4	.4	.4
.36	.3	.4	.4	.4	.4	.5	.5	.5	.5	.5	.5	.5	.5	.5	.5	.5	.5	.5	.5	.5
.38	.3	.4	.4	.5	.5	.5	.5	.5	.5	.5	.5	.5	.5	.5	.5	.5	.5	.5	.5	.5
.40	.4	.4	.5	.5	.5	.5	.6	.6	.6	.6	.6	.6	.6	.6	.6	.6	.6	.6	.6	.6
.42	.4	.5	.5	.6	.6	.6	.6	.6	.6	.6	.6	.6	.6	.6	.6	.6	.6	.6	.6	.6
.44	.4	.5	.6	.6	.6	.6	.7	.7	.7	.7	.7	.7	.7	.7	.7	.7	.7	.7	.7	.7
.46	.4	.5	.6	.6	.7	.7	.7	.7	.7	.7	.7	.7	.7	.7	.7	.7	.7	.7	.7	.7
.48	.5	.6	.7	.7	.7	.7	.8	.8	.8	.8	.8	.8	.8	.8	.8	.8	.8	.8	.8	.8
.50	.5	.6	.7	.7	.8	.8	.8	.8	.8	.8	.8	.8	.8	.8	.8	.8	.8	.8	.8	.8
.52	.6	.7	.7	.8	.8	.9	.9	.9	.9	.9	.9	.9	.9	.9	.9	.9	.9	.9	.9	.9
.54	.6	.7	.8	.8	.9	.9	.9	.9	.9	1.0	1.0	1.0	1.0	1.0	1.0	1.0	1.0	1.0	1.0	1.0
.56	.6	.7	.8	.9	.9	1.0	1.0	1.0	1.0	1.0	1.0	1.0	1.0	1.0	1.0	1.0	1.0	1.0	1.0	1.0
.58	.6	.8	.9	.9	1.0	1.0	1.1	1.1	1.1	1.1	1.1	1.1	1.1	1.1	1.1	1.1	1.1	1.1	1.1	1.1
.60	.7	.8	.9	1.0	1.1	1.1	1.1	1.1	1.1	1.2	1.2	1.2	1.2	1.2	1.2	1.2	1.2	1.2	1.2	1.2
.62	.7	.9	1.0	1.1	1.1	1.1	1.2	1.2	1.2	1.2	1.2	1.2	1.2	1.2	1.2	1.2	1.2	1.2	1.2	1.2
.64	.7	.9	1.0	1.1	1.2	1.2	1.2	1.3	1.3	1.3	1.3	1.3	1.3	1.3	1.3	1.3	1.3	1.3	1.3	1.3
.66	.8	.9	1.1	1.2	1.2	1.3	1.3	1.3	1.4	1.4	1.4	1.4	1.4	1.4	1.4	1.4	1.4	1.4	1.4	1.4
.68	.8	1.0	1.1	1.2	1.3	1.3	1.4	1.4	1.4	1.4	1.4	1.5	1.5	1.5	1.5	1.5	1.5	1.5	1.5	1.5
.70	.8	1.0	1.1	1.2	1.3	1.3	1.4	1.4	1.4	1.4	1.4	1.5	1.5	1.5	1.5	1.5	1.5	1.5	1.5	1.5

Contd.

TABLE 2.7 (*Contd.*)

ha / ft.	.02	.04	.06	.08	.10	.12	.14	.16	.18	.20	.22	.24	.26	.28	.30	.32	.34	.36	.38	.40
.72	.9	1.1	1.2	1.3	1.4	1.5	1.5	1.6	1.6	1.6	1.6	1.6	1.6	1.6	1.6	1.6	1.6	1.6	1.6	1.6
.74	.9	1.1	1.3	1.4	1.5	1.5	1.6	1.6	1.7	1.7	1.7	1.7	1.7	1.7	1.7	1.7	1.7	1.7	1.7	1.7
.76	.9	1.2	1.3	1.4	1.5	1.6	1.7	1.7	1.7	1.7	1.8	1.8	1.8	1.8	1.8	1.8	1.8	1.8	1.8	1.8
.78	1.0	1.2	1.4	1.5	1.6	1.7	1.7	1.8	1.8	1.8	1.9	1.9	1.9	1.9	1.9	1.9	1.9	1.9	1.9	1.9
.80	1.0	1.3	1.4	1.6	1.7	1.7	1.8	1.8	1.9	1.9	1.9	1.9	1.9	2.0	2.0	2.0	2.0	2.0	2.0	2.0
.82	1.0	1.3	1.5	1.6	1.7	1.8	1.9	1.9	2.0	2.0	2.0	2.0	2.0	2.0	2.1	2.1	2.1	2.1	2.1	2.1
.84	1.1	1.4	1.5	1.7	1.8	1.9	2.0	2.0	2.0	2.1	2.1	2.1	2.1	2.1	2.2	2.2	2.2	2.2	2.2	2.2
.86	1.1	1.4	1.6	1.8	1.9	2.0	2.0	2.1	2.1	2.2	2.2	2.2	2.2	2.3	2.3	2.3	2.3	2.3	2.3	2.3
.88	1.2	1.5	1.7	1.8	1.9	2.0	2.1	2.2	2.2	2.3	2.3	2.3	2.3	2.3	2.3	2.3	2.3	2.3	2.3	2.3
.90	1.2	1.5	1.7	1.9	2.0	2.1	2.2	2.2	2.3	2.3	2.4	2.4	2.4	2.4	2.4	2.4	2.4	2.4	2.4	2.4
.92	1.2	1.5	1.8	1.9	2.1	2.2	2.3	2.3	2.4	2.4	2.5	2.5	2.5	2.5	2.5	2.5	2.5	2.5	2.5	2.5
.94	1.3	1.6	1.8	2.0	2.1	2.3	2.3	2.4	2.5	2.5	2.5	2.6	2.6	2.6	2.6	2.6	2.7	2.7	2.7	2.7
.96	1.3	1.7	1.9	2.1	2.2	2.3	2.4	2.5	2.6	2.6	2.6	2.7	2.7	2.7	2.7	2.7	2.8	2.8	2.8	2.8
.98	1.4	1.7	2.0	2.1	2.3	2.4	2.5	2.6	2.6	2.7	2.7	2.8	2.8	2.8	2.8	2.8	2.8	2.9	2.9	2.9
1.00	1.4	1.8	2.0	2.2	2.4	2.5	2.6	2.7	2.7	2.8	2.8	2.9	2.9	2.9	2.9	2.9	2.9	3.0	3.0	3.0

CHAPTER 3

METHODS OF IRRIGATION

Introduction

India's and that of other countries, the agriculture is based on either rainfall or irrigation from man-made canals. In our country more than 50% of agricultural production comes from irrigated areas. In India 2.6 to 2.8 million hectares of land is brought under irrigation every year. It is therefore, vital to know about the entire irrigation system from development to efficient use as attempted in this chapter.

SURFACE IRRIGATION SYSTEM

The distribution of water with a surface system is totally dependent on the natural flow of water over the area to be irrigated. The land slope is, therefore, an important consideration besides intake or infiltration rate of the soil is another factor which would decide the choice of surface irrigation system for a particular area. Some types of systems are for level land only (Fig. 3.1) while other types of systems are for moderate to steepy soil slopes (Fig.3.2) present in the land. In both cases the choice is to made between the floor or furrow irrigation methods. However, before making the final decision regarding the installation of any system, the cost and returns of the various sytems are to be worked out. The following considerations should be made for finally selecting an irrigation system. These are :

(1) Basic units of surface system
(2) Working of different types of surface systems
(3) Land slope conditions of the area
(4) Infiltration rate characteristics of the area
(5) Field shape of the entire area to be irrigated
(6) Soil's physical and chemical conditions up to the rootzone and below, and
(7) Type of crops to be grown.

These are discussed categorically below.

Basic Units of a Surface System

There are 7 (seven) basic units to a field sized surface system that are common to all types (Fig. 3.3). These are following :

(a) A supply of water
(b) A field supply line
(c) Measuring devices
(d) A head ditch or pipelines
(e) Turnouts.

Besides these there are 2 more units to be considered :

(f) Structures for holding the water within a certain area like — dykes, levees or borders, and
(g) Arrangement of collecting excess runoff water into a tail ditch or a reservoir for reuse.

Water Supply : If the water supply is above the level of the field to be irrigated, the water can flow by gravity to other fields through an open ditch or pipeline. However, if the water level is below the level of the field, a pump would be required to raise the water to the field level and a ditch or pipeline to deliver it to the field. In case pipeline is more than a few feet long, a stand pipe or pressure relief valve has to be provided to control pressure in the pipelines.

Field Supply Line : This may be either an open ditch or a pipeline. This helps to deliver the water from the source to the field. The ditch may be unlined or lined with materials such as concrete or asphalt or plastic or any impervious material. For pipelines generally made of galvanized steel, aluminium, plastic, asbestos cement and concrete etc. are used.

Measuring Devices : These are installed to measure the amount of water applied to the field. If supply is delivered through an open ditch (water course), then Weir notch (Fig. 3.5) or a Parshall flume (Fig. 3.4) or cut throat flumes (Fig.3.6) are used. However, if water is being supplied through a pipe line, then flow meters (Fig. 3.7) are used. An orifice plate (Fig. 3.8) is also used for measuring the amount of water flowing through pumps.

A Head Ditch of Head Pipelines : These are constructed or installed from one end or one side of the field to be irrigated. It is the means by which water is delivered from the field supply line to the different parts of the field.

Turnouts : These are used for releasing the water from the head ditch or pipe line onto the land to be irrigated. These are in fact flood gates (Fig. 3.9) or siphon tubes (Fig. 3.10). In case pipeline system is installed the gated pipe (Fig. 3.11) or a hydrant valve (Fig. 3.12) can be used. In case automated surface system is to be installed, then the arrangement of providing type of checks and turnouts adaptable to automatic control system being put on has to be made (Fig.3.13).

Structure for Holding Water : In the area to be irrigated, certain structures are to be constructed to most of the surface systems. These are called "levees", "dikes" or "borders". Each one is essentially the same. These are simply earth ridge made from the field soil to encircle the area to be irrigated.

Reuse Reservoir of Tail Water Ditch : It is constructed for collection of excess water for reuse. This is essentially required so that higher flow rates through the irrigated strips which increases the uniformity of water application can be maintained. The excessive water saved through tail ditches can also be reused by pumping it back to the head ditch or head pipes or into another area to be irrigated. Fertilizers, pesticides etc. and salts that may wash from the irrigated fields are kept away from entering streams and polluting them.

DIFFERENT TYPES OF SURFACE SYSTEMS

Drip and Trickle Irrigation : Under favourable soil conditions and when water is extremely scarce, water can be supplied within rootzone through specially designed emitters or nozzles. The evaporation from water and soil surface is reduced and very high application efficiencies can be obtained. This system is also a type of sub-irrigation, but presently sophisticated for general application in India.

Surface Irrigation Methods : Any method adopted for surface irrigation must ensure uniform distribution of water in the crop rootzone and high water application efficiency. The suitability of the method is determined by water supply, soil type, land topography, nature of crops to be irrigated, climatic conditions and costs involved. Salient points for various methods of irrigations are given in Fig. 3.1.

In surface irrigation methods water is directly applied to soil surface from a channel constructed at the upper reach of the field and is spread by the gravity flow due to slope of the land. Water may be applied to crops in border strips or check basin or furrows. Irrigation efficiency in surface methods are about 35-38% on loamy sand, 45-50% on sandy loam, about 57-61% on loamy soils and 70-75% on clayey soils. For irrigating crops by surface methods, fields are usually laid out every time before or after crops are planted because these layouts are destroyed during preparatory tillage operations.

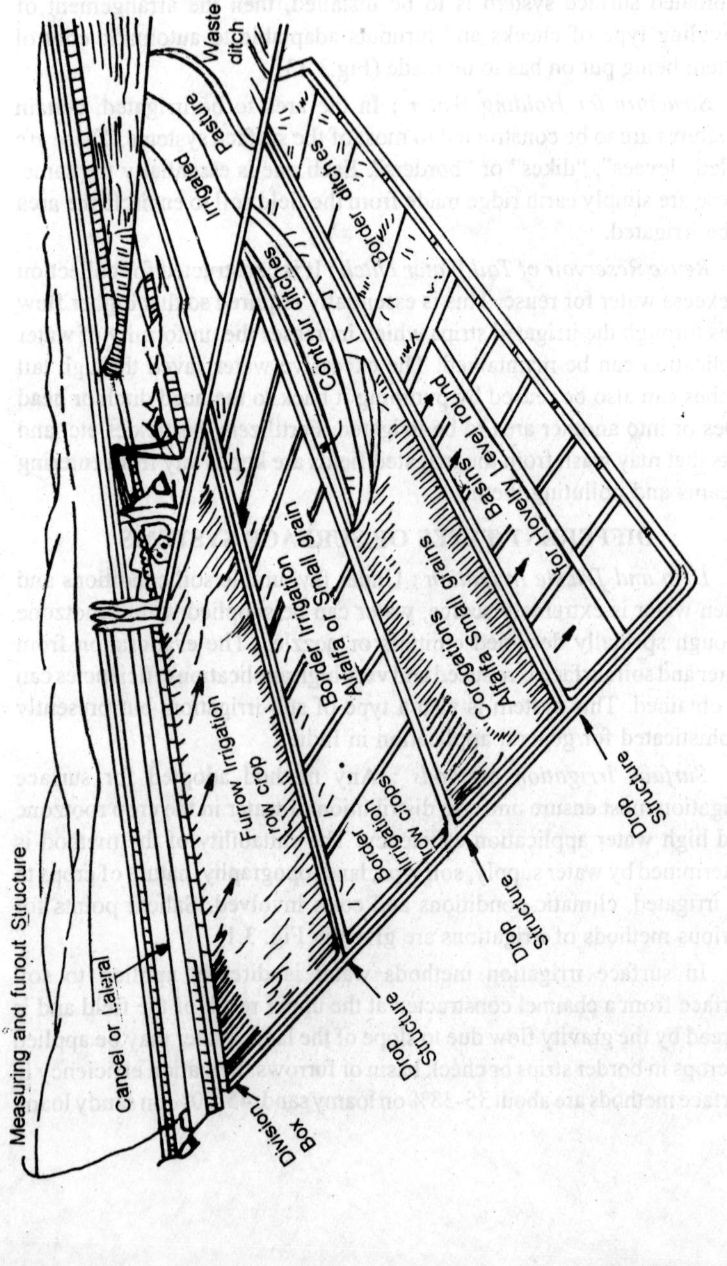

Fig. 3.1 : Various Methods of applying Irrigation water to field crops.

Border Irrigation : In border irrigation land is divided into a number of long parallel strips called borders, separated by low ridges and water moves in it as a uniform sheet down the slope. This method can be adopted to most soils that permit the required land levelling at a reasonable cost without permanently reducing its productivity. However, it is more suited to soils having moderately low to moderately high infiltration rates. In course sandy soils, very high infiltration rate poses stringent limitations in design, whereas for soils having very low infiltration rates to provide adequate infiltration opportunity time without surface runoff at the lower end. Irrigation stream may be too small to completely cover the border strips.

This method is suitable to irrigate closely spaced crops like wheat, barley, oilseeds, fodder crops, legumes, etc. except, rice which needs standing water. It has a number of advantages such as :

(i) border ridges can be economically constructed with simple farming instruments like bullock drawnband former or ridger to tractor drawn discridger,

(ii) labour requirement is low as compared to check basin,

(iii) high water application efficiencies are possible if properly designed,

(iv) large water stream can be efficiently used,

(v) operation of the system is simple and easy, and

(vi) adequate surface drainage is possible provided outlets are available.

Border strips have negligible or no cross slope but a uniform gentle slope with an even surface in the direction of irrigation to provide a nearly uniform depth of water application. Preparation of the field with desired slope is the main limitation under present conditions in India because mostly the operations are conducted with bullock power which is usually inadequate. Borders are laid along the general slope of the field (straight or down the slope) or laid across the general slope depending upon the general gradation of the fields. When fields can be levelled to desired slopes economically without permanently reducing its productivity, graded borders are easier to construct and operate. But when land slopes exceed safe limits, fields are undulating and levelling is not feasible, the borders are laid across the slope on contours. The design criteria of a contour border is the same as a straight border. Each contour border is levelled crosswise and has a uniform longitudinal gradient as in a straight border.

Border Specifications and Stream Size

Successful operation of the border method requires that the system is designed and operated properly. Proper design requires consideration of the hydraulics of flow in borders. However, some general suggestions on width, length and slope of borders and size of irrigation streams are presented here.

Width of Border Strip : The width of a border strip usually varies from 3 to 15 m depending on the size of irrigation stream and land slope. When size of the stream is small, width is reduced but it should not be less than 3 m otherwise too many ridges need to be prepared.

The length of border strips depend on the time required for uniform wetting of entire length, which in turn is influenced by infiltration rate of the soil, slope of the land and stream size available. For moderate slopes and small to moderate size irrigation streams, the following border lengths have been suggested :

Sandy to sandy loam soil — 60-120 m

Medium loam soils — 100-180 m

Clay loam to clay soils — 150-300 m

Border Slope : The border should have a gentle uniform longitudinal gradient because excessive slopes will make water to run to lower end faster resulting in erosion and insufficient irrigation at the upstream and water logging, deep percolation and breach in bunds at the downstream. On the other hand, too flat slopes will cause very slow movement of water resulting in deep percolations losses at the upper reaches and under irrigation downstream. General recommended safe limits of land slopes in borders are as mentioned below :

Sandy loam to sandy soils	—	0.25 to 0.6 per cent
Medium loam soils	—	0.20 to 0.4 per cent
Clay to clay loams soils	—	0.05 to 0.2 per cent

Size of Irrigation Stream

The size of the irrigation stream required is determined by the infiltration rate of the soil and width of the border strip. Coarse textured soils with high infiltration rates require large streams to spread water over the entire strip rapidly and avoid excessive losses due to deep percolation and water logging at the lower reaches. The size of the stream delivered into each border is the controlling factor in border irrigation which can be varied after the irrigation system has been installed to partly compensate for inadequacies in width or length of borders which have been selected as well as for change which may take place in soil infiltration rates with irrigations or depths of rooting of crops. The size of the stream required, however, should be determined as accurately as possible as a part of the design of the system. The large streams could be handled by letting in the water in several strips simultaneously. Metallic or plastic syphons, bamboo or earthen spikes may be used for diversion of water from the channels.

It is often convenient to express the irrigation stream in terms of the rate of water flow per unit width of the border, such as in litres per second per metre of border width. This value multiplied by the width of the border is the size of the irrigation stream that should be delivered into each border.

The depth of water applied to the soil can be regulated by the size of the irrigation stream. A larger stream is used to apply shallower and a smaller stream is used to apply greater depth of water. This is because the amount of water entering the soil is related to the infiltration opportunity time which in turn, is related to time needed to cover entire area of the border with the flow of water.

Values of stream sizes for different soil types and slopes based on available information are presented in Table 3.1.

TABLE 3.1

Some Values of Stream Sizes to Suit Varying Soil Characteristics and Border Slopes

Soil type	Border slope (Per cent)	Flow per metre width of border strip (l/sec)
Sandy soil infiltration rate 0.4 cm per hr.	0.20-0.40	10-15
Loamy sand infiltration rate 1.8 to 2.5 cm per hr.	0.40-0.40	7-10
	0.20-0.40	7-10
	0.40-0.60	5-8
Sandy loam infiltration rate 1.2 to 1.8 cm per hr.	0.20-0.40	5-7
	0.40-0.60	4-6
Clay loam infiltration rate 0.6 to 0.9 cm per hr.	0.15-0.3	3-4
	0.30-0.4	2-3
Clay infiltration rate 0.2 to 0.6 cm per hr.	0.10-0.2	2-4

Design of Border Irrigation Systems

A well designed border irrigation system provides for the application of desired amount of water nearly uniformly throughout the field. To obtain maximum water application efficiency, water should remain on the surface long enough to allow just the desired amount of water to infiltrate into the soil. The required infiltration opportunity time is obtained using the accumulated infiltration time relationship for the soil in question. Water distribution efficiency is governed mainly by the uniformity of the infiltration opportunity time obtained throughout the border length. When the behaviour of the irrigation system can be predicted from the measurable characteristics of the site, it is possible to obtain a nearly uniform infiltration opportunity time throughout the border by suitably adjusting the stream size, and the length of run or slope, of the border. In an existing field layout, where the length or slope of the borders cannot be altered, the main controllable variable is only the entrance stream size (Fig. 3.2).

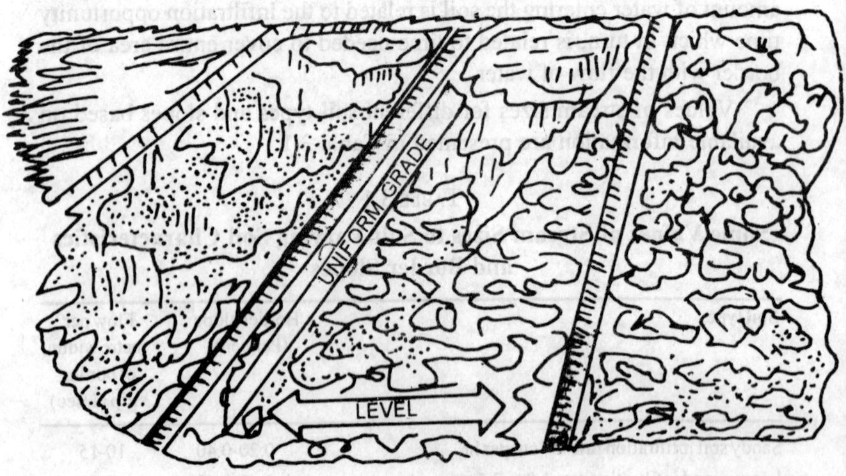

Fig. 3.2 : Graded Border

CHECK BASIN IRRIGATION

Check basin irrigation is the most common method of irrigation as it is simple in principle. There are, however, many variations in its use, but all involve dividing the field into smaller unit areas so that each unit has a nearly level surface. Bunds or ridges are constructed around the areas forming basins within which the irrigation is applied to the desired depth. When irrigating rice or ponding water for leaching salts from the soil, depth of water may be maintained for considerable longer periods by allowing water to flow continuously into basins.

Usually one field channel is provided for every two rows of check basins. The size of irrigation stream is not critical as long as it is sufficient to provide a coverage of the entire strip in a relatively small portion of the time required to apply the desired amount of water into the soil. As the infiltration rate of the soil increases, the stream size is increased or otherwise the size of basins reduced in order to cover the area within a short period of time. A large size irrigation system will permit a comparatively larger size of the basin.

Types of Check Basins Based on Size and Shape

The size of check basins may vary from as small as one metre square to as large as one or two hectares or more. The smaller size is preferred where smaller amount of water is required to be applied whereas a larger size is preferred for a crop like rice where more water is required to be applied. When the land can be graded economically into nearly level fields, the basins are rectangular in shape. In rolling topography the ridges follow the contours of the land surface. The contour ridges are connected by cross ridges at intervals. The vertical interval between contour ridges usually varies from 6 to 12 cm in case of upland irrigated crops like wheat and 15 to 30 cm in case of land irrigated crops like rice (Fig. 3.3).

The size of basins in rice fields vary with size of the irrigation stream available and the size of the land-holding. Large irrigation streams and large holdings permit larger basins. The size also depends on the infiltration characteristics of the soil. Sandy and sandy loam soils with high infiltration rates permit only small size basins while clay soils having low infiltration rates allow large basins.

In irrigation orchards, circular (also called ring) and/or square or contour basins may be used as in other crops. When the plants are widely spaced, ring or circular type of irrigation basin may be adopted. The ring basins are smaller in size when the plant is young and are made larger with the increase in the plant growth. An advantage of the ring method is that the entire area is not flooded and thus high water use efficiency is obtained.

Adaptability and Limitations of Check Basin Methods

Check basin irrigation is suited to smooth, gentle and uniform land slopes and for soils having adequate to low infiltration rate. Steep slopes require proper grading and land levelling. Both row crops and close-growing crops are adapted to be used with basins as long as the crop is not

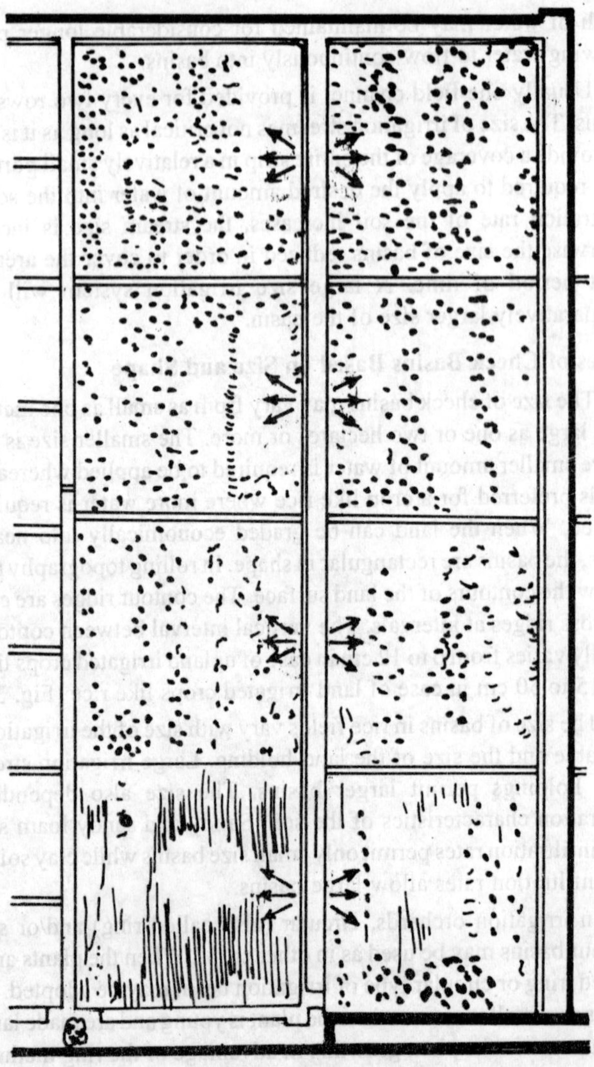

Fig. 3.3 : Check Basin

affected by temporary inundation or is planted in raised beds so that it will remain above the water level. It is also suitable for very permeable soils which must be covered with water rapidly to prevent excessive deep percolation losses at the upstream end.

The principal disadvantage of the check basin method of irrigation is that ridges interfere with movement of animal-drawn or tractor-drawn implements for interculture and harvesting of crops. Considerable land is occupied by ridges and lateral field channels and crop yields are substantially reduced on ridges and in the lateral channels. The method also impedes surface drainage as precise land grading and shaping are not required as in case of border strips. The labour requirement in land preparation and irrigation is much higher in check basin irrigation as compared to other methods, except when the basins are very large.

Design of Check Basin Irrigation Systems

In check basin it is possible to apply precisely needed amounts of water to fill the root zone moisture to field capacity if provisions are made to measure the rate of flow into the basin and control the duration of flow of the irrigation stream. This will result in high values of water application and water storage efficiencies. Water distribution efficiency is usually the limiting factor. A rough but useful rule in check basin design is that water should spread to cover entire basin in one-fourth the time required to infiltrate the net depth of irrigation water. By careful selection of the size of the check basin and the stream size to suit infiltration characteristics of the soil, it is possible to arrive at desired designs of check basins.

FURROW IRRIGATION

The furrow method of irrigation is used to irrigate row crops with moderate to large spacing. Furrows are made between the crop rows at the time of planting and, or during cultivating processes. The size and shape of the furrows depends on crops grown, equipment used and spacing between crop rows. Water is applied by running small streams in furrows. The time of water flow in furrows depends on the amount of water required to replenish the soil moisture deficit in the rootzone as well as the infiltration rate and the rate of lateral spread of water in the soil.

As compared to other methods of surface irrigation, the furrow method has several distinct advantages. The water in the furrows contacts only a small portion of the land surface and thereby reduces caking and crusting of the soil surface without affecting the direction of the soil. The erosion of the soil could be minimised on a wide range of natural slopes by carving the furrows across a sloping field rather than down the slope. The method reduces labour requirements in land preparation and irrigation. Compared to check basin method, there is no wastage of land in field ditches.

For furrow irrigation the land must be properly graded so that water can travel the entire length of the furrow without ponding. This means that high and low spots must be removed and the land given required slope to let the water flow down the furrows.

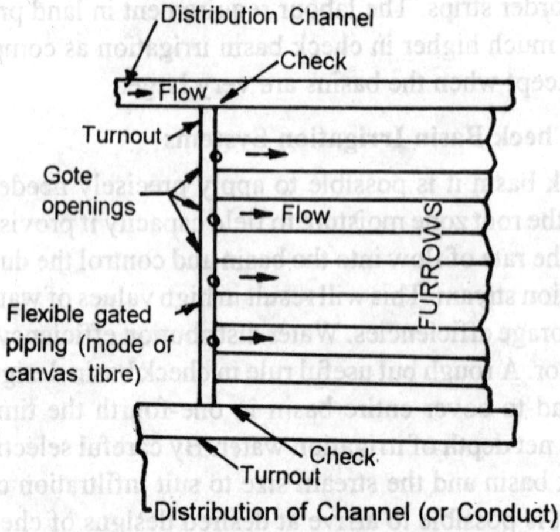

Fig. 3.4 : Furrow Irrigation by gated piping

Irrigation furrows based on their alignment may be classified into :

(a) 'straight furrows', and
(b) 'contour furrows'.

Based on their size and spacing, furrows may be classified as 'deep furrows' and 'corrugations'.

Straight furrows, like borders, are laid down the prevailing land slope. They are best suited to sites where the land slope does not exceed 0.75 per cent. In areas of intense rainfall, however, the furrow grade should not exceed 0.5 per cent so as to minimise the erosion hazard. The ranges in furrow slopes for efficient irrigation in different soil types are the same as these recommended for borders.

In fine textured soils having very low infiltration rates, the furrows are usually levelled lengthwise. With level furrows, the same stream size is maintained until the required amount of water is applied. The water is ponded in the furrows until it is absorbed by the soil.

Furrow Spacing

Furrows can be spaced to fit the crops grown and the type of machines used for planting and cultivation. Crops like potatoes, maize and cotton are planted 45 to 90 cm apart having furrows between the rows. Vegetable crops such as lettuce, carrots and onions etc. which have smaller spacing are planted on both the sides of ridges.

Furrow Length and Slope

The suitable length of a furrow is usually the longest furrow that can be safely and efficiently irrigated. Long furrows are an advantage in intercultivation. The length, however, should not be too long to result in over-irrigation at the upper end and under irrigation at the lower end. Short furrows require field supply channels to be spaced too close with consequent loss of land and increase in labour requirement.

Proper furrow length depends largely on the hydraulic conductivity of the soil. Furrows must be shorter on a porous sandy soil than on a light clay soil. The length of furrow which can be efficiently irrigated may be as short as 45 m on soils which takes up water rapidly, or as much as 300 m or longer on soils with low infiltration rates. In Table 3.2 general guidelines are given the maximum lengths of furrows for different soils, slopes and depths of irrigation.

TABLE 3.2

Length of Furrows for Different Soil Types, Furrow Slopes and Depths of Irrigation

Furrows slope per cent	Furrow length, metres soil type						
	Clay		Loams			Sand	
	Net depth of water application cm						
	7.5	15	5	10	15	7.5	10
0.05	300	400	120	270	60	90	150
0.10	350	440	180	330	90	120	190
0.20	370	470	220	370	120	180	250
0.30	390	500	280	400	150	225	280
0.50	380	500	280	370	120	190	250
1.00	270	400	250	300	90	150	220

Furrow Stream

The size of the furrow stream is the one factor which can be varied after the furrow irrigation system has been installed. The size of the furrow stream usually varies from 0.5 to 2.5 litres per second. To obtain uniform irrigation, the largest stream of water that will not cause erosion is used in each furrow at the beginning of the irrigation. The maximum size of the irrigation stream that can be used at start of the irrigation, is limited by consideration of erosion in furrows, overtopping of furrows and prevention of runoff at the downstream end. The maximum non-erosive flow rate in furrows is estimated by the following empirical equation :

$$qm = \frac{0.60}{s}$$

where qm = maximum non-erosive stream, litres per second

s = slope of furrow expressed as a per cent

The average depth of water applied during an irrigation can be calculated from the following relationship :

$$d = \frac{360\ qt}{wl}$$

where d = average depth of water applied, cm

q = stream size, litres per second

t = duration of irrigation (elapsed time), hours

w = furrow spacing, metres

l = furrow length, metres.

The surface irrigation systems are designed such that these may serve especially under two conditions of land slopes *viz.* (i) lands that are nearly level with slope less than 0.1 per cent slope (10 cms per 100 metres or 1.2 inch drop per 100 feet), and (ii) lands that are moderately sloping where slope is ranging from 0.1 per cent to 15% (10 cms to 15 metres per 100 metres or 1.2 inch to 15 feet per 100 feet). Under first slope level conditions of the ground (strips) the system designed is called as level systems (Fig. 3.4) while on second slope level conditions or sloping strips, the system designed is called as graded system. These systems are discussed as follows :

Level Systems

There are following types of level systems namely :

Level Border : It is also called check basin type as shown in Fig. 3.5. This type of surface system consists of a level area encircled by the earthen border ridges or levees (Fig. 3.6).

Fig. 3.5 : Contour Furrow Irrigation

The required quantity of water is released in the strip land for irrigation and is allowed to stand till it is soaked into the ground. The quantity of water may be increased depending upon weed infestation to avoid chances of short water supply to main plants *e.g.* rice or paddy crop. This helps to control weeds. The added water is allowed to stand for several weeks.

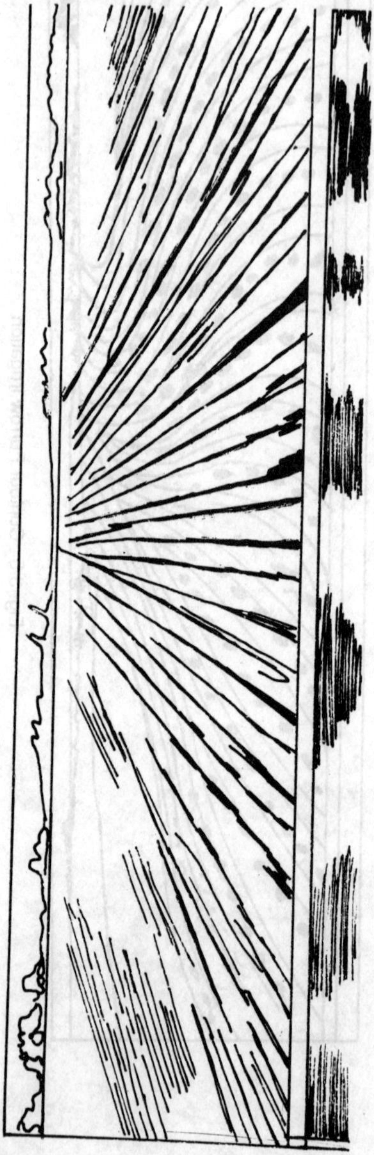

Fig. 3.6 : Level Furrow Irrigation

In order to attain the uniform distribution of water, as a thumb rule the quantity of water should be double than the cumulative infiltration rate of the soil *i.e.* twice the water quantity which can be absorbed by the soil up to the rootzone or more as may be decided. This helps to spread water over the strip as quickly as possible. Otherwise, more quantity of water will be absorbed than actually required to infiltrate near the head ditch. In view of this level border system should be constructed so that at least 1.7 cubic metres per minute (1.0 cubic foot per second) is available for each 8 hectare chak (20 acres) or strip. In general it has been experienced that around 6.7 cubic metres per minute (4.0 cubic foot per second) may serve the purpose of uniform application of water without loosing much at the head reach. Thus by keeping large stream size flooding would be quick and higher application efficiency.

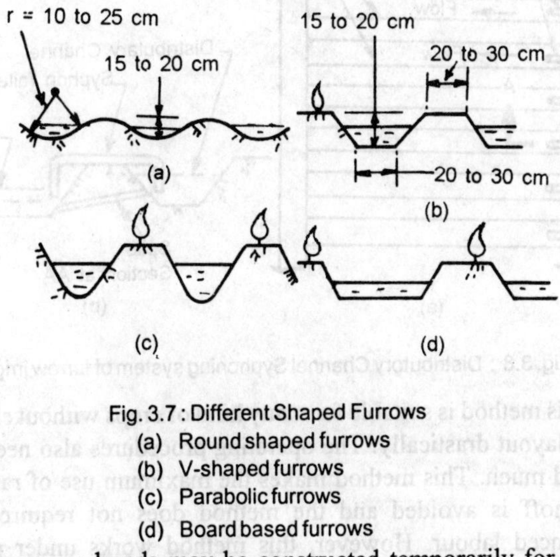

Fig. 3.7 : Different Shaped Furrows
(a) Round shaped furrows
(b) V-shaped furrows
(c) Parabolic furrows
(d) Board based furrows

The levees or bunds may be constructed temporarily for a single irrigation or for a cropping season or for permanent use for annual crops such as paddy. The bunds size would depend upon the depth of water to be impounded in the field as well as the stability of soil when wet or damaged by burrowing animals etc.

The supply channel should be aligned on the upper side of the area and the laterals are dug in between two rows of beds or check basins. The water from the channels is turned into the beds and supply is stopped (cut off) when the water level in the bed is as required. The provision of drains to remove excess rainfall water and latter to help to dry the field after maturity should be planned where the subsequent crops are to be grown without much delay.

The alternative to quick application of water as narrated above by which the speed of water can be increased across the strip is to construct a slight grade (total drop from one end of the strip to the other should not be more than one half of the depth of water to be applied). Also the provision of slight grade may also help the water collection in low lying spots which cause puddling or deterioration of structure and accumulation of salts and thereby resulting in salty patches at those places.

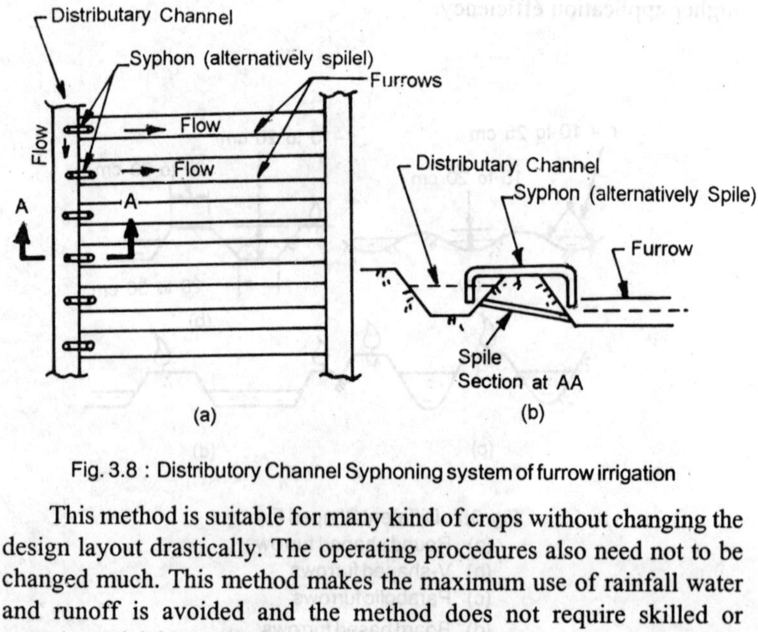

Fig. 3.8 : Distributory Channel Syphoning system of furrow irrigation

This method is suitable for many kind of crops without changing the design layout drastically. The operating procedures also need not to be changed much. This method makes the maximum use of rainfall water and runoff is avoided and the method does not require skilled or experienced labour. However, this method works under perfect and precise/accurate levelling and shaping of land in absence of which the application efficiency decreases. The dykes or bunds has to be kept high to check the overtopping of ridges by applied stream. Due to this reason it becomes more labour-oriented irrigation practice though the labour may not be experienced. The dykes or bunds interfere with the farm machinery (in case the check basins or level borders are small). These bunds also get damaged turning tillage operations and hence require recurring maintenance expenditure.

Basins Method for Orchards (Ring Method)

It is essentially the level border or check basin method except that for irrigating trees of orchards basins constructed are either squarely rectangular or circular shape (Fig. 3.9) of the size depending upon the quantity of water to be impounded as per age of the tree. This method works better in those soils which have moderate to slow intake rate and moderate to high available water holding capacity. This method also works efficiently for orchards under slopping lands. A basin may also serve more than one tree a group of few. However, this method has limitation on very slopy lands where deep cutting would be required for land preparation besides making special provisions for drainage.

Fig. 3.9 : Basin Method

Contour Levees Method

This is also a level system of irrigation and is alike level border method except it is more efficiently workable under sloping lands. In this, the strips are graded until they are level. But in this method the fields are bounded on the contour by levees at the lower edge of the strip (Fig. 3.10). The irrigation method is same as for level border *i.e.* from a head ditch or pipeline at one end or both ends of strip so that it spreads rapidly over the area where it remains until fully soaked except for extra water for weed control.

In this system since there are levelled areas on the side of a slope, there are often two or more such strips below the highest one. In such cases water can be released from the higher strips to the lower strips . The desired level of water on each strip is held with the help of small spillway or pipe/outlets in the levees. This arrangement helps to remove excess water from one strip to spill-over to other strip adjacent to each other. In case the quantity of water is considerable so as to hold by lower strip, it is taken out into a ditch or reservoir available at the lower end of the field which can be recycled again for use.

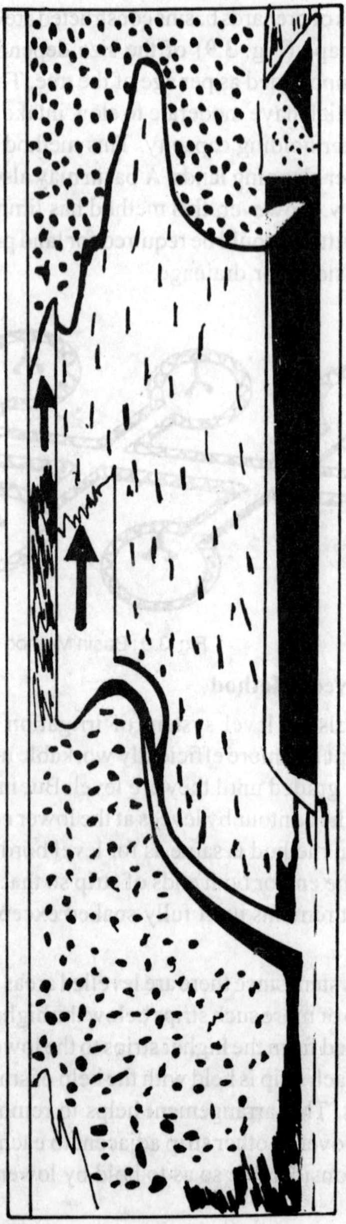

Fig. 3.10 Contour Ditch Irrigation

The spacing between channels is adjusted as per stream size available, slope and infiltration rate of the soil. Since minimum land grading is sufficient for working of this system and as such it can also work successfully on shallow depth soils.

However, this method requires careful location and spacing of the channels. This system is suitable for all types of close growing crops. In case of coarse and moderately light textured soils (sand, loamy sand, sandy loam), the ground slope should not exceed 4 per cent. This method can also be recommended for salt affected tracts with or without grass cover if plenty of water is available in that region. If lands are undulated, slight grading should be done to make the ground smooth to facilitate uniform distribution of water. This method is quite economical, less land preparation is needed on irregular topography. Easy working of farm and transport machinery is possible as the ditches can be easily filled.

Level Furrow Method

This method is similar to level border method but it has furrows on the ground. The slope of the ground is minimum (Fig. 3.11). The size and shape of the furrows depend upon the crops to be grown, the type of machinery being used and the spacing between the rows. The cross sectional area of the furrows should be of sufficient size to carry the amount of water needed to obtain uniform distribution of water throughout the length of furrows.

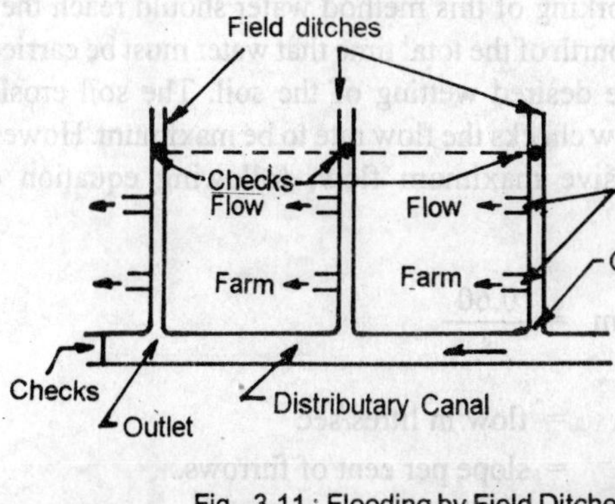

Fig. 3.11 : Flooding by Field Ditches

The wetting zone of the soil in this method is much less than level border (flooding method). This is because the water which flows in the furrows is absorbed in the soil vertically as well as laterally to irrigate the areas between furrows which decreases its vertical movement as occurs in flooding method. The time period for which water is continued to flow in furrows depends on the deficit quantity of water within rootzone, infiltration rate of the soil and the rate of lateral spread of water in the soil profile. It is essential that amount of water or stream size be designed such that it exceeds infiltration rate of the soil so that water advances rapidly in the furrow. However, the quantity of water should be reduced or cut off as soon as water is about to reach the last end of the field to avoid water losses or some reservoir be made to collect such excess for reuse (if not costly). In case of montmorillonite rich clayey soils which cracks on drying, it is not necessary to cutback the streams because the streams can be turned off when the water reaches the end of furrow.

The distribution of water can be uniform provided the initial stream size or water quantity released is large, of course as per carrying capacity of the furrow without erosion. If the furrows are short and flat, a large flow be released to quickly fill the furrow and shut off stream but if furrows are long and slopping the water quantity is to be regulated during the irrigation. The water into furrows can be delivered directly from unlined head ditch or with the help of syphon tubes or hose pipes etc. or gated pipe in line canal system. The water stands in the furrows until it is absorbed into the rootzone by soil below the furrows and in the ridges between the furrows. As a thumb rule about 15 per cent more water is required in this system as compared to that quantity of water actually needed to flow over the entire land strip.

For efficient working of this method water should reach the end of furrow within one-fourth of the total time that water must be carried in the furrow to obtain the desired wetting of the soil. The soil erosion and overtopping of furrow checks the flow rate to be maximum. However, for computing non-erosive maximum flow, following equation can be used :

$$Qm = \frac{0.60}{s}$$

where, Qm = flow in litres/sec

s = slope per cent of furrows.

The average depth of water applied during irrigation can be worked out by following equation :

$$D = \frac{W \times 3600}{Sm \times Lm}$$

where

D = average depth of water applied per hour
W = stream size in litres/sec
Sm = furrow spacing in metres
Lm = length of furrows irrigated in one hour in metres.

This method is suitable for all cultivated crops planted in rows including orchard and vineyard crops as well as vegetables.

Graded Systems

The graded systems are of 5 types, namely graded border, (ii) contour ditch, (iii) graded furrow, (iv) contour furrow, and (v) corrugation.

It has been expressed earlier that most graded system are designed for areas having gentle slopes *i.e.* 0.1 per cent and above but not exceeding 15 per cent. The choice of selecting irrigation system based on slope is given in Table 3.3.

Graded Border

This type of surface irrigation is the same as the level border one. However, the difference is that in this furrow has some slope in the flow direction.

This system is laid on contour on sloping fields by bench levelling. A slight grade is maintained in the contour direction. For irrigation the flooding is made into each strip. The quantity of water has to be kept large enough so that it equally spreads over the entire strip width between the border ridges or levees. The quantity of water depends upon the intake rate family characteristics of the area soils. Thus, if intake rate is low the quantity of water to be applied would be more because the soil cannot absorb required quantity of water at a time during flow and hence excess water to provide more opportunity time to wet these up to the desired depth. This excess water should be recollected for use otherwise it creates many problems and wastage of water.

Contour Ditch Type

This stystem is designed for sloping lands after the crop is planted (Fig. 3.10). For irrigation a temporary dam is constructed in the head ditch just below the contour ditch and in this ditch too, water is checked by a temporary dam or obstruction. The water is delivered from channels dug across or around the slope (approximately on contour). The full water collected in contour ditch flows further in the strips below. The first water obstructions is removed and so the water flows similarly across the second strip down and to the next contour ditch. However, in flowing water is simultaneously absorbed by the ground. The excess water thus, flows down ahead and collected again in another contour ditch and so on. This process is repeated till the entire field is irrigated. The excess water in last is collected at the end by a ditch or reservoir and can be pumped back either to the first ditch or to another field. The spacing between contour ditches varies from 24 to 914 metres (80 to 3000 ft.) depending upon slope, intake rate of the soil and amount of water to be applied to each irrigated area.

The other features and limitations of this method are that it can be used for saline and alkali fields and grass lands if sufficient quantity of water is available. It is quite economical, and field machinery can easily work on this system. However, the irrigation efficiency is low because uniform water penetration is difficult to achieve in this method. The crops at early growth stage may be damaged due to the soil bake or crust. If soils are susceptible to erosion, this method cannot be used on slopy lands.

Graded Furrow Type

This kind of surface system has a layout of small channels between rows or beds. It is planned so as to keep the slope uniform in the flow direction (Fig. 3.11). This type works like level furrow type and according to the crops to be grown, the furrows size and shape is selected. However, graded furrows are generally constructed straight down (along) the slope of the field. The maximum flow rate, and average depth of water to be applied can be determined emperically as given by equations given in level furrow. This method is suitable to irrigate all cultivated crops grown in rows, orchards, vineyards and vegetable crops. In sandy type soils (sand, loamy sand and sandy loam), wherein the vertical movement of water is sufficiently greater than lateral movement essential for water distribution between furrows. This method is not successful effectively but for other textured soil it works efficiently.

In this method since water remains in contact of the small portion of the soil. The problem of soil crusting and puddling is not faced. Also there is comparatively less evaporation losses than open surfaces exposed in other level systems. The size of furrow is not dependent on the stream size *i.e.* furrows can be used with any quantity of water by adjusting the water flow simultaneously to any number of furrows. This method can provide high efficiency of irrigation if proper irrigation management practices are adopted. In high rainfall regions, the furrows also work as drainage channels for taking care of surface runoff. This method does not waste land for construction of channels and bunds.

The important limitations of this method are as follows :

(1) It is not suitable for applying less quantities of water (light irrigation) as required for seed germination or for very shallow rooted crops grown on light textured or high infiltrating soils.

(2) Proper grading if not done, jeopardise the success of this method because proper and uniform distribution of water does not occur and there are chances of puddling of water in channels.

(3) The soil erosion is also an important limitation when furrow irrigation is practised which should be considered in designing the system.

(4) The land slope should not exceed 0.3 per cent if rainfall is erratic and high.

(5) Skilled and experienced labour is required to operate the system.

(6) It is costly due to high labour requirements.

Contour Furrow Method

This method is though similar to the graded furrow system but the furrows are to be laid across the slope on an uniform grade (Fig. 3.10) rather than down the slope. The contour furrows are curved to fit the land surface. Since the furrows follow the contour approximately, this method is called contour furrow method (difference between graded and contour furrow method). For irrigating a land the water is turned in the furrows from head ditches or pipelines or gated pipes. The water flowing in the furrows is absorbed by the soil both below the furrow and the ridge between the furrows. Head ditches or pipelines run down the hill or slightly across the slope to feed the individual furrows.

Contour furrow systems, in fact, are the series of small contour terraces. After the top furrow, each succeeding furrow is slightly lower than that above it. This method is adaptable to nearly all irrigable soils. However, it does not work in very light sandy soils and montmorillomitic soils which cracks on drying and results in severe erosion and water losses. In light textured soils, if the slope is more than 4 per cent the furrow may breach. Binding has to be provided for checking the possibility of breaches and damaging other fields where the soils are stable and are not cultivated as in orchards having steeper slopes. The land which is sloppy and furrow irrigation is to be designed, the better method would be to construct bench terracing first on which furrows can be constructed. This method is suitable to all row crops and vegetables which are planted in deep furrows. The size spacing and shape of furrow depends upon type of crops required to be grown. Grassed waterways and structures are generally needed to carry excess irrigation water and rainfall runoff from the rows. The method for efficiency should be supplemented with graded terraces to ensure against breaches.

The limitations of this method are as follows :

(1) It does not work on sandy and soils that crack.

(2) Rodents (rats) cause holes in furrows due to which water leakage may occur from higher to lower furrows.

(3) The furrow overflow and wash out may occur.

(4) In high rain storm, rainfall areas, the furrow breaches may harm land considerably if care is not taken at planning stage.

(5) The long length of furrow causes breaking of the furrows and thus leaking of water.

(6) If breaches are prepared and grass land waterways and structures are not present it may cause great damage.

Corrugation Type of Method

In this method water is applied in small furrows running down the slope from the supply channel. It is partially a surface flooding method and also a small graded furrow method for sown or sodded fields (Fig. 3.22). In this method irrigation water does not cover entire field but is applied in small channels or corrugations evenly spaced across the field. The water flowing in corrugations is absorbed into the soil and spreads laterally to irrigate the ridge areas between the corrugations or channels. The channels or corrugations are spaced so that water spreads laterally and sets the soil by infiltration in the ridges by the time the desired quantity has finished flowing in the furrows. The spacing should be closer on steep slopes than for flatter slopes and on sandy soils as compared to medium (loam etc.) and fine textured (clayey) soils. The corrugations are 'V' or 'U' shaped channels about 10 cm deep and spaced 40 to 75 cms apart. Corrugations are made after the crops are sown. Their slope depends upon the type of crops to be grown and erodibility of the soils.

The length of time for which water should be run in the channels depends on the amount of water required to meet the water deficit in the rootzone as well as infiltration rate of the soil. The stream size of water should be more so as to advance very quickly to attain the uniform distribution of water over the field. The corrugations should be kept full of water but not overflowing and the supply of water be cutoff as soon as water reaches the lower end of the field to avoid excessive wastage of water. The provision to collect this runoff water at the end should be made to reuse it.

This method is most suitable to close growing crops grown on smooth fields, having soils fine textured or medium textured but not sandy and that cracks (montmorillonitic). Corrugations are often used for preplanting irrigation within borders and later irrigation is given by border method. However, this method is not suitable in areas getting high rainfall during irrigation season. It is also not suitable when slope is even upto 1 per cent because very smooth surface is needed. But it is suitable for clayey soils which do not crack *i.e.* which do not have more proportion of montmorillonite clay material uncareful regulation of irrigation stream may also cause damage with this method.

INFLUENCING PARAMETERS OF SURFACE IRRIGATION

(a) The irrigation planning for a network distribution involves other parameters which influence irrigation system. These are :

(1) *Land Slope* : Based on this, irrigation system should be chosen and planned as given in Table 3.3.

(2) *Effect of Infiltration Rate* : If soils have low to moderate infiltration rate say upto 38 millimetres (1.5 inches/hr), then select any type of surface system (Table 3.3).

The system can be designed so that there is a minimum amount of excess water.

(b) If the infiltration rate is low say 2 mm, per hour which occurs in fine textured soils due to swelling of clay particles and fine grains of soil, fill the open pores or spaces between the large soil particles. This sealing effect does not allow water to penetrate. Under such conditions the infiltration rate may come down even below 2.5 millimetres per hour (0.1 inch per hour). This condition occurs less in furrow system, because there is more surface area to absorb water. Also in furrow system, since the sides of furrow do not compact as readily as if water were standing over the entire surface. Thus, for low intake rate soils furrow system can be employed more beneficially.

(c) In case soil has higher infiltration rates than above mentioned conditions and as listed in Table 3.3 the surface irrigation system would not work unless some artificial compaction with roller is created on the ground which would decrease infiltration rate.

TABLE 3.3

Maximum Length of Run for Surface Irrigation in Soils of Different Textured Soils (Ground Slope 0.1 to 0.2 per cent)

Soil texture	Max. length of run metres (feet)
Very coarse texture *i.e* very coarse sand	Not suitable
Coarse texture-coarse sands, fine sands and loamy sands	183 (600)
Moderately coarse texture-sandy loams and fine sandy loams	274 (900)
Medium texture-very fine sandy loams, loams and silt loams	366 (1200)
Moderately fine texture-clay loams, silty clay loams and sandy clay loams	549 (1800)
Fine textures-sandy clays, silty clays, and clayey	792 (2600)
Peats and mucks	Not suitable

Recommended furrow lengths vary in different parts of the country/ regions. The right length as per soil conditions, land slope and amount of water to be applied, data if available for area be used in absence. However, the above given data work as thumb rules.

(3) *Effect of Field Shape* : The level border and contour levee system works better when the field shape is irregular. The amount of water needed can be computed for such fields. This calculated amount of water can be turned into the strip and impounded in the field till that time it is totally absorbed by the soil.

In other types there is a problem to adjust the amount of water to the length of strip or the furrows. For instance, in furrows long rows require much more water to reach the end of the row than is true of short length rows. The same problem occurs with strips of irregular length.

Effect of Soil Conditions

There are two most specific conditions which influence the choice of a surface irrigation system, which are :

(i) Baking and cracking tendency of some soils.

(ii) Soils which are saline *i.e.* soil which contains excessive amount of soluble salts.

If the soil of the area in general has been classified to have a tendency to back and crack, it would be better to install the level furrow or level border system. This soil property has been indicated with different methods of irrigation particularly with methodology of contour furrows that the cracks in the soil function as path ways for the flowing water particularly during heavy rains. This is the main cause of ready erosion of the soil which washes the soil with run off water and as it extends more and more it results in gullies.

If the soils are highly saline, it is necessary to remove them by various methods (see Chapter 12). The most important is to leach the salts below rootzone. This can be accomplished effectively if level border and contour levee systems would be most effective. This is because the water is made to stand on the land until it has infiltered and leached the salt out of the top layer of the soil.

(4) *Effect of Types of Crops Grown* : The crops to be generally grown in the area after inception of irrigation would also decide the irrigation method suited to area in conjunction with other parameters discussed above. The crops can be classified into four categories as given below :

Group I – Row or bedded crops,
Group II – Close growing crops: sown, drilled or sodded,
Group III – High water tolerant crops — those which can stand flooding for 12 hours or more, and
Group IV – Orchards and vineyards.

If group I crops *i.e.* row crops in bed are to be sown it is advisable to practise one of the furrow systems. Level furrow or graded furrow — depending on which of the two fits well to the shape and slope of the area to be irrigated. The level border and contour levee systems cannot be used if the soils have low infiltration capacity for crops that cannot stand water for 12 hours or longer.

If crops to be grown are close growing *i.e.* Group II, any irrigation method except the contour furrow types is suitable. If crops which are high water tolerant are to be grown such as paddy and also it is intended to use water for weed control too, the irrigation method like border or contour levee system should be used. If orchards or vineyards are to be grown, any surface system that suits the shape of land and soil characteristics should be used.

BELOW-SURFACE IRRIGATION METHODS

This may be classified into two types namely (i) sub-irrigation, and (ii) sub-surface irrigation. These are discussed below :

Sub-irrigation Method

In this technique, the water is delivered to the rootzone by artificially the groundwater table level or height. In sub-irrigation, check dams and gates are used to maintain the water level in the soil from open ditches or from the jointed or perforated pipe. The water level is maintained below the rootzone (30 to 100 cm. or 12 to 40 inches). Water capillaries and its front travels towards rootzone due to the water suction head created between the wet and dry soil between the rootzone soil moisture and high water content in the saturated soil zone by surface attraction forces or surface tension. The direction of the said force may be in various directions such as upwards, sideways or downwards depending upon the presence of dry soil in any direction. The strict monitoring of water level can increase efficiency greatly.

In case deep rooted crops such as citrus, the water level may be raised periodically to near the surface to serve as irrigation and later the water level is brought down to provide aeration to roots which is necessary for their development.

It is necessary to provide an outlet for the drainage of the irrigated area particularly it is more essential in humid areas.

Sub-surface Irrigation Method

It is a method of irrigating the crops by applying water from below the surface by porous or perforated plastic pipe. This technique resembles to trickle irrigation method except that the pipeline position is reversed that is instead of putting it on surface it is placed within ground or under the row in the rootzone.

Advantages : Both the above BELOW SURFACE methods have many advantages over the surface method :

(i) It can be used effectively even for very light and coarsed textured soils having low water holding capacity and high infiltration rate where SURFACE methods cannot be used and the cost of sprinklers are considerably high.

(ii) The evaporation losses in these sub-surface methods is considerably less than surface methods.

(iii) Also weed problem is checked because their seeds are not carried over the surface by irrigation water.

(iv) The sub-irrigation distribution system can sometimes also be used as the drainage system. The feeder lines work better as drainage outlets than the open ditches.

(v) Labour requirements are low as it is needed only for regulating stream flow into the system.

(vi) The water level can be maintained at optimum depths for meeting crop requirements at various growth stages.

Limitations : The sub-surface method has the limited scope of installation due to following considerations :

(1) As this method requires unusual combination of natural conditions, it can be used in limited areas.
(2) The saline waters cannot be used.
(3) The sub-irrigation method may develop more intense salinity if drainage is not adequately provided.
(4) Leaching of salts if required either by rain water or by heavy surface irrigation would raise the permanent water table and hence water levels would be difficult to monitor.
(5) Crops' choice is limited in some areas.
(6) Deep rooted orchard trees cannot be sub-irrigated.

SPRINKLER IRRIGATION SYSTEM

The wastage of water is a common feature of surface irrigation method. Moreover, in view of the wide heterogeneity in soil types, topography, water supply, nature of crops, their water requirements and different management practices, different methods of irrigation have to be used. It is, therefore essential in order to attain the maximum water use efficiency by choice of a suitable irrigation method for a particular area. This would greatly reduce loss of costly water being harvested beside that of loss of various plant food ingradients due to excess and uncontrolled irrigation water application. The curse of water logging and heavy salt accumulation on soil surface and beneath it, would also be minimised causing land to go out of cultivation. The choice of irrigation method can be done from following methods *viz.* : (i) surface irrigation comprising of border or check or furrow, (ii) sprinkler or overhead irrigation in which less quantity of water is consumed, (iii) drip or trickle irrigation in which the limited soil area covered by plant is frequently supplied with water at an interval of 1-3 days in the form of water drops, and (iv) sub-irrigation in which water is consumed by plants under shallow water table depths or perforated underground pipelines without affecting surface of the soil. The general guideline of choosing method is given in tables (Agarwal, M.C. 1985).

Flow chart of sprinkler system of design

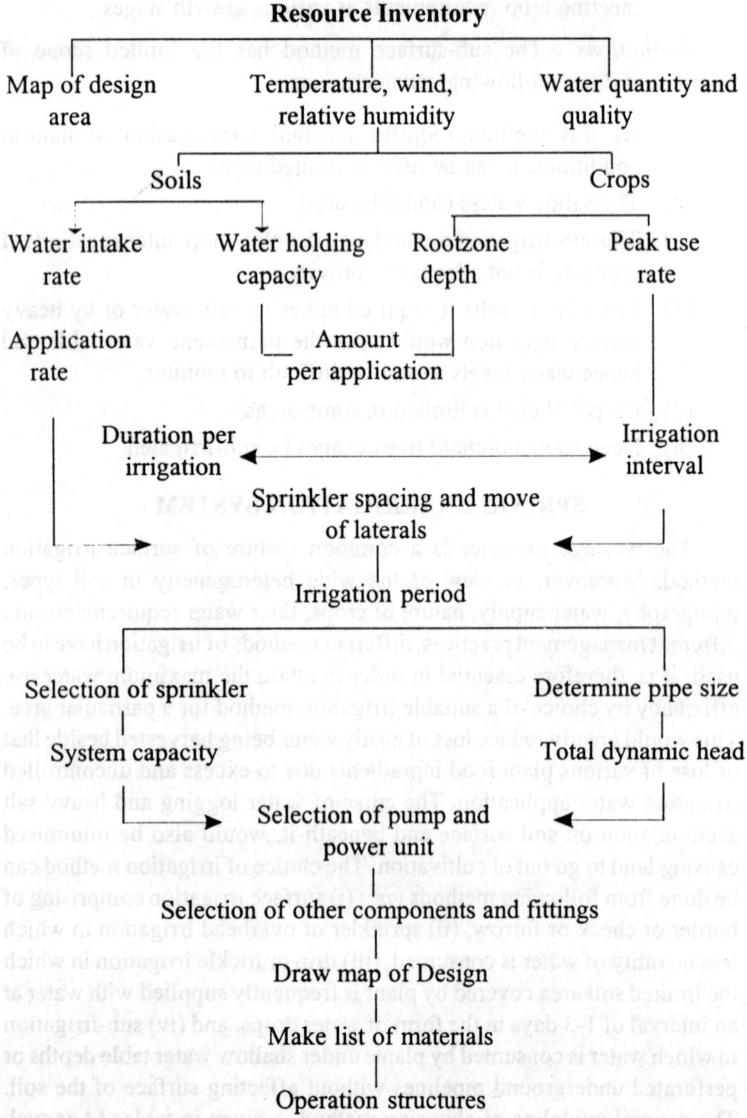

Sprinkler irrigation is a versatile method of irrigating different crops (except rice and jute) under different soil types and land relief. The aerial water spray developed through pumping under pressure through small orifices or nozzles of appropriate size have been found to be very useful.

The method of applying water to the surface of the soil in the form of a spray, somewhat as in ordinary rain, is known as sprinkling. It is a versatile means of applying water to any crop, soil, and topographic condition. Sprinkling is suitable for sandy soils or any other soil and topographic condition where surface irrigation may be inefficient or expensive, or where erosion problem may be particularly hazardous. Low rates and amount of water may be applied, such as are required for seed germination, pest protection and cooling of crops in hot weather. Even fertilisers that are dissolved by water can also be applied through this system. The flexibility of the sprinkler equipment and its efficient control of water application make this method adaptable to most topographic conditions without expensive land preparation. Specially, it is suited for steep slopes and irregular topography. Since this method does not call for construction of field channels, canals etc. more area is available for agriculture purposes and also this method does not create obstructions to movement of farm machinery.

As said earlier, sprinkler irrigation can be adopted to most climatic conditions where irrigated agriculture is feasible; however, extremely high temperatures and wind velocities present problems in some areas. Wind distorts sprinkler pattern and causes uneven distribution of water. The water to be used by sprinkling system should be free of sand, debris and dissolved salts. During hot winding days, it is not advisable to use sprinkler method because the evaporation losses increase tremendously. The major disadvantages of sprinkling system are high investment cost and high labour cost.

Types of Sprinkler Systems

Sprinkler systems are classified either on the basis of the arrangement for spraying irrigation water or on the basis of portability.

On the basis of former criterion following are the two types of the sprinkling system :

(i) *Rotating Head System* : Small size nozzles are placed on riser pipes fixed at uniform interval along the length of the lateral pipe. The lateral pipes are usually laid on the ground surface. In rotating type sprinklers, the most common device to rotate the sprinkler heads is with a small hammer activated by the thrust of the water striking against a vane connected to it.

(ii) *Perforated Pipe System* : In this system the lateral pipes are made perforated in a specially designed pattern. This system is usually designed for low operating pressures of about 1 Kg/cm^2 (10 m of water head). The sprays are directed on both sides of the pipe and can cover a strip of land from 10 to 15 metres wide. Since water by such system is applied at a relatively higher rate, it is suitable for soils having moderately high infiltration rate. This system is suited for irrigation of lawns, gardens and small vegetable fields.

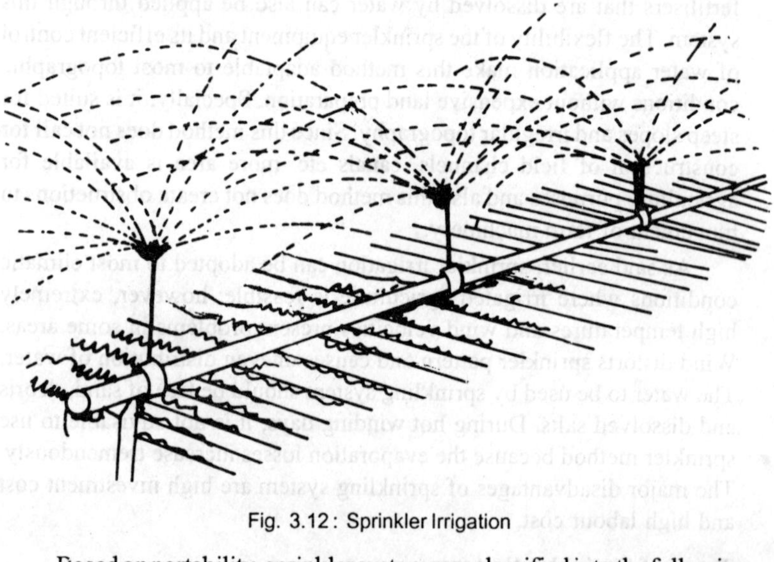

Fig. 3.12 : Sprinkler Irrigation

Based on portability, sprinkler systems are classified into the following types :

(i) *Portable System* : If the main lines, laterals and pumping plant are all portable, this system is referred as portable system. For portability the unit may be equipped with wheels.

(ii) *Semi-portable System* : It is similar to a fully portable system except that the location of the water source and pumping plant are fixed. Such a system can't be moved from field to field or from farm to farm except where more than one stationary pumping plant is utilised.

(iii) *Semi-permanent System* : A semi-permanent system has portable sprinkler lines, permanent main lines, and a stationary pumping plant. The main lines and sub-mains are usually buried, with risers for valves located at suitable intervals. These systems are used when the entire farm is to be sprinkler irrigated and field boundaries are fixed.

(iv) *Solid-set System* : A solid-set system has enough laterals to eliminate their movement. The laterals are positioned in the field early in the crop season and remain for the season. The system is used for crops requiring short frequent irrigations.

(v) *Permanent System* : A fully permanent system consists of mains, sub-mains, laterals and a stationary water source and pumping plant. Mains, sub-mains, and laterals are usually buried. Sprinklers are permanently located on each riser. Such systems are costly and are suited to automation of the system with moisture sensing devices. This type is used on permanently irrigated areas and for relatively high valve crops such as orchards, groves, berries, and nurseries. The most commonly used materials for buried pipe are asbestos-cement, concrete pressure pipe, and coated steel. Of late, plastic, fibre, glass and aluminium alloy pipe designed for underground use are being used.

Sprinkler System Components

The various components of all types of systems are similar in most respects. They mainly consist of the pump to provide the needed pressure, the main pipe lines and laterals, risers and sprinkler heads.

Pumping Set : A pump is required to overcome the elevation difference between the water source and the sprinkler nozzle, to counteract friction losses, and to provide adequate pressure at the nozzle, for good water distribution. The pump should be designed to lift the required amount of water from the source of supply to the highest point in the field and maintain an adequate operating pressure. Electric motors and internal combustion engines are used to drive the pumps operating the sprinklers.

Main Lines : These may be either permanent or portable. On farms where field boundaries are fixed and crops require full-season irrigation, permanent mains are more advantageous. Mostly these pipes are made of steel. For portable mainlines light weight aluminium pipes with quick couplers are used. Water is taken from the main either through a valve placed at each point of junction with a lateral or in some cases through either an L or a T-section that has been supplied in place of one of the couplings on the main.

Lateral Lines : The laterals are usually 5, 6 or 12 m lengths of aluminium or other light weight metal pipe connected with couplers. These lines are usually portable.

Sprinkler Head : For rotating sprinkler system, the sprinkler head is the most important component. When sprinkling is done by revolving head sprinklers, the water jet is thrown in a circular area. Sometimes, sprinkler heads have five nozzles, one to apply water at a considerable distance from the sprinkler and the other to cover the area near the sprinkler centre.

When to Use Sprinkling Irrigation

Sprinkling method of irrigation crops is found quite effective under following conditions (Pair *et al.* 1969, Schwale *et al.*, 1981) :

1. Uniform sandy soils or those which have good rate of infiltration. In organic and sandy soils, seeds of crops like onion, carrots, lettuce seeds are blown away or do not germinate being at more depth due to quick drying of soils.
2. In case of shallow depth soils.
3. Sand dunes or undulating lands or steepy lands where land levelling is expensive.
4. Soils susceptible to errosion or of dispersive nature.
5. Small quantities of irrigation water is available or canal net-work is designed for a low water application rate say 0.01 cm. per hr. and designed depth of irrigation at outlet is less than 2.5 inches (6.25 cm) or canal water application rates are less than 0.1 cm per day.
6. In case energy or power supply position is satisfactory (5 to 8 hrs. a day) and tube-wells exist in area.
7. Lands are to be cultivated immediately for crop production.
8. In case soil crusting is a frequent problem hindering seed emergence for which light and frequent irrigation is required.
9. The immediate safeguard against radiation, frost, high soil and atmospheric temperatures and humidity is required (application of water @ 2.5 mm/h, when temperature is recommended for removing ice from plants reaches zero).

10. The application of fertilizers, pesticides, herbicides and weedicides etc. have to be made urgently in view of crop conditions.
11. Soil salinity is to be leached with small quantity of water.
12. For spraying the fertilizers and chemicals simultaneously with irrigation.

When Not to Use Sprinkling Irrigation

Under following conditions the sprinkling irrigation should not be practised as it results in poor efficiency.

1. When the wind velocity exceeds 7/8 kmph.
2. When the atmospheric day temperatures are too high and it is not very much scorching to plants.
3. If the water to be used is not excessively saline having electrical conductivity 76 millimhos or above which would result in leaf burning especially when atmospheric temperature is 35°C (95°F) or more (the water up to 12 millimhos/cm has been used successfully).
4. Where warabandi or rotational water supply method is in vogue and construction of storage tanks for the said method is costly for frequent water storage.
5. When supply of electricity and water is irregular.
6. When lands have been levelled and on farm development works has been made.
7. At the flowering stage it cannot be used otherwise pollination and setting is affected.

Advantages

The beneficial advantages of sprinkler irrigation method may be summarised as follows :

1. Cutting down expenditure of land levelling works which may amount to Rs. 500 to 3000 per ha. as per job requirement.
2. Cutting down expenditure on cultivation practices since no land preparation etc. is required under this method.
3. *Saving in water* : Thus on account of the fact that exact quantity used to meet requirements of crop and that too evenly on all plant parts, hence less quantity of water per plant or per ha. is consumed. This saving may be of the order of 50 to 70 per cent as compared to surface irrigation.

4. *Cutting expenditure on labour* : It is done as no labour is required in sprinkler method due to its operation automatically without being attended to by a person except for shifting for very short time in a day.
5. *Saving of land for cultivation* : About 10 to 16 per cent land is otherwise wasted in construction of field water courses and drainage ditches can be utilised for cultivation. This also makes easier and effective interculture and weeding operations and easy mechanised farming.
6. *Better survival early seed emergence even crop growth and maturity* : In case of crops (chillies, onions, ragi, etc.) which are grown through nursery plantation, the survival under sprinkler method is much better than under furrow method. Higher seed bud emergence of certain crops (potato, sugarcane etc.). Similarly high production of certain vegetable crops particularly potato, radish, beans, peas, cabbage and groundnut and forage crops like berseem and plantation crops like tea and coffee etc.
7. *Better quality food stuff* : The quality of certain crops is improved such as tobacco and tomato. In sericulture plantation of mulberry is faster and its leaves are large, tender and clean which are better feed for silk worms.
8. *Higher returns* : The sprinkler method can irrigate more area of land with a particular amount of water as compared to surface irrigation. This results, therefore, more income per unit of land.
9. *Simultaneous fertilizer application* : The use of fertilisers through soil in surface method is costly and its efficiency is minimised due to leaching and deep percolation. In sprinkler method water soluble fertilizers can be safely applied through sprinkler system which saves time, labour cost and increases application and utilisation efficiencies besides being economical.
10. *Minimization of salty lands* : In surface irrigation methods excess and/or over-irrigation to crops above their water requirements is a common feature which results in salty and water logged lands. This serious threat is averted under sprinkler irrigation method.
11. *Control of pests and plant diseases* : It has been reported that occurrence of plant and root diseases and insect pest attacks are reduced under sprinkler method. The attack of aphids, thrips and mites have been particularly reduced to a considerable extent.

12. *Night irrigation* : Irrigations at night are more beneficial to crops, thus, it is easier with sprinkler method.
13. *Green manuring* : The introduction of green manure crops in crop rotations has been widely used but according to many reports it is being not practised either due to non-availability of water during May so that after its turning kharif crop may be taken to earn more profits. As such green manuring is hardly practised and if so that too only in rainy season. However, with sprinkler method, the green manuring practice can be easily taken well in time, turned and decomposed so as to improve physical conditions of the soil besides higher production.
14. *Salinity control measures* : The removal of soil salinity can be made through application of desired quantity of water for a calculated period to leach out salts below rootzone by fixing sprinkler system in the direction or towards salt affected area. Thus, it acts as salinity reclamation process.
15. *Easy post harvest tillage operations :* After a crop is harvested the land becomes too hard to till. As such one light irrigation with sprinkler method makes the soil easily tillable which saves hard labour of the farmer.
16. *Cooling of sheds :* Where the agriculture is being done simultaneously with dairy and poultry trade, the sprinklers are being used to cool down the roof temperature of livestock sheds reducing birds mortality and increasing quantity of eggs and milk. The roof temperature has been found to reduce by 10°F.
17. Environmental modification, frost protection, recreation purposes, cooling of fruit plants, waste water disposal and fire control device are other additional advantages of sprinklers.

1. Inventory of Resources and Conditions

(a) *Topographic features* : The size, shape and topography of the area giving details of fields are recorded. The locations of roads, buildings, trees irrigated areas, water source, and pumping site should be marked on the map.

(b) *Water supply* : Availability of sufficient size of stream for water supply is very important. The water available should be suitable chemically for irrigating the crop and soil of the area. Water should not have corrosive effects on sprinkling system. It should also be free of trash to avoid clogging.

(c) *Climatic conditions* : As the crop water climate, the knowledge of its variability will be helpful in determining the capacity of sprinkling system.

To achieve uniform sprinkling of water, it is necessary to overlap the sprinklers. The overlap increases with the increase in wind velocity.

(d) *Soily properties* : These will decide the maximum rate at which the sprinkler can discharge water. The discharge rate should be lower than the infiltration rate of soil. Suggested maximum application rates for sprinklers on average soil, slope and tilth are given in Table 3.4. The depth of water to be applied in a single irrigation will depend upon the available water holding capacity of the soil and the moisture depletion in different layers of the rootzone of the crop.

(e) *Power source* : The source of power to operate the pump is to be known in advance. Electric power is most convenient when pump is stationary. Electric pumping sets are cheaper in initial cost and maintenance cost. Diesel engines, when used in remote areas, should have the necessary facilities of service and fuel supply.

TABLE 3.4

Suggested Maximum Application Rates for Sprinklers for Average Soil, Slope and Tilth

Sl. No.	Soil texture & profile	0-5% slope (cm/hr)	5-8% slope (cm/hr)	8-12% slope (cm/hr)	12-16% slope (cm/hr)
1.	Coarse sandy soil to 2 m	5.0	3.7	2.5	1.3
2.	Coarse sandy soils over more compact soils	3.7	2.5	2.0	1.0
3.	Light sandy loam over more compact soils	2.0	1.3	1.0	0.8
4.	Light sandy loam to 2 m	2.5	2.0	1.5	1.0
5.	Silt loam to 2 m	1.3	1.0	0.8	0.5
6.	Silt loam over more compact soils	0.8	0.6	0.4	0.3
7.	Heavy textured clays or clay loams	0.4	0.3	0.2	0.1

2. Depth of Irrigation

On the basis of available moisture holding capacity of soil in its different layers and the soil moisture extraction pattern of the crop in its root depth, the depth of irrigation is calculated.

3. Capacity of Sprinkler System or Pump Capacity

This will be calculated by the equation :

$$Q = \frac{d \quad a}{f \times H \times E} \times 2780$$

Where,

Q = capacity of pump (lit/sec.)

d = depth of application (cm.)

a = area to be irrigated (ha)

f = irrigation interval, days

H = number of operating hammer per day

E = water application efficiency (per cent).

4. Optimum Water Application Rate

This is determined considering soil type, crop cover and slope of the land. These can be determined from Table 3.4.

5. Sprinkler Head Selection

The actual selection of the sprinkler is based largely upon design information furnished by manufacturers of the equipment. The choice depends primarily upon the diameter of coverage required, pressure available, and capacity to the sprinkler. Each manufacturer will recommend a combination of nozzle sizes and pressures to give the best break up of the stream and distribution pattern for uniform application.

6. Sprinkler Spacing, Nozzle Discharge and Operating Pressure

Sprinkler spacing is greatly influenced by wind run. Following table may be used as a guide :

Once the rate of application and the spacing of the sprinklers have been determined, the required sprinkler capacity can be computed by formula :

$$q = \frac{Sl \quad Sm \quad r}{1000}$$

Where,

q = required average discharge of individual sprinklers, m^3/hr.

r = rate of application (mm/hr.)

Sl = spacing between sprinklers along the lateral (m)

Sm = Spacing between sprinklers along the main (m).

TABLE 3.5

Spacing of Sprinklers Along and Across Laterals

Wind velocity (Km/hr)	Lateral spacing in per cent of diameter of coverage in m. Sm (along lateral)	Sm (along main)
0	50	65
6 or less	45	60
7-12	40	50
13 or more	30	30

The theoretical discharge of a nozzle may be computed from the orifice flow equation, which is :

$$q = a\,c\,\sqrt{2g\,h}$$

q = nozzle discharge, m^3/sec.

a = cross-sectional area of nozzle, m^2

h = pressure head at the nozzle, m

g = acceleration due to gravity, m/sec^2

c = coefficient of discharge which is a function of friction and contraction losses (for good nozzles C should be 0.95-0.96).

When the sprinkler has two nozzles, the total discharge is the combined capacity of both.

7. Number of Sprinklers

The number of sprinklers in a given sprinkling set will depend upon the spacings chosen. It is the most economical to select widest possible sprinkler spacing. Combinations of Sm × Sl are made, such as 18 × 12 metres, 18 × 9 metres, 15 × 12 metres and 15 × 9 metres. The best combination of Sl × Sm, suiting the application rate for the soil and wind conditions, should be selected.

Sprinklers are located just above the crops to be irrigated and, therefore, the height of the risers depend upon the maximum height of the crop. To avoid excessive turbulance in riser pipes the minimum height of risers given in following table should be selected.

TABLE 3.6

Minimum Riser Height for Different Riser Pipe Diameters

Riser pipe diameter (cm)	Minimum riser weight (cm)	
1.27	7.5	
1.90	15.0	
2.54	30.0	
7.6	90.0	(giant sprinklers)

8. System Layout

There are unlimited arrangements for the mains, laterals, and sprinklers in the field but the arrangement, once selected, should involve a minimum cost of irrigation pipe, a low labour requirement, and capable for providing water over the total area in the required period of time. If the field is odd-shaped with a variety of slopes in different directions, it becomes a complex engineering problem to design the complete system and will require a thorough analysis of various layout and pipe sizes, so as to achieve the most efficient combination. The best arrangement, in case of a fixed water supply, is to have the source of water in the centre of the field. If a well is to be drilled for the purpose of supplying water for a sprinkler system it is best to locate the water well near the centre of the area to be served. Following points should be kept in mind while planning a system layout :

(i) Main lines should be laid along the main slope of the field.

(ii) Lateral should be placed across the main slope or nearly on contour.

(iii) Laterals should be placed at right angles to the prevailing winds in high wind velocity areas.

(iv) Long laterals should be avoided. Shorter lengths will have small head loss and will result in a more uniform distribution of water.

9. Adjustments

The size of mains, laterals and sprinklers are determined on the basis of peak consumptive use. Adjustments are necessary in the duration of operation for other stages of plant growth, as it may not be necessary to operate the system of the maximum hours per day for which the system is designed.

10. Laterals — Numbers and Size

In the design of sprinkler laterals, the main objective is to maintain head losses or pressure differences within prescribed limits in order to hold sprinkler discharge variation to reasonable limits. The discharge of nozzle varies by about 10%, with a 20% difference in the pressure. Pressure variation of about 20% between the first and the last sprinkler nozzle on a lateral is permissible in design. ASAE (1978) recommended that the total pressure variation in the laterals, when practicable, should not be more than 10 per cent of the design pressure. If the lateral runs up or downhill, allowance for this difference in elevation should be made in determining the variation in head. If the water runs uphill, less pressure will be available at the nozzle, if it runs downhill, there will be a tendency to balance the loss of the head due to friction.

Water flowing in pipe is always accompanied by loss of pressure due to friction. The degree of loss depends upon the smoothness of the inside walls of the pipe, the viscosity of the liquid and the velocity of water flowing in the pipe. As the pipe ages, the interior surface of the pipe becomes rougher, because of corrosion and abrasiveness in the water.

Scobey's (1930) equation for friction or head loss in pipes may be expressed as :

$$Hf = \frac{K_s L Q^{1.9}}{D^{4.9}} \ (4.10 \times 10^6)$$

Where,

Hf	=	head loss, metres
Ks	=	Scobey's coefficient of retardation
L	=	Length of pipe, metres
Q	=	Discharge, lit/sec.
D	=	Inside diameter of pipe, mm.

Above equation is developed for pipes with full flow such as mains. In case of lateral at the distant end, the line is not full. However, the same equation may be adapted to lateral pipe with uniformly spaced sprinkler outlets by multiplying the friction loss Hf by a a factor F to obtain actual loss. The value of factor F will vary with number of sprinklers on the lateral. Suggested values of F are given in Table 3.7.

TABLE 3.7

Correction Factor F for Friction Losses in Aluminium Pipes with Multiple Outlets

No. of sprinklers	Correction Factor F	
	Ist sprinkler one sprinkler interval from main	Ist sprinkler one-half sprinkler interval from main
1	1.00	1.00
2	0.63	0.51
4	0.48	0.41
6	0.43	0.38
8	0.41	0.37
12	0.39	0.36
16	0.38	0.36
20	0.37	0.35
30 or more	0.36	0.35

The size of the lateral is selected so that the friction loss is within the allowable limits adjusted for elevation differences along the line. The selected pipe diameter should be closest nominal size available commercially.

Recommended values of Ks for design purposes are 0.40 for steel pipe or portable aluminium pipe and couplers, and 0.42 for portable galvanised steel pipe and couplers.

11. Pressure in the Laterals

The sprinkler pressure refers to the average pressure in the middle of the laterals. There is a loss of pressure in laterals due to friction losses. About 3/4th of the total frictional loss occurs in the first half of the line and 1/4th in the second half.

12. Economic Considerations in Pipe Selection

There should be a reasonable balance between the annual cost of owning the pipe and the annual pumping cost. This balance depends upon :

(i) the seasonal hours of operation, and

(ii) the cost of power used.

13. Pump and Power Units

In selecting a suitable pump, it is necessary to determine the maximum total head against which the pump is working. This head may be determined by :

$$Ht = Hn + Hm + Hj + Hs \quad ....(c)$$

Where,

Ht = total design head against which pump is working.

Hn = maximum head required at the main to operate the sprinklers on the lateral at the required average pressure, including riser height.

Hm = maximum friction loss in the main.

Hj = elevation difference between the pump and the junction of the lateral and the main.

Hs = elevation difference between the pump and the water supply after drawdown.

Once the total head and the pump capacity or discharge is known, horse power requirement of the pump may be known by :

$$H.P. = \frac{Q \times Ht}{75\ E_p}$$

$$KW = 1.34\ H.P.$$

Where,

Q = pump discharge, lit/sec.

Ht = total design head, m

Ep = Pump officiency (fraction)

K.W. = Wattage of motor.

14. Cost Estimate

After complete design of the system, an estimate of cost is made for following items :

(i) Well

(ii) Pump house

(iii) Power :

(a) electrical installation, transmission line, transformer, motor, switches etc.

(b) engine

(iv) Pump unit, suction and discharge pipes

(v) Main line and sub-mains

(vi) Lateral lines complete

(vii) Sprinklers and risers

(viii) Installation charges

(ix) Valve of form labour and equipment.

Design Problem

Design a sprinkler irrigation system based on following informations :

Location : Delhi — latitude 28° and longitude 78° (approximately)

Soil	:	Deep light sandy loam
Topography	:	Undulating, 5-8% slope
Water source	:	Tubewell, good water quality
Power source	:	Electricity
Crop	:	Wheat, Rabi season
Wind	:	7-10 Km/hr. from north east
Size of field	:	400 m long and 250 m wide field is to be irrigated when 50% of available moisture has been depleted.

Peak consumptive use of wheat	:	7.5 mm/day
Available moisture holding capacity of soil	:	1.20 mm/cm
Rootzone depth	:	150 cm
Operation hours per day	:	20
Solution	:	Depth of irrigation
A m c given	:	1.20 mm/cm.
So, A m c is 150 cm rootzone	:	1.2 × 150 = 180 mm
Depth of irrigation	:	180 × 0.5 = 90 mm

Shortest Irrigation Interval

Peak consumptive use given	:	7.5 mm/day
Interval	:	90/7.5 = 12 days

Capacity of the System

$$Q = \frac{d\,a}{f\,H\,E} \times 2780$$

TABLE 3.7A

Maximum Application Rates for Sprinklers for Average Soil, Slope and Tilth

Soil Texture and Profile	0-5% Slope	5-8% Slope	8-12% Slope	12-16% Slope
		cm/hour		
1. Coarse Sandy Soil to 2m	5.0	3.7	2.5	1.3
2. Coarse Sandy Soil over more compact soils	3.7	2.5	2.0	1.0
3. Light Sandy loams to 2m	2.5	2.0	1.5	1.0
4. Light Sandy loams over more compact soils	2.0	1.3	1.0	0.8
5. Silt loams to 2m	1.3	1.0	0.8	0.5
6. Silt loams over more compact soils	0.8	0.6	0.4	0.3
7. Heavy textured clays or clay loams	0.4	0.3	0.2	0.1

$a = 400 \times 250 = 10 \times 10^4 \text{ m}^2 = 10 \text{ ha}$

$d = 90 \text{ mm} = 9 \text{ cm.}$

$f = 12$ days, $H = 20$, Assuming $E = 70\%$

$$Q = \frac{9 \times 10 \times 2780}{12 \times 20 \times 70} = 14.9 \text{ Lit/Sec.}$$

Optimum Water Application Rate

From Table - 3.2a

For light sandy loam to 2 m deep for slope = 5–8%

Water application rate = 2 cm/hr.

Sprinkler Spacing, Nozzle Discharge and Operating Pressure

Choosing Sl × Sm = 12.2 × 18.3 m

Application rate = 1 cm/hr

$$\text{So, nozzle discharge} = \frac{\text{Sl Sm r}}{1000}$$

$$= \frac{12.2 \times 18.3 \times 10}{1000}$$

$$= 2.24 \text{ m}^3/\text{hr} = 0.62 \text{ lit/sec.}$$

Refer Voltas Sprinkler Tables :

Model No. 4 double nozzle

Nozzle size 5.16 × 3.17 mm

Pressure 2.46 Kg/cm^2

Discharge 0.62 lit/sec.

Number of Sprinkler Required

Width of field = 250 m

Hence, one lateral will cover 125 m when main line is at the middle of the width

Sl = 12.2

Length covered by 10 sprinklers = 122 m.

First sprinkler at half of Sl.

System Layout

Depth of irrigation = 9 cm/set

Peak consumptive use = 7.5 mm/day

Maximum irrigation interval	=	12 days
Pump capacity required at 70% of application efficiency and 20 hrs. opf working with 12 day rotation	=	15 lit/sec.

Design

Sprinkler spacing Sm × Sl	:	18.3 × 12.2 m
Type of sprinkler	:	model No. 4 double nozzle 5.16 × 3.17 mm
Make	:	Voltas
Main line	:	384 m long (63 pieces of 6.1 m long pipe having 22 tees)
Lateral	:	Two laterals of 115.9 m each having riser outlets at 12.2 m. First riser outlet will be at 6.1 m from main line. Total number required 38 of 6.1 m each
Sprinkler capacity	:	0.62 lit/sec
Application rate	:	1 cm/hr
Hours per lateral set	:	9 hrs.
Rotation	:	12 days with two lateral lines and two sets of each every day (18 working hours plus 2 hours for shirting *i.e.* 20 hrs.).

The total number of sets possible in a cycle of 12 days is 24. However, the required number of sets as per design is 22 which can be completed in 11 days. One extra day will be used for maintenance and breakdown, if any, of the system.

Number of laterals	:	Two
Flow in a lateral	:	10 × 0.62 = 6.2 lit/sec.

Refer Table 3.7 to find friction loss in lateral line of portable aluminium pipe with coupling.

From Table 3.7 :

Discharge 6.31 lit/sec for 7.5 cm dia. of pipe, friction loss 3.2 m/100 m. length. This is if the pipe is made of 9 m length of small pipes. For

6.1 m length of pipe the value is to be increased by 7%. Correction factor F from Table 3.7 = .365. Actual friction loss in a 116 m lateral

$$= \frac{3.2}{100} \times 1.07 \times .365 \times 116$$

= 1.45 m of water head

Average design pressure = 2.45 Kg/cm²

20% variation = .2 × 2.45 = .49 Kg/cm²

V 4.9 m water head

So, the head loss in lateral is within permissible limit.

Main Line

Length of main line : 192 m.

Discharge : 6.2 lit/sec.

Referring Table 3.7 for friction loss of portable aluminium pipe of diameter 10 cm and friction loss 0.9m/100 m for discharge of 6.2 lit/sec.

Loss in 192 m length
= 0.9 × 1.92 × 1.07
= 1.85 m of water
which is within permissible limits.

Total Head

Pressure at the last sprinkler :
= Average pressure - 1/4 × head loss in lateral
= 24.5 — .415
= 24.09 m of water
= 2.41 Kg/cm²

Total head = Pressure in last sprinkler
+ friction loss in lateral
+ friction loss in main line
+ elevation difference
+ riser height to other losses

Slope = 8% (let's take higher value)

Riser height = 60 cm (assume)

Assuming other losses = 2 m of water head

Total head = 24.1 + 1.66 + 1.85 + 15 + 0.6 + 2.0

Ht $= 45.21\text{m}$ say 46 meters

Pump horse power at 70% efficiency

$$= \frac{Q \times H_t}{75\ E_p}$$

$$= \frac{14.9 \times 46}{75 \times .7} = 13.05\ h_p.$$

The beneficial advantages of sprinkler irrigation method over surface irrigation are many such as effective water management through controlled irrigation, more land is irrigated with lesser quantity of water available, at least 10 to 16% land saved due to non-construction of water courses and drainage channels can be utilized for cultivation, easy mechanised farmings, very marginal conveyance and field application losses resulting in very high (about 82%) irrigation efficiency against surface irrigation, comparatively high production and quality of vegetable crops such as potato, radish, beans, peas, cabbage and groundnut and forage crops like berseem and plantation of tea and coffee.

Economics

The economics of sprinkler irrigation method has been worked out which has been reported to be about Rs. 863.00 per ha. per year which is profitable only when the rate of interest charged on capital is not more than 6% annually or the recovery period is not less than 6 to 8 years or the rate of Government subsidy is at least 25%. In absence of these official incentives *i.e.* (relief) possibly the use of sprinkler irrigation might not be very remunerative or profitable. However, community sprinkler irrigation projects may be quite economical if liked by group of farmers.

Design of Sprinkler Irrigation System

For designing a sprinkler irrigation system besides following considerations, the most important is environmental conditions (soil, crop and climate) of an area which greatly influence the performance and efficiency of system being designed. The design of the system should be considered from two viewpoints namely :

(i) Consideration of various parameters which would effect the designed system such as water source, crop grown and soil types, power supply, and weather conditions.

(ii) Pipe line layout which depends upon farm dimensions, elevations from pump to highest point in the field.

(iii) Choosing efficiently workable pipe diameters.

The other general rules pointed out by Schwab *et al.* 1981 are :

(a) Mains should be laid up and downhills.

(b) Laterals should be laid across slope or nearly on the contour.

(c) In case of multiple lateral operation, lateral pipe size should be limited to not more than two diameters.

(d) The water supply location should be nearest to the centre of the area.

(e) Balanced design lateral operation should be provided.

(f) Lateral movement should be minimum during season as per layout choosen.

(g) Provision of booster pumps be kept in case of need arises for arranging high pressures.

(h) The finalised layout should be self-sufficient to have provision for regulation of different rates and quantities of water to suit different soil types.

(i) Application rates should be less than intake rate to avoid runoff and stream pollution. As mentioned above the design is to be worked out as per pump and power units as such it is essential to calculate the maximum total head against which the pump has to operate. This is mathematically represented as

$$Ht = Hn + Hm + Hj + Hs$$

Where,

Ht = total design head against which the pump has to operate

Hn = maximum head required at the main to function the sprinklers on the lateral at the desired average pressure including the height to be attained

Hm = maximum friction loss in the main, the suction line and NPSH of the pump

Hj = the difference of height between the pump and the junction of the lateral and the main

Hs = the height difference between the pump and location of water supply after drawdown expressed in m or Kpa.

Hence, the quantity of water required will be the sum total of capacity of all sprinklers operating at the same time. Knowing total water head and consumption rate, the suitable pump may be chosen using standard rating curves or tables.

Different types of sprinklers may be used, namely, small one for gardens, lawns or nurseries which require low pressures, medium and large suitable for large area which can irrigate an acre of land at a time. Even bigger, huge boom type sprinklers mounted on giant trucks are designed to function in flat areas. Also single and double nozzle sprinklers, different types of nozzles and couplers, besides a plethora of accessories are available for different uses. Use of different materials for manufacturing sprinklers pipe such as steel, aluminium, PVC mild steel and fibre glass have been tried and are available. The modified sprinkler systems are also evolved such as (i) Perfo-spray system (for very low pressure operation) for sandy soils. (ii) Gated pipe system which is improvement over channel irrigation where aluminium pipes with gated spread at certain intervals varying from 18" to 36" are used. This method avoids percolation losses, effective regulation of flow and irrigation can be taken across a deep depression. (iii) Portable delivery pipelines system. In this portable aluminium pipes replace channels as laid for gated pipe system for supply of water. This saves 40 per cent water otherwise lost through channels. This is a very cheaper method.

It has been found that to provide one inch of rain over an acre through sprinkler about 25000 gallons of water is needed and hence this system of irrigation has many constraints for early popularization particularly in economically underdeveloped countries.

Examples

Given :

Area of the field	:	44 ha
Dimensions	:	440 m × 1000 m
Topography		
Location of the water source		
Crop factors		
Type of crop	:	Cotton
Rooting depth	:	0.75 m
Growing season		
Soil factors		
Soil type	:	Loam
Water holding capacity	:	150 mm/m
Infiltration rate	:	8 mm (.31 in)/hr.

Environmental factors

Wind speed	:	10 Km/hr
Peak water requirement	:	8 mm/day
Application efficiency	:	70%

With the above data, the following design information can be calculated :

Available water in the rootzone	:	150 mm/m × 0.75m = 112 mm
Gross application depth	:	(112/0-70) = 160 mm
Irrigation interval during the peak demand period	:	112 mm/(8mm/day) = 14 days
Duration of application	:	160 mm/(8 mm/hr)
		= 20 hours

In the first phase, the appropriate sprinkler characteristic are selected to achieve an application rate of 8 mm (0.31 in)/hr. The application rate is dependent upon the spacing of the sprinkler and the discharge rate from the sprinkler, *i.e.*

$$\text{Application rate} = K \; \frac{\text{discharge rate (pressure, nozzle size) } (m^3/hr)}{\text{Spacing of the sprinklers } (m^2)}$$

in which K is the unit conversion factor. Several combination of pressure, nozzle size, and spacing of the sprinklers can be used to achieve the desired application rate. If data on the radial distribution of water from a given nozzle at a given pressure is available, then an appropriate combination of spacing, nozzle size and pressure can be selected from the analysis of the above data. When actual data on the spray pattern of sprinklers is not available, the readymade tables can be used. These tables provide information on the required pressure, nozzle size and the spacing of the sprinklers to achieve the desired application rate. The following design specifications are obtained from the table.

Spacing of the sprinklers	:	9.1 m × 12.2 m (30'×40')
Nozzle size	:	3.6 mm (9/64")
Operating pressure	:	31 pascals (45 psi)
Flow rate	:	0.86 m^3/hr (3.8 Gpm)
Uniformity	:	85%
Radius of coverage	:	26 m (85')

This finishes the first phase of the design.

The layout of the pipes and the pipe sizes (the second phase of the design) depends upon the above information. First we will deal with the layout of the pipes. Since the irrigation interval is 14 days (336 hours) and the time required to apply the design depth is only 20 hours a decision must be made regarding the number of sets in the field: whether to irrigate the whole field simultaneously or to irrigate the different parts of the field in a rotation (or in sets)? To minimize the size of the mainline and the pump (and hence the cost of the system), it is always preferable to irrigate the field in sets, depending upon the time constraint. In this particular case, the irrigation interval is 14 days. Assuming that the farmer needs 2 days of free-time, and 4 hours to move the laterals during each set, the system can be designed to operate for 12 days out of the 14 days. The number of sets in the field during each irrigation is 12 (14-12) days/(20+4 hrs). The area irrigated by each set is 3.67 ha (44 ha/12 sets).

Design of a lateral : In the design of a lateral, the difference in the operating pressure of the sprinklers along the lateral must be less than 20% of the average operating pressure of the sprinkler. The average operating pressure head (in this case 31.7 m) is located about two-fifths of the lateral length downstream from the inset (for simplicity it assumed that the average operating pressure is located halfway down the lateral). This means maximum of about 6.34 m of headloss is tolerable in the lateral. The size of the lateral must be such that the total headloss in it would be less than 6.34 M.

Length of the lateral	:	250 M
Number of sprinklers on a lateral	:	250/9.1 = 27
Flow rate through individual sprinklers	:	$0.86 m^3/hr$ (0.238 lps)
Flow rate into the lateral	:	$0.86 \times 27 = 23.22 m^3/hr.$ (6.45 lps)

To calculate the friction loss in a pipe, the following equation (called the Hazen-William's equation) is used :

$$\frac{Q^{1.852}L}{C^{1.852}D^{4.87}\ F}$$

H = headloss, in m

Q = flow rate, lps

L = length of the lateral, m

D = inner diameter of the lateral, mm

C = friction coefficient for continuous sections of pipe

K = Units conversion coefficient, 1.21×10^{10}

F = Coefficient to compensate for the discharge along the pipe (tables are available to calculate the value of Fs function of the number of outlets on a lateral).

Using the above equation, the minimum pipe diameter can be calculated, for this problem

$$D^{4.87} = \frac{K\,(Q)^{1.852}}{C} \quad \frac{L}{H} \cdot F$$

$$D = 4.87\ 1.21 \times 10^{10}\ \frac{(6.45)^{1.852}}{130}\ \frac{(250)}{6.34}\ (0.37)$$

$$= 62.5 \text{ mm} = 2.5 \text{ inches}$$

Since the pipe diameters come in discrete sizes, an appropriate combination of length and diameters (around the above diameter) are chosen. A difference of 20% in pressure head would result in a difference of 10% in the flow rate from the sprinklers on lateral.

The design of a mainline is similar to the design of a lateral line. Information on the flow rate into an individual lateral, the number of laterals operating simultaneously and the inlet pressure into a lateral. In our case :

Flow rate into a lateral	:	23.2m³/hr (6.45 lps)
Number of laterals operating simultaneously	:	12
Inlet pressure into a lateral	:	31.7 m +.5(6.34) = 34.9m
Total flow rate into the mainline	:	(23.2 × 12) = 278.4 m³/hr 77 lps.

Once the system is designed, the mainline should deliver 23.2 m³/hr flow rate to each of the twelve laterals operating simultaneously at the required pressure of at least 34.9 m. In sizing the mainline, the cost of the

TABLE 3.8

Type of System	Maximum Slope	Water Application Rate Min. Max.	Shape of Field	Field Surface Conditions	Max. Height of Crop	Labour Required	Size of Single System	Approx. Cost	Adaptable To: Cooling and Frost Protect	Adaptable To: Chemical Application	Adaptable To: Fertilizer Application	Adaptable To: Liquid Animal Waste Distribution
	(per cent)	mm/hr (in/hr)[1]			m(ft)[2]	hrs/ha(a)[3]	ha (a)	$/ha (a)×100[4]				
Multi-Sprinkler Permanent	No limit	1.3(.05)50(2)	Any shape	No limit	No Limit	1-.25 (.05-.10)	4 or more (1 or more)	10-30 (4-12)	Yes			Not Recom.
Hand-moved: Portable set	20	2.5(.10)50(2)	Rectangular			1.2-3.7 (.5-1.5)	4-16 (1-40)	2-8 (.8-3)	No			Yes
Solid set	No limit	1.3(.05)50(2)	Any shape			.5-1.2 (.2-.5)	4 or more (1 or more)	10-30 (4-12)	Yes			Not Recom.
Tractor-moved: Wheel-mounted	10	2.5(.10)50(2)		Smooth enough for safe tractor operation		.5-1 (.2-.5)	8-20 (20-50)	4-8 (1.6-3)				Yes
Self-moved: Side-wheel-roll	10	2.5(.10)50(2)	Rectangular	Reasonably Smooth	1.2 (4)	.2-.7 (1-3)	8-32 (20-80)	4-8 (1.6-3)				
Side-move	10	2.5(.10)50(2)			1-2 (4-6)	.2-.7 (1-3)						

Self-propelled: Center-pivot	20	5.0(.20)75(1.5)	Circular, Square of Rectangular	Clear of obstructions, path for towers	2-3 (8-10)	.1-.4 (.05-.15)	8-80 (20-200)	5-10 (2-4)	No	Yes	
Central-move	20	5.0(.20)25(1)			2-3 (8-10)	.1-.4 (.05-15)	4-40 (10-100)				
Slope-Sprinkler Side-moved	20	6.4(2.5)50(2)	Any shape	Safe operation of tractor	No. limit	1.2-3.7 (.5-1.5)	8-16 (20-40)	2.5-5 (1-2)			Not Recom.
Tractor-moved: Wheel-mounted	No limit 5-15	6.4(2.5)50(2)				.5-1 (.2-.4)	8-16 (20-40)	5-10 (2-4)			Yes
Self-propelled	No limit	6.4(2.5)25(1)	Rectangular	Lane for winch and hose		.2-.7 (.1-.3)	8-16 (20-40)	5-10 (2-4)			
Boom-Sprinkler Tractor-moved	5	6.4(2.5)25(1)	Any shape	Safe operation of tractor	2-3 (8-10)	.5-1.2 (2-5)	8-16 (80-40)	5-10 (2-4)			
Self-Propelled	5	6.4(2.5)25(1)	Rectangular	Lane for boom and hose	2-3 (8-10)	.2-1.2 (.1-.5)					

[1]25.4 meters equals 1.0 inch.
[2] 1.0 meter equals 3.28 feet.
[3]1.0 hectare equals 2.5 acres.
[4] Does not include the cost of water supply, pump, power unit and mainline.

pipeline, and the friction loss must be minimized. The pressure variation along the mainline must be kept to a minimum, if pressure regulators are not going to be used in the system.

TRICKLE OR DRIP IRRIGATION SYSTEM

It has been assessed that water would be the major need in future of human society for meeting ever increasing development demand in all spheres of life. The cultivable area of the universe is a constant source. To meet both ends meet of food and fibre there is a urgent need of an expanding agriculture to achieve higher agriculture production per unit of land as well as per unit of water consumed. This in one way is possible through increasing crop intensity by growing high producing varieties of short duration as a cropping relays besides maintaining the proper water distribution most economically to just meet the crop water requirements. This goal is possible by reclamation of marginal soils for high production and conjunctive use of poor quality water. It has been estimated that even world's total harnessable water if brought to use by the year 2000 A.D. the irrigated area can hardly exceed 30-40%. This necessitates the search for advanced and more specialised ways in application and economy of scarce commodity, the water. During the last decade this search came out in the shape of Trickle irrigation which is being rapidly developed and expanded in many parts of the universe. Trickle irrigation method has been proved to be of high potential efficiency in water application, plant use effectiveness and economical high returns.

Definition

Tickle irrigation may be defined as a method of water and nutrient supply to crops rootzone depth through an especially designed tube emitter designed for very small flow rate of water. This is designated as trickler which helps three dimensionally and results in differential spread of water, maintaining low levels of soil-water tension.

Trickle irrigation is also called Drip irrigation or micro irrigation method and it is a major departure from the conventional surface irrigation methods which are in practice since long, the history of irrigation starts. This method of irrigation supplies just required crop water requirements at a very low pressure in the droplet form to wet the rootzone depth.

The wetted perimeter or zone around the plant on and inside the soil depth depends upon the rate of water application and permeability of the soil. This implies that with higher rate of water application in a less permeable or impermeable soil cover the broad spread wetted zone would

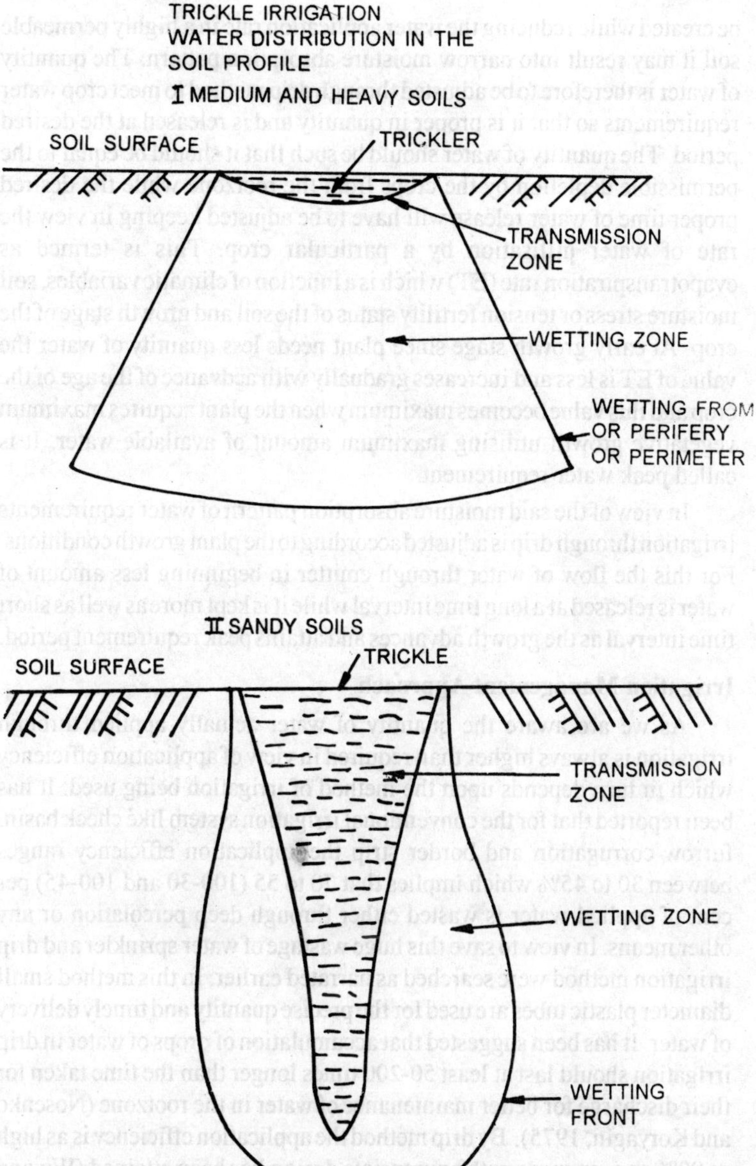

Fig. 3.13 (a) and (b) : Showing Trickle irrigation water distribution in the soil profile in
(a) Medium and heavy soils
(b) Sandy soils

be created while reducing the water application rate in a highly permeable soil it may result into narrow moisture absorption pattern. The quantity of water is therefore to be adjusted through drip method to meet crop water requirements so that it is proper in quantity and is released at the desired period. The quantity of water should be such that it should be equal to the permissible depletion by the crops from the rootzone while the desired proper time of water release will have to be adjusted keeping in view the rate of water utilisation by a particular crop. This is termed as evapotranspiration rate (ET) which is a function of climatic variables, soil moisture stress or tension fertility status of the soil and growth stage of the crop. At early growth stage since plant needs less quantity of water the value of ET is less and increases gradually with acdvance of the age of the crop and this value becomes maximum when the plant acquires maximum vegetative growth utilising maximum amount of available water. It is called peak water requirement.

In view of the said moisture absorption pattern of water requirements irrigation through drip is adjusted according to the plant growth conditions. For this the flow of water through emitter in beginning less amount of water is released at a long time interval while it is kept more as well as short time interval as the growth advances and attains peak requirement period.

Irrigation Management Approach

As we are aware the quantity of water actually applied through irrigation is always higher than required in view of application efficiency which in turn depends upon the method of irrigation being used. It has been reported that for the conventional irrigation system like check basin, furrow corrugation and border strip the application efficiency ranges between 30 to 45% which implies that 70 to 55 (100-30 and 100-45) per cent of applied water is wasted either through deep percolation or any other means. In view to save this huge wastage of water sprinkler and drip irrigation method were searched as narrated earlier. In this method small diameter plastic tubes are used for the precise quantity and timely delivery of water. It has been suggested that accumulation of drops of water in drip irrigation should last at least 50-200 times longer than the time taken for their discharge for better maintenance of water in the rootzone (Nosenko and Koryagin, 1975). By drip method the application efficiency is as high as 90% or even more with appropriate design has been attained (Wu and Gillin, 1975) which is about 20% more than sprinkler and 60-80 per cent more than conventional method (Sivanappan 1977-78). Hence it is a great breakthrough in irrigation management approach. Many countries are converting the land from conventional irrigation methods to drip method to manage extra land for cultivation besides less consumption of water and higher crop yields.

Special Advantages of Drip Method

There are various plus points of this method which makes it superior to other. The benefits of this method may be enumerated as follows :

1. Maximum use of irrigation water available.
2. Maximization of crop yield.
3. Less labour in tillage operations.
4. Product quality improvement.
5. Decreased incidence of bacteria, fungi pests and other diseases depending upon moist environment.
6. Higher fertilizer application efficiency.
7. Increasing crop intensity from 200% to much higher through multiple or relay cropping.
8. Less infestation of weeds in non-irrigated area.
9. Controlling of potential host population.
10. Minimized labour and operational costs.
11. Effectivity in undulating terrains avoiding levelling.
12. Possibility of use poor quality saline waters by keeping soil at high moisture level avoiding contact of water plant causing less damage to plants.
13. Increased intake of water in poorly drained soils.
14. Effectivity in green houses due to low pressure requirements.
15. Total control of run off, soil errosion and problem of short water supply to tail-end farmers.
16. Field edge losses and spray evaporation in other methods is considerably reduced.
17. Easy adjustment for automatic control of flow.
18. Mechanised farming easy and profitable.
19. Ir. trickle irrigation soil moisture pattern successfully facilitate aeration as compared to poor aeration by other methods.

Trickle irrigation effectiveness is unparalleled in marginal climate and soils especially with the use of poor quality water. It is also successful and economic yields, where other methods either displayed poor response (furrows) or totally failed (sprinkling).

There is also strong indication that in the case of trickle irrigation in high salt sensitive vegetable crop grew successfully even in comparison to sub-surface system.

Disadvantages

This method also has some limitations which are :

(1) Possibility of failure to clogging of system component by organic and biological matter etc.

(2) Moisture distribution problem.

(3) Accumulation of soil salinity at the fringes of the wetted surface strip.

(4) High initials cost of installation as compared to conventional ones.

(5) Possibility of wind erosion in dry soil portion due to dust formation.

(6) Non-suitability of emitters to certain crops.

(7) Root growth limitations only in moist soil volume.

(8) Specialised skill and training to design installation and operation of the system components.

Components of System

The arrangement and layouts of trickle system are designed so as to meet different requirements under field conditions for different crop species.

The components of the system may be divided into two main parts namely :

(1) Control head, and

(2) Distribution network.

Control Head : The control head of the system monitoring various activities comprises of various components as discussed below.

Pump/Overhead Tank : This component provides sufficient pressure in the system. The system requires low pressures which are generated through centrifugal pumps and are adjusted to supply constant pressures without creating overloading head characteristics. Pumps are utilised for spreaded area to be covered under drip system. These are also installed for undulating terrains, closely spaced crops and where large comparatively quantities of water are needed. The various types of centrifugal pumps with different heads and discharges suitable to specific system design are available. In case of small areas the pump may also be replaced by an overhead tank at about 3 metre height from the ground. This is generally practised in cases where water requirements are comparatively less such as orchard crops.

Filters

The function of emitters is an energy dissipators which occurs through reduction of the inlet pressure head (0.5 to 1.5 atm) to zero at the outlet to the atmosphere. The emitters are designed for low discharges and hence possess small, narrow flow passages which are prone to blocking or clogging. As such efficiently functioning filters should be employed for trouble free operation of the system. The various kinds of filters have been tried.

(a) *Gravel filters* : These filters are available in various sizes ranging from 500 to 900 mm diameter with an output of 15 to 30m^3 respectively. They consist of circular tank filled with alternate layers of coarse pond (0.2 mm dia) and different sizes and grades of gravels. The tank is provided with a flushing valves to clean the clogged materials. These filters have been successfully deployed to check the passing of organic matters such as algae, moss and other vegetative materials contaminating the water to be used. These must be used especially when the water source is pond, open well, canal and ditch etc.

(b) *Hydrocyclone* : The silted water carries sand particles in it. In case such water is used for drip system the filters of hydrocyclone type should be used to exclude the sand particles. Such type of filters are also called as vortex sand separator. These filters are used in conjunction with other filters. The output of such filters varies from 0.5 to 70 m^3 for 20 mm to 150 mm size pipelines.

(c) *Screen filters* : The water of certain resources is also contaminated with fine sand and partially soluble silica and dust particles which may also choke the working system. The filters to screen out these solid impurities through screen filters which are fitted simultaneously with gravel filters. These screening filters are single or double perforated cylinders placed in a plastic or metallic container to remove all suspended materials. The mesh size used in these filters varies from 80 to 150 mesh. Various types of filters are being manufactured which vary in size ranging from 20 mm to 75 mm and 4 to 60 m^3 discharge. In case voluminous quantity of water is required to be filtered a series of filters may be deployed. These filters have manual and automatic (electrically or hydraulically) cleaning facilities.

(d) *Volumetric filters :* These filters consist of concentric grooved rings which are mounted on a longitudinal shaft. The rings when are lightened together take a shape of cylindrical body.

The precise selection of filters should be used which has to be done based on the water quality and the anticipated discharge in the control head.

The process of filter cleaning is called back flushing. The method is known as back flushing system. This operates on the principle of reverse movement of suspended impurities and silt when flushed with stream of water. The valves are operated either manually or by a hydraulic system. The automatic cleaning system of filters is made through the created inlet/outlet pressure differentials through a accumulation of filtered mass resulting in blockage of the screen. For the self-cleaning process hydraulic valves working through hydraulic or electronic devices are generally used. In hydraulic system pre-set pressures differences provide pulse to hydraulic valve for opening and closing while in electronic method solenoid valve is used which transmits the electronic pulse into hydraulic pulse. The modified electronic systems are also available which are accompanied with timer which at a particular time and interval does the filter cleaning job. However, these though very effective but are costly. Different kinds of filters discussed above are being used in drip system.

Trickle irrigation method has serious handicap of clogging of the emitters which is due to suspended particles of organic matter of colloidal dimensions as well as the minute spores and separate cells of micro which infiltrate through ordinary filters reach the trickler. These under conditions or reduced velocity of water oxidation-reduction potentials, favourable temperature and aeration flocculate (colloids) or proliferate (micro-organisms) and result in gradual plugging of the outlets. Hence specific filters should be selected.

Fertilizer Applicators

The use of water soluble fertiliser through drip irrigation method is now being practised in many parts of the world. This method besides being very efficient is helpful in saving huge labour cost in advanced countries besides being economical. This is achieved either through by-pass pressure tank or by venturi pumps or direct injection system. In by-pass case the valve of main system is closed and partial or entire quantity of water is taken to fertilizer tank and the resultant mixture is used through drip system.

In venturi pump type a portion of the water is allowed through venturi (small diameter taper) which raises the velocity of flow at the junction of tube and venturi resulting in suction head causing flow of mixture in the system.

In direct injection type piston or diaphram pumps are used which operates through system pressure and utilise the fixed quantity of dissolved fertilisers through irrigation.

Pressure regulators : The decrease in higher pressure to lower pressure are managed by pressure regulators. The pressure regulators consist of spring loaded valve inside it to control the pressure which is attained through adjusting the stud of the tension spring. Variously designed pressure regulators workable under different situations such as for undulating terrain and steepy lands have been manufactured and used.

Control valves and water meters : The control valves having metering and totalizer devices and working automatically to deliver pre-set quantity of water are now available. These are made of gunmetal and their sizes generally varies between an inch to 6" for drip systems. These are employed for automatic computer control irrigation system.

Distribution network : In the drip irrigation system the water is conveyed through the source to near the plant rootzone via closed pipe network and regulated so as to release water drop by drop through drippers. The pipeline and drippers are called distribution network. The design of drip irrigation system varies with the type of soil, topography, crop variety and environmental conditions and accordingly as per requirements the distribution network is also changed. The main components of distribution network are main line, sub-main line, sub-sub-main line and laterals with dripper and other accessories.

Main line/sub-main line : The main lines are put under the ground. The pressure ratings for these main lines may be chosen to have range between 4 to 6 kg cm² while diameter should be between 60 to 65 mm. The material of these pipelines should be preferably rigid PVC (RPVC) and high density (HDPE). The life of these underground pipelines may be 20 years or more. In case of sub-main lines, besides above material, low density polythene (LDPE) may also be used. The diameter may be between 32 mm to 75 mm having pressure ratings of the order of 2.5 kg cm². These may be installed on the surface as well as in the sub-surface. However, if used on surface, these should be protected against ultraviolet rays by mixing carbon back material.

Laterals : The lateral pipelines manufactured from low density polythene (LDPE) having 2.5% carbon back are put on the ground. The use of better materials like linear low density polythene is replacing low density polythene which are more resistant to ultraviolet rays. The thickness of the pipelines varies from 1.0 to 3.0 mm while internal diameters range from 10 to 20 mm. The size and pressure ratings of pipes is kept as per design of the drip system being used.

Emitters/Drippers

The drippers are also made of polythene materials and are used to reduce inlet pressure varying from 0.5 to 1.5 atmospheres to zero to create suction. These are of many types namely :

(a) *Inline drippers* : These are fixed in between lines on cutting edges so as to make a continuous row after the drippers are fixed. The flow path of these inlet drippers are thread or labyrinth type. The latter helps to create a turbulent flow of water and have large cross section area. This avoids blocking of the drippers. The discharge rate of these drippers may vary from 2 to 8 litres per hour at one atmosphere. These are useful for the pipelines having internal diameter from 10 mm to 13 mm.

(b) *Online drippers* : These type of drippers are put directly on the pipeline by making hole of appropriate size. These are of two types namely :

(i) *Non pressure compensation type* : These are of simple type wherein the discharge is directly proportionate to the pressure. The flow paths are either thread or labyrinth or zigzag or vertex type to dissipate energy. The discharge rating at one atmosphere is generally 2, 3, 4, 8, 16 lits/hour. For pot type irrigation multiple openings are kept in emitters.

(ii) *Pressure compensating type* : These are designed to deliver uniform discharge at pressures ranging from 0.3 to 3.5 atmosphere. The discharge rate is 2, 3, 4, 8 lits/hr. at different pressures controlled by high quality rubber diaphragm which also monitor the quality of fertilizer if used. These drippers are used for undulating and steepy terrains and helps to have long laterals and fewer main lines. There is no need to use regulators in this kind and if suitable design is chosen it may be very economical too.

(iii) *Built-in dripper tube* : The recent system has been provided with built-in dripper tube which forms the part of the tube and are designed to avoid the chance of blocking the passage. The built-in dripper tubes may have spacing range of 0.6, 0.75 and one metre with discharge rate of 2 to 3.5 l/h at 0.5 to 4 atmosphere.

(iv) *Laser beam-perforated type* : Recently in Israel for row crops a dripper system having hole in place of dripper, drilled longitudinally at 5° to horizontal line by laser beam has been manufactured. The diameter of the pipelines may be 12, 16, 20 with capacity of discharge rate as 4 and 6 lit/hr at one atmosphere. The spacing interval in drip lines is kept from 0.3 to 1.5 metres.

(v) *T-type, twin well type drip hose* : The hose of this type is also made of thin polythin film with thickness of .250 to .500 mm on account of less thickness compared to other tubes it works out to be more economical, however, their life is also reduced (1 to 2 years). This can work under low pressures ranging between 0.4 to 0.8 atmosphere (0.4 to 0.8 kg/cm²).

Other Accessories

The remaining accessories of the system includes takeouts/starter, rubber, grommet, end plug, jointer, tees many folds etc. which are available in 4 to 20 mm sizes.

Automation in Drip System

The automatic working drip system based on computers are also now available for various jobs.

The automatically working volumetric valve for allowing fixed volume of water sequentially as per programmings are very useful for large areas without employing any human being.

Small and Large Scale Electronically and Computer Based System

Such type of units which are highly automatised through electronic network and master control units of computer working at remote distance are available and as per needs can control hundred of valves and the land area.

Efficiency of Distribution of Water Influence on Crop Yields

It has been reported (Grainer *et al.* 1976) that irrigation with drip system resulted in 5 to 16 kg per cubic metre increase in yields of crops like tomato, cucumber and melon. The tomato crop yielded 27.8 per cent more by drip irrigation as compared to furrow method (Channappa, 1979). Similarly yield increases in case of sugarcane crop were reported (Holl, 1977) high by drip method as compared to conventional 4.2 tons raw sugar, and, 20.3 tons cane/ha respectively high. Under some experiment it is reported that tomato gave 15%, bhindi (ladyfinger) 12%, beetroot 12%, raddish 15.%, papaya 11.%, cotton (CVS-156) 18%, sweet potato 20%, and sugarcane 15%, onion 25%, sugar beet 13%, and potato 18% and high economic returns were also observed in case of fruit crops increase in yields with drip irrigations compared to conventional methods. Similarly gourd gava 45 to 47% yield increase, 10 to 12% watermelon over sprinkler. About 10 to 38% increase is reported.

Factors Affecting Efficiency of Distribution of Water

The following factors affect the efficiency of trickle system :

(i) A maximum discharge variation of 10% from the average between all tricklers controlled simultaneously by the one header.

(ii) A sufficient initial pressure at the header in order to meet the cumulative head losses which is governed by :

- (a) the necessary head losses in the elements of the system
- (b) gains and losses due to topography
- (c) the head losses specific to the trickle type
- (d) the maximum value of head losses allowed at the filter
- (e) when flow regulators are introduced in the system the necessary energy required.

(iii) Effective checking of leakage and (logging).

A good designed system must consider the maximum balance of friction losses and topographical gains in the mains while most head losses occurring in the laterals along with blocking of the system due to suspended matter which may be organic materials, calcium carbonate precipitated by CO_2 and H_2O sand and silt, pipe rust due to corrosion (iron oxides) etc.

Number of Trickles Per Unit Area

The spacing between tricklers depends upon the main requirements of the project under consideration, type of soil crops to be irrigated. The following recommendations may be kept in view :

(i) there should be separate emitter for each plant
(ii) avoid too great overlap between wetted bulbs
(iii) tricklers should be as far apart as the width of the wetted bulb
(iv) plant spacing along and between rows
(v) soil characteristic and depth
(vi) root development
(vii) average discharge of trickler and pattern and pace of soil wetting
(viii) evapotranspiration rate in the area
(ix) interval between applications
(x) volumetric value of water application needed per unit area
(xi) required time period of application.

The various results of comparison between conventional and drip method of irrigation have been worked out. Maity (1985) has shown that results of the three cropping seasons which indicate higher per cent of total yields under drip system over furrow method as given in Table 3.9.

TABLE 3.9

Irrigation Method	Yield of Potato q/ha. 1979-80	1980-81	1981-82
Furrow	217.74	206.28	222.20
Drip	223.66	225.45	245.54
C.D. at 5%	12.91	13.08	3.93

Source : S.P. Maity, 1985.

[Paper presented in short term course on sprinkler and drip irrigation (25th Feb.–16th March, 1985) at New Delhi.]

The comparison of surface, sprinkler and drip method have been worked out by Patra (1985) on the groundnut crop. It was found that sprinkler out-yielded Border method while drip produced over and above both the methods. The results are given in Table 3.10.

The beneficial effect of drip irrigation in increasing yields of many crops over other methods has also been reported. Thus Taylor (1974) found higher yields of peech, Voth and Bringhust (1971) for strawberry, Walcher (1973) for grapes, Gibson (1975), Hill (1977) for sugarcane, Sierfert *et al.* (1975) for sorghum, Singh *et al.* (1978) for tomato and potato, Awardy and Amerhem (1976) for peas, Chavez and Andrews (1979) for grapevines when conventional surface irrigation method like

TABLE 3.10

Performance of Irrigation Methods *Vs.* Groundnut Yield in the Year 1981

Particulars	Method of irrigation		
	Border	Sprinkler	Drip
Quantity of water (cu/ha)	50	34	30
Yield (ponds)	1713	1954	2242
Relativeness			
(a) yield	100	114	166
(b) water	100	69	61
Production (kg/ha/ha.cm water)	34	58	95

Source : Patra, S.C. (1985).

furrow and check basin were replaced by drip method. The net amount of water required per irrigation is given in Table 3.11.

TABLE 3.11

Net Amount of Water Required Per Irrigation

Type of soil Profile	Net amount of moisture to apply for various root depths						
	12"	18"	24"	30"	36"	48"	72"
Coarse sandy soils uniform in texture 6 ft.	0.45	0.60	0.95	1.30	1.30	1.75	2.60
Coarse sandy soils over more compact sub-soils	0.45	0.60	1.50	1.75	2.00	2.50	3.00
Fine sandy loams uniform in texture to 6 ft.	0.85	1.30	1.75	2.20	2.60	3.00	4.00
Fine sandy loams over more compact subsoils	0.85	1.50	2.00	2.40	2.80	3.25	5.00
Silt loams uniform to 6 ft.	1.10	1.70	2.25	2.75	3.00	4.00	6.00
Silt loams over more compact subsoils	1.10	1.70	2.50	3.00	3.25	4.25	6.25
Heavy clay or clay loam soils	0.90	1.40	2.00	2.40	2.85	3.85	5.50

Source : "Sprinkler Irrigation" booklet published by Sprinkler Irrigation Association, Washington.

Influence on Root System

The drip irrigation system supplies continuous application of water which maintains a high soil water potential in a relatively small soil depth. This indicates that probably shallow root system would develop under this irrigation method. However, it would depend upon the rate, amount, frequency and salt concentration of added water.

Rema Devi (1980) reported that in an annual flower plant using good quality irrigation water by drip method on a sandy loam soil resulted in 70% root weight accumulation in the upper 10 cm soil layer while fewer roots at the edges of wetted perimeter and more near the drip nozzles. Earl and Jurry (1977) observed the distribution of roots as per wetted volume of the soil according to the differential frequency of irrigation. When the poor quality irrigation water (EC 3 and 10 mm hrs.) was used under drip system the potato roots distribution was maximum below the emitter. Over the entire wetted area which remains salt free was spreaded 20 to 30 cms from the crop (Singh *et al.* 1978).

It may thus be seen that with drip irrigation high soil water potential is created in the crop rootzone as such the availability of moisture as well as the nutrients needed by crop are easily met with. Besides this the effect of salts through osmotic pressure is also nullified. The soil also does not turn to hard compacted mass so as to produce mechanical impudence for the restriction of root growth. The root system may also be modified by monitoring the flow rate, quantity and frequency of irrigation. In the context of above discussion it may be inferred that under drip irrigation method the soils ceases to act the role of water reservoir as in case of other irrigation method.

It is thus very obvious that the drip method of irrigation is quite effective not only in saving scarce commodity water but in significantly increasing the yield of most of the crops. However, the economic feasibility of the method has also been very encouraging but its success very much depends upon the general acceptability by the farmers.

TRANSMISSION LOSSES IN IRRIGATION SYSTEM

Water being scarce and costly commodity has to be spent carefully and cautiously to avoid the unuseful drain of this resource. The wastage of this resource is through various losses which decrease the profits and benefits. These are discussed below.

A substantial part of the water which is released at head of canal system is lost during its travel from head of canal system to the field. In unlined canal system, it has been established that about 50% of the water is lost before it is utilised by crop.

Approximate ranges of water at various stages are as under :

Canal Water Losses

Main Canal System		In water courses	In the field
×		20-25%	25-30%
Main Canal & Branches	Disty. & Minors		49-60%
10-15%	5-10%		

Inadequately or improperly designed water courses and unscientific water application methods may result in huge water losses and deep percolation below rootzone.

Losses in the water course and in field are accounted for in fixing the outlet discharge factory but those in the irrigation canal system upto outlet head have to be considered in designing the channel capacity.

Channel losses : In the channels losses occur due to two main reasons :

(i) Evaporation from the surface.

(ii) Seepage through wetted periphery (perimeter) of the section of the channel.

Evaporation losses : Evaporation losses are usually very small in magnitude and depend upon water surface area, temperature, humidity and wind velocity. Evaporation losses cannot be helped out. Evaporation takes places 24 hours throughout the year and ranges between 3 mm to 10 mm per day, thus totalling to about 1500 mm a year.

Evaporation losses are insignificant as compared to seepage losses and are of the order of 1.5 to 2% of the total losses or about 0.25 to 1% of the total flow.

Seepage losses : Seepage losses constitute the major loss of irrigation water from a canal system, being of the order of 98-98.5%. As such "seepage losses" only are sometimes, termed as transmission losses in canals depending upon the position of water table. These losses are categorised as under :

(i) Permeability of the strata through which the canal passes. Percolation losses are maximum in sandy soil and less in heavy black soils.

(ii) Position of ground water table. If it is deeper the losses are less and *vice versa*.

(iii) Drainage condition of the sub-soil.

(iv) Condition of the canal.

(a) Seepage losses in a silted and old canal are less than that in a new canal.

(b) Losses are more in filling reach than in cutting reach.

(c) Losses are less if velocity of flow is more.

(d) Wetted perimeter of the canal–smaller the perimeter, lesser are losses.

(v) The amount of silt carried by the canal water. Silt free from water have greater losses.

(vi) Temperature of water. More the temperature, greater are losses.

(vii) Regulation of canal, losses are less in perennial canal than an intermittently run canals.

(viii) Lined section pore low seepage losses.

Design Criteria

Various methods are being used for design criteria of losses :

(i) Etcheverry and Harding have given losses in conveyance in cumec/million sq.m. of wetted perimeter in various types of soil-strata as under :

Impervious clay loam	=	0.9 to 1.2 cumec/mil.sq. mm
Ordinary clay loam or silty soil	=	1.2 to 2.7
Sandy loam	=	3.6 to 5.2
Loose sandy soil	=	5.2 to 6.1
Gravelly sandy soil	=	7.0 to 8.8
Porous gravelly soil	=	8.8 to 10.6

(ii) The other empirical formula being used is :

Q = 1/200 (B+D)2/3 cumec/km length of canal

Where B = Bed width in metre

Where D = Depth in metre

Punjab & Haryana, empirical formula used is K = 1.9 Q 1/10

Where K = losses in cumec/mill.sqm.

Where Q = Discharge in cumec.

(iii) For lined canals — Davis and Wilson formula can be used as under :

$$SL = 0.45\ C \frac{P_w L}{4\times10^6+3650\ v\ ½\text{-}D1/3}$$

Where

SL = seepage loss

V = velocity

L = length of canal

D = depth of flow

P_w = wetted perimeter

C = constant

Value of 'C' can be adopted as under :

Lining Types	*Value of 'C'*
Concrete lining	1
Man clay — 150 mm thick lining	4
Light bitumen lining	5
Cleared clay lining 75 mm	8
Bitumen or cement mortar	10

Dr. Lovasky's Formula :

S_L = seepage losses (cumec/km length of canal)

BW_s = canal width at water edge (M)

y = depth of flow, C1 cuft. of filtration in m/dy

Values of C are :

(i) Heavy loam 0.05, medium, light loam 0.5 -010

(ii) Sandy loam 0.10 - 0.50, losses 0.25 - 0.50, Disty. sand 0.5-1.0

Fine sand 1.0 to 5.0

Med. grained sand 5.0 to 20.0

MEASUREMENT OF SEEPAGE LOSSES FROM CANALS

Various methods are being used to measure the seepage losses from water resources. These are :

Direct Measurement Methods

The methods used to measure water losses from canals. The detailed procedure of each is discussed further :

(i) Ponding method.

(ii) Inflow-outflow methods.

(iii) Tracer technique.

(iv) Seepage meter method.

Ponding Method

As the name implies, seepage loss is determined by measuring loss of water from a ponded reach of a canal. For this purpose, a reach of channel is located by constructing temporary bunds or by bulk heads on existing control structure.

The method can be used even for large canals depending upon availability of material and equipment for the construction of bund and water for filling the pond. Methods can be used upto 150-200 cumec capacity canal. Seepage losses from the ponded reach are computed from :

(i) Rate of loss of water from the pond.

(ii) Dimension of the wetted perimeter.

(iii) This method works on the principal that to measure the rate of water required to be added to pond for maintaining a constant level in the pond. The method is reasonably accurate and particularly useful in measuring small seepage losses occurring in smaller reaches of a canal.

The following factors are considered while selecting the site for this test :

(a) A curved reach should be avoided.

(b) The reach should be so selected that the nature of material in the reach has small variation.

(c) Reach should be such that no structure which are sources of additional losses fall in it.

(d) It should have approach road to transport equipment.

(e) Length of the pond should be 100 times the bed width of the canal.

Procedure : The following steps are involved in this method :

(a) *Construction of ponded section* : The one of the following ways can be adopted as per situation :

(i) For small channels having upto 0.6 M depth of flow, a dam built of canvas is placed across the X-section with the help of timber and sealing the edges by earth, canvas can be replaced by heavy plastic sheets also.

OR

(ii) Pond be constructed by building earthen bund on either end and making it water proof by laying canvas or plastic sheets over it.

OR

(iii) Existing regulators be used to pond water and putting canvas/heavy plastic sheet cover over joints where edges can be packed by earth.

(b) *Equipment* : It consists of :

(i) two staff gauges and two hook gauges, and
(ii) evaporation pan.

The gauges are installed at either end of reach, hooks, capable of reading upto 0.1 MM with the aid of vernier, are fixed, with the help of survey instrument linked with survey Bench mark on the canal.

Procedure : (i) The pond can be filled by gravity flow or with the help of pump.

(ii) With the help of gauge fixed in pond. Water levels are recorded at intervals of 1 to 4 hours depending upon the rate of losses observed.

Following proformas may be filled in :

Seepage Loss Data - Ponding Method

Canal...
Chainage ....one end..............other end ....
Staff gauge chainage .....one end.......other end..................

Date	Time	Hook gauge		Staff gauge		Temperature	
		One end	Other end	One end	Other end	Air	Water

Analysis of results : Following tables be compiled with canal data and observations of losses done.

TABLE 3.11

Seepage Losses by Ponding Method

Table for water surface width :

Name of canal .... Pond No.......................................

Chainage........ one end............ other end.......

Chainage (km)	Water surface width required for various elevations			
	El.	El.	El.	Average

TABLE 3.12

Seepage Losses by Ponding Method

Table of wetted perimeters.

Name of Canals...................... Pond No...

Chainage (km)	Wetted perimeter for various elevation (E)			Average value
	El.	El.	El.	

Seepage rate (m^3/Sec/10^6m^2) is obtained by :

$$\text{Seepage rate } (m^3/s/10^6M^2) = \frac{\text{Total volume lost } (M^3) \times 10^6}{3600 \times \text{Average wetted} \times \text{Total} \times \text{length of pond Peri.(M) (m)}}$$

Limitation of the Method

(1) Normal running of canal is interrupted.
(2) Procedure of construction/demolition of dams are costly.
(3) Arrangement of large quantity of water is needed to fill the pool initially and subsequent replenishment.
(4) Though the result is accurate, it does not show variation reach-wise in the pond length.
(5) Though the result is accurate, it does not show variation reach-wise in the pond length.
(6) Actual running conditions are not simulated with standing pool. Suspended material mettles down reducing seepage losses.
(7) There may be variation in ground water table throughout the length of canal from that in ponded reach.

Merits

(a) Suitable for large canals.
(b) Suitable for more accurate results in small seepage.

Inflow-Outflow Method

This method utilises measurement of discharges at the upstream and downstream end of the reach under study and the difference is taken as seepage + evaporation losses. By deducting evaporation losses, the seepage losses can be ascertained. Discharge at either end can be measured by fixing partial flume V. notch, rectangular notch, even an existing weir/ fall can be also used. Where such facilities are not available, current meter gauging may be done.

Procedure : Following preliminary arrangements shall be made :

(a) As far as possible all the outlets from the canal shall be kept closed. In case they are required to be kept open, the opening size should be locked to ascertain constant discharge from it and arrangement to measure the same be done and their record maintained.

(b) All measuring devices should be checked for their dimensions and well caliberated.

(c) Constant discharge is released and maintained during the experiment.

(d) In addition to discharge, water levels should also be measured and record maintained.

(e) Water level be tried to be maintained at level where gauge discharge relationship is available.

Observations : Water level and discharge should be recorded at an interval of 3-6 hours in table given below :

TABLE 3.13

Proforma of Observation of Seepage Loss by Inflow-Outflow Method

Name of canal ....
Location ....
Type of gauge ....
Observer ....

Sl. No.	Date	Time	I Gauge at	II Gauge at	III Gauge at	IV Gauge at	V Gauge at	VI Gauge at	Remarks

Experiment closed at......................on.........................

TABLE 3.14

Statement Showing the Losses in Canals by Inflow-Outflow Method

Name of canal........................

Observer............................

Date ....

Sl. No.	Length of reach (M)	Averaged wetted perimeter (M)	Inflow M³/s	Outflow M³/s	Loss M³/s	Rate of M³/s for M/s of flow.	Loss M³/s for mill.Sq. metre of wetted perimeter.	Remarks

To the above values are added/deducted following :

(i) Evaporation losses.

(ii) Discharges through outlets which could not be closed.

Limitation of the Method

(i) Losses worked out are total losses in the reach for water table temperature, humidity of at the time of experiment.

(ii) Results will be not accurate for small discharges/seepage losses.

(iii) It is not possible to determine distribution of seepage losses in a reach.

(iv) Adequate arrangement may be required in large reach and for bigger canals for measurements of leakage and outflow from off-taking channels.

(v) Most of the outlets have to be closed during experiments.

Advantages

(i) Method can be applied without bringing canal out of operation, without not much effecting irrigation/power generation.

(ii) Seepage losses are obtained under normal running operation of the canal.

Tracer technique

A radio active tractor is a mixture of isotopes of an element which may be incorporated into a sample to make possible observation of course of that element. The observation may be made by measurement of its radioactivity. The isotopes generally used are Bromine-82, Iodine-131, Trituum, Irridium-192, Cobalt 60 etc. The method used in sub-surface flow are :

(a) *Double well method* : Where in tracer is injured in one well and observations done in another well.
(b) *Single well dilution method* : The tracer's injected in a single well and its dilution is noted with respect to time after injection.
(c) *Single well pumping method* : The method is best suited for deep canals with turbid, fast flowing water, canals with heavy weed growth and adverse bottom conditions.

Seepage Meter Method

They are suitable devices to measure local seepage. Design is based upon the assumption that rate of water loss for an isolated surface area of the canal can be measured. Various seepage meters have been developed. They are by Salinity Laboratory of Agriculture Department, Irrigation Research Institute, U.P.

CANAL LINING

Conservation of irrigation water supplies is highly important as the demand of water is increasing continuously and particularly where sources are limited. Principle of conservation requires optimum use of available water and most effective and promising being reduction in water losses through seepage (and sometime rodents or crabs burrows) during conveyance through the canals. It has been very well established that through installation of an impervious lining by some treatment of canal section, considerable quantity of water can be saved. Thus we see that lining offers a satisfactory solution to water conveyance besides controlling the menace of water-logging.

Thus principle objects of lining irrigation channels are :

(i) To minimise losses due to seepage.
(ii) Project the area prone to water logging.
(iii) Pass increased discharge through the same (existing section of canal).
(iv) Less maintenance cost.

The advantages of lining can be listed as below :

(a) Reduction in seepage losses from lined canals and thereby reduction of wastage of water and water-logging/water stagnation in canal adjoining areas.

(b) Conservation of water which otherwise would require construction of bigger reservoir for the same areas to be irrigated.

(c) Flatter slopes in lined canal again resulting low height of dam effecting considerable reduction in the cost of head work or to bring more area under command.

(d) The carrying capacity of canal (cd=VA) increases due to reduced friction (n) resulting in increased velocity (V) for the same slope (s) and same hydraulic mean depth corresponding to (R) as may be seen from manning formula $V=\frac{1}{n}R^{\frac{2}{3}}S^{\frac{1}{2}}$. Also the lined canal would have less cross sectional area width and depth of flow for the same capacity of unused canals thus stable channel section, thereby reducing maintenance cost. However, lining cost and labour factors are to be kept in consideration.

(e) Steeper side and bed slopes are possible as lined section is immune to erosion.

(f) Higher velocity, reduction in cross-sectional area for same discharge, reduction in earthwork quantities, lesser land acquisition, smaller length of pucca structures etc.

(g) Canal water does not pick up harmful salts from canal soil bed.

(h) Weed growth and scouring which is a noxious problem and requires huge expenditure every year is avoided by lining.

(i) Prevents theft of water by cultivators.

(j) Recurring expenditure on desilting of channel is reduced, since higher velocity does not permit silting of canal.

(k) In areas where topography is more slopy (slope more than 0.7%) the mean flow velocity is high unless appropriate number of falls are provided which increase expenditure of maintenance. This can be avoided by canal lining. This also reduces evaporation losses on account of decreased travelling time as well as reduced surface area from the head-reach to the tail-end of canal.

Contrary to above advantages, only disadvantages are higher cost, high cost of repair, besides the fact that if position of outlets are to be changed, extra cost is incurred.

Selection of Suitable Type of Lining

It is always advisable to adopt lining which :

(i) secures maximum reduction in seepage losses;

(ii) makes optimum utilisation of locally available material;

(iii) economical in cost; and

(iv) speedy in construction.

The type of lining is, however, governed by following considerations :

1. *Imperviousness* : It should ensure maximum degree of water tightness and shall develop minimum cracks, opening of points etc.
2. *Hydraulic efficiency* : Since capacity varies inversely with roughness, co-efficient, it is desirable to have smoother surface concrete lining which is most suited for the purpose.
3. *Durability* : With minimum thickness and cost it would be most durable.
4. *Structural safety* : It should be able to withstand differential sub-soil water pressure and should be safe against a difference in head of 15-25 cm which shall develop when canal is closed slowly.
5. *Economy* : Some of the lining though costly are more durable *e.g.* concrete lining whereas some, though cheaper, are less durable. We shall have to arrive at some compromise.
6. *High velocity* : It must permit high velocity to avoid silting.
7. *Life* : It should have good life *e.g.* C.C. lining has an age of 50 years.
8. *Weed growth* : It should be impregnable to roots of plants entirely eliminating possibility of weed growth.
9. Availability of construction material.
10. Availability of labour.
11. Operation and maintenance charges.
12. Nature of sub-grade *e.g.* for heavy soils rigid linings are less safe.
13. *Resistance to erosion* : It should be able to withstand abrasion due to sediments.

Types of Lining

Broadly lining can be categorised into following categories :

(1) Exposed lining.

(2) Burried membrance lining.

(3) Earth lining.

(4) Soil sealant lining.

Exposed lining : Exposed linings are linings (except earth-lining) in which water barrier is exposed to wear, erosion and deterioration. The category includes all hard surface (usually rigid type) lining constructing of asphaltic material, port-land cement, concrete, soil cement, masonry lining etc.

General design consideration of exposed lining are :

(i) Since cost of a hard surface lining is large, section with minimum perimeter should be adopted for which steeper bed slopes are of advantage. B.D. ratio ranging from 1 to 2.

(ii) A firm foundation base to lined surface is essential to avoid differential settlements and development of cracks in lining. Undisturbed sub-grade is often found to function satisfactorily. Expensive soils are hazardous to such type of lining and it is advisable to provide a 'sand' cushion below the lining.

(iii) Embankments should be well compacted and laid at O.M.C.

(iv) Back filling should be generally avoided, but if done, should be well compacted before lining.

(v) Suitable under drainage system should be provided to safeguard against sudden drawdown conditions which shall range between 0.15-0.25 M/sec when canal is closed.

Various types of lining falling under this category are :

(a) Cement concrete lining - Precast precase cast *in situ*.
(b) Stone brick masonary lining.
(c) concrete lining or gritting.
(d) Cement mortar lining.
(e) Asphaltic lining.
(f) Hydraulic lime lining.
(g) Soil cement lining (for water courses only).
(h) Soda-ash-clay lining (The mix ratio is 1:10)

In spite of the above, various combinations of two or more types of impermeable material membrances can be and have also been tried *e.g.* P.C.C. block lining overlaid on polythene sheets.

Other Water Carrying Devices

The various types of devices for carrying water are used as discussed below :

Stone Katla lining : Where cut stone slabs are available in plenty trench is cut in middle of the bank and cut stone slabs are erected and earth is puddled on either sides of them. Overlaps as shown in the figure are provided and sealed with C.M. 1:3.

Major advantage of stone Katla lining is that they are not susceptible to theft and no maintenance is required at later stage.

WATER LOSSES AND IRRIGATION EFFICIENCY OF CONVEYANCE SYSTEM

(A Case Study in Binayaka Minor Catchment of C.A.D., Kota was done by G.P. Nathani *et al.*, 1984 from paper, presented in workshop on water conveyance efficiency. Some details of the study are presented below.)

Introduction

The water loss study was conducted during Rabi 1980-81 in the O.F.D. area of 164.58 ha. in the Chambal command on 2.220 km. long Binayaka Minor to study the effectiveness of water resources use as being utilised in crop production.

Description of Area

Binayaka Minor is unlined and takes-off at Chain 105 from Bajer distributary of L.M.C. The command area of the minor is divided in four chaks, each commanded by separate earthen water course. The command area start after 750 meter length of minor. After 2.22 km. length, the minor turns into a water course. Four water courses receiving water from the minor are located at a distance of 750 m, 870 m, 1585 m and 2220 m. The detailed information regarding the command area and length of Channel are given in Table 3.15. The total length of water course varied from 1113 m to 2069 m with an average length of 1748 m. The first three water courses had two arms. The arms of water course No. 1 were 918 m and 1263 m long with a common arm of 112 m length between them. The arms of water course No. 2 were of 350 and 1522 m length with no common arm, whereas the arms of water course No. 3 were 533 m and 1567 m with a common arm of 212 m length. The tail-end water course was 1113 m long.

The area of chaks ranged from 30.05 ha. to 52.49 ha. with an average chak size of 41.14 ha. The network density was :

Minor	: 13.49 m/ha.
Water course	: 42.36 m/h.

Materials and Methods

The measurement of discharge of water was done by using Parshall measuring flumes. The flumes of 30 cm. throat width were used in the minor. In water courses, the measurement of flow of water was made with flumes of 15 cm. throat width. In the straight section of the minor, one flume was placed near the head and second at a distance of 2140 m from head. In the water courses, flumes were installed near the head and on the starting points of individual fields. The actual two hourly measurement of the discharge of water was recorded at the head and tail-end of minor. The chak outlets discharge and flow of water to the individual fields was regularly measured during day hours. The water losses were calculated and measured during day hours. The water losses were calculated by determining the difference in the discharge of water at different measuring points in the water courses and in the minor.

TABLE 3.15

Command Area of Chak, Channel Length and Network Density

Chak/ Outlet No.	Command area (ha)	Irrigated area (ha)	Channel length (m) Ist arm	IInd arm	Common arm	Total	Net work density (m/ha)
1.	52.49	30.63	918	1263	112	2069	39.42
2.	42.06	31.18	1522	350	...	1872	44.51
3.	39.98	23.21	583	1567	212	1938*	48.47
4.	30.05	21.68	1113	...	...	1113	37.04
Average	41.14	26.67	...	...	...	1748	42.36
Minor	164.58	106.70	2220	...	...	2220	13.49

* Effective length of second arm of water course No. 3 was reduced to 1167 as the farmers installed unauthorised outlet beyond this length.

Results and Discussions

The actual discharge of Binayaka Minor and that in the water-courses was measured every day from 27.10.80 to 30.4.81. The discharge in the minor varied from 6.79 cusec to 7.15 cusec with an average of 6.93 cusec (Table 3.16). These data indicate that the unit flow in the Binayaka Minor averaged about 16.84 cusecs/400 ha. which comes out about 2.80 times higher than the flow as proposed in the World Bank appraisal report. The proposed water allowance at the minor head for O.F.D. Area is 6.00 cusec/

400 ha (0.42 lit/8 ha.) at irrigated cropping intensity of 133% with Kharif and Rabi ratio of 57:76.

TABLE 3.16

Water Discharge at the Hard of Binayaka Minor in Rabi, 1981-82

Period	Hours of flow	Volume of water released (m)	Discharge	
			m^3/ha	Cusec
27-10-80 to 1-11-80				
8-11-80 to 25-11-80	294.80	208966.38	710.77	7.10
25-11-80 to 8-12-80	316.00	224565.35	710.65	7.10
18-1-81 to 27-2-81	958.50	650973.21	679.16	6.79
23-3-81 to 6-4-81	331.25	226094.20	682.55	6.82
17-4-81 to 30-4-81	321.75	230131.91	715.25	7.15
Total/Average	2221.50	1540731.05	693.55	6.93

Source : Nathani, G.P. (1984), Paper presented in workshop on water conveyance efficiency by Irrigation Management, Kota (Raj.).

The delivery flow to the chaks measured at water course heads varied from 1.05 cusec to 1.74 cusec with an average of 1.24 cusec. The unit flow in the courses varied from 10.37 cusec to 14.51 cusec with a mean discharge of 12.16 cusec/400 ha. which was about two times higher than the proposed water allowance (Table 3.17).

The water losses from 2.22 km. long minor averaged about 27.2%. The wastage of water to drain by cutting the minor at a distance of 2140 m by tail-end farmers averaged to 12.00%. The water losses from water courses varied from 43.76% to 6.14% with an average of 55.54%. The major losses occurred in the beginning of water courses which run for the longer duration. The water losses showed variation with the length of water courses. These were observed to be more with longer length of water courses. The wastage of water to the drains from water courses was about 5.20% of the total delivery of water during Rabi season.

The conveyance efficiency of minor came to 72.80 per cent with average losses of 27.2 per cent. The conveyance efficiency in the water courses varied from 34.86 to 56.24 per cent with an average efficiency of 44.43 per cent. The conveyance efficiency was maximum in the tail-end water course whereas minimum efficiency was obtained in the water course No. 1 located in the upper reach of minor.

TABLE 3.17

Command Area, Channel Length, Water Allowance as per CCA Conveyance Efficiency and Water Received for Irrigation Rabi Crops

Irrigation channel	C.C.A. (ha)	Area irrigated (ha)	Length of channel (m)	Hours of flow	Total inlet flow (m^3)	Total delivery to outlets (m^3)	Water losses %	Discharge cusec	Unit inlet-flow cusec/ 400 ha	Irrigation efficiency %
Binayaka Minor	164.58	106.70	2220	2221.50	1540731	1121651	27.20	6.93	16.84	72.80
Water courses										
1	52.49	30.63	2069	1581.50	275442	96030	65.14	1.74	13.26	34.86
2	42.86	31.18	1872	2115.65	231563	90674	60.84	1.09	10.37	39.16
3 A + 35	39.98	23.21	1538	1393.20	145860	69242	52.53	1.05	10.50	47.47
4	30.05	21.68	1113	953.00	104314	58667	43.76	1.09	14.51	56.24
Water course average	41.14	26.67	1648	1510.84	189295	78663	55.54	1.24	12.16	44.43

The field water application efficiency reported for Binayaka area has been 40 per cent (Report on Water Management Efficiency Study for Rabi Season, 1979-80). Under ideal and optimum irrigation practices, the attainable field application efficiency recommended is 60% for fine textured soils.

The efficiency data reveal that the minor irrigation efficiency achieved in the study area was 13 per cent only against 50 per cent as proposed by World Bank for O.F.D. areas. This indicates that for every 100 m^3 of water delivered from the distributary at the minor head, only 13 m^3 of water were actually utilised in the fields for crop production. The low irrigation efficiency in Binayaka catchment may be attributed to heavy water losses from the carrier system, deep percolation losses in fields, inadequate maintenance of water courses and poor land preparation.

Suggestions for Improvement

Since much of the water is wasted in unlined channels through seepage and/or leakage while conveying water to the fields, it lowers down the irrigation efficiency substantially. Certain suggestions for increasing the efficiency are given below :

1. The length of water course should be small, preferably limited to one kilometre.
2. First, 40-50 m. length of each water course could preferably be lined.
3. The fields are irrigated by wild flooding. This contributes to low T.E. and greater losses of water in field application. Farmers be advised for good land preparation for even application of water and made irrigation strips of suitable size.
4. Farmers be advised to seal the cracks and burrow pipings at the time of irrigation.

CHAPTER 4

IRRIGATION SCHEDULING

Water distribution *i.e.* conveyance of water from the source to the field is the most important link between the water supplier (Irrigation Deptt.) and the users (farmer). For effective distribution of water the tight management is also essential. This, however, is a two-dimensional problem *viz.* : (1) technical *i.e.* planning, design, and operation; and (2) social-illiteracy, lack of cooperation, leadership pressure from influencial farmers, vested interests etc. Factors influencing irrigation scheduling are weather, soil-plant, water relationships, soil moistures, irrigation water requirements and water management of irrigation system. The data are to be generated for implementation.

IRRIGATION SCHEDULING

Essential Exercise

Irrigation scheduling is an essential exercise to meet the water requirement of crops. This is a function of soil patterns, water requirement, climatic conditions and management practices, antecedent soil moisture, irrigation characteristics of soil (irrigability classes). As such to finalise the date and depth of irrigation the assessment of soil moisture contents, evapotranspiration, the soil moisture stress conditions of the soil type under study and the relationship between crop yield. The variability of water requirements for different growth periods of a crop is also important factor to be considered. These requirements for any area is also dependent on the type of crops and cropping pattern.

Need of the day

The ever increasing rate of growth population and continuously increased demand for food and fibre, there has arisen a gread need for very judicious consumption of irrigation water which is quite costly and scarce commodity in view of huge capital investments so far incurred on irrigation projects and yet the insufficient quantity of water harvested for various uses. Scheduling of irrigation water in irrigated commánds is therefore, very essential and call of today.

In many irrigation projects water quantity is limited and where it is not so there is serious problem of inequitable distribution of irrigation water at appropriate time to avoid over-irrigation or excessive watering particularly at head reaches, problem of water logging, runoff, erosion and many environmental problems besides decreasing the cultivable area and reduced crop yields.

REQUIREMENTS OF GOOD WATER DISTRIBUTION METHOD

These can be grouped as : (1) Appropriateness, (2) Equity, (3) Environmental stability, (4) Predicability, (5) Adequacy, (6) Timeliness, (7) Flexibility, (8) Incentive to users, and (9) Minimum scope for mal-practices.

The various approaches have been made to meet the above requirements by formulating different irrigation distribution policies such as different types of rotational water applications which are being used for a long time in many parts of the country such as flexible and rigid methods. The ethics of these approaches is the partitioning of available water resources equitable to each holding within the command based on a compromise between the supply and the demand. However, none of the approach adequately considers the different parameters that governs the depth of water application in each irrigation and its interval.

PRINCIPLES OF IRRIGATION SCHEDULING AND FACTORS

To arrive at some norms that can be used as broad guidelines about the system design and delivery schedule of irrigation below outlet certain principles have been laid down for deciding the depth and interval of irrigation in the commands of surface irrigation projects.

Water Requirement

Water requirements of the crop and capacity of rootzone soil to conserve water, predicts the time of irrigation and the depth of water to be applied. The crop water requirements depend upon the type of crop (Table 4.1), its age and climate. The quantity of water needed by a particular crop in terms of frequency if kept constant, the dose of water per rotation would need a change. Therefore, under irrigated agriculture the dose of water should vary considerably over the life cycle of any specific variety of crop. The frequency of irrigation would also depend

TABLE 4.1

Amount of Water Needed by Crops

Low water needing crops	Medium water needing crops	High water needing crops
Pomegranates Sitaphal Lisoda Mulberry Ber Avonla	Citrus Guava Papaya Mango Tamarind	Banana Kethal Tapioca
Gram Mustard Linseed Melons Cicirnot	Wheat Barley	Paddy Jute Sugarcane Fodder (Chari) Berseem Leucern etc.

upon the moisture holding capacity and the rate of deplation of moisture. Higher frequency is needed for soils having low moisture holding capacity.

Crop Rooting Characteristics

The rooting characteristics are very much different for different crops. The quiz when to irrigate with how much water application depends upon when and where the water is removed from the soil by plant roots. The rooting characteristics are governed by plant genetics. Thus vegetable crops have sparse rooting systems and therefore, are unable to use all the soil water within the rootzone. Forage crops, sorghum, maize etc. root travel very deep in the soil and therefore, utilize entire water present in the rootzone system from the wetted perifery. Shallow rooted crops as such cannot utilise the water in deeper soil depths and on account of this fact, require more frequent irrigation as compared to deep rooted crops. Soil conditions that hinder the growth of roots also influence the irrigation practices. Thus high water-table conditions, shallow depth soils and existence of impermeable soil strata or pans near the ground surface inhibit the root development. Conditions of soil fertility, contents of salts and the management has significant influence on rooting patterns. The scheduling of irrigation depends upon the effective rootzone depth, not necessarily on the maximum depth travelled by the roots particularly in the plants having tap root which travel far long way from the rootzone area. The volume and depth of soil in which the effective rootzone of a plant is present is depleted in soil moisture that is required to be replaced by irrigation soil once again attained the field capacity moisture status.

The approximate values of effective rootzone depth of certain important crops grown in medium textured and fine textured deep and well drained soils are given in Table 4.2 & 4.3 indicating that water requirements is affected by rooting depth.

TABLE 4.2

Rootzone Depth Limits Crops

Shallow rooted	Moderately deep rooted	Deep rooted	Very deep rooted
Deep of rooted zone			
60 cm	90 cm	120 cm	180 cm
Rice	Wheat	Maize	Sugarcane
Potato	Tobacco	Cotton	Citrus
Cauliflower	Caster	Sorghum	Coffee
Cabbage	Groundnut	Pearl Millet	Apple
Lettuce	Muskmelon	Soyabean	Grapevine
Onion	Peas	Tomato	Safflower
	Bean	Berseem	Lucerne
	Chilli		

TABLE 4.3

Rootzone Depth Limits Crops in Heavy Textured (Clay) Soils

Shallow rooted	Medium deep rooted	Deep rooted
Wheat Barley Vegetables Lentil Peas etc.	Cotton Mustard Gram Sugarcane	Plantation (Orchard) crops

The roots of a particular plant derive or extract more quantity of water in moist soil as compared to the conditions when the same attains the comparatively less moisture status. In other words the roots at first hand extract most of the soil moisture from the surface and after this soil gets drier, the moisture is extracted from lower depths till through subsequent irrigation surface is again wetted. Thus the deplation of moisture would occur between these two intervals of irrigation from different soil depths of rootzone. It has been understood that 40% of the total moisture utilised by plant is from the first quarter of effective rootzone depth, 30% from the second, 20% from the third quarter and 10% from the fourth quarter as shown in Fig 4.1 below :

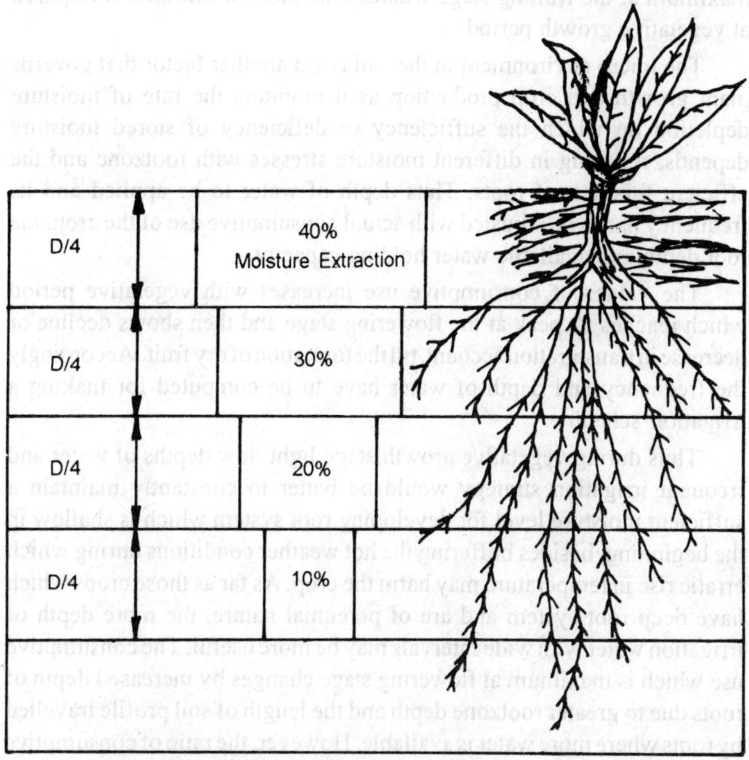

Fig. 4.1 : Average-moisture extraction pattern of plants growing in a soil without restive layers and with an adequate supply of available moisture throughout the rootzone

It has been reported that plant growth can be divided into three growth stages in respect of irrigation practices. These are : (i) vegetative, (ii) flowering, and (iii) fruiting. The fruiting stage has been further divided into two stages namely (a) the wet fruiting stage which is after flowering, and (b) dry fruiting stage which is after wet fruit formation. The harvesting stage which is the last but not the least important stage in scheduling of irrigation varies from crop to crop. Thus grasses, cabbage, spinach and other leafy vegetables are harvested at vegetative stage while flowers, cauliflower, fodder, maize, and sorghum during flowering stage, yet another crops like tomatoes, brinjals, green peas, melons and sugarcane during wet fruit stage while many other crops like rice, maize, sorghum, wheat, cotton, potato, onion etc. are harvested during dry fruit stage.

The requirements of nutrients by plant also varies with the crop growth stage. Thus plant's phosphorus and potash requirements are maximum at the fruiting stage whereas the most of nitrogen is required at vegetative growth period.

The micro environment in the soil is yet another factor that governs plant growth and crop production as it monitors the rate of moisture depletion on which the sufficiency or deficiency of stored moisture depends, resulting in different moisture stresses with rootzone and the efficient function of roots. Thus depth of water to be applied and its frequency has to be adjusted with actual consumptive use of the crop, the root depth and available water holding capacity.

The values of consumptive use increases with vegetative period which reaches its peak at the flowering stage and then shows decline or decrease in transpiration account, till the formation of dry fruit. Accordingly the frequency and depth of water have to be computed for making a irrigation schedule.

Thus during vegetative growth stage light /low depths of water and frequent irrigation strategy would be better to constantly maintain a sufficient moisture level for developing root system which is shallow in the beginning, besides buffering the hot weather conditions during which erratic rise in temperature may harm the crop. As far as those crops which have deep root system and are of perennial nature, the more depth of irrigation water with wide intervals may be more useful. The consumptive use which is maximum at flowering stage changes by increased depth of roots due to greater rootzone depth and the length of soil profile travelled by roots where more water is available. However, the ratio of consumptive use to depth of extraction for a proliferating and enlarging root system remain more or less constant. It is due to this reason that with increasing rooting depth the irrigation frequency for most of crops also remains constant during vegetative and flowering stages. Although special care has to be taken during flowering stage to avoid moisture stresses so that emerged flowers are converted to seeds of normal size, colour and quality. At the same time excessive moisture at flowering should also be avoided to control the vegetative growth in case of certain crops which reduce overall quantity of fruits or seeds. In order to avoid the need of irrigation after wet fruiting stage the heavy irrigation at this stage meets the further water requirements of the crop up to final development stage *i.e.* dry fruiting stage. It is because the water requirement or consumptive use declines considerably and no excess moisture in soil than already present is needed by the plants.

Soil Moisture Factors

As emphasised earlier the soil moisture patterns and storage capacity are most important characteristics that would influence the depth and frequency of irrigation which necessitates scheduling of irrigation. The available soil moisture values are calculated from the moisture hold between field capacity and permanent wilting point. Fine textured soils have a wide range of available moisture holding capacity and permanent wilting point values than coarsed soils is given in Table 4.4.

The soil moisture tension at field capacity depends upon soil type and varies between one-tenth to one-third bar atmosphere while at permanent wilting point ranges between seven to thirtytwo bar atmospheres the general accepted value is, however, 15 bar atmospheres. The wilting range represents progressive conditions from dropping of fresh leaves, drying of old leaves, to complete and irreversible drying or death of the plant.

TABLE 4.4

Estimated Available Soil Moisture Cm/Metre

(Dent and Young, 1981)

S. No.	Textural class	Available soil moisture (mm/m)
1.	Heavy clay	170
2.	Silty clay	190
3.	Loam	180
4.	Silt loam	210
5.	Silty clay loam	215
	General value for fine textured soils	195
6.	Sandy clay loam	180
7.	Sandy loam	170
8.	Loamy fine sand	110
	General value for medium textured soils	155
9.	Fine sand	110
10.	Medium and coarse sand	95
	General value for coarse textured soils	100

Available Soil Moisture in cms/metre

It is essential to determine moisture content by any method for the soil samples of different depths say up to 1 metre. The methods of soil moisture measurement have already been discussed. For example 110 gm moist soil sample when completely dried in oven at 105°C at constant weight is 100 gms. Then soil moisture per cent would be

$$\frac{(110 - 100) \times 100}{100} = 10.0 \text{ per cent (by weight).}$$

Then we should know the bulk density of the soil by any method say by core cutter method and if it comes out to be 1.4 gm/cc, then available soil moisture in cm per metre soil depth (by volume) is given as soil moisture per cent × B.D. or 10 × 1.4 = 14 cm per metre. For general idea bulk density values for fine textured clay soils may be assumed to be 1.0 gm/cc and for sand 1.8 gm/cc. The values of other textures fall in between these two ranges. The average value be taken as 1.5 gm/cc.

Climate

It is also a major factor in deciding the irrigation scheduling because it governs the rate of water used by crops. The parameters of climate are temperature, wind velocity, humidity and sunshine hours which influence consumptive use rate. The plants need more water during hot, dry, windy days with bright sunshine and less water during cool, humid, calm days with overcast sky. The rate of evapotranspiration for young age plants varies between 1.25 - 3.75 mm per day while at flowering and wet fruiting stages *i.e.* when they have attained maturity it varies between 3.75 to 7.00 mm per day. These values may have still wide variations if the climatic conditions of the different countries are taken.

IRRIGATION INTERVAL AND DEPTH OF WATER APPLICATION

It is very essential to know for any area, when the irrigation is to be supplied and how much quantity of water should be applied. This would decide the opening and closure period of the canal system as well as the flow discharge to be released.

The amount of water or net depth of water application is the difference between the total moisture holding capacity of the rootzone soil and the antecedent soil moisture present at the time irrigation is to be supplied.

This amount of water applied to soil bring it back to field capacity. The gross depth can be known by dividing the net depth of field application efficiency. Irrigation frequency interval is the difference of days between last and the subsequent irrigation. It has been seen that most of the crops thrives well if they are irrigated again after the average soil moisture depletion (M.A.D.) of 50% has taken place. The different crops of course have the different average level of moisture depletion as well as it varies at various stages of growth at which the irrigation should be supplied to help them to produce optimum production. This depends upon the available moisture holding capacity of the effective rootzone soil depth, allowable moisture depletion (M.A.D.) and consumptive use rate of crop. The relationship between these factors are given in Table 4.5.

The effective rooting depth of full grown crops is represented by the soil depth at a particular location. The available soil moisture is also dependent on this soil depth. The rooting depth of any crop may be assumed equal or less to the upper limit of soil depth in a given depth class of soil. In this way the soil depth is used for calculating available soil moisture in place of crop rooting depth in a given textural class of the soil.

Assuming available soil moisture as AW in per cent volume, PW as the allowable moisture depletion fraction of AW, and soil depth (Z) in mm the depth of water needed in the rootzone (hR) may be presented as

$$hR = \frac{AW\ PW\ Z}{100}.$$

Assuming the three broad textural classes and their available soil moisture holding capacities (mm), three soil depths classes namely upto 22.5 cm, upto 45.0 cm and upto 100 cm and four average soil moisture depletion values for 4 crops groups (Table 4.6) we get $3 \times 3 \times 3 \times 4 = 108$ values of depth of water needed in the rootzone (hR). The above basis has been used by Holsambre *et al.* (1983) the calculations for which are given in Tables 4.7 and 4.8.

Example :

Given

(*i*) Soil type = Fine Sandy loam

(*ii*) Crop = Wheat

(*iii*) Design moisture extraction depth = 91 cm

(*iv*) Total moisture extraction depth = 122 cm

(*v*) Design moisture use rate = 4.06 mm/day
(Based on peak period moisture use rate of 5.08 mm/day, 80% of which will be from design moisture extraction depth.)

(*vi*) Efficiency = 85%

Find out : (a) Moisture to be depleted at each irrigation.

(b) Design frequency.

TABLE 4.5

Effective Rooting Depth of Full Grown Crops and Allowable Depletion of Available Soil Moisture

Crop Cr. No.	Crop	Allowable depletion fraction	Effective rooting depth (cm)
1	2	3	4
I.	Potato	0.3	40
	Leafy vegetables		30
	Onion		30
II.	Banana		40
	Carrot		50
	Grapes		100
	Melons	0.4	100
	Peas		60
	Beans		50
	Cabbage		40
	Groundnut		50
	Tomato		70
III.	Sunflower		80
	Citrus		120
	Cucumber	0.5	70
	Orchards		100
	Soyabean		60
	Wheat		100
	Sugarcane		100
IV.	Sorghum		100
	Grains		90
	Cotton	0.6	100
	Maize		100
	Olive		120
	Safflower		100
	Sweet potato		100

Source : F.A.O. 24.

TABLE 4.6

Available Soil Moisture, mm Source Holsambre *et al.* 1983

Soil texture Group	Soil depth class groups		
	Shallow upto 22.5 cm	Medium upto 45 cm	Deep upto 100 cm
Fine textured	45	90	235
Medium textured	35	70	185
Coarse textured	25	45	120

TABLE 4.7

Depth of Water (hR) Needed in the Rootzone

Soil texture group	Allowable depletion of available soil moisture											
	Shallow 22.5 m				Medium deep 22.5-45 cm				Deep 45-100 cm			
	0.3	0.4	0.5	0.6	0.3	0.4	0.5	0.6	0.3	0.4	0.5	0.6
Fine textured	14	18	23	27	27	36	45	55	71	95	118	141
Medium textured	11	14	18	21	24	28	35	42	56	74	93	111
Coarse textured	8	10	13	15	14	18	23	27	36	48	60	72

The illustration of forgoing results and discussions has been given by Saksena and Saksena (1983) with following given data of the profile.

TABLE 4.8

Depth of soil sample	Textural class	Weight of moist soil sample (gm)	Weight of dry soil sample (gm)	Bulk density of soil (gm/cc)	Field application efficiency (%)
0—25	Loam	134.60	126.82	1.5	80
25—50	Silt loam	136.28	127.95	AV. value	
50—75	Clay loam	122.95	115.32	rootzone	
75—100	Clay	110.92	102.64	depth of one metre	

Solution :

(A) Net amount depth = 50 % of total available moisture in 91 cm.

Available moisture for 0-14 cms depth = 14 × .13 cm/cm = 1.82
(fine sandy loam soil)

For 14-40 cm depth = 26 × .14 = 3.64
(light sandy clay loam soil)

For 40-91 cm depth = 51 × 0.15 = 7.65
(sandy clay loam soil)

Total = 13.11 cm

Net amount of water depth (cm) for 91 cm.

= 13.11 × 50% (MAD) – 6.56 cm

= say 6.6 cm = 2.6"

$$\text{Gross amount} = \frac{\text{Net amount}}{\text{Efficiency}} = \frac{6.6}{.85} = 7.6 \text{ cm}$$

= say 7.8 cm or 3.0"

(B) Design frequency (How often to irrigate during period when crop is using maximum amount of moisture from the soil, also length of time allowed to irrigate the field — irrigation period).

Net amount of moisture between field capacity and start of irrigation

$$\text{(cm)} = \frac{(100\% - 50\%)\ 13.11}{.508 \times (80\%)}$$

Peak period moisture use rate of crop which must be met from design

$$\text{moisture extraction depth (cm)} = \frac{6.56}{.406} = 16.1 \text{ or say 16 days}$$

Example :

Calculate the interval of irrigation for a given soil in order to ensure sufficient irrigation to given crop :

Given : Field capacity of soil = 30% or 0.30

Permanent wilting point = 12%

Bulk density of soil = 1.25 gm/cc/or mgm m^{-3}

Effective depth of rootzone = 60 cm.

Daily consumptive use of water = 12.5 mm.

Assume readily available moisture = 80% of ASM

(It is 75 to 80% of av. soil moisture A.S.M.)

Solution :

Available soil moisture = F.C.(–) PWP = 30–12 = 18%

Readily available moisture @ 80% $= 18 \times \frac{80}{100} = 14.4\%$

Optimum moisture content = F.C.(–) Readily available moisture

(O.M.C.) = 30–14.4=15.6% or 0.156

It follows that moisture will be filled by irrigation between optimum moisture and field capacity (F.C.)

$$\text{Hence depth of water} = \frac{\text{Unit weight of soil} \times \text{rootzone depth}}{\text{Unit weight of water (density)}} \times (\text{F.C.–O.M.C.})$$

$$= \frac{1.25 \times 0.60}{10} \times (0.3 - 0.156) \left[\frac{\text{gm/cc}}{\text{gm/cc}} \times \text{m} = \text{m}\right]$$

= 0.108 metre or 10.80 cm.

Number of days after which water should be applied

$$= \frac{\text{Depth of water (cm/or mm)}}{\text{Daily consumptive use (mm/day)}} = \frac{10.80}{1.25}$$

= 9 days.

Example :

Calculate water depth and irrigation interval if given :

Field Capacity of soil = 25% or 0.25

P. Wilting Point = 10% or 0.10

Dry unit weight of soil = 1.4 gm/cc

Consumptive use = 10 mm/day

Rootzone depth = 100 cm

Assume no losses and soil moisture depletion 100%.

Solution :

Available soil moisture = FC – PWP = 25 – 10 =15% (0.15)

Optimum moisture is = 25 – 15 = 10% (0.10)

$$\text{Hence depth of water} = \frac{1.4 \times 1.0}{1.0} \times (0.25 - 0.10) = 0.21\text{m} = 21\text{cm}$$

$$\text{Number of days after which water should be applied} = \frac{21}{1.0}$$

= 21 days

Example :

Compute the depth and frequency of irrigation required for a certain crop from data given below :

Rootzone depth	= 100 cm
Field capacity	= 22% (0.22)
Wilting point	= 12% (0.12)
Apparent specific gravity (D.B.D.)	= 1.5 gm/cc
Consumptive use	= 2.5 mm/day
Efficiency of irrigation	= 50%

Assume 50% depletion of available moisture before application of irrigation water at field capacity.

Solution :

Available soil moisture = 22 – 12 =10% (0.10)

Readily available moisture at 50% depletion of A.S.M. $= \frac{10 \times 50}{50} = 5\%$

Optimum moisture = F.C.(–) Readily available moisture

= 22 – 5 = 17% (0.17)

Hence depth of water $= \frac{1.5}{1.0} \times 1.0\ (0.22 - 0.17)$

= 0.075 m or 7.5 cm

Field irrigation required at 50 % efficiency

$= \frac{7.50}{0.50} = 15$ cm

Water application frequency $= \frac{\text{Depth of water}}{\text{Daily consumptive use}}$

= 15/2.5 = 6 days.

Calculations of moisture content in the rootzone

0-25cm : $\frac{(134.60-126.82) \times 100}{126.82} = 6.14\% = 6.14 \times 1.5$

= 9.20 cm/m depth

$= \frac{9.20 \times 25}{100}$

= 2.30 cm

$$25\text{-}50\text{cm} : \frac{(136.28-127.95) \times 100}{127.95} = 6.52\% = 6.52 \times 1.50$$

$$= 9.76 \text{ cm/m depth}$$

$$= \frac{9.76 \times 25}{100} = 2.44 \text{ cm}$$

$$50\text{-}75 \text{ cm} : \frac{(122.95-115.32) \times 100}{115.32} = 6.6\% = 6.60 \times 1.50$$

$$= 9.90 \text{ cm/m depth}$$

$$= \frac{9.90 \times 25}{100}$$

$$= 2.47 \text{ cm.}$$

$$75\text{-}100 \text{ cm} : \frac{(110.92-102.64) \times 100}{102.64} = 8.06\% \times 1.50$$

$$= 12.10 \text{ cm/m depth}$$

$$= \frac{12.10 \times 25}{100}$$

$$= 3.02 \text{ cm}$$

Adding value for all soil depths we get

2.30 + 2.44 + 2.47 + 3.02 = 10.23 cm

Hence the net irrigation depth would be 17.75 – 10.25 = 7.5 cm

The gross irrigation depth would be $= \dfrac{7.5 \times 100}{80}$

$= 9.38$ cm

Calculations for available moisture (AW) : It is worked out in Table 4.9.

TABLE 4.9

Depth of soil cm	Thickness of soil layer cm	Textural class of layer cm	Available moisture holding capacity cm	Available moisture cm
0-25	25	Loam	14	4.25
25-50	25	Silt loam	19	4.75
50-75	25	Clay loam	18	4.50
75-100	25	Clay	17	4.25
				17.75

New Equation for Calculating Irrigation Scheduling

The Government Res. sta. Jyndevad Denmark* has given equation

$$1\text{-}ya/yp = K(1\text{-}Ea/EP)$$

where

ya = crop yields at the actual soil water status
Yp = The yields when water does not restrict plant growth
Ea = Actual Evapotranspiration
Ep = Evapotraspiration at field capacity of soils

The above equation has also been claimed to provide reasonably comparable results with various methods as discussed in this chapter.

Irrigation Scheduling by Monthly Computation — A Case Study

The interval of irrigation as well as depth of irrigation of a given crop varies with stage of growth. Based on this monthly water requirement to be supplied should be carried out and accordingly outlets or nakka points should be operated. This method would provide exact water needs and if we add losses (NIR + field losses) it provides field irrigation requirement (FIR). If conveyance losses are added, then we get gross irrigation requirement which would be actual quantity of water to be released to particular field for a given crop for a known duration with given outlet discharge. The case study of Gudha irrigation command, Chambal command area of Bundi Rajasthan has been worked out and given in Table 4.10.

Qualitative Methods of Scheduling

These methods are used in the absence of scientific data available and to some extent fulfils the demand to irrigate the field crops. These are discussed below :

(1) Feeling the soil colour as a measure of soil moisture stress. The soil colour change at drying and wetting by self-experience provides idea that time for irrigating crop has arrived.
(2) Change in colour of plants also helps to assess the moisture stress being experienced by plants.
(3) Counting days since last irrigation and supply irrigation at prefixed days interval to sustain crop growth.

These are human sensing and human identification methods to fix water demand periods for different crops. However, it does not provide exact computation and may affect crop growth.

---

* Thomson, P.C., Ins. of Irrig. & Agric. Metereology Jyandevad., Tinglev Denmark, 1986, proc. of a sympon Agric. Water managet, Netherlands, 18-29, June, 1985 Edited by A.L.M. Vanwijk & J. Wesseling.

TABLE 4.10

Soil Moisture at Field Capacity, Wilting Point and Available Soil Moisture in Various Soil Series of C.C.A., Rajasthan

S. No	Soil	Depth (cm)	Moisture % at			Average moisture % at			Bulk density
			F.C.	W.P.	ASM	F.C.	P.W.P.	A.S.M.	
1.	Kota series	0-19	27.8	13.4	14.4				
		19-32	28.0	13.6	14.4	27.5	13.6	13.9	1.40
		32-52	26.6	13.8	12.8				
2.	Kota variant	0-15	24.7	13.2	11.5				
		15-30	23.9	13.2	10.7	24.0	13.4	10.6	1.50
		30-45	23.4	13.8	9.6				
3.	Chambal series	0-18	27.1	14.8	12.3				
		18-44	26.9	15.4	11.5	27.3	15.0	12.3	1.35
		44-42	28.0	14.8	13.2				
4.	Bundi series	0-10	15.5	5.1	10.2				
		10-37	19.8	6.3	13.5	18.2	6.1	12.1	1.55
		37-75	19.3	6.9	12.4				
5.	Gudha series	0-13	15.6	5.9	9.7				
		13-36	15.6	5.9	9.7	16.2	6.1	10.1	1.60
		36-75	17.5	6.4	11.4				

(i) F.C. = Field capacity moisture at 1/3 bar.
(ii) PWP = Moisture at permanent wilting point at 15 bar.
F.C.–P.W.P. = A.S.M. (Available Soil Moisture).

TABLE 4.11

Yearly Average Net & Gross Depth and Interval of Irrigation at 50% M.A.D.

S.No.	Soil series	Net & gross depth and interval of irrigation at 50% M.A.D.											
		Rootzone 30 cm			Rootzone 45 cm			Rootzone 60 cm			Rootzone 75 cm		
		Depth (cm)		Interval days	Depth (cm)		Interval days	Depth (cm)		Interval days	Depth (cm)		Interval days
		Net	Gross		Net	Gross		Net	Gross		Net	Gross	
(1)	Kota series	2.92	4.05	5.4	4.38	6.09	8.1	5.84	8.11	10.7	7.30	10.14	13.5
(2)	Kota variant	2.39	3.32	4.4	3.58	4.97	6.6	4.77	6.63	8.8	5.97	8.28	11.0
(3)	Chambal series	2.49	3.46	4.6	3.74	5.19	6.9	4.98	6.92	9.2	6.23	8.65	11.5
(4)	Bundi series	2.82	3.92	5.2	4.22	5.86	8.2	5.63	7.82	10.4	7.04	9.77	13.4
(5)	Gudha series	2.43	3.37	4.5	3.64	5.05	6.7	4.85	6.74	9.0	6.06	8.42	11.2

Assumptions

(i)	Yearly average E.T.	=	5.4 mm (or 54 cm)
(ii)	Field application efficiency	=	72%
(iii)	50% M.A.D.	=	50% depletion of available soil moisture
	A.S.M.	=	Avaiiable soil moisture
	B.D.	=	Bulk density

Soil Details

	Soils	A.S.M.	B.D.
(i)	Kota series	13.9	1.40
(ii)	Kota variant	10.6	1.50
(iii)	Chambal series	12.3	1.35
(iv)	Bundi series	12.1	1.55
(v)	Gudha series	10.1	1.60

TABLE 4.12

Interval of Irrigtion at 50% M.A.D. in Diffrerent Months as Affected by Various Soils Series

D = Net depth of Irrigation at 50% M.A.D. in cms.
I = Interval of Irrigation in Days

Months	Average E.T. (cms)	Effect of soil on depth & interval of irrigation									
		Kota series		Kota variant		Chambal series		Bundi series		Gudha series	
		D	I	D	I	D	I	D	I	D	I
Rootzone 30 cms.											
January	0.27	2.92	10.8	2.39	8.9	2.49	9.2	2.82	10.4	2.43	9.0
February	0.38	2.92	7.7	2.39	6.3	2.49	6.5	2.82	7.2	2.43	6.4
March	0.60	2.92	4.9	2.39	4.0	2.49	4.2	2.82	4.7	2.43	4.1
April	0.79	2.92	3.7	2.39	3.0	2.49	3.2	2.82	3.6	2.43	3.1
May	0.96	2.92	3.0	2.39	2.5	2.49	2.6	2.82	2.9	2.43	2.5
June	0.91	2.92	3.2	2.39	2.6	2.49	2.7	2.82	3.1	2.43	2.7
July	0.57	2.92	5.1	2.39	4.2	2.49	4.4	2.82	4.9	2.43	4.3
August	0.44	2.92	6.6	2.39	5.4	2.49	5.7	2.82	6.4	2.43	5.5
September	0.47	2.92	6.2	2.39	5.1	2.49	5.3	2.82	6.0	2.43	5.2
October	0.49	2.92	6.0	2.39	4.9	2.49	5.1	2.82	5.8	2.43	8.0
November	0.34	2.92	8.6	2.39	7.0	2.49	7.3	2.82	8.3	2.43	7.1
December	0.28	2.92	10.4	2.39	8.5	2.49	8.5	2.82	10.1	2.43	8.7

(Contd.)

TABLE 4.12 (*Contd.*)

Months	Average E.T. (cms)	Effect of soil on depth & interval of irrigation									
		Kota series		Kota variant		Chambal series		Bundi series		Gudha series	
		D	I	D	I	D	I	D	I	D	I
Rootzone 45 cms.											
January	0.27	4.38	16.2	3.58	13.3	3.74	13.9	4.22	15.6	3.64	13.5
February	0.38	4.38	11.5	3.58	9.4	3.74	9.8	4.22	11.1	3.64	9.6
March	0.60	4.38	7.3	3.58	6.0	3.74	6.2	4.22	7.0	3.64	6.1
April	0.79	4.38	7.9	3.58	4.5	3.74	4.7	4.22	5.3	3.64	4.6
May	0.96	4.38	4.6	3.58	3.7	3.74	3.9	4.22	4.4	3.64	3.8
June	0.91	4.38	4.8	3.58	3.9	3.74	4.1	4.22	4.6	3.64	4.0
July	0.57	4.38	7.7	3.58	6.3	3.74	6.6	4.22	7.4	3.64	6.4
August	0.44	4.38	10.0	3.58	8.1	3.74	8.5	4.22	9.6	3.64	8.3
September	0.47	4.38	9.3	3.58	7.6	3.74	8.0	4.22	9.0	3.64	7.7
October	0.49	4.38	8.9	3.58	7.3	3.74	7.6	4.22	8.6	3.64	7.4
November	0.34	4.18	12.9	3.58	10.5	3.74	11.0	4.22	12.4	3.64	10.7
December	0.28	4.38	15.6	3.58	12.8	3.74	13.4	4.22	15.1	3.64	13.0

D = Depth of Irrigation.

I = Interval of Irrigation.

TABLE 4.13

Interval of Irrigtion at 50% M.A.D. in Differrent Months as Affected by Various Soils Series

D = Net depth of Irrigation at 50% M.A.D. in cms.
I = Interval of Irrigation in days

Months	Average E.T. (cms)	Effect of soil on depth & interval of irrigation									
		Kota series		Kota variant		Chambal series		Bundi series		Gudha series	
		D	I	D	I	D	I	D	I	D	I
Rootzone 60 cms.											
January	0.27	5.84	21.6	4.77	17.7	4.98	18.4	5.63	20.9	4.85	18.0
February	0.38	5.84	15.4	4.77	12.6	4.98	13.1	5.63	14.8	4.85	12.8
March	0.60	5.84	9.7	4.77	8.0	4.98	8.3	5.63	9.4	4.85	8.1
April	0.79	5.84	7.4	4.77	6.0	4.98	6.3	5.63	7.1	4.85	6.1
May	0.96	5.84	6.1	4.77	.0	4.98	5.2	5.63	5.9	4.85	5.1
June	0.91	5.84	6.4	4.77	5.2	4.98	5.5	5.63	5.9	4.85	5.1
July	0.57	5.84	1.2	4.77	8.4	4.98	8.7	5.63	9.9	4.85	8.5
August	0.44	5.84	13.3	4.77	8.4	4.98	8.7	5.63	12.8	4.85	11.0
September	0.47	5.84	12.4	4.77	10.2	4.98	10.6	5.63	12.0	4.85	10.3
October	0.49	5.84	11.9	4.77	9.7	4.98	10.2	5.63	11.5	4.85	14.3
November	0.34	5.84	17.2	4.77	14.0	4.98	14.6	5.63	16.6	4.85	14.3
December	0.28	5.84	20.9	4.77	17.0	4.98	17.8	5.63	20.5	4.85	19.3

(Contd.)

TABLE 4.13 (*Contd.*)

Months	Average E.T. (cms)	Effect of soil on depth & interval of irrigation									
		Kota series		Kota variant		Chambal series		Bundi series		Gudha series	
		D	I	D	I	D	I	D	I	D	I
Rootzone 75 cms.											
January	0.27	7.30	27.0	5.97	22.1	6.23	23.1	7.04	26.1	6.06	22.4
February	0.38	7.30	19.2	5.97	15.7	6.23	16.4	7.84	18.5	6.06	15.9
March	0.60	7.30	12.2	5.97	10.6	6.23	10.4	7.04	11.7	6.06	10.1
April	0.79	7.30	9.4	5.97	7.6	6.23	7.9	7.04	8.9	6.06	7.7
May	0.96	7.30	7.6	5.97	6.2	6.23	6.5	7.04	7.7	6.06	6.3
June	0.91	7.30	8.2	5.97	6.6	6.93	6.5	7.04	7.7	6.06	6.7
July	0.57	7.30	12.8	5.97	10.5	6.23	10.9	7.04	12.4	6.06	10.6
August	0.44	7.30	16.6	5.97	13.6	6.23	14.2	7.04	16.0	6.06	13.8
September	0.47	7.30	15.3	5.97	12.7	6.23	13.3	7.04	15.0	6.06	12.9
October	0.49	7.30	14.9	5.97	12.2	6.23	12.7	7.04	14.4	6.06	12.4
November	0.34	7.30	21.5	5.97	17.6	6.23	18.2	7.04	20.7	6.06	17.8
December	0.28	7.30	26.1	5.97	21.3	6.23	22.3	7.04	25.1	6.06	21.6

TABLE 4.14

Statement Showing Interval of Irrigation in Different Months for Wheat and Sugarcane in Various Soil Series
Interval of Irrigation at 50% M.A.D. in various soil series

Months	Rootzone (cms)		Interval of irrigation at 50% M.A.D. in various soil series									
	Wheat	Sugarcane	Wheat					Sugarcane				
			Kota series	Kota variant	Chambal series	Bundi series	Gudha series	Kota series	Kota variant	Chambal series	Bundi series	Gudha series
January	60	75	21	18	18	21	18	27	22	23	26	22
February	60	75	15	13	13	15	13	19	16	16	18	16
March	60	30 (sowing)	15	18	18	9	8	..	..	3	3	3
April	..	do	..	..	..	..	..	..	..	3	3	3
May	..	45	..	..	..	..	..	5	4	4	4	4
June	..	45	..	..	..	..	..	5	4	4	5	4
July	..	45	..	..	..	..	..	8	6	7	7	6
August	..	60	..	..	..	..	..	13	11	13	13	11
September	..	75	..	..	..	..	..	12	10	11	12	11
October	..	75	..	..	..	..	..	12	10	10	12	10
November	30 (days)	75	..	..	..	..	..	22	18	18	21	18
December	45	75	16	13	14	16	14	26	21	22	25	22

Agronomic Method

This method involves to calculate the ratio of amount of irrigation water given to crops based on outlet capacity (IW) to cumulative pan-evaporating values (CPE). Thus IW/CPE ratio is the time interval of irrigation. The depth of IW in this case is decided by the available water holding capacity of the soil and the probable moisture deficit before irrigation in view of existing irrigation efficiency can be worked out.

This method is also having some lacunae and does not provide much reliable results but is still used.

To sum up, the scheduling of irrigation is a complex phenomenon which is influenced by various factors.

Irrigation Time or Interval

Considering effective rootzone depth 1 metre and available moisture holding capacity of 17.75 cm/m, allowable moisture depletion (AMD) or maximum allowable depletion (MAD) of 50% and the consumptive use rate of 4.50 mm/day, irrigation be applied after 20 days of previous irrigation by formula :

$$\text{Irrigation interval} = \frac{\text{available soil water} \times \text{rootzone depth or Max allowable depletion (\%) (soil depth)}}{100 \times \text{crop evapotranspiration}}$$

$$= \frac{17.75 \times 50 \times 1}{100 \times 4.50} = \frac{1775 \times 5}{100 \times 45} = 19.72 \text{ say 20 days.}$$

It may be called designed irrigation interval.

Irrigation schedule should be so planned and designed so that crop could get water before it faces a moisture stress. The following critical limits be used for deciding depth and interval of irrigation based on soil, crop and climate.

TABLE 4.15

Showing Critical Depth of Water (cm) to be Applied During each Irrigation

Crop rootzone	Depth of application (cm)		
	Sandy soil	Loamy soil	Clayey soil
Shallow less than 60 cm	2.5 to 5.0	5 to 7.6	7.5 to 10
Medium 60-180 cm	5.0 to 7.5	10 to 15.0	15 to 20
Deep 180-240 cm	10 to 15	20 to 25	25 to 35

For calculation of interval of irrigation the crops may be grouped into three main categories :

Group I	:	paddy
Group II	:	onion, tomato, banana, cabbage, potato and like crops (vegetable)
Group III	:	maize, safflower, sunflower, sorghum, soyabean, tobacco, cotton, wheat, groundnut, sugarcane and similar crops.

The interval of irrigation should be kept less than the designed depletion level to avoid the chances of moisture stress to the crops. For this following considerations may be kept in view for above 3 groups.

Group I

In this crop group the soil moisture content should not be allowed to fall below saturation capacity of the soil and a depth of water 5.0 to 0.5 cm should be kept ponding during all stages of crop growth with each irrigation restoring the ponding depth to 5.0 cm (the new research, however, reveals that ponding only at booting stage is just enough for ponding).

Group II

Keeping into consideration the following division of evapotranpiration and depletion level factor, the irrigation interval be calculated :

Evapotranspiration demand	*Depletion level factor*
2.0 - 4.0 mm/day	0.50 of available moisture
5.0 - 7.0 mm/day	0.40 of available moisture
8.0 - 10.0 mm/day	0.30 of available moisture

Group III

For this group also the following limits of evapotranspiration and depletion level factor are listed so as to arrive at appropriate irrigation interval :

Evapotranspiration demand	*Depletion level factor*
2.0 - 4.0 mm/day	0.7 of available moisture
5.0 - 7.0 mm/day	0.5 of available moisture
8.0 - 10.0 mm/day	0.4 of available moisture

It is thus obvious that allowable moisture level (AMD or MAD) factor varies from 0.30 to 0.70 or 30 to 70 per cent of available moisture holding capacity or available soil moisture (A.S.M.) for all crops except paddy. Hence if a soil has available soil moisture 17.75 cm per metre of soil (effective rootzone), the irrigation interval should be kept between 12 days to 28 days or (2 weeks to 4 weeks) as per formula by putting

$$\text{MAD at 30 and 70} = \frac{17.75 \times 1 \times 30}{10 \times 45}$$

Instead of supplying water every 20th day (as calculated by taking 50% depletion) depending upon the evapotranspiration demand (*i.e.* corresponding depletion be taken for calculation). In case of paddy crop, the frequency of irrigation may be kept once in a week for heavy and medium textured while two or three in a week for coarse to very coarse textured soils (if paddy crop is to be taken at all as per local climate conditions, water availability, food habits etc. otherwise should not be taken). Based on above discussion, the irrigation interval be fixed at minimum period and would be the rotation period, from the number of intervals worked out. However, less than one week rotation should not be fixed except for paddy crop.

However, the quantity of water needed for land preparation, transplantation and lacking etc. should be found separately by actual determination for specific situations. The average values given below could be used as guideline (Table 4.16).

THE DELIVERY SCHEDULE

If the depth and intervals is fixed the next step is to decide the delivery of water and its rotation distribution below the outlet, through the outlet and above the outlet. These conditions are discussed below :

TABLE 4.16

Operation	Quantity of water
1. *Land Preparation*	
Light soil	50 mm
Medium soil	75 mm
Heavy soil	90 mm
2. *Transplantation*	
Rice light soil	300 mm
Rice heavy soil	200 mm
Other crop	75 - 100 mm

Delivery Below the Outlet

The equitable distribution of water is the cardinal principle of water distribution below the outlet. According to this each farmer in the area should get his due share (volume) of water as calculated by considering his holdings in the outlet command. This in turn would be possible if each ha. of land is spreaded with an equal quantity of water through its distribution system. The deviation from this principle occurs when the area has paddy or sugarcane or perennial crop growing in it. As such these areas are to be allocated extra water than their actual share for their survival. However, in such areas again the equity of distribution should be maintained. The time schedule within outlet command is computed by calculating unit time (*i.e.*time per unit area) of water availability at each rotation and along with the calculations of conveyance losses and travel time up to individual holdings in on-farm water distribution and their adjustment in the time interval as discussed below :

Maximum water requirement for design cropping pattern calculation :

1. Discharge in litre/sec./ha.

$$= \frac{\text{100 lits.} \times \text{for one cusec water requirement}}{\text{seconds of fortnight}}$$

2. In above discharge add 20% amount for losses for field application and 10% add for variation in water demand.
3. Since one cusec = 28.30 lits, the same is divided by the calculated discharge which will give duty of one cusec *i.e.* the area that can be irrigated by this flow.
4. As the above water requirement is for one fortnight hence 360 hrs divided by the area in ha. that can be irrigated by the above flow, which will give the hrs. per ha. per fortnight, which is

worked out for every season of average year and drought year and appeared in separate statement.

5. From the above base time the total hrs. required for completing the schedule is worked out by multiplying the area, base, time. The same is worked out in days.
6. Now the area of each system is divided in such a way that the group of area may not be more than the duty as worked out for each season and year.
7. Then total days worked out as above by dividing the Nos. of groups will give the period in days required for completing the irrigation of that area.

The unit time : This is a function of the period of rotation, the time of irrigation each day and the total area under the command of an outlet and is equal to

$$= \frac{\text{time of irrigation water availability (per rotation)}}{\text{Command area of the outlet}}$$

A weekly rotation with day and night (24 hrs.) irrigation would be equal to 168 hrs. of water availability ($7 \times 24 = 168$) or for 2 weeks rotation it would be $2 \times 168 = 336$ hrs. and if half a week rotation then $168/2 = 84$ hrs. rotation has to be fixed. Incidentally a weekly rotation with irrigation schedule only during the day time irrigation (12 hrs.) would also be equal to 84 hrs. of water availability.

The time interval : After determining the unit time for an outlet the time interval of individual cultivator can be calculated by multiplying the unit time with the farmers holding (area) in the outlet command.

Conveyance loss and travel time : There is a loss of water during conveyance in the time it has travelled. These both factors *viz.* conveyance and also the time of travel are directly proportional to the channel length which is covered by the water before it reaches to the field of the farmer. Whereas whole channel length filled up with water from the outlet to the field adds to the losses occurring during the travel of water. The travel time is that channel length in which water travels from one farmer field to the other adjoining field (or from the outlet to the first farmer field) and this will depend on the sequence (order) of turns. These orders among the farmers of outlet command may be grouped into three broad categories namely : 1. Head to tail, (2) tail to head or from the mid-point to tail and (3) head to mid-point. Therefore, the length of channel for computing the travel time will be different in each above case and shall have to be calculated from the field channel layout in the outlet command.

The travel time : It is the function of the velocity of flow which can be measured by float method or current meter or if the discharge and cross sectional area of a field channel are worked out (Q = AV).

The length of turn: The finalisation regarding the length of turn of each farmer in outlet command is made by calculating the conveyance losses in terms of time as well as the time to be taken by water to reach the farmer field. The total time for outlet command which would be thus calculated is matched with the total time available for distribution and necessary adjustments have to be made accordingly. The time turn to be fixed as calculated above has to be further added in the time which would be required in the depletion of channel. This depends upon the length of channel which is filled up to the farmer field and the area of holding. This is done so that the last farmer or last but one farmer should get enough water volume (in the channel itself) for the holding in spite of the condition that water supply is cut off or shut off at the outlet for other outlets.

Allocation of time interval : As discussed above the time length of turn for each farmer has to be converted to time interval in hrs. and minutes such that the fixed quantity of water on a fixed day be used by the farmer. A time schedule thus has to be drawn up for the rotation period. Also the opening time of the canal and time taken by water to travel from canal head to the outlet should also be considered in time schedule. Further to avoid the regular possibility of turn, falling at night for any particular farmer the time schedule every year is changed by 12 hrs. when irrigation is for 24 hrs. so that every year the night turn is converted to day turn and *vice-versa* to avoid any complaint from the farmers. This can also be done for alternate years or so.

Irrigation adjustments within outlet command : The supply of irrigation is to be adjusted as per need of the area crops. This can be done in two ways :

1. Water rotation between group of farmers within outlet distributaries and minor, definite section of canal command; and
2. Among each farmer of a group.

In case of individual farmers it is essential to record the actual discharge one gets due to excessive seepage from bed and bank, evaporation from water surface common to all and transpiration by aquatic weeds (these of course should be cleaned to avoid losses). Thus seepage is a major factor which decrease the designed discharge through losses depends upon total porosity of the soil through which the canal traverses, the depth of flow in the channel, the wetted perimeter of the channel, the flow velocity sediment proportion in the flowing water, the turgidity and temperature of water, the shape of the channel and age of the channel. Since the field channels do not carry water continuously like canals, the alternate wetting and drying wells, they have higher ratio of wetted area to the volume of water carried, the amount of seepage is more in these. The seepage losses should be determined for various channels based on soil type available in the area since this is the major factor which if could be checked can substantially reduce the seepage loss. Other factors add to this amount. The tentative values of seepage losses for various materials and with wetted perimeter are given in Table 4.17 (a) and 4.17 (b). These also provide idea of conveyance loss.

For fixing the intervals for water supply, four situations (zones) can be considered in the outlet command *viz.*

Zone I — The zone where maximum paddy is grown (paddy zone Gr. I).

Zone II — The zone where vegetable and other crops (Gr. I and Gr. II) are maximum (vegetable and other crops zone).

Zone III — The zone where soils of varying textures are available having different water holding capacities (based on soil survey classification or texture).

Zone IV — Lower reaches fields where the arrangement for continuous supply of water or supplement source is to be arranged. In the zone II the individual farmers on a subsidiary channel or two nearby subsidiary channels can be clubbed together to form groups, with each group and each farmer getting water once in a rotation. If any group of farmers need to apply irrigation for more than allocated period than this time of rotation for irrigation can be in its multiples, by either of two ways :

(i) The lands be divided in two or more parts and one portion be irrigated in first rotation and next portion in subsequent rotation and so on.

(ii) The irrigation arrangement could be made with one or two adjacent farmers of the same group who have nearly similar or multiple size of plots for example if the rotational interval/period has been given of one

TABLE 4.17 (a)

Values of Seepage Losses for Different Materials

Character of Material	Cubic metre per sq. metre wetter perimeter per day	Cubic feet per sq. feet wetted perimeter per day	Cusec per million sq. metres of wetter perimeter	Cusec per million sq. metres of wetted perimeter
Impervious Clay ioam	0.076-0.110	0.25-0.35	0.92-1.20	3.0-4.0
Medium clay loam underlined with hard pan at depth of over (net) 0.60 to 1.0 m below bed	0.11-0.15	0.35-0.50	1.2-1.8	4.0-6.7
Ordinary clay loam, silt soil or lavaah loam	0.15-0.23	0.50-0.75	1.8-2.7	6.0-9.0
Gravelly or sandy clay loam, cemented gravel, sand and clay	0.23-0.30	0.75-1.00	2.7-3.6	9.00-12.0
Sandy loam	0.30-0.46	1.00-1.50	3.6-5.2	12.0-17.0
Loose sandy soil	0.46-0.53	1.50-1.75	5.2-6.1	17.0-20.0
Gravelly sandy soil	0.61-0.76	2.00-2.50	7.0-8.8	23.0-29.0
Porous gravelly soil	0.76-0.91	2.50-3.00	8.8-10.6	29.0-35.0
Very gravelly soil	0.91-1.83	3.00-6.00	10.6-22.2	35.0-70.0

TABLE 4.17 (b)

Seepage Losses as Proposed by U.S.B.R.

Cemented gravel and hard pan with sandy loam	0.10 in 24 hrs	0.34 in 24 hrs	1.19	3.9
Clay and clay-loam	0.12	0.41	1.46	4.8
Sandy loam	0.20	0.66	2.35	7.7
Volcanic Ash	0.21	0.68	2.40	7.9
Volcanic ash with sand	0.30	0.98	3.47	11.4
Sand and volcanic ash or clay	0.36	1.20	4.23	13.9
Sandy soil with some rock	0.51	1.58	5.94	19.5
Sandy and gravelly soils	0.67	2.20	7.83	25.7
Concrete lining	0.10	0.33	1.16	3.8

week but the selected one in three weeks, this farmer has to make two farmers of the group as partners who has equal size of plots or one partner who has plot size double of his own plot to have the right partnership.

The another way of above partnership can be such that some of the group of farmers may use the time of other farmer of same group and the turn left by the farmer gets double time at the next turn *i.e.* he uses the time of his partner who used his time in first turn. Thus the time allotted to each farmer remains fixed but the time within the group changes and the time schedule is to be modified accordingly for groups without changing the time of individual farmer. This arrangement is called the use of water in multiples at the desired time between multiple 1-2 and multiple 2-3, the period of rotation.

For the Zone III the group of farmers has to be made on the basis of soil texture classes *e.g.* course, medium and or fine textured (this can be also made on the basis of soil series or clubbing similar mapping units and arbitrary boundaries can be drawn on soil map to make different sub-zones). These textural classes would have different water holding capacities which require water application at different periods and the depths or quantity to bring it every time to field capacity.

In Zone IV which are the lowlying fields *i.e.* at a lower reach of a slopy-outlet command, the seepage water accumulates there and if without considering the seepage amount the period is allotted to such farmers it may be sheer wastage and hence the time should be accordingly curtailed.

DELIVERY ABOVE THE OUTLET

While formulating the irrigation schedule the delivery schedule above the outlet should also be considered zone-wise. Thus for Zone I (paddy zone) the water distribution network has to be operated for continuously supply of water to outlet command say once or twice a week as the need may be.

For Zones II and III if the crops require irrigation at different times than date of sowing of the entire area is to be fixed up so as to cover all crops during the prescribed irrigation period. Also where the textural changes are much in the command of distributary channel the outlet should be regulated specifically for those plots/fields for specific different periods and water depth so as to meet the water requirements of crops of Gr. II & III. In case water supply is low which does not allow the water to reach distributary tail, the outlet be opened alternately so that once it is opened and next closed and so on. The designed discharge under low supply can be managed by providing cross regulating structures on the channels or through adjustment of the size of outlet vents by providing screw gates.

The running schedule of distributary has to be also made keeping in view the pressure of demand on different channels. Regulation of canal network should be done in multiples of the minimum time of irrigation computed in the command. To work out this exercise procedure for "bank account" or book keeping be evolved and followed.

The climatic conditions considering soils and crops may also provide a guide to fix up irrigation schedule. This avoids the measurement of moisture depletion in soil and average accordingly the irrigation supply. This is possible if evapotranspiration could be measured at different outlet commands and these can be fed to central station for computing consumptive use with the help of its relationship with evaporation or by using crop coefficients (KC). Besides this rainfall data are also processed. Based on these, gain or loss balances in soil moisture can be worked out using antecedent soil moisture data and irrigation interval, depth etc. are worked out and forecasted.

The distribution of water becomes only difficult when the demand is more than supply which can be managed only through rotational supply or warabandi. According to the situations the water supply is regulated so as to meet either the entire demands or tight the water supply so as to meet the maximum proportion of the all needies or close some of the minors/ distributaries by turn and allow water to others and then interchange the closure or decreasing the supply depth to save water for equal distribution or decreasing the irrigation interval etc. so that water at highly critical growth stage is only supplied fully or partially at all growth stages of the crop.

It is necessary that distributary should run on a cycle somewhat longer than that of tertiary system because some time is bound to elapse before the water reaches the last outlet. The statement of rotational running of canal system is called roster. It should be designed in such a way so that it can distribute equitably the available supply as also to suit the crop water needs in the commands of different distributary channels. The channels are classified in following ways :

(a) Alternate running

(b) One in two running

(c) Two in three running

(d) Three in five running.

If they run in alternate week, these are classed like run for one week in two weeks and so on in weekly rotation. In the cases when the demand is very high channel may be kept closed during alternate fortnights.

Hypothetical example for working out irrigation scheduling (Source : Saxena, RS and Saxena, KK, 1983) :

Given : (i) Command area = 30 ha

(ii) Irrigation season = Rabi (15th October to 31st March)

(iii) Crop pattern

Crops	Area per cent	Effective rootzone depth (cm)
Wheat	60	90
Berseem	10	120
Cauliflower	10	60
Sugarcane	10180	

(iv) Soils :

(A) *Top soil* : (a) upper reach, 40% of command area — clay loam; (b) middle reach, 20% of command area — loam ; (c) lower reach, 40% of command are — clay loam.

(B) *Horizons* :

Upper & lower reach	Middle reach
90 cm loam	90 cm clay loam
90 cm sand	90 cm sandy clay

(C) *Crop coverage* :

Upper reach — Wheat 30% of command or 9.0 ha., sugarcane 10.0% of command or 3.0 ha.

Middle reach — Cauliflower, 10% command or 3 ha., sugarcane 10% of command or 3 ha.

Lower reach — Wheat 30% of command or 9 ha., Berseem 10% of command or 3 ha.

(D) *Available water* :

(i) Upper reach and lower reach (clay loam soil) :

Depth	Layer thickness	Available moisture holding capacity (standard values for cm/m) (AHMC)	Total available moisture
0.0-0.9 m	0.9	17.0	15.3
0.9-1.9 m	0.9	15.0	13.5
	Total	32.0	28.8
	Average AHMC	= 32.0 = 16.0 cm/m	

(ii) Middle reach

0.0-0.9 m	0.9	18.0	16.2
0.9-1.9 m	0.9	14.0	12.6
	Total	32.0	28.8
	Average AHMC	$= \frac{32}{2}$ = 16.0 cm/m	

(iii) Available Moisture in effective rootzone depth (AV.AHMC × layer thickness of rootzone) :

Wheat	Upper reach	16 (cm/m) × 0.9 m = 14.40 cm
	Lower reach	16 (cm/m) × 0.9 m = 14.40 cm
Berseem	Lower reach	16 (cm/m) × 1.2 m = 19.20 cm
Cauliflower	Middle reach	16 (cm/m) × 0.6 m = 9.60 cm
Sugarcane	Upper reach	16 (cm/m) × 1.8 m = 28.8 cm
	Middle reach	16 (cm/m) × 1.8m = 28.8 cm

(iv) Climate :

(a) *Mean daily evaporation*

Month	—	Oct.	Nov.	Dec.	Jan.	Feb.	March	April
Evaporation mm/day	—	3.9	2.8	1.9	2.0	3.7	5.6	8.6

(b) *Consumptive use*/Evaporation* — (Ratio of $\frac{\text{Cu}}{\text{Evapo}}$)

Month	—	Oct.	Nov.	Dec.	Jan.	Feb.	March	April
Wheat	—	..	0.16	0.54	0.69	0.82	0.98	..
Berseem	—	..	0.71	0.76	0.80	0.95	0.77	0.58
Cauliflower	—	..	0.37	0.96	1.20	0.80	..	..
Sugarcane	—	0.57	0.54	0.51	0.49	0.48	..	..

(c) *Consumptive use* ** (mm/day) by standard methods

Month	—	Oct.	Nov.	Dec.	Jan.	Feb.	March	April
Wheat	—	..	0.45	1.10	1.40	3.00	5.50	..
Berseem	—	..	2.00	1.40	1.60	3.50	4.30	5.00
Cauliflower	—	..	1.00	1.80	2.40	3.00	..	..
Sugarcane	—	2.20	1.50	1.00	1.00	1.80	..	..

(d) *Monthly consumptive use (mm)*

Month	—	Oct.	Nov.	Dec.	Jan.	Feb.	March	Apri
Wheat	—	75.00	13.50	34.10	43.40	84.00	170.50	420.50
Berseem	—	75.00	60.00	43.40	49.60	98.00	133.30	609.30
Cauliflower	—	75.00	30.00	55.80	74.40	84.00	..	319.20
Sugarcane	—	68.20	45.00	31.00	31.00	50.40	..	225.60
Total	—	293.20	148.0	164.30	198.40	316.40	303.80	..

* Land preparation requirement.

** For easy calculations IW/CPE where IW = Irrigation Water, applied (cu) = ETC, CPE is cumulative pan evaporation in mm. (ETO) installed at suitable sites provides actual water requirement of crops or the consumptive use of water (however for tropical reasons, modified penmen method should be used).

$$\therefore \text{IW/CPE} = \frac{\text{ETC}}{\text{ETO}} = \text{KC (Crop factor)}$$

Quantity of water required :

Crop	Area (%)	Seasonal water depth (mm)			Peak period monthly water depth	Quantity of water required per ha.	
		For land preparation	For consumptive use	Total		Seasonal	Peak period
Wheat	60	75	345	420	84	2520	504
Berseem	10	75	535	610	98	610	98
Cauliflower	10	75	245	320	84	320	84
Sugarcane	20	..	225	225	51	225	51
Total	100	225	1350	1575	317	3675	737

Flow requirement : For a field application efficiency of 70% and distribution efficiency of 60%

(a) Seasonal - $\dfrac{3675\text{ m}^3 \times 1000\text{ lits/sec}}{166\text{ days} \times 24\text{ hrs.} \times 60 \times 60}$ seconds × 420 over all efficiency.

= 0.61 litre/sec/ha or per 30 lit/sec.

(b) Peak Period $\dfrac{737\text{m3} \times 100\text{ lits/sec}}{281\text{ days} \times 24\text{ hrs.} \times 60 \times 60}$ seconds × 4.2 overall efficiency

(mm) (sec)

= 0.72 lits/sec/ha. or 42 ha. per 30 lits/sec.

Design of the System

The system is designed for peak period requirement. As we have 30 ha. of command area under this example and for peak period it is calculated that discharge of 30 lits/sec for 42 ha and hence for 30 ha. it would be 21.42 lits per sec. or say 21.5 lits per sec. The above figures are for culturable command at an outlet or project as a whole. This water allowance would therefore irrigate the entire culturable command (CCA) assumed for calculations. There are two main constraints in water supply, firstly the supply is always in a limited quantity thus designed supply cannot be met with and so the compromise has to be made between the demand (calculated above) and the available supply. Also it is difficult to run the distributary channel continuously throughout the crop season. Secondly constraint is the danger or menace of development of salty lands and high water logging. The time leg therefore, comes to play for regulation of water supply. This is worked out as the ratio between the operational period of water supply through distributary to the crop period (season) and is called TIME FACTOR. In view of these two constraints the total CCA (100%) is not possible to be irrigated due to less discharge or supply and the decrease in the irrigated area of CCA occurs, the remaining area which is irrigated is called irrigation intensity. For example if out of 100% of CCA only 70% area (of CCA) is irrigated the irrigation intensity or intensity of irrigation is 70% and so on.

Thus if the discharge of 21.5 litres per second for peak demand as calculated above for 30 ha. CCA is not available and hence less than 30 ha. area would be irrigated that would determine intensity of irrigation.

Depth of Irrigation

Keeping into view the various influencing factors affecting supply the depth of irrigation can be kept 5-15 cm. The depth of application has to be manipulated or adjusted with respect of time *i.e.* if more depth is to be given the period of irrigation be extended and if less depth is to be supplied period can be reduced accordingly or water can be allowed to flow other direction of field (from over a field) in desired quantity, that would adjust the required depth of the two plots/fields in place of one which can be reversed in the next irrigation.

Interval of Irrigation upto February

Wheat : For this crop the consumptive use rate is 3 mm/day and maximum allowable depletion MAD is 0.7 or (70%) of total available moisture (TAW) = FC(–) PWP. The depth of rootzone = 1 metre or 100 cm.

The interval of irrigation can be found as follows :

B.D. = 1400 kg/m3 or 1.40m/cc/T = 14.40 cm, MAD = 0.7, consumptive use = 3 mm/day and factor 10 is conversion to mm.

Now maximum soil moisture depletion depth in this example is given :

$$(PW) = \frac{70}{100} \times 14.40 = 0.7 \times 14.40$$

apparent specific gravity (As) or Bulk density = 1000 Kg/m3 or g/cc

if rootzone depth D = 1.0 metre = 1.0 gm/cc.

Hence depth of soil moisture which can be safely depleted

$= PW \times As \times D = 0.7 \times 14.40 \times 1.0 \times 1.0 = 10.08$ cm

∴ frequency or interval of irrigation =

$$\frac{\text{depth of moisture depleted (mm)}}{\text{consumptive use (mm)}} = \frac{100.80}{3.0} = 33.60 \text{ or } 34 \text{ days}$$

3.5 mm/day, NAD = 0.50 of ASM, ASM =

19.2% BD = 1.0gm/cc

soil depth or rootzone depth = 1.0 metre,

$$\therefore \text{Irrigation Interval} = \frac{192. \times 0.5 \text{ cm}}{3.5 \text{ cm}} = \frac{192. \times 0.5 \times 10 \text{ mm}}{3.5 \text{ cm}}$$

$$= 27.43 \text{ days}$$

say 28 days

Cauliflower : The maximum consumptive use rate is 3 mm/day and MAD = 0.5% ASM (9.6%), BD = 1.0gm/cc and rootzone depth 1.0 metre

$$\therefore \text{Irrigation interval} = \frac{9.6. \times 0.5 \times 1.0}{3.5 \text{ cm}} = 16 \text{ days}$$

Sugarcane : The maximum consumptive use rate is 2.2 mm/day, MAD = 0.7 of ASM (28.8)

$$\therefore \text{Irrigation interval} = \frac{28.6 \times 0.7 \times 10}{2.2} = 91.6 \text{ days say 92 days}$$

Similarly in March from given data, the Interval of irrigation is calculated as under :

Crop — Wheat (Consumptive use rate in March = 5.5 mm/day & 4MAD = 0.50

$$\therefore \text{Interval of Irrigation (I.I.)} = \frac{14.40 \times 0.5 \times 10}{5.5} = 14 \text{ days})$$

Crop : Berseem (Consumptive use = 4.3mm/day and MAD = 0.40

$$\therefore \text{Interval of Irrigation} = \frac{19.2 \times 0.4 \times 10}{4.3} = 18 \text{ days})$$

In this way the maximum interval of irrigation is two weeks. Hence in example given above the farmer are to be supplied water once in two weeks. The time schedule at the rate of 16.8 hrs. (one week) of water availability can be worked out for the outlet command and the distributary channel can run in alternate weeks.

Thus net irrigation requirement (NIR)

(PW × As × D) = 10 cm = 100 mm

(effective rainfall nil)

and losses in field application = 20% of water applied.

Hence FAE (field application efficiency) = 100 — 20 = 80% = 0.8 cm

and Field irrigation requirement $\text{FIR} = 100 \times \frac{1}{0.8} = 125$ mm (20% loss)

$$\text{FIR} = \frac{\text{Net Volume}}{\text{FAE or Ef for Ea}}$$

The exemplary worksheet data are given in Table 4.18 to 4.21.

DURATION OF IRRIGATION RUN

It is defined as the time during which an irrigating source (canal outlet or turnout) must be kept open to supply the requisite amount of water to the area irrigated by the source. If Qo is the flow rate (outlet capacity) and 't' is the duration, then the total volume of water supplied is = Qo × t. This volume must be equal to the product of the area (A) irrigated and the depth of moisture (d) added to meet FIR *i.e.* A (d + field losses) = A × (FIR) where d = depth of irrigation.

Thus Qo × t = (A) × (FIR).

If all values except 't' is known, the duration of irrigation can be found. This can be illustrated by following example.

Example 1 :

Given is to be :

(i) area to be irrigated from canal outlet = 0.5 ha

(ii) capacity of canal outlet or flow rate = 50 lts/sec

(iii) the antecedent moisture (initial moisture content before irrigation) = 10%

(iv) desired moisture after irrigation = 20%

(v) dry unit weight of soil *i.e.* bulk density = 1300 kg/m^3 or 1.3 gm/cc

(vi) losses of water due to evaporation and percolation in the field = 20%

(vii) rootzone depth of the soil = 50 cm.

Note : 1. One cusec water in one hour over an acre supplies = one acre inch of water *i.e.* 1 cusec/hr/acre = one acre inch of water.

2. One kilometer of water course is sufficient to irrigate 40 to 45 acres of land as per soil texture.

Now Qo = 50 litres/sec = 50 × 1000 cc/second. If 't' seconds is the duration, then total volume supplied is given by Qo × t = 50,000 × 't' c.c.

Now soil moisture depletion = (20 — 10) per cent = 10%

soil depth = 0.50 metre

$$\therefore \text{The supply duration} = \frac{\text{FIR (volume)}}{\text{Discharge available at field head in outlet command}}$$

$$\therefore d\,(\text{cm}) = PW \times BD\,(As) \times D = 10 \times 1.3 \times 0.5 = 6.5$$

$$\text{Hence F.I.R.} = 6.5 \times \frac{1}{0.80} (20\% \text{ loss out of } 100\% = 100 - 20 = 80\%)$$

$$= 8.1 \text{ cm}$$

$$A = 0.5 \times 10^8 \text{ cm}^2 \; (1 \text{ ha. } 10{,}000 \text{ m}^2 = 10^4\text{m}^2 = 10^8\text{cm}^2)$$

$$\therefore A \times \text{F.I.R} = 0.5 \times 10^8\text{cm}^2 \times 8.1 \text{ cm}$$

$$= 0.5 \times 10^8 \times 8.1 \text{ cm}^3$$

$$\therefore t = \frac{0.5 \times 10^8 \times 8.1 \text{ cm}^3}{50{,}000 \text{ cc (cm}^3\text{)/sec}} = 8100 \text{ sec} = 2 \text{ hr } \& \text{ 15 min.}$$

Example 2 :

Given :

(1) Stream of 300 cubic metres per hour

(2) Soil depth to be wetted = 120 cms (Rootzone depth)

(3) Moisture before irrigation = 10%

(4) Moisture after irrigation = 15%

Calculate how many hours will be required to irrigate if spreading of water is assumed to be uniform and losses very negligible (nil).

Solution :

Using equation

$$t = \frac{PW \times As \times D \times a}{100\, q} \text{ (per meter soil)}$$

We shall get time = 2.34 hours would be needed by given stream to increase desired moisture level to 1 hectare-metre of soil.

Hence for soil depth of 1.2 metre soil to reach to field capacity the time required would be = 2.34 × 1.2 = 2.8 hours = 2 hours 40 minutes.

COMPUTER PROGRAMMING METHOD

If water scheduling is to be done by use of computer the flow-chart of computer programme can be made as follows :

This programme may be developed in Fortran as well as in Basic language. It can be run on Micro computer like HCL-1800 or any other similar computer. The flow chart notations are explained below :

Input

(i)	Number of crops in a season	...	N
(ii)	Discharge at the head of outlet	...	Q
(iii)	Field application efficiency	..	FAE or Ef
(iv)	Distance of the farthest farm from outlet	..	FD
(v)	Losses of discharge (fraction, *e.g.* 20%=0.2) in field channel upto farthest farm	..	QL
(vi)	Total growing period of all crops in days (Net time growing)	..	NTG
(vii)	Total number of farms in outlet command	..	M
(viii)	Reference crop evapotranspiration and effective rainfall for all outlets in a season	...	RE
(ix)	Age of crop (Midpoint) in days as on the first day of the first rotation	..	NAGE
(x)	Distance of farm from outlet	..	D
(xi)	Area under each crop	..	A

Output

For all rotations :

(1) Farmwise duration of supply in hours and minutes

(2) Total running time of outlet in days.

Case Study

This can be done any one or two of the minors :

STEP I — The season crops considered in season say Rabi, Wheat, Gram, Potato etc.

STEP II — Assumed rotation period taken as assumed in project design, say 14 days.

STEP III — Seasons total rotation divide whole season in number of rotations periods each of 14 days duration which comes say 11 rotation periods.

STEP IV — Probable reference crop evapotranspiration say 75% (ETo) as worked out by say modified Penman method based on local climatic data for 10-12 years or so.

STEP V — Total number of crops = 9.

STEP VI — Discharge of outlet given, Q = 1800 lits/sec.

STEP VII — Field application efficiency FAE or Ef = 0.75 (75%).

STEP VIII — Distance of farthest field from outlet, FD = 800 m.

STEP IX — Loss in water course in 800 m length, QL = 0.25 (25%).

STEP X — Total number of forms to be studied or M = 9.

STEP XI — Assuming the first rotation of Rabi season from which it starts say = 15th October.

STEP XII — The age of crop from date of start of Rabi (15 Oct.) is the boundary line before which the age of crop is given directly and for those sown afterwards are indicated as negative assuming normal date of sowing in the area.

STEP XIII — Make the table of crop coefficients 'K' for the each crop of area along with readings of Pan evaporimeter.

The programme should be run for complete Rabi season or Kharif season and water distribution schedules for all rotations fixed (ii) which would be printed out by the computer. The irrigation scheduling on computer worked out by Suryavanshi and Patwardhan (1983) are given as under to understand the data analysis.

Suppose 3 Schedules are as follows :

(1) Schedule for rotation No. 1 in which wheat is not sown.

(2) Schedule for rotation No. 5 in which all crops but onion are sown.

(3) Schedule for rotation No. 10 in which all other crops are harvested but not wheat.

The computer results of these 3 rotations are given in tables 4.22, 4.23, 4.24 along with the table which indicates abstract of total running time of outlet for all 10 rotations (Table 4.25).

TABLE 4.18

Crop Coefficients (ke) Adopted from FAO Irrigation and Drainage Paper 33

Crop	Crop Development Stages					Total Growing period
	Initial	Crop Development	Mid Season	Late Season	At Harvest	
Banana :						
Tropical	0.4 - 0.5	0.7 - 0.85	1.0 - 1.11	0.9 - 1.0	0.75 - 0.85	0.7 - 0.8
Subtropical	0.5 - 0.65	0.8 - 0.9	1.0 - 1.2	1.0 - 1.15	1.0 - 1.15	0.85 - 0.95
Bean Green	0.3 - 0.4	0.65 - 0.75	0.95 - 1.05	0.9 - 0.95	0.85 - 0.95	0.85 - 0.9
Dry	0.3 - 0.4	0.7 - 0.8	1.05 - 1.2	0.65 - 0.75	0.25 - 0.3	0.7 - 0.8
Cabbage	0.4 - 0.5	0.7 - 0.8	0.95 - 1.1	0.9 - 1.0	0.8 - 0.95	0.7 - 0.8
Cotton	0.4 - 0.5	0.7 - 0.8	1.05 - 1.25	0.8 - 0.9	0.65 - 0.7	0.8 - 0.9
Grape	0.35 - 0.55	0.6 - 0.8	0.7 - 0.9	0.6 - 0.8	0.55 - 0.6	0.55 - 0.75
Groundnut	0.4 - 0.5	0.7 - 0.8	0.95 - 1.1	0.75 - 0.85	0.55 - 0.6	0.75 - 0.8
Maize :						
Sweet	0.3 - 0.5	0.7 - 0.9	1.05 - 1.02	1.0 - 1.15	0.95 - 1.1	0.8 - 0.95
Grain	0.3 - 0.5	0.7 - 0.85	1.05 - 1.2	0.8 - 0.95	0.55 - 0.6	0.75 - 0.9
Onion :						
Dry	0.4 - 0.6	0.7 - 0.8	0.95 - 1.1	0.85 - 0.9	0.75 - 0.85	0.8 - 0.9
Green	0.4 - 0.6	0.6 - 0.75	0.95 - 1.05	0.95 - 1.05	0.95 - 1.05	0.65 - 0.8

Pea, fresh	0.4 - 0.5	0.7 - 0.85	1.05 - 1..2	1.0 - 1.15	0.95 - 1.1	0.8 - 0.95
Pepper, fresh	0.3 - 0.4	0.6 - 0.75	0.95 - 1.1	0.85 - 1.0	0.8 - 0.9	0.7 - 0.8
Potato	0.4 - 0.5	0.7 - 0.8	1.05 - 1.2	0.85 - 0.95	0.7 - 0.75	0.75 - 0.9
Rice	1.1 - 1.15	1.1 - 1.5	1.1 - 1.3	0.95 - 1.05	0.95 - 1.05	1.05 - 1.2
Safflower	0.3 - 0.4	0.7 - 0.8	1.05 - 1.02	0.65 - 0.7	0.2 - 0.25	0.65 - 0.7
Sorghum	0.3 - 0.4	0.75 - 0.75	1.0 - 1.15	0.75 - 0.8	0.5 - 0.5	0.75 - 0.85
Soyabean	0.3 - 0.4	0.7 - 0.8	1.0 - 1.15	0.7 - 0.8	0.4 - 0.5	0.75 - 0.9
Sugarbeet	0.4 - 0.5	0.75 - 0.85	1.05 - 1.2	0.9 - 1.0	0.6 - 1.7	0.8 - 0.9
Sugarcane	0.4 - 0.5	0.7 - 1.0	1.0 - 1.3	0.75 - 0.8	0.5 - 0.6	0.85 - 1.05
Sunflower	0.3 - 0.4	0.7 - 0.8	1.05 - 1.2	0.77 - 0.8	0.35 - 0.45	0.75 - 0.85
Tobacco	0.3 - 0.4	0.7 - 0.8	1.0 - 0.8	1.0 - 1.2	0.9 - 1.0	0.75 - 0.85
Tomato	0.4 - 0.5	0.7 - 0.8	1.05 - 1.25	0.8 - 0.095	0.6 - 0.65	0.75 - 0.9
Watermelon	0.4 - 0.5	0.7 - 0.8	0.95 - 1.05	0.8 - 0.9	0.65 - 0.75	0.75 - 0.85
Wheat	0.3 - 0.4	0.7 - 0.8	1.05 - 1.2	0.65 - 0.75	0.2 - 0.25	0.8 - 0.9
Alfalfa	0.3 - 0.4				0.05 - 1.2	0.65 - 1.05
Citrus clean						0.65 - 0.75
Weeding no						0.85 - 0.9
Weed control						
Olive						0.4 - 0.6

First figure : Under high humidity (RHmin 70%) and low wind (U 5 m/sec)

Second figure : Under low humidity (RHmin 20%) and strong wind (5 m/sec).

TABLE 4.19

Consumptive use (Evapotranspiration) Coefficients K, to be Multiplied by Estimated or Measured Class a Pan Evaporation

% of Crop Growing Season	Wheat	Wheat	Maize	Maize	Jowar	Cotton	Soyabeans	Small Vegetables	Shallow rooted vegetables
	Ludhiana	Poona	Ludhiana	Albama U.S.A.	Albama U.S.A.	Poona	Hargreaves	Hargreaves	Hargreaves
8	0.41	.30	.40	.40	.42	.22	0.15	0.25	0.10
5	0.17	0.40	0.42	0.40	0.44	.22	0.18	0.28	0.15
10	0.23	0.51	0.47	0.43	0.46	0.23	0.20	0.30	0.20
15	0.33	0.62	0.54	0.46	0.48	0.24	0.23	0.38	0.30
20	0.45	0.73	0.63	0.52	0.50	0.26	0.25	0.45	0.40
25	0.60	0.84	0.75	0.59	0.52	0.35	0.28	0.50	0.45
30	0.72	0.92	0.85	0.67	0.56	0.58	0.30	0.55	0.50
35	0.81	0.96	0.96	0.76	0.59	0.80	0.38	0.58	0.55
40	0.88	1.10	1.04	0.85	0.64	0.95	0.45	0.60	0.60
45	0.90	1.10	1.07	0.93	0.71	1.03	0.50	0.63	0.60
50	0.91	1.00	1.09	1.02	0.79	1.08	0.55	0.65	0.60

55	0.90	0.91	1.10	1.09	0.92	1.08	0.63	0.65	0.60
60	0.89	0.80	1.11	1.14	1.01	1.07	0.70	0.65	0.60
65	0.86	0.65	1.10	1.19	1.07	1.05	0.75	0.63	0.58
70	0.83	0.51	1.07	1.21	1.09	1.00	0.80	0.60	0.55
75	0.80	0.40	1.04	1.23	1.09	0.93	0.75	0.58	0.50
80	0.76	0.30	1.00	1.22	1.05	0.85	0.70	0.55	0.45
85	0.71	0.20	0.97	1.16	0.99	0.73	0.65	0.50	0.40
90	0.65	0.12	0.89	1.06	0.91	0.62	0.60	0.45	0.35
95	0.58	0.10	0.81	0.95	0.82	0.50	0.55	0.38	0.33
100	0.51	0.10	0.70	0.75	0.70	0.40	0.50	0.30	0.30
Seasonal K	0.61	0.86	0.86	0.86	0.75	0.68	0.48	0.50	0.44

TABLE 4.20

Consumptive use (Evapotranspiration) Coefficients K, to be Multiplied by Estimated or Measured Class a Pan Evaporation

% of Crop Growing Season	Sugarcane	Rice	Groundnut	Castor Beans	Sugarcane
	Hawaii	Los Banos	Israel	Hargreaves	Hargreaves
0	0.34	1.00	0.30	0.16	0.48
5	0.37	1.02	0.30	0.30	0.50
10	0.40	1.03	0.32	0.50	0.53
15	0.44	1.05	0.35	0.65	0.55
20	0.50	1.07	0.40	0.74	0.60
25	0.60	1.09	0.49	0.81	0.67
30	0.72	1.11	0.60	0.87	0.75
35	0.86	1.13	0.69	0.92	0.80
40	0.93	1.16	0.78	0.96	0.85
45	0.98	1.18	0.85	0.98	0.87
50	1.02	1.20	0.90	1.00	0.89
55	1.05	1.21	0.94	1.00	0.90
60	1.07	1.22	0.96	0.99	0.90
65	1.10	1.22	0.95	0.97	0.85
70	1.13	1.21	0.94	0.93	0.75
75	1.16	1.19	0.91	0.89	0.71
80	1.19	1.16	0.86	0.82	0.68
85	1.20	1.10	0.79	0.72	0.59
90	1.20	1.03	0.72	0.58	0.51
95	1.19	0.96	0.64	0.37	0.50
100	1.19	0.86	0.55	0.22	0.50
Seasonal k	0.89	1.10	0.68	0.73	0.69

TABLE 4.21

Relationship Between Consumptive use by Different Crops and Evaporation from Free Water-surface

Crop	Factor	Jan.	Feb.	March	April	May	June	July	Aug.	Sept.	Oct.	Nov.	Dec.
Berseem	Cu/E	0.80	0.95	0.77	0.58	-	-	-	-	-	-	0.71	0.76
Cauliflower	Cu/E	1.20	0.80	-	-	-	-	-	-	-	-	0.37	0.96
Cotton	Cu/E	-	-	-	-	0.16	0.37	-	-	-	-	-	-
Maize	Cu/E	-	-	-	-	-	-	0.56	0.81	0.70	-	-	-
Onion	Cu/E	0.60	0.79	0.94	0.98	-	-	-	-	-	-	-	-
Potato	Cu/E	1.34	0.44	-	-	-	-	-	-	-	-	-	-
Rice (Trans-planted)	Cu/E	-	-	-	-	-	-	0.94	0.97	0.91	-	-	-
Rice (Upland) (Drilled)	Cu/E	-	-	-	-	-	-	1.34	1.46	1.58	1.60	-	-
Sugarcane	Cu/Eo	0.49	0.48	-	0.53	0.70	0.78	0.80	0.78	0.68	0.57	0.54	0.51
Tobacco	Cu/E	-	-	0.29	0.54	0.30	-	-	-	-	-	-	-
Wheat (Dwarf)	Cu/E	0.56	0.69	0.82	0.28	-	-	-	-	-	-	-	0.56
Wheat (Tall)	Cu/E	0.69	0.82	0.98	-	-	-	-	-	-	-	0.16	0.54

N.B. :
1. Cu = Consumptive use
2. E = Evaporation from U.S. Weather Bureau Standard Pan Evaporiameter
3. Eo = Evaporation from a hypothetical lake surface (Penman, 1948)
4. Approximate relationship between E and Eo is 0.7 E = Eo.

TABLE 4.22

Rotation Number 1 (Wheat, not sown), Crop Areas in Ha.

Farm No. Khassa No. (Randomly)	Distance (m)	Wheat	Hy. Jowar	Gram	Potato	Onion	Hrs.	Mins.
1	2	3	4	5	6	7	8	9
A	800	0	1.5	0.25	0.15	0	12	8.64
B	514	0	0.0	0.0	0.0	0	0	0.00
C	464	0	0.6	0.0	0.2	0	4	23.72
D	411	0	0.0	0.3	0.0	0	0	30.31
E	396	0	0.75	0.1	0.1	0	5	12.51
F	306	0	0.50	0.2	0.2	0	3	51.37
G	230	0	1.0	0.2	0.15	0	6	41.73
H	208	0	0.5	0.1	0.1	0	3	22.38
I	10	0	1.2	0.2	0.2	0	7	27.55
		Total time = 181 days					43	38.24

Source : Suryavanshi, A.R. and Patwardhan, M.M. (1983).

TABLE 4.23

Rotation 110-5 Note (a) All Crops are Presented Exception Which Totally Absent in a Season, and (b) All the Areas

1	2	3	4	5	6	7	8	9
A	800	.8	1.5	0.25	0.15	0	29	2.3
B	514	.5	0.0	0.0	0.00	0	4	33.17
C	464	.0	.6	0.0	0.2	0	7	41.91
D	411	.2	.0	0.3	0.0	0	4	35.23
E	396	.4	.75	0.1	.1	0	12	25.48
F	306	.3	.5	.2	.2	0	10	43.26
G	230	.5	1	.2	.15	0	16	6.19
H	208	.3	.5	.1	.1	0	8	37.12
I	10	.4	1.2	.2	.2	0	16	2.14
						Total time	110 or 4.58 days	2.14

TABLE 4.24

Rotation Number 10 (Only Wheat is Present and Other Crops are Harvested)

Farm No. Khassa No. (Randomly)	Distance (m)	Wheat	Hy. Jowar	Gram	Potato	Onion	Hrs.	Mins.
1	2	3	4	5	6	7	8	9
A	800	.8	0	0	0	0	5	38.13
B	514	.5	0	0	0	0	3	8.82
C	464	.0	0	0	0	0	0	0.0
D	411	.2	0	0	0	0	1	12.74
E	396	.4	0	0	0	0	2	24.70
F	306	.3	0	0	0	0	1	45.15
G	230	.5	0	0	0	0	2	50.77
H	208	.3	0	0	0	0	1	41.71
I	10	.4	0	0	0	0	2	7.19
						Total time or 0.86 days.	20	49.24

TABLE 4.25

Abstract Table

Rotation No.	Total running period (days)
1	1.81
2	2.74
3	3.52
4	4.11
5	4.58
6	4.45
7	3.96
8	3.27
9	1.47
10	0.86

Important Features of the Programme

The following conclusions have been drawn from above programming :

(1) Once the basic data is supplied, farmwise supply time and total running time of outlet is obtained for all the rotations in a season before hand. Therefore, it is very easy to intimate the same to farmers in advance.

(2) If the crop is not sown in initial rotations, the area under that crop is automatically taken as zero until the rotation in which it is sown.

(3) The area of the crop harvested in any rotation is taken as zero for next rotations.

(4) Loss of discharge upto each field along the field channel is accounted for and correspondingly the supply time is increased.

The computer programme suggested above can be used for preparation of water distribution schedules to attain the object of scientific irrigation management.

HIGHLIGHTS OF ROTATIONAL WATER SUPPLY IN INDIA

Rotation method has been called by different local names in the country *viz.* Shejpali or Rigid Shejpali or RWS in Maharashtra.

— Warabandi in North India.

— Varavaram in Tamilnadu.

Warabandi

Rotational method of water distributions called warabandi is practised in Northern India *i.e.* in the states of Punjab, Haryana, U.P., Rajasthan, Bihar etc. In these states most of the irrigation schemes are runoff of the river schemes.

"Wara" means turns and Bandi means fixation *i.e.* warabandi is fixation of turns. In this method the available water is allocated to cultivators in equal proportions to their holdings. This imposes water scarcity condition. The utilisation of irrigation supplies is left entirely to the cultivators, who is under no obligation to grow any particular crop and area. In this system the water from the source is carried by main canal. The main canal feeds two or more branches which operate by rotation and may or may not be able to run full. This is the primary distribution system and run continuously throughout the irrigation season. Branch canals supply water to a large number of distributaries which must run at full supply level by rotation.

This is the secondary distribution system. Distributaries supply water courses (called gulls) through ungated, fixed discharge outlets generally semi-modular outlets water courses run at full supply level (FSL) when the distributary is running and the water is allocated between farmers on a water course by a time roster. This is tertiary distribution system.

Water Allocation Management

Each unit of culturable command area is allocated a certain rate of flow termed as water allowance. Distributaries and water courses are designed on the basis of this water allowance. The value of this water allowance at water course head is generally 2.5 to 3 cusecs per 1000 acres of CCA.

The distribution of water up to outlet is managed by government agency. The distributions are always run full in 8 days period. The distribution of water coming out of an outlet (called mogha) is changed by cultivators. The distribution of this water is done on a 7 days rotation basis with the help of an approved roster which divides 168 hrs. *(i.e.* 7 days) in the ratio of the holdings. The outlet have no gates and it is illegal to keep any of them closed when the parent distributary is running. The distributary is run for 8 days *i.e.* one day more for the filling of distributary so that all water courses can get water at least for 7 full days.

Along water courses (W.C.) the water distribution proceeds from head to tail. Each cultivator is entitled to receive the entire water in a water course only on a specific week day and at a specified time. There is no provision in this system to compensate any individual farmer who does not receive water in his turn because of the reasons for which he is not responsible like fault in operation or branches in canal etc. This system also does not compensate for the losses in the water course.

Roster of turns : When water is delivered in the water course, it requires some time to reach upto each delivery point (called Nakka). This time of filling is called *Bharai.* Thus total time of filling (bharai) is debited to the common pool time of hours and credited to the individual accounts of each farmer.

Filling of water courses starts from head and proceeds towards its tail. At the end of rotation, the whole length of the water course, which has been filled with common pool time is utilised by the last farmer. Hence part of total *Bharai* time considering sudden reduction of supply, is debited on the account of last farmer. This is called Jharai. The *Jharai* time is credited to the common pool. Thus :

$$\frac{\text{Net running time in hours per unit of CCA}}{\text{Total time for each farmer (hours)}} = \frac{168 \text{ total bharai + jharai total area}}{\text{Net running time per unit area his area + his Bharai} - \text{Jharai}}$$

(Bharai is zero for all farmers excepting the last.)

Shejpali : This method is practised in south-western states like Maharashtra, Gujarat and Karnataka. The method is described in nutshell as below :

(1) Preparation of Preliminary Irrigation Programme (PIP) before the start of Rabi season and deciding the area and crops to be grown on the basis of a water storage *(i.e.* water budgeting).

(2) Inviting water applications from the farmers and sanctioning them.

(3) Preparation and publication of rotation programme, *i.e.* days "off and on".

(4) Water indenting on the basis of AI/DC or ETc before the start of each rotation and supply of water accordingly (AI/DC means area irrigated per day/cusec).

(5) Preparation of Shejpali started by canal inspector and communicating the day and time to each irrigator by calling them at a predetermined place.

(6) Supply is rotated among farmers on each outlet, on the distributary among different distributaries and in different sections of canal.

(7) Actual supply of water is from tail to head of water course and main system.

(8) Field to field distribution of water from tail to head and checking of irrigation by canal inspectors and higher officers.

(9) Preparation of AI/DC statements at the end of each rotation (monitoring).

(10) Preparation of Completed Irrigation Programme (CIP) at the end of each season and evaluation of the performance.

Rotational Water Supply System (RWS) or Rigid Rotational System

On the established canals in Maharashtra, the Shejpali system of water distribution is practised. According to the sanctioned areas, the irrigators are supplied water, in turn from tail to head, as per the schedule prepared and communicated in advance. When the time allotted to each irrigator is rigidly prescribed. It is called Rigid Shejpali or Rotational Water Supply (RWS). This is the system proposed to be followed on Maharashtra irrigation projects.

Preparation of RWS Schedule : RWS schedule on the basis of ET requirement of crops. The schedule of RWS on an outlet command provides for the turns of the irrigators from tail to head. A constant discharge of 30 lit/sec (about one cusec) is maintained at the outlet head. Only one irrigator is to take water at a time. The time to each irrigator can be calculated on the basis of traditional practice of AI/DC or modern practice of Cu or ET requirements of crops during particular rotation. The time allotted to the farmers at the tail end is required to be adjusted to account for the conveyance losses in the field channels. Similarly while computing the total time required for the stream to fill the water course should be taken into account.

RWS Schedules on the basis of ET or Cu Requirement of Crops : When ET requirements are considered for preparation of RWS Schedule, then it becomes Rotation-cum-Demand method. Crop water requirement on the basis of Evapotranspiration Demand (ET) consumptive use varies as the stages of the crop growth. Fortnightly (14 days) crop water requirement can be calculated by modified penman method or evapotranspiration method, using climatological data. ET demand is calculated as mm/ha or cm/ha for the given period. ET demand in each rotation varies as per the growth of the crop. Hence in each rotation ET requirement will be different.

To satisfy the ET requirement in each rotation with fixed supply, time of supply will vary from rotation to rotation. Following steps may be taken for the preparation of RWS schedules on the basis of ET requirements for one rotation on particular outlet.

STEP I — Calculate ET of each crop in particular field or farm of one farmer.

STEP II — Calculate Net Irrigation Requirement (NIR) of all crops *i.e.* NIR = ET — Effective rainfall

STEP III — Calculate field irrigation requirement (FIR), considering field application efficiency; if 20% losses (0.2)

$\because$ Efficiency = 80% or $\frac{1}{0.8}$ of field application

STEP IV — Calculate time to satisfy FIR with fixed supply of water

$$\text{Time} = \frac{\text{F I R in ha. mm or ha. m}}{\text{Discharge rate in litres/sec (lps)}}$$

STEP V — Apply correction factor to time as worked out above to compensate for losses in field channel *e.g.* if the losses in field channel in longest length of last field are 20% instead of 30 lits/sec it will receive only 24 lit/sec (30 × 0.8 = 24). Hence time to last farmers must be increased by 30/24 = 1.25 times. Assuming linear variation of losses along the length of field channel correction factor for time to each farmer can be calculated.

For RWS schedule on the basis of ET of crops outlet No. DR-6, rotation No.4 (Jan. 1 to 14) capacity of outlet 30 lits/sec losses in FC= 20% in 700 m length (tail to head). The details of calculations are given in Table 4.26 and 4.27.

MERITS & DEMERITS OF ROTATIONAL SUPPLY OF WATER

The following are the salient merits and demerits of rotational water supply :

Merits

1. The closure period is beneficial in lowering the ground water table.
2. Similar cross section of main canal through more cross section of the distributary canals can be attained.
3. The engineer is helped to organise his time which enables him to supervise a bigger area.
4. The closure helps for periodical maintenance of sytsem.

Demerits

1. If rotation period is more it causes water stress in the growing crops which may decrease crop yields.
2. If time of individual irrigation is not controlled it may result in low field application efficiency.
3. Since closure is a discretion of the supplier the farmer has to adjust himself as per rotation schedule.

TABLE 4.26

Sl. No.	Survey No.	Farmer	Distance from outlet (m)	Demand Crop	Area (ha)	Total NIR for 14 days	NIR % ha m	FIR (NIR) 0.7 ha mm	Time Min.	C.F. correction factor	Corrected times Min.	Supply From	To
1	2	3	4	5	6	7	8	9	10	11	12	13	14
		A	700	Wheat	0.3	85	25	57	317	1.25	6-40	Mon. 8-00	Mon. 14-40
				Jowar	0.2	75	15						
		B	600	Wheat	0.4	85	34 } 109	156	867	1.22	17-40	Mon. 14-40	Mon. 8-20
				Jowar	1.0	75	75 }						
		C	600	Wheat	0.4	85	34 }	137	762	1.22	15-30	Tue. 8-20	Tue. 23-50
				Gram	0.3	75	22 } 96						
				Jowar	0.2	75	15 }						
				Sugarcane	0.2	125	25 }						
		D	450	Wheat	0.4	85	34 } 64	31	506	1.16	9-50	Tue. 23.50	Tue. 9-40
				Jowar	0.4	75	30 }						

(*Contd.*)

TABLE 4.26 (*Contd.*)

Sl. No.	Survey No.	Farmer	Distance from outlet (m)	Demand		Total NIR for 14 days	NIR % ha m	FIR (NIR) 0.7 ha mm	Time Min.	C.F. correction factor	Corrected times Min.	Supply	
				Crop	Area (ha)							From	To
1	2	3	4	5	6	7	8	9	10	11	12	13	14
		E	450	Wheat	0.3	85	24 } 74	106	590	1.16	11.25	Wed. 9-40	Wed. 21-05
				Sugarcane	0.4	125	50						
		F	250	Wheat	1.0	85	85 } 137	196	1090	1.09	19.50	Thu. 21.05	Thu. 16.55
				Jowar	0.7	75	52						
		G	150	Sugarcane	0.8	125	100	143	795	1.05	14.00	Fri. 16-55	Fri. 6-55
		H	100	Wheat	0.6	85	51	73	406	1.84	7.00	6.55	6.55
		I	0	Wheat	1.0	85	85 } 173	247	1373	1.0	23.00	Fri. 13.55	Sat. 12.55
				Sugarcane	1.7	125	88						

Marking of Distribution Boxes

The distribution boxes within chak may be coloured according to zones *e.g.* Zone 1 — Red; Zone 2 — Yellow; Zone 3 — White; Zone 4 — Green; Zone 5 — Pink; Zone 6 — Brown; Zone 7— Black; Zone 8 — Orange; Zone 9 — Blue, Zone 10 — Grey and so on. This helps farmers to recognise his zonal colour. For example, if zone 2 is being irrigated, it (yellow) should only get water and not other boxes. However, if two zones are getting water from the same box, the box may be painted in strips in both zone colours. Or if three zones are getting water from one box, it may be painted in 3 colours. The boxes are also numbered if not coloured. Keep display boards near heads of chak giving all details.

For more understanding some model calculations are given for illustration :

MODEL CALCULATIONS FOR WARABANDI

Say the total chak is 33.05 acres and the numbers of farmers are 37. The steps for working out Warabandi schedule are as follows :

Step 1 : Obtain ownership plan and design plan of chak including field channel lay out and distribution boxes.

Step 2 : From area-based zones within the chak having 6 to 10 farmers in a zone in consultation with the farmers. Four zones were formed in this example (as indicated in column 1 to 12 of Table 4.27.

Step 3 : The area of each individual holding within each zone has to be shown in column 3 of the table. If one farmer holds more than one piece of holding within a zone each holding has to be dealt with separately.

Step 4 : Since water requires time to travel from one distribution box to the next, this time is shared as loss by all farmers in the chak. The travelling time is a function of slope. Since slopes vary, care has to be taken in calculating the time. Column 4 shows the length of field channels from one box to the other. The first farmer in zone 1 has 290 feet of channel length.

Step 5 : Conveyance losses of water in the field channels to individual farmers holding have to be borne by all farmers. Losses accumulate from box to box. If for instance, the first farmer and the second farmer on a field channel have each 2% losses in their field channel stretch, the second farmer has to bear also the losses of the first farmer thus has actually 4% losses. The accumulation of length of channel for each individual plot is shown in column No. 5.

Step 6 : The slope of each field channel stretch is taken from the map and shown in column 6.

Step 7 : For easier calculation, the slope of 1:1000 has been adjusted as if it were a slope of 1:500. The adjusted length is 1.5 times longer if a slope of 1:1000 considered because the losses are 1.5 times higher. Column No.7 shows that the first farmer in the zonal one has an adjusted length of 435 feet which is 1.5 × 290 feet of column 5.

Step 8 : The conveyance time is calculated now by taking the appropriate slope into consideration. The first farmer of zone one has a slope of 1:1000 with a flow of velocity of 1 feet/second. Since his stretch is 290 feet long, 290 seconds or 0.08 hours is his conveyance time (see column 9).

Step 9 : Each farmer in the command area is allocated a 'basic time'. This is equal to the time of irrigation available divided by the total areas (acres) in the chak. Since the irrigation is for 24 hours a day in 7 days, in a week, 168 hours are available for irrigation.

In the example it would be 168/33.05 = 5.08 hours per acre. Therefore, the first farmer in zone one obtains a basic time of 5.08 × 0.45 = 2.29 hrs. for his plot of 0.45 acres (see column 8). The total of basic time allocated for the entire chak is 168 hours.

Step 10 : Using column 4, the conveyance time is now calculated. If for instance, the first farmer in zone one is considered, he has 290' of field channels to cover before the water reaches his field. The slope of the field channel is according to plan 1:1000 and thus the velocity time is 1 foot per second. Thus 290 seconds of transport time loss occur which is equal to 0.08 hrs. as shown in column 9. Since the second farmer of zone one uses the same box for irrigation he will not have any conveyance loss and thus column 9 indicates nil. The third farmer of zone one is having 100' of channel length from the second farmer, with a slope of 1:500 with a corresponding velocity of 1.5 feet per second. He thus has 66 seconds to bear which is equal to 0.02 hours as indicated in column 9.

Step 11 : The transmission losses during conveyance of the water in the field channel is 10 per cent for a slope of 1:500 and 15 per cent for a slope of 1:1000. Since however, in column 7, the lengths of field channels with a slope of 1:1000 have been adjusted to a slope of 1:500 with a loss of 10 per cent per 1000 feet for this slope for 435 feet the losses would be 4.35 per cent losses have to be considered for him (see column 10). Seventh farmer of zone one will have to bear the losses of all the previous farmers plus the losses occurring in the field channels which is only used by him. The total adjusted length of that farmer is 1160 feet, thus 11.6 per cent as total transmission losses is applicable to him.

Step 12 : Following the determination of transmission losses in percentage these have to be converted into time. If we consider 10 per cent loss over a certain length of time, only 90 per cent of the water will reach the field. In order to get 100 per cent of the volume into the field the water has to run more than 10 per cent longer, in fact

$$\frac{100}{(100-10)} = 1.11 \text{ times longer}$$

In case of the first farmer in zone one having a total transmission loss of 4.35 per cent and 2.29 hours basic time, the formula to be followed would be 2.29 × 4.35 /100 = 0.099 hours or 0.1 hour.

It can easily be seen from column 11 that total transmission losses increase with distance from the water source and that the tail-end farmers have the highest transmission losses to bear.

Step 13 : Each individual farmer is compensated for the losses due to conveyance in terms of time. Thus the first farmer in zone one will get 0.10 hours extra as shown in column 11 plus 2.29 hours from column which is equal to 2.39 hours (see column 12). Summing up column 12, total hours now needed by the farmers would be 181.74 hours, providing for the losses in conveyance converted into time equivalent (column 12). The availability time during one week is however only 168 hours minus the transport time (from column 9) of 0.90 *i.e.* only 167.10 hours are actually available. Column 12 is adjusted for this available time and shown in column 13.

Step 14 : Since now every plot is compensated with time for transmission loss, the transport time of column 9 can be added to column 13 resulting into column 14. For instance, the first farmer in zone one obtains 2.27 hours, this is his final time. Summing up of all final times will result in 168 hours (column 14).

Step 15 : Column 14 which indicates decimal hours is converted into hours and minutes as shown in column 15.

Step 16 : With this finally the time schedule with days are worked out as shown in column 16.

These steps have been shown in Table 4.27 for better grasping and convenience of use.

TABLE

Table for Calculation of Time Schedule for Introduction

Group No.	Name of the farmer	Area in Acres	Length of F.Cs from previous wet D.B. in feet		Slopes of F.Cs from previous D.B.I.	Adjusted length for calcula-tion in feet	Basic time allocated in hours
			Individual	Cumulative			
1	2	3	4	5	6	7	8
	Sarvashri						
I. (1)	Pogula Pedda Rajam	0.45	290	290	1000	435	2.29
(2)	Makunuri Bhumaiah	0.30	-	290	1000	435	1.53
(3)	Pogula Nadipi Rajam	0.87	100	390	500	535	4.42
(4)	Pogula China Hanmanthu	1.00	150	540	500	685	5.08
(5)	Nemuri Thuniki Sayebu	0.50	250	790	500	935	2.54
(6)	Beemanathula Rajakka	0.50	125	915	500	1060	2.54
(7)	Nemuri Thuniki Sayebu	1.52	100	1015	500	1160	7.73
	Group Total :	5.15					26.13
II. (1)	Makunuri Rajam	0.37	—	—	—	—	1.88
(2)	Errolla Rajam	0.90	200	200	500	200	4.58
(3)	Pogula Nadipi Rajam	0.65	150	350	500	350	3.31
(4)	Pogula Nadipi Rajam	0.82	—	350	500	350	4.17
(5)	Pogula China Rajam	0.60	100	450	500	450	3.05
(6)	Pogula Pedda Rajam	0.60	100	550	500	550	3.05
(7)	Nemuri Thuniki Rajam	0.50	—	550	500	550	2.54
(8)	Pogula China Hanmanthu	0.50	100	650	500	650	2.54
(9)	Bemanathuni Rajakka	0.63	70	720	500	720	3.20
(10)	Rajaiah	1.00	—	720	500	720	5.08
(11)	Gangaram	1.00	60	780	500	780	5.08
(12)	Bheemaiah	1.00	120	900	500	900	5.08
	Group Total :	8.57					43.56
III. (1)	Makunuri Bhumaiah	0.40	260	610	500	610	2.03
(2)	Makunuri Rajam	0.42	90	700	500	700	2.13
(3)	Makunuri Bhoomaiah	0.70	160	869	500	860	3.56
(4)	Makunuri Rajam	0.45	120	1980	500	1980	2.29
(5)	Ganganna	1.00	120	1100	500	1100	5.08
(6)	Bhumaiah	0.18	230	840	500	840	0.92
(7)	Rajanna	0.52	—	840	500	850	2.64
(8)	Ganga Ram	0.60	190	1030	500	1030	3.05
(9)	China Gangaram	0.77	—	1030	500	1030	3.92
(10)	Rajanna	0.52	180	1210	500	1210	2.64
(11)	Rajaiah	1.00	150	1360	500	1360	5.08
(12)	Bheemaiah	3.10	200	1230	500	1230	15.76
	Group Total :	9.56					49.10
IV. (1)	Pabbathi Rajakka	2.00	—	—	—	—	10.16
(2)	Pabbathi Rajakka	3.10	250	250	1000	370	15.76
(3)	Chaliganti Chinnanna	0.55	400	650	1000	975	2.80
(4)	Ganga Mallaiah	1.40	100	950	500	1075	7.12
(5)	Ganna Venkanna	1.15	175	925	500	1250	5.85
(6)	Ganna Linganna	1.58	130	1055	500	1380	7.52
	Group Total :	9.78					49.21
	Grand Total :	33.05					168.00

4.27

of Warabandhi Under Canal Areas

Transport time in hours	Total transmission losses in %	Total transmission losses in hours	Total time required if compensated in hours	Adjusted time per plot in hours
9	10	11	12	13
0.08	4.35	0.10	2.39	2.91
	4.35	0.07	1.60	1.47
0.02	5.35	0.24	4.66	4.27
0.03	6.85	0.35	5.43	4.98
0.05	9.35	0.47	3.01	2.76
0.02	10.60	0.27	2.81	2.58
0.02	11.60	0.90	8.63	7.91
0.22		2.40	28.53	26.16
-	-	-	1.88	1.72
0.04	2.00	0.09	4.67	4.28
0.03	3.50	0.16	3.47	3.18
-	3.50	0.15	4.32	3.96
0.02	4.50	0.14	3.19	2.92
0.02	5.50	0.17	3.22	2.95
-	5.50	0.14	2.68	2.46
0.02	6.50	0.17	2.71	2.48
0.01	7.20	0.23	3.43	3.14
-	7.20	0.37	5.45	4.99
0.01	7.80	0.40	5.48	5.02
0.02	9.00	0.46	5.54	5.08
0.17		2.48	46.04	42.18
0.05	6.10	0.12	2.15	1.97
0.02	7.00	0.15	2.28	2.09
0.03	8.00	0.28	3.84	3.52
0.02	9.80	0.22	2.51	2.30
0.02	11.00	0.56	5.64	5.17
0.04	8.40	0.08	1.00	0.92
-	8.40	0.22	2.86	2.62
0.04	10.30	1.06	4.11	3.77
-	10.70	0.42	4.34	3.98
0.03	12.10	0.32	2.96	2.71
0.03	13.60	0.69	5.77	5.29
0.04	12.30	1.94	17.70	16.22
0.32		6.60	55.16	50.56
-	-	-	10.16	9.31
0.05	3.75	0.59	16.35	14.98
0.07	9.75	0.27	3.07	2.81
0.02	10.75	0.77	7.89	7.23
0.03	12.50	0.73	6.58	6.03
0.02	13.80	1.04	8.56	7.84
0.19		3.40	52.61	48.20
0.90		14.34	182.34	167.10

TABLE 4.27 (*Contd.*)

Group No.	Final time per plot Hrs. Mts.	Hrs. Mts.	Time schedule Hrs. Mts.	Hrs. Mts.	Day
1	14	15	16	17	18
I. (1)	2.26	2-15	4-00	6-15	Monday
(2)	1.45	1-25	6-15	7-40	Monday
(3)	4.26	4-15	7-40	11-55	Monday
(4)	5.01	5-00	11-55	16-55	Monday
(5)	2.60	2-40	16-55	19-35	Monday
(6)	2.61	2-40	19-35	22-15	Monday
(7)	7.99	8-00	22-15	6-15	Tuesday
	26.18	26-15			
II. (1)	1.71	1-45	6-15	8-00	Tuesday
(2)	4.28	4-15	8-00	12-15	Tuesday
(3)	3.15	3-10	12-15	15-25	Tuesday
(4)	3.93	3-55	15-25	19-20	Tuesday
(5)	2.92	2-55	19-20	22-15	Tuesday
(6)	2.95	3-00	22-15	1-15	Wednesday
(7)	2.46	2-25	1-15	3-40	Wednesday
(8)	2.50	2-30	3-40	6-10	Wednesday
(9)	3.15	3-10	6-10	9-20	Wednesday
(10)	5.00	5-00	9-20	14-20	Wednesday
(11)	5.07	5-05	14-20	19-25	Wednesday
(12)	5.11	5-05	19-25	0-30	Thursday
	42.23	42-15			
III. (1)	2.03	2-00	0-30	2-30	Thursday
(2)	2.11	2-05	2-30	4-35	Thursday
(3)	3.57	3-35	4-35	8-10	Thursday
(4)	2.32	2-20	8-10	10-30	Thursday
(5)	5.22	5-15	10-30	15-45	Thursday
(6)	0.95	1-00	15-45	16-45	Thursday
(7)	2.62	2-40	16-45	19-25	Thursday
(8)	3.13	3-05	19-25	22-30	Thursday
(9)	3.97	4-00	22-30	2-30	Friday
(10)	2.76	2-45	2-30	5-15	Friday
(11)	5.39	5-20	5-15	10-35	Friday
(12)	16.44	16-25	10-35	3-00	Saturday
	50.51	50-30			
IV. (1)	9.28	9-15	3-00	12-15	Saturday
(2)	15.00	15-00	12-15	3-15	Sunday
(3)	2.88	2-55	3-15	6-10	Sunday
(4)	7.29	7-15	6-10	13-25	Sunday
(5)	6.11	6-05	13-25	19-30	Sunday
(6)	8.52	8-30	19-30	4-00	Monday
	49.08	49-00			
Grand Total	168.00	168-00			

Warabandi or Shejpali

The conveyance of water from the outlet head to the farmer's field turn by turn is an important parameter for judicious use and the management of available irrigation water. Besides different types of water distribution, the rotational type method is mostly used in India. It is the rigid method of water distribution. In this, the water is delivered at a fixed time on pre-arranged schedule. The rotation may be made between :

(a) Two farmers or water user
(b) Two or more group of farmers
(c) Outlets
(d) Distributaries and minors
(e) Definite sections of main canal

This method is called — Shejpali or RWS in Maharashtra
— Warabandi in North India
— Varavaram in Tamilnadu

Warabandi is practised in the state of Punjab, Haryana, Uttar Pradesh, Rajasthan and Bihar.

"Wara" means turn and "Bandi" means fixation. Thus Warabandi is a fixation of irrigation turns. In this method the available irrigation water is allocated to the area farmers in proportion to their land holdings. The utilisation of irrigation water is left to the farmers *i.e.* they decide their seasonal or yearly cropping sequences at their own will in one's holding. The full water supply in main canals and upto outlet is controlled by the irrigation department. Water supply level is maintained such that water courses run at full supply level, when the distributary is running and the water is allocated between farmers on a water course by a time roster. The farmer manages water drawn from an outlet (mogha).

Water Allocations and Management

The water allowance *i.e.* flow rate is fixed for each unit of culturable command area The water courses are already designed for given rate of water flows (2.5 to 3 cusecs per 1000 acres C.C.A.).

The water distribution is worked out on a 7 days (168 hrs.) rotation basis as per fixed roster which provides number of hours (time) to each farmer in the proportion of his holding. The outlets are ungated to have free flow of water. The distributary runs for 8 days *i.e.* one day more for filling of water in the water courses (W.C.), thus allowing them to supply full water for 7 days.

Along water course, the water distribution proceeds from head to tail. Each farmer gets total water allocated only on a particular week-day and at a given time. If there is any mishappening *e.g.* breach of canal, operational fault etc. Also the compensation for water losses in the W.C. is not provided.

Roster of Turns

The roster of turns is calculated considering the "Bharai" time *i.e.* time required for filling the W.C. from one Nakka (delivery point) to the next Nakka. The total time required for filling is debited to the common pool time of 168 hours and in turn added/credited to the individual water account of each cultivator.

Filling of W.C. begins from head and proceeds its tail. At the end of the rotation, the whole length of the W.C., which has been filled with common pool time is used by the end farmer. Therefore, the part of total Bharai (filling) time (due to any casual reduction of water supply) is deducted/debited to the roster account of the end farmer. It is termed as "Jharai" time and is added/credited to the common pool time.

The calculation of rosters are made as under :

1. Net running time in hours per unit of C.C.A. $= \dfrac{(168 - \text{Total Bharai}) + \text{Total Jharai}}{\text{Total Area}}$

2. Total time for each farmer (hours) = (Net running time per unit area × Farmer area) + his Bhari time (–) his Jharai time

Note : Jharai is zero for all farmers excepting the last.

Shejpali : It is common in Maharashtra, Karnataka and Gujarat. The various steps considered in Shejpali are :

(a) Preparation of Irrigation Programme (PIP) before on set of Rabi and fixing the area for different crops based on the water availability in the reservoir (*i.e.* water budgeting). A constant discharge of 30 lit/sec (about one cusec) should be maintained at the outlet head.

(b) Inviting water application from the farmers and sanctioning them (seasonwise).

(c) Preparation and notification of Rotation programme *i.e.* days off and on.

(d) Water indenting based on AI/DC or ET_c. before the start of each rotation and supply of water accordingly (AI/DC means — Area Irrigated per day cusecs or it is the area of mixed crops irrigated by one cusec of water flowing throughout the day (24 hours *i.e.* duty on day basis).

(e) Preparation of Shejpali Patrak by Canal inspector and communicating the day and time to each irrigator by calling them at a fixed place.

(f) Supply is rotated among farmers on each outlet, on the distributary, among various distributaries and in different section of canal.

(g) Accounting of the actual water supply from head to tail and main source.

(h) Field to field water supply (tail to head) checking.

(i) Preparation of AI/DC statements after completion of each rotation for monitoring (on a fixed format).

(j) Preparation of Complete Irrigation Programme (CIP) at the end of each season and carry out performance evaluation.

CHAPTER 5

WATER DISTRIBUTION AND DELIVERY SYSTEM — SOURCES OF IRRIGATION WATER

DISTRIBUTION STRUCTURES

The various modes of conveying irrigation water to the agricultural land through a proper network is called distribution work. This may be done through open channels (lined or unlined as per soil texture and other characteristics) or closed conduits either cast *in situ* or precasted by using concrete, asbestos pipes, PVC pipes etc. or tunnels (in case of hilly areas). The choice of the conveyance system depends upon the condition of terrain. There may be a single conveying method or mixture depending upon the area and length which is to be constructed and the purpose for which it is required.

Types of Irrigation Canals

Based on the layout, size and capacity, the canals to be used for irrigation may be broadly divided into following types :

(1) *Contour canals* : When canals are required to be constructed in hilly regions, these are made on contour lines so as to avoid excessive slope, cutting and filling.

(2) *Ridge canals* : The canals constructed on the highest elevation points of the terrain in order to facilitate irrigation on both side slopes are called ridge canals.

(3) *Side-slopping canals* : These are constructed across the contours and irrigate only one side of its path. Generally all canals start at the off-take point as a contour canal but later these are constructed along the ridge or sub-ridge line.

The various nomenclature have been given to the canals depending upon their size and water carrying capacities such as main branch, distributary, minors (laterals). The field channels are the water courses at farm gate which draw water from the canal distribution network for irrigating soil.

Gross Command Area (G.C.A.)

It is defined as the surface area which can be brought under the irrigation command of a canal or in other words it is the total area within the extreme limits set for irrigation. For instance the gross command area of a ridge canal would be the area lying within the two adjacent valley line. These different types are depicted in Fig. 5.1.

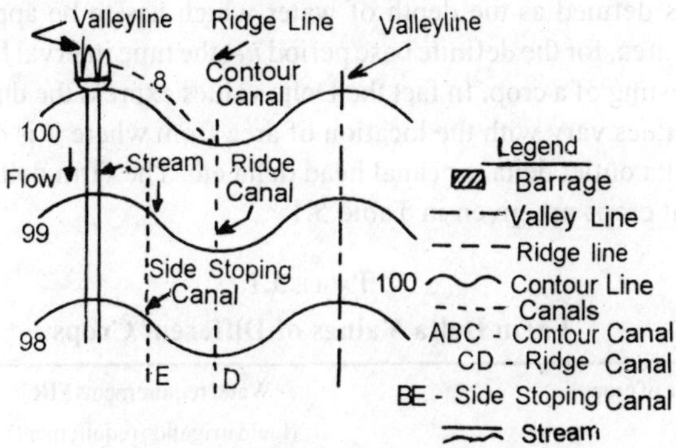

Fig. 5.1 : Different Layouts of Irrigation Canal

Culturable Command Area (C.C.A.)

It is that surface ground area which is actually under cultivation of crops which would be irrigated. Thus in other words it is the difference between gross command area and the area which is occupied by rocks, marshes, ponds, roads, houses and hence cannot be cultivated (non-C.C.A.).

Thus CCA = GCA – non-CCA.

Irrigation Intensity

It is defined as the ratio of the actual irrigated area to the culturable command area. This term is mostly used because of the limited availability of water resource in a country or state or any particular region or a canal system as the entire CCA is difficult to be irrigated and this shortfall in irrigation supply is measured in terms of irrigation intensity. For example the CCA is 100 ha and irrigated area by system is 80 ha. Hence, irrigation intensity (per cent) would be $\frac{80}{100} \times 100 = 80\%$

Crop Ratio

It is defined as the ratio between the anticipated cropped area (area covered by various crops) individually and on the whole to be irrigated per annum or during a year.

Delta

It is defined as the depth of water which has to be applied over a definite area, for the definite base period *i.e.* the time interval from sowing to harvesting of a crop. In fact the Delta values express the duty of water. Delta values vary with the location of area from where it is counted *e.g.* farm delta outlet delta, or canal head delta etc. The farm delta values for different crops are given in Table 5.1.

TABLE 5.1

Farm Delta Values of Different Crops

Name of crop	Water requirements FIR (Field irrigation requirement)
Rice (Kharif)	160
Maize (Kharif)	62
Jowar (Kharif)	50
Wheat (Rabi)	40
Gram (Rabi)	16
Mustard (Rabi)	16
Sugarcane (Perennial)	120 to 150 per variety

Duty

It indicates the relationship between the area to be irrigated and the quantity of water required for irrigation during a given base period. This term is expressed in various following forms :

1. Delta (depth of water in metres)
2. Area per unit rate of flow (usually in ha. per cumec)
3. Area per unit volume of flow (ha. per million cubic metre)
4. Volume of water required per unit area (ha. metre per ha.).

Alike delta the duty at any point of measurement is called against that location point such as canal head duty, farm duty, outlet duty etc.

Inter-Relationship between Duty and Delta

Assume one cumec of water supply released for irrigation for a base period of 'X' days in case of a particular crop for 'Y' ha. of land then Y = duty of water in ha. cumec.

Then if 'Q'* is the total quantity of water for the period of X days at the discharge of one cubic metre per second. Therefore, Q = (X × 24 × 60 × 60) × 1 cubic metre (24 hrs. converted to minutes and then seconds).

If 'Y' ha. of same land holds the 'Q' volume water the resulting depth m of water would be the value of delta.

Also 1 ha = 10^4 sq. metre

Y (in ha) = × 10^4 sq. metre

$$\Delta \text{ in meter} = \frac{\text{volume of water}}{\text{Area holding it}} = \times \frac{X \times 24 \times 60 \times 60 \times 1}{Y \times 10^4}$$

$$= 8.64\ X/Y \text{ or } Y = 8.64\ X/\text{Delta in metres.}$$

This equation provides inter-relationship between duty ('Y') expressed in ha. per cumec, and delta (Δ) expressed in metres and 'X' is the base period in number of days.

In case duty is to be expressed in number of ha. per million cubic metres (10^6) of water for any crop the calculations be made as follows :

Crop growing period = 'X' and duty for crop in question = Y ha/ cumec.

Therefore, volume of water supplied in 'X' days at the rate of 1 cumec = X × 24 × 60 × 60 × 1 cubic metres.

(The 'X' days are converted to seconds by taking one day = 24 hours, 1 hr. = 60 minutes and 1 minute = 60 seconds).

Now this volume of water can irrigate Y ha. duty. Therefore, total ha. which can be irrigated by a supply of one million cubic metres of water.

Hence duty = Z ha. per million cubic metres.

In case duty is to be expressed in terms of ha. m of water per unit area in ha. for any crop, then

---

$$^*Q = \frac{\text{Volume of Water (cubic metre)}}{\text{Time required to fill (sec.)}}$$

1 ha. m = 10^4 cubic metre

Hence 1 million cubic metre $= \frac{10^6}{10^4}$ ha. m = 100 ha.m (or 10^6 cubic m)

or 1 ha. of area would be irrigated by a water supply of

$$= \frac{100 \text{ ha.m}}{Z \text{ ha.}}$$

$$\text{Duty} = \frac{100 \text{ ha.}}{Z} \text{ m/ha.}$$

These values can be computed for different crops by substituting the values of total growing days (X) and total area to be grown under each crop (Y)

Thus for wheat	X = 120 days	
for rice	X = 140 "	
maize	X = 100 "	
jowar	X = 125 "	These are average values
gram	X = 175 "	which may change with
mustard	X = 100 "	variety of crop.
sugarcane	X = 300 "	

Canal Capacity (Full supply)

It is defined as the maximum rate of supply (cumecs) of water to be carried by the canal for supplying a certain depth of water in a certain time. This is also called full supply discharge capacity (or full supply discharge). This depends upon the area to be irrigated by the canal and schedule of irrigation application for the various crops. Since the schedule of irrigation depends upon crop type and stages of growth and in view of it canal capacity is to be developed as to cover all possible factors which consume quantity of water which is to be supplemented by canal water. These are :

(*i*) Consumptive water use requirement.

(*ii*) Effective rainfall which will delay irrigation.

(*iii*) Water losses through percolation, seepage and non-efficient use including conveyance and application.

(*iv*) Amount of water needed for land preparation, nursery beds etc.

(*v*) Soil parameters such as depth, water holding capacity etc.

It is, therefore, obvious that for the computation of canal capacity the above factors should be considered to meet the field irrigation requirements (FIR).

In order to work out the total designed capacity of a canal at head reach *i.e.* near offtake point, we adopt following method :

Step I — Assume crop ratio of different major crops in culturable command area of 'A' ha. say the crop ratio = X:Y:Z for three main crops.

Step II — Assume intensities of irrigation for three crops say — a%, b% and c% respectively monthwise.

Step III — Calculate monthwise field irrigation requirement (FIR) for every crop.

Step IV — Assume B% losses of water during conveyance as such efficiency = (100 — B%).

Step V — Calculate per cent loss of water stored in reservoir through evaporation say 'C' %.

Hence —

$$\text{Area under First Crop} = \frac{X}{(X+Y+Z)} \times \text{C.C.A. ha.}$$

$$\text{Area under Second Crop} = \frac{Y}{X+Y+Z} \times \text{C.C.A. ha}$$

$$\text{Area under Third Crop} = \frac{Z}{X+Y+Z} \times \text{C.C.A. ha}$$

From the above data make the data table— if the value of delta for the given crops are either given or taken the standard values of water requirements (FIR) of the crops in question and values of duty from the equation :

$$\text{Duty} = 8.64 \times \frac{\text{total growing period of base period of crop}}{\text{delta value of that crop}}$$

e.g. the following data are given for the crop in a particular month of growing season :

monthly consumptive use = value of pan evaporation × crop factor = 16.5 cm

monthly effective rainfall = 0. 5 cm

∴ Net irrigation requirement = consumptive use – eff. rainfall

Also total field losses such as = 16 cm

Percolation + application + land = 20% (B%). Hence efficiency is 80%, preparation if any.

$$\text{Hence F.I.R.} = 16 \times \frac{100}{80} = 16 \times \frac{10}{8} = 20 \text{ cm}$$

$$\therefore \quad \text{Delta} = \frac{10}{8} \text{ metre} = 0.20 \text{ m}$$

Calculate delta value for each growing month till harvest, calculate duty from above equation for each month for total growing period. Also calculate canal capacity value in cumec by formula — Area/Duty for every month and sum for overall growing period.

Hence design capacity at head reach (near offtake) considering 20% losses or 80% efficiency would be given by 100/80 × maximum value of 'Q' total for any wanted period or overall growing period for all crops of area, *e.g.* if the maximum value of canal capacity comes to 40 cumec, then by above formula the designing capacity of canal should be 100/80 × 40 = 50 cumec.

The entire values monthwise for different crops can be put in following proforma for calculations of design capacity of canal. (See Tables 5.2 and 5.3).

Live Storage

In case the losses are assumed to be nil then live storage is given by following relations (Fig. 5.2) :

For crop A = net area × total delta value for growing season of a crop

$$= \text{Net area} \times \sum \Delta$$

Similarly for crop B and crop C etc. may be calculated and added to get total gross live storage. If there are B% total losses, then net total live

$$\text{storage} = \frac{100}{B} \times \text{total gross live storage.}$$

TABLE 5.2

Computation of Design Capacity of Canal

Months*	Crops to be grown in area												Q total $Q=Q_1+Q_2+Q_3$ cumec
	Crop A				Crop B				Crop C				
	Net area X_1 total area × I.I (ha)	Delta Δ FIR/(cm) / 100 (m)	Duty 8.64 × Base Period / (ha/cum.)	Q_1= Net area / Duty (cumec)	Net Area X_2 Total × I.I (ha)	Delta FIR(cm) / 100 (m)	Duty = 8.64 × Base Period / (ha./cum)	Q_2= Net area / Duty (cumec)	Net X_3 T.Area × I.I (ha)	Delta FIR cm / 100 (m)	Duty 8.64 × Base Period / ha per (Cumec)	Q_3= Net Area / Duty (Cumec)	
* Jan.													Q Jan
Feb.													Q Feb
March													Q Mh
April													Q Ap
May													Q May
June													Q June
July													Q July
Aug.													Q Aug
Sept.													Q Sep
Oct.													Q Oct
Nov.													Q Nov
Dec.													Q Dec
		EA				EB					EC		

**Note* : For easiness of calculations assume each month of 30 days.

Sum of Δ Values for each crop for its growing period may be computed for other calculations as A, B, C.

TABLE 5.3

Computation of Design Capacity of Canal

Months	Crops to be grown												Q total
	Rice				Wheat				Sugarcane				$Q_1+Q_2+Q_3$
	X_1 ha	Δ m	Y ha per cumec	$Q_1 = \frac{X_1}{Y}$ cumec	X_2	Δ	Y	$Q_2 = \frac{X_2}{Y}$	X_3	Δ	Y	$Q_3 = \frac{X_3}{Y}$	cumecs
Jan.	-	-	-	-	21000	0.10	2592	8.10	9000	0.10	2592	3.47	11.57
Feb.	-	-	-	-	21000	0.10	2592	8.10	9000	0.10	2592	3.47	11.57
March	-	-	-	-	21000	0.10	2592	8.10	9000	0.10	2592	3.47	11.57
April	-	-	-	-	-	-	-	-	9000	0.10	2592	3.47	3.47
May	-	-	-	-	-	-	-	-	9000.	0.15	1728	5.21	5.21
June	-	-	-	-	-	-	-	-	-	-	-	-	0.00
July	36000	0.25	1036	34.75		-	-	-		-	-	-	34.75
Aug.	-do-	0.30	864	41.67	-	-	-	-	-	-	-	-	41.67

Sept.	-do-	0.15	1728	20.83	-	-	-	-	-	-	-	-	20.83
Oct.	-do-	0.15	1728	20.83	-	-	-	-	-	-	-	-	20.83
Nov.	-do-	-	-	-	-	-	-	-	9000	0.05	5184	1.74	1.74
Dec.	-do-	-	-	-	21000	0.10	2592	8.10	9000	0.10	2592	3.47	11.57
Total	$\Delta = 0.85$ m				Total $\Delta = 0.40$ m				Total $\Delta = 0.70$ m				Total Q = 174.78

$\therefore$ Q mean = 174.78 ÷ 12 = 14.56 cumec.

All Months are assumed to be of 30 days

Where - X_1, X_2, X_3 = Area in ha.

Δ = Delta in meter

Y = Duty in ha/cumec

and Q_1, Q_2 and Q_3 = Area/Duty in different crops

For illustrations it is advised to check the selected examples at the end of chapter.

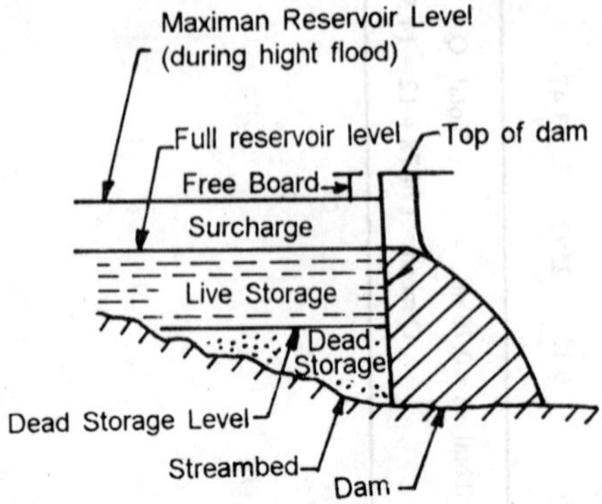

Fig. 5.2 : Showing section of a dam for different type of storages

Capacity Factor and its Importance

Capacity factor — It is defined as the ratio of the mean supply to the full supply capacity or design capacity of a canal.

Thus say Q mean = 12 (QJ + QF + QMch + QAp + QMy + QJn + QJu + QAu + QSep + QOct + QNov + QDcc)

= 15 cumec (per month)

Also suppose Q max = 45 cumec

$$\text{Hence capacity factor} = \frac{\text{Q mean}}{\text{Q max}} = 15/45 = 0.30 \text{ (or from Table 5.3} = 0.35)$$

Thus, if Q mean cumec/month is given

∴ The total volume to be supplied in a year = Q mean × 12

= 12 Q mean cumec per month

∴ Total volume supplied yearly = 12 Q mean × 30 (days) × 24 (hrs) x 3600 sec (60 × 60 *i.e.* minutes & seconds) cumec

(1 cumec = 24 × 3600 cum = (864) hectare metre per day

(by converting cubic metre to ha. metre)

It may be understood by following example :

Say Q mean = 15 cm

∴ Total volume supplied in 12 months = 15 × 12 = 180 cumec (per month)

Converting this to per day by multiplying by 30 and to hours by 24 and to cubic metre by 3600, we have — 180 × 30 × 24 × 3600 cumec

$$= 46656 \text{ cumec.}$$

If converted to ha. metre this would come equal to the gross live storage for all the crops in the area without considering any loss *i.e.* it is equal to Σ (area × delta) or sum total of net area of each crop multiplied with total delta value of total growing season of each crop growing in the area

$$i.e.\ X_1 \times \Sigma\, \Delta A + X_2\ \Sigma\, \Delta B + X_3 \times \Delta\, C \text{ are cropwise deltas.}$$

The ideal conditions of 100% canal utilisation are when Q max = Q mean or when crop factor is unity. This is difficult to achieve in practice which it means that it would not be possible for canals to close for any annual maintenance including repair, desilting and weed clearance. In practice it should be done in the month of June when canal water is generally not required. This also avoids the maximum losses which occur in this hot season due to surface evaporation and evapotranspiration by weeds.

The capacity factor approaching to unity can be attained for efficient utilisation of available water by proper selection of crops, crop ratio and intensity of irrigation. Thus, the higher is the capacity factor, less will be the peak supply (for the same volume of water) and accordingly the less investment on the project because the canal cross section can be reduced correspondingly.

Alignment of Canal

The best alignment of the canal is the ridge line so that it can irrigate on either side of the slope. As far as possible canal alignment should be straight unless either unproductive, or inhabitated area comes in its way. The curvature under the said conditions should be such that its radius is 10 to 15 times the width of the canal. The alignment may be shifted to some extent depending upon the contour, soil, land use conditions which helps to reduce cost of cross-drainage works, regulating works, bridges etc. It is also advisable to avoid deep cuttings as well as high embankments by filling by suitable detouring so as to have a check on breaching and heavy percolation loss, besides large right of way.

L -Section (Long section or Longitudinal section)

When the canal alignment is finalised, the centre line of the canal should be laid on the ground and along the central line level should be taken. These data along with other are plotted on a graph paper sheet having longitudinal scale between 1:10,000 or 1:20,000 and vertical scale of 1:100 is called L-Section. The various structures, ground surface, canal bed and full supply line (F.S.L.) top of banks, and details of outlets, regulators, bridges, drainage crossings, offtaking channel etc. are included in this L-Section sheet (Fig. 5.3).

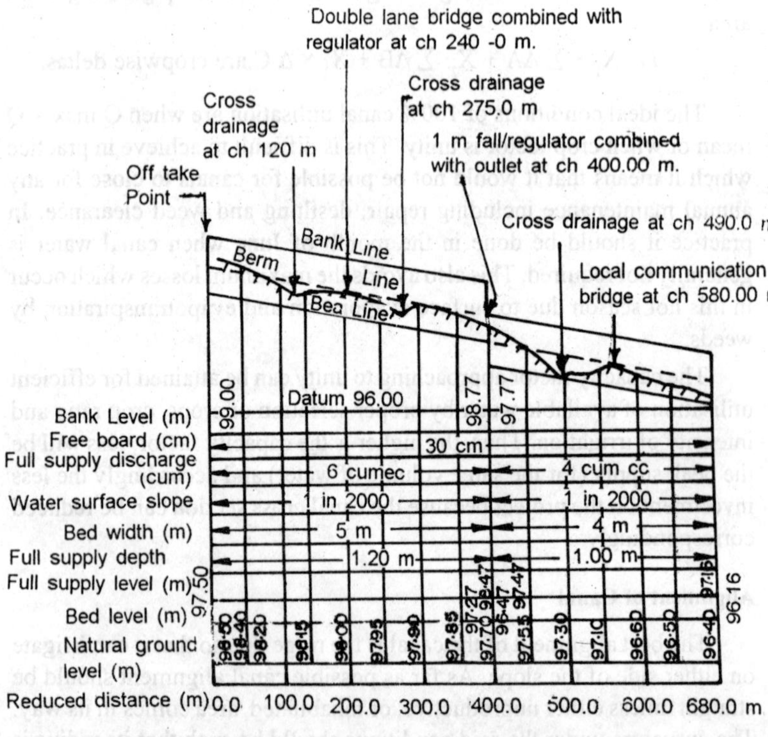

Fig. 5.3 : Typical Long Section Profile of an Irrigation Canal

Full Supply Level of Canal (F.S.L.)

The F.S.L. of a canal is always fixed w.r.t. the level of land to be brought under irrigation. Thus F.S.L. is a function of land relief or topography. This is calculated from the tail end of the canal. In the beginning of F.S.L. of minors or laterals from the offtake point is fixed and kept 15 to 30 cms above the ground level. Similar difference at offtake point is further maintained for distributaries *i.e.* 15 to 30 cms high than minor/lateral. Further 10 to 15 cms high at the offtake points are kept for branch and main canals.

High FSL should be avoided as this would result in excessive filling which would be costly and susceptible to breaches. For this balancing depth value 'd' is to be calculated. The two parallel lines at distance 'd' apart are then drawn on tracing paper sheet which is superimposed on L-Section such that the top line cuts the maximum number of lines on the ground surface. The position of canal on paper indicates its balanced section at different locations within its reach. Similarly on L-Section the bottom line drawn on tracing paper at a distance 'd' from the top is also transferred and this shows canal bed line.

In case the terrain of a particular canal reach has greater or steep slopes the provision of fall is shown in the L-Section after a certain reach of canal. If the full supply depth (FSD) is fixed, the FSL can also be decided.

The other important factor in making an earthen canal section is to keep optimum allowable slope which would check erosion of canal bed and banks due to the high velocity of running water along the slope. This factor does not come in picture if the canals are lined fully or in a reach where the slopes are kept considerably high, yet the slope values decided should be reasonable to create optimum flow velocity in the canal.

The designed FSL should be such that when the water availability is comparatively low or canal runs half capacity or there is a shortfall in the water demand in the area the command area outlets get the full or maximum discharge. In case as per calculation it is not possible to cover the entire command outlet to discharge the designed water quantity when canal is crossing half full or less FSL the provision of cross regulators may be made to raise the water level up to the FSL.

In spite of all the care taken to design a canal to cover maximum culturable area it is sometimes not possible to irrigate part of the CCA being at very high elevations in respect of flow of water by gravity. Such areas are excluded and in order to irrigate them, provision of lift irrigation should be kept in planning and accordingly FSL should be designed so that later on the cost of pumping water from canal to these areas may not come out to be too high which results in public grievances. Thus optimum FSL would be that by which at low cost irrigation canal is made to irrigate flow as well as lift area for which through consideration of bed level, location of offtake should be done at the planning stage. Otherwise there may be a huge investment of cost and still the project efficiency may be quite low. In general the highest elevation of lift areas should be kept preferably below 15 cms of canal FSL so that these can be easily irrigated by lift method.

Selected Examples

Example 1 :

Assuming following data calculate the delta and duty.

(i) Crop = wheat

(ii) Water depth required for irrigation or water requirement (FIR) = 40 cms or 40/100 = 0.4 metre

(iii) Base period (crop period) = 120 days

(1) Hence duty Y (for wheat) $= 8.64 \times \frac{X/X}{\Delta} = 8.64 \times 120/0.40$
$= 2592$ ha/cumec

(2) In case duty is to be expressed in number of ha. per million cubic metre of water for wheat crop then total volume of water (Y) supplied in base period 'X' (120 days) at the rate of 1 cumec. Therefore $Y = 120 \times 24 \times 60 \times 60 \times 1$ cubic metre. As calculated above this volume of water can irrigate 2592 ha. Hence 1 million cubic metre of water (10^6 cubic metres) would irrigate equal to $= \frac{10^6}{120 \times 24 \times 60 \times 60} \times 2592 = 250$ ha.
Hence duty = 250 ha. per million cubic metres.

(3) In case duty is to be expressed in terms of ha. metre (ha.m) of water per unit area in ha (for wheat)

1 ha. m = 10^4 cubic metre

Hence 1 million cubic metre = 100 ha. m

As calculated in (2) the number of ha. *i.e.* 250 ha can be irrigated by 100 ha.m of water.

Hence one ha. area would need a supply of = 100/250 = 0.4 ha.m of water.

Therefore, duty = 0.4 ha.m/ha.

Example 2 :

Calculate the designed capacity of the canal at head reach off the data given are :

(i) CCA = 90000 ha.

(ii) Crops to be grown — rice, wheat and sugarcane

(iii) Crops ratio of the crops to be grown = 3:2:1 (6) Total

(iv) Intensities of irrigation : for rice 80%
for wheat 70%
for sugarcane 60%

(v) Monthly FIR given for different crops are as under

(vi) Conveyance losses = 20%.

Rice : July 25 cm, August 30 cm, September 15 cm, October 15 cm.

Wheat : December to March = 10 cm every month.

Sugarcane : Nov. 5 cm, Dec. to April — 10 cm every month, May 15 cm.

Solution :

From above data we have

$$\text{Area under rice crop} = \frac{3}{6} \times 90000 = 45000 \text{ ha.}$$

$$\text{Area under wheat crop} = \frac{2}{6} \times 90000 = 30000 \text{ ha.}$$

$$\text{Area under sugarcane} = \frac{1}{6} \times 90000 = 15000 \text{ ha.}$$

Taking into account the cropwise given irrigation intensities, the actual different crop areas (X) under irrigation would be as follows :

Rice = 0.80 × 45000 = 36000 ha (X_1)

Wheat = 0.70 × 30000 = 21000 ha (X_2)

Sugarcane = 0.60 × 15000 = 9000 ha. (X_3)

The canal capacity (Q) is given by ratio of area to the duty (cumec)

Hence canal capacity Q = Z/Y (cumec)

The value of $Y = 8.64 \times \frac{X}{\Delta}$ (the base monthly period is taken as 30 days)

Taking different actual area values *i.e.* x_1, x_2 and x_3

From table 5.3 it is obvious that the highest value of canal capacity (Q) is 41.67 cumec for which canal must be designed. Considering 20% losses means, if 100 cumec flow is released at the offtake point it will be only 80 cumec in the field. As such the design capacity is to be increased accordingly *i.e* design capacity of computed 41.67 cumec is to be raised by 100/80 × 41.67 = 52.08 cumec near offtake.

Example 3 :

Calculate the annual live storage if 10% of the water stored is lost in evaporation as per data given and calculated in example 2.

Solution :

Live storage without losses for different crops would be as under :

For rice	=	36000 × 0.85 ($\Sigma\Delta$ for rice)	=	30600 ha.m.
For wheat	=	21000 × 0.40 ($\Sigma\Delta$ for wheat)	=	8400 ha.m.
For sugarcane	=	9000 × 0.70 ($\Sigma\Delta$ for sugarcane)	=	6300 ha.m.
		Total	=	45300 ha.m.

As the total % loss is 30% (including conveyance and evaporational losses *i.e.* 20 Y+ 10 Y = 30%).

$$\text{The total live storage} = \frac{100}{70} \times 45300 = 64714 \text{ ha.m.}$$

Selection of Sites

There are various number of factors which influence the site of storage reservoir. These are :

(i) Land relief or topography
(ii) Characteristics of foundation to be selected for dam construction
(iii) Surface and sub-surface soil characteristic
(iv) The amount of grouting involved for attaining the water tightness of the reservoir space
(v) Distance of agricultural land
(vi) Availability of construction material
(vii) Transport facilities
(viii) Diversion facilities for river water.

Project Works

The construction work of irrigation project till its completion involve following steps :

(i) Various types of surveys such as soil survey, survey about construction materials, topographic and transport to route, technical feasibility of the scheme. These are exploratory, detailed and location surveys which are carried out in phases.
(ii) Information collection such as climatic data, hydrologic data, geological and foundation data, agricultural land and crop data and data regarding power level, flood damage, wild life, forestry, sewage and industrial waste and likelihood of pollution and recreational facilities.
(iii) Selection of Type and Design of dams (Fig. 5.4)

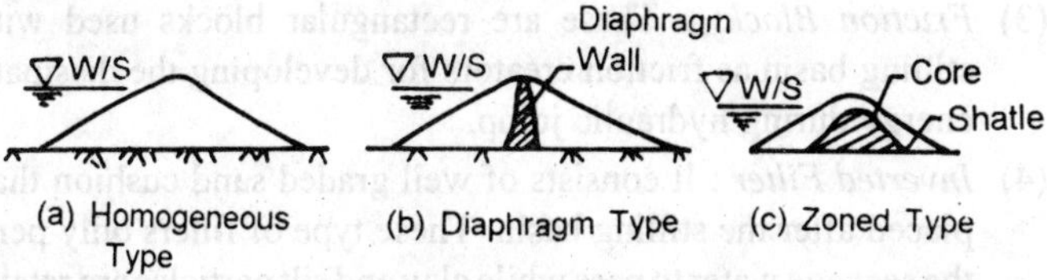

Fig. 5.4 : Types of earth fill dams

Diversion Works

The diversion or head works are related with the flow characteristics of a river and the stages through which it passes. These depend upon terrain topography and flow characteristics. The path of river can be depicted as follows :

The dams are always planned and constructed in mountaneous zone of river path, the different weirs/barrages/earth and rock fill dams are made in boulder or tough path as well as in the plain path of river. The respective reason for this is availability of natural barriers for storing water, easy availability of working material and proximity of the weirs to nearby agricultural lands. These water diversion structures carry the water to the desired destinations after completing the anticipated works such as irrigation through canals or conduits, generation of power, navigation, municipal and industrial uses, ground water storage. The storage capacity of these structures is also small and these function on the principle of gravity which is attained by raising the water level upstream.

Components of Weir

Weirs and barrages which are low height dams, have different components or parts namely :

(1) *Sheet Piles* : These are underground cutoff walls made of mild steel piles having on N type or ~ type cross section, driven on plumb by special types of hammers (vibro type) so that the interlocks (*i.e.* the joints in between two consecutive piles) are water sealed against leakage. Their main function is to protect the foundation and reduce seepage from it.

(2) *Stilling Basin* (*Energy Dissipator*) : These help to dissipate the excessive kinetic energy of flow due to sudden fall in the water level caused during the waterfalls allowed through weir gates

from the maximum water level upstream to the tail water level downstream.

(3) *Friction Blocks* : These are rectangular blocks used within stilling basin as friction creators for developing the dissipation energy during hydraulic jump.

(4) *Inverted Filter* : It consists of well graded sand cushion that is placed after the stilling basin. These type of filters only permit the seepage water to pass while clay and silt particles are retained back.

(5) *Masonry Block and Boulder Protection (Flexible Apron)* : This work is done to prevent any erosion of canal or river bed by high volume of flood water having some energy left after it has been carried through stilling basin. This help in the protection of the foundation immediately below the weir.

(6) *Vertical Gates* : These are mild steel gates fitted in the weir to resist the water pressure and can be operated both electrically and manually.

(7) *Counter Weights* : These are put to reduce the self weight of the gates so as to easily lift them through pulley action. Any material such as sand, gravels etc. may be filled in the boxes to act as counter weights.

(8) *Hoist* : It is an electric motor-driven winch for lifting the gates.

(9) *Gangway* : It is the bridge for the movement of the staff for operation and maintenance of gates.

(10) *Silt Excluder* : The silt or sediments deposited near the head regulator bay is retained back by a number of submerged box-culvert type tunnels called silt excluder which end at the sluice gates when water is released which comes out with high velocity through tunnels before it is released in the canals.

(11) *Fish Ladder* : A passage made for migratory fishes for convenient movement either upstream or downstream by manipulating the flow velocity favourable for moving fishes through a ladder is called fish ladder.

(12) *Head Regulator* : It is the device constructed at head of canal for the control of flow of water and sediments from the reservoir up to the main canal is called head regulator. These structural controls such as stop logs, trak rack (or screen) and gates are operated by means of hoists.

(13) *Scouring Sluices* : For scouring of silts and sands deposited near the head regulator the provision of gates is made which is called scouring sluices.

(14) *Divide Wall* : A masonry wall dividing the river into the weir bay (two ends of source) and the scouring sluices bay at the place from where canals offtake is called dividing wall. These are used for fish ladders and logchutes. If suitably designed the wall detracts the flowing sediments from the head regulator.

(15) *Afflux Bundhs* : The difference between the maximum reservoir level upstream and corresponding high level of flood at downstream is called afflux. The earthen embankments protected with stone pitching are made on the upstream of the weir at the level and elongated up to the length to which water would be ponded by a weir is called bundhs. The embankment looking after the anticipated afflux is called afflux bundh. This guide the river to flow through weir bays.

(16) *Logways* : A long passage made for easy movement of wooden logs through the barrage carried by upstream to downstream is called logway.

(17) *Navigation Lock* : The flow velocity braking structures to monitor the kinetic energy of flowing water in the river so that they may be used for navigation purposes are called navigation locks. These are special chambers controlled by gates on either side of the lock chamber which facilitate movement of boats and steamers to pass from the upstream of the weir to downstream side or *vice versa.*

REGULATING AND CROSS DRAINAGE STRUCTURES

The lowering down of the flowing water surfaces in order to check the excessive running of the canal in filling a balance has to be maintained in cutting and filling section. This is controlled by regulating and cross drainage structures at locations where canal falls or drops are decided (Fig. 5.5). The depth of drops may vary from a few centimetres to as high as 5 metres as per terrain topography and the job requirements such as generation of hydropower through propeller type tubular turbines.

The fall structures are combined with communication bridges and regulators. Also offtake and branches and distributaries are made upstream of a fall for efficient use of high level water and to bring more area under irrigation. The fall site should be choosen where down below the hard and impervious ground is available to have less wastage of water and cut down the cost of structure.

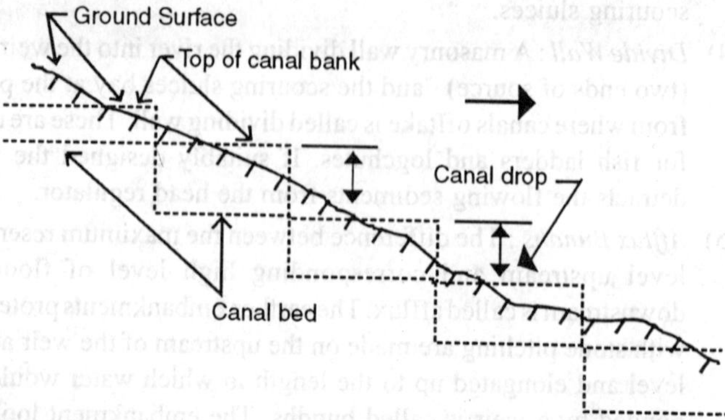

Fig. 5.5 : Canal Drops

Type of Falls

The various types of falls classified are :

(1) Sarda project type falls (U.P) and C.D.O. type falls (U.P.).

(2) Montagu (inventor name) falls which have its glacis shapes as half gravity parabola.

(3) Measurement falls such as rectangular notch, trapezoidal notch, standing wave flume type, curved glacis type, straight inclined glacis type, ostep type, ogee type, pipe type, well type, flumed type (laterally made), proportional type for storage discharge and Baffle type etc. The choice of fall depends upon discharge or maximum flow rate over the fall and height of fall to be provided.

(i) *Energy Dissipation* : The excessive kinetic energy of flowing water is dissipated by striking it against various medias such as friction through rough surfaces, through hydraulic jump impact, air entrainment, trapped eddies, through wiremesh or grids of brick or concrete to generate more turbulence. This mechanism reduce erosion hazard likely to occur through briskly flowing water falling from high elevation. The dimensions of energy dissipators and the appurchute and basin blocks tenances calculated from standard charts and curves.

(ii) *Crest Level* : This is made to balance the FSL which may take care excess water flowing above FSL. However, if it is made very high the water level in upstream would rise above

FS level and cause breaching of canal while if too low crest is made it would result in draw down (or lowering of water below FSL).

(iii) *Fluming* : The construction of canal laterally at the fall is called fluming. It is done to reduce cost of construction of a canal fall, regulating structure (*e.g.* gates) and the bridges (may be combined with fall).

(iv) *Transition* : In case of a flumed fall one set of transition consisting of two wings would connect to trapezoidal section of the canal with flumed section or throat. It is called contracting transition as it contracts flow. Similarly another set of transition is put downstream. This set connects the throat with the normal canal section. This set is called expanding transitions as it causes expansion of flow.

(v) *Uplift and Exist Gradient* : A failure of canal fall due to uplift and exist gradient conditions may be avoided by providing cuttoff on the upstream and downstream side, through adequate floor length, by inverted filter at the downstream end after expanding transition.

(vi) *Scour in the Canal Bed and Bank* : The scouring or erosional damage of canal bed and banks in spite of provision of crest and dissipation arrangement is avoided providing by two sets of cut off walls at the two extreme ends of the apron. Flexible stone pitching of bed and banks is also made to avoid scouring.

(vii) *Flow Metering* : For measuring of flow in the canal falls flumes can be employed. The discharge over the fall is given by equation

$$Q = Cd\, L_{eff}\, H^{3/2}$$

Where Q = full supply discharge in cumecs.

Cd = coefficient of discharge as found by current metre

Leff = effective length of the crest total length of water way (after deducting end contractions)

H = height between crest and FSL.

Considering flow through trapozoidal section as sum of the flow passing through rectangular (Q_1) plus triangular the total discharge (Q_2) can be found out. (See standard books on topic).

Coefficients of discharge are applicable only when the flow is free. For submerged flow, the Cd́ values will be reduced. Cd́ values are non-dimensional. The value of Cd́ (= Cd́ $\sqrt{g}$) are in meters and are to be used when Q is in cumecs and Leff is in metres.

$$Q = Cd\acute{}\sqrt{g}\ Leff\ H^{3/2} = Cd\ Leff\ H^{3/2}$$

Note : Flow over a Weir/Flume is free as long as the submergence (h_2/h_1) is less than the values of submergence limits given or less than one.

The calculation of Q_1 and Q_2 are given by formulae :

$$Q_1 = \frac{2}{3}\ Cd_1 \sqrt{2g}\ BoH^{3/2}$$

$$Q_2 = \frac{8}{15}\ Cd_2 \sqrt{2g}\ H^{5/2} \tan\theta$$

Discharge per notch,

$$Q = Q_1 + Q_2 = \frac{2}{3}\ \sqrt{2g}\ (BoH^{3/2} + \frac{4}{5}\ H^{5/2} \tan\theta)$$

Assuming $C \simeq Cd_1 \simeq Cd_2$

If Cd_1, Cd_2 C and 'n' number of notches are given — The total discharge will be n Q, the value of C varies between 0.6-0.65 depending on head.

(viii) *Proportionality* : Flume type or trapezoidal notch type falls are constructed so that normal depth at two different flows can be maintained in canal if silting does not occur. These are classified as proportional type falls cross drainage structures.

The canal run length has to cross many natural nalla or drains, rivulets, different streams, valleys and public works such as roads, railways etc. before it ceases to function. This long length at different obstruction points has to be provided with some structure to maintain canal length and flow. These bypass structures are called cross drainage structures.

The cross drainage structures are also constructed for disposing the natural run off from those areas which are intercepted by the canal. The cross drainage structures work just like culverts underneath disposing the accumulated runoff near the highway road embankment. Similarly the canal passes upwards and underneath the runoff way is constructed. However, it is tried to minimise the number of such works or by changing the alignment of canal or by providing the diversion of drains.

Structure Types

The different type of cross drainage structures and their functions are discussed below :

Aqueduct : This type of structure is constructed to pass runoff water etc. underneath canal section particularly when the highest level of runoff flood remains sufficiently below the canal bed of the running section passing above such drainage catching area. According to size of such areas the structure is designed. Thus if there are small drainage channel to be bypassed by canal the provision of pipe or masonry barrel below the canal bed and bank would serve the purpose for disposal of runoff. In case there is a river or very big nalla or drain it is a general practice to flume the canal and pass it over the river through a wooden or concrete trough. In case canal capacity is small the appropriate diameter pipeline be installed over the area to bypass the drain etc.

Super Passage : This condition is just reverse of the aqueduct in which canal section runs below the natural drain *i.e.* the runoff water has to be passed over the canal section, such construction arrangement is called super passage.

Inverted Syphon Aqueduct : In case the bed level of canal and that of drain happens to be at the same level such that aqueduct or super passage becomes meaningless, then the passage provided to canal water is called inverted syphon aqueduct. This is done by constructing a drain beneath the canal or putting a RCC box type barrel used for such purpose is usually 70 cm or more.

Inverted Syphon : In conditions if sometimes essential in view of levels of a terrain that canal has to be taken through an inverted syphon barrel below the drain, structure made is named as inverted syphon or canal syphon. The choice of construction regarding a syphon or syphon aqueduct depends upon the relative size of the drain and canal and also the relative levels. Syphoning a large sized drain/river/canal below its natural bed level is difficult.

Level Crossing : There may be such situations when the level of canal and drain may be nearly same and either of these possess water for only small period in a year, then drain and canal may be made so as to cross each other alike the crossing of rail track and road.

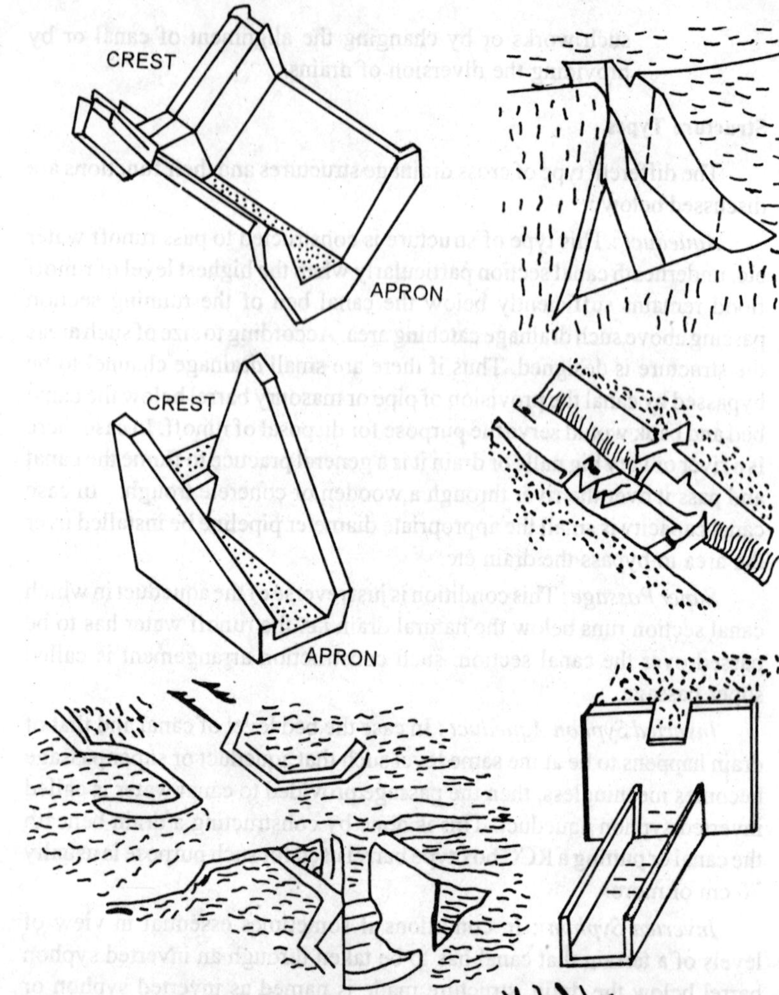

Fig. 5.6 : Drop Structures for Small Channels

The passage of drain through canal is provided with shutter gates (regulators) while the same arrangement is made in the bed of drain for canal passage. The drain regulators are generally kept closed while canal regulators are open. As per need and urgency the canal and drain regulators are used.

Inlets and Outlets : In areas where runoff intensity is generally very high and polluted, the run off is intercepted by a drain constructed parallel to canal and then letting this discharge to mix with canal water at specific points through inlets provided by energy dissipators and silt excluders. The increase in canal FSL due to high run off is likely to breach the canal. This possibility is avoided by canal outlets or escapes at fixed points which are constructed near to cross drainage structure such that extra water released from such canal is disposed off to the drain.

It is sometimes less costly to release canal in a natural stream, river or pond at one end and take it out from other end through separate head work. This helps in crossing as well the water of these resources are also utilised. For such arrangement generally a weir is constructed across the stream and through regulators the inlet and outlet of such system is monitored.

Failure Causes of Cross Drainage Structures

Any failureness of a cross drainage structure results in defunct of the canal system. The plausible reasons are discussed under :

(i) *Insufficient Water Way for the Run off Water* : In case the discharge capacity of any drainage network is insufficient to cater the needs of runoff in the area it will overtopple canal banks due to considerable afflux which causes breaching of the canal.

(ii) *Poor Construction* : In case any part of the constructed structure is made through non-genuine materials or the overhead concrete flume in case of aqueduct which collapse on account of bending, shear or bonding due to poor design of bottom floor, improper calculation of lateral thrust, and traffic loads the entire constructed structure fails. Similarly in case of syphon aqueduct when canal is not running as well as dry the internal pressure develops in the barrel which may burst it. Whereas in case the drain is empty and dry the vertical pressure as well as lateral earth pressure acts upon owing to overburdening and surcharge which may also lead to the barrel damage.

(iii) *Poor Foundation* : The thickness of foundation should be kept sufficient enough whenever cross drainage structures are constructed.

Thus piers and abutments in case of aqueduct should be quite strong and extended beyond the maximum possible depth of scour. The design criteria for abutment should take of the uplift pressure developing from seepage from the canal in addition to the usual earth pressure and hydrostatic thrust similarly while constructing inverted syphon aqueduct the uplift pressure owing to raised water table above the foundation should be considered in design lest it causes failure of the foundation. In such cases the barrel is either anchored to the foundation or foundation thickness is proportionately increased.

(iv) *Poorly Designed Transition* : It has been previously described that in view of economy the drains are flumed. This results in severe erosion and failure of the section of canal and drains unless properly and scientifically designed transitions are not used. The poorly designed transitions causes high head loss thereby afflux separation and are one side flow concentration causing erosion of bed and banks.

(v) *Scouring of Bed and Banks* : If uncontrolled flow of the flood is not properly checked and diverted it causes scouring of bed and banks. The different cross drainage structures should therefore be such as to avoid such situations. For example syphon aqueduct is protected with a cut off and pitching of the floor both at the upstream and downstream ends to safeguard the barrels. Thus in case of aqueduct the two ends are susceptible to procuring due to heavy filling and by putting masonry blocks and stone pitching along with cut offs at the end of the apron would safeguard the bed and banks from scouring.

(vi) *Leakage and Piping* : In case the joints provided for facilitating expansion of adjoining structures gets leaked the structure fails. The care should therefore be taken to seal all kinds of leakage by use of water sealents such as mixture of bitumen, sand and cement with jute or other fibrous materials. If piping or water creeping is a danger to structure the provision of ribs cut offs be made immediately.

(vii) *Supervision Negligence* : The strict supervision if maintained during the use of materials tested by quality control laboratories and inspected by site incharge along with derived specifications for filling concreting, curing, jointing can save the work failureness. Similarly negligence in planning, design and construction without considering all relevant factors such as natural forces due to thermal effect, wind, earthquake along with loading from flowing water may result in gross failure of high cost invested works.

Head Regulators and Cross Regulators

The water application to field varies with time and therefore, to monitor the required quantity to be released through canal needs regulating structures. The regulators provided at the offtaking points of any canal is called its head regulator all main, distributary and minor canals which are branched to distribute water to various directions are therefore provided with regulators to pass into them the required quantity of water in such a way so as to avoid low flow wastage of water either through seepage or evaporation or both. This is possible through upstream and downstream cross regulators which divert the flow into field channels.

The head and cross regulators also simultaneously control the flow of sediments passing into the canal as well as with their help the repair and maintenance of canals becomes feasible. The measurments of flow by providing suitable flume such as reprogal or other can also be made by provision of said regulators. In case of short storage of water when normal FSL cannot be maintained in canals, the regulators by suitable adjustment of opening helps to maintain water at any level of FSL as required. In this way the canal outlets which are provided at higher elevation of canal bed can get suitable quantity of water or as per their share and thus may not remain dry when limited water flows in a canal at the normal depth. The regulators are combined with bridges and falls at suitable locations to economise the construction cost.

Canal Escapes

The flow in canals sometimes gets much above the designed FSL and crest which can cause overtopping, outbanking and breaching of canals. To avoid such possibilities the provision of safety valves also called escapes is made within canal at certain locations. The escapes may serve any one or all of the following objectives :

(1) To protect the canal from any unknown situations which may cause damage.

(2) To empty the canal at particular sections for repair and maintenance.

(3) To remove the deposited sediments at any location.

To face the various problems which have occurred in past or anticipated, a particular escape of the following type may be provided during the canal construction :

(a) weir or surface escape and

(b) sluice escape.

The disposal of surface water from the canal is arranged by construction of surface escapes by either masonry or concrete work with or without crest shutters. The sluice escapes have arrangement of sluice gates which provide flush with the canal bed.

These escapes or scouring sluices workings as silt ejectors help to clean the deposited silt in the canal upstream as well as for emptying the canal for repair. These escapes are kept near to the natural drains. The silt which consist of fine and coarse fractions have to be cleaned fully otherwise the coarse fractions may damage the canal lining as well as chock the distributaries and laterals. These coarse fragments in power canals may totally damage the turbines and tunnels also. It is, therefore, essential to have extractors which are of following type :

(1) *Vane-type Extractor* : This is also called as vane diaphragm type silt extractor. This consists of a number of diaphragm walls made under the canal bed are constructed in curved form which end into the sluice gates. The accumulated coarse fractions by this method are drained out.

(2) *Vortex Tube-type Extractor* : This extractor is made of a number of tips circular tubes which have their top flush with the canal bed level and remove the accumulated silt through these tube elongated upto the sluice chambers as controlled by sluice gates operated as per requirement to flush the sediments into the drain.

IRRIGATION OUTLETS

These are the structures through which the flow of irrigation water from the distributaries or minors to the water courses or field channels can be controlled. In usual practice one outlet is provided for every 30 to 40 ha. of land to be irrigated. The location of outlet should be on the upstream of the fall and near the farm land such that water may flow due to gravity and losses due to percolation and evaporation may be minimum. The outlets are located at the head of the field channels excavated by farmers.

Essential Conditions for Outlets

The various requisites of the irrigation outlet may be following :

(1) An outlet should be static and strong.

(2) The interference of the farm should not be possible and, if so happens, can be easily detected.

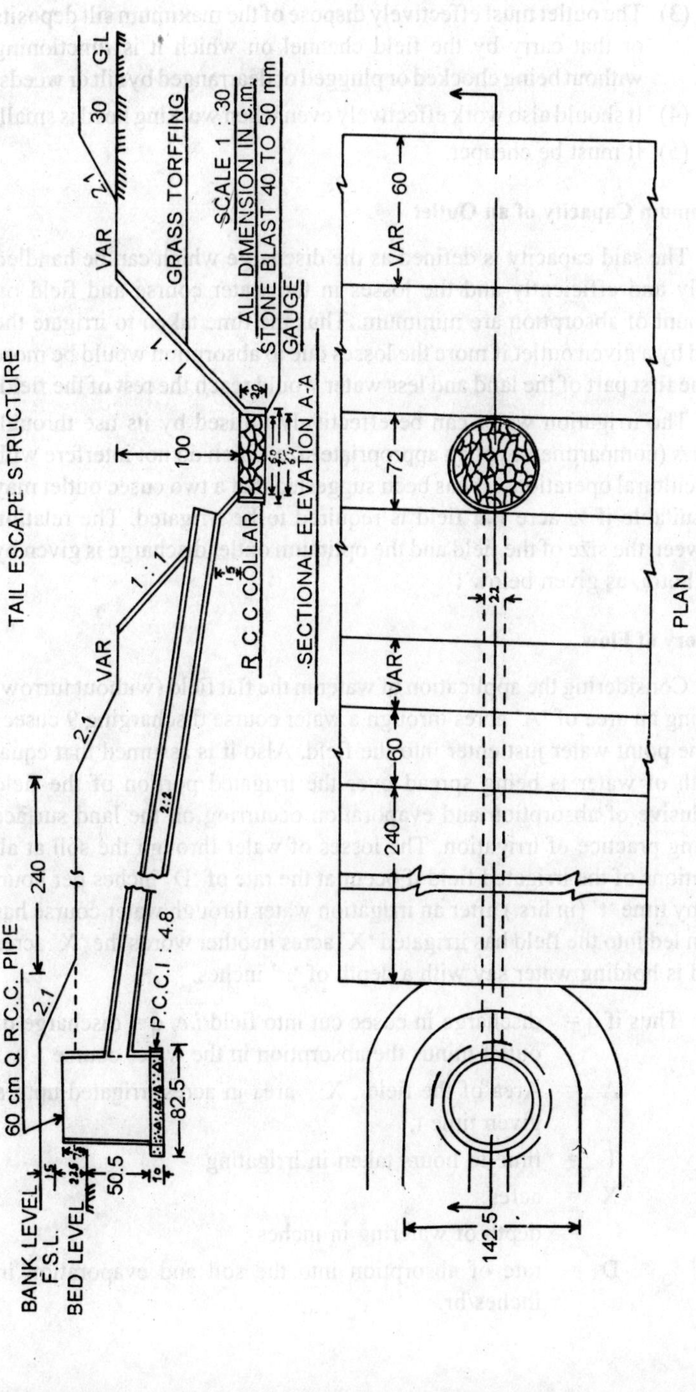

Fig 5.7 : Tail Escape Structure

(3) The outlet must effectively dispose of the maximum silt deposits or that carry by the field channel on which it is functioning without being chocked or plugged or dearranged by silt or weeds.
(4) It should also work effectively even when working head is small.
(5) It must be cheaper.

Optimum Capacity of an Outlet

The said capacity is defined as the discharge which can be handled easily and efficiently and the losses in the water course and field on account of absorption are minimum. Thus the time taken to irrigate the field by a given outlet if more the losses due to absorption would be more in the first part of the land and less water would reach the rest of the field.

The irrigation water can be effectively utilised by its use through *Kiaris* (compartments) of an appropriate size which do not interfere with agricultural operations. It has been suggested that a two cusec outlet may be suitable if ½ acre flat field is required to be irrigated. The relation between the size of the field and the optimum outlet discharge is given by Malhotra, as given below :

Theory of Flow

Considering the application of water in the flat field (without furrow) having an area of 'A' acres through a water course discharging 9 cusecs at the point water just enter into the field. Also it is assumed that equal depth of water is being spread over the irrigated portion of the field exclusive of absorption and evaporation occurring on the land surface during practice of irrigation. The losses of water through the soil at all locations of the irrigated field if occur at the rate of 'D' inches per hour, at any time 't' (in hrs.) after an irrigation water through water course has been led into the field has irrigated 'X' acres in other words the 'X' acres land is holding water say with a depth of '..' inches.

Thus if q_1 = discharge in cusec cut into field *i.e.* q = discharge of outlet minus the absorption in the water course

A = Area of the field., X = area in acres irrigated upto a given time t,

T = time in hours taken in irrigating

X = acres

= depth of watering in inches

D = rate of absorption into the soil and evaporation in inches/hr.

The volume of water entering the field in a subsequent small interval of time, dt hours is q_1 dt cusec-hours, or q_1 dt acre inches (one cusec hour = one acre inch). The quantity of water is being consumed in satisfying the absorption capacity of the soil over an area of 'X' acres at the intake rate of 'D' inches per hour. Also after irrigating entire 'X' acre area part of the applied water say also irrigated a very small area of dx acres ahead upto the same depth of inches then we have :

(i) The quantity of water used in absorption = DX dt acre inches.

(ii) The quantity of water used for irrigation = q_1 dt – DX dt

Hence $q_1 dt - DX\, dt = DX\, dt$

or $dt (q_1 - DX) = DX\, dt$

$$\therefore \quad \frac{dx}{q_1 - DX} = \frac{dt}{DX}$$

Integrating both sides, we have

$$\frac{dx}{q_1 - DX} \qquad \frac{dt}{DX}$$

or — $1/D \log (q_1 - DX) = 1/\ B$, where 'B' is a constant

when

$X = 0, t = 0$ and

when $X = A, t = T$

Therefore, $-1/D \log q_1 = B$

and $- 1/D \log (q_1 - DA) - T/ B$

Substracting

$$1/D \text{ long } (1 - \frac{DA}{q_1}) - T/$$

or

$$1 - \frac{DA}{q_1} - DT/$$

or

$$q_1 - DA\ (a - e^{-DT/D})^{-1}$$

This equation provides interaction of irrigation water discharge required in the field and the various factors such as field area, depth of watering, rate of evaporation and absorption into the soil and time needed to irrigate the field. It is thus obvious that to assess the discharge of the outlet the losses of water through absorption in the water course must be taken into consideration.

From the above equation it may be visualised that the term 'q' should not be less than 'DA' *i.e.* the quantity of water being discharged into the field through a water course should not fall short of the losses occurring through absorption over the entire field (or intake rate). Such a situation would stop the advancing of water front and it will never reach the destination *i.e.* end of the field or the anticipated distance to be travelled by it. Therefore, the optimum discharge being released should be fixed so that water front continuously and steadily advances ahead of the cut point of the water course and should stand at a minimum depth on the field. Suppose the such minimum depth is taken = 1 inch. The maximum area which is physically possible to irrigate by the discharge q_1 in one hour with D = 0.5 inch per hour is given from above equation and this will be A = 0.787 q_1

The maximum values of 'A' for different values of q_1 are given below :

q_1 (Cusecs)	(Maximum A) Acres
0.10	0.08
0.15	0.12
0.50	0.40
1.00	0.79
1.50	1.18
2.00	1.57
4.00	3.15

In case the area to be irrigated is ½ acre a minimum discharge of 0.64 cusec is essential. However, it has been experienced that the minimum discharge is not the economical concept. This may be understood if eq. given above is expanded in a series which is valid if DT is less than 2.

$$q_1 = DA \left[\frac{DT}{12} \quad \frac{DT^{2T2}}{2^2} \quad \frac{D^3T^3}{6^3} \right]^{-1} ....$$

From this equation if we assume D=0 then

$$q_1 = \frac{A}{T}$$

$$i.e.\ \text{Discharge} = \frac{\text{area} \times \text{depth}}{\text{time}}$$

In case the absorption or intake 'D' is small as compared with the discharge 'q' then

$$q_1 = \frac{A}{T} + \frac{DA}{2}$$

This equation explains that in addition to discharge which would be required to irrigate the given area up to the required soil depth in a fixed time more quantity of water would be needed which would be equal to the half of the absorption rate multiplied with area over which spreading has to be done (DA/2). In fact from the water course when water is released the water is first absorbed for whole time T before it goes ahead where at more distance the absorption is little. Half of the loss in the upper part of the field may be considered as an average for the whole field.

Influence of Field Shape

Although this parameter has not been included in the above equation but it does affect the irrigation velocity of the moving water. As we know the velocity of advancing front can be represented as follows with given discharge q_1 the velocity of advance water front

$V = \frac{q_1}{F}$ where F = sectional area of the water front. It indicates that if F the area of two rectangular fields is same but one has front is correspondingly decreased thereby covers shorter length of diagonal of the field.

Optimum Discharge for a Field

The discharge equation may be rewritten as follows :

$$1 - \frac{DA}{q_1} = e^{-DT/\Delta}$$

Taking logarithm of both sides we have

$$\log_e e^{\frac{DT}{\Delta}} = \log_e \left[1 - \frac{DA}{q_1} \right]$$

$$\text{or} \quad = \frac{\Delta}{DT} = \log_e \left[1 - \frac{DA}{q_1} \right]$$

$$\text{or } \log_e = \left[1 - \frac{DA}{q_1} \right] \quad X - \frac{\Delta}{D} = T$$

$$\text{or} \quad T = \frac{\Delta}{D} \log_e \left[1 - \frac{DA}{q_1}\right]$$

The values of water depth Δ and 'D' the infiltration or absorption rate of a particular field can be known, the substitution of their numerical values would reduce the equation with only notations of T.A. and q_1 from which different combinations of values of optimum discharge in respect of area of the field and time of irrigation of that field relationship can be worked out as per needs. (For details see examples on irrigation outlets at the end of this chapter.)

Various Types of Outlets

The types of outlets being used on any irrigation system has many considerations based on wide experience of field. The various factors kept in view for fixing an outlet are discussed below :

(1) **Location of an Outlet :** The criteria for fixing the outlet depends upon the land slope, contour positions of the field/fields to be irrigated and farmers' experience about the proper location to fully irrigate the command under the given outlet. The site of the outlet for each chak (area included in the irrigation boundary of an outlet) is fixed in respect of lie of the land in that chak. This position of outlet shall be at the highest point in the chak adjacent to the irrigation channel.

(2) **The Size of an Outlet :** This may be fixed as many criteria such as :

(a) *Based on Wet Land* : Some percentage of wet land (gross area, less unculturable area, less the area under well irrigation).

(b) *Based on Acreage (area to be irrigated)* : The pipe outlet of any appropriate diameter may be chosen which would supply irrigation to the entire area *e.g.* 6 inches diameter may be allowed for 100 acres of annual irrigation from the main distributary and for every 50 acres from the minor. The above difference in duties of the main distributary and the minor has been made for the following reasons :

(i) Minor would run only half the time while distributary would be in constant flow.

(ii) The less working head in minor as compared to distributary.

(iii) Water supply in the minor may be generally deficient on account of silt deposit at its head.

This above assumption that the duty of pipe or colaba (earthenware pipe fixed as outlet) on a minor would be half of that attained in distributary has wide acceptability. As we know the size of the water outlet is directly related to the area it has to irrigate. The working head of the outlet should also be taken into account for fixing such duties.

Based on the Capacity of an Outlet : The assumption based on hit and trial is made as to how much acres (A) would be irrigated by one cubic foot per second (cusec) per diem. From this turn (ward) of the outlet may be estimated as seven days. If the irrigation has to be provided for 'X' acres

then $D = \text{discharge} = \dfrac{X}{7 \times A}$

The area of the outlet (X) may be calculated from the formula

$$A \times 8.025 \sqrt{H} = D$$

where cd $= 0.62$

A $=$ Area of outlet

H $=$ head

Suppose one cubic foot (cusec) irrigates 6.8 acres (Kharif) per diem, head (H) = 0.5 ft. at full FSL. Hence gross area (X) under each outlet can be calculated. In general duty of one cusec varies from 250 to 450 acres in different systems.

Design of an Outlet : There is a general practice to put the outlets as one or more rows of pipes without collars inserted in banks without concrete, puddle or masonry work. These outlets are of the standard size 6 inches or 4.5 inch diameter or near to these as per needs of the particular area and its length to be irrigated. The following considerations are made :

(i) The mouth of outlet should be set back from the vertical plane passing through the junction of the bed and side slope. In practice the pipe may be set back 1, 1.5 and 2.0 feet depending upon the maximum depth of water in the channel varying from 3 feet between 3 to 4 feet and above 4 feet respectively.

(ii) The bottom of the pipe may be kept flush with the bed 0.5 foot and 1.0 foot above the bed of the distributary provided the top of the pipe exterior surface should never be above the natural surface. The position of outlet may also be shifted as per needs of area. The placing of outlets at bed level of the distributary so as to draw the maximum amount of silt has also been suggested but the controversy on this issue exists.

(iii) The use of modular and open flumes design outlets are now commonly used.

(iv) Other type outlets : The use of bend type, bell mouthed type, O.S.M. type, nozzle type, gibb's type are modular forms of outlets with certain modification in earlier one.

Flap Valves : In case when water is not required to be drawn from the outlets, these may be closed by cast iron or wooden lids of shutters which are called Flap valves. These arrangements save considerable amount of water. However, this practice has been now dropped because need of closure is now less required due to water shortage and cultivation of high water requirement crop varieties.

Tatiling (off days) : This term was used in connection with water supply which are used for the off days clearance of silt chocked outlets to get the fixed maximum discharge through these. In cases even when silt problem does not exist channel tatils are observed due to short water supply during winters distribution. However, now tatiling is used for distributaries in place of channels as used to be in earlier days which now is considered as sign of inefficient working of a system.

Remodelling of Outlets

The remodelling of outlets is necessary when the duty attained for each pipe outlet (colaba) vary appreciably on different outlets on the same channel as well as on different channels. The following considerations may be made in this regard :

(i) In such cases where the high duty attained is due to the very large head, the better way would be to change head correspondingly to needs without altering the size of pipe outlet which can be achieved either by relaying the pipes at more height from the bed or by constructing an uptake at the downstream end of the outlet.

(ii) In case the duty fixed for the outlet on a channel turns out to be high the fixed duty should be altered by keeping more frequent tatils (off days) without reducing the discharging capacity of the outlets.

(iii) In case permanent outlets are being built in the area the increased or decreased size pipe outlets may be fixed to have optimum head discharge and duty for the outlet.

Before fixing the outlet of a particular size, location as well as at certain height from canal bed the following considerations should be very clear in the mind of field engineer :

(1) The level of the floor or cell of the outlet with reference to the bed of the distributary channel and the natural surface outside.

(2) The position of the face of the outlet with respect of the line of the bank of the distributary.

(3) The height of the face and tail walls.

(4) The length of barrel of the outlet in the case of a road alongside the distributary and the method of carrying the road over the water course.

(5) The size of the barrel in relation to the correct size of the discharge orifice.

(6) The procedure for closing the orifice.

(7) The units of the discharging capacity of outlets.

(8) The use of clustered pipes or rectangular orifices.

(9) The need of construction of permanent outlets.

(10) The design of the face and rear walls of the outlets.

Selected Examples on Irrigation Outlets

Example 1 :

Suppose it is given that —

1. Depth of watering Δ = 2 inches
2. Rate of absorption loss into the field (D) = 1/2 inch per hour (for alluvial soils)
3. Time of irrigation of field T = 1 hour

From the equation $q_1 = \left[\frac{A}{T} + \frac{DA}{2} + \frac{D^2}{12} \times \frac{AT}{\Delta}\right]$

$q_1 = 3.257\ A$

If the area A is square of side 'b' ft then

$b^2 = 4840 \times 9 \times A$

or $b = 66\sqrt{10A} = 66\sqrt{3.070 q_1}$

$= 115.6\sqrt{q_1}$ or $116\sqrt{q_1}$ ft approx.

From this equation the value of A and field size for varying value of q_1 may be deduced as follows :

TABLE 5.4

q_1(cusec)	A (acres)	Field size in ft.	Remarks
0.10	0.03	36 × 36	Discharge from a
0.15	0.05	45 × 45	well worked by
0.50	0.15	81 × 81	persian wheel.
1.00	0.31	116 × 116	
1.50	0.46	143 × 143	
2.00	0.61	164 × 164	
4.00	1.23	232 × 232	

Example 2 :

Calculation of optimum discharge for a field for given values of area 'A' and discharge 'q' determine values of 'T' for irrigating a field given depth of watering (d) = 3 inches, D = 0.5 inch per hour.

Solution :

Take following equation to arrive at solution

$$T = \frac{\Delta}{D} \log_e \left[\frac{1 - DA}{q_1}\right]$$

Substituting values of Δ and D we have

$$T = \frac{-3}{0.5} \log_e \left[\frac{1 - 0.5A}{q_1}\right]$$

$$= -6 \log_e \left[\frac{1 - A}{2q}\right]$$

This equation has three unknown terms namely T, A and q_1. If values of two are given that of third can be found out. Assume the different values of q_1 (cusec) and A (area in acres), say q_1 = 0.15, 0.50, 1.00, 2.00 and A = 0.25, 0.50, 1.00 and 2.00 acres. The time T for each values may be tabulated as given in table 5.5.

TABLE 5.5

q_1	Area in acres			
	0.25	0.50	1.00	2.00
	Time in hours			
0.15	10.74	N*	N	N
0.50	1.73	4.15	N	N
1.00	0.80	1.73	4.15	N
2.00	0.39	0.80	1.73	4.15

N* —It means entire area of the field cannot be irrigated by the given discharge.

The following inferences may be drawn from above tabulated results.

Inferences

1. That for the same discharge, as area of the field increases, the time of irrigation increases proportionately more than the area. It is obvious from table that discharge of 2 cusecs from an outlet irrigates 0.25 acres in 0.39 hours while one acre (four times of 0.25 acres) is being irrigated in 1.73 hours which is thus much more than four times (about 11% more to total time) the time taken for 0.25 acres time *i.e.* 0.39 hrs ($0.4 \times 0.39 = 1.56$ hrs against 1.73 hrs).

2. The fields having same area if receive higher discharge allowed through water course would reduce the time of watering as well as reduce the time proportionately which would be more than the increase in discharge allowed. However, after a certain stage the reduction is not worth consideration. The said stage may be considered at value given by A = q¼. This may by clear if we consider following, say —

(a) the 3 inches of water is passed for irrigation.
(b) The absorption loss = 1/2 inch per hour.

Hence to achieve uniform distribution of water in the field, the discharge (cusecs) in the field to be allowed should be four times the area of the field in acres ($q_1 = 4A$).

3. If the losses due to absorption amount to 25 per cent of the discharge allowed (q_1), the quantity of discharge to be released would be

$$q_1 + \frac{q_1}{4} = \frac{5q_1}{4} = \frac{5 \times 4A}{4} = 5A$$

$$[\because q_1 = 4A];$$

i.e. five times of the area of the field in acres.

4. The optimum ratio between the discharge of an outlet and the field size can be worked out for different conditions in practice since the time of watering 'T' is proportional to the depth of watering. If the depth of watering is 6 inches, the time of watering for their depth (6") will be just doubled. Since there is no relative difference in the value of T, the optimum ratio of water course discharge to the area of field will remain the same as before.

5. This may also be seen from the statement that the value of time T for equal values of q_1/A are the same. In the above example where time of watering was found to be 1.73 hrs. for all the three following cases :

$$A = 0.25;\ q_1 = 0.50$$
$$A = 0.50;\ q_1 = 1.00$$
$$A = 1.00;\ q_1 = 2.00$$

If values of q_1/A are tabulated with different rates of absorption while depth of watering is kept 3 inches, the time 'T' in hours required can be calculated as given in Table 5.6.

TABLE 5.6

q_1/A	Absorption/Infiltration rate (D)		
	D = 0.3	D = 0.5	D = 0.7
	Time (hours)		
0.5	9.16	N	N
0.6	6.93	10.75	N
0.8	4.70	5.89	8.91
1.0	3.57	4.16	5.16
1.5	2.23	2.43	2.69
2.0	1.63	1.73	1.85
2.5	1.28	1.34	1.41
3.0	1.05	1.09	1.14
4.0	0.78	0.80	0.82
5.0	0.62	0.63	0.65
6.0	0.51	0.52	0.53
7.0	0.44	0.44	0.45
8.0	0.38	0.39	0.39

It is obvious from above tabulated data of Table 5.6 that if value of q_1/A exceeds 4.0 *i.e.* upto 8.0 the values of absorption at different rates *i.e.* 0.3 or 0.5 or 0.7 does not change appreciably. This infers that the time taken for irrigating the field is not affected much by the rate of absorption.

6. The volume of irrigation water needed per acre of the field can be

calculated by the values of the product of T q_l/A. Thus volume of irrigation water/acre = T × q_l/A.

The Table already given between different value of q_l/A and rate of absorption may also be tabulated in relation to the volume of water needed per acre (Table 5.7).

This Table infers that volume of water required for irrigation is not decreased much if q_l/A is increased after a certain value or stage. This value or stage for different ranges of infiltration/absorption rate (D) are given below :

D	q_l/A
0.3	3.0-4.0
0.5	4.0-5.0
0.7	6.0-7.0

TABLE 5.7

q_l/A	Absorption / Infiltration rate (D) D = 0.3	D = 0.5	D = 0.7
	Volume (acre inches)		
0.5	4.58	N	N
0.6	4.16	6.45	N
0.8	3.76	4.71	7.13
1.0	3.57	4.16	5.16
1.5	3.34	3.64	4.04
2.0	3.26	3.46	3.70
2.5	3.20	3.34	3.52
3.0	3.15	3.27	3.42
4.0	3.12	3.20	3.28
5.0	3.10	3.15	3.25
6.0	3.06	3.12	3.18
7.0	3.08	3.08	3.15
8.0	3.04	3.12	3.12

This indicates that if the soil porosity increases and the higher is the absorption rate, the quantity of water needed irrigation would be correspondingly high. The optimum value of q_l/A for different soil conditions *i.e.* textures or types or series can be fixed from the table and adjustment of q_l and A can be done accordingly.

PRINCIPAL SOURCES OF IRRIGATION WATER

The principal source of irrigation water varies from country to country. In India it is the natural precipitation or rainfall which constitutes the main source of water being conserved or flown into rivers. The sources conserving this are ground reservoirs, natural lakes and ponds and artificial reservoirs constructed to collect the runoff or river water for irrigation and other purposes. It is computed that the average intensity of irrigation in India does not exceed 30% which means that still 70% land is being cultivated by the natural rainfall. Thus major factor of our agricultural economy still rest on the balanced rainfall conditions. If it is uniformly distributed over a crop growing period and just meets the crop requirements by proper absorption of soil reservoir the crop production is good otherwise damage of crops either due to drought or water logging or flood results. The successful implementation of minor and medium irrigation projects also depends upon the average rainfall in the catchment area.

The other source of water is snowmelt which contributes substantial quantum of water especially during summers.

HYDROLOGY

It is the science which is related to the process of rainfall and runoff, snowfall and snowmelt, ground water, oceanography etc. The knowledge of this science helps to exploit the surface and sub-surface water resources judiciously as well as to understand the measures of control and abatement of flood damage.

Hydrologic Cycle

The hydrologic cycle governs the interrelation between rainfall, surface and sub-surface flows, storage, evaporation and transpiration. The natural ecological balance is maintained through this cycle. The cycle starts from atmospheric vapour to its condensation and precipitation. The part of precipitation infiltrates into the ground and that is not absorbed flows as runoff and joins streams, lakes and ponds. This is given by rainfall flow diagram.

The excessive water flowing into streams and accumulated in ground is finally discharged into the oceans. The ponding water in various reservoirs gets evaporated back to the atmosphere. The water transpired from the plants also goes to the atmosphere through gaseous form and in this way hydrologic cycle is completed.

Forms of Precipitation : The precipitation in a hydrologic cycle comes to the earth surface in number of ways *viz.* rainfall, snowfall, ice-storm drizzle, dew etc. The rainfall is most common form of precipitation in tropical countries.

Rainfall Characteristics

There are different characteristics of rainfall which becomes ultimately source of irrigation and gets connected to hydrology of surface waters.

Mean Rainfall : The mean rainfall has been divided into two main parts *viz.* (1) time mean, and (2) areal mean. The time mean is defined as the average of parameters computed for a certain period of time. In this way we get mean annual or mean monthly or mean daily and hourly mean which are used in many calculations. Thus in case of crop against probable drought the mean annual rainfall while for the design of storm sewer in a city, the values of hourly mean are used. The areal mean rainfall represents the average rainfall over a certain area or location in a certain quantity at a certain period.

Intensity of Rainfall : It provides the values of quantity of rainfall over unit time and is expressed as cm/hour. If the time lapsed (hr.) is plotted against cumulative rainfall (cm.) the curve thus drawn indicates the intensity of rainfall. These data are useful in flood and runoff computation.

Duration and Frequency of Rainfall : The duration of rainfall represents the time period of the water storm in which rainfall takes place. The time interval between the two consecutive water storms resulting in rain is termed as frequency of rainfall. These two parameters decide the irrigation requirement and extent of runoff.

Intensity Duration-Frequency Relation : Many times it has been observed that short term storms precipitate more intense rains than those of long terms. If a graph is plotted between duration or terms (hrs.) *vs.* intensity (cm/hr) in descending order of years this inter-relationship indicates relation between intensity duration and frequency of rainfall. Thus rainfall frequency of 1 in 1 year is higher than 1 in 10 years.

Depth of rainfall is given by equation :

Depth = mean intensity × duration (cms.).

Rainfall Measurement : The various years rainfall data are very important for successful operation of any irrigation project. Besides this prediction about flood, drought, irrigation requirement, recharge of ground waters are also interpreted from long term rainfall data.

The rainfall measurement is made with two types of gauges namely (a) non-recording type (Simon's gauge) and (b) recording type (continuous gauges). The former does not give any idea about the duration of the storm and intensity of rainfall except depth of rainfall (mm) in the last 24 hours. The recording type gauges are of three types *viz.* (i) tipping bucket, (ii) syphonic type (or floating type) and (iii) weighing type.

Measurement of Areal Mean Rainfall : There are different methods as given below :

(i) arithmatic mean, (ii) Theissen Polygon, (iii) Isohyetal method, (iv) Station weight method.

Rainfall-Runoff Relation : The runoff forms the part of the rainfall and is expressed as the depth of water over the basin. This depth of runoff is the ratio of the total volume of the stream flow from a water storm to the area of the basin. Mathematically,

$$R = P - \Sigma \text{ loss}$$

where R = Runoff, P = Total rainfall and Σ losses = the sum of various losses such as (i) evaporation and evapotranspiration, (ii) infiltration, (iii) interception by trees etc. and (iv) by surface storage in natural and man-made reservoirs.

GROUND WATER AND THEIR HYDROLOGY

The source of this water is the fraction of the rainfall infiltered into the ground through hydrologic cycle into deeper layers. The water passing from canals, reservoirs, ponds and lakes at higher elevations and altitudes deep into the ground also contributes to ground water reservoir.

Benefits of Ground Water

The ground water is collected after series of infiltrations through various earth top layers before reaching a permeable layer and as such it is extremely good to excellent quality except when it passes through a saline strata and if turns to bad quality. As such normally this water is suitable for all types uses. The underground water can be used by artificial lifting it from the ground through pumps or other suitable devices or by construction of artificial, underground cut-offs to raise the water table which reduce the pumping head. Where water in underground exists in artesian condition the water bearing strata if perched, the water comes up by natural hydrostatic pressure head. The use of underground water has many advantages over surface irrigation such as flexibility of use, at any required time for a required time and can attain a higher irrigation efficiency 80 to 90% as compared to surface (15 to 20%).

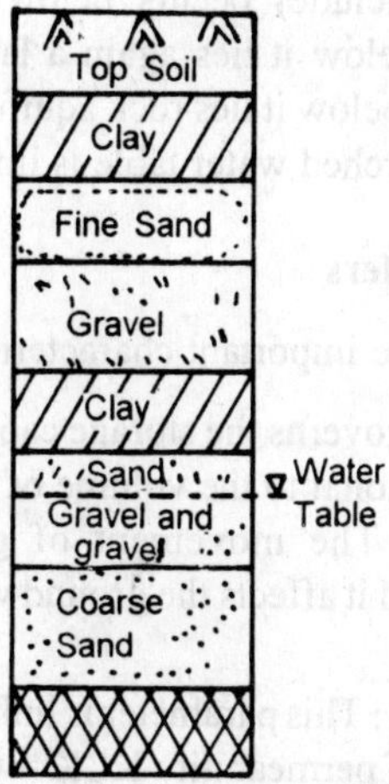

Fig. 5.8 : A Typical Well Log

DIFFERENT FORMS OF GROUND WATER

The different forms in which ground water may exist are :

(i) Soil moisture (up to rootzone depth).

(ii) Intermediate zone (below rootzone).

(iii) Capillary fringe (semi-saturated zone above the water table).

Aquifers

These are of two types : (i) unconfined, and (ii) confined.

The all water that is stored below the free water of saturation (water table) is called ground water. Aquifers are permeable rock mass strata reserving the water. The saturated loose mass deposits of sand and gravel lying below the water table are termed as unconfined aquifers. The first layer of sand and gravel below water table but above clay is called aquiclude is also an unconfined aquifer.

The deposition of pervious stratum of sand and gravel confined between two relatively impervious strata of aquiclude (clay) or between the aquiclude and aquifuge (rock) having storage of water under pressure are called confined aquifers. These aquifers depending upon the thickness and their areal extent store abundant amount of water which can be withdrawn for various purposes.

The local deposits of an aquiclude in some areas may create perched water table conditions. In old alluvium plain *i.e.* buried pedi-plain the deposition of clay (aquiclude) occurs below sand and gravel layer (unconfined aquifer). Below it lies again a layer of sand (and gravel (confined aquifer) while below it lies rock aquifuge. However, the water table found below the perched water table is limited.

Characteristics of Aquifers

The following are the important characteristics of the aquifer :

(1) *Porosity* : This governs the storage capacity of an aquifer and is directly proportional to the volume of water it will hold.

(2) *Permeability* : The movement of ground water is called permeability and it affects the ground water yield in a particular time period.

(3) *Transmissibility* : This parameter is linked to permeability factor or coefficient of permeability KCK = Q/iA, where

Q = rate of flow

$i = \frac{h}{L}$ or hydraulic gradient, A = cross sectional area

h = head loss and L = given length.

The transmissibility (T) is given by equation T = KD, where D = depth of aquifer and it indicates the flow per unit width (of aquifer surface) at right angles to flow direction having hydraulic gradient as unit. Its units are cubic metre per minute per metre or square metres per minute.

Artesian and Sub-artesian Aquifers

Any confined aquifer is always under a pressure which is more than hydrostatic pressure prevailing in unconfined aquifers and as such possesses piezometric surface or pressure head. The greater the piezometric surface more the upward velocity of ground water which flows as tapping water on earth surface. Such aquifer condition is termed as artesian well.

Specific Yield : It is the ratio of the volume of water which can be drained by gravity to gross volume of the aquifer. Thus water yield can be estimated by multiplying the aquifer volume by the specific yield.

Specific Retention : It is the volume of the water retained in the total voids of aquifer after drained by gravity force. The total voids or porosity of an aquifer is equal to the sum of the specific yield and specific retention.

Storage Coefficient : In case of confined aquifers, it is expressed as the volume of water which can be stored or yielded per unit volume of the aquifer with a unit change in piezometric head normal to its surface. However, in case of unconfined aquifers the storage coefficient is equal to the specific yield. The properties of different types of aquifers is given in Table 5.8.

TABLE 5.8

Aquifer material	Porosity %	Specific yield %	Specific retention %	Permeability cm/sec
Clay	40-55	1-10	30-54	0.000001 (1×10)
Sand	35-40	10-30	5-30	0.01 to 0.005
Gravel	30-40	15-35	5-25	1.00 to or more
Sand and gravel	20-35	15-25	5-20	0.06 to 0.03
Sandstone	10-20	5-15	5-15	0.005 to 0.01
Limestone	1-10	0.5-5.0	0.5-4.0	..

EXPLORATION OF GROUND WATER

The economical aspects of use of ground water for the purpose of irrigation has to be studied in detail considering following factors :

(1) Water table depth.

(2) Type of aquifer (confined or unconfined).

(3) Aquifer thickness and areal distribution.

(4) Movement characteristics of ground water (flow direction and velocity).

(5) Different properties of aquifer materials *viz.*, texture, porosity, permeability, specific yield etc.

(6) Ground water quality and suitability.

Methods

The sub-surface exploration of ground water for its possible location is made in two ways, namely : (i) indirect methods, and (ii) direct methods. In former one of the following ways are adopted *viz.* geological mapping; aerial photography and remote sensing; resistivity technique seismic method and tracer technique. The direct methods include — Auger bore holes (upto 9 m to 12 mts), drilled holes made either by cable tool or percussion method or hydraulic rotary method.

Quality of Ground Water Test : This test is made for following characteristics : (i) physical *i.e.* for colour, odour, turbidity and taste,

(ii) chemical total hardness, dissolved solids, alkalinity, chlorides, fluoride, sulphates, nitrates, nitrites, iron, manganese and dissolved gases, and (iii) bacteriological *i.e.* to estimate the degree of pollution due to the presence of bacteria of different kinds.

Lifting Ground Water

The methods which have been employed for lifting the ground water are as under :

(i) *Open Wells* : It may be done manually or mechanically. These are of two types (a) dug type and (b) sunk type, depending upon depth of water table available near or away from the surface.

(ii) *Tube Wells* : These are wells in which strainer or screens are used to artificially obstruct the flow of sand and silt under increased draw-down head the fall in water level inside the well measured below table when water is being pumped out. These screens only pass out water and retain aquifer material which increase draw-down head and water yield. The tube wells may be shallow and deep depending upon the depth to which it is installed.

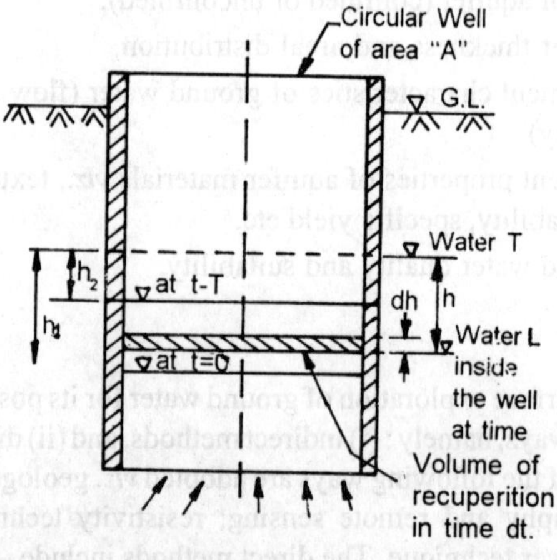

Fig. 5.9 : Recuperition test in an open well

Hydraulics of Ground Water Flow

This can be studied by Darcy's law according to which the velocity of flow (v) through an aquifer is directly proportional to the head loss (h) in a given length (L) and inversely proportional to length (L), mathematically it is expressed as :

$$V \propto \frac{h}{L} \text{ or } V = K\frac{h}{L} \text{ or } V = Ki;$$

where K is called the coefficient of permeability of the porous media and i (= h/L) is known as the hydraulic gradient.

If A is the cross-sectional area normal to the direction of flow, then the rate of flow (Q) through porous media would be expressed as :

$$Q = VA = KiA$$

Raynold's Number : Darcy's law holds good as stated above and is only applicable provided Raynold's number (Re) of flow remains usually below 2000 which is a critical limit. This number being non-dimensional is given by equation Re = Vd/v where d = diameter of porous media (depend upon texture) and V = Kinematic viscosity coefficient of water.

Steady Flow : In case water is withdrawn from an aquifer there is a reduction in water table near the well which develops cone of depression. If the aquifer has a unlimited volume of water stored in it which possesses some potential recharge the water yield may remain constant for a certain period of time. This constant water head where the cone of depression remains unchanged for a given yield is termed as steady flow.

Unsteady Flow : It has been generally observed that areal portion of most of the aquifers is not very large together with depth which on pumping causes variation in cone of depression for a given yield of the well. The continuous pumping from an aquifer will have increased cone of depression which causes greater draw-down that will result in unsteady flow.

Estimation of Yield

The reasonable amount of withdrawal of water (yield) of an open well depends on the permissible draw-down. This is calculated by difference between the water level inside the well at a steady state condition and that attained outside (h) draw-down head. The safe yield (Q) is given mathematically :

$$Q = Kh$$

where : 'h' is the draw-down head and K is the specific capacity of an open well having units as litres per minute per metre of draw-down or in cubic metres per second (cumecs) per metre of draw-down (difference of heads) *i.e.* m^3/sec.

The specific capacity is determined by Recuperation test given by equation :

dt = – Adh/kh. on integration between H_1 and h_2 and t=0, T = t

$$\int_o^T dt = \frac{-A}{K}\int_{h_1}^{h_2}\frac{dh}{h} \text{ or } K/A = 2.303 - \frac{A}{T}\log_{10}(h_1/h_2)$$

where T = time of recuperation in seconds, h_1 and h_2 in metres (the draw-down values before and after time T) and the area of section

$$(A = \frac{\pi}{4} \times D^2 \text{ where } D = \text{diameter of well}).$$

Yield of Tube-wells : The yield of tube-well for steady state flow in the well is the discharge 'Q' passing across any shell of height 'h' and wetted area A (=2 π rh) which must be the same as flow into the well. In other words under steady draw-down, the rate of inflow must be equal to the outflow. Mathematically it is given by Dupuit's eq. :

$$Q = VA = V \times (2\pi rh) = Ki\,(2\pi rh) = K\frac{dh}{dr} \times 2\pi rh$$

$$= Q = \frac{\pi K\,(h_1^2 - h_2^2)}{2.3\,(\log_{10}(Ri/rw))}$$

where rw = radius of the well pipe; Ri = radius of the base of the cone of influence given by volume of the aquifer contributing flow into the well and is contained in the volume lying between the piezometric surface and the water table h_1 = depth of water table, h_2 depth of water surface inside the well both measured from the bottom of the well.

Ground Water Budgeting

The ground water budgeting means the determination of total storage capacity, its utilisation and safe rate of withdrawal. In order to have effective management of ground water resource it is essential to measure annual input or addition of ground water in the basin and which is being withdrawn. The withdrawal less than annual input or recharge is called safe annual withdrawal or DRAFT.

The underground water reserve stock is influenced by following factors, *viz.* :

(1) Infiltration from rainfall

(2) Seepage from canals and reservoirs

(3) Sub-surface inflow into the given basin etc.

Withdrawals include :

(a) Evapotranspiration losses

(b) Yield of the wells and tube-wells

(c) Sub-surface outflow and leakage from the basin considered and also base flow to effluent streams, etc.

If the annual draft exceeds the annual recharge, it will result in lowering of the water table likewise an excess of recharge will lead to a rise in the ground water. The excess and lower table both are harmful to agricultural production because in former case water logging and other allied problems crop up while in the latter cost of pumping becomes very high. Thus proper budgeting of ground water is a proper management practice.

Artificial Recharge of Ground Water

In case there is an overdraft the depth of water table is maintained by carrying excess water from adjoining basins in the shape of link canals or recharging canals from diversion dams to the basin which recharges it. For this the spreading of water close on the ground surface is done which recharge low depth aquifers while for those lying deep the recharging is done through wells.

GROUND WATER TABLE BEHAVIOUR

The water added in excess of the crop requirement and soil capacity with various irrigation intensities, gets deposited in underground aquifers where the continuous recharge causes.

The rise in ground water table beyond a critical limit (usually 1.5 to 2 metre from the ground surface) is termed as water logging. The upper most fringe of the first saturated zone below the ground surface is defined as the sub-soil water table. The water of this zone is generally unconfined. This condition comes up on account of poor drainage and extensive surface irrigation practices. This condition of ground at surface creates high humidity, unhealthy climate which generates weed growth and enormous multiplication of insects, pests and mosquitoes, development of salinity and or alkalinity and many other disastrous conditions. The lands classification based on water table depth is given in Table 5.9.

TABLE 5.9

Showing Classification of Water Logging

Land classification	Depth of water table below ground surface
Good	Static water table below 2 m and upto 1.8 m for a maximum period of 30 days in a year
Fair	Static water table at 1.8 m and upto 1.2 m for a maximum period of 30 days in a year
Poor	Static water table at 1.2 m and upto 1.00 m for a maximum period of 30 days in a year
Bad	Static water table at less than 1 m depth

The basic cause of water logging is due to the excessive inflow recharge of water into soil (due to infiltration, seepage, sub-surface inflow etc.) into the ground water basin which in total volume is more than outflow of water (due to evapo-transpiration, ground water yields, sub-surface outflow) removed from the basin. This condition creates excessive storage resulting in static water table. If this storage is termed as 'S' then it can be expressed by equation

$$S = \Sigma \text{ inflow} - \Sigma \text{ outflow}.$$

Factors of High Inflow

The various factors responsible for excessive inflow are :

(1) *High Infiltration* : The area which gets high annual rainfall and are flat as well as having poor surface drainage gets more ground recharge.

(2) *Flooding* : The longer period spills from river banks infiltrate large quantity of water to ground.

(3) *Induced Seepage* : The constant seepage of water from different water resources acting as reservoirs causes large quantities of water to collect, in the ground. It is assumed that 40 to 50% of total volume of water diverted from the head works help to recharge ground water from unlined conveyance system carrying water.

(4) *Over-Irrigation* : The wrong method of irrigation and water application more than water holding capacity of soils and crops water requirements is called overirrigation and cause water logging.

(5) *Subsoil Flow* : The ground water recharge resulting due to irrigation or natural rainfall from the areas of higher elevations causes water logging in low lying areas.

Factors for Poor Outflow

The reasons for outflow are :

(a) *Poor or Insufficient Surface Drainage* : The natural drainage conditions of a particular area if cannot discharge the excess water from their catchment the outflow is said to poor and inadequate causing stagnation and water logging. Hence to have good water outflow, these should be properly cleaned and maintained.

(b) *Obstruction to Sub-Surface and Surface Outflow* : This may be due to geological obstruction like impervious clayey or rocky strata which does not allow excess water to pass from the area. Also artificial obstructions such as reservoirs, ponds, dams, deep foundations buildings, highways, flood and canal embankments etc. cause water logging.

(c) *Poor Topography* : Very flat areas having low lying depressions, inadequate land slope and impervious subsoil to lower depth (petrocalcichorzon) causes water logging.

CONJUNCTIVE USE OF SURFACE AND GROUND WATER

It has been generally noticed that the surface water is being largely consumed due to its excessive quantity, less cost of diversion and charging rates. This helps to recharge artificially the ground water storage basin and therefore increased water table. This may cause severe problems of water logging, salinity and/or alkalinity in command areas. This condition may be averted if the underground and surface irrigation waters are used in conjunction. It is advised that two-thirds of cultivable area should be irrigated with the use of surface irrigation water while one-third area with underground water in the same basin.

This would help to maintain balance between recharge and draft. This sharing of water depends upon :

(1) Extent of natural recharge
(2) Extent of artificial recharge
(3) Aquifer characteristics
(4) Surface water availability

(5) Fuel power availability

(6) Mobile repairing workshop facilities

(7) Economic and allied factors influence.

MERITS OF CONJUNCTIVE USE OF GROUND WATER

The use of underground water separately or along with canal irrigation water is called conjunctive use. It has many advantages as listed below :

(1) The underground water can be stored in higher volumes at low cost as compared to surface stored water and subsequent use through costly delivery and conveyance system to be provided for water application use and necessary disposal system to avoid soil losses and water logging etc.

(2) There is no risk of failureness of the system the chances of which might occur in surface storage dams built at huge cost investments.

(3) The underground water reserves serves as a big asset during any drought and if so it can be utilised to meet water requirements of crops which is not possible in minor and medium irrigation projects having small storage capacities.

(4) The well distributed well network in the area provides an efficient use of water due to self-sufficient and well-designed distribution system on each unit which is not feasible in canal system.

(5) The withdrawal of underground waters helps to control the rising water table a curse of surface irrigation storage system and thus acts an anti-water logging measure in canal irrigated areas.

(6) The removal of underground water especially in areas were drainage or disposal of excess water is not adequate resulting in the accumulation of harmful salts in the different depths of soil profile as well as at soil surface may be checked and leached below rootzone which provide favourable environment for plant growth.

(7) The infiltration rate of the soils is increased which averts the chances of flooding and other associated hazards.

(8) The enormous total period spent on the construction of a big storage capacity irrigation project and its distribution network and during this period the project remains idle as compared to the operation and execution of underground water use system, and

if harvested water is supplemented through a conjunctive use it can serve time of completion of project due to small size water storage and distribution network. This would also help to use underground water resource within a short period of time.

(9) The high evaporation losses occurring from a free and large surface area of surface irrigation are considerably reduced. At the same time a very small drainage network for control of rain storm, seepage would be needed to control surface runoff.

(10) The assured and equitable quantity of water as per crop water requirements can be managed for the farmers through effective water scheduling which is a major problem of many canal irrigation projects.

(11) A coordinated system of irrigation supply where both surface and sprinkler irrigation method is used can be put to use which effectively controls the use of irrigation water as per actual need of farmers. This helps in substantial saving of water.

(12) A substantial land holding occupied by bigger farmers, delivery, conveyance and disposal system can be saved by having smaller system in conjunction with underground system which can be put under cultivation.

DEMERITS OF CONJUNCTIVE USE OF GROUND WATER

Many arguments against the conjunctive use of underground water use are put forward, which are :

(1) Arrangement of huge quantity fuel for running pumps.

(2) Arrangement of capital cost of pumps and prime movers.

(3) Maintenance cost of machinery involved.

(4) Skill required for operation and repair of system.

(5) Low water discharge available to meet high crop water requirements in area.

Solutions

(a) The fuel problem may be partially solved by generating electricity from the low-head (bulb-type) turbines at those locations where there are falls in the canal network system.

(b) Solar and wind energy operated pumps can be tried and popularised in such areas.

(c) The government should invest the capital cost as a loan to the area farmers which may be recovered in long time scale easy instalments.

(d) For repairs a mobile workshop for entire area.

(e) The skill or professionals can be managed by intensive trainings in the technical institutes provided with infrastructure and other facilities required for trainers and trainees.

From environmental and topographic condition and cultural practices prevailing in any command area, the following main causes can be attributed to the problem of water logging :

(i) Defective land shaping and grading, which may expose permeable sub-soil layer, and provide more infiltration from rainfall and applied irrigation.

(ii) The canal alignment may pass through sandy loams and sandy soils and the canal may be partly in cutting and filling permitting seepage.

(iii) The canal system may be unlined.

(iv) Drainage network may not be constructed alongwith the canal network simultaneously.

(v) Severe drainage congestion may occur due to weed growth on the banks of nallas *e.g.* Eipomia and typha, the wild growth of which impedes the flow velocity in stream, needing eradication.

(vi) Low pace of ground water development in canal command, due to low water rates charges for canal irrigation.

(vii) Excessive application of irrigation due to water rates being charged on acreage basis and not on volumetric basis.

(viii) Conjunctive use of surface and ground water resources may not be adopted right from the time of project planning and design.

(ix) The farmers may not be using irrigation water in night and allow it to be wasted.

(x) The canals may not be kept closed for carrying out desilting operations. There may be severe leakage from head sluice causing deterioration faster.

(xi) The rate of growth of Kharif irrigation and perennial crop irrigation may be negligible, and only irrigation of only few crops be practised.

(xii) Proper Osrabandi and Warabandi may not be introduced in the canal system.

Some of remedial measures suggested for controlling water logging are as follows :

(i) Land grading and shaping should be judiciously done so as not to expose the underlying pervious layer if any, susceptible to high infiltration rates.

(ii) In highly undulating area with thin soil cover, sprinkler irrigation should be practised by laying of pipeline from minor etc. and pumping water through portable lines.

(iii) The canal system should invariably be lined, when it passed through pervious reaches and goes in cutting. For water logged villages, minors and water course should also be lined, besides the distributaries. The efficiency of the lining should be field tested by determining the losses in unlined and lined portions.

(iv) An effective network of drains should be provided with pump wells at different points and water pumped out and discharged into the natural outfall without permitting its recirculation in the area. Deep surface drains be constructed as also field drains, collector drains and effluent drains.

(v) Wild growth of weeds should be uprooted with weedicides (Harmless for fauna) or weed cutters and weed uprooters. The outfall drains should be dredged for removing silt and increasing the water way.

(vi) Cropping pattern under irrigation should be drastically altered. 5% of summer Zaid crop, 30% of Kharif paddy, soya, jowar, maize crops, 60% under high yielding wheat and 46% under gram and mustard be adopted giving about 140% intensity of cropping and irrigation. In higher fields soyabean may be taken in place of paddy.

(vii) Existing open wells may be deepened by 5-6 m for providing vertical drainage. These wells should be pumped and their discharge disposed off in proper manner outside the command area or dropped in the natural outfall channel.

(viii) Drilling of closely spaced shallow anti-water logging tube-wells and pumping from them to depress the water table.

(ix) Excessive irrigation should be discouraged through extension work and wastage of water should be penalised heavily.

(x) In water logged areas, the proportion of ground water and canal water use should be 60% and 40%. Lesson should be learnt from

Sareli area under Canal Command, Haryana, where Ground Water Development through hundreds of shallow tube-wells depressed the water table sufficiently to avert the water logging conditions for a decade or so.

(xi) Canal closure should be systematically implemented for periodic repairs and maintenance of the canal system for this, adequate financial provision should be made. The closure should start immediately after wheat irrigation is over in mid-April, so that 2 clear months (60 days) are available before the onset of the monsoons.

(xii) Canal operation manual be prepared for the major (main) canal, branches and distributaries and experienced and well trained, staff posted for canal operation.

(xiii) Water should be distributed equitably on 21 days turn for wheat irrigation.

(xiv) Canal roads and link roads should be well maintained to rush up men and materials for repairing canal breaches etc. causing flooding of the nearby fields and aggravating the problems of water logging.

(xv) The farmers whose fields are affected by water logging should be paid proper amount of compensation for crop loss, damage to their property like houses etc. Their rehabilitation and gainful employment should be the moral responsibility of Ayacut Development Authority.

(xvi) Geological mapping and shallow seismic survey should be done to determine depth to basement and sub-surface lithology on micro scale from Vindhyan era to recent pleistocene. This will greatly help in proper drainage measures to be adopted.

Use of Saline Waters Alone or in Conjunctive use

As discussed earlier the underground water if happens to be saline and is to be used either alone or to supplement for irrigation, then the resultant salinity of soil water extract should be determined and based on soil texture and salinity resistance of crops. The crop calendar should be planned to get sustained production. The guideline of these are shown in Table 5.10.

TABLE 5.10

Ec × 10^3 Limits of Tolerance

EX × 10^3 in 1:2 Soil Water Extract at 25^{oC}

Soil Texture	Limits for sensitive crops	Limits for semi-tolerant crops	Limits for tolerant crops
Clay	1.2	2.4	4.8
Clay loam	0.8	1.6	3.2
Loam	0.7	1.4	2.8
Sandy clay loam	0.6	1.2	2.4
Sandy loam	0.4	0.8	1.6

General Salt Tolerants of Crops

Sensitive	Mostly tolerant or semi-tolerant	Tolerant to high tolerant
Field beans	Soyabean	Wheat, Barley
Carron	Sensbania	Safflower
Raddish	Rice	Rye Cotton
Cucumber	Guar	Sunflower
Orange	Sorbhum	Sugarbeet
Lemon	Maize	Triticale
Apple	Oats (fodder)	Lucerie
Sugarcane	Potato, Onion	Muskmelon, Fig, Palm,
(at planning time)	Musklemon, Grape	Soo-babul, Coconut
	Eucalyptus, Grasses	

WATER ACCOUNTING

One of the most important aspects of irrigation management is Water Accounting. An Irrigation Engineer must have an assessment of water released from reservoir, actually consumed for various uses it is planned for such as for agriculture, power generation, drinking purpose or Industrial use as the case may be. He should also have information about the area actually irrigated and the crop pattern to enable him to work out actual delta and duty of canal system. He should thereafter make a comparative study of delta and duty actually attained with respect to the one actually designed. This study will give actual efficiency of the system, and attempt be made to examine the causes for lesser efficiencies and workout ways to improve it.

Since our water resources are limited and likely to be exhausted after some time, but demand for irrigation will always be increasing. To cater this ever increasing demand, optimal use of water will have to be practised. Water accounting is therefore, essential in this regard.

In order to work out water account, the following data, must be available or collected :

(i) Reservoir capacity at different levels with at least 1 Ft. interval.

(ii) Monthly evaporation losses chart generally issued by C.W.C. or meteorological department.

(iii) Surface area of reservoir at different levels, again at 1 Ft. interval.

(iv) Daily release of water into/through

 (a) Canals
 (b) Power generation if any
 (c) Water spilled (surplussed)
 (d) Any other consumptive use such as by industries or drinking (water supply).

(v) Daily release data in each canal, right upto minors.

(vi) Daily channel-wise details of outlets open and closed.

(vii) Designed or actual conveyance losses (if measured) expressed as cusec/million sq.ft. of wetted perimeter of (or cumec/million sq.m. of wetted perimeter) the canal.

(viii) Area under cultivation and that received irrigation water, alongwith crop pattern for each minor/distributary or branch canal which have direct outlets also.

(ix) Information about any unforeseen water losses such as due to piping/breaches etc.

The above collected data/information be compiled in the following proformas :

1. *Proforma I*: Containing water account for the whole system *i.e.* at Reservoir.
2. *Proforma II* : Containing water account for discharges released into canal system at head of Main canals — for left bank and right bank canals.

3. *Proforma III* : Containing water account for each branch canal, Distributary and minor.

The water account is generally recorded in terms of cusec-days or million-cubic ft. for medium/minor project. But for major projects such as Chambal system or Rajasthan canal, it can be in Acre ft. also.

It is advisable to work out water account on 10 day utilisation basis which can be summed up month-wise and season-wise.

DISTRIBUTION OF CANAL LOSSES FOR VARIOUS BRANCHES, DISTRIBUTARY AND MINORS

Major exercise, which is required to be done in water account is to debit losses in the Main canal (Parent channels) into branch canals, distributaries, minors, etc. For this, following methods can be used :

(i) Equitable basis

(ii) Cusec-mile basis

Equitable Basis : In this all the losses in Minors/Branches/Main canal are shared, equally and for working out duty of canal or delta, it is divided by the whole area under command.

Cusec-Mile basis : In this, the losses are distributed, reach-wise and losses are debited in the ratio of discharge utilised to the discharged passed on to d/s and losses d/s of the canal are not debited to channels upstream.

This method is more useful when water account of Main canal are utilised by two states or agencies such as for Chambal Right Main Canal where Madhya Pradesh and Rajasthan have to share, water of the Right Main Canal.

Prodedure

(i) Let total discharge at Head of parent channel be Q

(ii) Let total length be L.

(iii) And it is divided into 4 reaches with lengths L_1, L_2, L_3 and L_4

(iv) Let discharges utilised (by direct outlets/ offtaking channels in these reaches be Q_1, Q_2, Q_3 and Q_4 respectively so that

$$Q = Q_1 + Q_2 + Q_3 + Q_4$$

(v) Let seepage losses through the canal, reach-wise and total be

q_1, q_2, q_3, q_4 and q respectively, so that

$$q = q_1 + q_2 + q_3 + q_4$$

Then as per cusec mile basis

q_1 is to be shared in the ratio

$$q_1 : Q_2 : Q_3 : Q_4$$

q_2 is to be shared in the ratio

$$Q_2 : Q_3 : Q_4$$

q_3 is to be shared in the ratio

$$Q_3 : Q_4$$

Whereas q_4 is to be entirely bourne by reach L_4. Thus we see that reach L_1 does not have any share in q_2, q_3, q_4: L_2 does not share q_3 and q_4 and so on. This is sharing of losses in cusec mile basis.

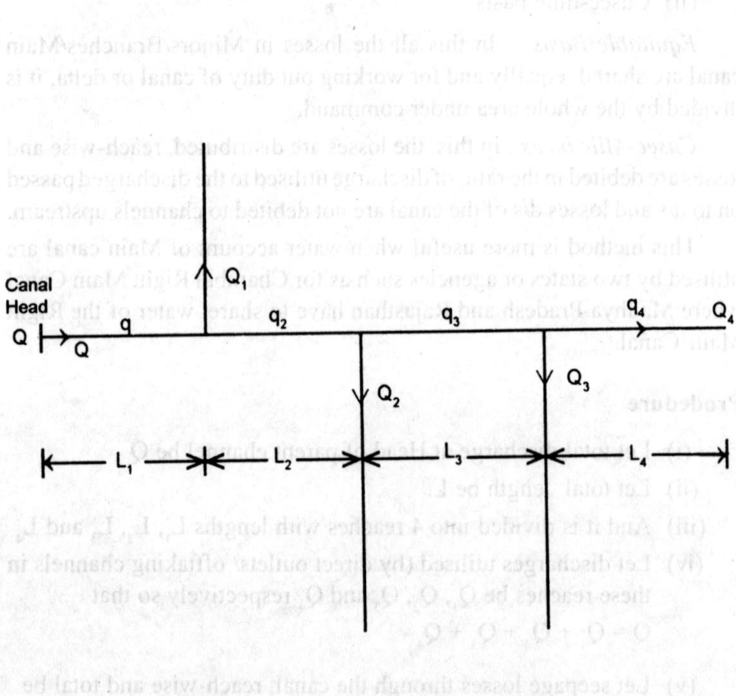

Fig. 5.10 : Line Diagram of Parent Channel

Proforma I — Water Account for the Whole Project at Reservoir and Canal Head

Sl. No.	Date	Reservoir level	Capacity	Water spread	Evaporation losses		Water Releases from Reservoir									Area irrigated	
					Rate per month	Evap. losses for 10 days	Spill D/S	Into canals: Left canal		Into canals: Right canal		Through machine (for power generation if any)		Any other use — Industry or drinking			
		MCF (MCM)	Sq. Ft.		in (cm)	MCF (MCM)	CS	MCF	MCF	MCF	CS	MCF	CS	MCF	CS	MCF	Ha.
1	2	3	4	5	6	7	8	9	10	11	12	13	14	15	16	17	18
Sub Total 'A'																	
10 days																	
10 days																	
Sub Total 'B'																	
10 or 11 days																	
Sub total 'C'																	
Grand Total A + B + C																	

Proforma II — Water Account for Main Canals

Name of Channel : Month

Designed Discharge at Head.. CS : Designed Duty..CS/1000 Ac

Sl. No.	Date	Discharge at Head	Seepage losses	Actual Utilisation of water		Area under Irrigation		Actual duty of channel
				Direct outlets	Offtaking channels	Direct outlets	Offtaking channels	
		Cusec-day	Cusec-day	Cs-day	Cs-day	AC cusec-day	AC Cs-day	Cusec/1000 AC
1	2	3	4	5	6	7	8	9

Proforma III — Water Account of Minor

NAME OF MINOR.............................DISCHARGE HEAD.............................DESIGNED.............................

DUTY OF MINOR.............................

MONTH.............................

S.No.	Date	Discharge at Head	Area Irrigated	Actual Duty

Example of Interstate Water Account

Statement enclosed as Annexure 1 is a sample statement of M.P. Rajasthan share of cater from Chambal system. The Right Main canal which has capacity of 6656 cs. at head is required to carry and release 3900 cs. at Rajasthan-M.P. border. In this canal design losses have been taken as 484 cs. The cost and losses are to be shared by M.P. and Rajasthan on cusec mile basis it works out to 75.6:24.4 in M.P.-Raj. Account. This is valid when the discharge in RMC is shared in ratio 3900 : (6656 – 484 – 3900) : 3900:2276

Ratio of due share of MP & Rajasthan :: – 3900:2276

:: 1.716:1

On cusec mile basis the losses as per design are to be shared on 3:1 Ratio :: 76.4 : 24.6

Thus when discharge Ratio is 1.716, the share of losses is 3:1

∴ if ratio is "X"

Then share of M.P. $\dfrac{X \times 3}{1.716} = 1.748\ X$

Thus if 5500 is discharge at head and delivery to M.P. is 3500 and losses are say 450 cs. Then share by M.P. $= \dfrac{3500}{(5500-450-3500)} \times 1.748$

$$= \frac{3500}{1550} \times 1.748 \text{ cs.}$$

$$= 394 \text{ cs}$$

and share of Rajasthan $= 4450 - 394$

$= 56$ cs.

Anticipated Evaporation Losses in the Chambal Reservoir

July	4½"
Aug.	3"
Sept.	3½"
Oct.	4"
Nov.	3½"
Dec.	3"
Jan.	3"
Feb.	4½"
March	8"
April	10"
May	13"
June	11"

TABLE 5.11

Example of Water Account from 1-10-82 to 6-1-83 (Rabi) in Chambal Command Area

Period	G.S.DAM Discharge in Cs-days	R.P.S. Dam Discharge in Cs-days	J.S. Dam Discharge in Cs-days	Indent placed to RSEB Ex. J.S.	R.M.C. Discharge Cs-days	L.M.C. Discharge Cs-days	Spillage from Kota Barrage	Discharge at Parwatgi Aqueduct Cs-days	Losses to MP A/c Cs days	Water to M.P.A/C Cs-days	Water to Raj. A/C Cs-days	Remarks
1	2	3	4	5	6	7	8	9	10	11	12	13
1-10-82 to 10-10-82	35738	49542	59957	67000	45519	14252	Nil	19970	2974.38	22944.38	36826.62	
11-10-82 to 20-10-82	35700	70322	70164	68000	50429	14851	466	24411	3234.93	27645.93	37634.07	
21-10-82 to 31-10-82	40074	56274	74040	74800	52744	14250	Nil	32609	4225.27	36834.27	30169.70	
1-11-82 to 10-11-82	19324	52088	48142	66000	41915	11836	Nil	17453	2945.50	20398.50	33353.50	
11-11-82 to 20-11-82	20179	29427	33400	38000	34019	Nil	7251	26311	4555.80	30876.00	3152.20	

(Contd.)

TABLE 5.11 (*Contd.*)

1	2	3	4	5	6	7	8	9	10	11	12	13
21-11-82 to 30-11-82	43486	17009	21793	40000	22734	Nil	Nil	15923	4519.00	20442.00	2292.00	
1-12-82 to 10-12-82	44025	42286	43832	65000	38044	5480	207	22574	3813.00	26387.00	17147.00	
11-12-82 to 20-12-82	61821	69356	71304	58800	50501	12085	5034	29574	3339.00	28912.00	33674.00	
21-12-82 to 24-12-82	73279	85708	90303	71500	57461	12021	14087	35148	4170.00	39318.00	30164.00	
25-12-82 to 26-1-83	32965	58916	52989	39000	32269	6600	14920	22531	2474.12	25005.12	13863.88	
Total 1-10-82 to 6-1-83	406582	530938	465964	588100	425645	91386	41965	242503	36251.00	278754.00	238277.00	
Total Maf.	0.8074	1.0544	0.9254	1.1679	0.8453	0.1814	0.0833	0.4816	0.0720	0.5536	0.4732	

Water to M.P. A/c = 0.5536 Maf.

Water to Raj. A/c = 0.4732 Maf.

CHAPTER 6

SOIL WATER-PLANT RELATIONSHIP UNDER IRRIGATED AGRICULTURE

Introduction

Water is essential for every living biological system. The bodies of living beings contain about 90 per cent of water and every physical and biochemical reaction taking place in the body is dependent on the presence of water in one form or another. Since ancient times, mankind took water as a gift of god and also recognised its importance as one of the basic elements of life. Most of the old civilization arose in the valleys and around the great rivers all over the world. The rivers did not only provide a means of transport, but also supported plant domestication, crop improvement and food production. In spite of the fact that several of the modern crops originated and diversified in semi-arid climates of the central and western Asia and Ethiopian centre of Africa, they evolved soil agronomically around the major rivers of the Indian sub-continent, China, Egypt and parts of Europe. Plant nutrition based on soil of region recognised the need of water as a medium for plant growth and as a source of hydrogen and oxygen. The unique properties of water including its dipolar character, hydrogen bonding and latent heat, make it biologically an important compound. The other significant properties of water which need mention are its characteristics as a solvent and its cohesive and adhesive properties.

WATER-PLANT RELATIONSHIP

Water is a unique liquid having properties unparallel with other solvents. Not only it is important as a good solvent, but also is involved in the organisation of organic molecules, cell organells, cells, tissue and organs. Most cells and tissues contain 80-90 per cent water of their weight. Once if cells and tissues are dehydrated, they look lifeless.

The amount of water varies in different plant parts. The apical portions of the roots and stems contain nearly 90 per cent or more water. Leaves and young fruits are other organs which are rich in water. When the organs mature their water content decreases. The woods of large trees may contain 50-60 per cent moisture whereas the stems of wheat and barley contain about 60-70 per cent water which at harvest time may decline to 5-10 per cent. Freshly harvested grains of most crops contain 10-15 per cent of water. Indeed it is the moisture content of these grains which determines their storage life, viability and germinability.

Crop plants are normally grown on the soil which must supply water to support their growth. A mere aerial spray of water to shoots does not lead to plant growth and crop production. If we enclose a small patch of crop under polythene sheet we find that water drops accumulate on its inner surface and the temperature of chamber also rises. Thus when a plant grows it partly dissipates its accumulated energy and also loses moisture to the atmosphere. In fact the soil is the source of water but the latter traverses through the plant and is released into the atmosphere as vapour. We can therefore, recognise three main phases of water-plant relationship as follows :

(1) Water absorption.
(2) Water conduction and transportation.
(3) Water loss or transpiration.

In determining the importance of water in crop productivity, we have to understand clearly all the three processes *viz.* absorption, transportation and transpiration and analyse their effects on plant growth and crop yield to recognise the steps which need regulation or modification to achieve the maximum water use efficiency.

PHYSIOLOGICAL ASPECTS OF WATER

It is a well recognised fact that the availability of water influence almost all biochemical and physiological processes in plants. This in turn affects the plant morphology. Plants growing in abundance of water (hydrophytes) tend to have enlarged cell size with small quantities of cytoplasm. This usually provides them a larger shape combine with fragile and weak structure. As against this plants growing under scarcity of water (xerophytes) are short statured, thick and succulent. Most of the crop plants (mesophytes) when subjected to low moisture regimes are reduced in size along with the reduction in reproductive capacity. In most instances, the crop plants have an onoptimal moisture regime. Any deviation from this optimum results in adverse effect leading to poor growth and yield. However, in order to fully appreciate the relationship of water and plant growth, let us examine the relationship of individual cells and tissues. A brief description of the structure of the plant is given below to make a few points clear.

PLANT STRUCTURE

Morphologically a plant consists of roots, stems and leaves. One belonging to grass family (monocotyledonous) like wheat, barley, maize, sorghum, millet etc. The other group of plants named dicotyledonous, includes, pea, redgram, gram, chickpea, and mustard, sesamum, tomatoes, potatoes, tapioca. Once these plants grow in field it is easy to distinguish them on the basis of their stems. The monocotyledonous plants give an appearance of leaves directly emerging from the soil because these plants have a very condensed stem during early stages of their growth. A typical stem can be noticed during later stages of growth. In dicotyledonous plants, on the other hand a distinct stem is visible from the very beginning.

The leaves are borne throughout the stem in all the plants. These organs are mainly responsible for the loss of water. If we examine the surface structure of leaves it may be seen that the surface of leaves has small pores surrounded by two cells. These pores are called stoma and the cells surrounding them are called guard cells. Similar pores are found on the surface of stem as well as fruit wall of many crops such as pea, mung, bean, cowpea, mustard etc.

The study of internal structure of a typical leaf (Figs. 6.1 & 6.2) reveals that the stomate have a cavity below them and have continuity with inter-cellular spaces which are filled with air. The stomate regulate the loss of water as vapour and exchange of carbondioxide from the air in the leaf and other organs. It is thus, the efficiency of these structures which possibly determine the water loss from the plant. The leaves maintain their continuity of structure with the stems which has conducting tissues called xylem and phoem. The former are the main channels of water transport. The stem maintains its continuity with the root which eventually is in contact with the water source, the soil.

The structure of root consists of a root apex which has three distinct zones namely,

(1) apical meristem with root cap,

(2) root hairs, and

(3) root maturation zone.

It is the second zone which is largely involved in water uptake. The transverse section of a root brings out clearly the relationship of root hairs with the remaining structure of the root. It is found that an outer most or an epidermal cell usually gets elongated into a long hair which has its continuity with the remaining cells.

Other epidermal cells are also capable of absorbing water but the root hairs provide the advantage of exploring more areas in their vicinity because of their enlarged surface.

THE MECHANISM OF WATER ABSORPTION AT DIFFERENT LEVELS OF ORGANIZATION IN PLANTS

Water Relations of a Single Cell

An ideal plant cell contains a cell wall enclosing a protoplast. A thin layer of cytoplasm is pressed against the cell well which contains nucleus, mitochondria, golgi apparatus, plastids and other cell inclusions. The inner layer of the cytoplasm called tonoplast surrounds a cell vacuole which contains cell sap. The sap is a water solution having some osmotic potential. When such a cell is placed in pure water, its functions are determined by the water potential gradient.

Pure water has zero water potential. When a solute is added, the water potential of the solution decreases below zero. This means that the cell sap has a lower water potential than pure water. When such a cell is placed in a pure water a gradient due to difference in water potential is caused. This results in the movement of water inside the cell. The effect of this is the creation of a new force, called turgor-pressure inside the cell. This pressure works against the force which is responsible for the movement of water inside the cell. However, simultaneously the concentration of sap also decreases which results in a decrease of the osmotic potential of pure water and cell sap gets reduced. This lowers the force by which water enters the cell. We can represent this relationship by the following equation :

$$\psi = \psi + \psi_q \text{ .... } (1)$$

where ψ is the total water potential of the system, ψ_s is the osmotic or solute potential and ψ_w is the cell wall pressure or turgor pressure.

The driving force F that causes water to move can be represented by the following equation :

$$F = \text{grad.} \quad (\psi_v - \psi_m) \quad \ldots\ldots\ldots\ldots\ldots\ldots \quad (2)$$

where F grad represents the gradient, ψ_p is the total water potential of the cell including that of the cell sap and ψ_m is the total water potential of the medium. If the later is pure water then this value will be zero. In that case the driving force will be equal to ψ_p. However, as the water will move into the cell ψ_p will be regulated by equation (1). In this relationship the elasticity of the cell wall would also play an important role. The volume of the cell would increase up to a certain limit with the dilution of the cell sap and this will lower the total osmotic potential. This in turn would influence the force developed due to the gradient between the cell and the medium.

Water Relations of a Tissue

In higher plants no cell exists in isolation from others. Even a root hair which is projected outside into the surrounding medium is attached with other cells on all the remaining sides. In a transverse section it would appear to be surrounded on the three sides by other cells. Thus the water relations of a root hair are governed on one side by the surrounding medium and on the other by other cells. Let us just consider two cells joined with each other through a common cell wall. If these two cells individually have the same total water potential, then there will not be any net exchange of water between them. This can be shown as follows :

The total water potential of a cell (ψ_s) equal to $\psi_s + \psi_w$. Let us say that for the cells A and B these values are :

$$\psi_a = \psi_{sa} + \psi_{wa} \text{ and } \psi_b = \psi_{sb} + \psi_{wb} \quad \ldots\ldots\ldots\ldots\ldots \quad (3)$$

Now, the driving force

$$F = (\psi_a - \psi_b) \quad \ldots\ldots\ldots\ldots \quad (4)$$

If ψ_a is = ψ_b the gradient will be zero and so will be the F. Therefore no net exchange of water will take place between the cells A and B. However, we must realise that the same value of a and b does not necessarily mean that the two cells have to have the same osmotic potential and the same turgor pressure or wall pressure.

On the other hand, if the total water potential of cell B is lower than that of cell A, a driving force will develop which would cause influx of water into cell B till the two cells attain the same total water potential. Now this example can be extended to a larger number of cells which are connected with each other in a tissue. If there are 20 cells beginning from I to 20, they will attain an equilibrium amongst themselves depending on their total water potential in the same way as discussed for the two cells attached with each other. Under such conditions there may come situation when water absorption and movement will come to a standstill.

Water Relations of a Plant

Let us now consider the water relations of a plant which has leaves, stem and roots providing a continuum for water in soil-plant environment. The total water potential in the environment could be very low, depending upon the temperature and humidity. The Table 6.1 provides an appro 'mate magnitude of water potential in the soil-plant atmosphere system.

TABLE 6.1

Approximate Magnitudes of Water Potential in the Soil Plant Atmosphere System

(Plaut and Moreshet, 1973)

Component	Water potential
Soil	— 0.1 to — 20
Leaf	— 5.0 to — 50
Atmosphere	— 100 to — 2000

It is apparent from the above Table 6.1 that the difference in total water potential in the soil-plant atmosphere system could generate a driving force for water movement from the soil through the plant to atmosphere. If this continuum is broken, the driving force would automatically disappear. We can assume and create such a system. Take an intact plant and cut its stem into two pieces. Join these two pieces again through a clean glass or tygon tubing in such a way which leaves an air gap between the two ends. Now we can put back the plant in open atmosphere, but it will not absorb water at the same rate and the upper part of the plant will wilt. Here an air column between two stem pieces does not provide a continuum. In plants the movement of water only takes place in liquid phase which can stand enormous pressure without breaking the liquid column.

ABSORPTION OF WATER IN SOIL-PLANT-ATMOSPHERE SYSTEM

The root system of different crop plants vary extremely in their depth of penetration, root length and horizontal distribution is influenced by environmental factors and the genetic constitution. Nevertheless, both the properties of the soil and the roots determine water uptake by plants. The cereal roots apparently occupy more surface area of the soil than other crops. For example, it has been shown that cereal roots have 200-4000 cm/cm^2 of soil surface area as against 15-200 cm/cm^2 for non-graminaceous plants (Newman, 1969).

Since the roots act as a dynamic system in their water uptake, it is difficult to include all the possible factors in a model. Yet some attempts have been made in this direction. Gardner (1960) proposed one such model which assumes a single root to be infinitely long and thin extracting water at a constant rate per unit length. However, a major limitation in this assumption is that the roots do not absorb at the same rate throughout their length and secondly, the absorption rate changes with the age (Kramar, 1969).

However, it would be important to consider water absorption in the total soil plant atmosphere system instead of the roots alone. In this system, one can partition the system in such a manner so that the involvement of different plant parts is taken into account. The flow rate of water in this system is given by the following equation :

$$\text{Flow Rate} = \frac{\psi\ \text{soil} - \psi\ \text{root surface}}{\text{r - soil}} = \frac{\psi\ \text{root surface} - \psi\ \text{xylem}}{\text{r - root}} = \frac{\psi\ \text{xylem} - \psi\ \text{leaf}}{\text{r-xylem + r-leaf}} = \frac{\psi\ \text{leaf} - \psi\ \text{air}}{\text{r-leaf + r-air}} \quad \text{..........} \quad (5)$$

where ψ is the water potential at various sites of the system and 'r' is the corresponding resistance.

This model is though not leak proof but is good in considering the water relation of the entire plant. This brings out the fact that the water potential of the atmosphere determines the flow of water or vapour from the leaves which in turn determines water flow in the plant. In fact one would expect a gradient in total water potential in different parts of the plant depending upon the water potential of the atmosphere. This can give an idea of the absorption and water flow in the system. Merit Meiri et al. (1975) conducted experiments under different trasnpiration conditions both in green house and growth chamber to determine water potential in leaves and shoot. These results are given in Table 6.2.

TABLE 6.2
Effect of Transpiration Conditions on the Water Potential Difference Between Leaves and Shoots

(After Meiri et al. 1975)

Growth site	Transpiration Condition	Water Potential Leaves	Shoots	Difference
Green House	High (Non-clouds)	-15.0 ± 0.7	-8.4 ± 0.7	7.5
	Low (Clouds)	-5.7 ± 0.4	-4.6 ± 0.3	1.1
Growth Chamber	High (High light intensity)	-14.3 ± 0.3	-8.5 ± 0.5	5.8
	Medium (Low light intensity)	-4.1 ± 1.0	-4.1 ± 0.5	0.0
	Low (High air humidity, dark)	-1.1 ± 0.1	-0.8 ± 0.2	0.3

It is clear from this data that high transpiration conditions reduced water potential more in leaves than in shoot resulting in a gradient of –7.5 bars. On the other hand low transpiration conditions caused a difference of only – 1.1 bars.

Inside the growth chambers at low light intensity or that high air humidity, there was hardly any difference in the water potential of leaves and shoot. Therefore, there was almost no gradient. In another experiment they further showed that the different regions of a leaf have different water potential, the apical portion being at the lowest level. The importance of air moisture or water potential on growth has been examined by Milford and Lawlor (1975) who have shown that a slight reduction in air moisture results in considerable reduction in dry matter accumulation.

Factors Affecting Water Absorption

The flow rate of water in the soil-plant-atmosphere system was given earlier in Equation 5. This includes both the physical as well as the biological components. The soil and the atmosphere are the chief physical factors which determine the flow rate of water through the plant. It is true that a high water potential in the atmosphere would reduce water loss from plants and consequently slow down the rate of water absorption. But it does not follow from this that water will be continuously absorbed if water potential of the atmosphere is very low and the soil is near drying when the equilibrium in the soil-plant-atmosphere system is disturbed either by change of the soil properties or of the atmosphere, the biological system responds and can exercise control over the entire relationship to a great extent within such limits that do not make it inactive.

Thus, it may be concluded that the rate of water absorption is controlled by the rate of transpiration as well as regulated by the size and distribution of roots and several soil factors such as soil temperature, soil water potential, soil water content, concentration of soil solution, aeration etc. Among the plant factors, resistance to flow of water and vapour in different plant parts provides another mechanism for the control of water loss. These are the major factors to be considered.

SOIL — A SYSTEM

Soil is a three phase system comprising the solid phase made of mineral and organic matter, the liquid phase called the soil moisture and the gaseous phase called soil air. The main component of the solid phase is the soil particles, the size and shape of which give rise to more space of different geometry. These are spaces filled with water and air in varying proportions depending on the amount of moisture present. The presence of solid articles liquid (soil solution) and gas (soil air) constitute a complex poly phasic system. To be more precise it is a heterogeneous, particulate, disperse and porous system, in which the interfacial area per unit volume can be enormously large.

The solid phase of the soil consists of mineral particles arranged in multiple ways and interspersed with organic material. The size of mineral particles ranges from a fraction of a micron to a few millimetres in thickness. The geometry of the particles and the pores influence the quantity of liquid flowing through the system. The common phenomena like swelling and shrinking, freezing and thawing and root action can alter the pore geometry which leads to change in water transmission characteristics. Water applied through irrigation makes ways to the pores and its further retention and transmission depend on the factors mentioned above. For efficient use of water in agriculture it is desirable to understand the different phenomena of the soil system as a whole and the soil water in particular.

It is difficult to separate the different phases of the soil system as they interact strongly upon one another. But for the sake of their quantitative proportion it is desirable to consider them as independent constituents.

BASIC PHYSICAL PROPERTIES OF SOILS

Soil Texture : It quantitatively refer to the relative proportions of various sizes of soil particles in a given soil. The three gradients are sand, silt and clay.

Soil Structure : The natural arrangement, organization and orientation of the soil particles give rise to soil structure. Generally, in the field, the soil particles are present in near the other form of aggregates as a result of a temporary or stable aggregation. It is very rare when the soil particles exist as such. This occurs when there is absence of aggregating, agents or the soil is just made of sand. Unlike texture, the structure of the soil is highly dynamic in nature, and changes in soil structure occur due to soil management practices. There are three main types of soil structure — single grained, massive and aggregated. On the basis of shape, the structure has been classified as columner, platy, prismatic, blocky etc. The stability or structure is imported by cementing agents like organic matter, clay, iron, and alluminium oxides. The aggregate size distribution of soil is determined by either dry or wet sieving method.

Soil structure is of great importance as it effects water, air and heat regimes in the filled in addition to mechanical properties. The formation of structure consequent to proper management of the soil brings about moderation of the distribution of solid-void proportion which might be skewed to extremes in case of unaggregated soils.

Volume and Mass Relationship of Soil Constituents

The above relationship may be represented diagrammatically as below. The three phases are shown in relative proportions both in masses and volumes.

Here :

M_a = Mass of air (negligible M)

M_w = Mass of water C

M_s = Mass of solid

M_t = Total mass ($M_a + M_w + M_s$)

V_a = Volume of air

V_w = Volume of water

V_f = Volume of pores $(V_a + V_w)$
V_s = Volume of solids
V_t = Total volume $(V_f + V_s)$

Based on the above designation, quantitative relations amongst the three soil phases can be meaningfully expressed.

Density of Solids

$$\rho = \frac{MS}{V_s} \rho_a (\rho_w = 1 \text{ density of water})$$

$$+ \frac{MS}{V_s}$$

Where : ρ = density, M= Mass of solid, S= V= Volume of solid.

Density of Some of the Minerals

Minerals	Density gram/C^3 $_m$ or gm/C.C.
Augite	3.2 to 3.6
Dolomite	2.8 to 3.0
Illite	2.6
Kaolinite	2.5 to 2.65
Montomorillonite	2.0 to 2.4
Quartz	2.62 to 2.65

Moisture *Vs.* Dry Bulk Density

The dry bulk density is dependent upon the soil texture and structure. In sandy soils it may be as high as 1.6 whereas in fine textured soils may be as low as 1.1 gm/cm^3. Besides, soil manipulation through ploughing compaction and shrinkage might alter the bulk density appreciably.

Total (wet) Bulk Density

(Net bulk density is the mass of moist soil per unit volume),

$$P_t = \frac{M_t}{V_t} = \frac{M_s + M_w}{V_s + V_w + V_a}$$

Moisture *Vs.* Porosity

It can be defined as the ratio of the volume of pores (voids) to the total soil volume as designated below :

$$N = \frac{V_f}{V_s} = \frac{V_a + V_w}{V_a + V_s + V_w}$$

Porosity is an index of the relative volume of pores, coarse textured soils have less total porosity as compared to the fine textured soils. Generally, it varies from 0.3 to 0.6 or 30 to 60 per cent. The total porosity does not describe the destruction of different pore sizes. The porosities of organic soil and well aggregated soils sometimes exceed 0.6.

Air Filled Porosity (N_A)

It is the ratio of pores filled with air or pores free from water to the total porosity. This is the measure of relative air content of the soil.

$$N = \frac{V_a}{V_t} = \frac{V_a}{V_a + V_w + V_s}$$

Void Ratio

The quantity expressing the ratio of the volume of pores to the volume of solids is termed as void ratio or relative porosity.

$$e = \frac{V_t}{V_s} = \frac{V_a + V_w}{V_s}$$

This index has certain advantages over porosity (n) in as much as in the later case, total soil volume also changes with the volume of change without voids, whereas in the former case volume of pores may change without change in the volume of solids. Therefore, a meaningful knowledge of dynamics of pores due to external load is possible with the information on void ratio.

Soil Wetness

Soil wetness refers to the relative water content in the soil. It can be expressed in the following ways :

Mass Wetness (W) : It is the ratio of mass of water to the mass of soil and is often referred to as "gravimetric water content" :

$$W = \frac{M_w}{M_s}$$

The index W is most commonly used. In mineral saturated soil, W, can range between 0.25 to 0.60 or 25 to 60 per cent depending upon the bulk density. However, in organic soils such as peat or muck the saturated water content on mass basis may exceed 100 per cent.

Volume Wetness : This is the relative water content to soil on volume basis of water and soil. It is the ratio of volume of water to the total soil volume :

$$\varnothing = \frac{V_w}{V_t} = \frac{V_w}{V_s + V_f}$$

It is also termed as volumetric water content. The use of ∅, over W is preferred as the former is more directly adaptable to the computation of fluxes and water quantities. The wetness at saturation varies from 40 to 50 per cent in sandy soils to 60 per cent in clayey soils.

Degree of Saturation

This relationship refer to the volume of water present in the total pore volume. It is also termed as degree of saturation :

$$\varnothing_s = \frac{V_w}{V_f} = \frac{V_w}{V_a + V_w}$$

Soil Water Energy Relations

Soil water or soil solution contains energy in different quantities and kinds like any other body in nature. The soil solution is confined between solid liquid and liquid air interfaces. It may occur as a thin film on the solid or as pore-water when in excess. Water properties, complex as such, are being further complicated by interaction within the soil framework. The physical tension, viscosity and vapour pressure change considerably when the pure water becomes a part of the soil water system. The dielectric coefficient of pure water is nearly to 88 and this decreases with impurities of added salts and changes with change in the concentration of electrolyte.

Examples

(a) $\psi_{TA} = \psi_g + \psi_p = + 30 — 30$ cm water lead

$= 0$ cm water lead.

$\psi_{TB} = \psi_g + \psi_p = + 20 — 20$ cm water lead

$= 0$ cm water lead.

$$V = -K - \frac{\psi_{TA} - \psi_{TB}}{L} = -K\frac{0 - 0 = 0}{10} = 0$$

No flow

(b) ψ_{TA} = $\psi_g + \psi_p$ = +30 — 40 cm Water Lead

= -10 cm

ψ_{TB} = $\psi_g + \psi_p$ = +20 – 266 cm

= – 6 cm

$$V = V = -K - \frac{TA - TB}{L} = -K\frac{-10 - (^{-6})}{10} = K\frac{(^{-4})}{10}$$

$$= k \times 0^{-4}$$

Flow in upward direction.

Moisture movement in unsaturated phase may be classified in three phases *viz.*,

(i) Infiltration, when water is being applied.

(ii) Redistribution, after application ceases.

(iii) Withdrawal as evaporation from soil surface, transpiration through plant system and deep-percolation beyond the rootzone depth.

The downward entry of water into soil may be predicted by the following relationship :

where, i = $a^{t^{-1/2}} + bt$

i = cumulative intake rate (c^m3/cm^2)

a = constant

t = time

b = basic intake rate.

HYSTERESIS

The soil moisture characteristic curve is not generally unique and single valued. It has been found that there are two moisture content values against the same suction value obtained through two-way description and absorption procedures. These are of great importance in case of wetting and drying process occurring simultaneously. This phenomenon is common in irrigated as well as rainfed agriculture. This phenomenon is termed as hysteresis.

Measurement of Soil Water

The measurement of soil water for moisture content as well as potential is important for efficient water management in irrigation. The amount of irrigation water to be applied is directly related to the water already present in the soil. The methods of measurement of soil water may be divided into :

(1) Measurement of water content in soil (wetness), and
(2) Measurement of water potential.

TABLE 6.3

Moisture Deficit Curves of Different Soil Types* at Various Soil Moisture Tensions (mm water/cm Soil Depth)

Soil type	Soil moisture tension (bar)					
	0.5	1.0	3	5	10	15 PWP
Loamy sand	0.50	0.73	1.10	1.21	1.32	1.34
Sandy loam	0.96	1.15	1.36	1.44	1.54	1.56
Sandy clay loam	0.95	1.11	1.37	1.48	1.63	1.68
Sandy Clay	1.35	1.56	1.78	1.88	2.00	2.02
Clay	0.63	0.99	1.55	1.86	2.27	2.52
Loam	0.70	1.60	2.29	2.50	2.70	2.75
Clay loam	0.95	1.55	2.20	2.54	2.87	3.03
Silty clay loam	1.15	1.60	2.47	2.89	3.26	3.34

* Soil types are based on U.S. System of Textural Classes.

Desert Soils						
Pali	A	40.1	29.8	19.3	8.0	11.0
	B	48.2	36.5	29.5	10.7	9.8
Beri Ganga	A	29.4	24.5	8.5	3.7	4.8
	B	24.4	20.8	6.0	2.7	3.3
Saline Soils						
Sonapur	A	52.2	45.4	38.1	11.9	26.2
	B	57.9	42.1	36.3	12.2	23.1
Mankhanda	A	50.7	42.3	33.6	10.5	21.5
	B	57.9	42.1	36.3	13.2	23.1
Ganning	A	55.6	54.2	41.9	15.5	26.4
	B	48.8	47.5	35.1	15.4	19.7

Water Content of Soil

There are different methods to estimate soil water contents namely :

(i) Gravimetric method

(ii) Neutron scatter

(iii) Rapid moisture meter, using calcium carbide

(iv) Infrared moisture meter etc.

MEASUREMENT OF WATER POTENTIAL

The measurement of soil water content or wetness is very important for investigation of soil properties. However, this does not reveal the energy status of soil water and it becomes difficult to deal with the soil water availability to plants in different soils on the basis of soil moisture content only. Therefore, it is essential to measure simultaneously, the energy status or the total potential or soil water. The different potentials are matric, esmatic and gravitational which when added provides total water potential.

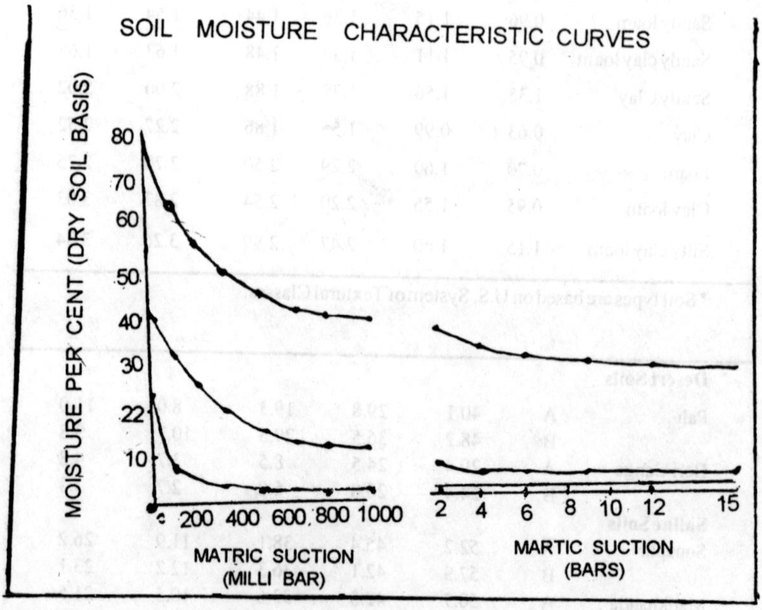

Fig. 6.1 : Soil Moisture Characteristic curves (Water Retention curves)

Matric Potential

The matric potential is the measure of the relative reduction in water potential as a result of the attraction of the soil matrix. A simple tool to measure this potential is called *tensiometer* or commercially irrometers.

Suction Plates or Tension Plates

There are gypsum blocks embedded at different depths of soil and the variation in tension is measured using a resistance meter against the caliberated against a range of moisture. The other materials used for making blocks are nylon fibre glass etc. The blocks may be rectangular or cylindrical. Resistance blocks are not useful for saline soils for the resistance reading is affected by salt concentration. However, gypsum blocks work better even in saline conditions, because of buffering, action, where nylon or fibre glass blocks cannot be used. Generally the resistance blocks should not be used for wet soil moisture range.

Soil Moisture Content

The different methods are hygroscopic coefficient.

MOISTURE EQUIVALENT AND MOISTURE PERCENTAGE AT ONE-THIRD BAR

Water Potential

The moisture equivalent is defined as the amount of water that will be retained in a soil of 1 cm depth when it is centrifuged at a speed intended to produce a force at the outflow boundary, 1000 times that of gravity (0.98 bar equivalent suction) for medium textured soils, the moisture closely corresponds to water potential of 1/3 bar equivalent suction as determined by pressure plate apparatus. Therefore, moisture equivalent and moisture percentage at 1/3 bar are equipotential.

Moisture Percentage of Fifteen Bar

It is the moisture content that is retained in the soil which is subjected to a pressure difference of 15 bar across a water permeable membrance. It is equipotential in the vicinity of permanent wilting point.

Field Capacity

It is expressed commonly as a upper limit of available moisture range. It is also defined as maximum force between soil particles and water molecules and are responsible for lowering potential energy of water in the soil compared with water in bulk.

Total Soil Water Potential

It can be defined as the amount of work that must be done per unit quantity of pure water in order to transport reversibly and is isothermally an infinitesimal quantity of water from a pool of pure water at a specified elevation at atmospheric pressure to soil water at the point under consideration (Aslyng *et al.*, 1963).

When expressed per unit amount of water the potential energy thus defined is referred to as the potential of water (YK) in the particular force field considered, or

$$Y_k = F_k\, d_1$$

In which F_k = Force per unit mass due to field 'K' the total potential can be represented by

in which

= Gravitational potential

= Pressure (or matric) potential

= Osmatic potential

There are other potentials like electric and temperature potentials which affect the system.

Soil Characteristics

Soil water content and soil water potential are important determines of water uptake. The relationships between soil-water potential (y soil), root surface water potential (y root) and leaf water potential (y leaf) were reported by Slatyer (1967) in a system where water supply was withheld but similar evaporation conditions existed before 5 days.

Fig. 6.2 showing probable changes in leaf water potential (ψ leaf) and root water potential (ψ roots) of a transpiring plant rooted in a soil allowed to dry from a water potential (ψ soil) near zero (wet soil) to a water potential at which wilting occurs (Slatyer, 1967).

Soil Moisture Characteristics

Release of water from a soil has a certain bearing with the size and volume of water filled pores. The suction causes release of water, in the beginning larger pores empty the water, as suction increases, the smaller pores release water. These can be represented by "soil moisture characteristic curve" in different soil textures and conditions.

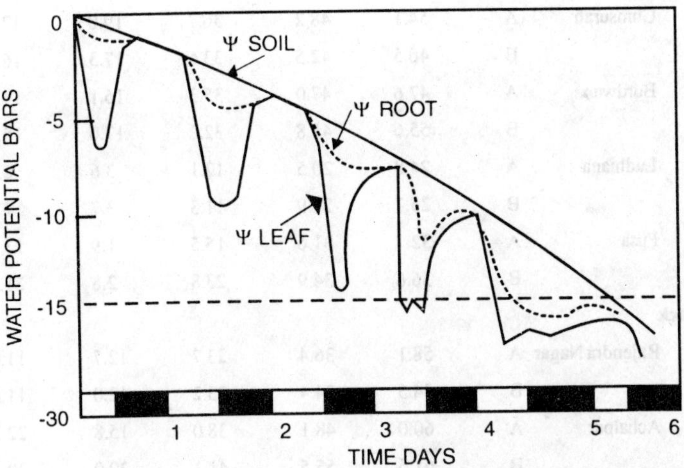

Fig. 6.2 : Diagram showing probable changes in leaf water potential (ψ leaf) and root water potential (ψ root) of a transpiring plant rooted in soil allowed to dry from a water potential (ψ soil) near zero (wet soil) to a water potential at which wilting occurs (After Slatyer, 1967).

It has been found that an increase in tension from zero to 1/3 atmosphere released more than 75 per cent of water in light textured soil but less than 50 per cent in a heavy textured soil. The moisture at various atmospheric pressures of tensions in different soil types in India has been given below by Ali *et al.*, 1966.

Soil		Atmosphere				Available moisture per cent
		0	1/10	1/3	15	
1		2	3	4	5	6
Alluvial						
Delhi	A	34.0	27.2	10.7	4.4	6.3
	B	37.4	29.9	17.7	7.7	10.0

1		2	3	4	5	6
Lucknow	A	47.0	42.1	29.2	8.1	21.1
	B	41.2	34.6	25.8	6.0	19.8
Chinsurah	A	54.1	48.2	36.7	19.0	17.7
	B	46.5	42.5	33.6	17.3	16.6
Burdwan	A	47.6	47.0	35.3	16.1	19.2
	B	55.6	41.8	32.2	17.0	15.3
Ludhiana	A	24.8	20.5	12.1	3.6	8.5
	B	25.7	21.9	11.3	3.7	7.6
Pusa	A	32.1	31.6	15.5	1.9	13.6
	B	36.6	34.9	23.8	2.8	21.0
Black						
Rajendra Nagar	A	58.1	36.4	23.7	12.7	11.0
	B	54.5	34.4	23.2	12.0	11.2
Achalpur	A	60.0	48.1	38.0	15.8	22.2
	B	61.5	55.5	41.1	20.0	20.1
Tharsa	A	50.1	45.8	30.0	16.1	13.9
	B	54.5	40.5	28.3	16.2	12.1
Padgaon	A	83.8	68.3	43.5	25.7	16.8
	B	76.3	68.8	43.3	27.2	16.1
Nagpur	A	8.1	54.4	38.9	21.1	17.8
	B	54.5	51.3	34.8	20.5	14.3
Red Soils						
Cheruvukomi	A	33.8	30.2	17.5	8.5	9.0
	B	41.4	34.9	28.0	12.3	10.7
Yemmiganur	A	34.5	31.4	19.8	8.2	11.6
	B	44.3	38.7	24.9	13.6	11.3
Tolukhal	A	35.0	27.4	13.4	8.8	4.5
	B	35.6	25.8	16.8	11.5	5.2
Raichur	A	31.4	26.2	13.7	7.4	6.3
	B	32.2	24.3	14.0	7.5	6.5
Laterite & Lateritic						
Midnapur	A	27.6	21.8	13.7	5.2	8.5
	B	37.2	27.9	18.2	9.1	9.1

1		2	3	4	5	6
Kuttapana	A	30.0	36.8	15.1	9.7	5.4
	B	43.0	33.8	25.6	19.9	5.7
Nerkodu	A	51.6	43.2	22.2	16.9	5.3
	B	55.0	43.4	29.4	21.1	8.3
Bhata	A	43.0	35.2	26.5	13.1	13.4
	B	48.5	36.9	27.5	15.5	12.0
Suri	A	24.0	22.5	14.2	4.3	9.9
	B	23.0	20.5	13.3	4.4	8.9
Mountain & Forest Soils						
Bhowali	A	56.2	44.9	32.3	9.1	22.9
	B	50.3	36.4	27./2	10.4	16.8
Ootacamand	A	49.7	42.0	30.5	18.7	11.8
	B	45.2	34.9	26.7	17.3	9.4
Dehradun	A	41.3	37.0	29.1	8.4	20.7
	B	43.7	35.0	26.8	9.8	16.9

However, when water potentials, in leaves, roots and soil become equal, water absorption becomes negligible.

In irrigated agriculture practices, we use two terms field capacity and wilting percentage to describe the water status of the soil. It is well known that the same amount of irrigation would not necessarily bring all soils to the field capacity (F.C.) because F.C. values differ for different soils. Similarly, the moisture content at which wheat shown permanent wilting, cannot be the permanent wilting percentage for other crops even in the same soil. This happens because some plants are prone to wilting at a fairly reasonable water content of the soil, whereas others wilt when the moisture content has been very much reduced. However, from the point of view of crop production, PWP is important because, if such a situation develops at a critical stage of plant growth the crop would be completely ruined. This warrants the classification of plants with respect to a particular soil type.

SOIL TEMPERATURE

The water absorption and transpiration are considerably influenced by soil temperature. In many plants water absorption below a soil temperature of 10°C is reduced sharply and has almost a linear function upto 25°C. Above this temperature limit uptake is again slowed down. In most instances temperatures above 40°C in the rhizosphere do not support water absorption and plant can show signs of wilting, usually low soil temperature are encountered in northern India during the winter season when crops such as wheat, barley, bengal gram, potatoes etc. are grown. Some of these crops are adversely influenced by frost injury. The plants show wilting and the crop is damaged. It was observed at Delhi that the soil temperature at 5 cm depth was generally lower by 2.5 to 4°C than the ambient temperature if the soil water content was near field capacity. In dry soil this difference was insignificant. However, the contribution of soil temperature to frost injury in crops like potatoes and peas is not known. The occurrence of gram wilt disease has been assumed to be due to wet weather, and low temperatures both which reduce soil temperature. A freezing temperature in soil cause finally wilting of the plants (I.A.R.I. Monograph No. 4, 1977).

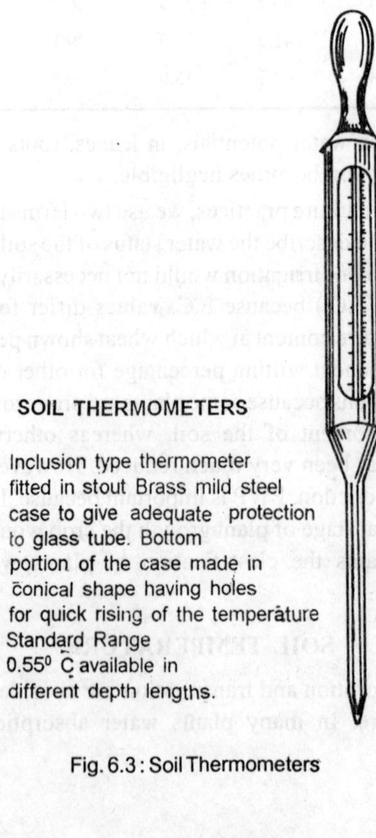

Fig. 6.3 : Soil Thermometers

The low soil temperature reduced water absorption due to following reasons, Kramer (1969) :

1. Decreased root growth occurs in dry soils having high temperature which limits the movement of water and hence reduced water uptake due to poor root growth.
2. *Increased viscosity of water*: The viscosity of water increases as the temperature decreases and is about twice as great near 0°C as at 25°C
3. *Increased resistance to movement of water into roots* : This is caused by decreased permeability of cell membrances and the increased viscosity.
4. *Decreased metabolic activity of root cells*: This has some effect on active water uptake because it results in decreased salt accumulation. It affects passive absorption only so far as it affects permeability of cell membrance of the root.

SOIL AREATION AND FLOODING

Some plants wilt when they are compelled to stand continuously in water. It is because they do not absorb water under waterlogged conditions. This wilting may be observed particularly in cowpea, mung and maize plants after continuous rains under bright sunshine conditions. In tobacco crop, this wilting is often termed as flopping. As against this a rice crop grows profusely when there is a standing water. Plant such as Typha-latifolia (cattail), para grass also grow profusely under standing water or water-logged conditions.

The injury to crops under water-logged or flooded conditions may be due to the following reasons :

(i) Poor availability of oxygen and occurrence of higher CO_2 concentration around roots.

(ii) Accumulation of toxic substances either in the submerged roots or around them.

(iii) Changes in the pattern of ion uptake resulting in the accumulation of some ions to toxic limits.

In water-logged conditions the availability of oxygen is reduced considerably. This has a direct bearing on the respiratory activity of roots and the "active water uptake" which although is only a small component of total water uptake, can be stopped. In addition, the increased concentration of CO_2 affects the permeability of membrances and consequently adversely influences water uptake (Sinha S.K. and Singh, N.P., 1977).

Another effect of reduced oxygen is through its influence on root growth. Once the plants are water-logged the roots become thick and dévelop larger air spaces. Further growth is almost inhabited. Therefore, the total surface area is reduced. These effects can be seen on the nodules which are enlarged but loose their nitrogen fixing capacity (Sprent, 1975). However, in some plants such as sorghum (Jowar), Sesbania etc. a large number of advertitious roots appear from the aerial parts. This apparently helps to meet their oxygen demand but the plants do not show normal growth even when the water-logged conditions are over. As against this rice thrives well under similar conditions because of larger intercellular spaces in leaves and stem which maintain continuity with roots. Thus in rice, oxygen transport throughout the plant is possible.

Among the toxic substances which are known to accumulate in the rhizosphere under water-logged conditions are the metabolities produces as a result of an aerobic respiration. These could be ethanol, aldehydes etc. Some plants such as rice have been shown to have a strong alcohol dehydrogenase system which could effectively eliminate the accumulation of alcohol. Epinasty in leaves of the plants standing in water has been known since long and various reasons were ascribed to it. Present evidences suggest that this could be due to the adverse effect of ethylene. Methods to eliminate ethylene accumulation can go a long way to overcome the adverse effects of water-logging.

Olomu and Raez (1974) reported that flax plants usually become chlorotic under water-logged conditions. They found that chlorotic plants contained lower concentration of iron (Fe) and higher concentration of manganese (Mn). It was further shown that the yield of flax decreased with increase in 'Mn' concentration and Mn: Fe ratio of plants. Apparently under wet conditions the reduction in translocation of iron from roots to tops contributed to chlorosis.

PLANT FACTORS

Among the plant factors directly related to the absorption of water from the soil is the root system. Assuming that the soil water potential, soil temperature and aeration are favourable then, it is the root system which can strongly influence the uptake of water. This happens because the root system of crops and varieties differ and the absorption of water by roots in different parts is different.

Root system has recently attracted more attention in past and attempts have been made to distinguish varieties with different root systems. In wheat and barley differences in root systems have been observed at the varietal level. There are, however, some reports which do not support this under field conditions, Hackett (1969) reported differences in the root pattern of two varieties of barley as given in Table 6.4.

TABLE 6.4

Root Pattern in Two Varieties of Barley

(Hackett, 1969)

Varieties	2 weeks	4 weeks	Ratio 4:2 weeks
Maris Badger			
No. of Members	187	2080	11.1
Length (cm)	439	5700	13.0
Surface area (cm²)	38	467	12.3
Volume (cm³)	0.30	3.77	12.6
Proctor			
No. of members	201	1210	6.0
Length (cm)	442	3850	8.7
Surface area (cm²)	39	312	8.0
Volume (cm³)	0.30	2.62	8.7

These data indicate that the rates of root growth in two varieties were different which may be done to some other factors too, like difference in top growth, which depends on root : shoot ratio. The real root growth is when this ratio is also changed.

The root growth under field conditions is very much influenced by the soil and therefore, soil and crop management can help to improve root growth and eventually water absorption. The root structure development and depth penetration is of much importance under dry-land agriculture than irrigated one. In fact it is only the spread of the root system between 15-30 cm zone which may play a more important role in crops like wheat.

Chaudhary and Parihar (1974) found following in sandy loam and loamy sands of Ludhiana :

(i) Straw mulch and cultivation inhibited root growth in the upper 15 cm of the soil and increased the lateral spread.

(ii) Inter-row compaction inhibited lateral spread of roots in the surface layers and caused downward growth of roots.

The rates of water absorption into roots of different plants differ with their stage of growth (Highest rates of water entry are associated with root hairs and unsuberized roots and lowest are suberized woody roots. Kramer, 1969).

Once water has entered the roots, its path is through the cortcal layers, pericycle and endodermis to the vascular bundle. It is only its passage through the endodermis which offers resistance.

In a plant which is losing water through leaves it is expected that it would have a difference in the water potentials of the xylem sap and the roots which act as a driving force. This has indeed been shown by several workers. The various theories of water movement from the roots to the leaves of tall plants have been worked out. The essential features of these theories are given below :

(1) Leaves and other aerial parts contain pores called stomata through which water is lost. The process is called transpiration.

(2) The loss of water vapour through stomata brings down the water potential of the surrounding cells, depending upon the water potential of the atmosphere.

(3) Drop in the water potential of the leaves creates a "pull" effect on the water column present in the xylem vessels and trecheids of the leaves and stem maintaining, continuity upto roots, greater the loss of water from the leaves higher will be the gradient, and higher will be the "pull" effect.

In this process the cohesive and adhesive properties of water play an important role in the maintenance of the water column, if the column is broken and the air gets into the xylem vessels or trecheids, the upward movement of water would stop. At the same time the xylem vessels and trecheids are not the continuous columns extending from the roots to the leaf. In fact they have septa which offer resistance to water flow. In tall plants this resistance can be enormous but in crop plants this apparently does not pose any serious problem. However, values of resistance to flow through the whole plant and its component have been worked out by Jensen *et al.* (1961) for sunflower and tomato as given in Table 6.5.

Transpiration

In the process of soil absorption it should be realised that transpiration plays the most significant role. It is this process that determines the gradient between the atmosphere and the plant through leaves. Though transpiration is essentially a process of evaporation and it is different from the latter in several respects. Evaporation from an open surface meets less resistance but when water evaporates through leaves there is considerable amount of resistance.

The main components offering resistance to water vapour diffusion from leaves to the atmosphere are (a) air boundary layer resistance and (b) leaf resistance. The component of leaf resistance are mesophyll tissue, cuticle, inter-cellular spaces and stomata of these components. The cuticular resistance is maximum and is followed by the stomatal and the boundary layer. The cuticle also offers resistance to carbon-dioxide essential for photosynthesis. Therefore, it is only stomata which regulate both water loss and exchange of carbon-dioxide. A plant which absorbs carbon-dioxide has possibly to lose water vapour once the stomata are open.

TABLE 6.5

Values Resistance to Flow Through Whole Plants and Their Components

(Jensen *et al.* 1961)

Measured components	Resistance (mb sec/g water)	
	Sunflower	Tomato
Whole plant	2.40	1.40
Stem and roots	1.50	0.81
Stem and leaves	0.88	0.42
Stem only	0.44	0.24

Principle of Stomatal Regulation

In the process of transpiration there are several factors which offer resistance. If the stomatal resistance could be enhanced through some mechanism it could possibly lead to decreased water loss and increased water use efficiency (WUE). This is the basis of several models and simulations, Cowan and Troughton (1971) derived the following relationship for water use efficiency :

$$w = \frac{r_m/r_a + 0.5}{0.66 + 0.58}$$

where :

w = The water use efficiency at saturated water vapour density with respect to change in temperature.

r_a = Boundary layer resistance to CO_2 diffusion of individual leaf surface.

r_m = Internal leaf resistance or mesophyll resistance of CO_2 diffusion.

They concluded that *the water use* efficiency could be improved through increased mesophyll resistance where it is already high ($r_m > 1$) as in C_3 plants.

WATER AVAILABILITY, PLANT GROWTH AND YIELD

The availability of water in the right quantity and at the right time is essential for good plant growth and yield. Both the amount of water as well as the time may differ in different crop plants. Thus what may be true for one crop may not necessarily be so for other crops, growing even in the nearby fields. When we talk of the amount of water, our concorn is both the shortage as well as the excess. However, sometimes we feel shortage of water for supply particularly during summers and even in winters when the preceding monsoons had been not enough to have enough water storage. In rainy season normally the water supply is in excess except a monsoon failures. The excess water problem may also come up when farmer gets water through public distribution system and he is more apt to apply excess water in spite of the fact that it may not do any good. Farmer commits this mistake firstly because he is usually unaware of the concept of optimal requirement and use of water as per soil conditions and crops selected. He usually feels that the application of water is helpful irrespective of its amount and other constraints, secondly the farmer is possibly not certain to receive water (non-assured water supply) when the crop needs it again.

All plants experience some amount of water deficit during their growth. One of the first effects is the loss of relative water content (RWC). Identified levels of stress are as follows :

(1) *Mild Stress* : Drop in RWC by 8-10% corresponding to values in well watered plants under mild evaporative demands. This corresponds to a drop of water potential by 5 to 6 bars.

(2) *Moderate Stress* : Lowering of water potential less than 12 to 15 bars corresponding to more than 100% but less than 20% change in RWC.

(3) *Severe Stress* : Resuction of water potential more than 15 bars and lowering of RWC by more than 20%.

The above classification serves as a good practical guide for field problems. However, there is a specific and generalised effect of water stress on various plant processes such as cell growth, wall synthesis, protein synthesis, nitrate reductase level, ABA accumulation, stomatal opening, CO_2 assimilation, respiration, proline accumulation and sugar accumulation.

The relationship of growth of a plant with time is normally sigmoid in nature. The evapotranspirative demand of the plant increases as the emerged plant develops due to start of photo synthesis, as well as due to development of root system. If we draw α curve for the water use throughout the plant life, it starts with germination, reaches the peak point when the canopy is thick and starts declining with the onset of senescence of leaves and other organs. Depending upon the time when water is in short supply the plant may enter the state in which division and cell growth would be either suspended or inhibited. If this happens to be the period when tiller differentiation or branching were occurring the process will be effected adversely. An example is first irrigation of wheat between 21 — 25 days when crownroot stage appears after sowing. Failure to irrigate at this stage suppress crown roots and yields. The same is true for other critical stages of growth where irrigation is a must. The water deficiency besides retarding growth of a crop affects the fertility of reproductive organs. However, the critical growth stage for irrigation varies from crop to crop and variety to variety and soil type.

It is therefore, essential that behaviour of different yield components under different irrigation management practices must be determined for predicting more precisely the water requirement of different crop varieties at different times.

SOIL WATER POTENTIAL

The water present in the soil is influenced by different force-fields, matrix, osmosis and body forces. The matric forces result from the solid phase case. When water is added to the soil the adhesive forces due to air water interface cause holding of water through well known capillarity phenomena. The surface tension of water at 25°C is as high as 72 dynes/cm. At 0°C it is 75.6 dynes/cm. The dielectric coefficient of pure water at 0°C is 88). The force of adhesion is related with the following equation :

$$W = O\,(1 + \cos\,\theta)$$

in which

O = Surface tension dynes/cm

θ = Liquid solid contact angle, degrees

Due to surface tension water rises in the soil pores formed by the soil matrix. The height of water is represented by following equation :

$$h = \frac{20\ \alpha\ \text{Cos}\ \theta}{\rho_{gr}}$$

where :

h = Height of water rise, cm

h = Density of water, gm/cm³

g = Acceleration due to gravity, cm/sec.

r = Radius of pore, cm

θ = Angle of contact between soil particles and water degrees.

Water is also held by the soil matrix through electrostatic fields of the solid surfaces (diffuse double layers).

All the forces are very strong, attractive forces between soil particles and water molecules and are responsible for the lowering of potential energy of water in the soil compared with water in bulk.

However, in view of the recent knowledge about soil water behaviour the field capacity is not a unique value that always occurs in soil. The equilibrium condition between the amount of water in the soil and the gravitational force field is hardly reached owing to the dynamic system of water removal by drainage evapotransportation, addition by dew, rainfall and irrigation. The hysteresis effect also gives different F.C. values. Texture, structure and temperature changes also cause variation in yield capacity values. In contrast to the definition the movement of water downward in the soil does not cease when the soil reaches the so-called F.C. In view of these facts, the filled capacity should be considered as a range of soil water contents over which the rate of water removal from the soil following and irrigation or heavy rain begins to reduce. Thus this term may be used precisely to indicate the general region of water percentages. Therefore, the definite values such as moisture percentage at 1/3 bar be used.

Available Water Capacity of Soils by Soil Texture Classes

In estimating the available water capacity of the groups of soils in this irrigation guide, the predominant soil textures of the major soil horizons for the soils in each irrigation group were used. The individual soils in the irrigation design groups will vary somewhat in total available water capacity because of minor differences in the texture of the soil horizons.

TABLE 6.6

Available Water Capacities

Soil texture classes	Surface soil 0-12"	Sub-soil 12 -36"	Lower horizons 36 - 60"
Coarse sand and gravel	.04 to .06	.03 to .05	.02 to .04
Sands	.07 to .09	.06 to .08	.05 to .07
Loamy sands	.10 to .12	.09 to .11	.08 to .10
Sandy loams	.13 to .15	.12 to .14	.11 to .13
Fine sandy loams	.16 to .18	.15 to .17	.14 to .16
Loams and very fine sandy loams	.20 to .22	.17 to .19	.17 to .19
Silt loams	.22 to .24	.20 to .22	.20 to .22
Silty clay loams	.21 to .23	.18 to .20	.18 to .20
Sandy clay loams	.18 to .20	.16 to .18	.15 to .17
Clay loams	.17 to .19	.15 to .17	.14 to .16
Silty clays	.12 to .14	.11 to .13	.10 to .12
Clays	.11 to .13	.09 to .11	.08 to .10

The ranges of available water capacities are the adjusted water retention difference between 1/3-bar and 15-bar tension for the medium and fine textured soils, and between 1/10-bar and 15-bar for the moderately coarse and coarse textures. Undisturbed clods were used to determine the bulk densities of the soils. Readily available capacity is influenced by soil texture, organic matter content, kind of clay, soil structure, minerology and other physical and chemical features. For this irrigation guide the figures shown for available water capacity (by foot increments) are estimates determined on the basis of the data shown in the above table.

Permanent Wilting Point

This term like F.C. was (P.W.P) considered as a constant value for a given soil where plant wilts permanently. It was also considered to be the lower limit of available water range. But in reality the permanent wilting point is dynamic in nature and so it must be explained as a range of water percentages over which the rate of water supply to the plant is not adequate to prevent wilting. The P.W.P. is also dependent upon profile features and Hydraulic Conductivity.

CHAPTER 7

ROOTS, THEIR MECHANISM OF WATER AND NUTRIENTS ABSORPTION IN DIFFERENT SOILS

Introduction

The plants like solids are also three phase system of solid, liquid and gas and development of both has relationship for the favourable plant growth.

The favourable plant growth is a major factor responsible for the soil profile differentiation or its development through the supply of organic matter, absorption of water which helps to translocate the plant nutrients through production of a specific root system and vegetative cover or canopy to the soil surface. Plants also help indirectly in the soil profile development through their occasional burning and wind falls.

The leaves maintain the plant structure with the stem having conducting tissues called xylem and phloem. The former are the main channel of water transport. The stem gets water from the roots in contact with water and soil. The air is passed through stomatas.

To design a successful irrigation system, the irrigation engineer must know the rooting characteristics of plants and how plants use moisture. Since a continuous supply of available moisture is necessary for good plant growth, the irrigation system for any given crop must be designed to supply the essential amount of water during that crop's peak use period. The size of the soil reservoir that holds available water for the use of plants is determined mostly by that plant's rooting characteristics. The distribution of its roots determine its moisture extraction pattern.

HOW PLANTS GET THEIR MOISTURE

There is an enormous root surface in most of the plants. Near the growing top of each root or root let, there are many root hair's in close contact with soil particles (collids) and with air spaces from which roots get their oxygen. Through osmotic and other forces, root hairs extract moisture from the film of water that surrounds each soil particle.

The intake and transpiration of water by plant roots may be explained by two important phenomenon :

(1) Capillary movement of water to plant roots, and

(2) Growth of roots into moist soil.

As roots take up moisture, tension around the soil particles increases and water moves toward these points of plant absorption. This depends on type of soils which decides capillary movement and delivery of water to the soil adjacent to the root system. This therefore, depends upon soil moisture holding capacity and replenishment of soil moisture through irrigation or by other source.

During favourable growing periods in a soil under very good structural conditions and adequate supply of moisture as per water requirement of the crops, the root system develops profusely and roots often elongate so rapidly that satisfactory moisture contents can be maintained even when the soil moisture content declines and without much help from capillary movement. Because under these conditions roots are able to derive soil moisture from deeper soil layers (provided no barrier layer exists). Thus even if the moisture in rootzone is reaching near wilting point, the moisture supply for plant growth is being maintained from below the rootzone soil where root system has developed during early favourable plant growth period.

TYPES OF ROOT SYSTEMS DEVELOPMENT

The type of root system developed in a soil depends upon (1) heredity character of plant, (ii) type of soil, and (iii) water table conditions.

Some plants have (a) A tap root system (dicot crops) which penetrates deeply into soil under favourable conditions and (b) slow growing plants develop, shallow primary roots and many lateral (fibrous) roots system (see Fig. 7.1). The depth root penetration is different for different crops.

(i) Thus crops like spinach and celery develop root system within one foot top soil.

(ii) Potato roots extend within the upper 2 feet.

(iii) Corn, cotton and tomato roots permeate an open soil to a depth of 4 feet or more.

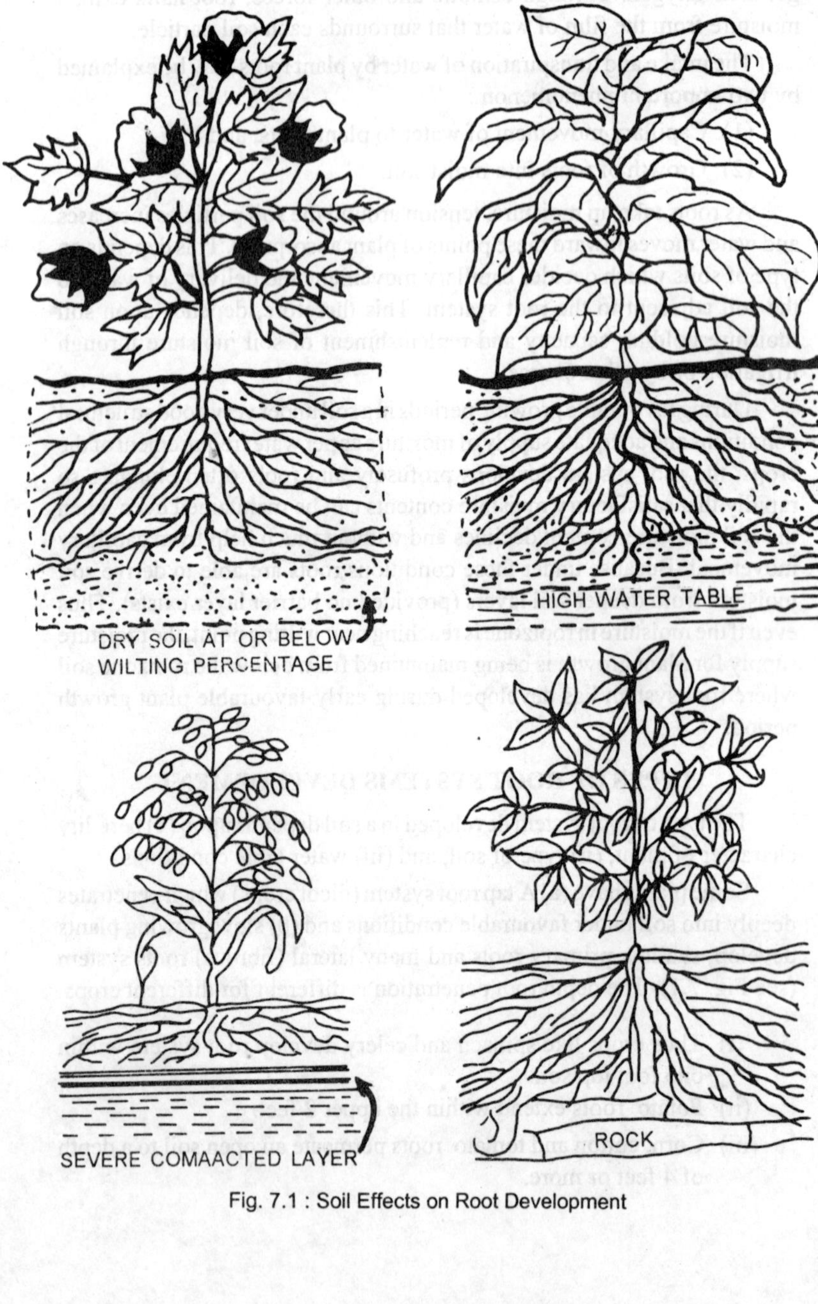

Fig. 7.1 : Soil Effects on Root Development

(iv) Alfalfa and Asparagus (fodder grass) roots penetrate into good soils to a depth of 8-10 feet or more.

(v) Cucumber roots extend laterally 5 or 6 feet in the ploughed layer.

The Fig.7.2 shows the root system of field and vegetable crops in deep irrigated soils.

Effects of Soil Texture on Root Development

Root penetration is seriously affected by a (i) Compacted layer in the soil at any soil depth due to any reason. The roots are therefore, confined to that layer due to the soil pressure being more than what roots can exert except in soil or any other cracks where roots may penetrate in search of moisture and plant nutrients. (ii) The soil texture is another factor in this regard. Thus root system develops more in medium to fine textured soils than sandy texture.

EFFECT OF TOPOGRAPHY (RELIEF) AND TIME OF GROWTH

(i) Soil moisture deficit in rootzone and below affects root growth in the initial growth period. Thus if soil at any time in rootzone reaches near wilting point, the root growth is hampered and that initial shock cannot be regained, even after excess moisture at later stage of growth. Thus topography of land determines intake and supply of moisture time of growth stage and life cycle is important.

(ii) A high water table limits root growth. A rising or fluctuating water table may kill roots that have previously grown in the initial water table conditions and developed system to adapt that particular conditions. Thus saturation of the soil above the normal rootzone depth of a plant restricts root development.

Effects of Organic Matter

Deficiency of plant nutrients and organic matter in the surface and sub-soil also limits the depth of root penetration.

The above effects have been shown in Fig. 7.3.

Effects of Climte on Root Development

Considering two important moisture regions of the universe namely (i) arid, and (ii) humid.

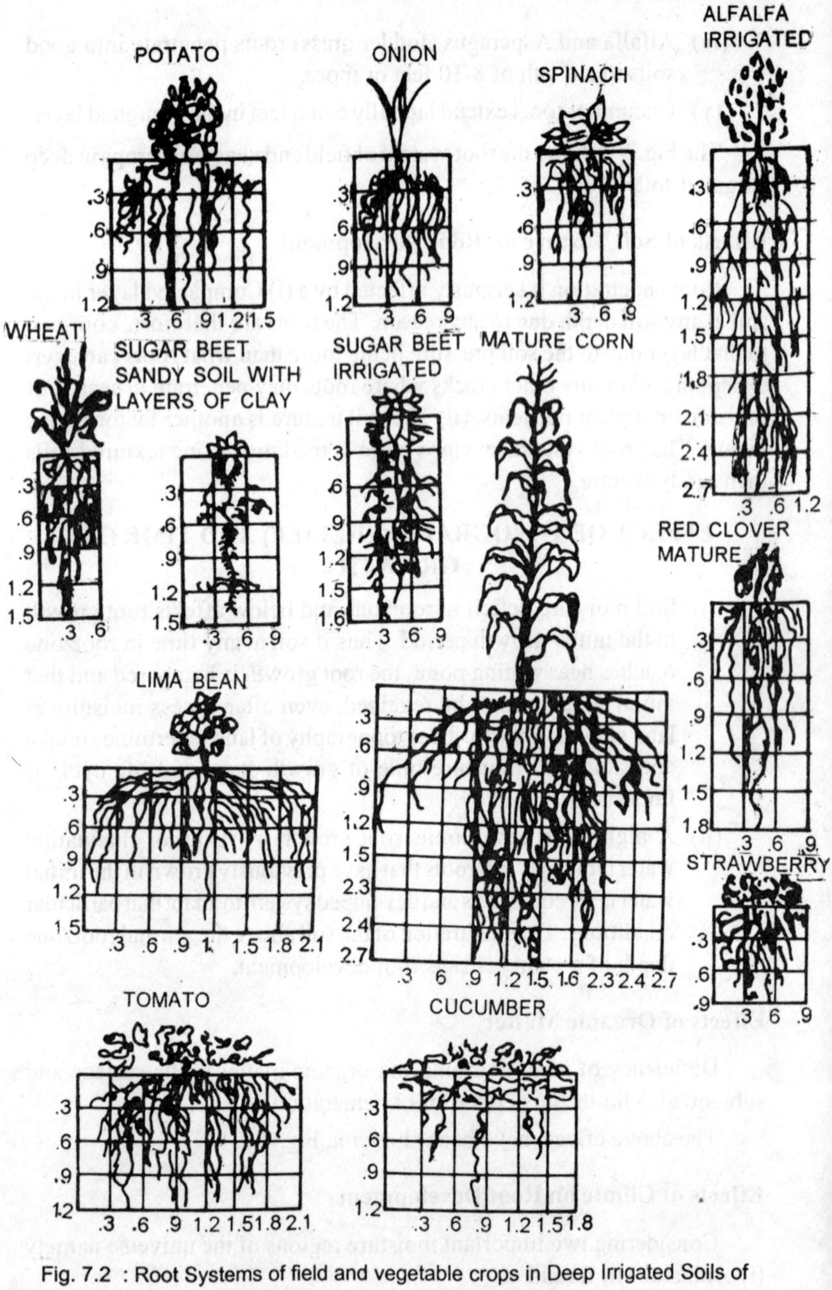

Fig. 7.2 : Root Systems of field and vegetable crops in Deep Irrigated Soils of Central United States. (Depth in metres)

Arid and Semi-Arid Tracts

In these regions the soils are generally permeable and aerated to a greater depth and have a fertile sub-soil as such the root development is profuse and satisfactory throughout the soil profile (uniform) unless otherwise the impermeable conditions created by bad soil and water management practices which limit root growth (non-uniform).

In the humid regions even at the beginning of the growing season, the upper part of soil may be at field capacity and the lower more saturated with high moisture content as a result of winter and spring rains. This results in a shallower root growth than in comparison to the irrigated tracts of arid and semi-arid regions.

This therefore, points out that the soil moisture reservoir is smaller in humid regions than in arid or semi-arid regions. The quantity of irrigation to meet the requirement of crops through root system therefore has to be calculated as per moisture needs which is changing or variable from zone to zone and soil to soil for favourable plant and root growth.

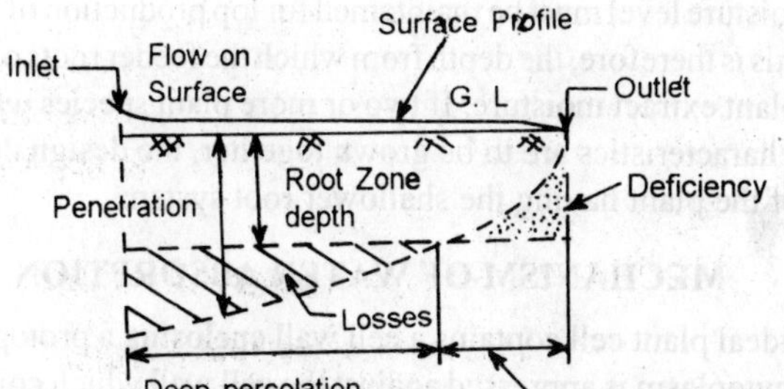

Fig. 7.3 : Non-Uniform distribution of moisture in rootzone (in surface flooding)

MOISTURE EXTRACTION PATTERN

The amount of roots responsible for absorbing roots is greatest in the upper part of the rootzone (usually in the top foot) and near the base of the plant. The extraction of water is maximum in the zone of maximum development of roots provided the conditions of temperature and aeration are favourable. The condition extraction of moisture is more from the upper few inches of soil till it is unable to supply required quantity of moisture and under these conditions the moisture is withdrawn or depleted from lower soil layers.

The moisture extraction pattern is different in uniform and non-uniform soils. In uniform soils the moisture extraction pattern is in general the same type. Thus about 40 per cent of moisture extracted is contributed by upper quarter of rootzone, 30% from the second quarter, 20% from the third quarter and 10% from the bottom quarter. Values for the different crops are within a range of 10 per cent.

In *non-uniform* soils, however, the amount of moisture available for crop growth may be determined by the soil layer that has the lowest amount of available moisture. If the top layer of a soil is coarsed texture having a low water holding capacity the supply of moisture to roots gets exhausted earlier than medium to fine textured soils. Hence if the moisture replenishment is not made early the plant and root growth is severely hampered causing reduction in yields.

Similarly the presence of compacted barrier layer also exhaust moisture earlier besides poor root growth and development. Thus shallow depth soils or deep soils with barrier layer or coarse textured soils behave more or less similar manner.

Design Moisture Extraction Depth : It is related to the soil depth used to calculate irrigation water requirement for design. It is the depth in which a high moisture level must be maintained for top production of agricultural crops. This is therefore, the depth from which the feeder roots of an average mature plant extract moisture. If two or more plant species with different rooting characteristics are to be grown together, the design depth should be that of the plant having the shallower root system.

MECHANISM OF WATER ABSORPTION

An ideal plant cell contains a cell wall enclosing a protoplast. A thin layer of cytoplasm is appressed against the cell wall which contain all cell inclusions.

The inner layer of the cytoplasm called Vacuole contains cell sap. The sap is a water solution having same osmotic potential when such a cell is placed in pure water its functions are determined by water potential gradient.

Now pure water has zero potential. When solute is added, the water potential of the solution decreases below zero. This means that the cell sap has a lower water potential than pure water. When such a cell is placed in pure water a gradient due to difference in water potential is caused. This results in the movement of water inside the cell which causes creation of turgor pressure or force which is responsible for the movement of water

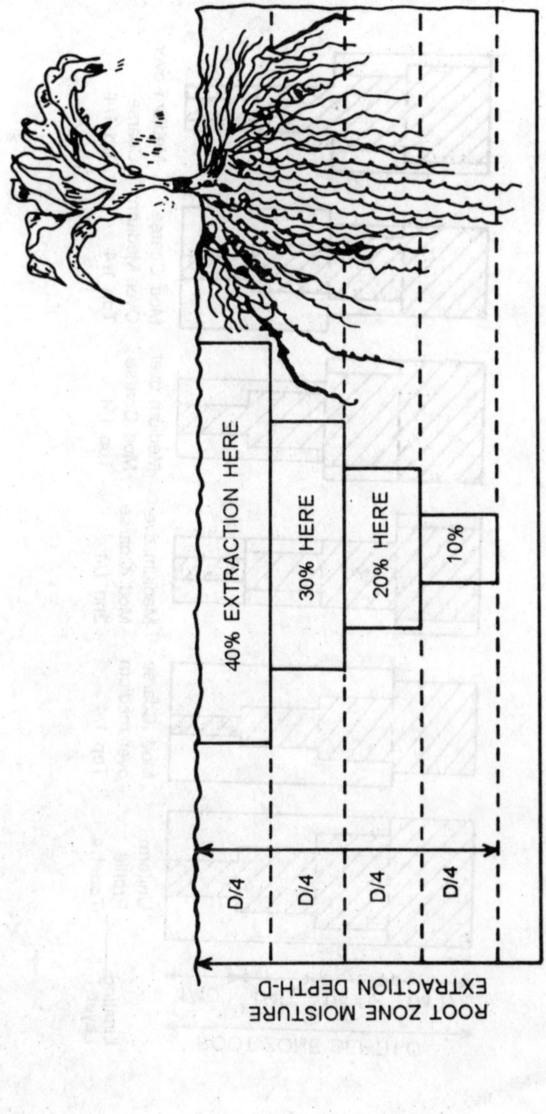

Fig. 7.4 : Average moisture extraction pattern of plants growing in a soil in uniform soil.

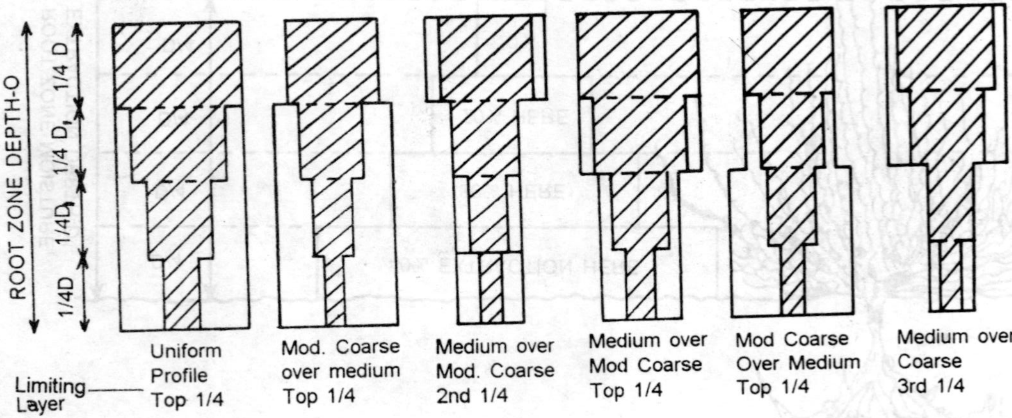

Fig. 7.5 : Moisture extraction patterns as determined by available moisture content represents in various parts of the soil profile. Width of each profile represents available moisture, gross area (height and width of each profile represents total available moisture in profiles, hatched area shows moisture-extraction pattern for each profile, Agri. Engin, 1955)

inside the cell. Since the concentration of sap also decreases, the osmotic potential of the sap is also decreases over time. Thus the difference between the potential of pure water and cell sap gets reduced. This lowers the force by which water enters the cell. (After Kramer, 1969). See Fig. 7.6.

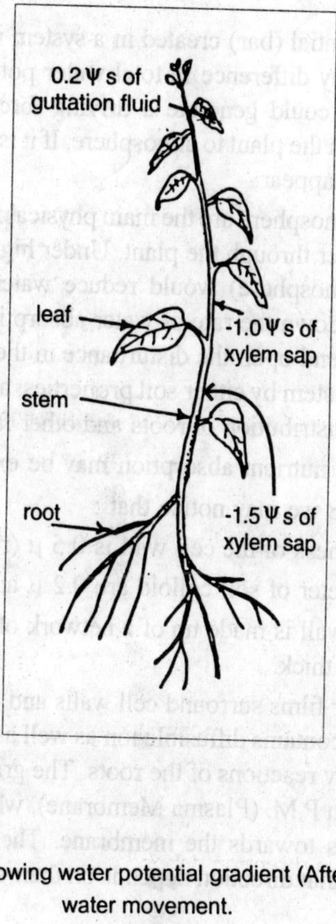

Fig. 7.6 : Plant parts showing water potential gradient (After Kramer, 1969) for water movement.

Factors Affecting Moisture Absorption by Roots

The following factors reduce moisture absorption of roots :

(1) Soil characteristic

(2) Soil temperature

(3) Soil aeration and flooding.

The root growth under field conditions is influenced by soil characteristics, hence soil management can help to improve root growth and eventually water absorption. The root structure and growth of course has more significance under dry land farming wherein a deep root system could provide some advantage. However, under irrigated agriculture, the spread of root system between 15-30 cm zone plays more important role in crops like wheat.

The water potential (bar) created in a system is different for soil, leaf and atmosphere. Any difference in total water potential in the soil-plant-atmosphere system could generate a driving force for water movement from the soil through the plant to atmosphere. If it is broken by a cut in stem the force would disappear.

The soil and atmosphere are the main physical factors which determine the flow rate of water through the plant. Under high-humidity (High water potential in the atmosphere) would reduce water loss from plants and consequently slow down the rate of water absorption by plants. However, this absorption depend upon the disturbance in the equilibrium in the soil plant atmosphere system by either soil properties, atmosphere or biological changes, size and distribution of roots and other factors discussed earlier.

The water and nutrient absorption may be explained by Fig. 7.7.

As per Fig. 7.8 we may notice that :

1. The thickness of the cell wall is 0.5 μ (range 0.1 to 3 m)
2. The diameter of soil colloid are 0.2 μ and less.
3. The cell wall is made up of a network of cellulose strands about 0.0005 μ thick.
4. The water films surround cell walls and soil colloids. This water (H+OH) contains diffusible ion as well as CO_2 produced from the respiratory reactions of the roots. The gradient for CO_2 and H^+ is away from P.M. (Plasma Membrane), while that of cations of the nutrient is towards the membrane. The movement of nutrients cation in that direction depends on their associated anions. Under

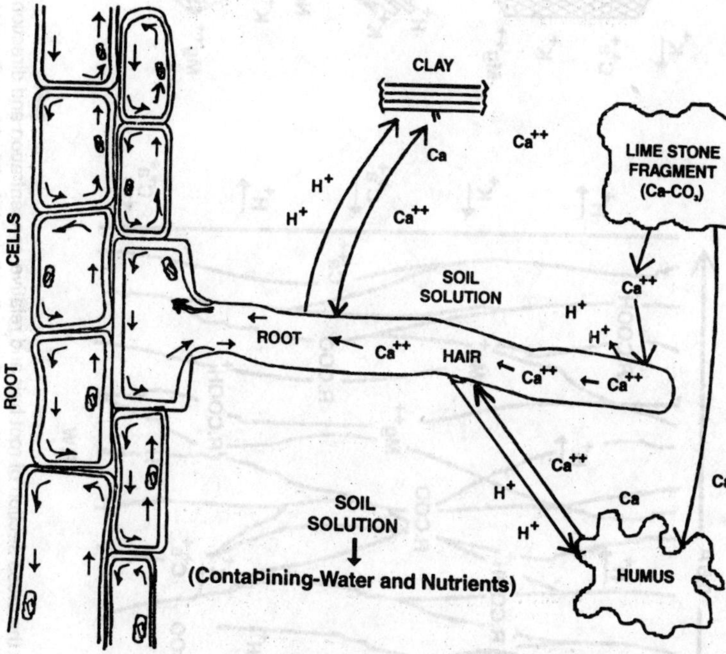

Fig. 7.7 : Root hairs obtain nutrients required for the plants by an exchange of cations and anions between the surface of the root hairs and the surfaces of clay and humus particles, and from the soil solution.

certain conditions, therefore, root absorbed cations may be lost to the outer medium (soil solution).

The ions absorption involves physio-chemical and metabolic-physiological processes. These are represented by RCOOH and RH respectively. The RCOOH is distributed throughout the cell wall and in the plasma membrane while RH is restricted to the membrane (P.M.).

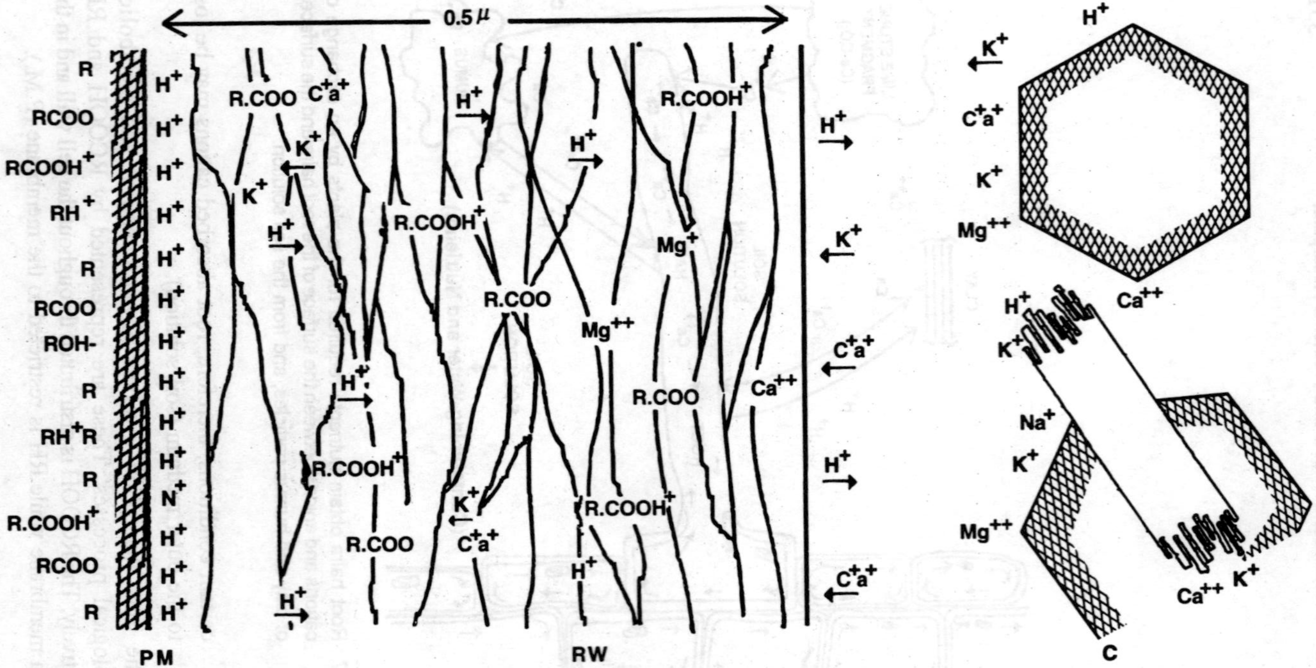

Fig. 7.8 : Schematic illustration of the cross section of root hair and relative concentration and direction of movement of ions. *PM* = plasma membrane; *RW* = root-cell wall; *C* = soil colloid. (*Modified from Frey-Wyssling*)

Mechanism of Ion Absorption by Plant Roots

The various ions present in soil solution are primarily absorbed through the roots. However, many plants are also capable of absorbing a variety of nutrient ions through the leaves, stems and other organs. Examples of latter absorption is a foliar spray of nutrients such as nitrogen, iron, zinc, copper and molybdenum. (Fig. 7.9)

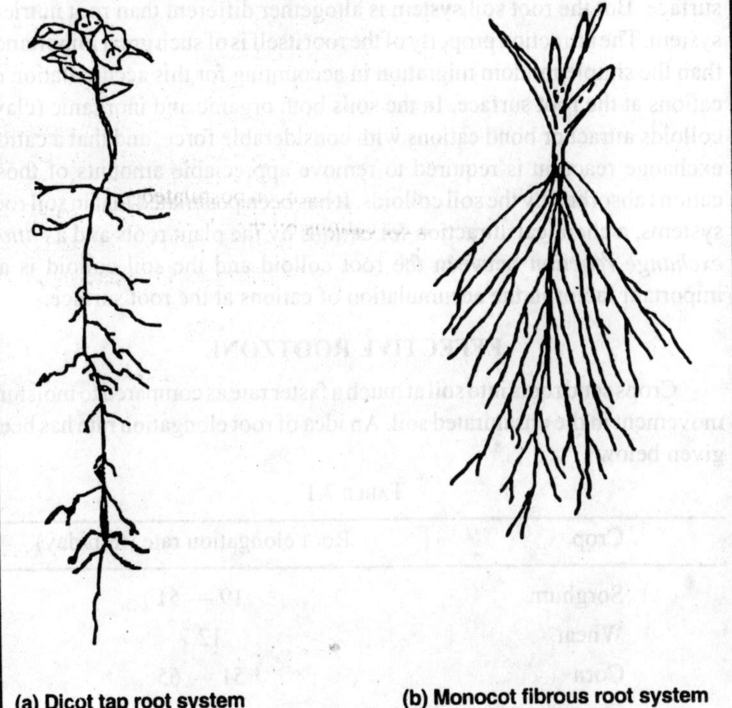

Fig. 7.9 : Root Pattern in Dicot and Monocot Plants.

The ions are absorbed by plant roots through an exchange process. The roots release cation H and absorbs in its place metal cations. Similarly OH and HCO_3 anions release cation H^+ in lieu of anions through exchange. The compounds responsible for cation and anion absorption as discussed earlier are designated by R.H. and R.OH respectively.

Jacoleson and Overstreet suggested that cations in plants may be bound in the form of chelated complexes since many plant substances such as amino acids, protines and organic acids are known to form chelated compounds notably with polyvalent cations. Stewart and Leonard (1950), observed that iron supplied as Fe. EDTA entered the roots and was translocated into plant leaves as the iron-chelate. The *Chlorophyll molecule* may by considered as a *magnesium chelate cation movement from Nutrition medium to Root Surface.*

The movement of cations occurs from the growth medium to the root surface. But the root soil system is altogether different than root nutrient system. The attraction property of the root itself is of such great importance than the simple random migration in accounting for this accumulation of cations at the root surface. In the soils both organic and inorganic (clay) colloids attract or bond cations with considerable force, and that a cation exchange reaction is required to remove appreciable amounts of those cations absorbed by the soil colloids. It has been postulated that in soil root systems, a chemical attraction for cations by the plant roots and a *cation exchange reaction* between the root colloid and the soil colloid is an important factor in the accumulation of cations at the root surface.

EFFECTIVE ROOTZONE

Crops send roots into soil at much a faster rate as compared to moisture movement in the unsaturated soil. An idea of root elongation rate has been given below :

TABLE 7.1

Crop	Root elongation rate (mm/day)
Sorghum	19 — 51
Wheat	12.7
Corn	51 — 65
Groundnut	28.4

In irrigation practice soaking the soil upto a depth where 80-85% active roots occur (or effective rootzone) will be enough to relieve the plant from soil moisture stress as deeper roots rarely experience any acute soil moisture shortage. Table 7.2 gives some idea about the effective rootzone depth of some crops at flowering stage and grown on sandy soil.

TABLE 7.2

Effective Rootzone Depth of Different Crops

Crop	Effective rootzone depth (cm)
Rice	30
Onion	30
Potatoes	45
Groundnut	45
Wheat (dwarf)	60
Jowar	60
Maize	60
Soyabean	60
Lentil	60

METHODS OF ROOT EXAMINATION

The root is the main organ of plant which absorbs moisture and nutrients from soil body. The more the root system is developed in respect of spread, depth and density, more would be the nutrient and water intake from the growing media. The characterisation of different plant genotypes and their growth pattern depending upon various edaphic and agro-climatic conditions differentiates their intake efficiencies.

The different classification methods have been reported as discussed under :

(i) Exacavation Method

In this method the root system is carefully excavated from the soil. This is also called as ''Skeleton method'' and is oldest one now used for ecological research (Weaver, 1926). The roots studies are made after removing shoot parts. The roots are excavated by digging a trench at a distance which would not damage laterally growing roots. The trench is about one meter wide and 20-30 cm deep. These dimensions, however, vary with plant species and soil type, *e.g.*, in very sandy soils the trench is kept more wide than clayey soils. The trench resembles half profile dug pit.

The soil should be removed as carefully as possible to avoid root damage. The tools used are : metal forks, screw drivers, forceps, spatulas, small dental picks and sharp pointed needles of different sizes, camel hair brushes etc.

In case soils are clayey, these are first little moistered over night before excavation.

There are many advantages but few disadvantages of this method being very laborious, time consuming and difficulty of selecting representative plant for study.

(ii) Monolith Method

This involves taking soil monoliths and separating soil from roots by washing. It is adopted when quantitative estimations are to be made. The size of monoliths may vary and range from 20 cm to 1 m in length, 8 to 15 cm wide and appropriate depth. The square monoliths of 10 × 10 × 10 cm to a large block of one ton in weight have been studied. However, the average volume of a common monolith varies from 1000 to 5000 cm^3. The soil wall should be nearly flat before taking monolith and use of metal knives and sharpened edge metal sheets to push into the soil are needed. The roots are then washed with water for their separation.

(iii) Needle Board Method

It is also called nail board or pin board method. In this a soil monolith is taken using special wooden board, while needles or nails in the board helps to retain roots *in situ* conditions. The soil is then washed. The board size of 50 × 50 cm with needles 5 cm long is often used, however bigger size boards of 60 × 100 cm with 20 cm needle or even larger can also be used if needed.

(iv) Auger Method

This is reported to be most suitable one for taking volumetric soil root samples. A hand auger is specially designed (Goede Waagen, 1971) having 15 cm high cylindrical tube with inside dia of 7 cm. Above the tube a hollow shaft about 100 cm long marked at every 10 cm is fixed for sampling to a depth of 100 cm. At the end of shaft, auger is provided with a T-handle so as to rotate the auger and for back pulling. The cutting edge is serrated. The hollow shaft has a rod with a disc at the bottom acting as plunger inside the tube to force the soil cores out of the auger. The replicated samples are taken. The peridic studies are done. The root production per hectare is calculated from root weights per boring.

(v) Trench Profile Method

In this method a thin layer of soil from smoothened profile walls are scrapped and exposed roots are counted (Thiel, 1892; Bohm, 1976). The dimensions of a profile depends upon the development stage of the plants under study, generally 1.2 to 1.5 m long, 1 m wide and 10-15 cm deep below the expected rooting depth but minimum one meter deep. The roots are cut by pair of scissors for study.

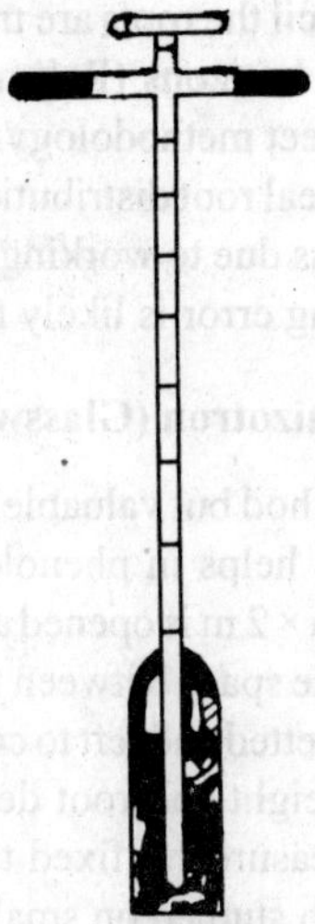

Fig. 7.10 : Hand auger for taking soil root samples

These roots are mapped and counted using wooden or metal frames (interior 100 × 100 cm) with 5 × 5 cm grid made up of copper or white nylon threads laid against profile wall. Kept moist during studies.

Example :

Root length can be determined directly at the profile wall considering uniform root distribution in the soil. Suppose 5 mm of soil depth has been washed from $100 \times 100\ cm^2$ area and there are 1000 root units in the whole profile corresponding to a root length of $1000\ m/m^3$ then estimated root length is equal to 10,000 Km root length/ha

$\therefore$ Counted root = 5 mm = 0.005 m

for, 1000 counts = 1000 × 0.005 = $5\ m/0.005\ m^3$

if the frame size is $100 \times 100\ cm^2$

$$\therefore \text{In } 1\ m^3 = \frac{5}{0.005} m = 1000 \text{ m } i.e. \ 1000\ m/m^3$$

However, the correctness of this method is only 50% as compared to root counting machine. It is due to the fact that fine roots stick to medium and coarse roots and are difficult to be counted. But not much difference is noticed in the relative densities (Bohm, 1976).

(vi) Foil Method

In this method a transparent plexiglass plate (5 mm thick) covered with transparent plastic foil (0.1 mm thick) is placed in front of the profile wall. Using special pencil the roots are traced on the sheet foil along with soil depth and structural horizons (Reijmerink, 1973). Some errors occur in counting due to indirect methodology used, however, it has advantage that natural look of the real root distribution may be visualised. The count of roots is somewhat less due to working indirectly on foil particularly in Ap horizon and counting error is likely to occur by the workers.

(vii) Rhizo or Mini-Rhizotron (Glasswall) Method

It is a bit costly method but valuable. The root growth is restricted in one direction and even helps in phenologic changes of roots and their decay. A pit 2 m × 3.5 m × 2 m is opened and glass wall is constructed over a concrete platform. The space between the glass and the pit is filled with a soil under study and wetted and left to come to tilth. Seeds are sown near glass wall and plant weight and root depth recorded periodically. The entire root length is measured at fixed time interval using map mileage reader. This can be also studied on small scale by using glass tubes into boxes containing soil. The 5 × 5 cm grids are marked on eight acrylic plastic tubes (185 cm long and 7.5 cm dia). Bucket auger are used to sample from 170 cm depth by taking 4 holes in the row and 4 midway between 100 cm wide rows in field. The holes done are back refilled with sieved soil with corresponding soil horizons from a dug pit. Roots growing at the soil tube interface are lightened using four 6 volts bulbs positioned around a concave mirror tightened to steel rod. Roots were studied by lowering the tube and recording their reflected images in the mirror (Waddington, 1971 and Bohm, 1974). Rooting densities are obtained as given by (Taylor *et al.*, 1970).

Indirect Methods

The previous mentioned were direct methods which are laborious and time consuming for roots study. Hence some of indirect methods based on changes in water or nutrient in different soil layers by successive sampling occasions to get root distribution in the soil profile. These are :

(i) *Soil Water Depletion Method* : This works on principle that correlation exists between soil water depletion rate and quality of roots present in the soil. In this 2 cm dia soil tube auger is employed to draw soil samples from depths 0-15, 15-30, 30-60, 60-90, 90-120, 120-150 cm and so on up to rooting depth. The gravimetric moisture determination is done starting from field capacity moisture level to nearly wilting. The method does not work in non-uniform soils, where capillary fringes to rootzone *i.e.* water logged soils.

(ii) *Neutron Method* : Based on Neutron scattering.

(iii) *Radioactive Tracer Method* : By placement of readily detectable radio-tracer at suitable soil depth *e.g.* P^{32}, Rb^{86}, I^{131}, K^{42} and Ca^{45}. A solution containing suitable isotope is injected at various distances and depths from the base plant into soil and the amount of isotope found in the above ground parts is determined which reflects root activity.

Techniques of Root Washing

Roots are separated by one of ways :

(i) *Floatation Methods* : The soil with plant is submersed in bucket of water and washing by nozzle pipe. The density of the dispersed soil root suspension can be increased upto 1.52/cc by adding pure calcium chloride. This will help to float roots and debris and can be skinned off with wire sieves.

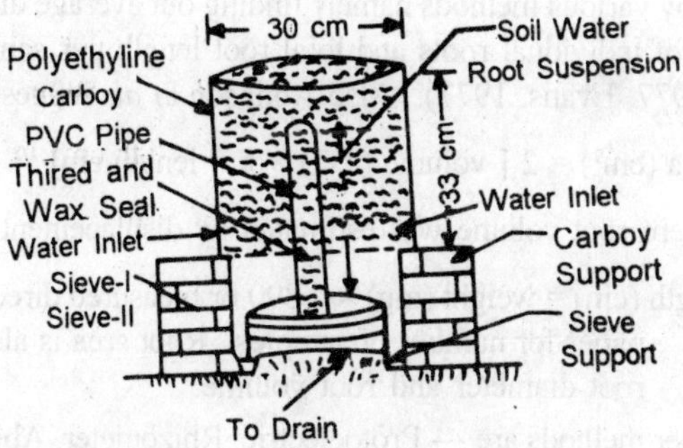

Fig. 7.11 : Root Washing Assembly (dot to scale)

(ii) *Using Root Washing Assembly for soil root cores* : In this method (Sharma *et al.*, 1981) a polythene carboy (inner dia 30 cm) of 20 litre capacity and its upper portion is cut off at 28 cm high from bottom. A hole is made at centre in which 4 cm dia PVC pipe is fixed protruding sealing joint with thread. The horizontal slanting holes at about 45° against wall are made on two sides of carboy at 2 cm height off bottom. These holes are used to push in jet tubes for washing roots kept on 2 sieves in this carboy. The roots are cleaned by tweezers.

ROOT PARAMETERS & MEASUREMENTS

The measurement of root growth and distribution are : number, weight, surface area, volume, diameter, length and the number of tips.

Root Number : This is done in one of the methods discussed in the different soil layers and provides idea about rooting density in profile. The careful count may provide total root length.

Root Weight : It provides relationship between root growth and environment. The air dried washed roots are weighed and redried in oven at 75°C for 10 to 20 hours. Also the air dried roots are heated at 650°C in muffle furnace and root ash after treating with HCl in filtered and dried at 105°C and weighed. This latter weight represents undissolved matter and is substracted from the root dry weight. The HCl treatment should not be done in calcareous soils.

Root Surface Area

This provides idea regarding nutrient and water uptake by plants. It is done by various methods namely finding out average diameter of a large number of individual roots and total root length per sample (Adepetu & Kapa, 1977, Evans, 1977). Also Atkinson *et al.* suggested the formula :

$$\text{Area (cm}^2\text{)} = 2\ [\text{ volume (c.c.)} \times \pi \times \text{length cm}]^{1/2}$$

Where root volume was estimated by displacement of water.

length (cm) = weight (mg) × 0.890 or measured directly on mm graph paper for number of samples. Root area is also be found from root diameter and root volume.

Other methods are — Protoelectric, Rhizometer, Absorption methods [methylene blue solution (0.02–5 mg/lit)] colouration and use of colorimeter).

Root Volume : From above methods and also by water displacement method using over flow spout. The quantity of water replaced by roots indicate their volume.

Root Diameter : By Formula : $\frac{\text{Area of surface}}{\text{Root volume}}$

It is indicated pore size and potential of root penetration. Use of microscope, hand lens, a micrometer, screw/calliper graduated to a tenth of a millimeter can be used.

Root Length : By keeping wet roots in a flat glass dish having some water and placing it above graph paper. The roots are elongated with forceps and length elongated and measured with underneath graph paper or grid of convenient size say 1 cm, 5 cm, 1 m or 5 m etc. Also by formula (Newman, 1966)

$R = \frac{\pi NA}{2H}$; where R = Root length

measured by counting the number of interceps (N) of roots in a regular area 'A' with oriented lines of total length (H) or $R = \frac{11}{14} \times N \times$ grid unit (Tennant, 1975).

Shoot-Root Relation : It is denoted by formula

$C = \frac{\text{Shoot weight}}{\text{Root weight}}$ where 'C' is coefficient.

This is being further explored for more precise interpretations.

CHAPTER 8

IRRIGATION (MOISTURE) REGIMES AND PLANT GROWTH

Water is the most abundant compound of the earth yet on a world-wide scale a deficit of water has been felt. It is the single most important input affecting crop yields. The crop response is a function of soil moisture regimes and is not only essential but very vital for its more efficient use. The moisture utilisation by plants has been explained by two ways namely : (i) the soil moisture available for plant growth equally over the range from field capacity (FC) to permanent wilting point (PWP) and (ii) the plant growth showing differential response as soil moisture declines from FC to PWP. The moisture is more readily available to plants at low soil moisture tension or near field capacity. These values are different in different textured soils. The crop response would be different if the soils were irrigated when available soil moisture drops to the 50 per cent level. However, if these soils are irrigated at soil moisture tension of 2 atmospheres, the comparable yields can be found. At this value, the A.M.C. in the clay is 75 per cent; in the loam, 50 per cent; and in the sand, 25 per cent. These are given in Fig. 8.1.

At 50 per cent level, the moisture tension for the clay is 4.5 Atmosphere, for the loam 2 Atmosphere and for the sand 0.75 Atmosphere.

Many soil plant and environmental factors affect the dynamic processes of water in the soil, plant-atmosphere continuum, perhaps in a number of ways. Thus the crop response observed in a light deep soil in the temperate climate would be different than the response in a shallow heavy soil in tropical climate. The source of moisture is either rainfall or well/canal irrigation. This meets evapotranspiration needs of plants to attain proper growth.

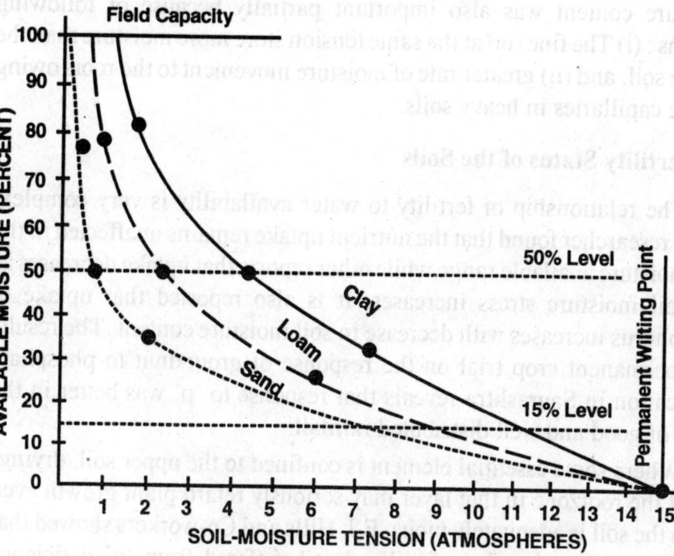

Fig. 8.1 : Moisture release curves for three textured soils (USDA, 1956)

FACTORS INFLUENCING PLANT GROWTH IN RELATION TO MOISTURE

(a) Soil Moisture Quantum and Movement

The universal truth is that plant growth would be slowed down if the water contents are less so as to move into the plant body. However, the symptoms of damage cannot be visualised unless the water used by plant is more than the water present in the soil. As discussed in previous chapters there is equal availability of soil moisture between FC and PWP which means that the rate of moisture uptake would not be a limiting factor in this range. The opposite theory, however, conceives that plant growth shows differential response as soil moisture declines from FC to PWP. It is assumed in this explanation that increasing moisture stresses decrease water uptake to a harmful degree. Peter (1957) reported that plants at the same tension grew better in heavy soils than in coarse soil, which implies that soil moisture tension was not the only factor affecting water availability, moisture content was also important partially because of following reasons : (i) The fine soil at the same tension store more moisture than the coarse soil, and (ii) greater rate of moisture movement to the roots owing to fine capillaries in heavy soils.

(b) Fertility Status of the Soils

The relationship of fertility to water availability is very complex. Some researcher found that the nutrient uptake remains unaffected in the soil moisture available range while other reports that uptake decreases as the soil moisture stress increases. It is also reported that uptake of phosphorus increases with decrease in soil moisture content. The results of a permanent crop trial on the response of groundnut to phosphate application in Saurashtra reveals that response to 'p' was better in the years of good and well distributed rainfall.

Where some essential element is confined to the upper soil, drying-out of the rootzone in that layer may seriously retard plant growth even when the soil is adequately moist. F.J. Hills and Co-workers showed that sugar-beat in a phosphate fertilized soil suffered from 'p' deficiency whenever the surface soil dried up even though deeper roots were obtaining sufficient water to maintain plant turgor. Therefore, increased yield from increased irrigation is not entirely attributable by simply correcting the moisture deficiency alone.

Similarly, it is found that low level of nitrogen would equally utilise available water between FC and PWP by the plant. However, when nitrogen level is high the yield may be substantially reduced by lighter irrigation treatment within the available moisture range. If irrigations are more than normal recommended, the crops yields may even decrease with increased water application at each level of fertilization mainly because of leaching.

(c) Stage of Growth

Optimal soil moisture requirement varies with the stage of the plant growth such as germination seedling, nursery, vegetative growth, flowering and fruiting (wet and dry) etc. An irreversible influence of soil moisture on the growth rate at any particular stage may effect subsequent growth and total yield at maturity. This explanation is of great importance. This means that moisture availability becomes so critical at certain growth stages that further growth can be checked at later stages, irrespective of growing conditions afterwards. The examples of critical growth stage for irrigating, the crop at these stages are recommended. Thus wheat at crown-root-initiation stage, maize just before tasseling and groundnut at pegging stage has been advised to be irrigated. The details of critical growth stages where these should be irrigated can be referred in standard books.

(d) Growth and Yield

Irrigation method and quantity differs from crop to crop. This depends upon the type of organ to be harvested. It is reported that in case of a clover crop, increasing soil moisture stress decreased the forage production but increased the yield of harvestable seed. Similarly, increasing soil moisture stress is reported to increase in sugarcane and beat, decrease sugar and increase nicotine and nitrogen in tobacco.

(e) Roots

The more the roots are far apart the greater would be the possibility of retarded growth, if irrigation is delayed. This is because the soil moisture stress in the vicinity of roots is higher than a little distance away.

(f) Climate

The climatic factors include temperature (soil and atmosphere) wind velocity, humidity, incipient solar radiation depending upon the latitude and total sunshine hours or cloudy days. The higher the level of light intensity the more corresponding decrease in soil moisture. Thus when climatic conditions favour greater water loss from the leaf surface, the rate of photo-synthesis would diminish due to decrease in the soil moisture. It is also believed that plant growth is controlled directly by plant water deficits and only indirectly by soil water deficits. In fact, with adequate water supply plant water deficits can occur as a result of increased evaporative demand by the atmosphere.

OPTIMUM MOISTURE REGIMES FOR DIFFERENT CROPS

The irrigation requirement determined for a specific crop is not universally applicable to different agro-climatic regions. Even within a given arid or semi-arid zone, the variations in climatic conditions are so high that value of evapotranspiration are not comparable. Also within the range of available moisture, each crop has its own characteristic range beyond which the growth and yield suffers. For maximum yield, irrigation

need be applied when moisture reaches the lower limits of the optimal moisture range.

The moisture regimes and water requirements of important crops have been given in Table 8.1.

TABLE **8.1**

Moisture Regimes and Water Requirements for Important Crops

Sl. No.	Crops	Average crop duration (days)	Range of optimum moisture regime (ASM)	No. of irrigations	Approximate amount of water required (m.m.)
1.	Paddy	120-160	3 to 5 cm standing water throughout (Drain water 10-15 days before harvesting)	Desired level of water to be maintained	1200-1500
2.	Bajra (Pearl millet)	90-110	100 to 40 ASM	2-3	200-300
3.	Jowar (Sorghum)	100-120	100 to 40 ASM	2-3	200-300
4.	Maize	100-125	100 to 50 ASM	3-4	350-400
5.	Cotton	150-180	100 to 40 ASM	5-8	550-700
6.	Groundnut	120-140	100 to 50 ASM	2-3	300-350
7.	Kharif pulses	100-120	100 to 40 ASM	2-3	200-300
8.	Wheat	125-150	100 to 50 ASM	4-7	500-600
9.	Barley	115-130	100 to 50 ASM	3-5	350-450
10.	Mustard	120-150	100 to 40 ASM	2-3	250-350
11.	Gram	130-150	100 to 40 ASM	1-2	200-300
12.	Berseem	140-180	100 to 75 ASM	8-12	700-1000
13.	Sugarcane	300-325	100 to 50 ASM	10-15	1200-1500

IRRIGATION AND CROP PRODUCTION

When crop stress from moisture shortage is eliminated by proper and timely irrigation, other factors become inhibitors to production. These factors include poor soil structure and tilth, low fertility, poor stands, weeds, insects and diseases. Much of the water applied through irrigation may be wasted unless sound farming practices are followed.

Soil structure and tilth must be favourable in order to have good aeration, good initial water intake, and good soil permeability. Good soil tilth prevents runoff and water waste. Tilth and structure can be maintained or improved by avoiding cultivation of wet fields, addition of manure or plowing under green manure crops, using grass and legumes in rotation, stubble mulch farming, and minimum tillage. On irrigated pastures, cattle should be excluded until surface soil is dry after irrigation.

Low fertility or an imbalance of nutrients are often the limiting factors on irrigated land. The well-fed plant uses water much more efficiently than a plant that is starved or lacking in some nutrient elements. Total water use by a healthy, well-fed plant is greater than for a plant deprived of plant food but the production per unit of water is much greater for the well-fed plant. Fertility problems should be corrected by the application of barnyard manure and commercial fertilizer. Soil tests, observations, and field experiences help determine the type and amount of fertilizers to use. Crop quality may be more important than crop production. Quality can be greatly improved by proper fertility.

Adequate moisture and fertility, and good soil physical conditions will not insure high production unless the irrigation farmer controls pests, uses high quality seed of adapted varieties, and uses timely operations. Weeds, insects, and diseases may be a greater problem on irrigated than on dry land. Crops and varieties should be selected to fit the soil and irrigation system. Plant population should be increased in most cases to take advantage of water added by irrigation.

For maximum production and most efficient use of water, plants must have ample moisture throughout the growing season. This is most important during critical periods of growth and development. Although plants indicate moisture stress by various symptoms, yields will usually be reduced by the time the plant shows stress. Time of irrigation should be determined by examination of the soil for moisture content. The feel and appearance of the soil at various moisture contents are given in Part I. Symptoms of serious moisture stress, critical water requirement periods and other irrigation considerations are listed in Table 8.2.

CONSUMPTIVE USE (EVAPOTRANSPIRATION) AND NET IRRIGATION REQUIREMENT

Soil moisture withdrawal from the rootzone depth takes place in the form of (i) evaporation from soil surface, (ii) transpiration through leaves, and (iii) as deep-percolation beyond the reach of root.

Evaporation of water from soil is a rather complex process in which water may be moving in either the vapour or liquid phase and which, in the general case, will involve the combined transport of heat and water.

TABLE 8.2

Moisture Stress Symptoms and Critical Growth Period for Irrigated Crops

Crop	Serious moisture stress	Critical growth period	Other considerations
Alfalfa	Bluish green color, then wilting	Seedling and immediately after cutting	Soil kept moist in upper 5 feet. Avoid over-irrigation. Fall irrigation is desirable.
Corn	Leaf curl by 10.00 a.m.	Tasseling; soil stage until grain becomes firm	Sensitive to over-irrigation. Needs adequate moisture from germination to dent stage.
Sorghum	Leaf curl by 10.00 a.m.	Boot, bloom, and milkdough stages	Need adequate moisture-germination through dough stage. Reduced yields when moisture is short during heading and seed development.
Grass Pasture	Dull green color, then wilting	Seedling stage, for seed production boot to head formation	Late fall irrigation is necessarry. Frequent light applications. Irrigate at end of grazing period in a rotation system.
Sugar Beets	Leaves wilting during mid-day	From seedling stage through root enlargement	Shallow, frequent irrigation. Avoid over-irrigation tion. Late fall irrigation. Lowers amount of sugar.
Small Grain	Dull green color, then firing of lower leaves	Boot, bloom and early head stage	Fall grain, irrigate before planting to top 4 feet. Last irrigation at milk stage. Spring small grain as a nurse crop, irrigate for needs of grass seedlings.
Dry Beans & Soyabeans	Dull color, then wilting.	Early bloom, seed forming.	Very sensitive to over-irrigation. Last irrigation at time of first set of pod maturity.
Potatoes	Darkening of leaves, then wilting.	Tuber swelling period	Water should not stand around tubers. Do not over-irrigate. Lower tuber quality if plants go into serious moisture stress. Last irrigation 3 to 4 weeks before harvest.

When the soil is relatively wet, the rate of evaporation is controlled by external conditions *i.e.* by the energy available for evaporation. Under such condition water movement to the soil surface usually takes place in the liquid phase. In case of dry soil condition, movement mainly occur in vapour phase.

Process of Consumptive Use

The consumptive use, often called evapotranspiration includes water used by plants in transpiration and growth and that evaporated from the adjacent soil and from precipitation intercepted by plant foliage. It is expressed in mm per hectare or cm per hectare or in depth in mm or cm.

Transpiration is the process by which water is removed from the soil by a plant, moved through the plant to the leaves, and lost to the atmosphere in vapour form. For irrigation, the moisture used in plant growth and that retained by the plant is included. Evaporation from the soil surface is not included in transpiration but included in the consumptive use.

Transpiration occurs mostly from the leaves of the plant, but a small part of moisture is also evaporated from the younger stems. It occurs mostly during the day light hours, and only a small amount, possibly 5 to 10 per cent, occurs during the night. The rate of transpiration is the lowest just before sunrise and usually reaches maximum during noon. Transpiration accounts for a substantial part of the total consumptive use of a crop.

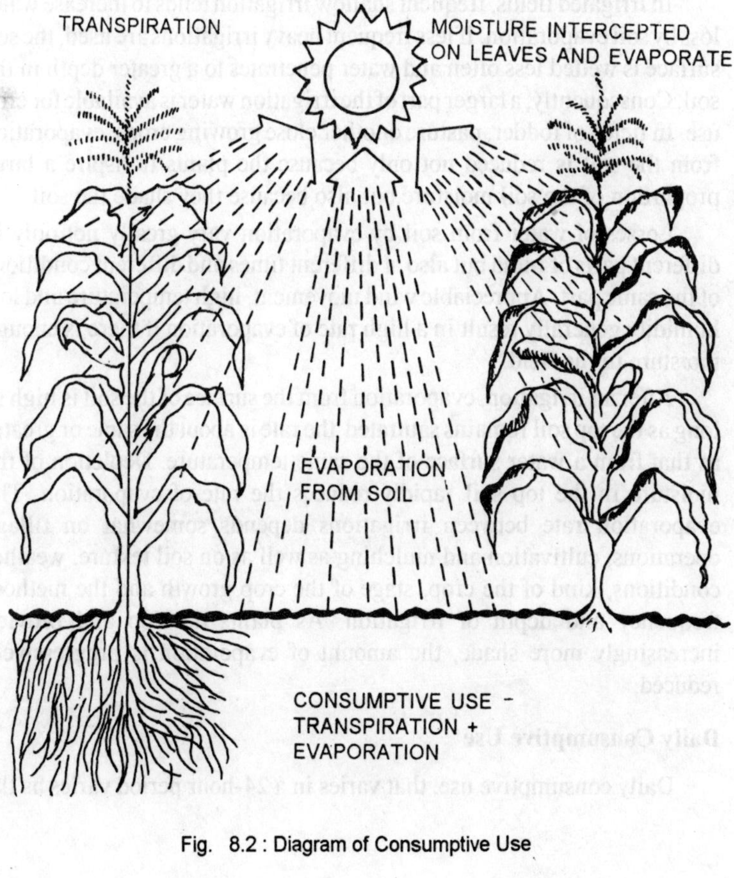

Fig. 8.2 : Diagram of Consumptive Use

Some of the factors that affect the rate of transpiration are moisture available in the soil, kind and density of plant growth, amount of sunshine, temperature, humidity and wind velocity etc. In summer, when exceedingly hot winds blow over a field, transpiration may take place more rapidly than moisture can be absorbed by plant roots even when the soil contains ample supply of moisture. When this occurs plant wilts. In some cases, the foliage may be dried beyond recovery.

Evaporation is the diffusion of water as vapour from a surface into the atmosphere. Factors that affect the rate of evaporation are : the nature of the evaporation surface and differences in vapour pressure as determined by temperature, wind and atmospheric pressure. In determining the consumptive use, evaporation included both evaporation from the ground surface and evaporation of the water intercepted by vegetation.

In irrigated fields, frequent shallow irrigation tends to increase water loss by soil evaporation. If less frequent heavy irrigations are used, the soil surface is wetted less often and water penetrates to a greater depth in the soil. Consequently, a larger part of the irrigation water is available for crop use. In fields of fodder, pasture or other close growing crops, evaporation from the soil is reduced not only because the plants transpire a large proportion of the soil moisture but also because they shade the soil.

Losses of water from soil by evaporation vary greatly not only in different parts of India but also at different times and different conditions of the same part. Appreciable wind movement, high temperature and low humidity generally result in a high rate of evaporation if there is enough moisture in the field.

After an irrigation, evaporation from the surface of the soil is high so long as the top soil remains saturated the rate is about the same or greater as that from a water surface of the same temperature. Depletion of the moisture in the top soil rapidly reduces the rate of evaporation. The evaporation rate between irrigations depends somewhat on tillage operations, cultivation and mulching as well as on soil texture, weather conditions, kind of the crop, stage of the crop growth and the method, frequency and depth of irrigation. As plants develop and provide increasingly more shade, the amount of evaporation is progressively reduced.

Daily Consumptive Use

Daily consumptive use, that varies in a 24-hour period varies as the factors that influence evaporation and transpiration vary. Consumptive use is low at the start of the growing season, increases as plant foliage develops and days become longer and warmer, generally reaches a peak during the fruiting period and then rapidly declines to the end of a crops growing season. From the time seed is planted until plants emerge, soil moisture loss is by evaporation. As plant emerges, transpiration begins and increases in amount as they develop. After the plants die, transpiration ceases and further soil-moisture loss is by evaporation. If all the physical and climatic conditions remain the same, daily consumptive use drops in fodder and pasture fields immediately after cutting or gazing because of the reduction in transpiration. If the field is irrigated immediately after cutting, however, there is no reduction in daily consumptive use and the rate may increase because of high evaporation.

Seasonal Consumptive Use

The amount of water used in evaporation and transpiration by a crop during its growing season is called seasonal consumptive use. It is expressed usually as cm per hectare or depth in cm (or acre-inches per acre or as depth in inches). Seasonal consumptive use values are needed to evaluate and determine seasonal irrigation water supplies.

Peak Period Consumptive Use

The average daily water use rate during 6 to 10 days of the highest consumptive use of the season is called the peak period use rate and the design rate to be used in planning an irrigation system. The peak use period generally occurs when the crop is starting to produce its harvest, vegetation is most abundant and temperatures are high.

Since the average consumptive use rate is higher for a very short peak-use period (2 or 3 days) than for a longer peak-use period, the design rate varies with the amount of water that can be used from the rootzone (for normal depth of water application per irrigation). In shallow soils, in soils with a low water holding capacity or for plants with shallow root systems, the depth to which water is applied is shallow and irrigation frequency during the peak use period during Kharif ranges from 3 to 6 days. The peak use period for plants with a moderately deep root system growing in deep soil with a good water holding capacity may range from 8 to 15 days during Kharif. The average use rate for those short period is considered higher than the average rate for the month of the greatest moisture use and is generally less than the peak daily use rate.

Estimating Consumptive Use (Evapotranspiration)

In planning and designing of the irrigation systems an estimate of water requirement of crops is required. Since the beginning of this century, a considerable amount of work has been done on soil, water, plant relationship and on computation and determination of evapotranspiration for different crops. The objective of this work was to obtain practical answers to the main problem of knowing the quantity of irrigation water that is needed for growing certain crops in an area. The emphasis was given in these studies to the need of developing useful concepts and different methods which could be reliably used, based on the knowledge gained in one climatic zone to another climatic zone or agro-climatic zones.

APPROACHES FOR ESTIMATION OF CROP WATER REQUIREMENT

Crop water requirement involves a knowledge of plant-soil-water relationship under any given climatic conditions. It may be defined as the quantity of water, regardless of its source required by a crop or diversified pattern of crops in a given period of the time for its normal growth under conditions at a place. Water requirement includes the losses due to evapotranspiration or consumptive use plus the losses during the application of irrigation water and the quantity of water required for special operations. Estimation of seasonal, monthly and short period water requirements for various crops is needed for a scientific planning and management of irrigation.

Techniques employed for estimation of water requirements of different crops can be broadly grouped into six classes as follows :

(1) Transpiration ratio approach
(2) Depth-interval-yield approach
(3) Soil moisture deficit approach
(4) Water at critical stages of crop growth approach
(5) Estimation of crop water requirements from open pan evaporation
(6) Climatological approach

Transportation Ratio Approach

At the beginning of this century, the entire water requirement was taken as transpiration ratio. This is the amount of water transpired by a crop in its growth to produce a unit weight of dry matter. Based on this approach, work was initiated at Pusa, Bihar, as early as 1906. Similar approach was also adopted in these days in U.K., U.S.A. and other countries for determining water requirements of crops. In such trials, the values of transpiration ratios varied tremendously from place to place. For wheat, values varying from 200 to 1000 and for sugarcane from 250 to 1500 were reported. Now it is known that the transpiration and the dry matter production by a plant are not related in simple manner as in the transpiration ratio. Several soil plant and atmospheric factors influence growth of crops. The knowledge of transpiration ratio is, therefore, of little value in planning irrigation practices under field conditions. This approach therefore, is no more in use.

Depth-Interval-Yield Approach

Several workers in the Irrigation and Agriculture Department in the country carried out field trials to find out optimum water requirements of crops. Different depths of irrigation such as 100, 150 & 200 mm were applied at different intervals such as 2, 3 and 4 weeks. The irrigation treatments which gave the maximum yield with the minimum delta of water was taken as the optimum water requirement of that particular crop. Bulk of the work conducted in the field of irrigation in India falls in this category. These depths and intervals were fixed arbitrarily without taking cognizance of soil characteristics and weather conditions which caused either under-irrigation or over-irrigation.

Soil Moisture Deficit Approach

The depth-interval-yield approach was further improved by soil moisture deficit approach. This method involved measurement of soil moisture from various depths at a number of times throughout the growth period.

Later it was realised that relative availability of soil moisture is available moisture range from field capacity wilting point and that the crop yields are affected long before the soil moisture reaches the wilting point. The intervals of irrigation were therefore, fixed on the degree of depletion in the available moisture range to find out the optimum regimes. The degree of depletion of soil moisture was measured with different criteria such as percentage availability, tensions, resistance etc.

Experiments of this nature have been in progress from 1956 onwards at the IARI, New Delhi and at certain Agriculture colleges and Universities. This technique is satisfactory for all practical purposes. Such trials are, however, very few and inadequate taking into account varying soil types, weather conditions and vast dimensions of the country. Lysimeters were employed and caliberated to estimate water requirements (Fig. 8.3).

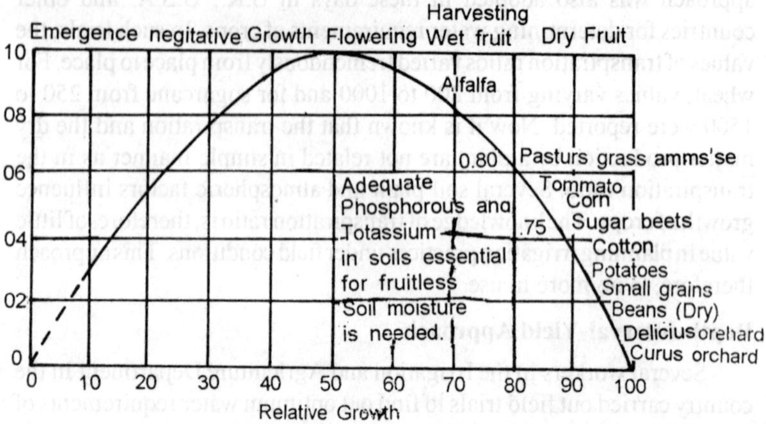

Fig. 8.3 : Generalized Curve Computing Consumptive use evaporation ratio to relative growth of crop. (Bell Type curve)

Water at Different Stages of Growth Approach

It has been observed that water requirement of crops vary with the stages of its growth. When water supply is limited, it is necessary to take into account the critical stages of crop growth with respect to moisture. The term critical stage is commonly used to define the stage of growth when plants are most sensitive to shortage of water. Each crop has certain critical stages at which if there is shortage of moisture the yield is reduced drastically. For example, the growth stages of cereals are germinations, tillering, jointing, sheething, booting, heading, flowering and grain formation. When there is a shortage of water, it is better to take care of the critical stages first to obtain increased water use efficiency.

Estimation of Crop Water Requirement From Pan Evaporation

The other important method for evapotranspiration estimation is by using evaporimeters which are exposed to the same environmental conditions as that of the crop. Proper correlations could be established between crop evapotranspiration and evaporation from evaporimeter for scheduling irrigation. Several types of evaporimeters for scheduling irrigation like open pan, sunken pan, screened pans and small pan can be used to determine evaporation values.

But USWB class open pan is recommended as its values are available from many meteorological observatories in the country. The ratio of the amount of irrigation water (IW) to cumulative pan evaporation (CPE) can also be used for scheduling irrigation. The depth of irrigation water (IW) in this case is decided by the available water holding capacity of the soil and the probable deficit before irrigation and the irrigation efficiency that can be achieved.

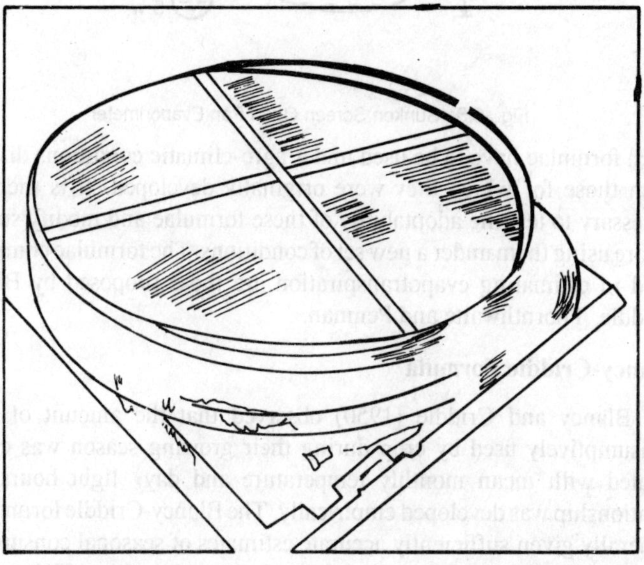

Fig. 8.4 : USPW Class-A Pan Evaporimeter

Climatological Approach

Evapotranspiration is predominantly governed by the climatic factors. The approach followed is to relate the magnitude and variation of evapotranspiration to one or more climatic factors such as temperature, day length, humidity, wind velocity, and sunshine hours. By these methods crop water requirements can be determined much more accurately incorporating some crop factors along with the developed relation. Many formulae have been developed and used from time to time and have been critically reviewed by various workers. Broadly these approaches fall into two classes :

(1) Purely empirical attempts.

(2) The application of more theoretical approach.

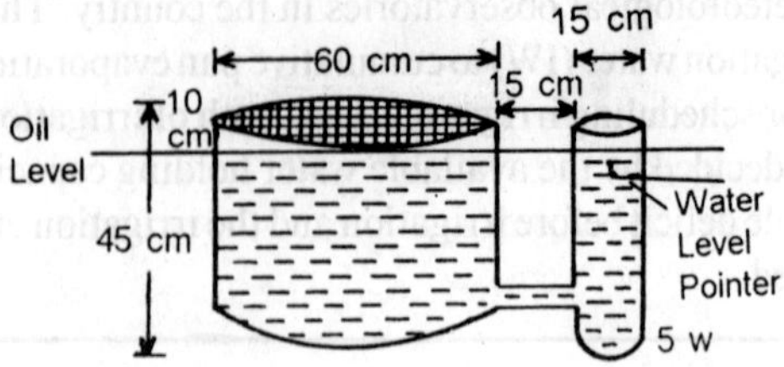

Fig. 8.5 : Sunken Screen Open Pan Evaporimeter

Such formulae have to be used under agro-climatic conditions different from those for which they were originally developed. It is therefore, necessary to test the adoptability of these formulae and modify suitably before using them under a new set of conditions. The formulae commonly used in estimating evapotranspiration are those proposed by Blancy-Criddle, Thornthwaite and Penman.

Blancy-Criddle Formula

Blancy and Criddle (1950) observed that the amount of water consumptively used by crop during their growing season was closely related with mean monthly temperature and day light hours. The relationship was developed empirically. The Blancy-Criddle formula has generally given sufficiently accurate estimates of seasonal consumptive use owing to the inclusion of locally developed crop coefficient. This formula considers that the consumptive use of water is dependent only on temperature and day length, which is not fully true. Crop water requirements have been found to vary widely between climates having similar air temperature but different humidity and wind condition.

Thornthwaite Formula

Thornthwaite (1948) assumed that an exponential relationship existed between mean monthly temperature and mean monthly consumptive use. The relationship was based largely on experience in the central and eastern United States. No allowance was made for different crops or other land use. The formula was originally developed for the purpose of rational classification of broad climatic patterns of the world. Suitable co-efficients should, therefore, be developed locally for reliable estimation of crops evapotranspiration value. The Thornthwaite formula gives a reasonable estimate of potential evapotranspiration in the temperature continental climate or North America where the formula was originally derived because there the temperature and rediation are strongly correlated. In other parts of the world this approach has been less successful.

Modified Penman Formula

Penman (1948) proposed an equation for evaporation from open water surface based on combination of energy balance and sink strength. Since the Penman equation estimates evaporation from a free water surface, the result must be modified to pre-provide evapotranspiration estimates for crops. Based on intensive studies of the climate and measured gross evapotranspiration ratio data from various research stations in the world and the available literature on prediction of evapotranspiration or potential evapotranspiration are used. Docrenbes and Pruitt (1977) proposed a modified Penman method, as below, for estimating fairly accurately the reference crop evapotranspiration and gave tables to facilitate the necessary computations.

$$Eto = C \{\underbrace{W.\ Rn}_{\text{Radiation term}} + \underbrace{(1-W)\ f(u)\ (ea-ed)}_{\text{aerodynamic term}}\}$$

Where

Eto = The reference crop (gross) evapotranspiration in mm/day (not adjusted).
ea = Saturation vapour pressure in m bar at the mean air temperature in °C.
ed = Mean actual vapour pressure of the air in m bar = ea×RH% mean/100.
f(u) = wind related function.
w = A temperature and elevation related weighing factor for the effect of radiation on ETc.
Rn = Net radiation, mm/day = Rns – Rnl.

Where

Rns = Net incoming short wave solar radiation

and

Rnl = Net long wave radiation
RH = Relative Humidity
C = Adjustment factor to compensate for the day and night weather effects.

The actual evapotranspiration can be determined by adjusting evapotranspiration obtained from modified Penman equation. It is adjusted for day and night time weather condition with the help of figure developed by Docrenbes & Pruitt. The modified Penman relationship gives very satisfactory values of crop evapotranspiration and widely used for the determination of crop water requirements accurately.

The details of these and other methods are discussed below :

(a) *Lower-Johnson Method Year 1941*

This method is based on the assumption of a linear relationship between consumptive use and "Effective Heat". Originally the equation is in f.p.s. system of units but converting it into equivalent metric, effective heat can be defined in the accumulated degree days of maximum daily temperature above 0°C.

$$U = 0.244 + 0.0856\,F$$

where U = Yearly potential evapotranspiration in metres

F = Effective heat in thousands of day degree (centigrade) accumulated for the whole year

$$= \frac{1}{100} \frac{m}{1\ td}$$

where t is the monthly mean maximum temperature, d is the no. of days in the month and it represents the no. of months of the year.

The method is used for calculating consumptive use of a valley on an annual basis but can also be adopted to get an idea of monthly values by proportion.

(b) *Thornthwaite Method, Year 1944, 1948*

Thornthwaite equation is based on the assumption of an exponential relationship between mean monthly temperature and mean monthly consumptive use.

$$\mu' = 1.6\,(10\,t/I)^a$$

where U = unadjusted monthly consumptive use in cm.

t = mean monthly temperature in degrees centigrade

I = temperature-efficiency index or annual heat index, which is equal to the sum of 12 monthly values of heat index,

$$I = \left[\frac{t}{5}\right]^{1.514}$$

$$a = 0.000000675\,(I)^3 - 0.0000771(I)^2 + 0.01792\,I + 0.492339$$

This value (μ), however, gives only unadjusted rates of potential evapotranspiration. Owing to the ariations in the number of days in a month and in the number of sun light hours during a day with season and latitude, it becomes necessary to multiply the calculated value by a correction factor m, so that corrected value of evapotranspiration U = mú. The value of correction factor m is the ratio of average to actual day length in a month so that

$$\text{PET or } U = \acute{U} \quad \left[\frac{d}{5} \times \frac{n}{10}\right] \qquad \left(m = \frac{d}{5} \times \frac{n}{10}\right)$$

where d is the average of actual lengths of days in hours and n is the actual number of days in a month. Values of m for different locations and months are given in Table 8.3. It is because unadjusted values are based on 12-hour day (h) and 30 days month (M). Hence actual $\text{PET} = e \left(\frac{h}{12}\right)\left(\frac{M}{30}\right)$.

TABLE 8.3

Mean possible duration of Sunlight for the Thornthwaite method in the Northern hemisphere expressed in units of 30 days of 12 hours each or the correction factor for potential evapotranspiration computed by Thornthwaite method

[After Criddle (9)]

Latitude Month	0	10	20	30	35	40
January	1.04	1.00	0.95	0.90	0.87	0.84
February	0.94	0.91	0.90	0.87	0.85	0.83
March	0.04	1.03	1.03	1.03	1.03	1.03
April	1.01	1.03	1.05	1.08	1.09	1.01 (11)
May	1.04	1.08	1.13	1.18	1.21	1.24
June	1.01	1.06	1.11	1.17	1.21	1.25
July	1.04	1.08	1.14	1.20	1.23	1.27
August	1.04	1.07	1.11	1.14	1.16	1.18
September	1.02	1.02	1.02	1.03	1.03	1.04
October	1.04	1.02	1.00	1.98	0.97	0.96
November	1.01	0.98	0.93	0.89	0.86	0.83
December	1.04	0.99	0.94	0.88	0.85	0.81

Thornthwaite method can be more conveniently used graphically with the help of a monograph as illustrated in examples.

(c) *Blancy-Criddle Method, Year 1950*

Blancy-Criddle equation, due to its simplicity, has been extensively used. It is given as :

$$U = K^m F = \Sigma\, kf = \Sigma\, u$$

This method has been modified and is used for areas where available climatic data cover air temperature data only :

$$ET_o = C\ [(P\ (0.46\ T + 8)]\ \text{mm/day}$$

where,

ET_o = reference crop ET in mm/day for the given month.

T = mean daily temperature in °C over the given month.

C = adjustment factor which depends upon minimum relative humidity, sunshine hours and daytime wind estimates.

U = potential evapotranspiration, in inches for m months.

m = number of months in a growing season.

p = per cent day light hours of the year.

t = mean monthly temperature in Fahrenheit degrees.

K = seasonal or monthly consumptive use coefficient.

k = monthly use consumptive use coefficient. AV value are 0.60 for potato, 0.80 for wheat

f = monthly consumptive use factor = (t × p)/100

F = Σf fortal time,

u = kf = monthly consumptive use

Values of P can be computed from U.S. Weather Bureau ''Sunshine tables''. Values of normal seasonal consumptive use coefficient, K, for some crop are shown in Table 8.4 during the growing season of any crop an average value of K can be taken but actually K value changes with the stage of growth, peak value being at the beginning of flowering and at the end of the vegetative stage of growth.

The above equation is in British units which on converting it into metric units is given as :

$$\mu = 2.54\ K \sum_{1}^{m} F \quad (1.8t + 32)$$

In the above equation μ is in meter and t is in centigrade degrees.

TABLE 8.4

Normal Seasonal Consumptive Use Coefficients for use in Blancy-Criddle Equation for Some Important Irrigated Crops

[After Criddle (9)]

Sl. No.	Crop	K
1.	Beans	0.60 to 0.70
2.	Cotton	0.65 to 0.75
3.	Maize	0.75 to 0.85
4.	Orchard	0.50 to 0.65
5.	Potatoes	0.65 to 0.75
6.	Rice	1.00 tc 1.25
7.	Small grains	0.75 to 0.85
8.	Sorghum	0.70
9.	Small vegetables	0.60
10.	Tomatoes	0.70

TABLE 8.5

Per cent Day-Light Hours 0 to 40° North

Month Latitude	0	5	10	15	20	25	30	32	34	36	38	40
January	8.50	8.32	8.13	7.94	7.74	7.53	7.30	7.20	7.10	6.99	6.87	6.76
February	7.66	7.57	7.47	7.36	7.25	7.14	7.03	6.97	6.91	6.85	6.79	6.72
March	8.49	8.47	8.45	8.43	8.41	8.39	8.38	8.37	8.36	8.35	8.34	8.33
April	8.21	8.29	8.37	8.44	8.52	8.61	8.72	8.76	8.80	8.85	8.90	8.95
May	8.50	8.65	8.81	8.98	9.15	9.33	9.53	9.62	9.72	9.82	9.92	10.02
June	8.22	8.41	8.60	8.80	9.00	9.23	9.49	9.59	9.70	9.82	9.95	10.08
July	8.50	8.67	8.86	9.05	9.25	9.45	9.67	9.77	9.88	9.99	10.10	10.22
August	8.49	8.60	8.71	8.83	8.96	9.09	9.22	9.27	9.33	9.40	9.47	9.54
September	8.21	8.23	8.25	8.28	8.30	8.32	8.33	8.34	8.36	8.37	8.38	8.39
October	8.50	8.42	8.34	8.26	8.18	8.09	7.99	7.95	7.90	7.85	7.80	7.75
November	8.22	8.07	7.91	7.75	7.58	7.40	7.19	7.11	7.02	6.92	6.82	6.72
December	8.50	8.30	8.10	7.88	7.66	7.42	7.15	7.05	6.92	6.79	6.66	7.52

(d) *Penman's Method, (24, Year 1948)*

Penman's method is based on theoretical analysis indicating that consumptive use is dependent upon the radiant solar energy. The method uses the following three formulae :

1. $H = R_a (1-r)(0.188+0.55\, n/N) - OTa4\,(0.56-0.092\sqrt{ed})$
2. $E_a = 0.35(e_a - e_d)(1+0.0061\, U_2)$ and
3. $E_c = \dfrac{H + 0.27\, E_a}{+ 0.27}$

where

H = Daily heat budget at surface in mm H_2O/day (Table 8.9)

R_a = Mean monthly extra terrestrial radiation in mm H_2O/day (Table 8.6).

R = Reflection co-efficient of surface

n = Actual duration of bright sunshine

N = Maximum possible duration of bright sunshine

O = Boltzman constant

= 2.01×10^{-9} mm/day

e_d = Saturation vapour pressure at mean dew point (*i.e.* actual vapour pressure in the air) mm Hg

E_z = Evaporation in (mm) H_2O/day

ea = Saturation vapour pressure at mean air temperature in mm Hg.

U_2 = Mean wind speed at 2 metres above ground (km/day) (Table 8.8)

E_t = Evapotranspiration in mm H_2O/day

Ta = Average temperature, °Kelvin (Table 8.7)

= Slope of saturated vapour pressure curve of air at air temperature (mm Hg/O_f)

Thus in the above equation it may be seen that all terms are in metric units excepting which is mm of Hg per °F. Converting into corresponding metric units *i.e.* mm of Hg. per °C this equation can be written completely in metric units as

$$E_t = \frac{H+0.486\ Ea}{+0.486}$$

Since Penman equation gives evaporation as would occur from free water surface, the computed value must be multiplied by a coefficient, C so that actual consumptive use, $U = C\,E_t$

The value of C ranges from 0.6 in winter to 0.8 in summer and depends upon the location of the place, growing season and crop characteristics.

(e) *Vanbavel Method*

Vanbavel suggested a nomograph for simplified solution of Penman evapotraspiration equation. The nomograph can be conveniently used with fair degree of accuracy. He gave that :

$$ET\ (PET) = \frac{\frac{\Delta}{Y} Rn + Ea}{\frac{\Delta}{Y} + 1}$$

where :

$$Ea = 0.262\ (ea - ed)\ \frac{\mu a}{\left(\ln \frac{za}{zo}\right)^2}$$

μa = Wind run in miles/day & (la–ld) = Deficit vapour pressure (mm of Hg)

Zo = Roughness parameter

Za = Height above surface.

Example :

R = 16.7 mm/day
= 0.65 inches/day

$\frac{n}{N}$ = 70 %

Ta = 25°C = 77°f

Then E_t = 0.165 in/day
= 12.97 cm/month

(After Vanbavel, taken from Chow)

(f) *Hargreave Method, Year 1956*

Hargreave established a relationship between evaporation and the relative humidity of the air. Hargreave's equation originally in British units can be written as

$$E_t = d\ (0.38 - 0.0038\ h)\ 9t - 32$$

where

E_t = Potential evapotranspiration in inches per month

d = Monthly day time coefficient dependent upon latitude.

h = Mean monthly relative humidity at noon in per cent

t = Mean monthly temperature in °F.

This Eq. can be written in metric units as follows :

$$E_t = 3.56\ d\ (0.38 - 0.0038\ h) \times t$$

where E_t is in cm and t is in centrigrade units.

Actual consumptive use for a specific crop is assumed to vary according to crop characteristics.

$$\mu = K\, E_t$$

where μ is the actual consumptive use for a crop with a consumptive use co-efficient K.

(g) *Radiation Method* (Makkink, 1957)

This method is used for areas where data on air temperature sunshine, cloudiness or radiation are available but on wind and humidity are not. The latter are extrapolated from nearby areas. The equation used is — ET_o = C(W.Rs) mm/day

where

ET_o = reference crop ET in mm/day for the periods considered.

RS = solar radiation in equivalent evaporation in mm/day. It is measured by solar monitor with Pyremometer sensor or by eq. Rs = (0.25 + 0.50 n/N)Ra

where

n = Actual measured bright sunshine hours and are available locally (mean daily values in hours)

N = Maximum possible sunshine hours (See standard tables on mean daily percentage (p) of annual daytime hours for different latitudes) — Mean daily values in hours.

Ra = (mm/day). See standard tables for different months and latitudes. The constants 0.25 and 0.50 are used for practical purpose.

Example :

Ra = 8.6; =10.2, n (Sunshine mean) = 8.69 hrs/day

$$\therefore \text{Rs} = (0.25 + 0.50 \times \frac{8.69}{10.2})\ 8.6 = 5.81 \text{ mm day.}$$

(h) *Quackenbus and Phelan Method*

They proposed modification of Blancy and Criddle formula where the product of Kc and Kt equals to K. The Kc denotes crop growth stage coefficient while Kt, the temperature coefficient. Thus K = Kc × Kt and Kt = 0.0173 × t – 0.314. The Blaney and Criddle used crop factor to be developed for each crop under the environmental conditions of the particular area. At present this information is not available in India. Further this formula does not take into consideration such factors as humidity, wind velocity, elevation and the like. These aspects therefore make it necessary to try other methods which can give reasonably accurate estimation of irrigation water requirement.

Computing Pan Evaporation

In recent years much work has been done on correlating evapotranspiration with evaporation as measured in an Evaporimeter. The ratio between evapotranspiration (E_t) and pan evaporation (E_p) is usually termed K.

Christiansen *et al.* (5) provided an empirical formula to permit the estimation of pan evaporation from climatic data when reliable measured pan evaporation is not available. Hargreaves has developed a similar formula for estimating pan evaporation.

Unfortunately, class A pan evaporation is not available in many places where estimates of evaportranspiration are needed. Also because of variations in size and shape of pans, exposure, the presence or absence of algae, the specific methods of measuring the loss of water from the pans, and the protection against use of the water by birds and animals, available pan evaporation data may need to be standardised before it should be used in order to obtain reliable estimates of evapotranspiration. Pan evaporation estimated by means of a reliable formula may give more reliable results than reported pan evaporation.

The Christiansen Method

Christiansen and Co-workers have developed the following pan evaporation equation :

$$E_p = 0.459\, RC_t\, C_w\, C_h\, C_s\, C_e$$

in which E_p is computed pan evaporation equivalent to class A pan evaporation, R is extra-terrestrial radiation in the same evaporation units as E_p, C_t, C_w, C_h, C_s and C_e coefficients for temperature, wind velocity, relative humidity, per cent of possible sunshine, and elevation. Equations for these coefficients are as follows :

C_t = $0.393 + 0.02796\, T_c + 0.0001\, 189\, T_c 2$ (Table 8.7)
where T_c is expressed in degrees centigrade

C_w = 0.708 + 0.0034W — 0.0000038W = 2 (Table 8.8)
where W is the mean wind velocity at 0.5 metre above the ground in kilometres per day.

C_h = 1.250-0.0087H + 0.75 × 10⁴H² – 0.85 × 10 – 8H⁴ (Table 8.9)
where H is the mean relative humidity at noon, or average relative humidity at noon, or average relative humidity for 11 and 18 hours.

C_s = 0.542+0.0080 S — 0.78 × 10–4S²+0.62 × 10–6S³ (Table 8.10)
where S is the mean sunshine percentage.

C_e = 0.970 × 0.00984 E (Table 8.11)
where E is expressed in hundreds of metres.

R = Extra-terrestrial radiation (Table 8.6) may be expressed in millimetres or inches.

All these coefficients are given in attached tables.

Sample Calculations No. 1

Location : Bellary, Mysore State

Latitude : 15°09'N Elevation : + 449 metres

Month : April

Mean Temperature : 31.8°C

Wind Velocity at 2 feet : 183 Kilometres per day.

Mean Relative Humidity : 40%

Sunshine per cent : 89

R (Table 8.6) for April, Lat. 15°09'N — 473 millimetres.

C_t (Table 8.7) for 31°C — 1.403

C_w (Table 8.8) for 183 millimetres per day 1.200

C_h (Table 8.9) for 40% — 1.000

C_s (Table 8.10) for 89% — 1.073

C_e (Table 8.11) for 449 metres — 1.014

$$E_p = 0.459\, RC_t\, C_w\, C_h\, C_s\, C_e$$

$$= 0.459\,(473)\,(1.403)\,(1.200)\,(1.000)\,(1.073)\,(1.014)$$

$$= 398 \text{ millimetres.}$$

Relationship Between Evapotranspiration and Evaporation as Means for Computing Evapotranspiration

The relationship of evapotranspiration to pan evaporation has long been used in the computation of irrigation requirements. Many research stations are now reporting consumptive use data by relating evapotranspiration (consumptive use) to pan evaporation. This relationship is available for some crops from many diverse parts of the world such as Israel, the Philippines, the United States and India. Table 8.12 shows evapotranspiration coefficients for vegetative cycle percentages for various crops.

Where specific data are not available, average 'K' values can be used as recommended by Hargreaves. Table 8.13 and 8.14 shows consumptive use coefficients K, for computing evapotranspiration (E_t) from either computed or measured evaporation (E_p). These coefficients are suggested as representing in average conditions and are proposed for use in the formula $E_t = KE_p$. The eight crop groups are listed given below :

Crop Group A : These crops fits fairly even in bell type curve and have a model grouping of maximum E_t/E_p ratios in the range of 0.80 to 1.10. An average value of 1.00 is used. The more important crops include beans, maize, cotton, potatoes, sugar beets, jowar and peas.

Crop Group B : This group consists of the deciduous fruits and some field crops. Some group A crops that fail to produce maximum vegetative cover and maximum growth ratios will best fit in this group. It includes : dates, olives, plumes, walnuts, tomatoes, and hybrid Jowar.

Crop Group C : The crops include melons, onions, carrots, hops, and grapes with a maximum E_t/E_p ratios of about 0.60. This general pattern is again that of a bell type curve. (Fig. 8.3)

TABLE 8.6

Mean Monthly Values of Extraterrestrial Radiation [(R) in Christiansen formula]

Lat. Degrees	Expressed as equivalent evaporation in inches and millimetres per month											
	January		February		March		April		May		June	
	Inches	mms.	Inches	mms.	Inches	mms.	Inches	mms.	Inches	mms.	Inches	mms.
North												
45	6.15	156.21	7.87	199.90	12.58	319.53	16.17	410.72	19.81	503.17	20.53	521.46
40	7.72	196.09	9.21	233.03	13.79	350.27	16.90	429.26	20.08	510.03	20.53	521.46
35	9.27	235.46	10.50	266.70	14.91	378.71	17.50	444.50	20.23	513.84	20.44	519.18
30	10.79	274.07	11.73	297.94	15.91	404.11	17.98	456.69	20.26	514.60	20.23	513.84
25	12.26	311.40	12.87	326.90	16.79	426.47	18.33	465.58	20.16	512.06	19.91	505.71
20	13.67	347.22	13.93	353.82	17.54	445.52	18.55	471.17	19.92	505.97	19.46	494.28
15	15.00	381.00	14.89	378.21	18.16	461.26	18.63	473.20	19.55	496.57	18.89	479.80
10	16.24	412.50	15.75	400.05	18.64	473.46	18.57	471.68	19.05	483.88	18.21	462.53
5	17.37	441.20	16.49	418.85	18.98	482.09	18.37	466.60	18.42	467.87	17.41	442.21
0	18.40	467.36	17.12	434.85	19.17	486.92	18.04	458.22	17.67	448.82	16.50	419.10

TABLE 8.6 (*Contd.*)

Lat. Degrees	Expressed as equivalent evaporation in inches and millimetres per month											
	July		August		September		October		November		December	
	Inches	mms.	Inches	mms.	Inches	mms.	Inches	mms.	Inches	mms.	Inches	mms.
North												
45	20.64	524.26	18.15	461.01	13.86	352.04	10.13	257.30	6.65	168.91	5.45	138.43
40	20.76	527.30	18.70	474.98	14.87	377.70	11.54	293.12	8.15	207.01	7.02	178.31
35	20.76	527.30	19.12	485.65	15.77	400.56	12.86	326.64	9.63	244.60	8.59	218.19
30	20.65	524.51	19.40	492.76	16.55	420.37	14.10	358.14	11.06	280.92	10.15	257.81
25	20.41	518.41	19.56	496.82	17.20	436.88	15.24	387.10	12.43	315.72	11.67	296.42
20	20.04	509.02	19.57	497.08	17.72	450.09	16.26	413.00	13.74	349.00	13.14	333.76
15	19.55	496.57	19.45	494.03	18.11	459.99	17.17	436.12	14.95	379.73	14.53	369.06
10	18.93	480.82	19.18	487.17	18.35	466.09	17.95	455.93	16.07	408.18	15.85	402.59
5	18.18	461.78	18.78	477.01	18.46	468.88	18.60	472.44	17.09	434.09	17.07	433.58
0	17.32	439.93	18.25	463.55	18.43	468.12	19.11	485.39	17.99	456.95	18.18	461.77

TABLE 8.7

Mean Temperature, T and T, Co-efficient of Temperature, $C_{T,}$ and Log C_T (Christiansen Method)

T °F	T_C °C	C_T	Log C_T	T °F	T_C °C	C_T	Log C_T	T °F	T_C °C	C_T	Log C_T
				56	13.33	.787	–.1040	81	27.22	1.243	–.0944
32	0.00	.393	–.4060	57	13.89	.304	–.0946	82	27.78	1.262	–.1010
33	0.55	.408	–.3891	58	14.44	.622	–.0853	83	28.33	1.281	–.1076
34	1.11	.424	–.3727	59	15.00	.839	–.0761	84	28.89	1.300	–.1141
35	1.67	.440	–.3569	60	15.56	.857	–.0671	85	29.44	1.320	–.1205
36	2.22	.455	–.3415	61	16.11	.874	–.0583	86	30.00	1.339	–.1269
37	2.78	.471	–.3267	62	16.67	.892	–.0495	87	30.56	1.359	–.1332
38	3.33	.487	–.3122	63	17.22	.910	–.0410	88	31.11	1.379	–.1394
39	3.89	.503	–.2982	64	17.78	.928	–.0325	89	31.67	1.398	–.1456
40	4.44	.519	–.2843	65	18.38	.946	–.0242	90	32.22	1.418	–.1517
41	5.00	.536	–.2712	66	18.89	.964	–.0160	.91	32.78	1.438	–.1577
42	5.56	.552	–.2582	67	19.44	.982	–.0080	92	33.33	1.458	–.1637

43	6.11	.568	−.2455	68	20.00	1.000	−.0000	93	33.89	1.478	−.1696
44	6.67	.585	−.2332	69	20.56	1.018	−.0078	94	34.44	1.498	−.1754
45	7.22	.601	−.2211	70	21.11	1.037	−.0156	95	35.00	1.518	−.1812
46	7.78	.618	−.2093	71	21.67	1.055	−.0232	96	35.56	1.538	−.1870
47	8.33	.634	−.1978	72	22.22	1.073	−.0307	97	36.11	1.558	−.1927
48	8.89	.651-	−.1365	73	22.78	1.092	−.0382	98	36.67	1.579	−.1983
49	9.44	.668	−.1755	74	23.33	1.110	−.0455	99	37.22	1.599	−.2039
50	10.00	.684	−.1647	75	23.83	1.129	−.0527	100	37.78	1.620	−.2094
51	10.56	.701	−.1541	76	24.44	1.148	−.0599	101	38.33	1.640	−.2149
52	11.11	.718	−.1437	77	25.00	1.167	−.0670	102	38.89	1.661	−.2203
53	11.67	.735	−.1335	78	25.58	1.186	−.0739	103	39.44	1.682	−.2257
54	12.22	.753	−.1235	79	26.11	1.205	−.0808	104	40.00	1.702	−.2311
55	12.78	.770	−.1137	80	26.67	1.224	−.0876	105	40.56	1.723	−.2364

$C_T = 0.0678 + 0.0132T + 0.0000367T^2$

$C_T = 0.393 + 0.02796T_c + 0.0001189T_c^2$

TABLE 8.8

Wind Velocity W and Wk, Coefficient of Wind, C_w and Log C_w (Christiansen Method)

W mi/day	Wk km/day	C_w	Log C_w	W mi/day	Wk km/day	C_w	Log C_w	W mi/day	Wk km/day	C_w	Log C_w
0	0	.708	–.1500	56	90	.982	–.0077	86	138	1.104	.0423
5	8	.735	–.1337	57	92	.987	–.0058	87	140	1.107	.0443
10	16	.762	–.1183	58	93	.991	–.0039	88	142	1.111	.0457
15	24	.788	–.1057	59	95	.995	–.0020	89	143	1.115	.0472
20	32	.813	–.0893	60	97	.995	–.0020	89	143	1.115	.0472
20	32	.813	–.0893	60	97	1.000	.0000	90	145	1.118	.0486
25	40	.838	–.0766	61	98	1.004	.0017	91	146	1.122	.0500
30	48	.863	–.0641	62	100	1.008	.0035	92	148	1.126	.0514
33	53	.877	–.0569	63	101	1.012	.0053	93	150	1.129	.0528
34	55	.882	–.0545	64	103	1.016	.0071	94	151	1.133	.0542
35	56	.887	–.0521	65	105	1.021	.0089	95	153	1.136	.0555
36	58	.892	–.0498	66	106	1.025	.0106	96	154	1.140	.0569
37	60	.896	–.0475	67	108	1.029	.0124	97	156	1.144	.0582
38	61	.901	–.0453	68	109	1.033	.0141	98	158	1.147	.0596
39	63	.906	–.0430	69	111	1.037	.0158	99	159	1.151	.0611
40	64	.910	–.0408	70	113	1.041	.0175	100	161	1.155	.0626

41	66	.915	–.0386	71	114	1.045	.0192	110	177	1.188	.0747
42	68	.920	–.0364	72	116	1.049	.0209	120	193	1.219	.0861
43	69	.924	–.0342	73	117	1.053	.0225	130	209	1.249	.0965
44	71	.929	–.0320	74	119	1.057	.0242	140	225	1.276	.1060
45	72	.933	–.0299	75	121	1.061	.0258	150	241	1.302	.1146
46	74	.938	–.0278	76	122	1.065	.0274	160	257	1.326	.1224
47	76	.943	–.0257	77	124	1.069	.0290	170	274	1.347	.1294
48	77	.947	–.0236	78	126	1.073	.0306	180	290	1.367	.1357
49	79	.952	–.0216	79	127	1.077	.0322	190	306	1.384	.1413
50	80	.956	–.0195	80	129	1.081	.0337	200	322	1.400	.1461
51	82	.960	–.0175	81	130	1.085	.0353	210	338	1.144	.1503
52	84	.965	–.0155	82	132	1.088	.0368	220	354	1.425	.1539
53	85	.969	–.0135	83	134	1.092	.0383	230	370	1.435	.1568
54	87	.974	–.0116	84	135	1.096	.0398	240	386	1.442	.1591
55	89	.978	–.0096	85	137	1.100	.0413	250	402	1.448	.1608

$C_w = 0.708 + 0.328\,(W/W_c) - 0.036\,(W/W_c)^2$

W_c = 60 miles per day or 96.56 Kilometres per day

Ht. of Anemometer	Factor	Ht. of Anemometer	Factor
0.5 (in metres)	1.00	5.0	0.72
2.0	0.82	10.0	0.65

TABLE 8.9

Relative Humidity H, Coefficient of Humidity C_H, and Log C_H (Christiansen Method)

H %	C_H	Log C_H	H %	C_H	Log C_H	H %	C_H	Log C_H	H %	C_H	Log C_H
0	1.250	.0969	26	1.071	.0296	51	.944	–.0251	76	.738	–.1317
2	1.233	.0909	27	1.065	.0275	52	.938	–.0277	77	.726	–.1391
3	1.225	.0880	28	1.060	.0253	53	.933	–.0303	78	.713	–.1469
4	1.216	.0851	29	1.055	.0232	54	.927	–.0331	79	.700	–.1551
5	1.208	.0822	30	1.050	.0210	55	.921	–.0359	80	.686	–.1638
6	1.200	.0794	31	1.045	.0189	56	.914	–.0389	81	.671	–.1730
7	1.193	.0766	32	1.039	.0168	57	.908	–.0419	82	.657	–.1827
8	1.185	.0738	33	1.034	.0147	58	.902	–.0450	83	.641	–.1930
9	1.178	.0710	34	1.030	.0126	59	.895	–.0483	84	.625	–.2040
10	1.170	.0683	35	1.025	.0106	60	.888	–.0517	85	.609	–.2156
11	1.163	.0657	36	1.020	.0085	61	.881	–.0552	86	.592	–.2280
12	1.156	.0630	37	1.015	.0064	62	.873	–.0588	87	.574	–.2412
13	1.149	.0604	38	1.010	.0043	63	.866	–.0626	88	.555	–.2553
14	1.143	.0579	39	1.005	.0022	64	.858	–.0666	89	.536	–.2705

15	1.136	.0554	40	1.000	–.0001	65	.850	–.0708	90	.517	–.2867
16	1.129	.0529	41	.995	–.0020	66	.841	–.0751	91	.496	–.3041
17	1.123	.0504	42	.990	–.0042	67	.832	–.0796	92	.475	–.3229
18	1.117	.0480	43	.986	–.0063	68	.823	–.0844	93	.454	–.3432
19	1.111	.0456	44	.981	–.0085	69	.814	–.0893	94	.431	–.3653
20	1.105	.0432	45	.976	–.0108	70	.804	–.0945	95	.408	–.3893
21	1.099	.0409	46	.970	–.0130	71	.794	–.1000	96	.384	–.4156
22	1.093	.0386	47	.965	–.0153	72	.784	–.1057	97	.359	–.4446
23	1.087	.0363	48	.960	–.0177	73	.773	–.1117	98	.334	–.4767
24	1.082	.0341	49	.955	–.0201	74	.762	–.1180	99	.307	–.5125
25	1.076	.0318	50	.949	–.0226	75	.750	–.1247	100	.280	–.5528

$C_H = 1.250 - 0.0087\,H + 0.75 \times 10^{-4}H^2 - 0.85 \times 10^{-8}H^4$

$H_2 = 113 - 4.5\,\Delta t$, where Δt = T. Max – T.Min, where H_n = Mean Relative Humidity.

TABLE 8.10

Sunshine Percentages, Coefficient of Sunshine C_s and Log C_s (Christiansen Method)

S %	C_s	Log C_s	S %	C_s	Log C_s	S %	C_s	Log C_s	S %	C_s	Log C_s
0	.542	–.2630	26	.708	–.1499	51	.829	–.0813	76	.972	–.0125
2	.553	–.2336	27	.713	–.1467	52	.834	–.0787	77	.979	–.0094
3	.565	–.2477	28	.718	–.1436	53	.839	–.0761	78	.986	–.0063
4	.573	–.2429	29	.724	–.1405	54	.844	–.0736	79	.993	–.0031
5	.580	–.2365	30	.729	–.1375	55	.849	–.0710	80	1.000	.0000
6	.567	–.2311	31	.734	–.1346	56	.854	–.0684	81	1.008	.0033
7	.594	–.2259	32	.738	–.1317	57	.859	–.0658	82	1.015	.0066
8	.601	–.2209	33	.743	–.1288	58	.865	–.0632	83	1.023	.0099
9	.608	–.2160	34	.746	–.1260	59	.870	–.0606	84	1.031	.0133
10	.615	–.2112	35	.753	–.1232	60	.875	–.0579	85	1.039	.0167
11	.621	–.2066	36	.758	–.1204	61	.880	–.0553	86	1.047	.0201
12	.622	–.2021	37	.763	–.1177	62	.886	–.0526	87	1.056	.0236
13	.634	–.1973	38	.767	–.1150	63	.891	–.0499	88	1.064	.0271

14	.640	–.1965	39	.772	–.1123	64	.897	–.0472	89	1.073	.0307
15	.647	–.1894	40	.777	–.1096	65	.903	–.0444	90	1.082	.0343
16	.653	–.1854	41	.782	–.1070	66	.908	–.0417	91	1.091	.0379
17	.659	–.1814	42	.786	–.1044	67	.914	–.0389	92	1.101	.0416
18	.664	–.1776	43	.791	–.1018	68	.920	–.0361	93	1.110	.0454
19	.670	–.1739	44	.796	–.0992	69	.926	–.0332	94	1.120	.0491
20	.676	–.1702	45	.801	–.0996	70	.932	–.0304	95	1.130	.0529
21	.681	–.1666	46	.805	–.0940	71	.939	–.0275	96	1.140	.0568
22	.687	–.1631	47	.810	–.0915	72	.945	–.0245	97	1.150	.0607
23	.692	–.1597	48	.815	–.0889	73	.952	–.0216	98	1.160	.0646
24	.698	–.1564	49	.820	–.0864	74	.958	–.0186	99	1.171	.0686
25	.703	–.1531	50	.825	–.0838	75	.965	–.0156	100	1.181	.0725

$C_s = 0.542 + 0.0080 - 0.000078\, S^2 + 0.0000062\, S^2$

TABLE 8.11

Elevation E, Coefficient of Elevation, C_E and Log C_E (Christiansen Method)

Elev. 1000 feet	Elev. metres	C_E	Log C_E	Elev. E 1000 feet	Elev. metres	C_E	Log_{CE}	Elev. E 1000 feet	Elev. metres	C_E	Log C_E
.0	0	.970	–.0132	2.6	792	1.048	.0204	5.1	1554	1.123	.0504
.1	30	.973	–.0119	2.7	823	1.051	.0216	5.2	1585	1.126	.0515
.2	61	.976	–.0106	2.8	853	1.054	.0228	5.3	1615	1.129	.0527
.3	91	.979	–.0092	2.9	884	1.057	.0241	5.4	1646	1.132	.0538
.4	122	.982	–.0079	3.0	914	1.060	.0253	5.5	1676	1.135	.0550
.5	152	.985	–.0066	3.1	945	1.063	.0265	5.6	1707	1.138	.0561
.6	183	.988	–.0052	3.2	975	1.0666	.0278	5.7	1737	1.141	.0573
.7	213	.991	–.0039	3.3	1006	1.069	.0290	5.8	1768	1.144	.0584
.8	244	.994	–.0026	3.4	1036	1.072	.0302	5.9	1798	1.147	.0596
.9	274	.997	–.0013	3.5	1067	1.075	.0314	6.0	1829	1.150	.0607
1.0	305	1.000	.0000	3.6	1097	1.078	.0326	6.5	1981	1.165	.0663
1.1	335	1.003	.0013	3.7	1128	1.081	.03338	7.0	2134	1.84	.0719

1.2	366	1.006	.0026	3.8	1158	1.084	.0350	7.5	2286	1.195	.0774
1.3	396	1.009	.0039	3.9	1189	1.087	.0362	8.0	2438	1.210	.0828
1.4	427	1.012	.0052	4.0	1219	1.090	.0374	8.5	2591	1.225	.0881
1.5	457	1.015	.0065	4.1	1250	1.093	.0386	9.0	2743	1.240	.0934
1.6	488	1.018	.0077	4.2	1280	1.096	.0386	9.0	2743	1.240	.0934
1.7	518	1.021	.0090	4.3	1311	1.099	.0410	10.0	3048	1.270	.1038
1.8	549	1.024	.0103	4.4	1341	1.102	.0422	10.5	3200	1.285	.1089
1.9	579	1.027	.0116	4.5	1372	1.105	.0434	11.0	3353	1.300	.1139
2.0	610	1.030	.0128	4.6	1402	1.108	.0445				
2.1	640	1.033	.0141	4.7	1433	1.111	.0457				
2.2	671	1.036	.0154	4.8	1463	1.114	.0469				
2.3	701	1.039	.0166	4.9	1494	1.117	.0481				
2.4	732	1.042	.0179	5.0	1524	1.120	.0492				
2.5	762	1.045	.0191								

$C_E = 0.970 + 0.030\ (E/E_c)$.

E_c = 1000 feet or 305 metres.

TABLE 8.12

Consumptive Use (Evapotranspiration) Coefficients K, to be Multiplied by Estimated or Measured Class-A Pan Evaporation

*% of Crop Growing	Wheat Ludhiana	Wheat Poona	Maize Ludhiana	Maize Albama, U.S.A.	Jowar Albama, U.S.A.	Cotton Poona	Soyabeeans Hargreaves	Small Vegetables Hargreaves	Shallow rooted Vegetables Hargreaves	Sugarcane Hawaii	Rice Los Banos	Groundnut Israel	Castor Beans Hargreaves	Sugarcane Hargreaves
0	.14	.30	.40	.40	.42	.22	0.15	0.25	0.10	.34	1.00	30	.16	.48
5	.17	.40	.42	.40	.44	.22	0.18	0.28	0.15	.37	1.02	.30	.30	.50
10	.23	.51	.47	.43	.46	.23	0.20	0.30	0.20	.40	1.03	.32	.50	.53
15	.33	.62	.54	.46	.48	.24	0.23	0.38	0.30	.44	1.05	.35	.65	.55
20	.45	.73	.63	.52	.50	.26	0.25	0.45	0.40	.50	1.07	.40	.74	.60
25	.60	.84	.75	.59	.52	.35	0.28	0.50	0.45	.60	1.09	49	.81	.67
30	.72	.92	.85	.67	.56	.58	0.30	0.55	0.50	.72	1.11	.60	.87	.75
35	.81	.96	.96	.76	.59	.80	0.38	0.58	0.55	.86	1.13	.69	.92	.80
40	.88	1.10	1.04	.85	.64	.95	0.45	0.60	0.60	.93	1.16	.78	.96	.85
45	.90	1.10	1.07	.93	.71	1.03	0.50	0.63	0.60	.98	1.18	.85	.98	.87

50	.91	1.00	1.09	1.02	.79	1.08	0.55	0.65	0.60	1.02	1.20	.90	1.00	.89
55	.90	.91	1.10	1.09	.92	1.08	0.63	0.65	0.60	1.05	1.21	.94	1.00	.90
60	.89	.80	1.11	1.14	1.01	1.07	0.70	0.65	0.60	1.07	1.22	.96	.99	.90
65	.86	.65	1.10	1.19	1.07	1.05	0.75	0.63	0.58	1.10	1.22	.95	.97	.85
70	.83	.51	1.07	1.21	1.09	1.00	0.80	0.60	0.55	1.13	1.21	.94	.93	.75
75	.80	.40	1.04	1.23	1.09	1.93	0.75	0.58	0.50	1.16	1.19	.91	.89	.71
80	.76	.30	1.00	1.22	1.05	.85	0.70	0.55	0.45	1.19	1.16	.86	.82	.68
85	.71	.20	.97	1.16	.99	.73	0.65	0.50	0.40	1.20	1.10	.79	.72	.59
90	9.65	.12	.89	1.06	.91	.62	0.60	0.45	0.35	1.20	1.03	.72	.58	.51
95	.58	.10	.81	.95	.82	.50	0.55	0.38	0.33	1.19	.96	.64	.37	.50
100	.51	.10	.70	.75	.70	0.70	0.50	0.30	0.30	1.19	.86	.55	.22	.50
seasonal k	.61	.61	.86	.86	.75	.68	0.48	0.50	0.44	.89	1.10	.68	.73	.69

*Stage of Crop growth in % of growing season.

1. Based on a 13 months crop length.

Source : Michael, 1978, Based on Water Management Division (1971)

TABLE 8.13

Mean Values of 'K' Based on Growing Period (Hargreaves Method) for Computing Et

Per cent of crop growing season	Crop Factor K to be multiplied by Class — A Pan Evaporation (or computed PET) for the various groups of plants and rice							
	GR-A	GR-B	GR-C	GR-D	GR-E	GR-F	GR-G	Rice
0	0.20	0.15	0.12	0.08	0.90	0.60	0.50	0.80
10	0.36	0.27	0.22	0.15	0.90	0.60	0.60	0.95
20	0.64	0.48	0.38	0.27	0.90	0.60	0.70	1.05
30	0.84	0.63	0.50	0.40	0.90	0.60	0.80	1.14
40	0.97	0.73	0.58	0.52	0.90	0.60	0.90	1.21
50	1.00	0.75	0.60	0.65	0.90	0.60	1.00	1.30
60	0.99	0.74	0.60	0.77	0.90	0.60	1.00	1.30
70	0.91	0.68	0.55	0.88	0.90	0.60	0.90	1.20
80	0.75	0.56	0.45	0.90	0.90	0.60	0.80	1.10
90	0.46	0.35	0.28	0.70	0.90	0.60	0.70	0.90
100	0.20	0.20	0.17	0.20	0.90	0.60	0.50	0.20

Names of crops :

GR -A Beans, Maize, Cotton, Potatoes, Sugarbeets, Jowar, Peas, Mustard

GR-B Dates, Olives, Walnuts, Tomatoes, Hybrid Jowar

GR-C Melon, Onion, Carrots, Grapes

GR-D Barley, Flax (linseed), Wheat, Gram

GR-E Pastures, Orchards, Cover crops

FR-FCitrus crop, Orange, Lime, Grape fruit

GR-G Sugarcane, Alfalfa

Source : Irrigation Research Institute, Roorkee (U.P.).

TABLE 8.14

Net Irrigation Application (I) (mm)	Computed Peak Monthly Consumptive Use Rate (Um) in mm (Hargreaves)										
	100	125	150	175	200	225	2̈0	275	300	325	350
	Peak Period Daily Use Rate (U_p) In millimetres per Day										
25	3.9	5.1	6.2	7.4	8.5	9.6	10.8	11.9	13.1	14.2	15.4
38	3.6	4.8	5.9	7.0	8.1	9.2	10.3	11.5	12.5	13.5	14.5
50	3.5	4.6	5.7	6.7	7.8	8.8	9.9	11.0	112.0	13.0	14.0
63	3.5	4.5	5.5	6.5	7.5	8.5	9.5	10.5	11.5	12.5	13.5
75	3.4	4.4	5.3	6.3	7.2	8.3	9.3	10.3	11.2	12.2	13.2
88	3.4	4.3	5.2	6.2	7.1	8.2	9.1	10.1	11.0	12.0	13.0
100	3.3	4.3	5.2	6.1	7.1	8.1	9.0	10.0	10.9	11.9	12.8
113	3.3	4.3	5.1	6.0	7.0	7.9	8.8	9.7	10.6	11.6	12.6
125	3.3	4.2	5.1	5.9	6.8	7.7	8.6	9.5	10.5	11.4	12.4
138	3.3	4.2	5.1	5.9	6.7	7.6	8.5	9.4	10.3	11.3	12.2
150	3.3	4.2	5.0	5.8	6.7	7.6	8.5	9.4	10.3	11.2	12.1

Um = Use rate monthly

Up = Use rate at Peak period of crop growth per day.

TABLE 8.15

Crop Consumptive Use Coefficients (Hargreaves Method)

Per cent of Crop Growing Season	Consumptive Use (Evapotranspiration) Coefficients, K, to be Multiplied by Class-A Pan Evaporation or Calculated E_p (PET)							
	Group A	Group B	Group C	Group D	Group E	Group F	Group G	Ricc
0	0.20	0.15	0.12	0.08	0.90	0.60	0.50	0.80
5	0.20	0.15	0.12	0.08	0.90	0.60	0.55	0.90
10	0.36	0.27	0.22	0.15	0.90	0.60	0.60	0.95
15	0.50	0.38	0.30	0.19	0.90	0.60	0.65	1.00
20	0.64	0.48	0.38	0.27	0.90	0.60	0.70	1.05
25	0.75	0.56	0.45	0.33	0.90	0.60	0.75	1.10
30	0.84	0.63	0.50	0.40	0.90	0.60	0.80	1.14
35	0.92	0.69	0.55	0.46	0.90	0.60	0.86	1.17
40	0.97	0.73	0.58	0.52	0.90	0.60	0.90	1.21

45	0.99	0.74	0.60	0.58	0.90	0.60	0.95	1.25
50	1.00	0.75	0.60	0.65	0.90	0.60	1.00	1.30
55	1.00	0.75	0.60	0.71	0.90	0.60	1.00	1.30
60	0.99	0.74	0.60	0.77	0.90	0.60	1.00	1.30
65	0.96	0.72	0.58	0.82	0.90	0.60	0.95	1.25
70	0.91	0.68	0.55	0.88	0.90	0.60	0.90	1.20
75	0.85	0.64	0.51	0.90	0.90	0.60	0.85	1.15
80	0.75	0.56	0.45	0.90	0.90	0.60	0.80	1.10
85	0.60	0.45	0.36	0.80	0.90	0.60	0.75	1.00
90	0.46	0.35	0.28	0.70	0.90	0.60	0.70	0.90
95	0.28	0.21	0.17	0.60	0.90	0.60	0.55	0.80
100	0.20	0.20	0.17	0.20	0.90	0.60	0.50	0.20

Group Crop D : The maximum E_t/E_p ratio is about 0.90 and usually occurs at about 75 to 80 per cent completion of the crop vegetative cycle. The crops included are barley, celery, flax, wheat and other small grains.

Crop Group E : These crops have fairly flat curves. Ratios of E_t/E_p range from 0.70 to 1.10. The usual or modal group ratio is about 0.90. The crops include pastures, orchard with cover crop and plantain.

Crop Group F : This group includes the citrus crops — oranges and grape fruit. The E_t/E_p ratios are fairly constant throughout the year and average about 0.60.

Crop Group G : Group G includes sugarcane and alfalfa. E_t/E_p values increase with crop and generally vary from 0.66 to 1.00.

Rice : The E_t/E_p ratios present a fairly flat curve. A maximum value of 1.30 and a minimum of 0.80 is representative of average conditions.

Since these coefficients are average values, some care must be taken in their use. Frequently for a given crop considerable variations in E_t/E_p ratios may exist. Sugar beets are shown as fitting a typical bell curve with maximum ratios at 50 to 55 per cent completion of the crop growing season. This is frequently the true relationship. However, in highly productive fields, growth and evapotranspiration have been maintained until shortly before harvest.

Other factors may cause the evaportranspiration to be greater or less than the average value. Taller and more uneven vegetation tends to result in greater turbulence and more efficient utilisation of radiation in the production of water use. Dark green vegetation produces higher rates of absorption of solar energy and hence the rate of evapotranspiration will be higher than that for light green vegetation. Plant diseases that produce yellowing of the leaves of the plants greatly reduce evapotranspiration. Assuming that factors for crop roughness and crop colour are comparable, then evapotranspiration is roughly a function of crop cover.

Under similar climatic conditions, there is little difference in the rate of evapotranspiration by various crops or types of vegetative cover provided equal densities, roughness and colour of vegetation are compared and the crop is in an active stage of growth.

Computing Evapotranspiration (Consumptive use)

The following sample calculation (Table 8.16) show the computations of consumptive use and net irrigation requirement for jowar at Bellary, Mysore State. These estimates are made on a monthly basis.

TABLE 8.16

Dates	Mid-point	% G.S.	E_t/E_p (k)	PE or E_p	CU	Perc. L	R_e	NIR
1	2	3	4	5	6	7	8	9
October								
16-31	8	7	.44	84.9	73.4	...	34.2	3.2
November								
1-30	31	28	.54	155.7	84.1	...	21.9	62.2
December								
1-31	62	56	.94	165.9	155.9	...	5.4	150.5
January								
1-31	93	85	.99	191.0	189.1	...	1.5	187.6
February								
1-2	109	99	.73	15.4	11.2	...	.2	11.0

Source : Technical Series No. 2 and 3 published by the Water Management Division, Ministry of Agriculture (Department of Agriculture), New Delhi (1971).

Column 1 — Months and fractions of months.

Column 2 — Number of days from planting to mid-point of each monthly period.

Column 3 — Percentage of the growing season to the mid-point of the monthly period, *i.e.* column 2 divided by number of days required for crop.

Column 4 — E_t/E_p ratio for jowar at specific growth periods as shown in Table 8.16.

Column 5 — Pan evaporation, E_p, as computed by Christiansen Method for Bellary, Mysore (millimetres).

Column 6 — Consumptive use (evapotranspiration) of jowar by monthly periods (Column 5 times column 5) (millimetres).

Column 7 — Percolation losses.

Column 8 — Effective rainfall.

Column 9 — Net irrigation requirement is determined by substracting effective rainfall from consumptive use (millilitres).

Examples on Evapotranspiration (Many other Methods are Covered as Examples)

Example

Blancy-Criddle Approach : ETo or $U = KF = \Sigma kf = \Sigma u$

Let us compute the evapotranspiration for corn at latitude 41°-30'N for the month of July using Blancy-Criddle equation (1950). Assume for Palato U = 0.58 inches

$$\therefore \text{Crop coefficient } K = \frac{u}{f} = \frac{0.580}{0.963} = 0.06$$

$$(\text{if } t = 58.8 \text{ and } p = 1.64 \therefore f = \frac{t \times p}{100} = 0.963$$

Now say for the area given is

(i) Average monthly temperature 't' (Av. of daily minimum and maximum values) = 23.90°C (75°F)

(ii) Average percentage of the day time hours of the year for July = 10.32

∴ The monthly evapotranspiration by modified Blancy-Criddle equation is given by :

$$\text{ETo or } U = K\left[P\ 0.46\ t + 8\right]$$

where

U = monthly evapotranspiration in mm

K = monthly evapotranspiration coefficient (consumptive use function of crop and temperature) for total period.

t = mean monthly temperature in degrees Fahrenheit

p = monthly per cent of total day time hours of year

f = $\frac{t \times P}{100}$ = monthly evapotranspiration (consumptive use) factor.

Total evapotranspiration for the growing season or other period is the sum of the monthly totals. For temperature in 0°C, the above equation becomes :

$$\therefore U = Kp\,(0.46\,t + 8.0)$$

On substituting values we get

$$\therefore U = 0.6 \times 10.32\,(0.46 \times 23.9 + 8.0) = 117.61$$

Say = 118 mm/mo (4.64 in)

Example

Penman Approach

To calculate for data in Example 1 the evapotranspiration by Penman equation with G = 0 and the radiation coefficient of 0.2 for green crops :

As we represent net radiation energy by Eq.

$$R_n = Ra\,(1-r)\,(0.18 + \frac{0.55n}{N})$$

$$- \sigma\, Ta^4\,(0.56 - 0.09\,\sqrt{ed})\,(0.10 + \frac{0.9n}{N})$$

where

Rn = Net radiant energy available at the earth surface in cal cm^{-2} day^{-1}

Ra = Mean extra-terrestrial radiation mm H_2O/day

r = Radiation reflection coefficient (0.05 for water surface and 0.2 for green crops)

n/N= ratio of actual to possible hours of sunshine (n = actual duration of bright sunshine and N = Max. possible duration of bright sunshine)

σ = Stefan-Boltzmann constant (11.71×10^{-8} Cal cm^{-2} day^{-1}) or 2.01×10^{-9} mm H_2O/day

Ta^4 = Air temperature K° [°C+273 (Absolute temp.)]. See Appendix Table 8A.

ed = Actual vapour pressure of air mb (also saturated vapour pressure at dew point temperature evapotranspiration).

Also by using Rn = 937 cal cm^{-2} day^{-1} for given latitude of 41½° from standard table computed from formula

Extraterrestrial radiation in Cal cm^{-2} day^{-1}

$$= 889 \left[\frac{\text{Value from Brunt}}{\text{days per month}}\right]$$

The av. mean temperature for area = 18.9°C (es 21.9 mb)

The av. maximum temperature = 28.9°(es = 39.9 mb) for area

The average monthly relative humidity = 65.5 per cent and n/N = 0.745

$\therefore$ Rn = 937 (1–0.2) (0.18 +0.55 × 0.745)

(–) (11.71×10^{-8}) (297^4) (0.56–0.08)

(30.9 × 0.655) (0.1 + 0.9 × 0.745)

= 302 Cal cm^{-2} day^{-1}

Also if wind velocity at a height of 21.3 metre (70 ft) = 9.75 km/hr (6.1 mph or 234 km/d).

Assuming wind variation with height is logarithmic at 2 metres height.

Assuming a roughness height for corn in July of 1 m.

V_2 234 × $\ln_2$ / In 21.3 = 53 km/d

Substituting in Equation Potential ET given by Penman (1963)

$$ETp = \frac{\Delta}{\Delta + r} (Rn - G) \frac{r}{\Delta + r} 15.36\,(1 + 0.0062\, r_2)\,(la - ed)$$

where

ET = Potential Evapotranspiration in Cal cm^{-2} day^{-1}

Δ = Slope of saturation vapour pressure curve in mb/°C at mean air temperature

r = Psychrometric constant in mb/°C

ET = (0.723 × 302) + 0.277 × 15.36 (1+0.0062 × 53) (30.9 – 0.655 × 309) = 279 Cal cm^{-2} day^{-1}

or 2.79 × 10/590 = 4.7 mm/d

= 4.7 × 31 = 146 mm/mo

= (5.74 in/mo)

Example

Solar Radiation Approach (Rs) :

Calculate total evapotranspiration for the month of August for irrigated grain sorghum near a location where crop data are as follows :

Planting date	June 10	0 days
Heading date	August 15	66 days

For working out the above exercise given Rs (0.25 + 0.50 n/N) Ra = 10.2 mm/day from standard table on mean measured daily total solar and sky radiation (short wave) Rns.

For August 1 is say (51/66) 77 per cent of time planting to heading and August 31 is 16 days after heading. For August read an average crop coefficient of about 0.7 from figure on crop coefficient for the solar radiation method in relation to stage of growth of crop.

Assuming mean August temperature of 25°C and substituting in eqs.

PET or ET = C_t(tc-tx) Rs = 0.025 (tc+3) RS

where

ET = Potential evapotranspiration in mm/d

Ct = Temperature coefficient say 0.025

t_C = Mean air temperature in °C say 25°C

t_X = Intercepts of ET/Rs Vs t regression line with the temperature axis

R_s = Solar radiation as equivalent depth of evaporation in mm/d. Say 10.2

U = ETp or Consumptive use at crop coefficient 0.70

Where the coefficient Ct and tx can be obtained from accurate ET and climate data for a local area and actual ET_c = Potential ET [or ETo or PET] × crop coefficient × number of days of the month

∴ PET = 0.025 (25+3) 10.2 = 7.1 mm/day

∴ U = 0.7 × 31 × 7.1 = 154 mm/mo

Example

Calculate ET_o by Blancy and Criddle method from following data :

(i) T daily mean = $\Sigma \frac{T\ mean}{31} = 28.5°C$

T_{max} daily values/31 = 35°C

T_{min} daily values/31 = 22°C

$$T_{mean} \text{ daily} = \Sigma \frac{T_{mean}}{31} = \left[\frac{\Sigma T_{mean}}{31} + \frac{\Sigma T_{mean}}{31} \right] \div 2$$

(ii) Latitude = 30°-0" N

(iii) Longitude = 30°

(iv) Month = July

(v) Altitude = 95 M

(vi) RH Min = Med 20 — 50%

(vii) P for 30°N = 0.31 mm/day [from standard table of mean daily percentage (P) of annual day time hrs for different latitudes]

(viii) Max. possible sunshine hours n/N = High to medium (0.9)/(0.7)

(ix) Day time wind condition at 2 m height

(x) Say crop coefficient Kc = 0.45

(xi) U_2 day time = Moderate

The air humidity refers to minimum day time humidity and that wind refers to day time wind. If estimates of 24 hour mean wind are available, these are converted to day time wind. Generally U day/U night ≅ 2 and mean 24 hr. wind data should be multiplied by 1.33 to obtain mean day time wind. For areas with either predominantly night or day time wind, the following factors may be used :

U day/ U night ratio	1.0	1.5	2.0	2.5	3.0	3.5	4.0
Correction factor for U day	1.0	1.2	1.33	1.43	1.5	1.58	1.6

Source : FAO Bulletin 24.

$$ET_o = C\,[P\,(0.46T + 8)]\text{ mm/day \& ET crop} = Kc\,ET_o$$

where

ET_o = Reference crop evaporation in mm/day for the month in question.

T = Mean daily temperature in °C over the month in question.

P = Mean daily percentage of total annual day time hours obtained from standard tables for a given month and latitude.

C = Adjustment factor which depends on minimum relative humidity, sunshine hours and day time wind estimates.

Hence by calculation

$$P\,(0.46\,T + 8) = 6.6\text{ mm/day }[0.31\,(0.46 \times 28.5 + 8)]$$

The correction factor C is found from graphs to estimate ET_o by plotted as P (0.46T+8) on X-axis and the values of ET_o on Y-axis. Thus for this example on reading P (0.46T+8) = 6.6 on X-axis and RH Med. (20-50%) with sunshine n/N high/medium (= 0.9) 0 = 0.7 the values of ET_o from n/N medium on graph is 7.5 and at high is 8.5. Hence average is 8.0 mm/day. Since the correction factor 'C' (Block/line) = 1.4. Also from calculations

ET_o = 1.4 + 6.6= 8.0 mm/day ∴ ET crop = 0.45 × 8 = 3.60mm/day

Example

Calculate Solar radiation (Rs) and equivalent evaporation in mm/day. Here ETo = C (W. Rs) mm/day.

W = Weighing factor depending on temperature and altitude

Given :

(i) Latitude = 30°N
(ii) Month = July
(iii) Sunshine (n) mean = 11.5 h/day
(iv) Ra = 16.8 mm/day for 30°N (From table)

[Ra from Standard Extra-terrestrial Radiation (Ra) table expressed in equivalent evaporation in mm/day for different months and hemisphere at different latitudes.]

Also if

N = 13.9 h/day

[From table of mean Daily Duration of maximum possible sunshine hours (N) for different months and latitudes.]

Hence as Rs is given by equation

Rs = (0.25 + 0.50 n/N Ra)

∴ Rs = (0.25 + 0.50 × 11.5/13.9) 16.8

= 11.2 mm/day mean equivalent evaporation for the month in question for sun shine condition.

In case of cloudiness expressed in Oktas (0 to 8) and sometimes in tenths (0 to 10) which must be first converted to the n/ratio by following table :

Cloudiness (Oktas)	0	1	2	3	4	5	6	7	8
n/N ratio	.95	.85	.75	.65	.55	.45	.35	.15	–

Cloudiness (tenths)	0	1	2	3	4	5	6	7	8	9	10
n/N ratio	.95	.85	.80	.75	.65	.55	.50	.40	.3	.15	–

Example

To calculate the Rs values taking into consideration cloudiness.

Given :

Ra = 16.8 mm/day, latitude = 30°N

Month = July, Cloudiness, (Oktas) = 1

Conversion factor for n/N = 0.85 for cloudiness oktas = 1

∴ Rs (0.25 + .50n/N) Ra = (0.25 + 0.50 × 0.85) 16.8

= 11.3 mm/day

Example

To calculate weighting factor (W) : Since the factor W reflects the effect of temperature and altitude on the relationship between Rs and ET_o**, the values of W are related to temperature and altitude as given in table on values of weighting factor (W) for the effect of radiation on ET_o at different temperatures and altitudes.

If given are
Altitude = 95 m, T_{mean} = 28.5°C

Hence, from the appendix table 8G.
W = 0.77

Example

To find out adjustment factor (c). Since the adjustment factor (c) is expressed by the relationship between the radiation term (WRS) and reference crop evapotranspiration (ET_o) which is represented graphically as in Appendix (Prediction of ET_o from WRS) for different conditions of mean RH and day time Wind. It depends greatly on general levels of mean relative humidity (RH mean) and day time wind (07.00-19.00 hours) at 2 metre height above the soil surface.

Say given is T_{mean} = 28.5°C, Re = 16.8 mm/day

(i)	Latitude	=	30°N	
(ii)	Altitude	=	95 m	Also
(iii)	Month	=	July	n = 11.5
(iv)	Rs	=	11.2 mm/day	N = 13.9
(v)	W	=	0.77	n/N= 0.83
(vi)	WRS	=	8.6 mm/day	
(vii)	Wind day time	=	Moderate (0.700–19.00 hrs)	
(viii)	RH mean	=	Medium	

Thus from Fig. of Prediction of ET_o from WRS for different conditions of mean relative humidity and day time wind :

RH mean = Medium
U day = Moderate
ET_c mm/day = (8.7 + 8.0)/2 = 8.4 mm/day
(For WRs = 8.6 mm/day)
Also Rs = (0.25 + 0.50 n/N) by calculation = 0.67

Examples

Calculation of (ea–ed)

The form of the Penmen (1977) equation is given by :

$$ET_o = \underset{\text{Radiation term}}{\underline{WRn}} + \underset{\text{Aerodynamic term}}{\underline{(1-W)\, f\, u\, (ea-ed)}}$$

where

ET_o = Reference crop evapotranspiration in mm/day

W = Temperature related weighting factor

Rn = Nét radiation in equivalent evaporation in mm/day

f(u) = Wind related function

(ea–ed) = Difference between the saturation pressure at mean air temperature and the mean actual vapour pressure of the air, both in m bar

C = Adjustment factor to compensate for the effect of day and night weather conditions

If given

Altitude = 0 metre

$T_{maximum}$ = 35°C

$T_{minimum}$ = 22°C

$RH_{maximum}$ = 80% & RH_{max} = 30%

T_{mean} = (35 + 22)/2 = 28.5°C

$$RH_{mean} = \frac{(80 + 30)}{2} = 55\%$$

ea at 28.5°C from 'ea'
Table of Saturation
Vapour pressure (ea)
in m bar as function of mean air temp. T in C°** = 38.9 m bar.

(Also ed may be obtained from 'ed' table using T dew point data *e.g.* T dew point is 18°C, ed = 20.6 m bar.)

ed = ea × RH_{mean}/100 = 21.4 m bar

Hence

ea-ed = 17.5 bar

(ii) Also say

T dry bulb = 24°C

T wet bulb = 20°C

∴ ea from table = 38.9 m bar

ed at T dry bulb at 24°C

From table on vapour pressure (ed) in m bar from Dry and Wet bulb temperature Data in °C (Aspirated psychrometer) and at T wet bulb from above table = 20.7 m bar

Hence (ea-ed) = 18.2 m bar

(iii) Also given T dew point at depr. 0°C = 18°C

∴ ea at 28.5°C from table = 38.9 m bar

ed at dew point = 20.6 m bar

∴ (ea–ed) = 18.3 m bar

(iv) Calculation of wind function f(u) is given by :

f(u) = 0.27 (1 + U/100)

when U = 24 hr. wind run in km/day at 2 metre height

It is valid when (ea–ed) is given in m bar

Hence if given

(i) Wind speed at 3 m height = 250 km/day

(ii) U by above conversion = 232 km/day

(iii) fu from appendix table 8E = 0.90

Example

Calculation of weighing factor (1-w) :

Here = W $\Delta/(\Delta+\alpha)$;

[Δ = Rate of change of Saturation V. Pressure

α = Psychrometric constant

It is a factor for the effect of wind and humidity on ET_o.

Values of (1-W) as related to temperature and altitude are given in appended table 8F. For temperature use $(T_{max} + T_{min})/2$.

Hence, for altitude 95 m, T_{max} = 35°C & T_{min} = 22°C

i.e. T_{mean} = 28.5°C

(1-W) from appendix table 8F = 0.23

Example

To calculate weighing factor (W), for altitude of 95 m and T_{mean} = 28.5°C

∴ W from appendix table 8G = 0.77

Example

To calculate Net radiation (Rn)

Given latitude = 30°N, Altitude = 95m

month July, T_{mean} = 28.5°C & RH_{mean} = 55% and sun shine mean 11.5 hr/day

Hence Ra from appendix table 8B = 16.8 mm/day

α = 0.25 (crop surface reflectivess correction factor)

Also given n = 11.5 hr

N = 13.9 hr; n/N = 0.83

∴ Rs (0.25 + 0.50 n/N) Ra = 11.2 mm/day

Rns (1 - α) Ra from appendix table 8B = 8.4 mm/day

Rnl f_t f(ed), f(n/N) = 1.8 mm/day

If from appendex table 8I f_t = 16.3

from appendix table 8J fed f (ed) = 0.13

from appendix table 8K n/N f(n/N) = 0.85

∴ Rn = Rns – Rnl = 6.6 mm/day

Example

Calculation of adjustment factor (C)

Given : Month — July, & latitude 30°N and altitude 95 m

Rs = 11.2 mm/day

RH maximum = 80%

U day = 3.2 m/sec

U night = 2.1 m/sec

U day/U night = 1.5

∴ C value from appendix table 8L = 1.01 (by interpolation)

Hence from above the ET_o by Penman method with following data *i.e.*

Month = July

W = 0.77

Rn = 6.6

1-W = 0.23

f(u) = 0.90

(ea-ed) = 17.5

C = 1.01

∴ Putting values in equation :

$ET_o = C\ [W\ Rn + (1-W).fu\ (ea-ed)]$

$ET_o = 1.01\ (0.77 \times 6.6 + 0.23 \times 0.90 \times 17.5)\ 8.8$ mm/day

Example

To calculate ET_o by Pan evaporation method. Now Reference crop evapotranspiration is given by :

$ET_o = Kp \times E\ Pan$

where,

E Pan = Pan evaporation in mm/day and represents the mean daily value of the period considered

Kp = Pan coefficient

The value of Kp are given in appendix table 8M.

If given :

Month	= July
E pan for a cropped area	= 11.1 mm/day
RH mean	= Medium
Wind	= Moderate

For moderate wind and medium humidity value of KP = 0.75

∴ $ET_o = Kp \times E\ pan = 0.75 \times 11.1 = 8.3$ mm/day

Example

To calculate 'E Soil' from fallow, essentially weed free soil.

Given :

	Nov.	Dec.	Jan.	Feb.	March
ET_o mm/day	3.2	2.3	2.7	3.8	5.0
Frequency of rain, days	7	7	5	7	10
If K factor (from standard figure plotted against Kc Vs ET_o mm/day)	0.6	.65	.7	.55	.3
∴ E Soil mm/day = K ET_o	1.9	1.5	2.1	1.5	

Example

Compute the evaporation for the month of June from a shallow pond if the surface water temperature is 15.6°C(60°F), the average wind velocity W is 4.8 km/h (3 m.p.h.) and the average temperature and relative humidity at 7.6 m (25 ft) height are 21.1°C (70°F) and 40 per cent respectively.

Solution :

As we know from Dalton's law that evaporation from free-water surface may be given by

E = C (es – ed)

where,

es	=	the saturated vapour pressure at the temperature of the water surface in mm of mercury
ed	=	The actual vapour pressure of the air (es times relative humidity) in mm of mercury
E	=	The rate of evaporation
C	=	a Constant, evaluated by Rohwer (1931), and is given as C = (0.44 + 0.073W) (1.465–0.00073P) with W as average wind velocity in Km/hr at a height of 0.15 m (6 in) and P is atmospheric pressure in mm mercury at 0°C. With these units E is in mm/d. To find the evaporation from reservoirs, the calculated E has to be multiplied by 0.77.

Also value of constant 'C' for pans and shallow ponds (E as mm/mo) given by Meyer (1942).

(E as mm/mo) given by Meyer (1942) is C = 15+0.93 W and for small lakes and reservoirs C = 11+0.68W.

Hence,

$$E = \left(\frac{15 + 0.93 \times 4.8}{\text{'C' by Meyer}}\right)\left(\frac{13.0}{\text{es}} - \frac{18.5 \times 0.40}{\text{ed}}\right)$$

= 109 mm/mo (4.3 in/mo)

(Using vapour pressure for 60°F = 13° & for 70°F = 18.5) from saturation vapour pressure curve as a function of temperature — Glenn *et al.*, 1981 by John Wiley and Sons. Inc., Canada.)

The total and daily water requirement of crops based on growing season is given in Table 8.17.

TABLE 8.17

Water Requirements of Crops

Crops	Growing season* (No. of days)	Total water requirements (acre inches)	Daily water requirement (acre inches)
Barley	88	14.1	0.18
Chilli	202	34.8	0.19
Cotton	202	42.2	0.21
Groundnut	124	26.1	0.21
Jowar	114	25.7	0.23
Linseed	38	12.7	0.14
Maize	100	17.8	0.18
Mustard	88	10.6	0.12
Oats	88	14.4	0.16
Pea	88	12.0	0.14
Potato	88	26.7	0.30
Ragi	127	29.8	0.23
Rice	98	41.7	0.43
Sugarcane	365	95.0	0.26
Tobacco	132	39.2	0.30
Wheat	88	14.8	0.17

* Includes water lost in transpiration and by evaporation and seepage. (Source hand book of Agriculture, I.C.A.R.)

The net amount of water required per irrigation for different textured soils in acre inch/acre are shown in Table 8.18.

TABLE 8.18

Net Amount of Water Required Per Irrigation

Type of soil profile	Net amount of moisture to apply AC in/AC						
	12"	18"	24"	30"	36"	48"	72"
	— for various root depths						
Coarse sandy soils uniform in texture 6 ft.	0.45	0.60	0.95	1.30	1.30	1.75	2.60
Coarse sandy soils over more compact sub-soils	0.45	0.60	1.50	1.75	2.00	2.50	3.00
Fine sandy loams uniform in texture to 6 ft.	0.85	1.30	1.75	2.20	2.60	3.00	4.00
Fine sandy loams over more compact subsoils	0.85	1.50	2.00	2.40	2.80	3.25	5.00

Silt loams uniform to 6 ft.	1.10	1.70	2.25	2.75	3.00	4.00	6.00
Silt loams over more compact sub-soils	1.10	1.70	2.50	3.00	3.25	4.25	6.25
Heavy clay or clay loam soils	0.90	1.40	2.00	2.40	2.85	3.85	5.50

Source : "Sprinkler Irrigation" booklet published by Sprinkler Irrigation Association, Washington.

Another Aspects of Irrigation Requirements (I.R.)/Consumptive use

Using basic data of meteorological stations *i.e.* solar radiation, temperature, relative humidity, wind speed, open pan evaporation and rainfall, the irrigation requirement of a crop can be worked out using following formulae :

$$\text{I.R.} = \frac{100\,(\text{ETa} + \text{LR})}{\text{E}} - (\text{Peff} + \text{M.C.} + \text{Mg}) + \text{LC}$$

where

ET_a	=	Actual evapotranspiration by pan evaporimeter
L.R.	=	Leaching requirement
$(ET_a + LR)$	=	Net irrigation water to be given to crop for meeting demands at Kc = 1 if less than from standard tables take equivalent value of ET_c and use $(ET_c + LR)$
Peff	=	Effective rainfall
M.C.	=	Carried over/Antecedent soil moisture
Mg	=	Ground water moisture contribution
L_c	=	Losses through conveyance and operation etc.

The values change from place to place and particularly are dependent on rainfall pattern of area which is widely variable over a small range of distance.

LYSIMETER APPROACH

These are also called evapotranspiration meters approach. These equipments are tanks filled with soil where crops are grown and irrigated. The amount of water is measured by the amount of water lost by evaporation and transpiration to get direct readings of ET and is used to study climatic effects on ET. Although these methods do not exactly represent the field conditions but if lysimeters are properly filled with identical field situations as per soil horizons and depths of profile of a given field and values of bulk density layer-wise is maintained, fair accurate results are obtained. Also the crop in lysimeter should be the same as in outside field. The lysimeters may be installed at least 100 metre from the edge of the field. The rim or border of the lysimeter should be as small as possible and heat flux and soil temperatures in the lysimeter should have equal values typical for the surrounding field.

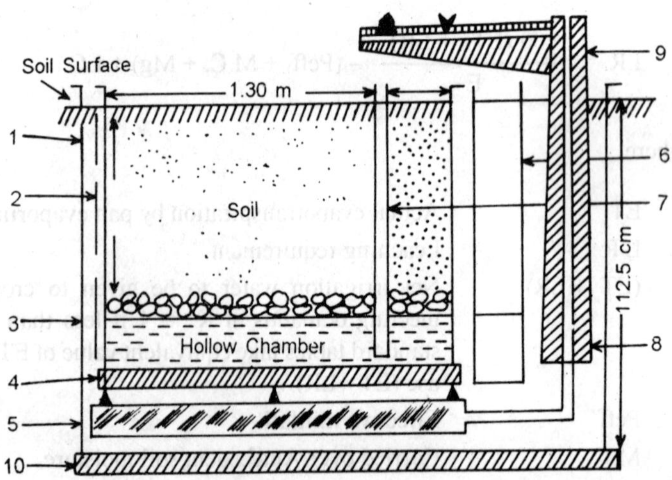

Fig. 8.6 : Schematic diagram of a Mechanical Weighing Lysimeter

Lysimeters are categorised as follows :

(1) Non-weighing types; and

(2) Weighing types.

The difference between the water supplied to the lysimeter and that which drains is measured. The changes in soil-water in the lysimeter (δθ/

area) and measured by any moisture measurement procedure (*e.g.* gravimetric, neutron etc.). The value of weekly actual ET values are found out and PET is calculated after irrigating the crop having adequate drainage. If irrigations are done daily, the moisture profile remains fairly constant and measurements over a week period is calculated. The ET is found by equation : ET = I+P–R–D; where ET = Evapotranspiration; I=Water supplied from over head tank; P=Rainfall/Precipitation, R=Surface runoff and D=Water collected in the overflow collector container.

The standard design and construction of lysimeter is pre-requisite for their installation and caliberation is done using formula :

$$ET \quad \frac{(\pi r_o^2 - \pi r_i^2)}{A} \times \frac{\Delta h}{\Delta t} \quad \text{or} \quad \frac{Sh}{St}$$

where ET is evapotranspiration (cm^3/cm^2 per hour); r_o = Inner radius of the outer tube (cm); r_i = outer radius of the inner tube (cm); A=effective surface area (cm^2) of each plant hill; h=change of height of water column in the reservoir (cm) in Δt or time (hr). The effective area of cylinder (say 314 cm^2) equals inner cross sectional area of cylinder when the leaf area index (LAI) is unity. If canopy covered more ground surface (LAI>1), the effective area become 400 cm^2 equivalent to an area represented by each hill in a 20 × 20 cm planting pattern. The design of lysimeter is given in Figs. 8.6 and 8.7 for the use of readers.

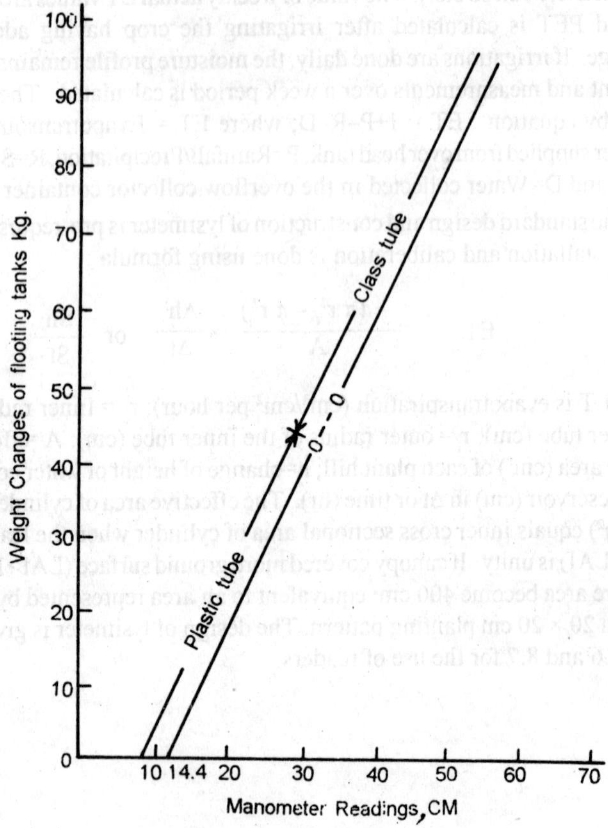

Fig. 8.7 : Calibration of Lysimeter

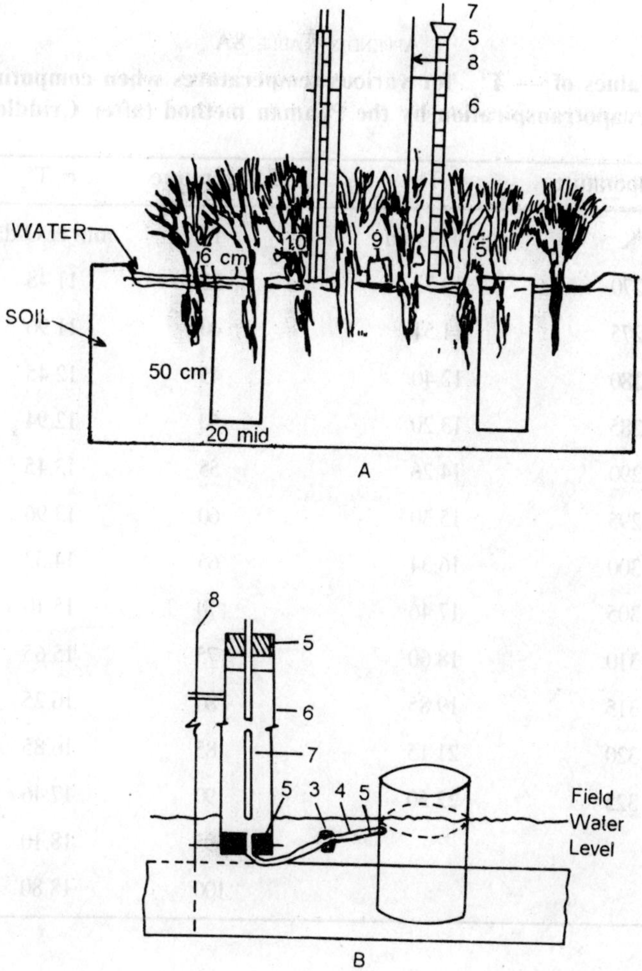

Fig. 8.8 : Cross section of field installed microlysimeters for measuring evapotranspiration (A) and details of mariotte system (B) (From Tomer and O' Toole 1980) (1. Bottomed and PVC pipe; 2. Cover; 3. Stopcock; 4. Flexible clear tubing; 5. Rubber stopper; 6. Reservoir/manometer; 7. Bubble Tube; 8. Stand; 9. Wakway.

APPENDIX

APPENDIX TABLE 8A

Values of — T_a^4 for various temperatures when computing evapotranspiration by the Penman method (after Criddle)

Temperature	σT_a^4	Temperature	σT_a^4
°K	mm H_2O/day	°F	mm H_2O/day
270	10.73	35	11.48
275	11.51	40	11.96
280	12.40	45	12.45
285	13.20	50	12.94
290	14.26	55	13.45
295	15.30	60	13.96
300	16.34	65	14.52
305	17.46	70	15.10
310	18.60	75	15.65
315	19.85	80	16.25
320	21.15	85	16.85
325	22.50	90	17.46
		95	18.10
		100	18.80

APPENDIX TABLE 8B

Extra-terrestrial radiation (*RA*) expressed in equivalent evaporation in mm/day

Northern Hemisphere

Lat.	Jan.	Feb.	Mar.	April	May	June	July	Aug.	Sept.	Oct.	Nov.	Dec.
1	2	3	4	5	6	7	8	9	10	11	12	13
50°	3.8	6.1	9.4	12.7	15.8	17.1	16.4	14.1	10.9	7.4	4.5	3.2
48	4.3	6.6	9.8	13.0	15.9	17.2	16.5	14.3	11.2	7.8	5.4	3.7
46	4.9	7.1	10.2	13.3	16.0	17.2	16.6	14.5	11.5	8.3	5.5	4.3
44	5.3	7.6	10.6	13.7	16.1	17.2	16.6	14.7	11.9	8.7	6.0	4.7
42	5.9	8.1	11.0	14.0	16.2	17.3	16.7	15.0	12.2	9.1	6.5	5.2
40	6.4	8.6	11.4	14.3	16.4	17.3	16.7	15.2	12.5	9.6	7.0	5.7
38	6.9	9.0	11.8	14.5	16.4	17.2	16.7	15.3	12.8	10.0	7.5	6.1
36	7.4	9.4	12.1	14.7	16.4	17.2	16.7	15.4	13.1	10.6	8.0	6.6
34	7.9	9.8	12.4	14.8	16.5	17.1	16.8	15.5	13.4	10.8	8.5	7.2
32	8.3	10.2	12.8	15.0	16.5	17.0	16.8	15.6	13.6	11.2	9.0	7.8
30	8.8	10.7	13.1	15.2	16.5	17.0	16.8	15.7	13.9	11.6	9.5	8.3

(Contd.)

APPENDIX TABLE 8B (*Contd.*)

1	2	3	4	5	6	7	8	9	10	11	12	13
28	9.3	11.1	13.4	15.3	16.5	16.8	16.7	15.7	14.1	12.0	9.9	8.8
26	9.8	11.5	13.7	15.3	16.4	16.7	16.6	15.7	14.3	12.3	10.3	9.3
24	10.2	11.9	13.9	15.4	16.4	16.6	16.5	15.8	14.5	12.6	10.7	9.7
22	10.7	12.3	14.2	15.5	16.3	16.4	16.4	15.8	14.6	13.0	11.1	10.2
20	11.2	12.7	14.4	15.6	16.3	16.4	16.3	15.9	14.8	13.3	11.6	10.7
18	11.6	13.0	14.6	15.6	16.1	16.1	16.1	15.8	14.9	13.6	12.0	11.1
16	12.0	13.3	14.7	15.6	16.0	15.9	15.9	15.7	15.0	13.9	12.4	11.6
14	12.4	13.6	14.9	15.7	15.8	15.7	15.7	15.7	15.1	14.1	12.8	12.0
12	12.8	13.9	15.1	15.7	15.7	15.5	15.5	15.6	15.2	14.4	13.3	12.5
10	13.2	14.2	15.3	15.7	15.5	15.3	15.3	15.5	15.3	14.7	13.6	12.9
8	13.6	14.5	15.3	15.6	15.3	15.0	15.1	15.4	15.3	14.8	13.9	13.3
6	13.9	14.8	15.4	15.4	15.1	14.7	14.9	15.2	15.3	15.0	12.2	13.7
4	14.3	15.0	15.5	15.5	14.9	14.4	14.6	15.1	15.3	15.1	14.5	14.1
2	14.7	15.3	15.6	15.3	14.6	14.2	14.3	14.9	15.3	15.3	14.8	14.4
0	15.0	15.5	15.7	15.3	14.4	13.9	14.1	14.8	15.3	15.4	15.1	14.8

APPENDIX TABLE 8C

Extra-terrestrial radiation (*RA*) expressed in equivalent evaporation in mm/day

Southern Hemisphere

Lat.	Jan.	Feb.	Mar.	April	May	June	July	Aug.	Sept.	Oct.	Nov.	Dec.
1	2	3	4	5	6	7	8	9	10	11	12	13
50°	17.5	14.7	10.9	7.0	4.2	3.1	3.5	5.5	8.9	12.9	16.5	18.2
48	17.6	14.9	11.2	7.5	4.7	3.5	4.0	6.0	9.3	13.2	16.6	18.2
46	17.7	15.1	11.5	7.9	5.2	4.0	4.4	6.5	9.7	13.4	16.7	18.3
44	17.8	15.3	11.9	8.4	5.7	4.4	4.9	6.9	10.2	13.7	16.7	18.3
42	17.8	15.5	12.2	8.8	6.1	4.9	5.4	7.4	10.6	14.0	16.8	18.3
40	17.9	15.7	12.5	9.2	6.6	5.3	5.9	7.9	11.0	14.2	16.9	18.3
38	17.9	15.8	12.8	9.6	7.1	5.8	6.3	8.3	11.4	14.4	17.0	18.3
36	17.9	16.0	13.2	10.1	7.5	6.3	6.8	8.8	11.7	14.6	17.0	18.2
34	17.8	16.1	13.5	10.5	8.0	6.8	7.2	9.2	12.0	14.9	17.1	18.2
32	17.8	16.2	13.8	10.9	8.5	7.3	7.7	9.6	12.4	15.1	17.2	18.1
30	17.8	16.4	14.0	11.3	8.9	7.8	8.1	10.1	12.7	15.3	17.3	18.1

(*Contd.*)

APPENDIX TABLE 8C (*Contd.*)

1	2	3	4	5	6	7	8	9	10	11	12	13
28	17.7	16.4	14.3	11.6	9.3	8.2	8.6	10.4	13.0	15.4	17.2	17.9
26	17.6	16.4	14.4	12.0	9.7	8.7	9.1	10.9	13.2	15.5	17.2	17.8
24	17.5	16.5	14.6	12.3	10.2	9.1	9.5	11.2	13.4	15.6	17.1	17.7
22	17.4	16.4	14.8	12.6	10.6	9.6	10.0	11.6	13.7	15.7	17.0	17.5
20	17.3	16.5	15.0	13.0	11.0	10.0	10.4	12.0	13.9	15.8	17.0	17.4
18	17.1	16.5	15.1	13.2	11.4	10.4	10.8	12.3	14.1	15.8	16.8	17.1
16	16.9	16.4	15.2	13.5	11.7	10.8	11.2	12.6	14.3	15.8	16.7	16.8
14	16.7	16.4	15.3	13.7	12.1	11.2	11.6	12.9	14.5	15.8	15.5	16.6
12	16.6	16.3	15.4	14.0	12.5	11.6	12.0	13.21	14.7	15.8	16.4	16.5
10	16.4	16.3	15.5	14.2	12.8	12.0	12.4	13.5	14.8	15.9	16.2	16.2
8	16.1	16.1	15.5	14.4	13.1	12.4	12.7	13.7	14.9	15.8	16.0	16.0
6	15.8	16.0	15.6	14.7	13.4	12.8	13.1	14.0	15.0	15.7	15.8	15.7
4	15.5	15.8	15.6	14.9	13.8	13.2	13.4	14.3	15.1	15.6	15.5	15.4
2	15.3	15.7	15.7	15.1	14.1	13.5	13.7	14.5	15.2	15.5	15.3	15.1
0	15.0	15.5	15.7	15.3	14.4	13.9	14.1	14.8	15.3	15.4	15.1	14.8

APPENDIX TABLE 8D

Saturation vapour (e_a) in mbar as function of mean air temperature in 0°C

Temperature 0°C	0	1	2	3	4	5	6	7	8	9	10
e_a mbar	6.1	6.6	7.1	7.6	8.1	8.7	9.4	10.0	10.7	11.5	12.3
Temperature 0°C	11	12	13	14	15	16	17	18	19	20	
e_a mbar	13.1	14.0	15.0	16.1	17.0	18.2	19.4	20.6	22.0	23.4	
Temperature 0°C	21	22	23	24	25	26	27	28	29	30	
e_a mbar	24.9	26.4	28.1	29.8	31.7	33.6	35.7	37.8	40.1	42.4	
Temperature 0°C	31	32	33	34	35	36	37	38	39		
e_a mbar	44.9	47.6	50.3	53.2	56.2	59.4	62.8	66.3	69.9		

Appendix Table 8E

Values of wind function, f(u) = 0.27 $\left(\frac{1 + U_2}{100}\right)$ for wind run at a 2 m height, in km/day

Wind in km/day	0	10	20	30	40	50	60	70	80	90
	—	0.30	0.32	0.35	0.38	0.41	0.43	0.46	0.49	0.51
100	0.54	0.57	0.59	0.62	0.65	0.67	0.70	0.73	0.76	0.78
200	0.81	0.84	0.86	0.89	0.92	0.94	0.97	1.00	1.03	1.05
300	1.08	1.11	1.13	1.16	1.19	1.21	1.24	1.27	1.30	1.32
400	1.36	1.38	1.40	1.43	1.46	1.49	1.51	1.54	1.57	1.59
500	1.62	1.65	1.67	1.70	1.73	1.76	1.78	1.81	1.84	1.90
600	1.89	1.92	1.94	1.97	2.00	2.02	2.05	2.08	2.11	2.15
700	2.16	2.19	2.21	2.24	2.27	2.29	2.32	2.35	2.38	2.40
800	2.43	2.46	2.48	2.51	2.54	2.56	2.59	2.62	2.64	2.65
900	2.70									

Where wind data are not collected at 2 m height the appropriate corrections for wind measurements taken at different heights are given below :

Measurement height, m	0.5	1.0	1.5	2.0	3.0	4.0	5.0	6.0	10.0
Correction factor	1.35	1.15	1.06	1.00	0.93	0.88	0.85	0.83	0.77

APPENDIX TABLE 8F

Values of weighing factor (1—*W*) for the effect of wind and humidity on ET_o at different temperatures and altitudes

Temperature °C	2	4	6	8	10	12	14	16	18	20
(1—*W*) at altitude m										
0	0.57	0.54	0.51	0.48	0.45	0.42	0.39	0.36	0.34	0.32
500	0.56	0.52	0.49	0.46	0.43	0.40	0.38	0.35	0.33	0.30
1,000	0.54	0.51	0.48	0.45	0.42	0.39	0.36	0.34	0.31	0.29
2,000	0.51	0.48	0.45	0.42	0.39	0.36	0.34	0.31	0.29	0.27
3,000	0.48	0.45	0.42	0.39	0.36	0.34	0.31	0.29	0.27	0.25
4,000	0.46	0.42	0.39	0.36	0.34	0.31	0.29	0.27	0.25	0.23

Temperature °C	22	24	26	28	30	32	34	36	38	40
(1—*W*) at altitude m										
0	0.29	0.27	0.25	0.23	0.22	0.20	0.19	0.17	0.16	0.15
500	0.28	0.26	0.24	0.22	0.21	0.19	0.18	0.16	0.14	0.14
1,000	0.27	0.25	0.23	0.21	0.20	0.18	0.17	0.15	0.14	0.13
2,000	0.25	0.23	0.21	0.19	0.18	0.16	0.15	0.14	0.13	0.12
3,000	0.23	0.21	0.19	0.18	0.16	0.15	0.14	0.13	0.12	0.11
4,000	0.21	0.19	0.18	0.16	0.15	0.14	0.13	0.12	0.11	0.10

Appendix Table 8G

Values of weighing factor *W* for the effect of radiation on ET_o at different temperatures and altitudes

Temperature °C	2	4	6	8	10	12	14	16	18	20
W at altitude m										
0	0.43	0.46	0.49	0.52	0.55	0.58	0.61	0.64	0.66	0.68
500	0.44	0.48	0.51	0.54	0.57	0.60	0.62	0.65	0.67	0.70
1,000	0.46	0.49	0.52	0.55	0.58	0.61	0.64	0.66	0.69	0.71
2,000	0.49	0.52	0.55	0.58	0.61	0.64	0.66	0.69	0.71	0.73
3,000	0.52	0.55	0.58	0.61	0.64	0.66	0.69	0.71	0.73	0.75
4,000	0.54	0.58	0.61	0.64	0.66	0.69	0.71	0.73	0.75	0.77

Temperature °C	22	24	26	28	30	32	34	36	38	40
W at altitude m										
0	0.71	0.73	0.75	0.77	0.78	0.80	0.82	0.83	0.84	0.85
500	0.72	0.74	0.76	0.78	0.79	0.81	0.82	0.84	0.85	0.86
1,000	0.73	0.75	0.77	0.79	0.80	0.82	0.83	0.85	0.86	0.87
2,000	0.75	0.77	0.79	0.81	0.82	0.84	0.85	0.86	0.87	0.88
3,000	0.77	0.79	0.81	0.82	0.84	0.85	0.86	0.87	0.88	0.89
4,000	0.79	0.81	0.81	0.84	0.85	0.86	0.87	0.88	0.90	0.90

APPENDIX TABLE 8H

Conversion factor for extra-terrestrial radiation *RA* to net solar radiation *Rns* for a given reflection *a* of 0.25 and different ratios of actual to maximum sunshine hours (1—*a*) (0.25 + 0.50 *n/N*)

n/N	0.0	0.05	0.10	0.15	0.20	0.25	0.30	0.35	0.40	0.45	0.50	0.55	0.60	0.65	0.70	0.75	0.80	0.85	0.90	0.95	1.00
(1—a) (0.25 + 0.50 *n/N*)	0.19	0.21	0.22	0.24	0.26	0.28	0.30	0.32	0.34	0.36	0.37	0.39	0.41	0.43	0.45	0.47	0.49	0.51	0.52	0.54	0.56

APPENDIX TABLE 8I

Correction for temperature *f(t)* on longwave radiation *Rnl*

t= 0°C	0	2	4	6	8	10	12	14	16	18	20	22	24	26	28	30	32	34	36
$f(t) = 6Tk^4$	11.0	11.4	11.7	12.0	12.4	12.7	13.1	13.5	13.8	14.2	14.6	15.0	15.4	15.9	16.3	16.7	17.2	17.7	18.1

Appendix Table 8J

Correction for vapour pressure *f(ed)* on longwave radiation *Rnl*

ed mbar																	
6	8	10	12	14	16	18	20	22	24	26	28	30	32	34	36	38	40
f(ed) = 0.34 - 0.444 *ed*																	
0.23	0.22	0.20	0.19	0.18	0.16	0.15	0.14	0.13	0.12	0.12	0.11	0.10	0.09	0.08	0.08	0.07	0.06

Appendix Table 8K

Correction for the ratio actual and maximum bright sunshine hours *f(n/N)* on longwave radiation *Rnl*

n/N																				
0	0.05	0.1	0.15	0.2	0.25	0.3	0.35	0.4	0.45	0.5	0.55	0.6	0.65	0.7	0.75	0.8	0.85	0.9	0.95	1.0
f(n/N) = 0.1 + 0.9*n/N*																				
0.10	0.15	0.19	0.24	0.28	0.33	0.37	0.42	0.46	0.51	0.55	0.60	0.64	0.69	0.73	0.78	0.82	0.87	0.91	0.96	1.0

APPENDIX TABLE 8L

Adjustment factor (C) in presented Penman equation

Rs mm/day	RH_{max} = 30%				RH_{max} = 60%				RH_{max} = 90%			
	U day m/sec											
	3	6	9	12	3	6	9	12	3	6	9	12
	U day/*U* night = 4.0											
0	0.86	0.90	1.00	1.00	0.96	0.98	1.05	1.05	1.02	1.06	1.10	1.10
3	0.79	0.84	0.92	0.97	0.92	1.00	1.11	1.19	0.99	1.10	1.27	1.32
6	0.68	0.77	0.87	0.93	0.85	0.96	1.11	1.19	0.94	1.10	1.25	1.33
9	0.55	0.65	0.78	0.90	0.76	0.88	1.02	1.14	0.88	1.01	1.16	1.27
	U day/*U* night = 3.0											
0	0.86	0.90	1.00	1.00	0.96	0.98	1.05	1.05	1.02	1.06	1.10	1.10
3	0.76	0.81	0.88	0.94	0.87	0.96	1.06	1.12	0.94	1.04	1.18	1.28
6	0.61	0.68	0.81	0.88	0.77	0.88	1.02	1.10	0.86	1.01	1.15	1.22
9	0.46	0.56	0.72	0.82	0.67	0.79	0.88	1.05	0.78	0.92	1.06	1.18

(Contd.)

APPENDIX TABLE 8L (*Contd.*)

	RH_{max} = 30%				RH_{max} = 60%				RH_{max} = 90%			
	U day m/sec											
Rs mm/day	3	6	9	12	3	6	9	12	3	6	9	12
	U day/*U* night = 2.0											
0	0.86	0.90	1.00	1.00	0.96	0.98	1.05	1.05	1.02	1.06	1.10	1.10
3	0.69	0.76	0.85	0.92	0.83	0.91	0.99	1.05	0.89	0.98	1.10	1.14
6	0.53	0.61	0.74	0.84	0.70	0.80	0.94	1.02	0.79	0.92	1.05	1.12
9	0.37	0.48	0.65	0.76	0.59	0.70	0.84	0.95	0.71	0.81	0.96	1.06
	U day/*U* night = 1.0											
0	0.86	0.90	1.00	1.00	0.96	0.98	1.05	1.05	1.02	1.06	1.10	1.10
3	0.64	0.71	0.82	0.89	0.78	0.86	0.94	0.99	0.85	0.92	1.01	1.05
6	0.43	0.53	0.68	0.79	0.62	0.70	0.84	0.93	0.72	0.82	0.95	1.00
9	0.27	0.41	0.59	0.70	0.50	0.60	0.75	0.87	0.62	0.72	0.87	0.96

APPENDIX TABLE 8M

Mean daily maximum duration of bright sunshine hours (*N*) for different months and latitudes

Northern Lats. Southern Lats.	Jan. July	Feb. Aug.	March Sept.	April Oct.	May Nov.	June Dec.	July Jan.	Aug. Feb.	Sept. Mar.	Oct. Apr.	Nov. May	Dec. June
50°	8.5	10.1	11.8	13.8	15.4	16.3	15.9	14.5	12.7	10.8	9.1	8.1
48	8.8	10.2	11.8	13.6	15.2	16.0	15.6	14.3	12.6	10.9	9.3	8.3
46	9.1	10.4	11.9	13.5	14.9	15.7	15.4	14.2	12.6	10.9	9.5	8.7
44	9.3	10.5	11.9	13.4	14.7	15.4	15.2	14.0	12.6	11.0	9.7	8.9
42	9.4	10.6	11.9	13.4	14.6	15.2	14.9	13.9	12.6	11.1	9.8	9.1
40	9.6	10.7	11.9	13.3	14.4	15.0	14.7	13.7	12.5	11.2	10.0	9.3
35	10.1	11.0	11.9	13.1	14.0	14.5	14.3	13.5	12.4	11.3	10.3	9.8
30	10.4	11.1	12.0	12.9	13.6	14.0	13.9	13.2	12.4	11.5	10.6	10.2
25	10.7	11.3	12.0	12.7	13.3	13.7	13.5	13.0	12.3	11.6	10.9	10.6
20	11.0	11.5	12.0	12.6	13.1	13.3	13.2	12.8	12.3	11.7	11.2	10.9
15	11.3	11.6	12.0	12.5	12.8	13.0	12.9	12.6	12.2	11.8	11.4	11.2
10	11.6	11.8	12.0	12.3	12.6	12.7	12.6	12.4	12.1	11.8	11.6	11.5
5	11.8	11.9	12.0	12.2	12.3	12.4	12.3	12.3	12.1	12.0	11.9	11.8
0	12.1	12.1	12.1	12.1	12.1	12.1	12.1	12.1	12.1	12.1	12.1	12.1

APPENDIX TABLE 8N
Δ/γ (Dimensionless) versus *T* in °C

T	Δ/γ	T	Δ/γ	T	Δ/γ	T	Δ/γ
1	2	3	4	5	6	7	8
0.0	0.67	11.5	1.34	23.0	2.51	34.5	4.43
0.5	0.69	12.0	1.38	23.5	2.58	35.0	4.53
1.0	0.72	12.5	1.42	24.0	2.64	35.5	4.64
1.5	0.74	13.0	1.46	24.5	2.71	36.0	4.75
2.0	0.76	13.5	1.50	25.0	2.78	36.5	4.86
2.5	0.76	14.0	1.55	25.5	2.85	37.0	4.97
3.0	0.81	14.5	1.59	26.0	2.92	37.5	5.09
3.5	0.84	15.0	1.64	26.5	3.00	38.0	5.20
4.0	0.86	15.5	1.68	27.0	3.08	38.5	5.32
4.5	0.89	16.0	1.73	27.5	3.15	39.0	5.45
5.0	0.92	16.5	1.78	28.0	3.23	39.5	5.57
5.5	0.94	17.0	1.82	28.5	3.31	40.0	5.70
6.0	0.97	17.5	1.88	29.0	3.40	40.5	5.83
6.5	1.00	18.0	1.93	29.5	3.48	41.0	5.96
7.0	1.03	18.5	1.98	30.0	3.57	41.5	6.09
7.5	1.06	19.0	2.03	30.5	3.66	42.0	6.23
8.0	1.10	19.5	2.09	31.0	3.75	42.5	6.37
8.5	1.13	20.0	2.14	31.5	3.84	43.0	6.51
9.0	1.16	20.5	2.20	32.0	3.93	43.5	6.65
9.5	1.20	21.0	2.26	32.5	4.03	44.0	6.80
10.0	1.23	21.5	2.32	33.0	4.12	44.5	6.95
10.5	1.27	22.0	2.38	33.5	4.22	45.0	7.10
11.0	1.30	22.5	2.45	34.0	4.32	45.5	7.26

APPENDIX TABLE 8N (*Contd.*)

T	Δ/γ	T	Δ/γ
46.0	7.41	53.5	10.1
46.5	7.57	54.0	10.3
47.0	7.73	54.5	10.5
47.5	7.90	55.0	10.8
48.0	8.07	55.5	11.0
48.5	8.24	56.0	11.2
49.0	8.42	56.5	11.4
49.5	8.60	57.0	11.6
50.0	8.77	57.5	11.9
50.5	8.96	58.0	12.1
51.0	9.14	58.5	12.3
51.5	9.33	59.0	12.6
52.0	9.52	59.5	12.8
52.5	9.72	60.0	13.1
53.0	9.92		

(See *Smithsonian Meteorological Tables*, 6th Edition, 1958, p. 365, equation 2, and p. 372, Table 103).

Ref: Van Bavel, C.H.M., 1966, "Potential Evaporation : The combination concept and its experimental verification", *Water Resources Research*, 2 (3) : 455-467.

APPENDIX TABLE 8O

Monthly consumptive use crop coefficients (*kc*) for use in Blancy-Criddle formula

Crop	Months											
	Jan	Feb.	Mar.	Apr.	May	June	July	Aug.	Sept.	Oct.	Nov.	Dec.
Rice	—	—	—	0.85	1.00	1.15	1.30	1.25	1.10	0.90	—	—
Maize	—	—	—	0.50	0.60	0.70	0.80	0.80	0.60	0.50	—	—
Wheat	0.50	0.70	0.75	0.70	—	—	—	—	—	0.70	0.65	0.60
Sugarcane	0.75	0.80	0.85	0.85	0.90	0.95	1.00	1.00	0.95	0.90	0.85	0.75
Cotton	—	—	—	0.50	0.60	0.75	0.90	0.85	0.75	0.55	0.50	0.50
Vegetables	0.50	0.55	0.60	0.65	0.70	0.75	0.80	0.80	0.70	0.60	0.55	0.50
Berseem	0.50	0.70	0.80	0.90	1.00	—	—	—	0.60	0.65	0.70	0.60
Citrus	0.50	0.55	0.55	0.60	0.60	0.65	0.70	0.70	0.65	0.60	0.55	0.55

(Dastane, 1972)

CHAPTER 9

INFILTRATION CAPACITY AND MEASUREMENT METHODS

What is Infiltration ?

Infiltration is the vertically downward entry of water into soil through the soil surface and is numerically equal to the hydraulic conductivity (k) when the soil is saturated to a sufficient depth. However, when the soil is relatively dry at a lower depths, the rate of infiltration may greatly exceed the hydraulic conductivity because capillary and absorption forces at the wetting front make the gradient for flow behind the wetting front larger than the gravity gradient. Nearly all water which enters the soil enters via infiltration, either from rainfall or from water directed to the soil surface via irrigation. Knowledge of the infiltration characteristics of a soil is basic information required for designing efficient irrigation systems or

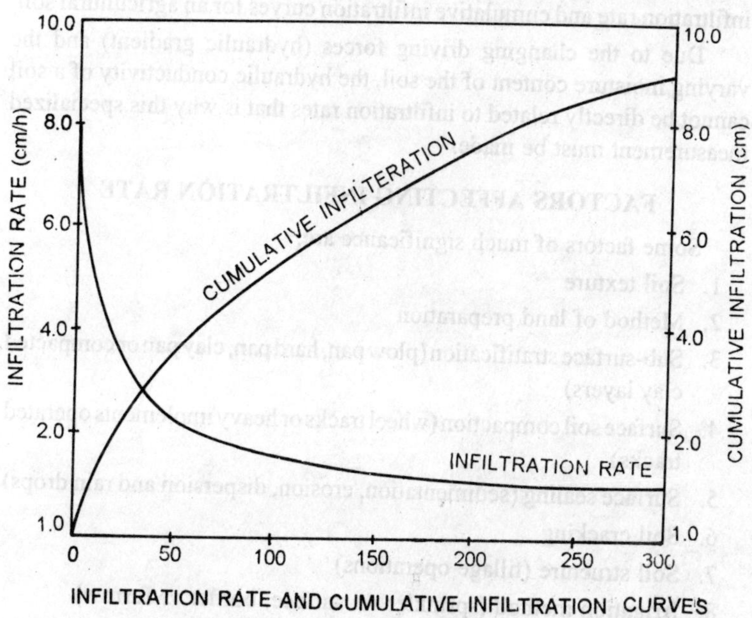

Fig. 9.1 : Infiltration Rate and Cumulative Infiltration Curves

predicting runoff. The soil infiltration rate will affect advance times and tail water runoff in furrow and border systems, ponded time in level borders (basins) and maximum allowable application rate for sprinkler or drip irrigation systems.

The time rate of which water is absorbed by the soil is the infiltration rate, "I" which has units of volume per unit area per unit time, $Cm^3/Cm^2/$ min., or equivalently depth per unit time, cm/min. The cumulative inflitration, 'Z' is the total accumulated depth infiltrated in a given time period, cumulative infiltration is thus the integration of the inflitration rate and conversely, I is the derivative of "Z".

$$Z(t) = \int I dt \quad ...(1)$$

$$I(t) = \frac{dz}{dt} \quad ...(2)$$

The rate at which water infilterates into soils usually decreases over time until a relatively steady state or basic infiltration rate is asymptotically approached. The decrease is caused by the decreasing capillary pressure of the soil as it becomes wet. The constant rate is due to the constant gravity force, the second component of the driving force. Fig. 9.1 shows typical infiltration rate and cumulative infiltration curves for an agricultural soil.

Due to the changing driving forces (hydraulic gradient) and the varying moisture content of the soil, the hydraulic conductivity of a soil cannot be directly related to infiltration rates that is why this specialized measurement must be made.

FACTORS AFFECTING INFILTRATION RATE

Some factors of much significance are:

1. Soil texture
2. Method of land preparation
3. Sub-surface stratification (plow pan, hard pan, clay pan or compacted clay layers)
4. Surface soil compaction (wheel tracks or heavy implements operated tracks)
5. Surface sealing (sedimentation, erosion, dispersion and rain drops)
6. Soil cracking
7. Soil structure (tillage operations)
8. Irrigation method (sprinkler *vs*. surface, border *vs* furrow)
9. Crops and surface mulches or vegetative cover

10. Soil and water salt concentrations (high sodicity)
11. Soil and water temperature.

CLASSIFICATION OF INFILTRATION RATES

Infiltration is a dynamic and quite variable character of the soil and can be fairly well controlled by management practices. Infiltration rates may be classified as follows :

1. *Very Slow*: Soils with infiltration rates of less than 0.1 inch per hour are classified as very slow. It is found in heavy clays.

2. *Slow*: Infiltration rates of 0.1 to 0.5 inch per hour are considered low. This includes soils high in clay, soils low in organic matter, or shallow soils.

3. *Moderate*: Rates of infiltration of 0.5 to 1.0 inch per hour are classified as medium. Loams, sandy loams and silt loams fall under this category.

4. *Rapid*: High rates include soils with greater than 1.0 inch per hour fall in this group. Deep sands and deep well integrated silt loams exhibit this rate.

Influence of Texture

Infiltration rates are generally lower in soils of heavy textured as compared medium and coarse textured soils (Fig. 9.1).

This has been found experimentally that during surface irrigation increased head (water depth) increases initial infiltration slightly but head has negligible effect after prolonged irrigation. It is noticed that infiltration rate decreases continuously during irrigation. This decrease is more initially but later it tends to attain constant readings/values. The rate under this equilibrium is termed as "Basic Infiltration Rate" (Fig. 9.1) curve II.

The Basic Rate of Infiltration

The basic rate of infiltration is defined as the rate of water entry or intake into the soil media after lapse of several hours when the change infiltration rate values is quite less.

Cumulative Infiltration (Y)

It is defined as the total quantum of water which enters the soil in a given time.

For design purposes the relationship between cumulative infiltration and elapsed time are expressed empirically by equation.

$$Y = at^{\alpha}$$

where Y = cumulative infiltration intime 't'

t = elapsed time or infiltration opportunity time a and α are characteristic constants.

The values of these constants are to be determined from the observed data of infiltration test.

The infiltration at any time 't' is determined by differentiating equation

(1) as below – $y = at^{\alpha}$ $\therefore$ $\frac{dy}{dy} = a\alpha t^{\alpha-1}$

Average Infiltration (IA)

It is equal to the cumulative infiltration divided by the time since infiltration started.

Method

Several methods are used to determine the infliltration characteristics of a soil under field conditions. Methods frequently used for basin and border irrigation are:

(1) Cylinder (ring) infiltrometer, and
(2) Basin infiltrometer.

The two common methods used for furrow irrigation are:

(3) Blocked/furrow infiltrometer, and
(4) Inflow-outflow measurements on a segment of the furrow.

An additional method applicable to both border and furrow irrigation is:

(5) Volume balance techniques based upon the rate of advance of the volume of water in surface storage. Cylinder blocked furrow infiltrometers.

Cylinder or Ring Infiltrometer Method

The cylinder or ring infiltrometer (Fig. 9.2) is a metal cylinder which is driven into the soil. It measures primarily the vertical rate of water movement into the soil surface (one dimensional) from the pond it encloses. Cylinder infiltrometer infiltration data is obtained by measuring the depth of ponded water inside of the cylinder at periodic intervals.

$$\text{Thus I.R.} = \frac{\text{Volume of water entering the inner ring (ml)}}{\text{Cross sectional areas of the inner ring} \times t}$$

$$\text{or } \frac{V\ (ml)}{A \times t}$$

After water penetrates the soil to the depth of the bottom of the cylinder, it will begin to spread readily as well as vertically and the infiltration rate will change accordingly.

Equipment

This equipment consists of two concentric cylinders. The cylinders are usually 25 cm deep. The diameter of inner cylinder is 30 cm while that of outer making buffer zone for minimizing lateral or horizontal movement is about 50 to 60 in diameter. The cylinders are installed 10 cm deep in the soil. (Fig. 9.2).

Fig. 9.2 : A Cylinder being used to measure intake rate of the soil

The water is added in inner and outer cylinder upto desired level through plastic sheet covering soil surface say 10 cm above the ground. After the initial reading point gauge measurements are taken at frequent intervals say 5 minutes to determine the amount of water that has infiltered during the time interval. Water is added quickly after each measurement so that a constant average infiltration head could be maintained. The average depth of water maintained in the cylinder is 7 to 12 cm which is approximately equal to the expected water level in the border or a basin during irrigation.

The buffer pond is filled with water immediately after filling the inner cylinder to maintain the same depth in both cylinders. The data are tabulated in the form as given in Table 9.1.

It is necessary to conduct at least 4 tests at suitable locations in the field having uniform soil. The average values of cumulative infiltration Y and average infiltration rates are plotted as a function of elapsed time as given below.

This curve represents by

$Y = at^{\alpha}$

However, when the observations of intake extends over a long period, the following relationship be used.

$Y = at^{\alpha} + b$

Here α is negative, Y decreases with increase in T. The intake rate Y will approach a constant value 'b' as time increases. The constant rate

TABLE 9.1

Cylinder Infiltration Test Data

Location ....

(S.N./Canal No.)... Observer..................

Soil type ....

Soil moisture content before the test crop history

Time			Infiltration (Y)			
Watch	Dift. min.	Cumulative min.	depth with reference point cm	Dift. cm	Cumulative cm.	Remarks
0800	...	...	11.00	...	...	Indicate
0805	5	5	9.30	1.70	1.70	the depth
0810	5	10	8.30	1.00	2.70	when water
0815	5	15	7.40	0.90	3.60	is refilled
0825	10	25	5.70	1.70	5.30	to new
0820	...	...	11.00	...	...	depth.
0840	20	45	8.80	2.20	7.50	
0900	15	60	5.80	1.50	10.50	
0915	...	...	11.00	...	...	
0930	15	90	9.50	1.50	12.00	
0950	20	110	7.50	2.00	14.00	
1010	20	130	5.50	2.00	16.00	

Source: Walmi-Aurangabad.

denotes final intake rate. Altention should be paid in using final intake rates for irrigation design. If light frequent irrigations are applied due to variations in beginning and constant intake rates. The amount of water entering as a function of depth is simplified as

$$\text{Yave} = \frac{a}{a+1} T^{\alpha} + b$$

This function plotted on ordinary co-ordinate paper gives a parabolic curve.

When the data are plotted on log-log paper a linear, relationship is indicated below :

$$Y = at^{\alpha}$$

Taking log of both sides

$$\log Y = \log a + \alpha \log t$$

Knowing the values of a and ∝ we can use the equation $Y = at^{\propto}$ or finding out cumulative Infiltration or Infiltration rate at any time t.

Comparison of Swelling and Non-swelling Soils

It must be brought in mind that in case of swelling soils water movement varies significantly as compared to non-swelling or rigid soils water movement in rigid and swelling soils may, however, be differentiated as under :

1. In swelling soils water moves in response to a potential gradient which includes the overburden potential.

2. Darcy's law applies to flow relatives to the soil particles which, in general, are in motion.

3. The hydrodynamic characterization of the soil requires, in addition to various relationships, a knowledge of the dependence of the void ratio, moisture content or moisture ratio.

Further, infiltration rates have been generally obtained using either buffered or unbuffered infiltrometers, in which flow may be to a large extent three dimensional. This adds considerably to the difficulty of interpretation of infiltration data for the one dimensional case. The kind of soil profile where determinations are made needs to be carefully understood *i.e.* dry, semi-dry, moist or water-logged.

Further equilibrium condition of the moisture profiles of sweiling and non-swelling or rigid soils have marked differences. There is often, decreasing water content below the water table in swelling clay soils which is wrongly interpreted as a "perched" water table condition, which may occur in non-swelling, layered soils.

Similarly, in hydric profiles, the hydraulic conductivity above the water table is higher than below and shows a gradual decrease with depth (Philip, 1969) Such behaviour, below the water table, in uniformly textured soils was claimed by Talsma and Flint (1958).

There is also a variation from Classical behaviour during steady flow in swelling soils. Such behaviour would not be possible to be interpreted in terms of classical hydrological concepts developed for rigid soils, *e.g.* medium, light textured or low montmorillonitic clay soils. For example, when infiltration occurs from buffered infiltrometers, the average quantity of water which may be found below the infiltrometer may be only 70 to 75% of the added water, indicating insufficient buffering and a three dimensional flow component.

The end filtration rate values found would show that water was still added to the soil even after saturation have occurred which have been in excess and needs to be considered for actual basic infiltration. This happens due to lateral movement and not vertical and hence needs correction of about 20 to 25% of values got in the examples of I.R. as given in this chapter for various fields under different crops on swelling "vertisols" of Chambal command area, Rajasthan, the correction to the tune of 25% have been made as —

$$(\text{total volume} \div \pi r^2) \times \frac{3}{4} = \text{I.R.}$$

The analysis of unsteady, vertical flows *e.g.* I.R. and capillary rise also is different for 2 type of soils discussed. The time course of infiltration has analogies with that of capillary rise into non-swelling soils and capillary rise may show typical infiltration behaviour. This means that a swelling soil would be better fitted to sub-irrigation techniques than an otherwise similar non-swelling one. However, field date on these aspects are yet to be collected.

The infiltration behaviour of cracking soils depends upon the *in situ* moisture contents at the time of data collection. When their moisture content is reduced beyond certain limits, extensive cracks develop. This causes initial, rapid, infiltration as discussed and obvious from data incorporated. It may be, however, added here that very marked increase in infiltration rate would be observed in swelling soils, once their moisture content corresponds to a mositure potential, equivalent to a pF-Value around 4.5. Apparently gross cracks which in Chambal command vertisols are 5 to 12 cm wide and 40 to 80 cm deep, are capable of rapid water conduction and are found mostly during end of April to middle of June when the soils are rather dry. This depends upon the limit between "normal" and "residual" shrinkage to occur around this moisture level in a poorly structured black earth. Hence under permanent irrigation as C.C.A. Kota-Rajasthan, over a period of time, it is likely that gross cracks would not be more large rather decrease in size. This means that under such conditions the beneficial effects of cracks on soil conductivity would not persist for long. In general an average of 70 to 75 of total water intake during 4 hours infilters during first 10 minutes. As the I.R. values of swelling soils are of magnitude of 3 to 5 mm/hr and the subsoil conductivity is about 10^{-7} m S^{-1}.

This is an equation of straight line and the values of a and α can be found out by plotting the values of Y and t on log-log or by fitting the straight line by the method of least squares. Eq. $Y = at^{\alpha} + CT$

Precautions in Ring Infiltrometer Method

1. Select a representative location for each cylinder and examine carefully for signs of unusual surface disturbances, such as stones that might damage cylinders, cracks which might give non-representative readings, etc. Avoid areas that may have been affected by unusual animal or machinery traffic. Note the soil type and condition (tillage).

2. Drive the infiltrometer cylinder to a depth of at least 15 cm. The cylinder should be installed as vertically as possible. This can be assured by checking the alignment frequently during the installation procedure. Do not drive the cylinder into the soil irregularly so that first one side then the other goes down. This method produces poor contact between the cylinder wall and the soil, and may disturb the soil core within the cylinder. If the cylinder gets out of alignment while driving, remove it and reset it in a comparable area nearby.

3. Set the buffer cylinder around the infiltrometer and drive it into the soil. The outside cylinder need not be driven as deep as the cylinder infiltrometer generally, 5 to 10 cm into the soil will be adequate.

4. Place a plastic sheet or other water proof membrance on the soil within the cylinder infiltrometer so that it forms a "bowl" to hold the water. The plastic should be in contact with the soil at the bottom of the infiltrometer and extend up the walls of the infiltrometer at least 10 to 15 cm.

5. Fill the buffer pond with water to a depth roughly equal to the depth desired in the inner ring. Maintain roughly equivalent depths throughout the period of observation.

6. Fill the cylinder infiltrometer with water to a depth of about 10 cm. In extremely porous (high intake) soils, a greater depth may be needed.

7. Set the water level gauge in place (the tip of the hook gauge is set at the water level) and measure the distance to the water level from some datum. On the gauges, a simple reading from the top edge of the clip is sufficient. This is initial depth reading, corresponding to the initial time reading.

8. Quickly, but gently, remove the plastic membrane. Record the time at which this is done. This is the initial time reading. Take a hook gauge reading as soon as the water surface is still enough to do so and compare this reading to the plastic.

9. Take additional hook gauge readings at periodic intervals between observations. It should be short (2 to 5 min) at the start of the test. After five measurements the intervals may be increased (10 to 20 minutes). After about 2 hours, measurement made at 30 to 60 minute intervals, which will usually be sufficient.

10. When the water level has dropped 4 to 5 cm in the cylinder, carefully add sufficient volume of water to return the water surface to the approximate initial level. The known volume of water added, divided by the cross-sectional area of the cylinder, gives the depth of water added, to the cylinder. If a volumetric container is not available, the added depth can be closely estimated by plotting the depth readings over time just before and after the water was added and determining the projected depth increase at the time the water was added. This equivalent depth added should be noted on the data collection sheet.

11. Where abnormally high or low infiltration values are indicated by the test results, the infiltrometer should be dug out and the soil examined for possible causes. While running the test, an obvious cause for a high rate of infiltration can be seen, such as water rising outside the cylinder, the test should be terminated immediately and the cylinder moved to a nearby location and reinstalled.

12. The measurement should be continued until the change in depth over time becomes fairly constant. The time required will generally vary from 3 to 6 hours, depending on the pre-existing moisture conditions and soil hydraulic conductivity.

The experimental data of infiltration rate at two locations of KOTA (Rajasthan) along with soil descriptions are given in Table 9.2. The effect of soil manipulation with equipments and irrigation use are given in Fig 9.3.

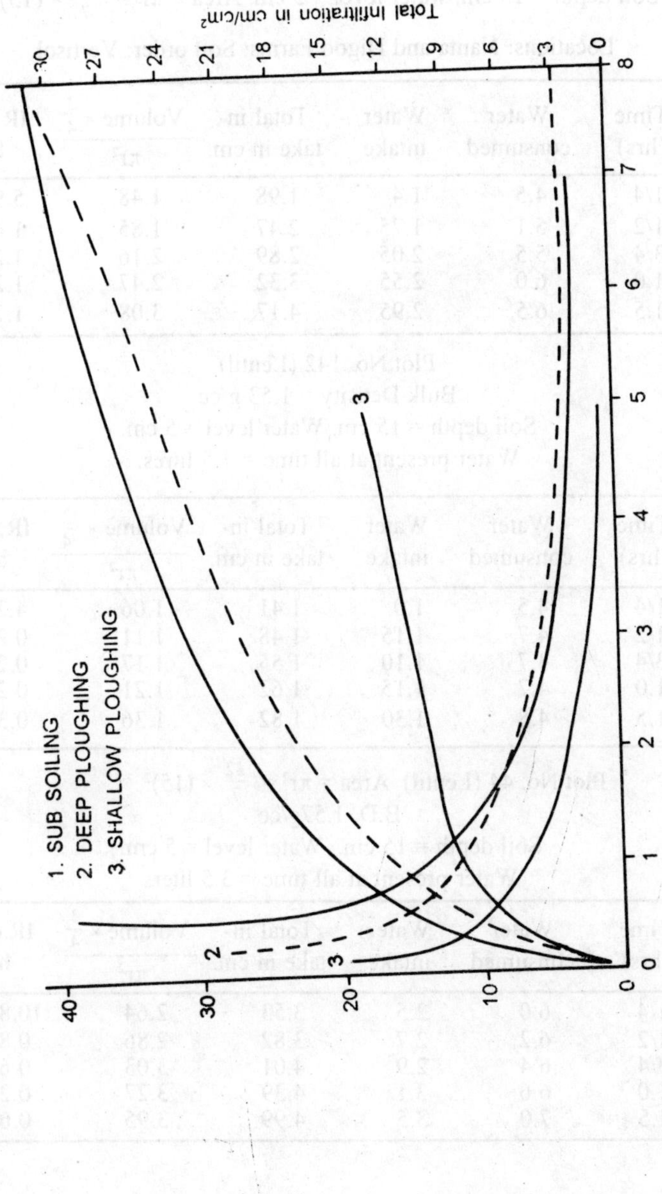

Fig. 9.3 : Time in Hours

TABLE 9.2

Double Ring Method

Exemplary Calculation of Infiltration rate of C.C. A Kota Soils Plot No. 95 (Wheat)

Soil depth = 15 cm, water level = 5 cm. Area = $\pi r^2 = \frac{22}{7} \times (15)^2$

Locations: Nanta and Digod Farms: Soil order: Vertisol

Time (hrs)	Water consumed	Water intake	Total in-take in cm.	$\frac{\text{Volume} \times \frac{3}{4}}{\pi r^2}$	IR.cm/hrs
1/4	4.5	1.4	1.98	1.48	5.92
1/2	5.1	1.75	2.47	1.85	1.48
3/4	5.5	2.05	2.89	2.16	1.24
1.0	6.0	2.55	3.32	2.47	1.28
1.5	6.5	2.95	4.17	3.08	1.24

Plot No. 142 (Lentil)
Bulk Density = 1.53 g/cc
Soil depth = 15 cm. Water level = 5 cm.
Water present at all time = 3.5 litres.

Time (hrs)	Water consumed	Water intake	Total in-take in cm.	$\frac{\text{Volume} \times \frac{3}{4}}{\pi r^2}$	IR.cm/hrs
1/4	4.5	1.0	1.41	1.06	4.24
1/2	4.7	1.15	1.48	1.11	0.20
3/4	4.7	1.10	1.55	1.17	0.20
1.0	4.7	1.15	1.62	1.21	0.20
1.5	4.8	1.30	1.82	1.36	0.30

Plot No. 44 (Lentil) Area = $\pi r^2 = \frac{22}{7} \times (15)^2$
B.D. 1.57g/cc
Soil depth = 15 cm. Water level = 5 cm.
Water present at all time = 3.5 liters

Time (hrs)	Water consumed	Water intake	Total in-take in cm.	$\frac{\text{Volume} \times \frac{3}{4}}{\pi r^2}$	IR.cm/hrs
1/4	6.0	2.5	3.53	2.64	10.86
1/2	6.2	2.7	3.82	2.86	0.88
3/4	6.4	2.9	4.01	3.03	0.68
1.0	6.6	3.1	4.39	3.27	0.2½
1.5	7.0	3.5	4.99	3.95	0.66

Plot No. 6 (Corriender)
Bulk Density = 1.57g/cc

Soil depth = 15 cm. Water level = 5 cm. Area = $\pi r^2 = \frac{22}{7} \times (15)^2$

Water level present at all time = 3.5 litres (volume)
r = Radius of inner cylinder

Time (hrs)	Water consumed	Water intake	Total in-take in cm.	$\frac{\text{Volume} \times \frac{3}{4}}{\pi r^2}$	IR.cm/hrs
1/4	4.5	1.0	1.41	1.05	4.20
1/2	5.0	1.35	1.90	1.42	1.48
3/4	5.0	1.50	2.12	1.59	0.68
1.0	5.1	1.60	2.26	1.71	0.48
1.5	5.1	1.75	2.47	1.86	6.30

Plot No. 74 (Corriender)
B.D. = 1.44g/cc

Soil depth = 15 cm. Water level = 5 cm. ∴ Area = $\pi r^2 = \frac{22}{7} \times (15)^2$

Water level present at all time = 3.5 litres.

Time (hrs)	Water consumed	Water intake	Total in-take in cm.	$\frac{\text{Volume} \times \frac{3}{4}}{\pi r^2}$	IR.cm/hrs
1/4	7.4	3.90	5.51	4.14	16.56
1/2	7.5	4.00	5.65	4.22	0.36
3/4	7.50	4.10	5.80	4.35	0.40
1.0	7.7	4.20	5.94	4.45	0.40
1.5	7.9	4.40	6.22	4.65	0.40

Plot No. 133 (Wheat)
B.D. = 1.48g/cc

Soil depth = 15 cm. Water level = 5 cm. ∴ Area = $\pi r^2 = \frac{22}{7} \times (15)^2$

Water present at all time = 3.5 litres

Time (hrs)	Water consumed	Water intake	Total in-take in cm.	$\frac{\text{Volume} \times \frac{3}{4}}{\pi r^2}$	IR.cm/hrs
1/4	5.3	1.8	2.5	1.86	7.44
1/2	6.6	3.1	4.4	3.30	5.76
3/4	7.0	3.5	4.9	3.60	1.20
1.0	7.3	3.8	5.3	3.90	1.20
1.5	7.5	4.0	5.6	4.20	0.60

Plot No. 90 (Wheat)
B.D. = 1.7g/cc Soil depth = 15 cm. Water level = 5 cm.
Water present at all time = 3.5 litres

Time (hrs)	Water consumed	Water intake	Total in-take in cm.	$\frac{\text{Volume} \times \frac{3}{4}}{\pi r^2}$	IR.cm/hrs
1/4	6.4	2.9	4.0	3.0	12.00
1/2	6.5	3.0	4.2	3.15	0.60
3/4	6.5	3.10	4.38	3.28	0.52
1.0	6.6	3.15	4.45	3.33	0.20
1.5	6.8	3.35	4.59	3.45	0.20

Plot No. 60 (Corriender)
B.D. = 1.59g/cc
Soil depth = 15 cm. Water level = 5 cm.
Water level present at all time = 3.5 litres.

Time (hrs)	Water consumed	Water intake	Total in-take in cm.	$\frac{\text{Volume} \times \frac{3}{4}}{\pi r^2}$	IR.cm/hrs
1/4	6.1	2.60	3.68	2.76	11.64
1/2	6.4	2.80	4.10	3.07	1.24
3/4	6.6	3.10	4.38	3.28	0.84
1.0	6.8	3.3	4.66	3.48	0.80
1.5	7.0	3.5	4.95	3.72	0.48

Plot No. 4 (Safflower)
B.D. = 1.6g/cc
Soil depth = 15 cm. Water level = 5 cm.
Water present at all time = 3.5 litres

Time (hrs)	Water consumed	Water intake	Total in-take in cm.	$\frac{\text{Volume} \times \frac{3}{4}}{\pi r^2}$	IR.cm/hrs
1/4	5.1	1.6	2.26	1.68	6.72
1/2	5.3	1.8	2.54	1.90	0.88
3/4	5.0	1.9	2.68	2.01	0.44
1.0	5.5	2.0	2.82	2.11	0.40
1.5	5.7	2.2	3.11	2.31	0.40

Plot No. 9 (Safflower)

Bulk Density = 1.6 g/cc Soil depth = 15 cm. Water level = 5 cm.

Water present at all time = 3.5 litres

Time (hrs)	Water consumed	Water intake	Total in-take in cm.	Volume $\times \frac{3}{4}$ / πr^2	IR.cm/hrs
1/4	5.0	1.5	2.12	1.59	6.36
1/2	5.3	1.7	2.40	1.80	0.84
3/4	5.4	1.9	2.68	2.01	0.84
1.0	5.6	2.1	2.97	2.22	0.84
1.5	5.75	2.35	3.32	2.41	0.54

Plot No. 139 (Safflower)

B.D. = 1.54g/cc

Soil depth = 15 cm. Water level = 5 cm.

Water consumed at all time = 3.5 litres

Time (hrs)	Water consumed	Water intake	Total in-take in cm.	Volume $\times \frac{3}{4}$ / πr^2	IR.cm/hrs
1/4	5.7	2.1	2.97	2.22	8.88
1/2	6.0	2.4	3.39	2.55	1.32
3/4	6.2	2.7	3.81	2.85	1.20
1.0	6.5	3.0	4.24	3.18	1.32
1.5	6.8	3.5	4.95	3.92	1.08

Two problems may take infiltration rates measured by cylinder infiltrometers unrepresentative of true infiltration rates (1) is that the soil may be disturbed when the rings are driven into the ground and (2) the ponded water may not duplicate real conditions.

Example

Although infiltration rates are not too sensitive to the water pressure at the surface, or equivalently the depth of water on the surface, water pressure will have some effect. The infiltration rate measured with an infiltrometer with 20 cm of ponded water will not be equivalent to that in a border with 5 cm water depth, or to that under a sprinkler where no water is ponded. Also air which is trapped under a level basin may escape laterally from around the infiltrometer. Finally, under real conditions, water usually moves across the soil surface re-arranging surface particles. This erosion and aggregation which does not occur in ponded infiltration tests to seal soil surface reduce infiltration rates. Further test is conducted in the similar manner as given for cylinder (ring) infiltrometer test.

Basin Ponding Method

Generally this is conducted in clay soils, because of their swelling property. Ring basin (inner and outer) can be constructed by building levies (bunds). Point gauge is fixed outside of the inner basin.

Blocked Furrow Method

This test is carried out for furrow irrigation method because infiltration characteristics in case of furrow are different. This method measures the infiltration of water into the soil profile from a short segment of a furrow (about 1 metre).

Border/Basin Method

In this method two plates are driven into the furrow to dam the water in a reach about 1 metre long (Fig. 9.4). The soil in the isolated reach of furrow is covered with plastic sheet and water is introduced into the section so formed to the level which would occur under normal operation of the furrow. At zero time (that is at start of expt) the plastic sheet is removed and the furrow is continuously supplied with water to maintain the original depth in the furrow. The volume required to maintain this depth is recorded as a function of time and from this data, the infiltration rate of the soil can be determined. The constant depth of water is attained by Merriott syphon device.

Steps for Blocked Furrow Method

1. Drive two metal sheets about 1 metre apart vertically into the soil to a depth of approximately 15 cm. with a minimum disturbance of the soil surface.

2. Install metal sheets or build earthen dams in the parallel buffer furrows. If every row irrigation is being used, the adjoining furrows would be the buffer furrows. If alternate furrows are integrated, the second furrow on each side would be buffer furrow.

3. Cover the furrow bottom with a plastic sheet or other impermeable material.

4. Fill the furrow with water to the level at which water would normally flow in the furrow during irrigation.

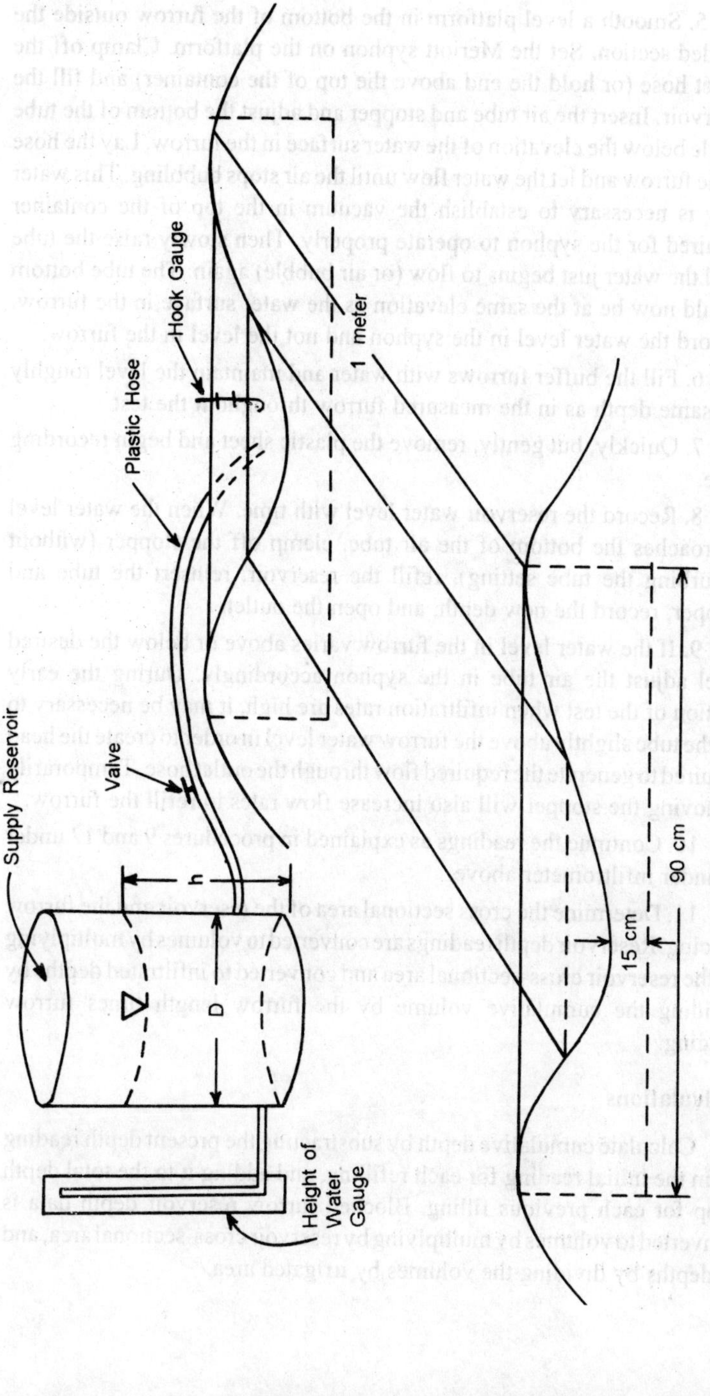

Fig. 9.4: Blocked furrow infiltrometer

5. Smooth a level platform in the bottom of the furrow outside the ponded section. Set the Meriott syphon on the platform. Clamp off the outlet hose (or hold the end above the top of the container) and fill the reservoir. Insert the air tube and stopper and adjust the bottom of the tube a little below the elevation of the water surface in the furrow. Lay the hose in the furrow and let the water flow until the air stops bubbling. This water flow is necessary to establish the vacuum in the top of the container required for the syphon to operate properly. Then slowly raise the tube until the water just begins to flow (or air bubble) again. The tube bottom should now be at the same elevation as the water surface in the furrow. Record the water level in the syphon and not the level in the furrow.

6. Fill the buffer furrows with water and maintain the level roughly the same depth as in the measured furrow throughout the test.

7. Quickly, but gently, remove the plastic sheet and begin recording time.

8. Record the reservoir water level with time. When the water level approaches the bottom of the air tube, clamp off the stopper (without disturbing the tube setting), refill the reservoir, reinsert the tube and stopper, record the new depth, and open the outlet.

9. If the water level in the furrow varies above or below the desired level adjust the air tube in the syphon accordingly. During the early portion of the test when infiltration rates are high, it may be necessary to set the tube slightly above the furrow water level in order to create the head required to generate the required flow through the outlet hose. Temporarily removing the stopper will also increase flow rates to refill the furrow.

10. Continue the readings as explained in procedures 9 and 12 under cylinder infiltrometer above.

11. Determine the cross sectional area of the reservoir and the furrow spacing. Reservoir depth readings are converted to volumes by multiplying by the reservoir cross-sectional area and converted to infiltrated depths by dividing the cumulative volume by the furrow length times furrow spacing.

Calculations

Calculate cumulative depth by substracting the present depth reading from the initial reading for each refilling, and adding it to the total depth drop for each previous filling. Blocked furrow reservoir depth data is converted to volumes by multiplying by reservoir cross-sectional area, and to depths by dividing the volumes by irrigated area.

Both blocked furrow and cylinder infiltrometer data (cumulative infiltrated depth *vs.* elapsed time) should be plotted on both rectangular and log-log paper. The general equation should be fitted to both data sets graphically and, if possible using the power curve regression techniques.

Infiltration rate will be determined by taking the derivative of the cumulative depth curve graphically, and of the derived equation mathematically. The graphical derivation is the slope of the curve (in rectangular co-ordinates) at a given elapsed time. The differentiated equation should be plotted with the graphically derived curve to compare the methods.

Note: One should complete the graphical analysis, and as many as possible, the regression analysis (*i.e.* those with access to programmable calculators or a computer).

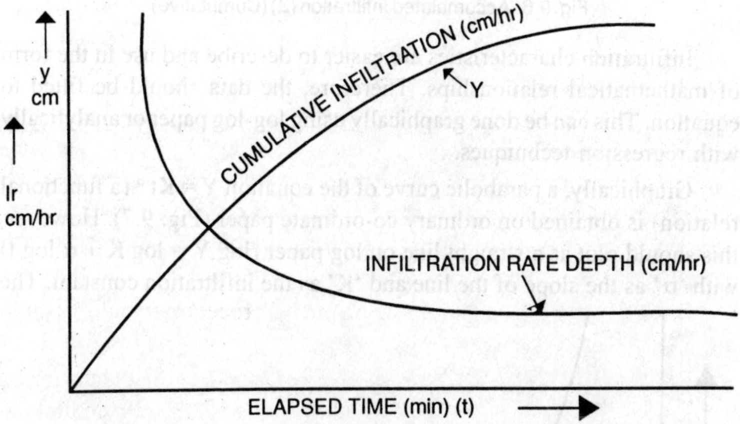

Fig. 9.5

Infiltrated depth or volume over time is measured (Fig. 9.5). The volume infiltrated into the blocked furrow length and row spacing (or if every second row irrigation is being practised by double the row spacing). The data should be plotted in the form of a cumulative infiltration curve, or a plot of the accumulated infiltrated depth Z, *vs.* time from the start or the intake opportunity time. This plot will indicate obvious errors in the data. The infiltration rate at any time, which is the derivative of the cumulative infiltration, can be determined from the slope of the 'Z' *vs.* 't' curves at any time. Both types of curves are shown in Fig. 9.6.

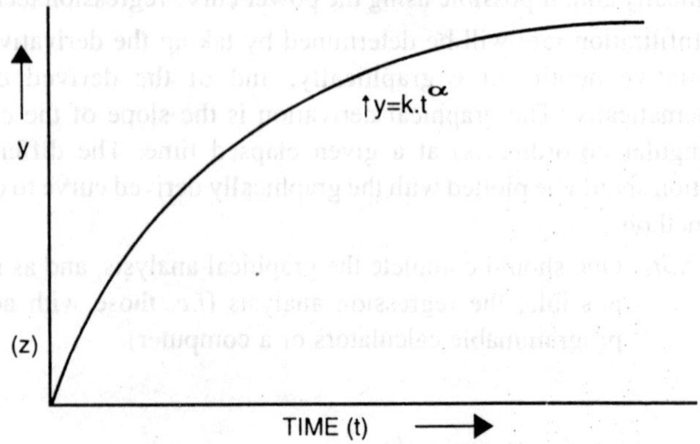

Fig. 9.6 : Accumulated Infiltration (Z) (Cumulative)

Infiltration characteristics are easier to describe and use in the form of mathematical relationships. Therefore, the data should be fitted to equation. This can be done graphically using log-log paper or analytically with regression techniques.

Graphically, a parabolic curve of the equation $Y = Kt^{\alpha}$ (a functional relation) is obtained on ordinary co-ordinate paper (Fig. 9.7). However, this should plot as a straight line on log paper ($\log Y = \log K + \alpha \log t$) with '$\alpha$' as the slope of the line and 'K' as the infiltration constant. The

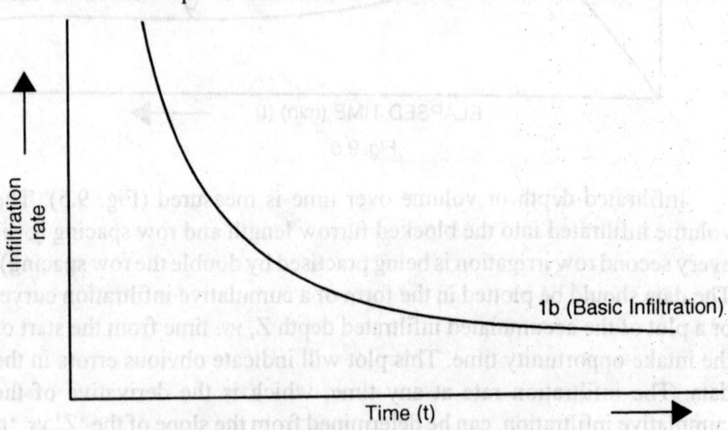

Fig. 9.7 : Effect of Time on Infiltration Rate

value of 'α' and 'K' can be found out by plotting the values of 'Y' and t on log-log paper (Fig. 9.11B) or by fitting the straight line by the least squares method. This helps to determine cumulative infiltration or infiltration rate at any time, t.

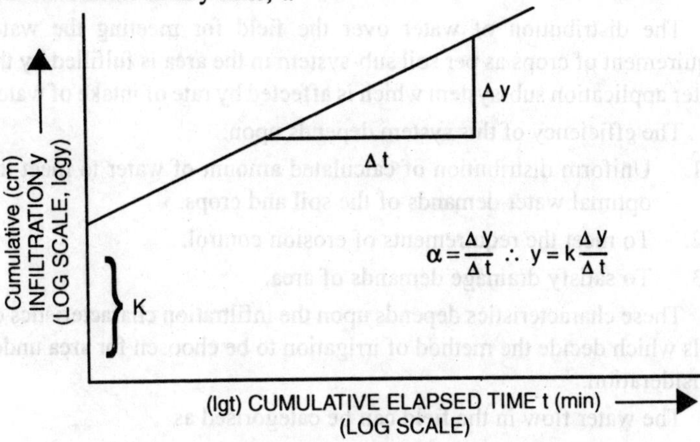

Fig. 9.8

Consequently, a value for Ib must be estimated before the data can be plotted. As was stated, Ib is the basic infiltration rate, so the first estimate for Ib is the infiltration rate after a long time, which can be determined from the infiltration rate plot, or the slope of the cumulative infiltration *vs.* time curve after a long time. From this initial estimate. the value of Ib should be adjusted by trial and error until the (Z-Ibt) *vs.* t data plots as near a straight line as possible on log-log paper. A plot which curves upward, or is concave upwards, especially at longer times, indicates in Ib value which is too small, and *vice-versa.* This graphical adjustment procedure is illustrated in figure. If the line curves at short times, a constant probably needs to be substracted from (if concave upwards) or added to all 'Z' values. The need for such a correction would indicate that the initial experimental conditions were off *i.e.* (plastic sheet not down tight).

If a calculator with a regression analysis capabilities is available this curve fitting process can be done analytically. By regressing in (Z-Ibt) *vs.* log t, the derived slope value will be the exponent, α will and the exponential of the intercept will be the coefficient K. The Ib value should be adjusted until the minimum coefficient of determination r^2, is achieved. Regression determinations should always be checked graphically.

The main problem with blocked furrow infiltrometer measurements is that they are made with ponded water. Water running down furrows will erode and deposit surface infiltration characteristics to change.

FIELD IRRIGATION METHOD

The distribution of water over the field for meeting the water requirement of crops as per soil sub-system in the area is fulfilled by the water application sub-system which is affected by rate of intake of water.

The efficiency of this system depends upon:

1. Uniform distribution of calculated amount of water to meet the optimal water demands of the soil and crops.
2. To meet the requirements of erosion control.
3. To satisfy drainage demands of area.

These characteristics depends upon the infiltration characteristics of soils which decide the method of irrigation to be choosen for area under consideration.

The water flow in the field can be categorised as

(a) advance time (for movement of water front or flux),

(b) storage and depletion of water in soil system,

(c) tail water recession phases.

Advance Time

The time taken by the water front to reach a particular point under gravitational flow from the initial time within outlet was opened for irrigation is called advance time. The curve drawn between distance travelled by water front *vs*. elapsed time is called advance curve (Fig. 9.9A and Fig. 9.9B).

Recession Time

The time taken when the disappearance of water from the soil surface of border strip at any particular length occurred is called recession time. If the values of recession distance are plotted against elapsed time the curve developed is called recession curve (Fig. 9.10).

Infiltration Opportunity Time (Ponding Time)

The difference between recession and advance time at the same particular point is called infiltration opportunity time or the ponding time *i.e.*

Infiltration Opportunity time = Recession time – Advance time

= Cutt off time.

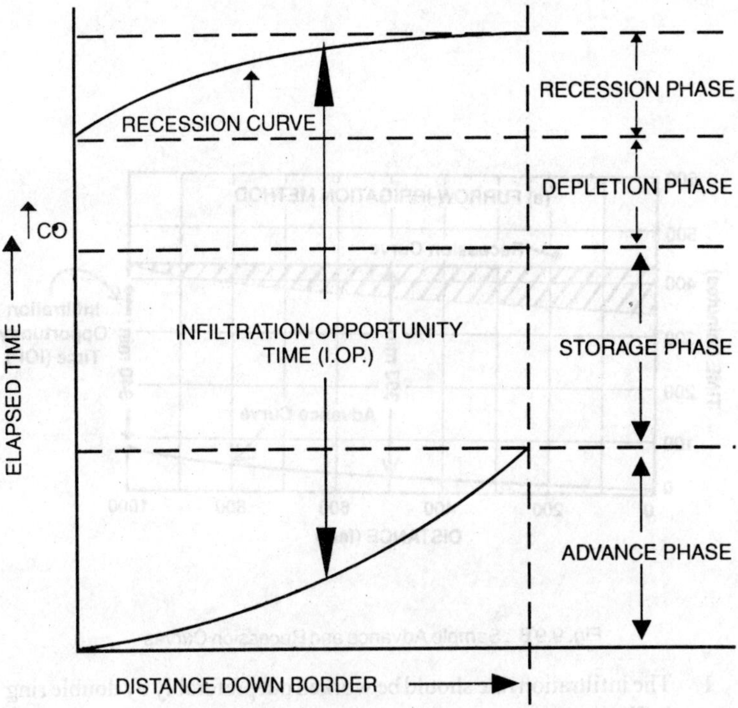

Fig. 9.9A

The difference of time between last recorded time when stream is stopped or cut off and the initial time is called cut off time.

EVALUATION OF BORDER IRRIGATION

The basic variables which influence the hydraulics of flow in borders are to be primarily determined and the characteristics of flow be measured for evaluating border irrigation. The computation of various efficiencies such as application efficiency, water requirement efficiency, distribution uniformity and deep percolation ratio have to be made.

The consideration of soil series and management practices to be adopted on the soil series for different crops have to be made for fixing up the criterias for efficient designing of the irrigation method. This is a phased procedure as listed below :

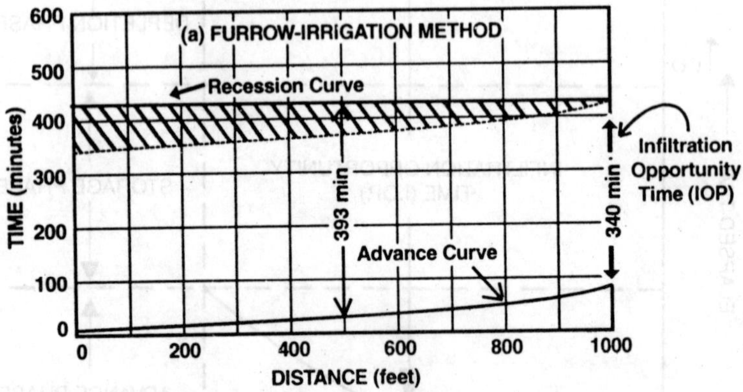

Fig. 9.9 B : Sample Advance and Recession Curves

1. The infiltration rate should be worked out preferably by double ring infiltrometers.
2. The wooden pegs or stakes be fixed 50 cm away from ridge in the field under study at an equal distance so as to represent equal area.
3. The water measurement device may be installed at the upper portion of the border.
4. The selected stream size should be released into the border.

After the water is turned on in border, following observations be taken :

1. The time when the water starts to flow into the border.
2. The time of advance of the water front when the water front reaches each station.
3. The time at which water application is stopped.
4. The rate of recession of tail water is determined by noting the

time at which water just disappears from the upstream end and recedes past each successive station downstream.

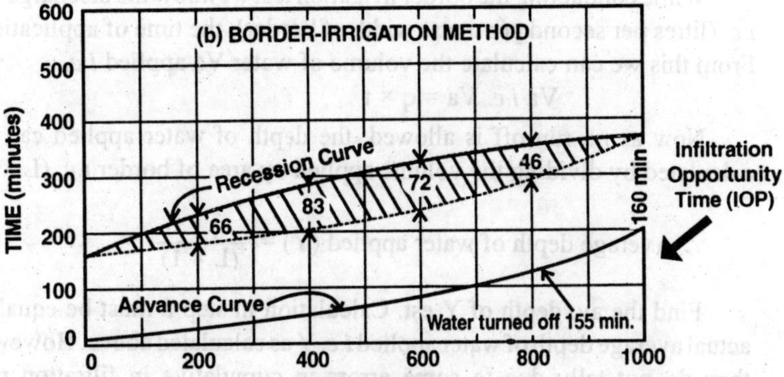

Fig. 9.10 : Sample Advance and Recession Curves

Analysis Data

(i) *Infiltration*: Data from ring infiltrometer test are analysed to obtain the functional relationship between cumulative infiltration and elapsed time

i.e. $Y = at^{\alpha}$.

(ii) *Advance Curve*: The plot of measured values of advance distance against elapsed time provides this curve.

(iii) *Recession Curve*: The plot of measured values of recession distance against elapsed time provides recession curve.

(iv) *Infiltration Opportunity Time (Top)*: The vertical distance between advance and recession curves is the opportunity time.

(v) *Estimated Depth of Water:* Knowing cumulative infiltration equation and opportunity time at each station, the depth of water infiltration is calculated from following equation :

$Y = at^{\alpha}$ – cumulative infiltration equ.

Y est. at any station = a (top of that station)

Calculate Y est at each station and find out the average depth of estimated (est) Y.

(vi) *Corrected depth of water infiltered* (Y corr): The cumulative infiltration equation *i.e.* $Y = at^{\alpha}$, may contain some error due to error in taking measurements during cylindrical infiltrometer test. Hence the value of depth infiltrated estimated by this equation (*i.e.* Y est) may not be correct. Hence it may be corrected as explained below.

While conducting the border irrigation test we know the discharge 'q' *i.e.* (litres per second per metre width of border), the time of application. From this we can calculate the volume of water Va applied *i.e.*

$$\text{Va } i.e. \text{ Va} = q \times t$$

Now as no run off is allowed, the depth of water applied can be calculated by dividing the volume applied by area of border *i.e.* (L × 1)

$$\therefore \text{ Average depth of water applied (Y)} = \frac{q \times t}{(L \times 1)}$$

Find the av. depth of Y est. Calculation in step 5 must be equal to actual average depth of water applied *i.e.* Y as calculated above. However, they do not tally due to some errors in cumulative in filtration rate equation. Hence Y est. must be corrected by applying correction factor R.

Now calculate corrected depth of water infiltration (Y error) by multiplying Y est. by correction factor R.

Example: Let cumulative infiltration eq. is

$$Y_{cm} = 0.5\ t^{0.55}\ (\text{min})$$

Discharge of 3 lit/sec per metre width of border is applied for 29 minutes in the border. Length of border is 100 m. Advance time and Recession time are noted and infiltration opportunity time (top) at each station is calculated by taking the difference between two and are given in Table 9.1. From these top, estimated depth of water infiltrated at each station is calculated by

Y est = 0.5 $(\text{top})^{0.55}$ (AV. Y est. = 41.44 mm)

correction factor 'R' is calculated as below:

$$\text{Actual volume applied} = \frac{3 \times 60 \times 29}{1000} = 5.18\ \text{cm}^3$$

Area of border = 100 × 1 = 100 cm²

∴ Actual average depth applied (Y) = 5.180 × $(10)^3$ = 51.80

$$\text{Correction factor } R = \frac{51.80}{41.44} = 1.25$$

∴ correct the depths infiltred as shown in table 9.2.

Performance Parameters (on farm efficiencies)

Four Irrigation performance parameters are defined as below (See Fig. 9.11) :

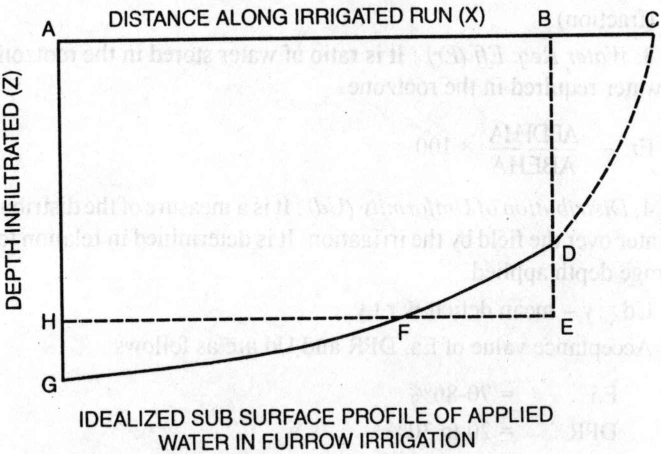

Fig. 9.11: Idealizes Sub-surface Profile of Applied Water in Furrow Irrigation

1. *Water Application Efficiency (Ea)* : It is the ratio of water stored in the root-zone to the total water applied

$$Ea = \frac{ABDFHA}{ACDGA}$$

2. *Deep Percolation Rate (DPR)* : It is the ratio of water lost due to deep percolation to total water applied

$$DPR = \frac{FGHF}{ACDGA}$$

where :

AB	=	Length of furrow
ACDGA	=	Total volume of applied water
ABEHA	=	Total volume of water requirement per furrow.

ABDFHA	=	Total volume of actual root zone storage per furrow
FGHF	=	Total volume of deep percolation/furrow
BCDB	=	Total volume of runoff water per furrow
DEFD	=	Total volume of rootzone deficit after irrigation per furrow

As no runoff is allowed the surface of Eq (fraction) and DPR is unity *i.e.*

Ea + DPR = 1

(fraction)

3. *Water Req. Eff (Er)* : It is ratio of water stored in the rootzone to the water required in the rootzone

$$\text{Er.} = \frac{\text{ABDFHA}}{\text{ABEHA}} \times 100$$

4. *Distribution of Uniformity (Ud)* : It is a measure of the distribution of water over the field by the irrigation. It is determined in relation to the average depth applied.

Ud = y – mean deficit w.r.t.y.

Acceptance value of Ea, DPR and Ud are as follows:

Ea	= 70-80%
DPR	= 20 to 30%
Er	= 90%
Ud	= 90%

Let us complete exp. 1

Table 9.4 is prepared to find out performance parameters.

Av. "Y" = 51.80

$$\text{Ea} = \frac{484.24}{518.06} \times 100 = 93.47\%$$

$$\text{DPR} = \frac{33.82}{518.06} \times 0.0653\ (6.53\%)$$

$$\text{Er} = \frac{484.24}{500} \times 100 = 96.85\%$$

$$\text{Ud} = \frac{51.8 - 2.296}{51.8} \times 100 = 95.6\%$$

TABLE 9.3

Station	Dist-ance	Advance time watch	Reces-sion time watch	Oppor-tunity time top min.	Estimated depth infiltrated Y est	correc-tion factor R	corrected depth infiltrated Y corr m.
1.	5	1103	1136	33	34.10	1.25	42.62
2.	15	1106	1142	36	36.00	...	45.00
3.	25	1110	1150	40	37.70	...	47.12
4.	35	1114	1157	43	39.6	...	49.50
5.	45	1119	1205	46	40.96	...	51.20
6.	55	1124	1213	49	42.20	...	52.75
7.	65	1128	1220	52	45.40	...	50.75
8.	75	1132	1228	56	45.70	...	57.12
9.	85	1140	1236	56	45.60	...	57.0
10.	95	1144	1244	60	47.20	...	59.0
		AV	–	–	41.44	–	AV. 51.8 (YS)

TABLE 9.4

Station	Hr. mm	Depth water infiltrated mm (Y corr)	Depth water stored in root zone mm	Depth deep per-colation (DPR)	Deficit w.r.t. Y mm
1	50	42.62	42.60	...	9.18
2	50	45.00	...	6.80	
3	50	42.12	47.12	...	4.68
4	50	49.50	49.50	...	2.30
5	50	51.20	50.00	1.20	0.60
6	50	52.75	50	6.75	0.00
8	50	57.12	50.00	7.12	0.00
9	50	57.0	50.00	7.00	0.00
10	50	59.0	50.0	9.00	0.00
Total	500	518.06	484.24	33.82	22.96

EFFECT OF SOIL ADDITIVES ON INFILTRATION

The addition of soil additives influence the physical characteristics of the soil including infiltration capacity. There are two types of additives: firstly those materials which bring about stable soil aggregation by improving soil structure which results in higher infiltration and percolation rates while other may be those wetting agents that do not cause the change in soil characteristics but instead change angle of contact of the soil-water with the soil surface causing change in the rate of intake *i.e.* water movement at depths greater than the application zone. However, these materials are to be added repeatedly as these are leached after irrigation. There are also some soil additives which decrease infiltration by causing swelling of soil particles *i.e* through inducing hydro phillic characteristic *e.g.* fine clays, petroleum or plastic films. It is required for reservoirs, irrigation canals and to have increased runoff for direct use of ground water recharge.

Analysis and Discussion

It is likely that in these tests the under-estimate values of infiltration rate are received then actual under normal field conditions. It is also likely that due to season of climatic variations the temperature of water would vary as given in Table 9.5.

TABLE 9.5

Temperature, T(°C)	Absolute viscosity (centipoise)
0	1.79
5	1.51
10	1.31
15	1.14
20	1.00
25	0.89
30	0.80
35	0.71

The wetted area of a furrow is less per unit area irrigated than that of a totally wetted surface as represented by a cylinder infiltrometer test. This smaller wetted surface should cause lower measured infiltration rates by the blocked furrow method (check the actuality of a case). If so, check the reduction in wetted surface area. After the results are obtained check, how much longer must water run in a furrow to achieve the same irrigation as would be achieved by border irrigation.

In case a sprinkler is used (2 cm/hr) you must calculate how much time would be required to penetrate 8 cm soil depth. At what time the water would pond on the surface under these conditions should also be recorded.

TABLE 9.6

Approximate Infiltration Rate of Soils (adopted from IARI monograph No. 1)

Type of soil	Basic infiltration rate mm/hr.	Approximate or say
Coarse sand	10.0 to 25.5	15 to 25
Fine sand	12.5 to 19.0	15 to 20
Fine sandy loam	12.5	15
Silty loam	10.0	10
Clay loam	7.5	5

Infiltration under Unsaturated Conditions

Infiltration into unsaturated soil is defined by the differential equation (Klute, 1952) as expressed below:

$$\frac{\partial \theta}{\partial t} = \frac{\theta}{\partial z}\left(K \frac{\partial \phi}{\partial Z}\right) + \frac{\partial}{\partial Z} (Kg)$$

where θ = the moisture content in volume of water per unit volume of soil

K = the unsaturated hydraulic conductivity (LT^{-1})

ϕ = the capillary potential (L)

g = gravitational constant (LT^{-2})

Z = the coordinate in the vertical direction (L).

A general solution to above equation cannot be obtained due to the fact that both K and ϕ are functions of θ. However, graphical solutions have been worked out and numerical solution with the help of computers.

MATHEMATICAL MODELS

Several mathematical relationships or models have been proposed for infiltration rates and cumulative infiltration, including the empirical Kostia-Kov-Lewis equation :

I. $Z = Kt^a$

The theoretically based approximation developed by Phillips:

II. $Z = St^{1/2} + At$

The empirical relationship used by U.S. Soil conservation/service:

III. $Z = Kt^a + c$

IV. The more general imperial equation (sometimes called the modified Kostia-Kov-Lewis)

$Z = Kt^a + Ib$

where

K and a	=	empirical determined coefficients
IB	=	basic infiltration rate,
S & A	=	theoretically determined values,
C	=	0.6985, and
t	=	time excess water is available at the surface.

V. *U.S. Soil Conservation Service Equation Model* : The following mathematical relationship has been tested and approved (U.S. Soil Conservation Service) after many cylinder infiltration tests.

$Z = Kt\alpha + c$

where $C = 0.6985$ cm.

Which fits best in data and catagorises soils into the various intake families shown in fig. 9.12. These can be used as design parameters for irrigation systems. You should plot your on data (a few) on the intake appropriate family curve and check up the results accordingly.

VI. *Richards Equations or Model*: It is based on the basic relationship of principle of conservation of mass, which, assuming the density of the water to be constant, may be expressed for a given point in the soil medium as :

$$\frac{\partial \theta}{\partial t} = \nabla . q \quad .... (1)$$

where q = flux of water

t = time

θ = volumetric soil water content

For flow in the vertical direction `Z' the equation 1 may be expressed as

$$\frac{\partial \theta}{\partial t} = \frac{\partial q}{\partial z} \quad .... (2)$$

Combining equation 1 and 2 and putting $H = h + z$ where he = matric or pressure potential expressed as a head, H = hydraulic head and Z is gravitational head (Vertical distance of the point of measurement above the reference plane. In case the measurement point is below reference plane the value of 'Z' is negative) provides equation termed as Richards' equation as given under :

$$C(h)\ \frac{\partial h}{\partial t} = \frac{\partial}{\partial Z}\left[K(h)\frac{\partial h}{\partial Z}\right] + \frac{\partial k}{\partial Z} \quad \ldots (3)$$

where C(h) = Soil water Capacity (denotes slope dθ/dh of the Soil water characteristic curve at any point drawn as soil water pressure head (cm water–h) on abscissa and water content θ (per cent by Volume) on ordinate. For more details about this refer A.S. A.E. (1963) monograph No. 3 on Design and Operation of Farm irrigation systems.

Horten (1940) Formula

The infiltration capacity of the soils according to Horten (1940) is given by

$$f = fc + (fo - fc)e^{-kt}$$

where

f = the capacity rate of infiltration at any instant mm/hr

f = the time measured from the beginning of the infiltration

fc = the constant rate at which 'f' is approached systematically as time continues

fo = the initial capacity infiltration rate 'f' where the soil moisture status of the water shed is equal to zero.

In this equation the parameters 'fc' and 'fo' represent the basic and initial infiltration rate respectively. The parameter 'K' defines the rate of decrease of the infiltration capacity 'f' from initial infiltration rate 'fo' to the final infiltration rate 'fc'.

For alkali soils this equation has been corrected with exchangeable sodium percentage by Karnal workers as follows :

fc = Exp. (1.90 – 0.07 E.S.P.)

fo = Exp. (3.46 – 0.04 E.S.P.)

K = 0.15 Pn E.S.P. + 0.24

These values are put in Horten's basic equation to get the universal infiltration equation for alkali soils with different E.S.P. values.

In alkali soils the infiltration decreases with increase in E.S.P. values. The same decreasing trends also holds good between the 'fo-fc' (difference between initial and basic infiltration). Thus it may be concluded that the initial infiltration rate is more affected with increasing E.S.P. values. So is the trend when relationship between the rate of decrease of infiltration and E.S.P. This has been attributed to the fact that the soil aggregates of high E.S.P. are easily broken to the particles (weak stability) due to the combined effect of gravity and capillary forces. This results in clugging of the voids of soil and drastically reduce infiltration. The addition of soil amendments reverse this phenomenon.

Example

Considering soil as reservoir, the depth of water to be applied based on infiltration the equation to be used is : qt = 28 ad

where : q = size of stream in litres per second.

t = time in hours required to irrigate are a

a = area irrigated (ha)

d = depth in cm that the volume of water used would cover the land irrigated, if quickly spread uniformly over its surface.

Also : qt = ad if q in cubic metres, t in hrs, a in ha, and d in metres.

$$\therefore \text{Yave} = \frac{d}{t} = \frac{q}{28a};$$

where Yave = average intake in cms/hr that would result if actual intake occurring in the furrow (lps) was spread over, the area between furrows (ha.). Example: If 0.2 lps enters the soil in 30m furrows, 50m apart, Yave = 4.8cm/hrs.

INTAKE FAMILIES

Different types of soils have their particular intake characteristics. The difference of intake may be small to high based on soil textures and other physical parameters. Based on these eight intake families have been constituted designated from A to H as given under:

Intake family Symbol	Intake characteristics
A	Very slow
B	Slow
C	Moderately slow
D	Moderate

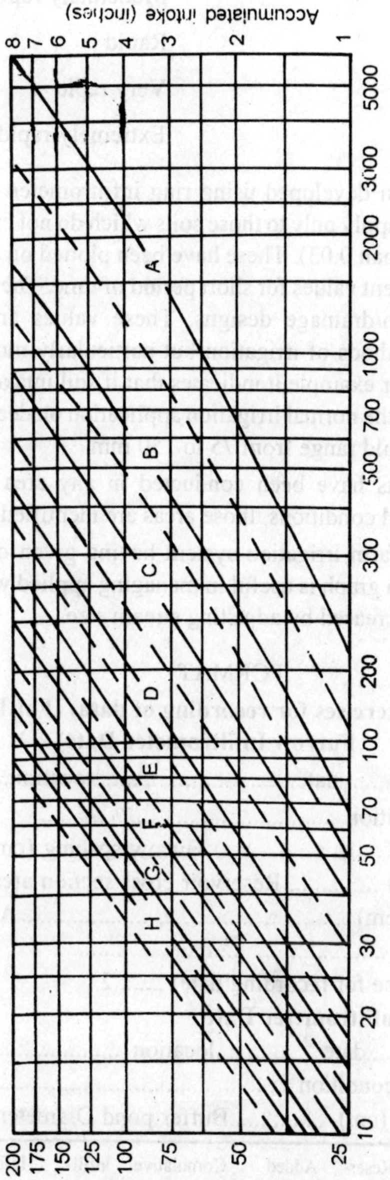

Fig. 9.12 : Intake Families for Surface Irrigation Design

E	Moderately rapid
F	Rapid
G	Very rapid
H	Extremely rapid.

These have been developed using ring infiltrometer method (Fig. 9.12). These curves apply only to those soils which do not crack much on drying (COLE less than 0.03). These have been plotted on a logarithmic scale to better represent values for short period of time. These are used as a tool for irrigation/drainage designs. These values are in general applicable to all methods of irrigation but particularly more to surface flooding method. For example it indicates that if soil intake rate is 63 to 200 mm (F-family), the normal irrigation application on deep silt loan for the crops grown would range from 75 to 150 mm.

If series of tests have been conducted in any area which show variability due to soil conditions, those areas are identified and mapped.

For designing farm irrigation system having given or determined intake rate, the given graph is useful in managing applied water and thus efficiency can be increased by adjusting stream size.

FORMAT

Sheet (Exercises for recording of data) (For blocked Furrow Infiltrometer Date)

Name........................... date........................... location................

Soil type and condition ....

Furrow length (cm) ...., Furrow spacing (cm) ....

Area Irrigated (cm^2) ...., Reservoir cross section area (cm^2)........

Wetted perimeter (cm) ...., ..., ..., Av(cm)....

Wetted area (cm^2) ....

Time Sheet (Exercise for recording date) 2

For cylinder Infiltrometer Date

Name ....date ....location ....

Soil type and condition ....

Ring Diameter (cm). ....Buffer pond Diameter (cm) ....

Time hr./min	Elapsed time (Min.)	Reser-voir level reading	Added depth (cm.)	Comulative Depth (cm.)	Infill-trated volume Cm^3	Infill-trated depth Z cm.	Comments

FORMAT

(Exercise for recording date)...........2
For Cylinder Infiltrometer Date

Name.......................................date.............................location.........................
Soiltype and condition..
Ring Diameter (cm.)........................Buffer pond Diameter (cm.)...............

Time (hr./ Min.)	Elapsed time t (Min.)	Cylinder depth (cm.)	Volume Added Cm^3	Equivalent depth (cm.)	Cumula-tive depth infil-trated Z (cm.).	Comments

EFFICIENCIES *Vs.* INFILTRATION

Irrigated agriculture is a game of water availability from the water resevoir to the field in first phase and its use by crops at second phase. Various kinds of efficiencies have been expressed under :

Irrigation Efficiencies

This can be divided into two parts as discussed below :

1. Off Farm-efficiency
2. On Farm-efficiency

Off Farm-Efficiency

It is the ratio of output to input. In case the irrigation system, water is conveyed from source to the field through distribution network. *i.e.* canal distributary, minor and field channel. While conveying the water, loss occurs on account of seepage, spillage, dead storage in the channels, evaporation from water surface, operation losses etc.

Water distribution net work of gravity irrigation system is shown below :

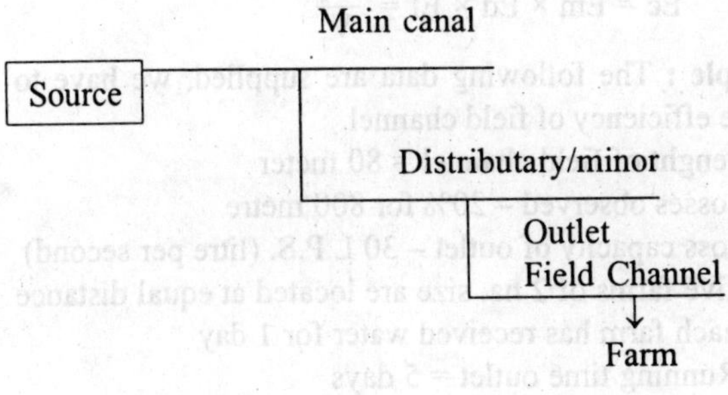

Off farm efficiency is expressed from canal head to field head. It can be divided into:

(a) *Conveyance efficiency of main canal (Em)* : It is the ratio of total volume of water delivered at Distributary/Minor head to the total volume of water diverted from canal head.

$\therefore$ Em = $\frac{V_2}{V_1}$, where V_2 = volume of water delivered at Dy/Minor head and V_1 = vol. of water diverted at canal head.

(b) *Conveyance efficiency of Dy/Minor (Ed)* : It is the ratio of total volume of water delivered at outlet head to the volume of water received at Dy/Minor head

$$\text{i.e. Ed.} = \frac{V_3}{V_2}$$

where

V_3 = vol. of water delivered at outlet

V_2 = vol. of water received at Dy/Minor head.

(c) *Conveyance efficiency of field channel (Ef)* : It is the ratio of total volume of water delivered at field head to the volume of water received at outlet head *i.e.*

$$\text{Ef} = \frac{V_4}{V_3}$$

where

V_4 = vol. of water delivered at field head

V_3 = vol. of water received at outlet head.

(d) *The overall conveyance efficiency of distribution network (EC)*: It can be defined as the ratio of total volume of water at field heads to the total volume of water diverted from main canal head *i.e.*

$$\text{Ec} = \text{Em} \times \text{Ed} \times \text{Ef} = \frac{V_4}{V_1}$$

Example : The following data are supplied, we have to find out conveyance efficiency of field channel.

– lenght of field channel = 80 meter
– losses observed – 20% for 800 metre
– loss capacity of outlet – 30 L.P.S. (litre per second)
– five farms of 2 ha. size are located at equal distance
– each farm has received water for 1 day

Running time outlet = 5 days

30 × 5 = 150 litre per second (l.p.s.) total volume of water received at farm head is as below :

Farm No.	Distance	Losses	Water received (lps)
5.	800 m	20%	24.0
4.	600 m	15%	25.5
3.	400 m	10%	27.0
2.	200 m	5%	25.5
1.	100 m	0%	30.0
		total	135.0

∴ Conveyance efficiency of field channel

$$Ef = \frac{135}{150} \times 100 = 90\%$$

On Farm Efficiency

The following efficiencies are defined on farm :

(a) Field application efficiency (Ea)

(b) Deep percolation ratio (DPR)

(c) Water requirement efficiency (Er)

(d) Distribution efficiency (Ed)

The details of these can be read in books on irrigated agriculture.

CHAPTER 10

RUNOFF CHARACTERISTICS

Introduction

The various conservation structures and channels are designed to take care of the natural flows of water from rainfall or melting snow. Runoff is the hydraulic 'head' which musţ be taken care by the various structures or channels.

The term runoff denotes that portion of the rainfall which flows towards stream channels, lakes or oceans either as surface or sub-surface flow. However, it constitutes a surface flow. The designing of channels or structures are made so as to withstand the peak rates of runoff, its voiume and temporal distribution of runoff rates and volumes.

OCCURRENCE

The runoff occurs when the rainfall is so much that even after the evaporation, interception, infiltration, surface and channels storage and retention, the water is still left to flow. Thus light rainfall is usually intercepted greatly which may even not allow the wetting of ground soil. This interception on account of storage capacity is usually due to dense cover of forests or shrubs. This has been on the average about 25 per cent of the annual rainfall. Thus a well grown maize crop may intercept about 0.5 mm (0.02 in), trees to the extent of 13 mm (0.5 in). The retention of rainfall by the interception process greatly reduce the runoff.

The runoff actually becomes significant only when the rate of rainfall exceeds the infiltration of the soil. The excess water collected on soil surface after filling the small and large depressions, the overflow starts flowing on the ground. This also occurs when at surface sufficient depth of water is built up. The same process occurs when this water flows through channels by retention. The retained water, however, in last, contributes to the subsided runoff conditions. The water infiltered into the shallow depth of soil is lost by evaporation.

INFLUENCING FACTORS

There are two important conditions which influence runoff. These are firstly from the rainfall and other from watersheds.

Rainfall

The rate and volume of runoff depends upon the total period of rainfall, its intensity and areal distribution. Infiltration characteristics of the soil are such that after some time it decreases with time and hence short term heavy rainfall may not produce runoff but if the duration of the same intensity is more it results in runoff. One of the important deteriorating effects is sealing of soil pores which cause considerable decrease in infiltration and results in runoff.

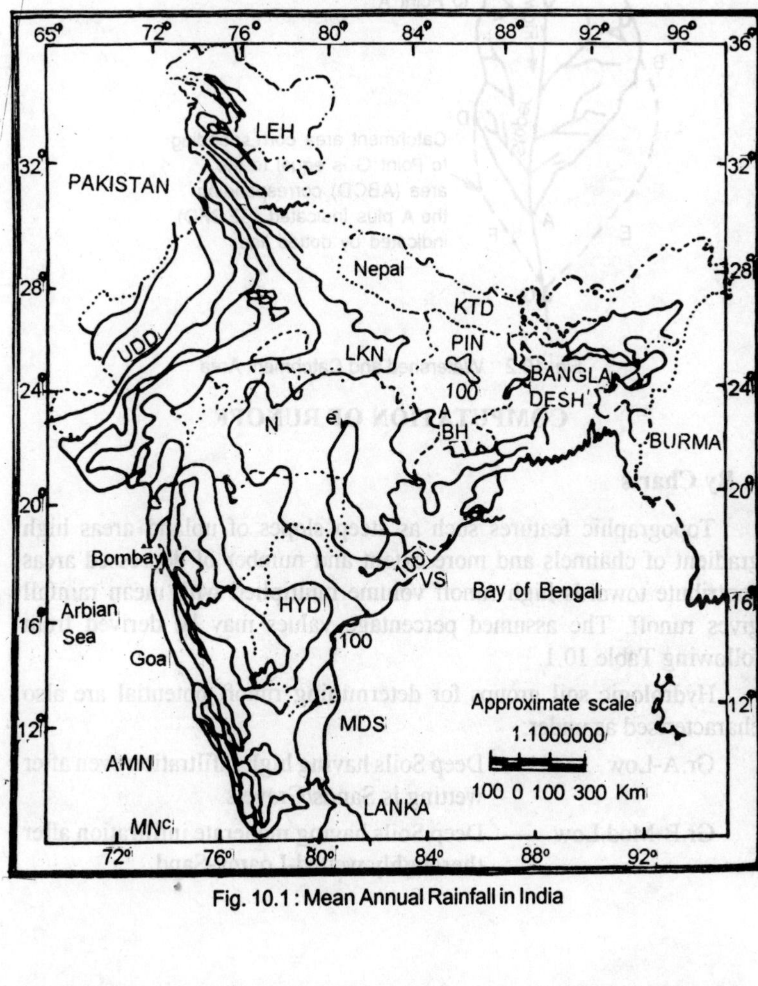

Fig. 10.1 : Mean Annual Rainfall in India

Watersheds

In case of a watershed the factors influencing runoff are size, shape, orientation, topography, geology and surface culture. The runoff volume and rates both increase if the watershed is of large size which also predicts the season at which it is either likely to occur or would be high.

It has also been observed that long, narrow watersheds may have lower runoff rates as compared to compact watersheds of the same size.

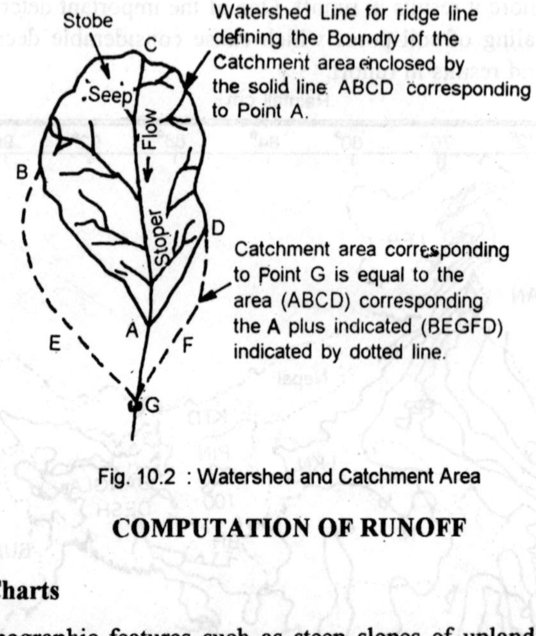

Fig. 10.2 : Watershed and Catchment Area

COMPUTATION OF RUNOFF

1. By Charts

Topographic features such as steep slopes of upland areas high gradient of channels and more extent and number of depressed areas contribute towards high runoff volume multiplied with mean rainfall gives runoff. The assumed percentage values may be derived from following Table 10.1.

Hydrologic soil groups for determining runoff potential are also characterised as under:

Gr.A-Low — Deep Soils having high infiltration even after wetting is Sands/Gravels.

Gr.B-Mod.Low — Deep Soils having moderate infiltration after thoroughly wetted-Loamy-Sand.

Gr.C-Mod.High — Soils having below average infiltration after presaturations *i.e.* shallow, sufficiently clayey and colloidal contents.

Gr.D-High — Soils having very slow infiltration after thoroughly wetted swelling clays, waterlogged, clay pan, shallow with impervious layers.

TABLE 10.1

Description of catchment of various classes	Class of catchment	Percentage values to be multiplied with rainfall to get runoff values			
		Types of rainfall*			
		N	L	M	H
A. Flat cultivated absorbed land	A	0	1	10	20
B. Flat partly cultivated stiff soil	B	0	3	15	33
C. Average catchment	C	0	5	20	40
D. Hills and Plains with little cultivation	D	0	10	25	55
E. Very hilly and steep with very little or no cultivation	E	0	15	33	70

* N = Negligible — All rainfall below 12.5 mm/day unless continuous for several days. Also isolated rainfall between 12.5 mm and 25 mm a day not preceded or followed by any rain.

L = Light — All rainfall upto 25 mm/day when continuous or followed or preceded by similar or heavier rainfall. Also isolated fall between 25 and 37.5 mm a day.

M = Medium — Fall between 25 and 37.5 mm a day when preceded by similar or heavier fall. Also isolated fall between 37.5 and 50 mm a day.

H = Heavy — All falls above 75 mm a day.

Source: Barlow, T.G., Classification of Catchment and Rainfall.

2. By Empirical Formula

The various relationships between rainfall and runoff expressed empirically be used as given below:

(a) Lacey's Eq. $$R = \frac{P}{1 + \frac{3038\,F}{PS}}$$

(b) Inglish $$R = 0.85P - 304.8 \text{ (For ghat areas)}$$

$$R = \frac{(P - 177.8) \times P}{2540} \text{ (For non ghat areas)}$$

(c) Khosla $$R = P - 4.811\,T$$

where:

R = Runoff expressed in mm

P = Rainfall in mm

S = Catchment factor (varies from 0.25 for flat land to 3.45 for very hilly area)

F = Monsoon duration factor (varies from 0.50 for very short duration monsoon to 1.50 for prolonged monsoon)

T = Temperature in °C

However, these formulae provides very tentative ideas about runoff.

3. Infiltration Method

The infiltration method for computing runoff is based on the principles that during monsoon period due to high relative humidity, evaporation, transportation interception, surface storage, soil moisture deficiency etc. *i.e.* all outflow factors are heavily minimised except the infiltration and if this is estimated during this period, the runoff can be computed by deducting infiltration loss from the rainfall. For this object the open-end tubes driven into the soil and filling them with a given depth of water, the fall in the water surface in the installed tube can be measured in a day or in an hour which gives infiltration rate per unit time wanted.

The infiltration capacity also called infiltration index is very high in beginning (Potential rate) but attains constant value (Steady-state) after the lapse of some time when the added water has satisfied the soil water requirement or demand. If the infiltration curve is superimposed over the depth of rainfall, the depth of rainfall excess over the given period can be found as indicated by the hatched area in figure which lies above the infiltration. Capacity (f) curve.

Example

Time (hr.)	Observed rate of flow (m^3/sec)	Mean rate of flow during the interval of hours (m^3/sec.)
0	6	8
6	10	15
12	20	...
18	28	24
24	20	24
30	15	18
36	10	13
42	8	9
48	6	7
	Total	118

Calculations:

Hence total volume of flow $= 118 \times 6 \times 3600$

$= 25.5 \times 105 m^3/m^3$

$\therefore$ Net volume of surface runoff $= \dfrac{90}{100} \times 25.5 \times 10^5$

Area of catchment $= 50 \times 10^6 m^2$

Hence depth of surface runoff $= \dfrac{23 \times 10^5}{50 \times 10^6} \times 100$

$=$ 4.6 cm Ans.

$\therefore$ The total loss $= 10 - 4.6 =$ 5.4 cm.

Rate of infiltration (W-index) $= \dfrac{5.4}{6} =$ 0.9 cm/Gr.

$=$ $= 9$ mm/hr **Ans.**

4. By Curves Method

The data of runoff (cm) *vs.* rainfall (cm) are plotted as curves. These data are collected through storm rainfall and stream discharge corresponding to given storm. (The total volume of the stream flow corresponding to a given storm divided by area of catchment gives the depth of run off).The catchment conditions change the shape of the said curve.

5. Stream Gauzing Method

It is the most dependable method to calculate the runoff arising out of the storm rainfall in a basin is to measure the discharge in the stream at any point. The depth of surface runoff (rainfall excess) is:

$$\text{depth of surface runoff} = \frac{\text{Total volume of streamflow (–) Vol. of subsurface flow}}{\text{Area of catchment}}$$

6. W-Index and ϕ Index Method

Here rate of infiltration is assumed to be constant. The former indicates average rate when multiplied by the duration of the storm (Thrs) will provide the total depth of water actually lost in infiltration during the period of storm. The ϕ index is that constant rate of infiltration above which all storm rainfall will produce a runoff equal to the rainfall minus the ϕ index.

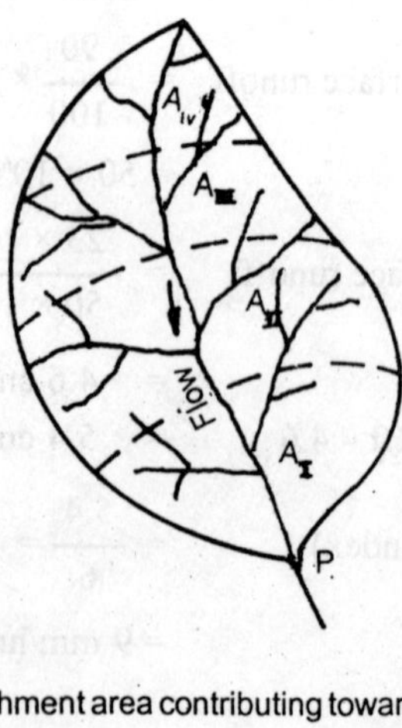

Fig. 10.3 : Catchment area contributing towards stream Flowat P.

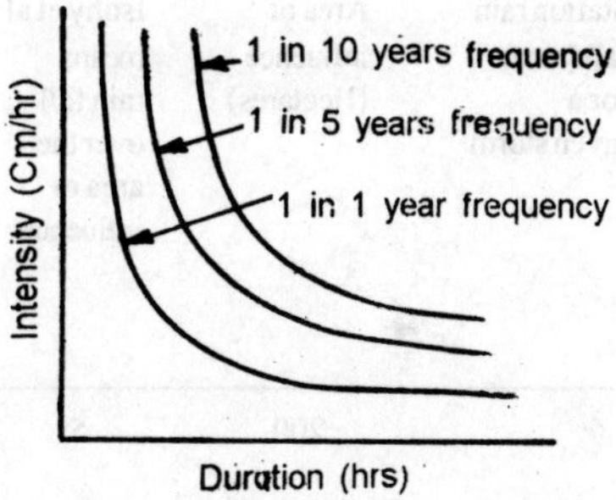

Fig. 10.4 : Intensity duration frequency relation for Rainfall

Examples on Runoff

Example 1: To calculate the station weight of the rainfall, influenced area and mean rainfall over the area of influence are given. The second rainfall shows 10, 12, 8 and 6 mm (P_1, P_2, P_3 and P_4) downpour at station.

Mean rainfall from the other storm

$$= W_1P_1 + W_2P_2 + W_3P_3 + W_4P_4$$

$$\therefore Pm = 0.167 \times 10 + 0.075 \times 12 + 0.360 \times 8 + 0.300 \times 6$$

$$= 1.67 + 0.90 + 2.88 + 1.80 = 7.25 \text{ mm}$$

Example 2: Given in table are mean rainfall of a storm and the corresponding runoff was 10 mm. Find the value of ϕ index and W index values.

where,

ϕ index = constant rate of infiltration above which all storm rainfall will produce a runoff equal to the rainfall minus the ϕ-index

W index = Average rate which when multiplied by the duration of the storm (T hours) will give the total depth of water actually lost in infiltration during the period of storm (Area of rainfall histogram lying below the infiltration capacity curve is the loss in infiltration).

Prepare following table for an area:

Locations	Station rain fall (mm) for a given storm	Area of influence (Hectares)	Isohy et al means rain fall over the area or influence	Station weight W= Mean rainfall station rainfall $\times \frac{\text{(Area of influence)}}{\text{Total area}}$
1	6	200	5	$W_1 = \frac{5}{6} \times \frac{200}{1000}$ = 0.167
2	8	100	6	$W_2 = \frac{6}{8} \times \frac{100}{1000}$ = .075
5	25	300	6	$W_3 = \frac{6}{5} \times \frac{300}{1000}$ =.360
4	4	400	3	$W_4 = \frac{3}{4} \times \frac{400}{1000}$ =.300
		Total Area = 1000		

Example 3 : To calculate W and ϕ Indexes.

Rainfall data

Time	Storm rainfall`	Rainfall Excess of P-ϕ for assumed ϕ index values		
		ϕ (10 mm/hr)	ϕ (12mm/hr)	ϕ (13 mm/hr)
0-1	14	4	2	1
1-2	22	12	10	9
2-3	12	2	0	0
	Total	18	12	10

$\therefore$ ϕ index = 13 mm/hr

and W index = $\frac{13 + 13 + 12}{3} = \frac{38}{3}$ = 12.7 mm/hr.

DESIGN RUNOFF RATES

It is defined as the capacity to safely carry runoff by a structure or channel. These are planned to carry runoff which may occur within a specified return period. Thus if runoff occurs within a small span of period say once in 10 years vegetated controls and temporary structrures are usually designed for taking care of runoff. However, if it is made to look after runoff which occurs once in 50 or 100 years, permanent and expensive structures are designed. Selection of the design return period also called recurrence interval depends on the economic balance between the cost of periodic repair or replacement of the facility and the cost of providing additional capacity to reduce the frequency of repair or replacement (Schwale et al., 1981). The damaging potentiality resulting from failure of the structure on downstream size should be considered for design frequency.

Different Methods

The various methods have been given depending upon various considerations and situations. The important ones are discussed here.

(i) Rational Method : A design peak runoff rate can be predicted if the rainfall intensity of a specified time and watershed area is known. This relationship may be given by equation:

$$q = 0.0028\ ciA$$

where

q = the design peak runoff rate in m^3/s.

c = the runoff coefficient which is ratio of peak runoff rate to rainfall intensity and is dimensionless.

i = rainfall intensity in mm/h for the design return period and for a duration equal to the 'time of concentration' of the water.

A = the watershed area in hectares.

The term 'time of concentration' of a watershed is defined as the time required for water to flow from the far distant point (in terms of time) of the area to the outlet when the soil has become fully saturated. It has been postulated that if the time for which rain has occurred is equal to the time of concentration then the water flow is occurring from entire portions of the watershed which would be discharged at the outlet. Kirpitch (1940) gave widely accepted equation for computation of time of concentration.

$T_c = 0.0195\ L^{0.77} S^{-0.385}$ (the explanation of various terms is given in the solution of example 1).

Mockus (1961), however, suggested a monograph for calculating time of concentration considering length of main channel, topography, vegetal cover and infiltration rate. Horn and Schwale (1963) consider this monograph as most satisfactory.

U.S. Soil Conservation Services Staff (U.S.S.C.S.S.) (1972) suggested 'Upland Method' in which the time of travel of flow is calculated by dividing length of flow by estimated velocity of flow. The sum of travel time occurred as sheet flow runoff and for entire channels flow was assumed to be time of concentration. However, it is applicable to watersheds having areas less than 800 hectares. Manning's formula is used for computing flow velocities. U.S. S.C.S.S. (1972) has also prepared velocity slope curves for various conditions of watersheds.

The rational method depends upon the assumption that frequency of rainfall and runoff are similar (Larson and Reich, 1973). It is an over-simplified attempt to view the complicated phenomenon.

Soil Conservation Service Method

This was published by U.S. Soil Conservation Services in 1973 considering uniform rainfall patterns for a biangular hydrograph. The time to peak flow was expressed in equation form:

$$T_p = D/2 + T_c = D/2 + 0.6\ T_c$$

(Notations explained in example 2)

Flood Frequency Analysis Method

This method depends upon the existence of a number of years of runoff/floods record from the basin. These data are then analysed statistically to interpret the probable frequency of recurrence of floods of given magnitudes.

Through extrapolation of the frequency curves hydrologist interpret flood peaks for different range of return periods.

Other Methods

Chow (1962) based on rainfall, soil and cover conditions computed runoff. In a simple form this was expressed by equation:

$$q = KA^x$$

where

q = the magnitude of the peak runoff.

K = a coefficient related to characteristics of a watershed.

A = Area of watershed

x = Constant depend upon local conditions.

Potter (1961) predicted peak runoff rates through deliberation of major geological zones based on topographic index.

The losses of soils through runoff is measured by water stage level recorder and wheel silt sampler with different gears. These equipments are available for different time periods for taking samples of runoff water. The values are obtained through a float connected to a clock and graph plotting drum device.

RUNOFF VOLUME ESTIMATION

The total volume of runoff in a watershed is determined for the design of flood control reservoirs. Various methods are available for this estimation.

(i) *Soil Conservation Service Method:* The relationship evaluated through consideration of many years storm flow records for agricultural watersheds was suggested by U.S. S.C.S. as given by equation:

$$Q = \frac{(I - 0.25)^2}{(I + 0.85)}$$

(The meaning of notations given in Example 4.)

In this method a rainfall I mm(in) is plotted on axis x and direct runoff Q mm (or in) on y-axis. This graph provides values of 'S'. It may be noticed that runoff decreases as 'S' or infiltration increases. The initial abstraction Ia = 0.2S takes into account interception losses, surface storage and water that infiltrates into the soil prior to runoff.

(ii) *Land Use and Per cent Area Method:* Weighted runoff for the watershed is calculated as below:*

Land Use	Area%	Q*(mm) calculated	Weighted runoff (Q × Per cent area)
Fallow Land	31	15.37	476.47
Paddy	24	15.37	368.88
Other Crops	45	96.80	4356.00
		Total	5201.35

∴ Weighted Q = 5201.35 ÷ 100 = 52mm

Volume of Runoff = 10 × Q × Area, ham = 10 × 52 × 1600 = 832000 ham.

$$* \; Q = \frac{(P - Ia)^2}{P - Ia + S},$$

$$G = P - Ia - Q$$

where
- Q = Runoff (mm)
- P = Precipitation (mm)
- Ia = Initial abstraction
- S = Potential maximum retention (mm)
- G = Precipitation less initial abstractions and runoff (mm).

WATER YIELD

The annual volume of water coming through total runoff and stored in ponds or reservoirs if measured through gauge is termed as annual water yield or simply water yield. Brakensick (1959) used runoff data for a water year instead of calendar year to arrive at satisfactory results of water yield. The data for beginning the water year varies with geographical location but in general it coincides with the season of maximum runoff. In India for example the maximum runoff season is monsoon period which extends from 1st July to 30th September and the irrigation year is considered from 1st July to 30th June while in U.S.A. from 1st October to 30th September. The water yield records may by extended to other similar agro-climatic or more precisely to hydrologic conditions.

Estimation of Minimum Water Yield

The minimum yield has been defined as the least flow (dry year) which decreases with the return period unlike rainfall and storm runoff which increases with the return period. It has been found that minimum yield increases with watershed size due to the greater contribution of the flow of ground waters. It is true particularly for humid regions.

Nixon and Schwale (1961) proposed watershed ratings for arriving at the estimation of water yields from other similar watersheds. This was made on the assumptions on climate, land use degree of slope, soil series and type and management practices.

The snowmelt in the ungauged watersheds has been recommended to be worked out from equation M = 45.72 KD, where M = depth of snowmelt water from watershed in mm/d, K = a constant for watershed and climatic conditions (0.02 for low runoff potential, 0.06 for average and 0.30 for high runoff potential), D = Degree days for a given day in °V.C° (A day with an average temperature of 15°C has 15 degree-days).

RUNOFF HYDROGRAPHS

The runoff hydrograph is a graphical or tabular illustration of the runoff rate (Y-axis) with respect to lapse of time (X-axis). These are developed for agricultural watersheds from stream flow records. Their characteristic is that for a particular watershed the duration of flow is nearly constant for individual storms regardless of the peak flow. Sherman (1932) developed a hydrograph representing one inch of runoff and is called unit hydrograph. Commons (1942) and others developed dimensionless hydrographs.

Triangular Hydrographs

The triangular runoff hydrograph is considered to be the simplest one among all hydrographs. They are used for (a) sub-areas of a watershed and/or (b) to know the time variations of rainfall. In both the above conditions the cumulative flow rates for the given time periods are worked out from several hydrographs. This results in curvilinear hydrograph which has been found to be a good side curves of a graph are considered to be or plotted as straight lines. This simplifies calculation of the variables. It has been considered to have 100 units of flow for the peak and 100 units of time for the duration of flow. Using the data of peak flow and the runoff volume of the desired return period of rainfall the design of a hydrograph can be worked out from the dimensionless hydrograph by using conversion factors. The various factors used are given by various relationships as discussed below:

Factor (u) : It is the ratio of the total runoff volume to the area under the dimensionless hydrograph. Thus if area under hydrograph is say 2620 square units, then each square unit value (u) for the design rainfall (storm) with total runoff volume Q is given by u = Q/2620.

Factor (w): It is the ratio of peak runoff for the design rainfall (q) to the peak flow of 100 considered on dimensionless hydrograph and the each unit of which is given as *w-q*/100.

Factor (K): It is also the value of each unit of time on the dimensionless hydrograph as represented in design hydrograph.

It is essential that on the design hydrograph 1/100 of the peak flow (w) times 1/100 of the duration of runoff (K) must equal to 1/2620 (u) of the flood volume just as it does on the dimensionless hydrograph. Therefore the equation developed is WK = u or K = u/w.

If runoff rate has been worked out in cubic metres per second, runoff volume in hectare-metres and time in minutes, the value of 'K' factor is given by following relationship:

$$K = \frac{u(\text{ha.m.}) \times 10{,}000\ (\text{m}^2/\text{ha})}{w(\text{m}^3\text{s}) \times 60\ (\text{sec/min})} = 167\ \frac{u}{W}$$

Dimensionless Hydrographs

This kind of hydrograph is also called Synthetic hydrograph due to its idealized shape. The shape which is a smooth curve indicates the flow from high rainfall in the watershed of small catchment area. It is under certain conditions similar to triangular hydrograph.

Other Hydrographs

Although many synthetic hydrographs have been suggested by various hydrologists but none so far has been widely accepted which is due to the limited flow records the accurate estimation of peak flow has not been possible through them.

An attempt has also been made on different statistical frequency distributions to develop several types of theoretical hydrographs but so far these need recognition. Dodge (1959) suggested a unit hydrograph using probability function approach. Gray (1970) used two parameter gamma distribution. Reich (1962) used three parameter Pearson type III function. Linsley et al. (1975) suggested many approaches for developing unit hydrographs. He also developed a hydrograph for overland flow. The unit hydrograph was defined as the hydrograph of one inch (or 1 cm) of direct runoff from a storm or rainfall of a particular period.

SELECTED EXAMPLES OF RUNOFF

Example 1: To calculate the design peak runoff rate for a 50 year return period storm from a 40.5 ha (100 ac) watershed having maximum length of flow, 610 m (2000 ft) and the difference in elevation along this path 3 m (10 ft) and the following data by rational method.

ha	Sub-area (ac)	Topography per cent slope	Soil group*	Land use treatment and hydrological condition
24.3	60	Flat	C	Row crop, contoured
16.2	40	10 to 30	B	Good wood land, good

* A = Lowest runoff potential. Includes deep sands with very little silt and clay also deep, rapidly permeable loose (silt).

B = Moderately low runoff potential. Mostly sandy soils less deep than A and loose less deep or less aggregated than A, but the group as a whole has above average infiltration after thorough wetting.

C = Moderately high runoff potential. Comprises shallow soils and soils containing considerable clay and colloids, though less than those of group D. The group has below average infiltration after presaturation.

D = Highest runoff potential. Includes mostly clays of high swelling per cent, but the group also includes some shallow soils with nearly impermeable sub-horizons near the surface.

Source: U.S. Soil Conservation Service. National Engineering Handbook, Hydrology Section 4 (1972) and U.S. Deptt. Agr. ARS 41-172 (1970).

Solution : The watershed gradient is (10/2000) 100 now from eq. Tc = 0.0195 L0.77 S-0.385 = 20 min. For a 50-year return period the 20 min rainfall = 97 mm/h (3.8 iph). The runoff coefficient C from table of Horn & Schwab (1963) for row crops, good practice & wood land is given 0.56 and 0.10 respectively and the correction factor for hydrologic soil group from C to B for the 24.3 ha sub-area from table is 1.09.

Hence, C = (24.3/40.5) × 0.56 × 1.09 + (16.2/40.5) × 0.10 = .41. Putting value in Eq. q = 0.0028 CiA (predicting a design peak runoff eq.)

q = 0.0028 × 0.41 × 97 × 40.5 = 4.51m^3/s (159 cfs)

Problem 1

Using SCS method determine the peak runoff rate from a 100 ha (247 ac) watershed from a uniform 36-min. (0.6 h) storm that produced 10 mm (0.39 in) of runoff volume. Assuming T_c for watershed 0.5 h.

Problem 2

Using SCS method determine the peak runoff rate from a 100 ha (247 ac) watershed from a uniform 36-min (0.6 h) storm that produced 10 mm (0.39 in) of runoff volume. Assuming T_c for watershed 0.5 h.

Solution: Using SCS equation, Tp = D/2 TL = D/2 + 0.6T_c

where:

Tp = time to peak
D = Duration of excess rainfall
TL = time lag
Tc = Time of concentration
Tp = 0.6/2 + 0.6 × 0.5 = 0.6 h

Putting values in eq. q = 0.0021 QA/TP

where,

Q = runoff volume in mm depth (area under the hydrograph)
q = runoff rate in m_3/s.
A = watershed area in ha
Tp = time of peak in hours

Hence q = 0.0021 × 10 × 100/0.6 = 3.50m³/s (124 cfs)

Problem 3

To calculate the estimated maximum volume of runoff during the growing season for a 50-year return period that may be expected from the watershed of example 1. Assuming antecedent moisture 5 days prior to the storm to be 40 mm (1.6 in) of rainfall and the critical duration of the storm 6 hours.

Solution: Say rainfall for a 6 hr. storm is 107 mm (4.2 in). Also between the point rainfall and area rainfall the reduction is less than 1 per cent, so no correction needed, also given data are as follows:

Sub-area, A, ha (ac)	Soil group	Land use treatment condition	Curve No. N	NA
24.3(60)	C	row & crop contoured good	82	1993
16.2(40	B	Wood land good	55	891
40.5(100 ac)			Total	2884

Hence weighted curve number = 2884/40.5 = 71.2

Putting in S.C.S. Eq. for evaluating antecedent moisture, soil conditions, land use and conservation practices.

$$\left[S = \frac{25400}{N} - 254\right]$$

where:

N = an arbitrary curve number varying from 0 to 100

Hence

$$S = \frac{25400}{71.2} - 254 = 103 \text{ mm}$$

$$Q = \frac{(107 - 0.2 \times 103)^2}{107 + (0.8 \times 103)} = 39 \text{ mm } (1.54 \text{ in})$$

$$Q = \frac{39 \times 40.5}{1000} = 1.58 \text{ ha.m. } (12.8. \text{ acft})$$

Problem 4

If 51 mm (2.07 in) of rainfall occurred the day after the 50-year storm in Problem 3 above. Calculate the expected runoff.

Given the antecedent rainfall condition as (107+40)>53 and the new curve number (71.2) (1.20) = 86 and S=41 mm.

Solution: Putting the above values in following equation for runoff volume given by S.C.S.

where

$$Q = \frac{(I - 0.2S)^2}{1 + 0.8\,S}$$

where

Q = Direct surface runoff in depth in mm

I = Storm rainfall in mm

S = Maximum potential difference between rainfall and runoff in mm starting at the time the storm begins.

Therefore, we get Q = 22 mm (0.87 in). Although rainfall was less than half that in Problem 3, the runoff was 56 per cent of the previous amount which indicates the importance of antecedent moisture.

Problem 5

To determine the minimum water yield volume from a 86 ha watershed for a driest year in 25 years span. Given minimum annual water yield for return period 25 years for 31 ha as 130 mm and for 141 ha as 178 mm.

Solution: By interpolation method half way between 130 and 178 mm (86 ha is half way between 31 ha & 141 ha) is 154 mm.

$$\left[\frac{178 + 130}{2} = \frac{308}{2} = 154\right]$$

Minimum volume = 86 × 154 × 10^{-3} = 13.25 ha.m.

Problem 6

To develop a runoff hydrograph for a design return period of 50 years for the watershed of 40.5 ha (100 ac) assuming ancedent moisture 5 days prior to the storm as 40 mm (1.6 in) of rainfall and the critical duration of the storm as 6 hours (as given in Problems 1 & 3).

Solution:

The peak runoff = 4.51 m^3/s

Flood volume = 1.58 ha.m.

Now from Eqs. $u = \frac{Q}{2620}$

$W = q/100$

$K = u/w$

and $K = \frac{u(ha - m) \times 10000\ (mr^2/ha)}{w(m^3S) \times 60\ (Sec/min)} = 167\ \frac{u}{w}$

where

Q = Total runoff volume.

w = Ratio of peak runoff for the design, runoff for the design. storm to the peak flow of 100 on the dimensionless hydrograph.

K = a factor the value of each unit of time on the dimensionless hydrograph as per design hydrograph.

u = The factor which is ratio of total runoff volume to the area under the dimensionless hydrograph.

q = Peak runoff for the design runoff.

Hence substituting value in equation with

u = 1.58/2620 = 0.0006 ha.m./unit

w = 4.51/100 = 0.0451 m^3/s. per unit

k = 167 × 0.0006/0.0451 = 2.22 min/unit.

Ordinates and abscissa of the design hydrograph are obtained by multiplying the values of q and t from figure of dimensionless and triangular flood hydrographs given by U.S. Soil Conservation Service (1972) by W and K respectively. The calculated coordinates are worked out at different points and values of Kt, Wq.

QUALITY OF RUNOFF WATER

The runoff water either from upper elevations or from cultivated fields dissolves various types and amounts of salts which are either used for irrigation at certain locations or are disposed of into rivers. The quality of these waters has a great bearing to agriculture sector as a whole as well as environment and human health. Various studies made in the country and abroad indicates that the pollutants and contaminations added to the flowing streams may have these sometimes above the tolerable quantities for human beings, mammals, and plants which erodes their health besides other environmental hazards.

Dungian and Shamsuddin (1972) reported different amount of losses at each interval of fertilization to crops which may get collected in underground waters as well as in drainage waters of the area. The losses of nitrogen ranged from 0.71 - 1.3 per cent, phosphorus 2.3 - 2.4% and potash 1.3 to 1.8%. Kolenbrander (1972) reported that the drainage waters were enriched with 0.22 kg. nitrogen per hectare per year while that of runoff 0.5 kg. phosphorus per hectare per year. The concentration of nutrients, however, was depending upon the soil texture and it was seen that about 4.5 kg. nitrogen/ha/year was lost from sandy while 5 kg. N/ha/yr from clayey soils. Carter et al. (1971) found that in return flow of Calcareous silt loam soils irrigated with river water increased down stream total soluble salts and nitrates nitrogen (NO_3-N) loads but decreased the downstreams PO_4-P. It was found that 50 per cent of total input water returned to the river as sub-surface drainage, net total soluble salts output was 25 quintals per hectare and NO_3-N was 35 kg/ha and only 30 per cent as much PO_4-P left the area in drainage waters as entered in the irrigation water. Thus from alluvial clay soil receiving 946.70 mm/year rainfall contributed soluble silica (SiO_2), organic matter suspensions, lime ($CaCO_3$), soluble cations from dissolved salts such as Magnesium, Sodium, Potassium, Chlorine, Nitrogen and Sulphur. The amount of which estimated was respectively 42.22; 24.33; 1343.91; 119.96, 572.73, 15.18, 70.30, 1267.03 and 89.85 killograms per hectare.

Matocha and Rouquette (1972) reported nitrogen, phosphorous and potash losses in runoff waters to the tune of 26 milligram per litre, 3 milligrams per litre and 18 milligrams per litre respectively.

Darra and Nagar (1985) conducted study in Chambal Commanded area of Kota (Rajasthan) and reported that the paddy runoff waters in two different soil series (Table 10.2 to 10.7) the losses occurring through runoff waters per total flushings of an acre field comes to 5 per cent of nitrogen, 22 per cent of phosphorus pentaoxide (P_2O_5) and 12 per cent of Potash (K_2O). The amount of salts added to runoff waters during each crop season were estimated to range between 50 to 150 kg/acre from two type of soils. The results of the findings are given in the following tables.

Thus the discharge of runoff waters either in irrigation canals or rivers or other water resource needs to be analysed for the different chemical and biological loads before being discharged into these resources to avoid complications.

Some Selected Examples on Erosion and Runoff

Example 1: Suppose a soil has intake rate of 0.25 inches per hour and has adequate water storage capacity and it gets a rainfall of 2 inches in 2 hours, what would be the runoff.

Now, if the rainfall occurs continuously then in 2 hrs soil can absorb only $0.25 \times 2 = 0.5$ inches of water. Hence out of total rainfall of 2 inches only 0.5 inches is absorbed which is only 25 per cent. Therefore 1.5 inches or 75 per cent of rainfall would result in runoff. But if the intake rate of the soil is 1 inch per hour then it will absorb all the rainfall and there would be no runoff.

TABLE 10.2

Morphological Description of Non-Calcareous and Calcareous Profiles in Chambal Commanded Area of Kota-Raj.

Depth Cms	Colour	Texture	Structure	Consistency (moist)	Root distibution	Drainage	Reaction with HCL.	Remarks
				Non-Calcareous Group				
Uncultivated Unirrigated (Nanta Farm Soils)								
0-17	10yr 4/4	Clayey	Angular blocky	Friable	Few thin roots	Moderately	Very mild.	...
17-70	10yr 3/3	Clayey	Angular blocky	V.Friable	Few thin roots	Moderately	Very mild.	..
70-110	-do-	Clayey	Angular blocky	Friable	Few thin roots	Moderately	Very mild.	...
Cultivated Irrigated (Nanta Farm Soils)								
0-17	10yr 3/4	Clayey	Angular Blocky	Friable	Few thin roots	Moderately good	Mild	—
17-68	10yr 3/4	Clayey	Blocky	Friable	Few thin roots	Poor	Mild	—
68-108	10yr 3/4	Clayey	Massive	Firm	No roots	Poor	Profuse	...
				Calcareous Group				
Uncultivated Unirrigated (Digod Farm Soils)								
0-11	10yr 3/2	Clay loam	Angular Blocky	Friable	Few thin roots	Moderate	Profuse	Mottings observed from 30 cm onwards
11-39	10yr 3/2	Clayey	Prismatic	Friable	Few thin roots	Moderate	Profuse	
39-58	10yr 3/2	Clayey	Prismatic	Friable	V. few thin roots	Poor	Profuse	
58-100	10yr 3/4	Clayey	Massive	Friable	V. few thin roots	Poor	Profuse	
Cultivated Irrigated (Digod Farm Soils)								
0-12	10yr 4/2	Clay Loam	Angular Blocky	Firm	Many thin roots	Moderate	Profuse	Clay films slightly visible
12-42	10yr 4/1	Clayey	Angular Blocky	Friable	Few thin roots	Moderate	Profuse	
42-63	10yr 4/1	Clayey	Angular Blocky	Friable	Few thin roots	Moderate	Profuse	
63-83	10yr 3/3	Clayey	Angular Blocky	Friable	No roots	Poor	Profuse	

Source : D.L. Sharma, B.L. Darra, G.P. Nathani and P.N. Sharma
Ind. Jr. Agri Res. 8(2) : 77-82, 1974

TABLE 10.3

Physical Make Up of Non-Calcareous Soils of Chambal Area, Kota (Rajasthan)

Depth	Sand%	Silt	Clay	$CaCO_2$	B.D.	Pore Space Total	Non-Cap.	Capilary	V.E.%	W.H.C.%	Hydraulic	O.C.
(1) *Fallow uncultivated irrigated (Nanta farm soils)*												
00-17	31.44	20.45	45.35	2.5	1.42	47.40	14.02	32.63	20.24	40.44	0.82	0.36
17-70	27.32	28.27	38.20	2.5	1.37	49.31	11.36	37.97	19.01	40.08	0.82	0.26
70-110	27.01	23.23	47.12	2.5	1.40	45.91	10.91	35.00	16.16	40.12	0.82	0.28
(2) *Cultivated irrigated (Nanta farm soils)*												
00-17	32.62	17.07	45.22	1.00	1.49	47.09	10.92	37.17	19.72	34.20	0.38	0.28
17-68	30.24	18.72	45.62	0.50	1.45	50.28	12.25	39.03	16.56	39.25	0.36	0.28
68-108	25.62	24.89	43.00	0.50	1.54	50.35	10.47	37.88	20.56	45.72	0.28	0.32

(Contd.)

Table 10.3 (*Contd.*)

Depth	Sand%	Silt	Clay	$CaCO_2$	B.D.	Pore Space Total	Non-Cap.	Capilary	V.E.%	W.H.C.%	Hydraulic	O.C.
(1) *Fallow uncultivated unirrigated (Digod farm soils)*												
00-11	30.14	23.50	42.45	12.00	1.33	54.40	8.40	46.00	18.54	43.85	0.61	0.34
11-39	24.57	20.90	40.45	12.00	1.33	56.90	12.70	43.90	19.31	42.30	0.70	0.45
39-58	25.10	21.00	40.75	13.00	1.34	56.70	12.60	44.10	21.57	41.96	0.80	0.34
58-100	25.43	16.05	45.50	13.00	1.31	60.23	...	...	20.36	40.34	0.11	0.22
(2) *Cultivated irrigated (Digod farm soils)*												
00-12	30.76	17.35	38.05	12.00	1.48	51.25	6.80	44.45	20.30	41.30	0.31	0.30
12-42	24.87	19.22	38.32	15.50	1.37	52.19	10.13	42.06	15.29	43.25	0.15	0.30
42-63	27.55	16.65	38.25	16.50	1.46	51.72	8.11	43.61	20.80	43.50	0.09	0.20
63-83	21.57	21.27	36.80	18.50	1.40	52.05	6.45	45.60	18.34	46.00	0.05	..

Source : D.L. Sharma, B.L. Darra, G.P. Nathani and P.N. Sharma, *Ind. Jr. Agri Res.* 8(2) : 77-82. 1974.

TABLE 10.4

Salt Removal in Paddy Fields at Digod and Nanta of Command Area, Kota (Raj.)

(B.L. Darra and R.P. Nagar, 1985)

Sl. No.	Location	Plot No.	Surface Soil (0.20 cm) E.C.×102(1:2) before sowing	Surface soil (0.20 cm) E.C. × 103(1:2) after harvesting	Flushed out water, EC × 103 (Average)	Salt removed by flushed out water kg/acre	Salt removed by canal water kg/acre	Salt gained by water during crop growth kg/acre	Actual salt reduction kg/acre
1.	Digod	6	0.48	0.22	0.63	358	168	185	364
2.	Soils	2A	0.58	0.47	0.43	240	168	72	144
3.		2B	0.58	0.49	0.42	235	168	67	126
1.	Nanta	2	0.28	0.22	0.36	202	168	34	84
2.	Soils	4	0.20	0.15	0.37	207	168	39	70
3.		7	0.22	0.16	0.38	213	168	45	84
4.		11	0.41	0.25	0.39	274	168	106	224

(1) Average conductivity values of canal water received at water head = 0.30 mmhos/cm.

(2) No. of flushing used in whole crop period of paddy = 8.

TABLE 10.5

Nutrients Loss From Paddy Fields Flushed Out Water in Soils of Digod & Manta of Chambal Command, Kota

(B.L. Darra and R.P. Nagar, 1985)

S. Locations No.	Plot No.	Months	No. of flushing	Nutrient contents P.P.M. (As per analysis) (Average values of total flushing)					Per cent loss of applied nutrients (AV. values)		
				HN_4-4	NO_3N	Total	P	K	N	P	K
1. Digod Soils	6	Aug.	3	0.09	2.35	2.44	1.24	1.56	1.8	3.7	3.3
		Sept.	3	0.14	4.40	4.54	0.80	2.73	3.4	2.4	6.2
		Oct.	2	0.28	1.48	1.76	0.93	1.56	0.9	1.8	2.2
		Total						6.1	7.9	11.7	
2.	2A	Aug.	3	0.09	3.78	3.87	1.07	1.56	2.8	3.1	3.3
		Sept.	3	0.41	3.28	3.69	1.75	1.56	2.7	5.2	3.3
		Oct.	2	0.41	0.31	0.49	1.09	1.95	0.2	2.1	2.7
		Total							5.7	10.4	9.3
3.	2B	Aug.	3	Traces	0.68	0.68	1.05	0.78	0.5	3.1	1.8
		Sept.	3	0.18	1.36	1.54	1.08	0.90	1.1	3.2	2.1
		Oct.	2	0.18	0.68	0.86	0.99	1.95	0.4	1.9	2.7
		Total							2.0	8.2	6.6
		Total Average						4.0	9.0	9.0	

(Contd.)

TABLE 10.5 (*Contd.*)

S. No.	Locations	Plot No.	Months	No. of flushing	Nutrient contents P.P.M. (As per analysis) (Average values of total flushing)					Per cent loss of applied nutrients (AV. values)		
					HN_4-4	NO_3N	Total	P	K	N	P	K
1.	Nanta Soils	2	Aug.	3	Tr.	3.10	3.10	0.45	1.95	2.30	1.3	3.5
			Sept.	3	0.28	1.24	1.92	2.55	1.95	1.20	7.0	3.5
			Oct.	2	0.62	0.40	1.02	0.77	0.39	0.50	1.5	0.5
										4.0	9.8	7.5
2.		4	Aug.	3	Tr.	3.47	3.47	0.93	2.18	2.6	2.7	4.8
			Sept.	3	0.25	4.51	4.76	1.24	2.90	3.4	3.7	6.6
			Oct.	2	0.11	0.49	0.60	0.93	0.39	0.3	1.8	0.5
										6.3	8.2	11.9
3.		7	Aug.	3	Tr.	1.55	1.55	1.82	2.75	1.20	5.4	4.7
			Sept.	3	0.34	2.17	2.15	2.17	1.11	1.80	6.3	3.3
			Oct.	2	0.12	0.49	0.61	5.50	0.39	0.30	11.2	0.5
										3.3	22.9	8.5
4.		11	Aug.	3	0.18	2.72	2.90	0.31	1.58	2.20	0.9	3.5
			Sept.	3	1.44	1.10	2.54	1.02	1.56	1.90	3.1	3.5
			Oct.	2	0.23	0.40	0.72	1.0	3.72	0.40	2.1	4.3
			Total							4.5	6.1	11.3
			Total Average							5.0	12.0	10.0

TABLE 10.6

Some Physical and Chemical Properties of the Digod & Nanta Soils

Sl. No.	Soils	Soil characteristics	Digod & Nanta Soils
1.	Series	Chambal Series	Kota Series
2.	Classification	Typic, pellustert, mixed, Hyper-thermic	Hyper-thermic mixed, hyper-thermic family
3.	Colour	Dark Grey	Grey
4.	Texture	Clay to clay loam predomination clay minal montmorilloonits followed by illite & Kaolinite	Clay to clay loam predominating clay mineral is montmonite followed by illite & kaolinite
5.	Calcium Carbonate %	Calcareous, on surface, it is 3 to 15% while in deeper layers it is 10 to 35%.	Non-calcareous 1 to 3% upto 150 cms depth.
6.	Organic Carbon	0..2 to 0.62%	0.3 to 0.60%.
7.	Bulk density	1.45 to 1.64 gm/cm^3	1.40 to 1.60 gm/cm^3
8.	Infiltration rate	0.2 to 0.62 cm/hr	0.12 to 0.50 cm/hr
9.	[H (1:2 soil water ratio)	8.2 to 8.3	7.8 to 8.3
10.	E.C. × 10^3 (1:2 ratio)	0.84 to 1.780 mmhos	0.20 tto 0.40 mmhos
11.	Cation Exchange	29 to 33 meq/100 gms	30 to 35 meq/100 gms
12.	Exchangeable	20 to 22 sodium percentage	4.5 to 10.8
13.	Available soil Nitrogen	100 – 150 kg./ha.	100 – 170 kg/ha.
14.	Available soil Phosphorous	18 – 50 kg./ha.	30 – 40 kg./ha.
15.	Available soil Potash	36 – 89 kg./ha	100 – 200 kg./ha.

Source: Darra B.L. and Nagar R.P.(1985): Quality of Surface Runoff Waters from Paddy Fields in Chambal Commanded Area, Kota (Rajasthan). Published in Journal of *Indian Water Resources Society*, Vol. 5, October, 1985.

TABLE 10.7

Quality of Flushed Out Waters, During Paddy Cultivation

(B.L. Darra and R.P. Nagar, 1985)

Location	Plot Nos.	Time	pH	EC × 10^3	CO_3	Anions (Meq/l) HCO_3	SO_4	Cl	Cations (Meq/l) Ca^{++}	Mg^+	$+Na^+$	K^+	S.A.R	S.S.P	R.S.C.	Class	Average E.C. mmhos/Cm
Digod Farm	6	Aug. 72	8.25	0.55	0.40	4.75	0.70	1.70	1.82	0.06	2.89	0.043	2.6	53.3	2.68	C2S1	0.63
		Sept. 72	8.27	0.79	0.62	3.99	0.70	1.92	2.68	1.13	4.50	0.072	3.4	53.6	0.80	C3S1	
		Oct. 72	8.25	0.59	0.69	3.92	1.10	1.92	2.48	1.03	3.26	0.045	2.5	47.8	1.10	C2S1	
	2 A	Aug. 72	8.80	0.32	0.60	2.30	0.30	1.00	1.50	0.77	1.74	0.025	1.74	43.1	0.63	C2S1	0.43
		Sept. 72	8.33	0.44	0.47	2.56	0.66	0.81	2.43	0.90	1.95	0.023	1.50	36.7	Nil	C2S1	
		Oct. 72	8.30	0.51	0.60	4.00	0.56	0.89	2.40	1.10	2.95	0.050	2.2	45.2	1.10	C2S1	
	2B	Aug. 72	7.50	0.34	0.40	1.90	2.10	0.70	1.66	0.89	3.46	0.04	3.1	57.1	Nil	C2S1	0.41
		Sept. 72	8.30	0.35	0.45	2.09	1.45	0.26	1.40	0.20	2.34	0.06	2.6	58.7	0.90	C2S1	
		Oct. 72	8.30	0.50	0.64	3.28	1.65	0.60	1.90	0.50	5.13	0.05	4.6	67.6	2.52	C2S1	

(Contd.)

TABLE 10.7 (*Contd.*)

Location	Plot Nos.	Time	pH	EC × 10^3	CO_3	Anions (Meq/l) HCO_3	SO_4	Cl	Cations (Meq/l) Ca^{++}	Mg+	$+Na^+$	K^+	S.A.R	S.S.P	R.S.C.	Class	Average E.C. mmhos/Cm
Nanta	2	Aug. 72	7.60	0.32	0.56	0.52	0.50	2.38	2.00	0.50	0.69	0.056	0.6	18.4	...	C2S1	0.36
Farm		Sept. 72	8.32	0.37	0.46	1.96	0.32	1.10	1.56	0.92	1.52	0.056	1.4	37.5	...	C2S1	
		Oct. 72	8.05	0.39	1.30	2.03	0.30	0.40	2.02	0.80	1.52	0.100	1.1	34.7	0.49	C2S1	
	4	Aug. 72	7.50	0.30	0.96	1.12	0.60	0.80	1.85	0.92	0.83	0.31	0.6	21.2	...	C2S1	0.37
		Sept. 72	8.25	0.46	0.30	2.64	0.44	0.98	2.11	0.70	2.08	0.05	1.6	42.1	0.13	C2S1	
		Oct. 72	8.10	0.29	0.68	2.03	0.24	0.36	1.45	0.35	1.22	0.05	1.3	39.7	0.91	C2S1	
	7	Aug. 72	8.50	0.56	1.20	4.90	0.30	1.20	1.70	1.80	3.42	0.14	2.0	48.4	2.60	C2S1	0.38
		Sept. 72	8.06	0.31	0.40	1.86	0.30	0.83	1.95	0.40	0.76	0.09	0.7	23.7	...	C2S1	
		Oct. 72	8.15	0.28	0.92	1.62	0.22	0.30	1.10	0.45	1.10	0.06	1.0	40.5	...	C2S1	
	11	Aug. 72	7.85	0.44	...	4.74	0.40	0.84	2.10	1.10	0.85	0.04	0.6	16.6	0.54	C2S1	0.49
		Sept. 72	8.07	0.55	0.30	4.20	0.30	0.80	2.30	0.60	3.30	0.087	2.7	52.5	1.60	C2S1	
		Oct. 72	8.15	0.48	...	4.60	0.20	0.44	2.63	0.81	2.58	0.061	2.3	42.4	1.16	C2S1	

Example 2: A soil that can hold 2 inches of available water per foot at field capacity will require how much rain to wet the soil to a depth of 3 inch.

Solution: It will require 1/2 inch of rain to wet soil and any high proportion or less would be lost by evaporation during the growing season in case the surface soil is dry to the wilting point at the time of rain.

Selected Examples on Soil Losses

Example 1: Calculate the soil losses from the contoured field if soil erodibility factor (K) = 0.1 t/a, slope length (l)= 122 metre (400 ft), field slope (s) = 10 per cent, cropping management factor (c) = 0.18 and the rainfall erosion index (R) = 310 (figure), LS = 2.7 Pc = 0.6.

Solution: The soil loss is given by equation and on substitution of values.

$$A = 2.24 \times R \times K \times LS \times C \times P$$

$$= 2.24 \times 310 \times 0.1 \times 2.7 \times 0.18 \times 0.6 = 20.2 \text{ mg/ha } (9.0\text{t/a})$$

Example 2: In case the soil loss tolerance for the conditions given in Example 1 is 3.0 (t/a) suggest practices to reduce the said soil loss.

Solution: As we have discussed only C&P are the practices that could be changed the following chart we may obtain by substituting appropriate factors in equation of soil loss given in Example 1.

(1) If P = 0.3, C=0.18: Hence soil loss = 4.5 t/a under strip cropping. This indicates very high rate of soil loss. Hence conservation practice needs to be changed as it is not adequate.

(2) If P = 0.3; C = 0.12 for terracing practice: Hence soil loss = 3.0 t/a under strip cropping. This much soil loss is satisfactory but still needs care by reducing crop management factor class than 0.12.

(3) If P = 0.12; C = .18: Hence soil loss = 0.7 t/a under terracing. It indicates quite less soil losses than permissible t/a from field or that from the terrace channel with up slope ploughing. It shows that by terracing practice.

(4) If P= 0.12, C = 0.18 under terracing: Hence soil loss = 3.0 t/a. This shows that for allowable soil loss from field *i.e.* 3 t/a the factor 'C' may even be increased upto 0.81.

(5) If P = 0.60, C = 0.16 under terracing: Hence soil loss = 3.0 t/a. It indicates Pc for soil loss to terrace channel.

(6) If P = 0.30, C = 0.32 max. under terracing: Hence soil loss = 3.0 t/a. It shows Pc for farm planning. As regards practices giving values of pounder 5 & 6, it may be said that with assumption of terrace slope length of 60 feet, the L.S. values may be reduced to 1.0. As such if it is decided to maintain soil loss upto 3 t/a or less, 'C' factor under condition 5 should be maintained.

Example 3: Suggest crop management practices if the soil conservation practice selected or recommended for any area is strip cropping.

Solution: As seen in Example 2, the maximum allowable soil loss is 3 t/a and under strip cropping this could be achieved by fixing value of C to 0.12 max. Let us assume a maize-barley oats-pasture cropping sequence or rotation.

The calculation can be made if the per cent of annual erosion are taken from a standard curve having relationship between monthly distribution rainfall and runoff erosivity index for different locations and part of the country. In this case use of data provided by Schwab et al. (1981) has been made. Similarly the data of Smith and Wischmeier (1960 & 1962) has been used to calculate ratio of soil loss from crops to corresponding loss from continuous fallow lands.

Using the yield values for maize, small grain with meadow and alone meadow (pasture land) for different growth periods or months and monthly rainfall data relationships to soil loss, we get the value of 'C' factor under different rotations as given in Table 10.8.

TABLE 10.8

Crop	Month	Soil loss in per cent of continuous fallow	Per cent of annual erosion	Col. 3 × 4 values of C factor
Maize Ist year (Hybrid) (twice a year)	Jan.-May	15	43	0.065
	June	30	13	0.039
	July	27	10	0.027
	Aug.-Sept.	15	22	0.033
	Oct.-Dec.	22	12	0.026
Oats (small grain) with meadow seeding	Jan.-Feb.	22	13	0.029
	March	30	9	
	April	18	10	
	May-Oct.	3	63	
	Nov.-Dec.	0.4	5	
Meadow	Jan.-Oct.	0.4	95	
	Nov.-Dec.	22	5	

Since C value 0.100 < 0.12 solutions, is satisfactory/Average 'C' for 3 years = 0.298/3 = 0.099. The different combinations of crops and management practice can also be selected. If the various terraces as given in Example 2 are chosen continuous maize crop can be grown keeping value of factor 'C' above 0.81. Also besides soil loses the cost of terracing should be considered.

CHAPTER 11

WATER USE EFFICIENCY IN CROP PRODUCTION

The rapid expansion and increase in world population has resulted in industrialisation and commercialisation of agriculture which has necessitated the increased demand for water. To meet the fresh water requirements of various sectors the water resources are to be tapped at one hand and the control or restraint has to be practised in water use. The latter is termed as water use efficiency. Rao (1975) and Darra et al. (1971) have warned that the water quality of the main streams of resources is being constantly polluted through different effluenting materials drained from industrial, farm and agricultural inputs. The increase in salinity and nitrates are one of the important pollutants. Consequently the quantity of water for irrigation is being curtailed which may result in less food and fibre production. There would also be a problem ahead if the deterioration of the water quality is not checked in near future.

It has been reported (Singh and Sinha, 1977), that about 65 cm of ground water is used to irrigate one ha. of land. The corresponding value in case of surface water is 90 cm because of higher conveyance losses and being relatively cheaper, it is also used with less care. The two together give an average of about 80 cm per ha. Nag and Kathpalia (1975) reported that on the basis of water resources available in India when fully utilized would suffice only for irrigating about 96 million ha. The various findings have been shown that the available water supply on most of the canal system in India is not adequate to meet the requirements of intensive agriculture.

Recently there was a hot discussion throughout the world whether the quantity of irrigation water being used for different crops is really sufficient or high. It is being probably agreed that there is luxurious and wasteful consumption of water by the all categories of farmers in the world (Nag and Kathpalia, 1975, Hagan et al. 1973, Jensen, 1972). It has been found that the actual consumption of irrigation is even sometimes double than the net irrigation requirements of a crop to irrigate that up to the rootzone depth. Also the quantity of irrigation water being applied is generally not according to soil irrigability class as well as physical and chemical properties of the area soils. This has resulted in havoc through considerable increase in water table, salinization and sodicization and constant decrease in the yield production of a particular crop variety. This larger gap in yield reduction has been partially recovered through high yielding strains of various crops being released. However, it would not be a final solution to overcome the problem.

This, therefore, warrants the efficient use of our water resources without affecting crop production to sustain an increasing human population and ensure their survival and standard.

IRRIGATION EFFICIENCY

The general concept of efficiency means higher output obtainable from the same system given input through effective management only. In irrigated agriculture it means that from the same available water resources more or higher crop production. Efficient utilization of water resource may be defined and evaluated through following approaches:

(i) Engineering and planning approach which is mainly concerned with the evaluation of the hydraulic performances at different levels in any irrigation project.

(ii) The detailed study of soils through soil survey approach and impact of soil irrigability classes and then physical and chemical characteristics on the engineering planning, hydraulic performances and agronomic aspects in relation to irrigation and drainage.

(iii) The agro-economic approach based on selection of crops and their yields in relation to water used.

The efficiency index may be defined in two ways: (i) it is the net amount of water allowed to saturate the rootzone, and (ii) it is the amount of water consumed through evapotranspiration by a crop as a fraction of the water being supplied through some source.

These efficiency indices indicate the different ways of water losses either during conveyance or application or both. It would be dependent upon the particular system which could be entire irrigation project or its part or an individual farm or a field.

In view of economist the irrigation efficiency of any system is the net financial return per unit of water used or the amount of finances invested on that system. This is found out from interim rate of return (IRR) or benefit, cost ratio (B:C ratio) during the phase of planning and estimation. However, the same has been found to vary considerably according to the economic conditions prevailing in time at a specific period. Clark (1970), suggested to have economic calculations based on the ratio of additional crop produced from further watering to the number of cubic metres of additional water used. From these the production functions are correlated with the marginal products.

The real water use efficiency may be determined under the field conditions where the assumptions made at the time of project planning and execution may come out to be satisfactory or poor which reflects the success or failure of any administered system.

This evaluation may be worked out by following ways:

1. Total area covered under irrigation and match it with the earlier planning.
2. Cropping intensities after inception of irrigation.
3. Estimated production and actual production.
4. Water application with minimum wastage by avoiding unnecessary runoff and evaporation losses.
5. Crop and soil aspects of water use.

The water use efficiency is mainly described as the water used by crops under particular soil type/series and agro-climatic conditions (Viets, 1962, 1966).

Water Use Efficiency

This term has been described in two ways, namely:

1. Crop Water Use Efficiency or Consumptive Use Efficiency (Ecu): It is defined as the ratio of crop yield (Y) to the sum of the amount of water taken up and used by the crop in growth (G), transpired through foliage (T) and evaporated directly from the soil surface (ES) or consumptive use (Cu).

$$E\,cu = Y/(G + T + Es) = Y/Cu \quad \text{........(1)}$$

2. Field Water Use Efficiency (Eu): It is also a ratio of crop yield (Y) to the amount of water used under the particular set of field conditions (WR), for example growth (G), transpiration (T), soil surface evaporation (Es) and heavy percolation losses:

$$(D)\ Eu = Y/(G + T + Es + D) = Y/WR \quad \text{........(2)}$$

The above described two indices are being widely used. However, the former is of academic interest while the later is of much practical use for planners as well as applied field research work and irrigationist including farmers.

The various workers have worked out these indices for better planning as well for use of water. Pande et al. (1970) used these indices only based on total dry matter production without considering soil moisture balance in the rootzone of crops in a particular type of soil. In latter years more work was carried out in this direction for various crops under different agro-climatic conditions (Berg et al. 1973, Hagan et al. 1973, Shmueli, 1971, 1973). It was concluded that since every soil has a different moisture retention capacity or in other words different available water per cent (AWP) which is a difference of moisture held at field capacity (F.C.) minus moisture held at permanent wilting point (PWP), the same crop if grown on such soils, the crops would derive different amounts of moisture to meet their requirements. It may also be remembered that since the rate of evaporation from the soil surface is different in case of different type of soils, the evapotranspiration or nett water requirement of the particular crop always varies from soil to soil. Conversely the nett water requirement of the different crops would be different on the same type of soil under similar agro-climatic or micro-climatic conditions for maximum production under specific conditions of growth and practices adopted. The term "optimum water requirement" was introduced by Hagan et al. (1973) which was defined as the seasonal amounts (depth) of water required by crops that would result in maximum production. Water requirement of crops is a sum total of soil moisture contributed through natural precipitation (rains), by ground water in way of capillary fringes, if within the vicinity of rootzone and by any water resource created for irrigation. The maximum value of the ratio of crop production to the seasonal depth of irrigation water applied to a particular crop under a particular set of agro-climatic or under any fixed controlled conditions has been designated as "optimum irrigation efficiency" by Shmueli (1973). This indice, however, should be used only under irrigated conditions.

In terms of economic terminology the concept of water use efficiency or optimum irrigation efficiency, means the economically viable or optimum profits which may be obtained optimum use of water for optimum crop production.

However, this economical approach has certain limitation as outlined by many workers (Beringer, 1961, Clark, 1970, Clawson and Landsberg, 1972, Stewart and Hagan, 1973, etc.)

As narrated above the water use efficiency is a ratio of crop production to the depth of water table. Both the values are affected by various constraints. The production constraints are seed and plant diseases, insect and pest attack and climatic hazards, the availability of water amount in catchment for supply of irrigation at the normal and critical stages of growth. Thus if constraints are more the water use efficiency would decrease. However, if the incidence of constraints is minimum the water use efficiency would be high. In other words if through research the genetic and environmental conditions can be adjusted or manipulated to suit crop requirement, the water use efficiency can be increased.

CONSTRAINTS INFLUENCING WATER USE EFFICIENCY

There are various factors infuencing water use efficiency which are enumerated below:

Environmental

The various environmental conditions such as climate and air pollution greatly influences the water use efficiency. The former is utmost important since it governs the water supply both in way of natural precipitation and the irrigation supply through created water reserves. The latter factor, however, governs the condition of climatic factors and has become very substantial in recent years.

The prefix or numerator of ratio that is production since it is bound to be affected by water supply *i.e.* suffix or Denominator of the ratio, the water use efficiency would vary accordingly (Dastane, 1972). Thus atmospheric temperature, day length, rainfall, relative humidity and their interactions would vitally affect the physiological and metabolic activities of the plant including rate of photo synthesis which is a function of solar radiation, also interacts with the said factors and influences the potential as well as maximum yield.

Among the factors enumerated above, the relative humidity is inversibally proportional to water use efficiency. Thus conditions of low relative humidity means high evapotranspiration without corresponding higher yields. The factors such as sun light and temperature depending on their intensity may either increase or decrease water use efficiency due to their relationship with rate of photosynthesis *i.e.* dry matter production and evapotranspiration. Krishnamurthy et al. (1973), found higher grain yields of maize under monsoon than in summer which may be on account of more leaf area index (LAI) and larger leaf area duration (LAD) in the former season. The man has been so far not very successful in controlling and modifying the climatic or weather conditions, therefore, the only way left is to manage, amend and adopt other factors of crop production to achieve higher water use efficiency.

Genetic Factors

Type of Crops: The genetic constitutions and the environmental conditions in which the plant grows and the interaction of these influence the growth and development of a particular crop species. This is the reason as to why the different plant species have great difference in the growth habits as well as different capacities of dry matter production off water requirements (Hsiao, 1973, Hsiao and Acevedo, 1974). This explains as to why the unit weight of dry matter of different crops is produced through different amounts of water for different crops. This fact may be obvious from Table 11.1

TABLE 11.1

Categorisation of Crops in Terms of Water Use Efficiency (Singh and Sinha, 1977)

Crop	Class of water use efficiency
Millets	
(Maize, Sorghum, Pearl Millet,	High
Sugarcane /Ragi) Cereals	
(Wheat, Barley, Oats)	Medium
Leguminous Pulses	
(Moong, Arhar, Soyabean, Peas)	Poor

The following new categorisation or ratings have been suggested for higher plants including crop plants:

(1) C3 plants

(2) C4 plants and

(3) CAM plants.

This classification depends essentially on the mode of primary carboxylation reaction during the process of photosynthesis. These rating characteristics are now being correlated with water use efficiency. It has been concluded that C3 plants indicated low rates of photosynthesis as well as low values of water use efficiency. This crop category grow favourably in an optimal range, of 20-25°C. The higher plants C4 in comparison to C3 indicate higher rate of photosynthesis as well as higher water use efficiency. Their optimal growth occurs in the temperature range of 35-40°C. The plants such as pulses, oilseeds and cereals like wheat, barley and oats fall under C3 category of plants. In C4 plant category, the crops like maize, sorghum and millets, amaranthus and sugarcane have been classified. In CAM *i.e.* crassulacear acid metabolism are also the plants falling under high plant group. These have normally succulent nature and unique pathways and are generally found in desert areas. The water requirement of these plants is much less due to their very low growth rate. The pineapple is a characteristic plant of CAM category. The characteristics of these plants are shown in Table 11.2. It may thus be concluded that C3 and C4 plants are only agriculturally important crops. The water use efficiency of these crops is given in Table 11.3.

The results of water use efficiency under the influence of temperature in C3 and C4 plant species are recorded by Downes (1969) which are given in table 11.4.

Slatyr (1971) conducted study on two species of Atriplex which belong to C4 and C3 plants and concluded that former crop class exhibited higher water use efficiency. Similar findings were reported by Bjorkman (1971). A study concluded by Teare et al. (1973) on water use efficiency of soyabean (C3 plant) and in sorghum (C4 plant) confirmed the sorghum had higher water use efficiency throughout the growth period as compared to soyabean crop.

Crop Species

The genetic constitution is responsible for major variations in yield amongst all crop varieties. The specific built up is also reflected in morphological and anatomical characteristics which control transpiration and water absorption rates by roots from the particular soil profile type. The rate of photosynthesis, respiration, translocation storage of photosynthates are also correspondingly different due to different physiological functions occurring in plant body of varying crop varieties. The different crops also exhibit different adaptation characteristics under different agro-climatic conditions, soil groups occurrence of disease and pest and agronomic practices.

The physiological analysis of yield difference based on varietal difference was suggested by Boonstra (1929, 1931). Such type of study was also conducted by Asana (1966, 1975), on effect of water stress and

TABLE 11.2
Carbondioxide Fixation of Primary Type
(Singh and Sinha, 1977)

	Characteristics	Plant type C3	Plant type C4
1.	Maximum rate of net photo-synthesis mg CO_2/dm²/hr	15-40	40-80
2.	Drymatter production tons/ha/yr	22.0 ± 3.3	38.6 ± 1.7
3.	Optimum day temperature	15-25°C	30-47°C
4.	CO_2 compensation, p p,m CO_2	30-70	0-10
5.	Response to light intensity	Saturation 1/4 to 1/3 full sun-light	Propor-tional or tending to saturate at full sun-light
6.	Photo respiration	Present	Difficult to detect
7.	Maximum growth rate gram dry matter/dm² leaf area/day	0.5-2.0	4.0-5.0
8.	g/m² of land area/day	19.5 ± 3.9	30.3± 13.8
9.	Sensitivity to oxygen from 1% to 2%	Yes	No
10.	Major carboxylating sequence	RuDP carboxylase	PEP carbo-xylase then, Ru DP carboxylase
11.	Energy requirement (CO_2: ATP:NADPH)	1:3:2	1:5:2
12.	Water use efficiency	Low	High

TABLE 11.3
Water use efficiency in C3 and C4 plants
(Downes, 1969)

Crop group	Water use efficiency (mg drywt/ g water)	
	C4	C3
Dicotyledenous	3.44	1.59
Monocotyledenous	3.14	1.49

TABLE 11.4
The effect of temperature on water use efficiency in C3 and C4 grass species
(Downes, 1969)

Temperature	A.V. water use efficiency* (mg dry out per gm water)		
	Class		
	C4	C3	C4/C3 ratio
20	4.0	2.4	1.7
25	3.1	1.7	1.8
30	3.6	1.1	3.3
35	2.3	0.2	11.5

* *Source*: *Water Requirement and Irrigation Management of Crops in India,* 1977.

temperature on yield of wheat. These studies paved a way for plant breedness for evolving large number of improved high yielding varieties and hybrid which created a new era of grain production in the world. Similarly the crop strains of short duration, smaller water requirement have been worked out which not only save the scarce commodity water but also permits to increase irrigated area as well as reduce increase in water table and salt accumulation problem in irrigated commands.

The green revolution of India may be attributed to introduction of screened dwarf high yielding and hybrid strains of various prevailing crops in the country based on their adaptation and other physiological basis. Singh et al. (1970) concluded that tall growing varieties of wheat although had same consumptive use of water under similar waterings as compared to dwarf varieties but latter had higher water use efficiency in terms of grain yield. Also these were more responsible to higher use of inorganic fertilizers. The different varieties of a same crop may also have different degree of resistance to water stress and water use efficiency (Reitz, 1974, Ferguson et al., 1972, 1973, 1974) due to different morphological characteristics which might be responsible for variability in sensible heat transfer.

Trenbath and Angus (1975) emphasised to utilise isogenic lines of crops with electrophilic leaf character over the planophillic. According to Rackle (1960) Crop canopy intercepts wide spectrum of insolation, both visible and thermal and this along with transpiration and other components of energy balance determines the leaf temperature. Miller (1972) through a complex simulation model explained the interactions between leaf angle, leaf temperature, canopy synthesis and transpiration of red mangrove. It was concluded that under certain environmental conditions higher leaf inclinations (from horizontal) would have lower maximum and higher minimum leaf temperature during day and night respectively. It was found that when the leaf area index was high the expected leaf temperature difference between prostrate leaved canopy and erect leaved canopy was about 11°C higher in the former one. In electrophillic canopy the daily canopy synthesis has been assumed to be high considering the influence of temperature on respiration while that of transpiration on leaf water potential as evidenced by his experimental results. However, Sinclair (1971) reported that in electrophillic canopy the temperature of the leaf would be high in mid-day.

The water stress has been exhibited more by prostrate leaves than those leave hold upright in the same plant. Similarly isolines of horizontal leaves of soyabean showed less resistance than its electrophile isolines which might be due to more loss of water in early part of day (Stevenson and Shaw, 1971).

Miller (1972), however, did not consider the water loss from beneath the canopy. It was found by Danmead (1973), that greater evaporation occurs from wet soil surface when there are steeply inclined leaves of the canopies. Donald (1962), however, reported that in case of above conditions, when the soil dries out it forms a dry mulch or crust which diminish the rate of evaporation. These discussions led to believe that soil-water plant atmosphere system is complex one and needs to be attempted from many angles to predict water use efficiency of plant system.

SOIL AND AGRONOMIC ASPECTS OF CROP MANAGEMENT

The crop growth and development has to be linked up with particular and larger per centage based on soil and survey, soil mapping unity rather than alone surface texture of soil being hitherto conducted. It alone is not responsible to share the overall effects on the life cycle of crop husbandry. In fact right from the tillage operations to the harvest of a crop, the reference of a mapping unit should be indicated to fully understand the effect of the soils on the growth and development of crops particularly when water use efficiency is referred. It is a must.

The climatic conditions in any area decides the optimum time of sowing of the crops to ensure the optimum utilisation of soil moisture. This also creates favourable conditions of the optimum crop growth by maintaining the physical conditions of the soils at appropriate soil and atmospheric temperatures. The time and method of sowing, pattern of crops etc. is to utilize the maximum advantage from solar energy by a crop by maintaining optimum crop canopy which may avoid shading effect. It is judged by leaf area index (Av. 4-6 for most of crops). The incidence of occurrence of plant diseases and attack of insects and pests have a positive relationship with time of sowing. This is due to fast competition between growing crops and field weeds of a particular season. The delayed sowing of Jowar was exposed to more and severe attack of insects, pests and diseases resulting in poor yields (Singh et al. 1975, Bhum, 1972, AICMIP, 1968). According to Howard (1924) the germination, growth and harvesting of wheat is affected by the soil temperature of seed bed. The various growth stages and total growth period in fact depends upon soil temperature which in turn depends upon atmospheric conditions. The time of sowing is no doubt a function of soil temperature and atmospheric conditions but it also depends the genetic character of a seed of any crop. This is evident from the fact that tall wheat varieties have to be sown in October but the dwarf ones needs more cool temperatures and hence are sown in November to 15th December for optimum crop growth and yields. Long duration and tall varieties on account of lodging characteristics many times result in poor yields thus decreasing water use efficiency (Wright, 1968, Pande et al., 1974, Sandhu et al., 1975, Sewaram et al., 1973 and Sumbali and Sharma, 1974).

The emergence force exerted by the growing seedling differs from crop to crp and their varieties (Jensen et al., 1972). This force depends upon the optimum depth of sowing for a particular crop. The shallow depth hampers the proper seed germination on account of deficit moisture while under deeper depth the seed if strong either takes more time to emerge or does not succeed to come up on the surface at all. This results in poor germination which affects overall crops yields. Thus if the seed is sown below 5 cms in Kharif it is usually rot and fails to germinate. It was found experimentally by Singh et al., (1971), that in case of soyabean when depth of seeds was more than 5 cm and the available soil moisture was at 60 there was a considerable decline in germination. The similar results have been observed by many workers on different type of soils and under different agro-climatic conditions for different crops showing that for optimum seed germination the seed has to be placed on the optimum soil depth (Taylor and McCall, 1936, Singh and Dastane, 1971, Peifferetal, 1972, AICWIP).

The water use efficiency or dry matter productivity is also indirectly affected by plant population and orientation due to interception and utilization of incident solar energy. The crop yields and water use efficiency under water stressed conditions are also effected by row spacing and canopy coverage (Singh & Sinha, 1977) and the direction of sowing in north-south direction provided more yields than it sown in east-west direction (Dungan et al., 1955) (Shekhawat et al., 1966, Pendleton and Dungan, 1958, and Singh, 1964). It has been reported by Gates and Harks 1967), that with 50% or more crop cover the evaporation is more or less equal to that of full cover under sufficient moisture regime.

ANTI-EVAPOTRANSPIRATIONAL TECHNIQUES

The absorption of water by plant roots to the stem and leaves meets the water requirements of a crop *i.e.* evapotranspiration. This may be minimized to some extent by the use of anti-transpirants, growth retardents, mulches and wind breaks. This may result in the increased crop production and water use efficiency.

Taylor and Ashcroft (1972) in the soil-water-plant atmosphere system the steepest potential gradient exists between water vapour in the stomatal cavity and the outside atmosphere. The chemical which can enhance stomatal resistance to the diffusion of water vapour or in other words vapour pressure gradient would act as an anti-transpirant substance. Many chemicals such as phenylmercuric acetate, alkenyl succinic acid and abscisic acid when applied in micro-milli or micro-molar concentration have been reported to inhibit stomatal openings which causes decreased transpiration activity. However, these chemicals also decreased photosynthesis activity because it occurs through stomatal pores by diffusion of water and carbondioxide.

Certain fatty alcohols and waxy or plastic emulsions which when applied produces thin films on canopy, also acts as anti-transpirant by producing external physical barrier, increases the resistance to water vapour diffusion. However, the effect depends upon the nature of the film formed. The substances like natural rubber, polyethelyne, cellulose acetate, polyvinyl chloride and cellophane have been tried but their overall effect was to increase resistance to CO_2 diffusion in comparison to water vapour causing more reduction in photosynthesis than transpiration (Waggoner, 1966). The waxy and plastic emulsions also were found to behave similarly (Prashar, 1967).

It was reported by Fisher and Lyon (1972) and Albrigo (1972), that if foliage is not properly covered with anti-transpirants the transpiration values were found to be higher than unsprayed plants. This was explained to be due to overtime opening of stomata because covered leaves remains turgid for more time (Brouwer, 1961). It was argued by Davenport and Hagan (1975) that in deciding the overall impact of anti-transpirant materials on water use efficiency is a function of stress to which plants are subjected under controlled untreated conditions. According to them the film producing substances provides reliable results when the crop is growing under natural moisture available conditions so that chances of leaf water deficit due to excessive soil drying and/or high evaporation or poor sunlight conditions does not exist. The effectiveness of these film producing materials, however, decreases as per variations in environment, nature of crop, new growth in same plant and depth of rooting. Many other substances have been tried for the reduction of transpiration. These are silicon and white materials like hydrated lime, chalk, kaolin. Ray (1968), reported that above mentioned white substances reduced transpiration on account of their more capacity to reflect incident solar energy resulted in decreased water offtake leaf temperature and vapour pressure gradient from stomatal pores. Patil (1974), concluded that the anti-transpirants which closed stomatas increased the leaf temperature through reduction of evaporative cooling. However, it is not of much significance. According to Poljackoff Mayber and Gale (1972), up to the 40% reduction in transpiration could result in about 3°C rise in leaf temperature which is not detrimental to plant.

It was reported by Ray (1969), that if the leaves of bean, citrus and wheat are white-washed if the photosynthesis and crop yield were not affected and at the same time, the water use efficiency increased by 30 to 78% respectively. The decreased rate of transpiration was attributed to increased leaf albedo and correspondingly decrease in leaf temperatures.

Similar results were recorded by Reddy and Shah (1973) by spray of 2% Raoli solution on wheat, decrease in transpiration rate was from 11 to 21 per cent under wetting and drying in moisture cycles of 25 days. It was reported by Paul (1974) that the spraying of chemical phenyl mercuric acitate (PMA), kaolin and tob leaf (a wax emulsion of Mobil Oil Co. of USA) on rapeseed (Brassica Compestris var. Brown Sarson) leaves caused increase in seed yield and water use efficiency (in respect of dry matter and seed production). The results are presented in Table 11.5.

TABLE 11.5

Water Use Efficiency as Effected by Anti-Tanspirants (Patil, 1974) On Grape Seed Crop

S. No.	Treatment	Water use efficiency (Kg/ha.cm water used)			
		1973-74		1973-74	
		Grain	Total dry matter	Grain	Total dry matter
1.	Control (Water spray)	6.6	22.0	16.8	55.8
2.	PMA one spray at 50 day @1 × 10^4M	7.4	23.8	18.1	60.6
3.	PMA 50 and 70 days @ 1 × 10^{-4}M	7.8	24.6	20.4	67.0
4.	Kaolin @ 6% suspension in water*	7.8	25.3	18.9	64.7
5.	Mobi leaf @ 1:10 (V:V) commercial was suspension	8.5	25.8	20.5	72.3

*0.2 per cent emulsion of teepol was used in Kaolin suspension as spreader sticker.

It was suggested by Davenport and Hagan (1975), that in areas where water is scarce and costly the use of anti-transpirants on watershed and riparian vegetation increased water yield. However, in areas where ground water is salty and brackish and these waters are to be used for irrigation, the spray of anti-transpirants on crop leaves would result in less quantity of these waters by crops and also avoid salt burning effect on leaves. The use of these chemicals may also increase water use efficiency in perennial and horticultural crops by reducing the frequency and number of irrigations.

The application of anti-transpirants on transplanted crops at the time of transplanting have been found to decrease water loss and check setback to seedlings due to transplanting particularly when roots are unable to absorb moisture from the soil. Singh and Sinha (1977), however, are of the opinion that the beneficial effects of anti-transpirants on annual field crops which are dependent on current photosynthesis for their growth and yield is less unless the crop is subjected to high moisture stress and/or high evaporation rate during the moisture sensitives critical stage of growth.

Effect of Growth Retardents and Hormones

The decrease in vegetative growth along with increase in yield is bound to increase water use efficiency. This effect has been induced in plants by the use of specific concentrations of same organic chemicals called growth retardents such as cycocel (2-chloroethyl trimethyl ammonium chloride or CCC) and 2, 4 dichlorobenzyl-tributyly phosphorium (phosphon). They maintain leaves turgidity for comparatively more time under moisture stress conditions either by missing irrigation or otherwise and decrease chances of lodging and more production of dry weight in cereal crops responsible for decreased water use efficiency. Halevy and Kessler (1963) proved above conditions in case of bean crop. Livne and Vaadia (1972) put forward the hypothesis that the effects of growth retardents might be due to the interference of these chemicals in bio-synthesis and reduced level of gibberellic acid that reduced stomatal opening and lowered transpiration. The findings of Plaut et al. (1964), however, showed that there was no decrease in rate of transpiration per unit treated leaf area by these chemicals.

The beneficial effects of CCC in respect of increase yields of various crops have also been recorded by Pinthus and Rudich (1967), Humphries (1968), Papadakis (1972); Lowe and Carter (1970), Srivastava et al. (1968), Srivastava and Bansal (1975), Gill et al. (1973), Singh and Sinha (1970), Hunsigi and Hummikeri (1973), Cheema et al. (1975), N.K. Jain (19....).

The use of growth hormones like Indole acetic (IAA), Gibberellic acid (GA), Indolebutyric acid and NAA also have been found to increase the leaf roots area and dry matter and grains yield of maize and wheat if used at specific concentrations by increased utilization of water underfield conditions in vertisols (Darra et al.). However, the use of only optimum concentration provided significantly beneficial results.

The Tables 11.6 to 11.9 indicate the affect of various hormones used at various concentrations on the various biometric parameters of hybrid Maize (Gauge 3) and Wheat.

The various hormones discussed above induce high root growth in plants at all depths deep and prolific root system developed due to hormonal treatment results in more water absorption from the soil during normal and moisture stress conditions to plants do not wilt for a longer period than otherwise. This results in more dry matter production and high water use efficiency. (Hams, 1967, Singh & Singh, 1970).

According to Armon (1975), however, the beneficial effect may be attributed to reduction of respiration rate of treated plants.

Effect of Mulches

The crop growth is also influenced by the use of mulches which besides acting as moisture preserver also act as anti-erosive, temperature bufferer, diseases and pest infestation monitor and mineral and organic matter supplier and regulator.

The nature and type of soil decides the total voids, capillary and air pores in a soil system sustaining a crop. Therefore, the rate of evaporation and transpiration is also affected correspondingly. The bare or uncultivated or fallow lands are major contributors towards loss of applied water. It is felt that nearly 25 to 50% of evapotranspiration includes loss of moisture from the bare or partially canopy covered soil surface due to evaporation depending upon the agro-climatic conditions of the area. The loss of vapour from the surface of the soil is a function of evaporation rate also termed as 'Sink Strength' of the atmosphere and water transmissibility or hydraulic conductivity of the soil profile.

Evaporation mechanism of a soil profile occurs in three phases. In case of uniform wet soil under first phase there, the capillary conductivity or water transmissibility is not hindered in any soil layer resulting in constant evaporation rate depending upon the evaporativity of the atmosphere. Under such conditions, enough soil moisture level, the evaporation rate is equal to potential evaporation or open pan evaporation. In second phase there is a continuous reduction in hydraulic conductivity due to drying of soil surface, resulting in low evaporational loss. Under this stage the intrinsic soil factors govern the major moisture flow to the soil surface, atmospheric factors have only minor influence. Under different temperature gradients either due to variation in soil or atmosphere the mechanism of moisture flow is a bit more complicated. The periodical

TABLE 11.6

(Darra, 1971)

Name of chemical and concentration of hormone used for presoaking treatment	Maize crop							
	AV leaf area cm^2	AV plant girth cms	AV Number of inter-nodes per plant	AV Length of cob cms	AV circumference of cob cms	AV No. of grains line per cob	AV stalk yield gtls/ha	AV grain yield gtls/ha
Control	1283.9	9.63	8.51	18.65	14.98	17.17	160.25	53.40
IAA 50 PPM	1393.7	10.23	8.75	22.21	15.40	18.03	169.07	60.90
IAA 100 PPM	1476.7	10.85	9.07	22.86	16.93	19.53	178.40	61.50
IAA 200 PPM	1395.9	10.05	9.00	20.20	15.47	19.49	172.32	58.25
IAA 300 PPM	1259.1	9.11	8.95	19.30	15.06	17.00	165.15	53.82
NAA 50 PPM	1391.1	10.38	9.26	19.49	15.23	18.87	169.08	56.95
NAA 100 PPM	1475.9	10.88	9.50	20.39	15.80	19.46	171.65	56.90
NAA 200 PPM	1408.9	9.78	8.75	19.63	14.52	17.61	167.86	55.23
NAA 300 PPM	1390.1	9.09	8.75	18.93	13.96	17.03	160.57	52.15

(*Contd.*)

Name of chemical and concentration of hormone used for presoaking treatment	Maize crop							
	AV leaf area cm^2	AV plant girth cms	AV Number of inter-nodes per plant	AV Length of cob cms	AV circumference of cob cms	AV No. of grains line per cob	AV stalk yield gtls/ha	AV grain yield gtls/ha
GA 50 PPM	1425.9	9.95	9.50	19.42	15.25	19.41	170.47	56.83
GA 100 PPM	1540.5	10.17	9.87	20.63	15.99	20.30	180.58	56.57
GA 200 PPM	1496.4	10.07	9.50	19.66	14.78	19.34	176.00	55.05
GA 300 PPM	1262.4	9.02	8.75	19.46	13.42	18.14	168.65	54.25
IBA 50 PPM	1363.8	10.05	9.02	19.81	15.08	17.23	168.22	56.75
IBA 100 PPM	1442.8	10.14	9.37	19.93	15.52	18.80	174.09	55.75
IBA 200 PPM	1412.8	9.74	9.03	18.53	14.88	17.15	170.65	53.38
IBA 300 PPM	1338.0	9.16	8.75	18.39	13.27	16.69	163.75	52.63

IAA = Indole-acetic acid.
NAA = Napthyl-acetic acid.
GA = Gibberellic acid.
IBA = Indole-butyric acid.

TABLE 11.7

Effect of Growth Hormones on Various Biometric Data of Wheat

(Darra, 1971)

Name of chemical and concentration	AV plant height cm	AV No. of total tillers	AV length of ear cms	AV No. of grains per year	AV strain yield qtls/ha	AV grain yield qtls/ha
Control	90.51	11.96	11.76	76.60	56.08	36.53
IAA 50 PPM	101.30	12.98	13.85	80.79	69.20	42.69
IAA 100 PPM	101.95	13.58	14.98	81.96	70.90	44.72
IAA 200 PPM	98.02	12.16	13.65	79.69	69.22	41.15
IAA 300 PPM	94.90	10.01	11.04	76.16	66.42	39.10
IBA 50 PPM	99.07	13.24	12.79	78.19	69.98	43.23
IBA 100 PPM	100.52	13.68	13.68	79.89	70.32	45.28
IBA 200 PPM	98.31	13.08	12.76	77.93	69.48	43.83
IBA 300 PPM	92.08	11.76	11.86	72.26	66.45	38.12

TABLE 11.7 (*Contd.*)

Name of chemical and concentration	AV plant height cm	AV No. of total tillers	AV length of ear cms	AV No. of grains per year	AV strain yield qtls/ha	AV grain yield qtls/ha
NAA 50 PPM	100.31	13.11	12.86	79.68	68.55	42.35
NAA 100 PPM	100.93	13.96	13.64	80.69	69.48	43.12
NAA 200 PPM	99.93	12.98	12.64	77.62	67.58	39.85
NAA 300 PPM	90.03	12.16	9.07	70.30	63.00	36.45
GA 50 PPM	98.20	13.66	12.98	79.76	68.95	43.55
GA 100 PPM	99.41	13.96	13.92	80.17	71.85	46.55
GA 200 PPM	100.10	13.08	12.91	79.09	68.95	40.02
GA 300 PPM	97.91	10.53	12.39	76.91	68.35	38.58

TABLE 11.8

Effect of Various Concentrations of IAA on the Total Uptake and Accumulation in Straw and Grain Yield (Kg/ha) of Wheat at Different Salinity Conditions

[Source: B.L.Darra & S.N. Saxena, (1971)]

Constituents. (Kg/ha.)	Low salinity (E1) IAA PPM						Medium salinity (E2) IAA PPM						High salinity (E3) IAA PPM					
	C	50	100	200	300	LSD 0.05	C	50	100	200	300	LSD 0.05	C	50	100	200	300	LSD 0.05
Nitrogen	126.8	129.9	127.5	127.4	125.1	N.S.	120.2	123.0	126.0	127.9	121.3	4.28	106.9	118.7	120.9	124.0	115.3	3.89
Phosphorous	80.2	85.0	84.0	84.0	81.1	4.17	64.5	70.3	72.6	74.9	70.2	5.89	50.1	52.8	54.0	55.9	50.4	3.85
Potassium	102.7	106.7	105.0	104.0	100.7	2.65	97.7	98.4	102.3	104.6	96.1	4.55	80.7	91.6	94.9	96.1	92.3	3.96
Calcium + Magnesium	48.1	52.9	56.5	54.0	50.7	N.S.	22.6	25.0	26.7	27.0	23.5	3.53	10.1	15.6	27.7	29.9	20.0	2.96
Sodium	61.2	55.6	53.0	49.6	44.1	9.27	67.4	65.6	65.3	63.6	4.67	79.2	73.2	63.7	60.4	57.2	6.98	
Iron	2.6	2.5	2.5	2.4	2.3	0.2	2.5	2.3	2.2	2.1	2.0	0.3	2.0	2.0	2.0	1.6	1.7	0.14
Boron	1.98	2.23	2.21	2.35	1.90	N.S.	1.91	1.68	2.04	2.69	1.95	0.53	1.06	1.35	1.64	1.79	1.31	0.29
Straw yield	6508	6920	7090	6922	6642	453	5685	5768	6083	6895	5618	514	2886	3212	3993	4253	2962	329
Grain yield	3990	4269	4472	4155	3910	373	3395	3600	3652	3853	3245	310	2170	2395	2550	2707	2265	478

Low salinity: pH, 8.2, E.C. × 10^3, 2.35, S.A.R., 10.15 and boron, 1.26 ppm.

Medium salinity: pH, 8.4, E.C. × 10^3, 5.35, S.A.R., 18.73, and boron, 2.00 ppm.

High salinity: pH, 8.4, E.C. × 10^3, 8.20, S.A.R., 17.83, and boron, 1.45 ppm.

All analyses corresponds to saturation extract of the soil.

TABLE 11.9

Effect of Various Concentrations of IAA on the Mineral Accumulation in Grains of Wheat at Different Salinity Conditions

(Darra, 1971)

Constituents	Low salinity (E1)						Moderate salinity (E2)						High salinity (E3)					
	IAA PPM						IAA PPM						IAA PPM					
	C	50	100	200	300	LSD 0.05	C	50	100	200	300	LSD 0.05	C	50	100	200	300	LSD 0.05
Nitrogen per cent	1.81	1.97	2.28	2.20	1.98	0.22	1.35	1.66	1.74	2.01	1.64	0.37	0.98	1.16	1.36	1.44	1.22	0.32
Phosphorus mg/100 gm.	843.95	849.62	850.46	858.43	844.41	12.90	640.38	642.88	646.60	644.41	640.93	4.02	630.31	639.52	640.56	642.96	638.03	2.32
Potassium meq/100 gm.	6.69	7.87	7.96	8.86	8.11	1.21	7.31	7.93	8.10	9.13	8.45	0.77	5.92	6.76	6.92	7.18	6.94	0.74
Calcium + Magnesium meq/100 gm.	22.42	23.41	23.12	18.30	13.20	N.S.	10.41	10.50	10.30	12.91	12.01	3.10	10.19	13.41	13.90	14.94	13.94	2.61
Sodium meq/100gm	8.99	4.85	4.80	3.89	3.55	1.59	13.64	10.49	10.08	8.55	8.69	2.21	23.25	16.11	14.52	10.38	10.60	4.09
Iron mg/100 gm.	10.18	9.91	9.43	9.58	9.38	0.89	7.82	8.16	7.52	7.26	6.92	1.60	6.72	7.16	6.83	6.05	6.16	0.94
Boron P.P.M.	9.46	9.80	10.00	10.07	10.00	1.13	10.50	8.40	9.30	10.81	10.91	0.93	10.50	11.09	11.33	12.01	12.63	1.17

The abbreviations are same as in Table 11.8.

drying of soils, the vapour flow and its condensation in the top soil layer becomes more important than liquid flow. Under these conditions the rate of water loss from the soil is effected by vapour diffusion occurring through dried soil layer which is a few cm below the soil surface. The third phase of moisture losses is quite slow and constant which depends on the nature of absorptive forces acting upon water molecules of dried soil particles and on the length of water vapour diffusion path from the wet soil layers to atmosphere. Hence the mulches effect on soil moisture movement depends on their skilled use in view of selection of them, time and mode of application which modifies the energy and matter transport in the mechanism of evaporation (Lemon, 1956, Penman, 1956, Philip, 1957, Gardner, 1960, Bhatia et al. 1966, Hillel, 1968, Wendt, 1971, Ungar 1975).

The research conducted on the use of mulches indicates that depending on crop and soil type 10 to 50 per cent water may be conserved and economised. The other factors which influence the moisture conservation are agro-metereological or atmospheric (Ali & Prasad, 1975, Bansal et al. 1971, Chowdhary and Chatterjee, 1967, Dheshi et al. 1964, Dixit and Agarawal Patil et al. 1972, Prihar et al. 1968, Rajput and Singh, 1970, Singh et al. 1967). The use of either organic mulches (stovers, straw, rice husk, sawdust etc.) or light coloured and light reflecting mulches such as aluminium foils reduce the soil temperature while dark coloured black or grey or transparent mulches (polyethylene emulsions) considerably increase the average soil temperature from 6°C to as high 17°C which may be harmful to plant growth. The water use efficiency of many crops have been tried through various kinds of mulches. It has been experienced that finer the plant residues (rice-husk, saw dust) the more is water conservation. Organic mulches are additionally advantageous since they also provide nutrients after decomposition in the soil besides moisture conservation.

Plantation of Shelter Belts

The cropped and uncropped areas create a different pressure gradient of head and due to this sensible heat transfer or advection occurs to equalize the difference in micro-climates in adjacent small areas. This phenomenon helps to create a measurable difference in sensible heat transfer between up wind and down wind points. It has been reported that due to drier air adjacent to the unwind points the more evapotranspirational loss of water occurs while decrease near down wind points (Pruitt and McMillan, 1962, Rider et al. 1963), Miller 1964, Davenport and Hudson, 1967a, 1967b). This phenomenon warrants that when such conditions exists in the field the evapotranspiration of cropped area becomes high (sometimes results in sunburn or sunscald which should be maintained by supplying enough moisture through irrigation to avoid moisture stress due to high water demand of plants). This, naturally results in lower water use efficiency. This therefore, necessitates the plantation of shelter belts to minimise and modify the adverse effects of climate (Rosenberg, 1966, Skidmore and Hagen, 1970, Vander linde, 1962, Van Eimern et al. 1964, Sturrock, 1975, Saraf and Dastane, 1970).

IRRIGATION AND SOIL MOISTURE BALANCE

Soil Moisture Distribution

Irrigation supply is made to maintain a soil moisture balance for optimum or favourable growth and yield of crops. The timely water supply to the plants balances evapotranspiration demand as well as looks after sensible heat advected from the nearby uncropped areas. The demand of evaporation and transpiration is met out by optimum water supply during grcwth period of the crop. The irrigation demand by crops varies with their growth stage. In the beginning, the irrigation meets the more demand of evaporation by maintaining favourable moisture balance within soil but when enough crop canopy has developed the demand of transpiration becomes more which are to be supplemented through irrigation. Even at later stage when the root development is sufficient the roots draw soil moisture from lower layer of soil profile but with increasing depth the root density decreases which results in more resistance to water movement within the roots. When the plant is fully developed the water needs of plant increases further and to cope up with atmospheric evaporativity and avoid moisture stress, plants often close their stomata to economise water use. At this condition the actual evapotranspiration is less than the potential.

It has been found that water use efficiency of a crop increase under field conditions except when either fresh or green vegetative portions are used after harvest. Also it happens so due to decline in moisture supply of the soils, the plants actively try to minimise the water use in the rain between wilting moisture to optimum moisture conditions. The decrease in soil moisture below optimum level causes decline of total production per unit area or per unit of water consumed.

According to Dastane et al. (1973), the water use efficiency may be enhanced through irrigating the crops at their most critical physiological stages of growth. There is a general consciousness among the researchers that at maximum physiological activity of the plant *i.e.* when the plant is just entering to its reproductive stage the moisture stress seriously affects the crop production. Thus for cereals and grain crops the critical stages are crown root initiation (CRI) or secondary root initiation (SRI) and flowering where moisture stress seriously affects plant growth and production. The choice of irrigation and its frequency under limited water availability is for the first stage (CRI or SRI) while the next irrigation if available has to be managed at flowering. For pulses or dicot as well as vegetable and fruit and cotton crops the moisture deficit must be avoided during flowering and pod filling or fruiting stages. For tuber crops like potato sugar beet etc. the critical stages for sufficient availability of water are stolomization and tuberization (Dastane et al., 1970, Yusf, 1973).

Quantum and Mode of Water Application

The quantum of water supplied at every irrigation is lost through surface runoff and deep percolation below the rootzone depth of crops. The quantity of water applied at each irrigation from a suitable stream size as per soil conditions and crop should be such that it always wets the rootzone depth. It therefore, suggest that it should neither be less and nor in excess because under both conditions the losses are more but optimum to have greater water use efficiency (Shmueli, 1973, Gautam et al., 1966).

The maximum percolation to the tune of 50 to 60 per cent or even more of the total water applied has been recorded in case of rice crop and to reduce it, puddling or compaction of the soil which reduces its permeability or hydraulic conductivity is practised (Pande and Mitra, 1970, 1971, Vamadevan and Dastane, 1968, Varade and Ghildyal, 1967 and Rao et al., 1972).

The water requirement of rice crop may be decreased by reducing the level of submergence during transplanting, maximum tillering and gradual disposal of field water 10 to 15 days prior to attaining the dough stage (Kung, 1971). The economy in water use may also be attained without significant decrease in yields when the rice fields are maintained just at moisture saturation level and even up to field capacity moisture (Hukkeri and Sharma, 1974, Mane, 1970, Vamadevan and Dastane, 1972, Rao, 1971, reports of the All India Coordinated Scheme for Research on Water Management and Soil Salinity, 1975). However if the water table is below 2.0 metres the rice grown at field capacity moisture may show significant decrease in yields. Hukkeri and Sharma (1974), tried cultivation of rice under different methods as given in Table 11.10.

TABLE 11.10

Effect of Method of Sowing/Transplantation of Kharif Paddy on Grain Yield and Production Efficiency of Irrigation Water

(Hukkeri and Sharma, 1974)

Method	Grain yield Q/ha.	Irrigation amount (mm)	Production efficiency of Irrigation water (Kg/ha-cm)
Transplanting	48.8	1826	26.7
Direct sown on puddled soil at the time of nursery sowing	45.1	2335	19.8
Direct sown on puddled soil at the time of transplanting	25.6	2192	11.6
Direction sown in lines on un-puddled soils with sprouted seeds at the time of nursery sowing	35.5	2308	15.3
Direct sown in lines on unpuddled soils with un-sprouted nursery sowing	32.9	2308	14.2
C.D. 5%	5.3	...	...

Various methods of irrigation have provided different amount of water losses, application and field water use efficiency. There are various factors *viz.*, land preparation, grading, topography, variability in soil characteristics, quantity, quality and cost of irrigation water zonal agro-climatic conditions, type and rooting characteristics of the important area crops, efficiency of irrigation system etc. should be considered well design and efficient irrigation system which would provide water use economy by crops.

Amongst the different methods of irrigation sprinkler method attains higher field water use efficiency in comparison to surface except under fine textured soils which reduce infiltration due to swelling. Also the presence of uncropped area which results in large amount of advected heat may also minimise the water use efficiency of sprinkling method. The drip irrigation method also provides higher water use efficiency because of less evaporation from wetted area and elimination of deep percolation losses as well as less pressure or energy needed to run the drip system in comparison to sprinkler. However, drip method has been found to be overall more yielding and beneficial for different crops under medium and coarse textured soils where the water quality is not satisfactory and/or water is scarce and costly. Trickle irrigation method in light and fine textured soils provided higher to identical yield respectively also water use efficiency values were higher in drip in comparison to sprinkler and furrow irrigation method (Singh, 1974, Bucks et al. 1974). These studies, however, proved that consumptive water uses was more or less equal in the different irrigation methods. It is thus apparent that drip irrigation may reduce the irrigation water requirement but values of consumptive use on an average remains unaltered.

Lal (1973), reported that in furrow irrigation method the wetting of alternate furrows resulted in higher total production per unit quantity of water due to more coverage of area. Also it has been found that water use efficiency of crops was maximum under flooding followed by borderstrip, check basin, basin and furrow irrigations.

Shainberg (1975), reported that surface irrigation may add 100 to 1000 grams of salts per cubic metre of added water. These salts are distributed in the entire soil profile and due to irrigation of crops are always below rootzone depth due to their continuous leaching or downward movement with water. However, the salinity problem comes up when the actual ground water table rises above 1.5 — 2.0 metres the irrigation water is just not enough to percolate below rootzone as in case of sprinkler and drip irrigation methods. In Chambal command area of Rajasthan there is highly compacted calcic horizon in sub-stratum which restricts the rise of existing high ground water table but this soil strata functions to create pseudo or pearched water table conditions which helps in sending salt saturated capillary fringes upwards and due to constant fluctuation of this kind of water table with opening and closure of canal the salinity and/or sodicity has cropped up in considerable area after inception of canal irrigation and in spite of some drainage network it has not gone down (Darra et al., 1971).

The reclamation of saline and/or sodic soils is feasible with the leaching and/or flushing of excessively accumulated salts on soil surface along with use of cultural and/or chemical amendments (Darra et al., 1971). The cultivation of crops under such salt infestation conditions have to be preceded by leaching for which the quantity of water required would be more than actual crop water requirements. The allowance of this demand is made hardly during the planning of any irrigation project and, also the regulation of conveyance system and water distribution strategy do not consider this vital factor through this has become a major problem of at least all major and medium irrigation projects which now seems to have attracted the attention of irrigation planners. However, reclamation process though initially decreases or lower down water use efficiency, it improves gradually and increases after a few years.

Fertilizer-Irrigation Relationship

The balanced use of inorganic and organic fertilizers under optimum soil moisture conditions results in higher crop yields which provides the high values of water use efficiency because for the same crop under fertilized or non-fertilized conditions consume more or less same quantity of water unless there is a considerable variation in crop surface roughness and the high advection. This is because once the soil surface is fully covered with foliage or crop canopy the under-fertilized conditions will not change the rate of water absorption by a crop, however, the photosynthesis is enhanced due to increased intensity and duration of solar radiation received by increased canopy.

Sengupta (1972), reported that limitation of either water or fertilizer severly affected the production efficiency of each other. The use of fertilizers under dry farming conditions have resulted in higher crop yields under favourable soil moisture availability through rains particularly at the critical growth stage because otherwise due to early vegetative growth as stimulated by fertilizers would exhaust the stored soil moisture and the plant would not only face moisture stress but also restrict the absorption of nutrients at this critical growth stage which would result in less yields (Olson et al. 1962, Viets, 1966).

The results of AICWIP (All India Coordinated Wheat Improvement Project), coordinated trials during 1970-71 indicate the production of gram per kg. of nitrogen applied was higher under irrigated than unirrigated one.

The placement of inorganic fertilizers under dry farming system has been recommended to be at 10 cm or deeper in the rootzone (Singh & Sinha, 1974). This is because under droughty conditions the availability of plant food decreases from dry soil surface which does not occur in deeper layers at the same time being moisture.

Weed Impact

The value of water use efficiency of a crop are also influenced by the intensity weeds since the weeds grow faster than crop seedlings therefore, the higher the weed infestation the lesser the yields and hence lesser water use efficiency. This is due to competition of weeds with the native crop in sharing and exhausting available nutrients, soil moisture and solar radiations which either results in lower crop yields or its failure (Singh et al., 1971, De Datta and Ross, 1955). The effect of weed under farmer's and improved practices on grain yields of rice under Philippines conditions as reported by IRRI 1973 are shown in the figure. The early establishment of crop competes the weed growth through its high foliage density and leaf area index by utilising more portion of moisture and nutrients and particularly with the light or shade sensitive grasses and sedge, which further suppress the weed growth and results in high water use efficiency. Stainforth and Weber (1956) and Stainforth et al. (1963), concluded some increase of soyabean crop. Chowdhary and Mani 1973, reported efficient utilization of water by decreasing the weed infestation through application of weedicides. Hence control of weed growth is a dominant factor for increase of water use efficiency.

Aquatic Weeds Problem in Irrigated Tracts

The inception of canal irrigation in any irrigated area is bound to develop heavy growth of aquatic weeds. The project canal system gets infested with equatic weeds. The weeds can be broadly grouped into the following three categories:

1. Floating weed : Water hyacinth, Pistia, Lemnoi, Azolla, Nelumbium etc.
2. Emersed weed : Fistulosa Typha, Phargmites, Ipomea.
3. Submersed weeds : Hydrilla, Vallisneria, Najas, Potomogeton, Ceretophyllum.

In addition to the checking of the water body, the floating and emersed weed cause physical loss of water through evapotranspiration which is reported to be ten times higher in case of typha and water hyacinth as compared to that occurs from free water surface under equivalent conditions. It has been found that approximately 7×10^6 inches litres water is lost for typha infested area alone, which can irrigate about 43000 ha additional cultivable area. In case of submersed weeds there is, however, no loss of water through evapotranspiration, but these weeds may reduce the flow velocity of water in the canals to the extent of 80 per cent as a result the designed discharge may not pass through the conveyance system even though the delivery system may even run above F.S.L. This is one of the major causes of unequitable distribution of water which denies the farmer of specially tail end to use his desired share of water. The reduction in water flow may be about 20 per cent after manual cleaning of the canals while after lapse of a month, it may rise to 40-50%. The weed obstruction in the flow raises the F.S.L. of water in the canals which may result in over topping the designed free board thereby submersing the adjoining land. This helps in creating another water hazards such as water-logging, salinity and/or alkalinity and allied agricultural problems.

CONTROL MEASURES

Various control measures may be employed as discussed below:

1. Physical : Lining, periodical drying (closure) of the canals.
2. Mechanical : Manual removal or cutting of weeds, use of weeds, cutters, week buckets, modest etc.
3. Chemicals : Use of herbicides.
4. Biological : Release of grass carp-fish, plantation of paragrass (Bracharia Mutica) in typha infested reaches.
5. Utilization : Use of weeds as raw material for compost, paper, biogas and some other articles.

Physical Method

Lining is an expensive, but very effective method to control submersed, as well as emersed weeds, if proper canal bed maintenance is done to remove the silt depositing. This is necessary because weed can grow in 5-7 cm thick bed silt, periodical drying (closure) of the minors and field channels for about 7-10 days have been found to keep check on the growth rate of the submersed as well as floating weeds. However, emersed weeds are not killed in such short closures. This method is effective only if uniform bed gradient of the canals is available for quick runoff, intake and evaporation of stagnant water so as to have totally dry bed. This method would not be effective for main canal system which needs still more time for their complete drying than the allowed scheduled closure period for the canals in many irrigated areas.

Mechanical Method

Manual cleaning of submersed weeds is effective and economical only in small canals but in main canals and tanks it requires closure for 6-8 weeks and still is not very effective. The remaining plants get better environment for their proper growth, therefore, the condition of the water body becomes the same within 2 months, as it is before manual weeding.

Manual removal of floating weed (water hyacinth) may be economic if it is done at the start of the problem, but becomes very expensive and time consuming if done after its heavy infestation. Cutting of typha weed is effective only for about a month if done in any season and above water level, but if their under water cuttings are done in rainy season at one month interval, the effect lasts for about a year and 90% plants are killed after the continuous submergence of the cut stamps for about 4 months. Use of weed cutters is effective only for a short period hence repeated operations after every 2-3 months are very necessary, which makes this method very expensive.

Chemical Control

Foliar Spray of 2,4-D @ 3.5-4 kg/ha or by paraquet @ 1 lit/ha or Amitrol @ 2 lit/ha can kill almost all the floating weeds. This method costs about Rs.450 to 1000/ha depending on the infestation and is cheaper as compared to manual removal which costs about Rs. 500 to 2000/ha.

Emersed weed typha can be controlled by folier spray of dalapan @ 25 kg/ha + 30 lit emulsified diesel oil, Amitrol @ 8 kg/lit/ha. The herbicides should be sprayed at flowering & post-flowering stage respectively. After one spray about 80% plants are killed, for the remaining plants second spray with the same dose must be done. With that two sprays about 95-93% plants are killed. The cost of both the sprays is about Rs.1500 to 1800/ha.

Submersed weeds can be controlled within a week by applying aculein, xylene or hydrothol, but these pesticides are very much toxic to the fish and may also be injurious to the crops. The method is expensive also. Another herbicide Fenac alone 7.5 to 10 kg/ha or with copper sulphate (2 ppm) when sprayed on the muddy, exposed bottom of the canal keeps the area weed free for about a month.

Biological Method

For controlling submersed weeds biological method proved very effective, economic and safe. Grass carp fish which consume all types of weeds equal or twice of their body weight within 24 hours are released in some of the minors. The growth rate of this fish in these agro-climatic conditions is very high and its induced breeding has also been done successfully. This is an edible fish and can profitably be sold in the market and may fetch revenue to meet the expenses incurred on its rearing and release.

Control of typha weed by replacing it by paragrass, which is a very nutritious fodder, is also very effective and economic method. In this way, waste water-logged fields, where at present typha and other grasses are growing can be converted to fodder production centres and an additional income of Rs. 3000 per ha/annum can be taken by selling paragrass.

Utilization

A very good compost can be prepared by using water hyacinth which is many times richer in nitrogen and potash contents than F.Y.M. and town compost. Many types of papers, biogas, silage can also be prepared with water hyacinth. Typha can be utilized to some extent for making huts, ropes, aasans, curtains, mats etc. and can also be used as a surface mulch in crops having wide spacing and as a soil amendment with pressmud for improving the problematic soils.

All the control methods depend on the type of weed and location of the infested site and it is not possible to control all types of weeds by one method only. Therefore, an integrated management approach to control these weeds, just at the starting stage of the problem, rather than after its full infestation is very necessary in any aquatic weed control programme.

Influence of Insects, Pests and Diseases

The considerable reduction in crop yields is also due to attack of insects, pests and various plant diseases. If there is a epidemic attack by a particular insect or pest or plant disease there is either a crop failure or very poor yields. This decreases the water use efficiency significantly. Therefore it appears that there is a positive correlation between the intensity of above three factors on water use efficiency, it is further borne out by the fact that the values of evapotranspiration or water requirement of crops do not indicate significant variation under infested or non-infested conditions. However, not much data are available which may establish any relationship between applied water or soil moisture *in situ* and the intensity or degree of infestation due to either of the three factors and water use efficiency except some informations provided by Kloster Meyer (1967) and Menzies (1967) on disease in relation to water application. Singh et al. (1974), however, concluded that yield losses due to insect or pest infestation can be reduced by appropriate crop management practices which provided higher water use efficiency. The control or severity of insects or pests has been related with soil moisture level under field conditions by Choudhary and Sharma (1960), who found higher infestation of wheat steam borer with excessive irrigation. Also the intensity of fruit flies and leaf hoppers was high under these conditions while shoot borer of sugarcane and stalk borer of maize along with other soil born insects attack was found to decrease under flood irrigation due to lack of aeration.

The high level of nitrogen and water application 0.3 and 0.8 atmtension were found to increase in gall number per tobacco plant was reported by Prasad et al. (1965). The excessive moisture conditions coupled with poor surface and sub-surface drainage have been found to multiply the growth of fungi like "Phytophothora and Pythium responsible for root and stem rots of the crops. The ground contact of plants like tomato and cucurbits resulted in fruit roots. The crops having close canopy and growing densely under warm and humid conditions are also more prone to virus and foliage diseases. The low moisture regimes and dry weather also creates favourable conditions for appearance of diseases like wilting disease of crops caused by species of Fusarium and Verticillium.

It is, therefore, imperative that water use efficiency can be increased by attaining high crop production and/or reduction in overall losses of water either by percolation, runoff or evapotranspiration. This can be achieved by screening the crop varieties adapted to an agro-climatic conditions and proper crop management practices which include good quality seeds, optimum time of seed sowing and depth in right directions, balanced quality of fertilizers, optimum quantity of irrigation water to maintain favourable soil moisture regime under adequate surface and internal drainage provisions and control of weed insects, pests and all type of soil and plant borne diseases through judicious application of general or specific weedicides, herbicides, insecticides or pesticides. The water use efficiency can further be increased by reducing deep percolation losses such as in paddy crop in which 60 to 70 per cent water losses occur by growing paddy either in soils which are suitable to it or by creating highly compacted strata within rootzone. For other crops use of anti-transpirants growth retardents, mulches and shelter belts along with switching over to sprinkler and drip irrigation methods to minimise amount of water for crop growth and application of water at critical growth stages only.

CHAPTER 12

FIELD DRAINAGE

Irrinage

The drainage is an integral part of irrigated agriculture. Therefore, it is rightly to use word IRRINAGE planning than the planning of irrigation for any project. The irrigation and drainage should, therefore, be planned and executed together for introducing irrigated agriculture in any area. The primary aim and object of drainage operations is to maintain the favourable soil moisture regime in root-zone for optimum growth of the crops to be grown, while secondary object is to lower the water table below critical level to avoid salt efflorescence within and on the soil surface. This results in favourable air-water ratio in a particular soil. The drainage facilities to soil provides access of air which contains oxygen necessary for roots and their exchange for the proper metabolisation of plants and subsequently higher and desired crop yields. Also the carbon-di-oxide produced by roots, soil organisms or by chemical reactions in the soil can diffuse through the air filled pores to the surface.

The need of field drainage varies with soil type, nature and quality of underground waters. The drainage schemes made in the offices without appropriate field traverse, and soil studies are likely to fail. In fact no two drainage schemes are exactly alike. Even in adjoining fields, two entirely different factors may be causing the water-logged condition.

TYPES OF WATER MOVEMENT

The ground water exists in many forms. The rainfall on earth can move in many different ways under ground after penetration into surface soils. The path ways can be:

(1) cause a high water table or water-logging;
(2) move along underground and form seepage line;
(3) move horizontally and make spring on hindrance;
(4) very slow infiltration into ground, turn land saturated;
(5) stored in pockets of varying permeability.

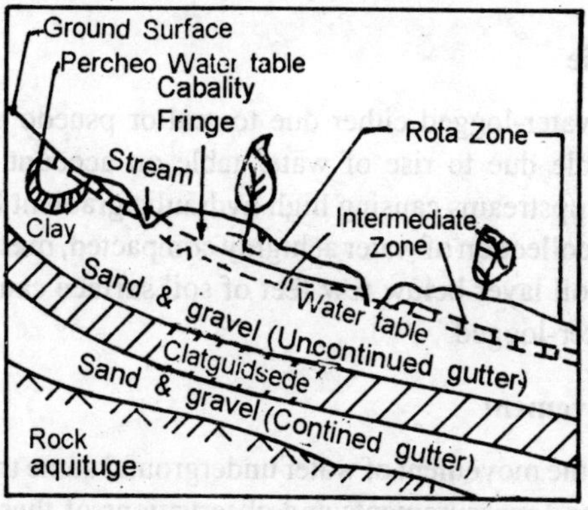

Fig. 12.1 : Different forms of ground water

The field engineer should locate either of the above possibility or group of few existing and work for the planning, designing and execution of job. A few schemes have been found in jeopardise due to incorrect diagnosis of the water movement. The failureness of tile drainage network in some parts of the world was attributed to the lack of planning to allow for water moving underground and breaking to the surface because of a barrier of soil of low permeability. Simply designing a system by fixing tile drains say 3-4 metres apart could not solve the problem unless the design is made so that drains run along the edge of the barrier. If they are designed so as to cut across and into it the possibilities are that after heavy rainfall the water will rise to the surface between the laterals before reaching the drain and run through the barrier as shown in Fig. 12.2.

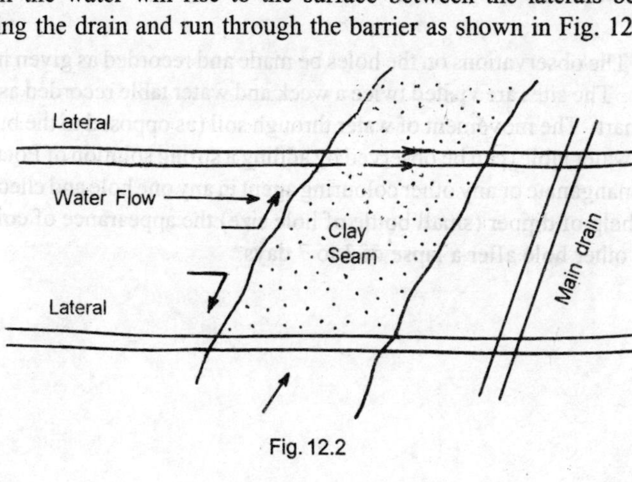

Fig. 12.2

Thus through study of the soils in respect of sub-soil and substratum is quite essential besides other which may be trouble shooter.

A High Water Table

The fields are water-logged either due to real or psuedo artificial (Pearched) water table due to rise of water table on account of high hydrostatic pressure upstreams causing high hydraulic gradient between the two points or the collection of water at highly compacted, massive and most impermeable soil layer below few feet of soil surface causing the fields to become water-logged.

Tracing Water Movement

For the study of the movement of water underground some trial holes are dug in the area and measurements and observations of these over a period of time provides data on movement and fluctuation of water table. If the field is flat and does not indicate visible drainage problem on the surface, such as rising springs, peaty pockets or seepage from high areas, then series of auger holes are dug to a depth of 150 cm or more depending upon the nature of study. In case solid bed of impervious strata (*e.g.* murram or petro calcic or calcic horizon in Chambal command of Rajasthan), the excavation should be up to that extent. The holes are made so as to uniformly distributed over study area. About 6 to 8 may be found enough for 2 to 4 hectares field. As each hole is dug, the tiles of 4 inches (10 cm.) tiles on end until the top one projects from the ground. This is done to keep the hole open during the observation period. The soil around the hole should be consolidated to reduce to entry of surface water into the hole.

The observations on the holes be made and recorded as given in table 12.1. The sites are visited twice a week and water table recorded as given in chart. The movement of water through soil (as opposed to the build up of a water table) can be observed by adding a strong solution of Potassium Permanganate or any other colouring agent in any one hole and check with the help of dipper (small bottle of hole size) the appearance of colour in any other hole after a lapse of 3 to 7 days.

TABLE 12.1

Date	Hole Numbers						Rainfall observations
-	1	2	3	4	5	6	
-	2'0"	2'0"	2'6"	2'6"	2'0"	2'0"	Dry
-	1'6"	1'3"	1'8"	1'7"	1'6"	1'4"	Drizzle
-	1'0"	1'0"	1'0"	1'6"	1'6"	1'6"	Heavy rain
-	1'6"	1'6"	1'6"	1'6"	1'6"	1'6"	Snowfall
-	1'9"	2'0"	1'10"	2'6"	2'6"	2'0"	Snowfall
-	1'0"	1'0"	1'0"	1'6"	1'6"	1'0"	Thaw

Figures indicates water table from ground level to top of water

Observation chart (Courtsey Livesely, C. 1960).

Ditch level
50,000

1 0 ground level 53.5	2 0
4 0 55.5	3 0 55.3
5 0 55.4	6 0 55.0

The data recorded after few months as per fixed intervals would show the levels of water table and possibilities of water-logged conditions during any period over a year time in any part of the field or area of zone etc. It would also indicate deep percolation of loss of water level in any area.

INTERPRETATIONS OF DRAINAGE BY SOIL COLOUR

Soil colours do help in recognising high water table conditions. Thus lands having good drainage would have oxidised iron and hydrated iron oxides, providing red and yellow colours in the sub-soil. These colours, however, also show the absence of organic matter and if rich in humus then blended or shaded brown colours. However, if soil is affected due to water-logging iron is reduced and with decay of organic matter (deoxynated) grey and drab shades are seen. In clayey soils, usually colours with grey background with small areas of orange and fawn may be found indicating fluctuating water table. It may also show deteriorated soil structure due to impeded drainage or poor percolation.

Soil degradation is possible either with good or poor quality irrigation water to soils of impaired drainage due to accumulation of soluble salts both of neutral and alkaline nature. Insufficient irrigation, however, may also result in similar type of soils.

Crop Responses

The excessive moisture due to inadequate drainage affects crop production due to deficient aeration. These conditions influence soil processes, plant metabolism, enhancement of phytological processes, optimal soil temperature etc. These conditions cause extremely slow rate of gaseous diffusion into soil causing deficiency of oxygen. This affects oxidation-reduction potential. Field drainage alone is not sufficient to provide optimum fertility and productivity from a given land, unless attention is also paid to various parameters *e.g.* healthy soil system, selected crop species, agronomical practices, proper amount of water for irrigation at critical growth stages and methods of irrigation, regulation and distribution etc. The main aim of field drainage is to provide farmers land in cultivable tilth conditions at the desired time to grow their crops. The wet lands delay sowing as well as harbour diseases, husk and liver fluke, weeds of anaerobic conditions, malarial spreading mosquitos etc.

The inadequate and faulty drainage adversely affects the:

(1) fertilizer efficiency

(2) puddling causing deterioration of structure

(3) reduction in soil temperature

(4) reduction in cultivable land

(5) excessive runoff

(6) reduction in population of earth worms and useful bacteria, flora and fauna.

(7) increase in weeds
(8) reduced workability
(9) poor root growth
(10) reduction in salt affected areas
(11) decreased plant deficiencies and diseases
(12) reduction in public and animal health.

which for well aerated soils in terms of EMF be 0.5 volts and come down to 0.30 volt in waterlogged conditions measured at pH 5.0. The dissolved oxygen under waterlogged conditions after consumed by plants causes complete decomposition of organic matter resulting in the production of incompletely oxidized and reduced organic compounds and complexes aldehydes. Mineral substances are reduced (deoxidized) as below:

Oxidized state	Reduced state
Nitrate ions (NO_3	Ammonia, nitrite, nitrous oxide and nitrogen
Sulphate ions (SO_4)	Sulphide ions or Hydrogen sulphide
Ferric ions (Fe^{+3})	Ferrous ions (Fe^{+2})
Manganic ions (Mn^{+7})	Manganous (Mn^{+5} or Mn^{+4})
Phosphate ions (PO_4^{-3})	Phosphite

Plant Adaptation

Plants naturally growing under anaerobic conditions develop artificial rooting system on soil humps which adapt to deoxinated conditions. These roots are slender type and also grow in well aerated pockets like cavaties and channels. The plants show yellowing or red dening or leckes or a scorched or stippled appearence and wilted. The translocation of auxins and carbohydrates through plant is hindered upwards and canveyed down the food as far as the plant is areated *i.e.* to the water level, where an accumulation of these substances results in abnormally luxuriant cell growth and the formation of adventitious roots.

In cereal crops flooding at flowering and milking stage causes total loss of crop even upland rice after 15 to 20 days of transplanting.

CHARACTERISTICS OF DRAINAGE GROUPS

These characteristics depend upon type of soils present in the area to be investigated. In Chambal command area of Kota, Rajasthan having mostly vertisols (heavy inverting clays), five drainage groups were recognised (Lovas, 1971). The groups were developed by evaluating five principles of hydrogeological factors namely:

A — Permeability of the soil,

B — Permeability of the base rock.

C — Depth to ground water in monsoon time.

D — Recharge to the ground water.

E — Natural drainage of the ground water.

Each of these factors may be further sub-divided in three conditions namely:

A. Topsoil

(1) Pervious (Permeability over 0.1 meter/day).

(2) Semi-Pervious (Permeability between 0.1 to 0.001 m/day).

(3) Impervious (Permeability less than 0.001 m/day).

B. Base Rock

(1) Pervious (lime stone and lime stone with intercalacation).

(2) Semi-Pervious (Weathered sand stone and shale).

(3) Impervious (Sound quartzitic sand stone and shale).

C. Ground Water Table in Monsoon

(1) Deep (Below 3.0 metre).

(2) Shallow (Between 3.0 to 1.5 metre).

(3) High (Above 1.5 metre).

D. Ground Water Recharge

(1) Through the top soil (downward movement).

(2) Through the alluvium (lateral movement).

(3) Through the base rock (upward movement).

E. Natural Drainage of Ground Water

(1) Good (Evenly sloping base rock surface).

(2) Poor (Undulating base rock surface).

(3) Bad (basin like, cupshape, base rock surface with level shoulder).

Based on these assumptions the correlation of drainage method and hydrogeological classification can be worked out for suggesting where drainage is not necessary and where surface, subsurface or coupled with surface, surface plus ground water lowering, surface plus vertical wells in the base rock etc. is worked out. The visual observations and the discovered sub-surface geological trends the drainage groups may be extra polated in the unsurveyed area (60% of the total). However, the survey may continue but work can be also started.

Initiation Studies and Works

The initiation of drainage work is started as follows after above studies.

(1) Training and cleaning of the existing natural drains (nallahs).

(2) Deepening and aligning of nallas to 0.6 to 0.9m lower than the proposed ground water table.

(3) Widening of the nallas.

(4) Providing proper grades.

(5) Provision of structures to cheque retrogression.

(6) Excavating new drains or regarding existing drains.

(7) Land levelling and providing field drains.

TYPE OF DRAINS AND DESIGN PARAMETERS

The field drains may be classified as:

(1) Surface drains and (2) Sub-surface drains. The following are the steps taken to provide field drainage in a particular area:

(1) Land Development

The smoothening or land levelling is pre-requisite of drainage programme. It helps to control soil erosion. It is done by—

(a) reducing the slope by terracing;

(b) reducing erodibility by proper plant canopy;

(c) reducing run off by damming or bunding;

(d) making storage ponds or *nadis* or tanks;

(e) reducing the rediment amount in water by making silting basins and using the deposits for reclaiming eroded soil.

Classification of Surface Drains

The surface drains are of following types:

(i) Storm water or surface drains;

(ii) Seepage drains;

(iii) Surface-cum-Seepage drain.

Fixing Alignment of Surface Drains

The alignment is fixed straight in the natural flow of water course. If the alignment passes through or crosses the pond, the drain is diverted to near the pond because of excavation of earth. The feeder drain is constructed or only a inlet is constructed to drain the water from pond to main drain.

Drainage Structures

The most common drainage structures used are :

(1) Pipe outlets;

(2) Road culverts;

(3) Drop structures.

Pipe Outlets and Design

If adequate disposal arrangement is not made, the chances of gully formation at disposal point are high. This is due to considerable difference between the bed level of the collecting drains and the main drains which results in high energy to be dissipiated while maintaining drain section. A pipe outlet is made of R.C.C. pipe of suitable diameter connects these two drains and results in safe disposal after rebatement to cheque scouring.

The design is based on formula —

Q = AV *e.g.* if velvity (V) = 8ft/sec and discharge Q = 25 cusecs, then, A = 25/8 = 3.12ft^2

Also $Q = cd \times A \sqrt{2gh} = 0.7 \times A/4 \times d^2 \sqrt{2 \times 32.2 \times 2}$

$g = 32.2$ or $d^2 = 3.1 \therefore d = 1.76$ (d = diameter of pipe)

The apron wall is made using base width = 0.75 × h *i.e.* 2.65 or say 3' – 0". Foundation depth = $\frac{h}{10+1}$ 1ft below GL. *i.e.* 3.5/10 + 1 =1.35 say 1' – 6"

Road Culverts

Where a drain has to cross a road for various uses road culverts are constructed over a drain. The culvert consists of wing walls which besides retaining the earth fill in the road also support the pipe. Enough cushion is provided to protect the pipes from the impact of heavy loads.

DROP STRUCTURES

It is also a drainage structure which is constructed where the land topography shows sudden fall. This is to be adjusted with drop in the bed level of the drainage or irrigation channel. The structure has a masonry head wall with a sloping down stream face and an opening in the form of a trepezoidal notch to provide smooth passage to water. Apron for protecting the bed and slopes as per design calculations are provided in these falls.

The design of a fall of notch type is given by equations—

$$Q = \frac{2}{3} c \sqrt{2g} \times (LH^{3/2} + \frac{2}{5} NH \times 2^{5/2})$$

where:

Q = Discharge = capacity of the notch

C = coefficient of discharge = 0.70

L = Length of the sill of the notch = 1 ft say

N = 2 tan, where 'θ' here is angle of inclination of the sides of the notch to the verticle.

H = Depth of water above 'sill' of notch say 2 ft

$$\therefore Q = \frac{2}{3} \times 0.7 \sqrt{2 \times 32.2} (1 \times 2^{3/2} + \frac{2}{5} \times 2 \tan 45^{o} \times 2^{5/2})$$

$$= \frac{1.4}{3} \times 8.02 (1.0 \times 2.95 + \frac{4}{5} \times 5.66)$$

$$= \frac{1.4}{3} \times 8.02 (2.95 + 5.66) = 35 \text{ cusecs approx.}$$

∴ This notch can carry discharge maximum up to 35 cusecs

Bodywall

For bodywall, the length kept is $\frac{7th}{8}$ of width or maximum equal to the width.

If top width of the bed is 6 ft and key allowed on both sides of the bunds is 2 ft. We can fix the length of body wall at 10 ft. Now assuming thickness of the body wall at the top as 1'-6" and d/s batter of 2/3 : 1 may be provided. The height of body wall is calculated as under :

H = Fall + depth of cushion = 4'+6" = 4.5ft

∴ Total height of the body wall = 4.5 ft ÷ depth of pier notch = 4.5 ft + 2.5 ft = 7 ft

Side Slopes

The side slopes of the drains are as under:

Firm soils (clay, clay loam, silty clay)	—	1:1 (H:V)
Loam soils	—	1.5:1
Sandy soils	—	2.5:1

However, it is desirable to design the side slope of a channel based on angle of repose of the soil.

Apron

Thickness of apron depends upon the nature the foundation should be so as to resist uplift. The nimimum thickness of the apron is given as:

Thickness of apron = $\sqrt{H + fall}$

As per example = $\sqrt{4+2.5}$ = $\sqrt{6.5}$ = 2.55ft say 2.5ft

Hence provide 2.6 ft thick apron.

As regards length of apron it is given as:

Lc + width of body wall at base + offset

where

Lc = Length of cistern

As per example : Lc = 2 × 2.5 + 2 $\sqrt{2.5}$ × 4

= 5+2 $\sqrt{10}$ = 10.16 say 10 ft

Length of apron = 10'+5'+0.6" = 15.' 6" (15½ ft).

Hence provide 15 ft long d/s apron also provide a toe wall at the end of the d/s. Apron with a section of 2 ft × 2 ft and length equal to that of body wall. This should project by 6 inches above the bed level to help dissipate the energy. The u/s & d/s rebating be done as per standards.

Maximum Allowable Velocities in Channels

This may be designed based on soil texture as given in table 12.2.

TABLE. 12.2

Soil Texture	Maximum Allowable Velocity m/sec
Silty sand	0.30
Loose sand	0.50
Coarse sand	0.75
Sandy loam	0.75
Silty loam	0.90
Firm clay loam	1.00
Stiff clay/gravelly	1.50
Coarse gravel	1.50
Soft rock, shale, hard pan	1.80
Hard cemented conglomerated	2.50

Capacity of Drains

The capacity of the drain may be calculated considering runoff say 0.75 inch per day and hence the total discharge passes through the drain may be calculated as:

$$Q = \frac{(0.40) \times (5280)^2}{12 \times 24 \times 3600} \text{ cusecs per square mile.}$$

Section Design of Drain

Based on capacity of the drain the desired section is found to pass the required discharge capacity. In given areas the discharge capacity is assumed between 10 mm to 15 mm runoff. By using manning formula:

$$V = \frac{1.486}{N} \times R^{2/3} \times S^{1/2}$$

where

V = Velocity in ft/sec.

N = Rugosity coefficient *e.g.* 0.03

R = Hydraulic mean depth infeet

S = Bed gradient

The surface drains are always in cutting (F.S.L. at least 1.0 ft below ground level). Side slopes are 1:1 (in medium textured or light textured) 1.5:1 in heavy soils and based on water hydraulic line.

The sections are designed for N = 0.03.or permissible occurring velocity (velocity ratio above 1.0) and bed gradient as per outfall.

Cross Section

The gradient of 1:1500 to 1:3000 is generally considered. The road width is at least 12 to 15 ft. For high grounds it may be on natural surface and for low grounds at least 1 ft above natural surface. The spoil bank away from road leaving a drain at least 2 ft wide and 1 ft deep below ground.

EFFICIENCY OF DRAINAGE CHANNEL

The drainage discharge should be decreased by adjusting the values of depth, or bottom width or both on higher side which increases the section of the drain. This is done by sacrificing the optimum efficiency section of the drain. Thus when the cross sectional area is fixed with the permissible velocity the calculations may be made further about the design discharge carrying capacity of this drain if it cannot the cross section may be increased further.

It has been proposed that the surface drains should always be cutting, the depth of cutting should be sufficient to keep the F.S.L. at least 1.00 ft below the ground level as far as possible. The side slopes may vary as per soils which is ranged between 1:1 to 1:1.5.

A typical cross section/used in MRBC area of Gujarat with gradient of 1:15000 to 1:30000 is given below (Fig. 12.3).

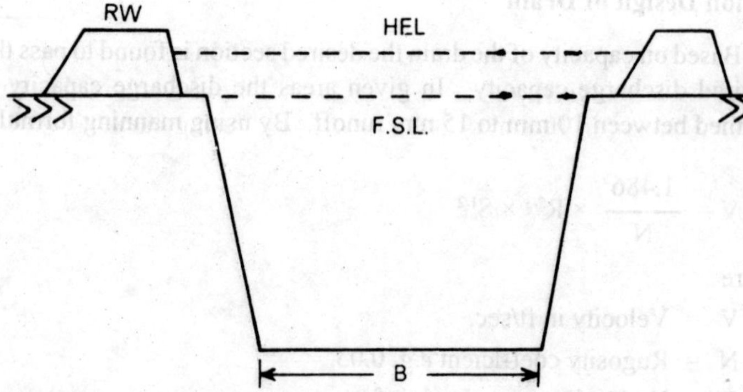

Fig. 12.3

The road width is kept between 12-15 ft. If the natural elevation of the ground is high the natural surface is maintained while in the low lying areas the surface may be raised by 1 ft above natural surface. The spoil bank should be always from the road leaving a drain at least 2 feet wide and one feet deep below the road surface. The slope of the sections for all earth work should be kept to be 1.5:1 to 1:1.

The inner slopes of the drain sections are usually considered 1:1 but in case of seepage it may be flatter according to the soil conditions particularly with occurrence of morrum or gypsic horizon exposed at a particular soil depth which are massive structure and easily erodable resulting in damage to the designed cross section.

Open Lateral Drains

The lateral drains are in the cultivable area which connects the main surface drains for disposal purpose. The nearest available nallah is also used as main drain. The main collecting drains run along the general slope of the field whereas the lateral generally run a cross the slope. The distance between two lateral drains varies from 200 to 400 ft depending upon topography and field boundaries. The alignment is kept straight as far as possible. The minimum depth of laterals is 2 to 2.5 ft. Pipe outlets are provided for safe disposal of surplus water into main drains. The earth excavated from laterals is used for constructing field irrigation channels adjacent to drains.

Design of a Drainage channel for 50 acres (Chambal command area, Kota, Rajasthan)

Example: Assuming maximum intensity of rainfall in Chambal command as 3 inches and 6 inches per hour, the drainage channel was designed to dispose rain water in 24 hours *i.e.* 6" rainfall to be carried in 24 hours. The calculations are as under :

∴ Quantity of water collected (6") per acre = C × I × A

where

C = Drainage coefficient taken as 1 for water-logged soils.

I = Per day rainfall intensity

A = Area in acres

∴ Per acre rain water storage = 1 × 6 × 1 = 6 cusecs/acre to be disposed off within 24 hours.

∴ Designed discharge of D.C. = 6/24 cusec = 0.25 cusec/acre

Design of D.C. for 50 acres: Given: Discharge = 0.25 × 50 = 12.5 Side slope-1:1, Bed slope 1.5 in 1000, section 2 feet deep & 6" free Book cusecs

$\therefore V = \sqrt{A/P \times 3/2 \times h}$

$V = \sqrt{6/524 \times 3/2 \times 7.9} = 3.69$ ft/second

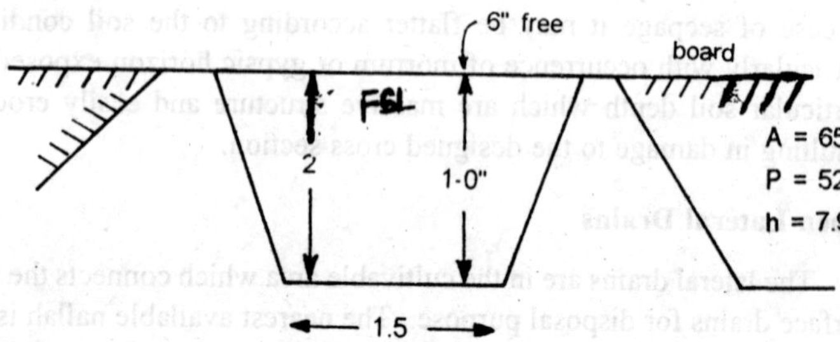

Fig. 12.4

Capacity of the Drain

$Q = A \times V = 6 \times 3.68 = 22$ cusecs

The free board of 6" was allowed and section adopted.

Design of Drainage Channel for 100 Acres

For 100 acres area the design of drainage channel was worked out similarly for section of 2' 6" deep with free board.

Designed discharge = 6/24 = 0.25 cusecs/acre with above assumptions and substitutions

$V = \sqrt{A/P \times 3/2\, h} = \sqrt{8.75/6.66 \times 3/2 \times 7.9} = 15.6$

$= 3.95$ ft per second

$\therefore Q = A \times V = 3.75 \times 3.95 = 34.5$ cusecs

The capacity of this channel is more than designed discharge *i.e.* 25 cusecs and hence allowed 6" free board between the section as shown below may be adopted.

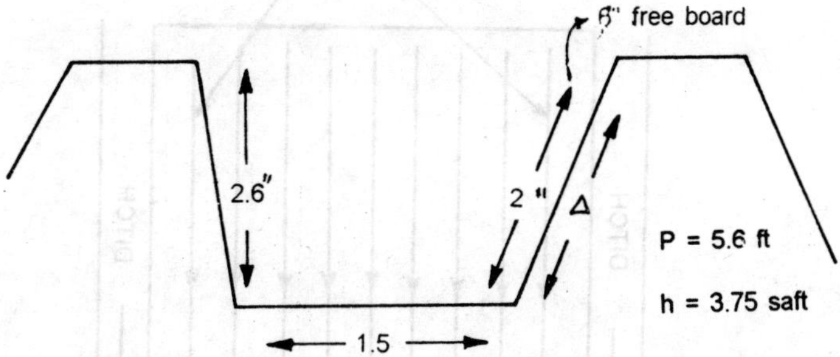

Fig. 12.5

Full Tile Drainage System

It is also known as "through system". In this main drain is excavated nearly parallel with the ditch to prevent too many outfalls liable to blockage. The laterals are then connected to main drain. The distance between laterals is governed by: (a) Percolation rate, (b) Average rainfall, (c) Type of crops. In some cases these are 20 feet to 30 feet apart. However, tile drains are very costly. However, if sub-soiling or chiesling is done simultaneously the space between them be kept 40 to 50 ft.

The tile outlets are provided with Sump also to take observations of effluent from laterals.

Sub-soiling

This helps to resort to the artificial creation of cracks or channels in the ground. It is done with a narrow blade to which there is attached a wedge shaped device, either attached to the plough if there is sufficient power to pull both by direct pull after a crawler tractor or by a winch. This implement helps to lift surface and cause cracks in the top soil thereby increasing water intake up to sub-surface. It also breaks all type of hard pans within rootzone depth and helps to increase moisture storage for growth period of plants. However, alone it is effective for 2 to 3 years only but if coupled with some other drainage system it can improve surface drainage for pretty good period. The spacing between two sub-soiler blades is found out by formula : $S = 1.5 \times d$; where S = spacing (meter); d = depth of sub-soiling (m). The length of strips be 100m or less. The moisture should be 5% less than plastic limit.

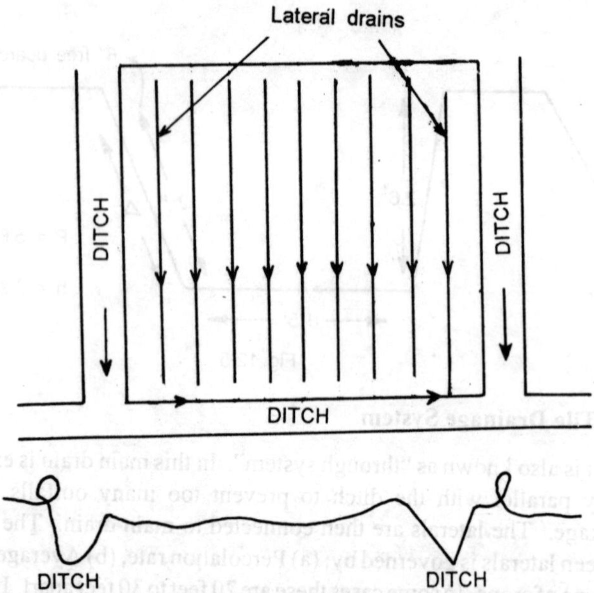

Fig. 12.6 : Full system tile drainage

In clayey soils this system may be installed. The distance apart of the lateral drains would depend upon:

(1) The rate of percolation of water through the soil.

(2) Average rainfall of the area.

(3) The type of cropping and farming to be carried out on the field.

In some cases 2 metres while in other 3 to 5 metres distance apart between the laterals have to be provided depending on type of lands and other considerations. However, it is a expensive system.

Mole Drains

The mole drainage system has been proposed for clayey soils. This is a cylindrical channel formed in the sub-soil by pulling through of a bullet shaped device at the bottom of a narrow blade. Such a channel if made in the sub-soil at appropriate soil moisture conditions with better designed mains may work for several years after insertion. It is a very cheap method and very effective and also after 5-10 years if repeated may further function for a very long time. The diameter of mole may vary from 5 to 7.5 cms, slope .3% to 3% (1% optimum).

The main drain is constrcted to this by using few pipes at the end of each mole drain as given in fig. 12.7. A turf may be placed on the tile to prevent entry of silt into the main. This silt mixed with fire clay or material from permeable material particularly if clinker is used would cause blockage in the main. The direct connection to the main with a few tiles is essential so as to avoid the breakdown of mole drainage schemes. The author worked out this reason of mole drain system failure installed in Chambal irrigation system under auspices of United Nations development programme at Digod Government Farm Kota, Rajasthan (India) in the years 1969-71. The other reasons which decrease the life of mole drainage system is that many times in clays having less percentage of sand some silt may be washed down the mole channel which may fill the holes in the clinker and causes retardation of water to the main drain. Also the water should not be allowed to stand within mole drain for long, which may decrease the stability and thereby function of mole drains.

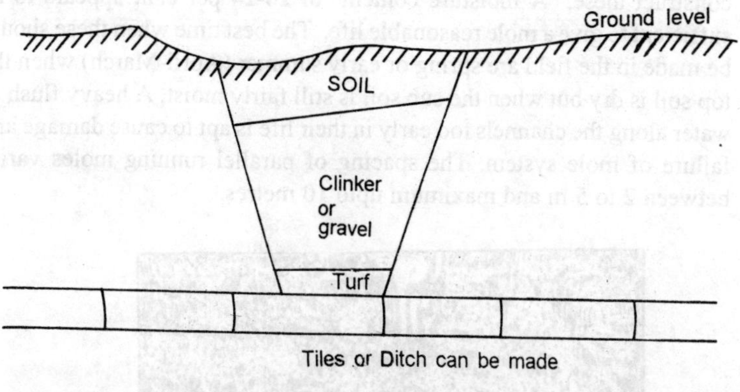

Fig.12.7 : Mole drainage connection box

The moles may be constructed by winch-pulling the mole plough or by direct pull with a crawler tractor. The 15 H.P. tractor with a pull, a 2 inches mole at about 15-18 inches deep may serve purpose. The use of heavy machinery should be avoided to avoid frequent and heavy wheel spin and movement which damage the surface structure and may retard the drainage.

The mole drains may be installed neither too deep nor too shallow. The appropriate depth may be kept between 45 to 60 cms. so as to collect or catch surface water easily and removed. The distance apart may vary as per land conditions, however, the distance of 75 metres may be useful for clayey soils. This may be reduced if:

1. The percentage of sand in the clay is high.
2. The fall is slight (3 inches to 1 ft. per chain).
3. The area has a high average rainfall.

In a levelled field with a steady fall to the main, normal practice is to have the moles 3-4 metres apart but in ridge and furrow land, where the water would collect in furrow land, where the water would collect in furrows 2-3 moles per each furrow may suffice. Maximum velocity of water flowing in the mole may be 0.35m/.sec in light clays; 0.4m/sec in heavy clay and minimum 0.30m/sec.

The time of year and condition of the ground when the operation is carried out has a direct bearing on the lasting nature of the work. If the soil is moist and plastic (moisture 2% above plastic limit), the walls of mole channels would be smooth and less force would be required to construct these. A moisture content of 20-24 per cent appears to be sufficient to give a mole reasonable life. The best time when these should be made in the field are spring or early summer (April-March) when the top soil is dry but when the sub soil is still fairly moist. A heavy flush of water along the channels too early in their life is apt to cause damage and failure of mole system. The spacing of parallel running moles varies between 2 to 5 m and maximum upto 10 metres.

Fig. 12.8 : Sub-surface drainage water being discharged into an outlet ditch.

D.C. in Clay loam soil texture : (27 to 40% clay, 20-45% sand and rest silt)

This texture contains more proportion of sand in comparison to clayey as such it needs different drainage system. In such soils mole drainage system will have short life. It is because more the sand content less the life of mole drains. In such type of soil textures a skeleton system is installed with sub-soiling of the ground every three or four years for improving the drainage of these soils which has resulted in better results. This may be coupled with the provision of sub-mains and laterals at an interval of 6-7 metres.

The installation of the tiled mains and sub-mains may be laid diagonally across the ridge and furrow lay out with outfalls into the surrounding ditches. The layout design of tile plus mole system for a typical ridge and furrow field is shown in Fig. 12.9 and may be appropriate in clayey to clay loam textured soils.

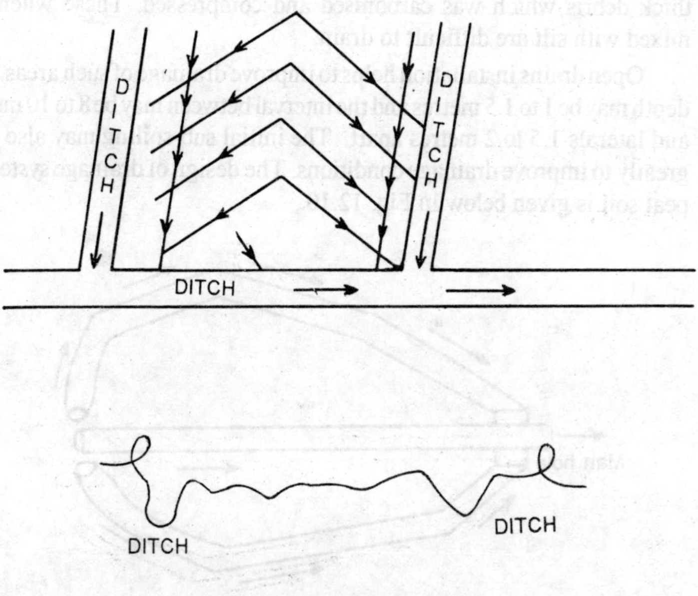

Fig. 12.9 : Tile plus mole system

D.C. in Sand Loams and Silty Clay Loams Texture

The sandy loam soils contains sand about 50% and clay less than 20% while in silty clay loams contain clay 40%, sand 20% and is slightly plastic when wet and has a tendency to make clods which are difficult to break on drying.

Spacing of Laterals

In these conditions of soil texture a long and narrow field may be provided with drains down the centre in sandy loam while laterals in addition in silty clay loam soils. The spacing may be kept more apart than clayey soils. In these soils very deep and widespread drains are made. The spacing is 5 to 6 times of its depth.

Peat Soils

In these type of soils which are more rich in decaying vegetation mixed with silt. These are basically formed from aquatic plants growing in swampy basin of impervious strata which due to the action of moist air conditions, bacteria moulds and fungi the top growth rotted became water-logged and sank to the bottom and with lapse of time made considerably thick debris which was carbonised and compressed. These when are mixed with silt are difficult to drain.

Open drains installation helps to improve drainage of such areas. The depth may be 1 to 1.5 metres and the interval between may be 8 to 10 metres and laterals 1.5 to 2 metres apart. The initial sub-soiling may also help greatly to improve drainage conditions. The design of drainage system in peat soil is given below in Fig. 12.10.

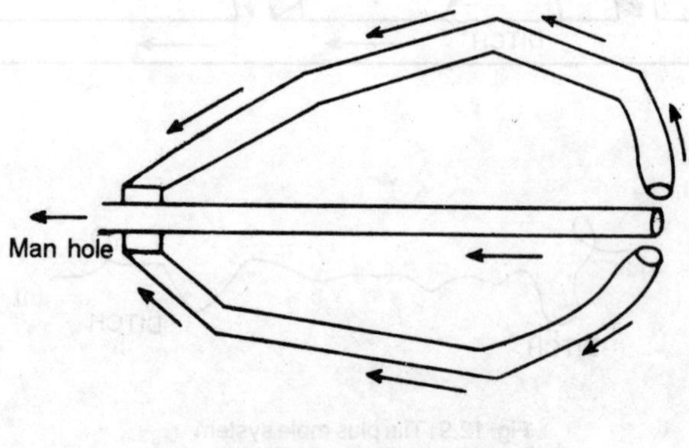

Fig. 12.10 : System in peat soil

Sandy and Chalk Soils

In sandy soils the problem is of excessive permeability unless these have hard compacted sub-stratas at lower depths. In fact in these soils the conservation of the surface water in rootzone instead of their disposal and removal is a problem which has to be given more attention. However, the rate increase of water table @ metre per year and salinity in deserts of Rajasthan elsewhere need the remedial measures for which drainage measures are to be installed. The provision of vertical drainage by pumping out the excessive ground water and leaching of salts by conjunctive use is the answer to these problems in such areas. The occurrence of silty clay sub-stratum in part of these areas also warrants the provision of some kind of drainage is also to be considered in such top sandy areas for which an outfall to allow water to enter the permeable surrounding lands as shown in Fig. 12.11 may also be considered for certain areas.

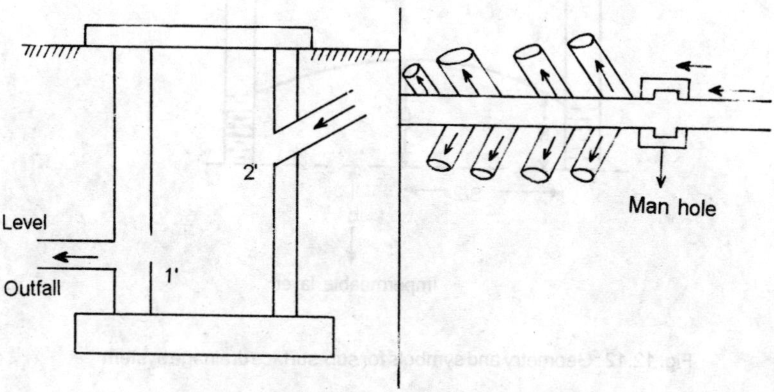

Fig. 12. 11 : Drainage Soakway

The main drain should empty into the manhole at least 60 cm above the bottom and outlet pipe 30 cm from the bottom for collecting silt of drainage system as is designed for a small septic tank and design as given below:

$$S^2 = \frac{4k\,(H^2 - h^2 + 2dH - dH)}{V}$$

where

S = spacing between parallel drains.

K = hydraulic conductivity of the soil.

H = height of the water in the sub-surface drain or the height of the water level above the tile line.

h = depth of the water in the sub-surface drain or the height of the water level above the tile line.

d = depth of impermeable layer below the drain bottom.

v = replenishment rate or rainfall intensity.

If the drain is considered empty the Hooghoudt's equation is given as

$$S^2 = \frac{4kH}{V} \times (2d + H)$$

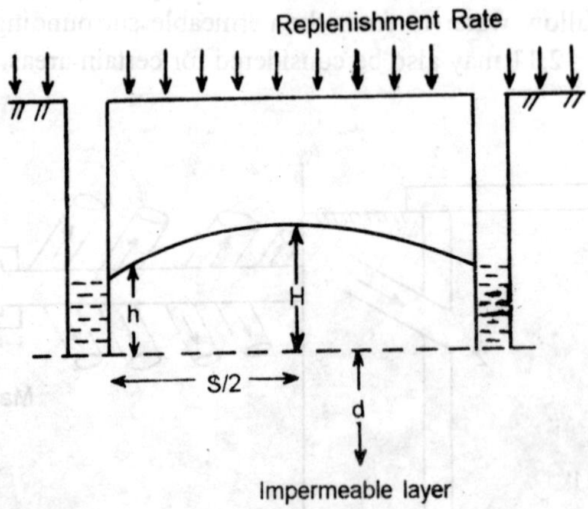

Fig. 12.12 : Geometry and symbols for sub-surface drainage system

If the soil is layered the hydraulic conductivity of which is given by Ka above the drain line and Kb for below the drain line the equation may be expressed as :

$$S^2 = \frac{4}{v}(K_a H^2) + (\frac{8}{v} K_b d H)$$

For multilayered soil profile above or below the drain line the equation may be expressed as :

$$K = \frac{K_1 L_1 + k_2 L_2 + \ldots\ldots\ldots + K_n L_n}{L_1 + L_2 + \ldots\ldots\ldots + L_n}$$

where

K = weighted mean of the hydraulic conductivities while $K_1 \ldots K_n$ of different layers having thickness depth of L_1, $L_2 \ldots L_n$ etc.

The more details can be seen from following design in which the construction of drains upto the impermeable layer is considered with following assumptions:

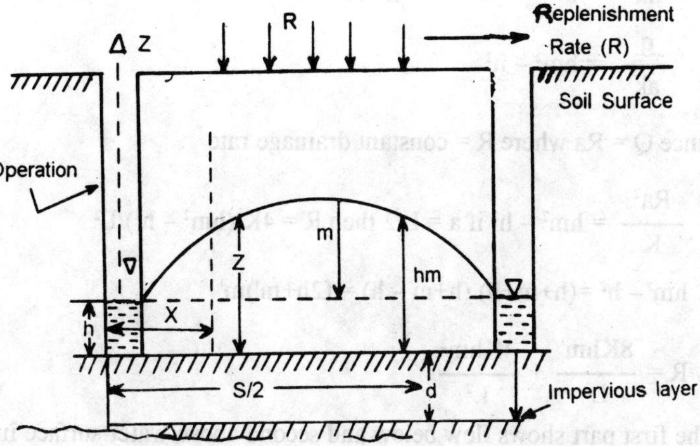

Fig. 12.13

In above diagram the hydraulic conductivity is say K; half drainage discharge per unit length of drain if assumed as Q, flow crossing the section per unit length at distance 'X' from the drain as q_x, hence $q_x = - V.Z.$

Since $V = -K \dfrac{dz}{dx}$ (Basis Darcy's law and dupit Forchheimer assumptions)

$$\therefore q_x = Kz \frac{dz}{dx} \quad \text{... (i)}$$

Also $q_x = \dfrac{(a-x)}{a} Q$ ... (ii)

Equating equation (i) & (ii)

$$Kz \frac{(dz)}{dx} = \frac{(a-x)}{a} Q$$

$$\text{or} \quad \frac{Q}{ak}(a-x)\, dx = Z\, dz$$

Integrating both sides we get

$$\text{or} \int \frac{q}{ak} \int_0^a (a-x)\ dx = \int_h^{hm} Z\,dz$$

$$\text{or} \quad \frac{q}{ak} = hm^2 - h^2$$

Since Q = Ra where R = constant drainage rate

$$\therefore \quad \frac{Ra^2}{K} = hm^2 - h^2 \text{ if } a = L/2 \text{ then } R = 4K\,(hm^2 - h^2)/L^2$$

$$\therefore\ hm^2 - h^2 = (h+m+h)\,(h+m-h) = (2h+m')m'$$

$$\therefore\ R = \frac{8Khm'}{L^2} + \frac{4Khm^2}{L^2}$$

The first part shows flow below and second above water surface in drain.

a = 1.0 for sulphate carbonate salinity/alkalinity

a = 1.1–1.2

For open channels where drains with sand and gravel filters or porous trench backfill materials are used and minimum of restriction of flow at the drain itself or where the convergence of flow at the drain is slight the Ellipse equation

$$L = \frac{\sqrt{4K\,(h^2 + 2Dgh)}}{q}$$

has been above suggested with different nomenclature used by different authors has been given, be used. In this formula:

R = Recharge rate per unit surface area (m/day).

q = drain discharge per unit surface area (m/day).

K = hydraulic conductivity of the soil (m/day).

H = height of impervious flow above the groundwater table midway between two drains.

D = Thickness of aquifer below drain level (m).

L = drain spacing (m).

g = H–D.

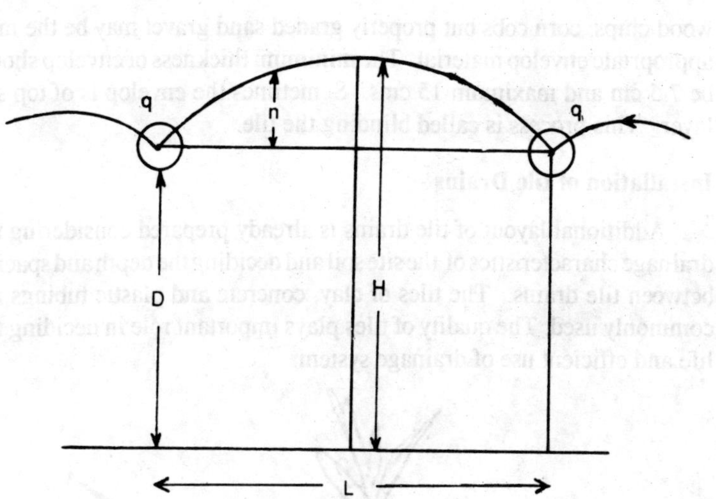

Fig. 12.14

Convergence of Flow

Where the land/soil indicate following conditions *viz.*:

(i) when deep homogeneous soils at surface and below exists without horizontal stratification;

(ii) the barrier layer if exists should be at a depth twice the depth of drain chosen;

(iii) when drains are constructed without porous filter and the soil samples several days after the steady state water table is attained. The soil moisture tension head at the point of sampling is taken to be equal to the vertical depth above the water table.

Envelop

In title drains water enters into the tile line through cracks between successive tiles through holes in pipes or for easy entrance of water porous materials are provided around the tile line. This helps in retaining the soil particles and silting of the tile line is avoided besides maintaining the proper alignment.

Envelop Material

These envelop of filter materials generally used are straw, sawdust, wood chips, corn cobs but properly graded sand gravel may be the most appropriate envelop material. The minimum thickness of envelop should be 7.5 cm and maximum 15 cms. Sometimes the envelop is of top soil layer. This process is called blinding the tile.

Installation of tile Drains

Additional layout of tile drains is already prepared considering the drainage characteristics of the site soil and deciding the depth and spacing between tile drains. The tiles of clay, concrete and plastic tubings are commonly used. The quality of tiles plays important role in deciding the life and efficient use of drainage system.

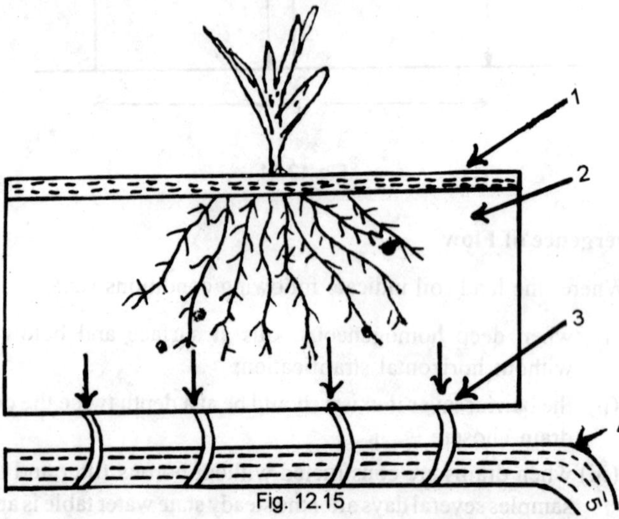

Fig. 12.15

(1) Irrigation water, (2) Salts, (3) Saline water coming out of tile drains, (4) Tile drains, (5) Drainage Outlet

It is suggested that tile should be regular, dense, strong and sound. Also the water absorption capacity of these tiles should not be more than needed to keep them on working. Thus a clay tile should not absorb water more than 16 per cent while concrete more than 11 per cent and be free from all imperfections, such as cracks, soft spots least they become brittle. The check on proper grade to be maintained throughout length of tile drain is also very essential. The use of perforated plastic pipes has been found to be highly satisfactory installed in vertisols of Chambal command area of Rajasthan and working even after over 15 years. However, the cost factor is still a problem for their economic use but in due course it may be a popular system in India.

Determination of Drainage Coefficient

This parameter is calculated by assessing the quantity of water to be disposed off in a certain period if rainfall analysis is available for monthly maximum, one day rainfall with return period of 10 to 15 years. Consequently runoff is calculated. Also tolerance of crop due to submergence and saturation should also be known. The hydraulic conductivity (H.C.) of the soil (upto rootzone depth) is determined by auger hole method. It is found that H.C. of heavy clay varies from 0.3 metre/day to 1.75 metre per day at depths of 75 cm to 2 metres from soil surface. However, the general value of 0.5m per day can be used. Some authors have given other values based on soil texture (Table 12.3). The spacing of open ditches for surface drainage system can be found out by Ernst equation:

$$h = \frac{qL2}{8\,KD} + q\,\frac{L}{K}\,\log\frac{Do}{\mu}$$

where:

h = Water table height above drain level at mid point.

q = Drainage coefficient.

L = drain spacing.

K = Hydraulic conductivity.

Do = Depth of impermeable layer from bottom surface of ditch where $D = Do + \frac{Do}{\mu}$

μ = Wet perimeter = $b+2y\sqrt{S^2+1}$

b = bottom width of ditch

y = Water depth in ditch

S = Side slope of the ditch

TABLE 12.3

Soil Texture		Hydraulic Conductivity (m/day)
Clay	-	Less than 0.01
Silty Clay	-	0.01 to 0.015
Silty Clay loam	-	0.015 to 0.024
Clay Loam	-	0.024 to 0.012
Sandy clay loam	-	0.012 to 0.019
Silt loam	-	0.019 to 0.213
Loam	-	0.213 to 0.427
Sand	-	3.658 to 4.877
Coarse sand	-	4.877 to 7.315

Source : Drainage book, [MT]

Drainage Coefficient for Crops

The calculations of D.C.for crops has been worked out for the whole country and zones are made for the purpose (Gupta et al. 1971). However, average D.C. has been suggested to be 0.25. Thus, the state-wise values are:

State	Average D.C. mm/day		
	Grains	Vegetables	Rice
Andhra Pradesh	14	13	8
Arunachal Pradesh	25	22	16
Assam	34	32	12
Bengal	35	30	4
Gujarat	32	18	6
Himachal Pradesh	10	10	2
Jammu & Kashmir	14	13	8
Kerala	19	20	12
Karnataka	16	19	10
Bihar	34	27	23
Maharashtra	21	26	14
M.P.	36	38	27
Nagaland	25	21	16
Orissa	37	26	24
Punjab, H.P. & Haryana	10	10	2
Rajasthan	12	11	2
Tamilnadu	19	20	12
Tripura	25	21	16
U.P. (Including Delhi)	29	23	10

NOTATIONS

The following notations have been used in this book unless otherwise stated in the text:

A	=	The cross-sectional area of a stream at a stated point
Ap	=	The cross-sectional area of a pipe or barrel outlet or the area of a circular orifice
A.O.S.M.	=	Adjustable orifice semi-module
A.P.M.	=	Adjustable proportional module
B	=	The length of a channel bed transverse to the direction of flow *i.e.* width
Bt	=	The width of the throat of a weir, flume etc.
C	=	An empirical coefficient
D	=	The depth below the surface of a stream at a given point
d	=	Diameter of a pipe, or a pipe outlet
di, do	=	Depth of flow at inner (i) and outerwalls (o) in a Gibb's module
E	=	Efficiency of an outlet
Ef	=	Energy of flow
F	=	Flexibility of an outlet
F.S.D.	=	Full supply depth
F.S.L.	=	Full supply level
G	=	A gauge reading (Zero of gauge must be specified) or the depth of water over a crest
g	=	The gravity constant
H	=	The head or energy required to produce a velocity: $H = \frac{V^2}{2g}$

Ha	=	The head or energy equivalent to the velocity of approach
Hc	=	The head measured from the water surface to the centre of an orifice
Hi, Ho	=	The head at the inner and outer wall respectively in a Gibb's module
Hi	=	The head lost at a fall, difference in elevation between the total energy line above and below a fall
Hm	=	The minimum working head required between two points for modularity
Hs	=	The head measured from the water surface to the soffit of an orifice
Hw	=	The available working head
J	=	Head recovered
K	=	The constant in the free fall discharge formula, theoretically $K = \sqrt{g\,(2/3)^{3/2}} = 3.08$
L	=	The length of a channel or work measured along the centre line parallel to the direction of flow between two points
Lt	=	The length of crest in the direction of flow
m	=	Index of H in the formula for discharge of the offtake
n	=	Index of D in the formula for discharge of a channel
O.F.	=	Open flume outlet
O.S.M.	=	Orifice Semi-module
q	=	The discharge in cusecs of an outlet
Q	=	The discharge in cusecs of a distributary
R	=	Depression ratio (Hs/Y)
Ri, Ro	=	Radii of inner and outer circumferences in a Gibb's module
S	=	Sensitivity
S_1	=	Sensitiveness
S.M.M.O.	=	Semi-modular meter outlet
S.W.O.	=	Standing wave outlet
V	=	The mean velocity in feet per second of a stream at any given point

W	=	Setback of the upstream face of an outlet equal to the q/Q of the water way of the channel
Y	=	The elevation of the roof block above the crest of an O.S.M. or the vertical dimension of a rectangular orifice.

INDEX